D1368144

14/8

B R I E F

THE
HARPER & ROW
READER

Liberal Education Through
Reading and Writing

MARSHALL W. GREGORY
Butler University

WAYNE C. BOOTH
The University of Chicago

E D I T I O N

1817

HARPER & ROW, PUBLISHERS, NEW YORK

Grand Rapids, Philadelphia, St. Louis, San Francisco,
London, Singapore, Sydney, Tokyo

Sponsoring Editor: Lucy Rosendahl
Project Editor: Susan Goldfarb
Text Design: Maria Carella
Cover Coordinator: Mary Archondes
Cover Design: Delgado Design, Inc.
Production: Beth Maglione

The Harper & Row Reader: Liberal Education Through Reading and Writing, Brief
Edition

Copyright © 1990 by Harper & Row, Publishers, Inc.

Acknowledgments begin on page 537.

All rights reserved. Printed in the United States of America. No part of this book may be
used or reproduced in any manner whatsoever without written permission, except in the
case of brief quotations embodied in critical articles and reviews. For information address
Harper & Row, Publishers, Inc., 10 East 53d Street, New York, NY 10022.

Teacher Edition: ISBN 0-06-040436-1
Student Edition: ISBN 0-06-042515-6

Library of Congress Cataloging-in-Publication Data

The Harper & Row reader : liberal education through reading and
    writing / [compiled by] Marshall W. Gregory, Wayne C. Booth. —
    Brief ed.
        p.   cm.
    Includes indexes.
    ISBN 0-06-042515-6
    1. College readers.   2. English language—Rhetoric.   I. Gregory,
Marshall W., 1940– .   II. Booth, Wayne C.   III. Title: Harper and
Row reader.
PE1417.H276   1990   89-33466
808'.0427—dc20   CIP

89 90 91 92 9 8 7 6 5 4 3 2 1

Contents

Preface

The Harper & Row Reader has met with the kind of success that supports our belief that many writing teachers want a reader to offer students an education at the same time that it helps them improve their writing. It was our conviction when we prepared the first two editions, and now in preparing this Brief Edition, that the aims of both general education and writing are most successfully fulfilled when they are intertwined. That they *can* be intertwined is the foundation upon which the Reader stands.

What's Different About the Brief Edition

One of the wishes consistently expressed by both confirmed and potential users of the Reader, especially those who teach on quarter or trimester systems, is for a shorter edition of the Reader, one that retains the basic format of the first and second editions but that contains fewer readings. The Brief Edition of the Reader, which reduces the full-sized Reader by one-third, is designed to satisfy the wishes of these teachers. In all other respects—philosophy, format, variety, levels of difficulty, and so on—the Brief Edition is identical to the first and second editions.

Six new pieces are introduced in the Brief Edition: a selection by Adrienne Rich on education (Chapter 1); a selection by Ursula K. Le Guin on imagination (Chapter 4); a selection by Lorraine Hansberry on equality for men (Chapter 5); a selection by Mary Midgley on the excesses of both optimism and pessimism based on evolutionary science (Chapter 10); a selection by Walter T. Stace on the nature of religious feeling (Chapter 11); and finally a selection by Joyce Carol Oates that raises disturbing questions about greed and materialism in American society (Chapter 12). That five of these inclusions are by women—and by women writing on a variety of topics, not just on feminist issues—is consistent with our commitment to make the Reader an equal-opportunity forum for the best thinking on a wide range of topics by both men and women. We think that users may especially like the

selections by Lorraine Hansberry and Mary Midgley, the former because few
occasional pieces by the brilliant author of *Raisin in the Sun* have ever been
reprinted and the latter because Mary Midgley is not a familiar name in
undergraduate anthologies, yet she writes with an elegant ease that will
immediately make her a welcome addition to the profession's pool of best-
liked writers.

   Other innovations introduced in the Second Edition of the Reader have
been retained: the inclusion of a few selections of poetry and fiction that have
an argumentative cast; the addition of the rhetorical index; and the substantial revisions in the chapter on language (Chapter 3).

   One of the first edition's most successful features—the inclusion of a
number of essays which "spoke" to each other from opposite sides of a
topic—was extended systematically throughout the second edition and has
been retained in this Brief Edition. Each chapter now has at least one such
pair of essays, sometimes two pairs, set apart under the heading "Ideas in
Debate." Paul Goodman and Karl Popper disagreeing about the value of
utopian thinking, Plato and Maxim Gorky disagreeing about the ethical value
of reading stories, Paul Johnson and four respondents disagreeing about the
value of capitalism, and C. S. Lewis and Bertrand Russell disagreeing about
the authority of Christianity—these are the voices of reasoned opinion and
civilized controversy. Lively, opinionated, rich, searching, and inquisitive,
these voices do not compel assent in every case, but they do command
attention and respect. In chorus they exemplify the educated mind at work,
inquiring with energy and moral responsibility into a diverse range of important issues. We firmly believe that both teachers and students will enjoy the
education that attends the study of these controversies.

   A frequent request received from users of the first edition was to include more fiction and poetry in subsequent editions. This we have done,
taking care to make these additions consistent with the character of the
book as a whole. We have not turned *The Harper & Row Reader* into a literature text, nor will the teacher be required to change the focus of the course
in order to use the literary pieces. Fiction and poetry are included here
mainly as argument. (It should be clear, however, that teachers who prefer
to use literature in the freshman class will find more to work with in this
edition than in the first edition.) We have chosen stories and poems that
have a strong argumentative slant, such as Mary McCarthy's "Artists in
Uniform" and Shirley Jackson's "Flower Garden." Such works allow students to see the rhetorical, argumentative, and polemical dimensions of
such "literary" features as metaphor and narrative. This will not only enrich
students' knowledge of how arguments actually get advanced in the world,
but will also offer them and their teachers a welcome change of pace without throwing the course into confusion.

   We have added a rhetorical index specifically designed for student use.
We have not indexed all of the ideas, concepts, and themes in the essays, but
we have indexed all of the references to, and most of the examples of,
rhetorical devices and strategies. Thus if students are unclear, for example,

about the meaning or use of analogy, a quick glance at the index will take them to a number of places where analogy is either discussed or exemplified. (As a further aid, a rhetorical table of contents is included in the Instructor's Manual.)

Finally, Chapter 3, on language, has been heavily revised and somewhat expanded in order to provide the student with better discussions of language as the fundamental milieu of human existence, and to present a sharper view of the political and educational controversies involved in language usage and study.

Purpose of the Course

We have assumed from the beginning that it is not only wasted effort in practice but indefensible in theory to attempt to train students to write without educating them. We assume, in other words, that writers must have something to say in order to have something to write, and that what they have to say will depend mainly on what they know, how they think, and who they are, not just on their mastery of isolated skills. We assume, further, that we write not just as thinkers but as moral agents attempting to do something in or to the world. Any attempt to teach writing as if it were something separate from our character, or to reduce writing instruction to the status of a "service course," insults our students and shortchanges our culture.

Obviously, we cannot offer decisive proof for these assumptions—as opposed to views that we think are cynical, impoverished, or unjust—but we have not chosen them blindly. In what we know of empirical research and learning theory, we find no justification for believing that learning to write well can be divorced from the daily nourishment of trying to understand what other writers have said and then trying to respond with something worth saying.

None of this means that we should fail to teach what are sometimes called "skills." But whatever skills we teach should be taught because they are important to achieving larger goals. Education, after all, is not just for abstract performance but to obtain wisdom. That term may seem moralistic or pretentious to your ears, but surely it describes the ends of education better than such modern equivalents as "maturity," "integrated selfhood," or "effective functioning as a critical and creative adult." But whatever your terms, we here invite you to join us in the unending quest for a liberal education. When courses in "composition" or "rhetoric" or "communication" are viewed in this light, they are for us without question the most important in any curriculum. If this claim seems extravagant to you (as it will almost certainly seem to your students), we hope that working through this book will justify it.

The notion of "working" cannot be dodged. We were convinced from the beginning that the job we wanted to do would require a reader with a fair number of pieces both longer and harder than those in most of the recent anthologies. Toughness for its own sake would no doubt be silly, but students cannot be stretched by what is already within easy reach. In each chapter we have thus included substantial essays, some of them once popular in readers but now abandoned, many of them never anthologized before.

Not all of our selections are hard, however; we have provided a range of both difficulty and styles. Nor have we made our selections with any sense that we are self-appointed guardians of an aristocratic tradition that the barbarian hordes have been neglecting. The distinction between aristocrats and barbarians seems to us absurd, especially when thinking about American education. The education we try to serve here is the kind that we think would be defensible for any group of young people in any historical period—a mixture of the best thinking that people are doing now with the best thinking from other periods.

The result, we believe, is a distinguished and engaging collection of essays. It is a controversial collection. In each chapter some essays confront others directly, while others address issues shared by other essays. Disagreement is found everywhere. The collection is also unusually wide-ranging. Even so, we obviously do not offer a complete list of topics important to liberal education, or a survey of the entire range of possible views about any one topic. Any critical reader will find that entire disciplines are either ignored or underrepresented; among the liberal arts, for example, we talk little about logic or grammar, but much about rhetoric. More particularly, many political, religious, and philosophical views go unmentioned. But we hope that our recommended approach to the readings will itself provide a way to compensate for our omissions and biases. In our introductions and questions, we have tried hard to avoid the suggestion, found in too many anthologies these days, that the authors and their editors are somehow privy to the one right way of looking at the world. And we assume that the kind of critical thinking we encourage throughout this book will in itself compensate, in the long run, for the inevitable gaps and distortions in our choice of selections.

Methods

Thinking of the difficulties presented to beginners by many of our pieces, we have asked ourselves what kind of guidance we would have welcomed when we were beginning college students. The result is that we offer more extensive commentary than any other reader we have seen. Of course we have tried to modulate our editorial voice, according to the difficulty of the selections, by limiting our introductions to a paragraph for some simpler pieces, while demonstrating how to perform extensive analyses of some of the more difficult works. For those to whom our commentary seems excessive, the format makes it easy to skip our words and work exclusively on our selections.

The introductions to the readings provide only a minimum of biographical and bibliographical information; we concentrate instead on grappling with the issues. "Grappling" is the word, because we do not conceal our own inability to solve many of the issues raised. These works have stretched us as we have performed our editing, and they do so still. Too many anthologies

have seemed to us to imply that their editors now have the whole of education taped, and that the students' task is to discover what the editors claim
to know already.

Similarly, we have not hesitated to raise questions for discussion that
we ourselves cannot answer, though we hope to have raised none that would
leave us tongue-tied. We have tried to strike a balance between relatively
determinate questions about the authors' procedures and open-ended questions about the issues.

In our suggested essay topics we have, in contrast, suggested no topics
that we could not happily write on ourselves. This has meant avoiding assignments that seem canned, arbitrary, abstract, or impossibly ambitious. (No
doubt we have not always succeeded, even after much probing and pruning,
but most of our topics *have* been tried out in the only crucible that counts in
such matters: the classroom itself.) Generally, our assignments place students
in situations where they can aim for concrete objectives directed at specific
audiences, choosing appropriate strategies and dealing with ideas raised or
suggested by the piece they have just read. If they take our suggestions
seriously, they will discover that learning to write well has become their own
goal, not just the instructor's or the editors'.

Organization

Our selections offer great flexibility to both students and teachers. Teachers
and students can enter *The Harper & Row Reader* at any of several levels of
reading difficulty. For example, a class might well move through the whole
text using mainly the shorter and less ambitious pieces, or a term could be
built mainly on the longer and harder essays. Or a class of "middling" preparation might well choose to read all or most of the readings in a few chapters,
beginning with the epigraphs that introduce a chapter and working right
through to the toughest arguments at the end. Some classes might want
entirely to ignore the sequence of our chapters, and the order within them,
though we hope—since our discussion material in general builds upon itself—
that most classes will profit from following our organization.

We have, then, worked throughout in the conviction that reading, writing,
and thinking are integrally related. No doubt every student will at some point
need to pay special attention to isolated skills; some will profit from drill—in
grammar, in reading techniques, in sentence combining. They will profit, that
is, provided they have learned why the drill is important, and why learning
to write well is something they should want for themselves, not something
they do just for their teachers, their grades, or their parents.

To educate is always harder than to train, and the world will no doubt
always find demonstrable uses for those who are trained without knowing
what they have been trained *for*. But neither students nor their teachers
should have to choose between a "useful" practical training and a "useless"

liberal education. Anything truly liberating is also useful, and anything truly useful, when done well and with joy, is also liberating. The best versions of liberal and practical education are ultimately inseparable.

Regardless of any mistakes we have made in our own theory and practice, we feel quite sure about one thing: the required freshman composition course (whatever it is called and however it is staffed) can provide the most important experience of any student's college years and a continuing experience of self-education for the teacher. It can do so, that is, when it enables students and teachers together to repossess for themselves what others have learned in the past and then to engage each other pointedly and eagerly, sharing their thoughts about who they are and how they should try to live, here and now.

We would like to thank the following reviewers of the second edition, on which this Brief Edition is based, for their helpful comments and suggestions: Nancy Baxter, Butler University; Sam Dragga, Texas A&M University; Gwendolyn Gong, Texas A&M University; Lynn M. Grow, Broward Community College; Jack Hibbard, St. Cloud State University; James R. Payne, New Mexico State University; Linda Peterson, Yale University; Richard Reid, Grand Rapids Junior College; Nancy Smith, Iowa State University of Science; Mary Soliday, University of Illinois; and Mary Wallum, North Dakota State University.

We would also like to acknowledge the help of the following reviewers of the new material for this Brief Edition: Edward Black, San Jacinto College South; Mary Comfort, Lehigh University; Mary Dietz, New York University; Mimi Still Dixon, Wittenberg University; Anne Matthews, Princeton University; Georgia Rhodes, University of Louisville; and Janet Streepy, Indiana University Southeast.

Special thanks must go to Phyllis Booth and Valiska Gregory, whose support and criticism have been both constant and nourishing, and to those many students and teachers who have contacted us over the past five years with suggestions and criticisms. They have helped sustain our energy and improve our work.

Marshall W. Gregory
Wayne C. Booth

PART

TOWARD A LIBERAL EDUCATION

ONE

1

EDUCATION

Images, Methods, and Aims

Ignorance is the night of the mind.
Efe Pygmies of Zaire

Never lose a holy curiosity.
Albert Einstein

Knowledge is capable of being its own end. Such is the
constitution of the human mind, that any kind of knowledge,
if it be really such, is its own reward.
John Henry Cardinal Newman

The pleasure of learning and knowing, though not the
keenest, is yet the least perishable of all pleasures.
A. E. Housman

Where there is much desire to learn, there of necessity
will be much arguing, much writing, many opinions; for opinion
in good men is but knowledge in the making.
John Milton

Whoso loveth instruction loveth knowledge: but he that
hateth reproof is brutish.
Proverbs 12:1

A little learning is a dangerous thing.
Alexander Pope

Human history becomes more and more a race between
education and catastrophe.
H. G. Wells

Authors Ethos — His personality coming through.

Norman Cousins

Norman Cousins (b. 1912) has for some decades been one of America's most widely read critics and journalists of ideas. As a columnist and longtime editor of the influential Saturday Review, *he has consistently prodded us into hard thought about how to improve our lives by improving how we write. Here we meet him as advocate for a controversial educational idea.*

Following the essay we offer a short "demonstration" of how one might go about reading this piece. As with our other demonstration of how to read an argument (pp. 70–73) and our introductory comments throughout this book, we urge you both to follow them carefully and to resist taking them as any kind of final word. Every reading is partial; every reading can be improved. We hope only to suggest useful ways of reading, not to kill the text and mount it neatly in a specimen case.

HOW TO MAKE PEOPLE SMALLER THAN THEY ARE

From *The Saturday Review*, December 1978.

Three months ago in this space we wrote about the costly retreat from the humanities on all the levels of American education. Since that time, we have had occasion to visit a number of campuses and have been troubled to find that the general situation is even more serious than we had thought. It has become apparent to us that one of the biggest problems confronting American education today is the increasing vocationalization of our colleges and universities. Throughout the country, schools are under pressure to become job-training centers and employment agencies. 1

Thesis

The pressure comes mainly from two sources. One is the growing determination of many citizens to reduce taxes—understandable and even commendable in itself, but irrational and irresponsible when connected to the reduction or dismantling of vital public services. The second source of pres- 2

4

sure comes from parents and students who tend to scorn courses of study that do not teach people how to become attractive to employers in a rapidly tightening job market.

It is absurd to believe that the development of skills does not also ³ require the systematic development of the human mind. Education is being measured more by the size of the benefits the individual can extract from society than by the extent to which the individual can come into possession of his or her full powers. The result is that the life-giving juices are in danger of being drained out of education.

Emphasis on "practicalities" is being characterized by the subordination ⁴ of words to numbers. History is seen not as essential experience to be transmitted to new generations, but as abstractions that carry dank odors. Art is regarded as something that calls for indulgence or patronage and that has no place among the practical realities. Political science is viewed more as a specialized subject for people who want to go into politics than as an opportunity for citizens to develop a knowledgeable relationship with the systems by which human societies are governed. Finally, literature and philosophy are assigned the role of add-ons—intellectual adornments that have nothing to do with "genuine" education.

Instead of trying to shrink the liberal arts, the American people ought ⁵ to be putting pressure on colleges and universities to increase the ratio of the humanities to the sciences. Most serious studies of medical-school curricula in recent years have called attention to the stark gaps in the liberal education of medical students. The experts agree that the schools shouldn't leave it up to students to close those gaps.

. . .

The irony of the emphasis being placed on careers is that nothing is ⁶ more valuable for anyone who has had a professional or vocational education than to be able to deal with abstractions or complexities, or to feel comfortable with subtleties of thought or language, or to think sequentially. The doctor who knows only disease is at a disadvantage alongside the doctor who knows at least as much about people as he does about pathological organisms. The lawyer who argues in court from a narrow legal base is no match for the lawyer who can connect legal precedents to historical experience and who employs wide-ranging intellectual resources. The business executive whose competence in general management is bolstered by an artistic ability to deal with people is of prime value to his company. For the technologist, the engineering of consent can be just as important as the engineering of moving parts. In all these respects, the liberal arts have much to offer. Just in terms of career preparation, therefore, a student is shortchanging himself by shortcutting the humanities.

But even if it could be demonstrated that the humanities contribute ⁷ nothing directly to a job, they would still be an essential part of the educational equipment of any person who wants to come to terms with life. The humanities would be expendable only if human beings didn't have to make decisions that affect their lives and the lives of others; if the human past never existed or had nothing to tell us about the present; if thought processes were irrelevant to the achievement of purpose; if creativity was beyond the human mind and had nothing to do with the joy of living; if human relationships were random aspects of life; if human beings never had to cope with panic or pain, or if they never had to anticipate the connection between cause and effect; if all the mysteries of mind and nature were fully plumbed; and if no special demands arose from the accident of being born a human being instead of a hen or a hog.

Finally, there would be good reason to eliminate the humanities if a free 8 society were not absolutely dependent on a functioning citizenry. If the main purpose of a university is job training, then the underlying philosophy of our government has little meaning. The debates that went into the making of American society concerned not just institutions or governing principles but the capacity of humans to sustain those institutions. Whatever the disagreements were over other issues at the American Constitutional Convention, the fundamental question sensed by everyone, a question that lay over the entire assembly, was whether the people themselves would understand what it meant to hold the ultimate power of society, and whether they had enough of a sense of history and destiny to know where they had been and where they ought to be going.

Jefferson was prouder of having been the founder of the University of 9 Virginia than of having been President of the United States. He knew that the educated and developed mind was the best assurance that a political system could be made to work—a system based on the informed consent of the governed. If this idea fails, then all the saved tax dollars in the world will not be enough to prevent the nation from turning on itself.

How to Read an Argument: Demonstration I

As you may have learned already, it 1 *is never easy to write about complicated matters, especially in a short space. Writers who try to say a great deal in a few words often wind up sounding pompous, desperate, vague, or wildly opinionated.*

Since your own papers will usually be short like Cousins's, you can profit from 2 *studying how he organizes his argument. Try to postpone any decision about whether you agree with him until you have worked out precisely what he is claiming.*

A good way to begin is to read the whole piece through once, fairly fast, slowing 3 *down only to circle any troublesome words or phrases. Then read through again, dictionary at hand, scribbling helpful definitions in the margin. Once you have done this, you will have gone further than most people ever do in ordinary reading, but you will have only begun to read at a serious college level.*

Much of the writing we run into is not worth the trouble of this second step. 4
The art of reading is in part that of knowing how and when to skim and when to dig in with hard study. Ordinarily you will have to decide for yourself whether to take the later, harder steps, but here we will assume that your first quick reading has led you to see Cousins as someone you would like to converse with for a while. How might the conversation be conducted?

On the basis of our first reading, we know Cousins's purpose: *He wants us* 5
to believe not only that the "humanities"—whatever they really are—are being neglected but that they are the most important part of the curriculum. And we know from the final paragraph that he sees the humanities as the source of the "educated and developed mind." Since this is obviously a controversial claim, one that would be questioned by many people, our next step is to ask him, "Exactly what reasons have you offered us for going along with your argument?"

There are many good ways to perform the careful reading that will uncover 6
Cousins's answer to that question. Some people can do it lounging in an armchair, reading and thinking; some can do it entirely in their heads, referring to the text with photographic memory. We (Gregory and Booth)—at least when we are feeling virtuous and energetic—do this kind of reading while sitting up at a desk, pencil in hand, marking the text frequently.

There is no use in underlining a great many passages unless your clues clearly 7
show why some passages are important and how the different sections relate to each other. It is useful to develop some sort of brief code that tells at a glance what statements you view as conclusions *and what statements you view as* reasons, *what words give evidence about* organization, *and what terms reveal the relative weight of different points.*

You may then want to distinguish different kinds of reasons: appeals to facts 8
(examples, statistics, commonsense experience) and appeals to general beliefs or
principles *("Everybody knows that . . ."; "All modern science teaches that . . .";
"Our country is founded on the principle that . . ."; "Nobody who has thought about this issue for more than five minutes has ever denied that. . . .") Some students use different pencil colors for the different kinds of attempts at proof. We find it even more useful to create an outline in the margins of the text, using roman numerals or capital letters to flag the major conclusions and a's and b's and 1's and 2's to flag the supporting points. It often helps to draw arrows from the evidence to the conclusion, underlining in the text the key* connecting terms *that show the relationship:*
because, but, therefore, thus, on the other hand, finally. *If it is important to us to decide whether to accept an argument (because we face an examination or must write something about the passage, let us say, or because we must decide how to vote or whether to invest our immense fortune), we may then even make a written outline on a separate sheet.*

Consider for a moment how Cousins supports his claim that "the American 9
people" (meaning you, of course) "ought to be putting pressure . . . to increase the ratio of the humanities to the sciences" (¶5). His first reason *comes in paragraph 6: because "nothing is more valuable" than the skills he then lists. (Note that as we move in*

this way, we begin to get a clearer and clearer notion of what he means by "the humanities": they are those studies that cultivate these skills.) Then, having introduced his first reason, he provides evidence for the because: first, the doctor's need for the humanities; then the lawyer's; then the business executive's; finally the technologist's. The result is that when we come to his therefore, three lines before the end of the paragraph, we see that he has worked hard to earn his right to use it with his four examples of vocations that depend on the humanities.

It is important to see that each of his claims about these vocations could in turn   10 be questioned, and that it would take him many pages to develop a full argument for any one of the four. (You will later find examples of much fuller development; see our analysis of Popper's "Utopia and Violence," pp. 82–90.) But Cousins counts on our finding each of his examples at least probable or plausible, and he goes on to show, by the way he moves into his next reason (¶7), that he knows how much more might have been said in paragraph 6: "But even if it could be demonstrated . . ."—that is, even if you are still skeptical about all that, I have even stronger reasons to offer: the humanities are "essential" for "any person who wants to come to terms with life." He can assume that every reader will want that, and he can thus move on to show why this second main reason is itself sound.

We leave it to you to determine how much evidence he provides for his second   11 reason and move on to the third one (¶8). (Note that Cousins has not numbered his reasons for you, but he has given you clear clues by beginning paragraphs 7 and 8 with "But even" and "Finally.") In paragraph 8 he moves from our private desire for "coming to terms with life" to society's "absolute dependence" on citizens educated in the humanities. Like his first two reasons, this one might require a long essay, or even a book, for its full support. In a short piece, Cousins can only suggest the line that he would follow in a longer proof: a consideration of our "underlying philosophy" as revealed by our national history. He ends with an argument that could be considered either as an extension of his third reason or as a new kind of reason altogether, an "appeal to authority." "Jefferson knew . . ."—knew what? Well, in effect, Jefferson knew that what Cousins is arguing for is true. The humanities are even more important than the points raised in the third reason: They are what government (and tax dollars) are for.

What we have just given is by no means a complete analysis of Cousins's   12 argument, but it is a good start toward knowing how to argue with him in a way that would make him sit up and take notice. At least we can now look him in the eye and say such things as, "What you claim is that P is true because A, B, and C are true and that each of those is true because X, Y, and Z are true. But at B I have serious questions [or it might be at every step]. Tell me more about why you think . . ."; or "You're flatly wrong about C. Just last week a report was issued showing that. . . ."

In a dialogue of this kind, either with someone in person or with the author   13 who lives before us (in a sense) in the text, we learn to read by learning to think and learn to think by learning to read. The process yields its reward when we sit down to write out the results of our "conversation," saying in effect: "Now see here, Mr.

Cousins, I've considered your case with full respect, and I've thought about your reasons. But I must conclude that. . . ."

Of course we seldom make up our minds only on the basis of carefully thinking 14 through an author's patterns of reasoning. At every point in our encounter with Cousins we are inferring his quality as a person, his character—what is sometimes called his ethos. Does he seem to be trustworthy, likable, a valuable friend and guide? Writers like Cousins who are skillful at creating an appealing character for themselves will be trusted (not by every reader but by those who like the ethos) even when the reasoning is vague or incomplete. You will find many authors in this book whom you like and some whom you dislike. As you work on your own writing, you will find it useful—though sometimes disturbing—to experiment in "sounding like" different writers you admire. There's nothing dishonest about practicing imitations of an author's style as long as you don't claim as your own what you have simply copied.

We might call this whole process, borrowing from Cousins's title, "How to 15 Re-make a Text So That It Is as Large as Its Author Intended It to Be." It will prove valuable in all of your college work. But of course it will not work at all in reading texts that are not organized as arguments. The questions we have asked of Cousins may prove entirely inappropriate when we approach other kinds of texts. But the technique of using marginal notes and underlinings to flag interrelationships (rather than simply to emphasize something you happen to like or, worse, to prove to yourself that you are working hard) should be useful in all kinds of difficult reading. Obviously there are many texts that will be destroyed if we read them with pencil in hand. Sometimes we have even been known to lie back in our hammocks, detective story or sci-fi thriller in limp hand—and fall asleep.

Malcolm X

Malcolm X (1925–1965) was a famous and powerful leader in the push for equal rights for blacks in the 1950s and 1960s. In The Autobiography of Malcolm X, *he describes the dramatic sequence of events that transformed him from Malcolm Little, street hustler and convicted thief, to political leader and outstanding evangelist for the Temple of Islam. In his devotion to Muslim teachings he journeyed to Mecca, and while there he became convinced that many of the teachings of the Temple of Islam were not true to the Muslim faith. On his return to America, he expressed his new convictions with characteristic forthrightness and power. He was assassinated in New York City in 1965 while preaching his new views. Some members of the Temple of Islam were convicted of the murder, but there is still controversy over who in fact killed him.*

The Autobiography *continues to be read as a passionate document expressing both private and public commitment to a cause. In the following selection, Malcolm X gives one of the most moving accounts we know of what it is like to engage in self-education. Although many people these days might scoff at the method he chose, his description of how he felt, once reading changed from merely deciphering words to understanding ideas, is vivid, indeed gripping. It is impossible to doubt that, for him, his strange method worked.*

FREEDOM THROUGH LEARNING TO READ

From chapter 11, "Saved," of *The Autobiography of Malcolm X* (1964). The title is ours.

It was because of my letters that I happened to stumble upon starting to   1
acquire some kind of a homemade education.

I became increasingly frustrated at not being able to express what I   2
wanted to convey in letters that I wrote, especially those to Mr. Elijah
Muhammad.* In the street, I had been the most articulate hustler out there—I
had commanded attention when I said something. But now, trying to write
simple English, I not only wasn't articulate, I wasn't even functional. How
would I sound writing in slang, the way I would *say* it, something such as,
"Look, daddy, let me pull your coat about a cat, Elijah Muhammad—"

Many who today hear me somewhere in person, or on television, or   3
those who read something I've said, will think I went to school far beyond
the eighth grade. This impression is due entirely to my prison studies.

It had really begun back in the Charlestown Prison, when Bimbi first   4
made me feel envy of his stock of knowledge. Bimbi had always taken charge
of any conversations he was in, and I had tried to emulate him. But every
book I picked up had few sentences which didn't contain anywhere from one
to nearly all of the words that might as well have been in Chinese. When I
just skipped those words, of course, I really ended up with little idea of what
the book said. So I had come to the Norfolk Prison Colony still going through
only book-reading motions. Pretty soon, I would have quit even these motions, unless I had received the motivation that I did.

I saw that the best thing I could do was get hold of a dictionary—to   5
study, to learn some words. I was lucky enough to reason also that I should
try to improve my penmanship. It was sad. I couldn't even write in a straight
line. It was both ideas together that moved me to request a dictionary along
with some tablets and pencils from the Norfolk Prison Colony school.

I spent two days just riffling uncertainly through the dictionary's pages.   6
I'd never realized so many words existed! I didn't know *which* words I needed
to learn. Finally, just to start some kind of action, I began copying.

*Elijah Muhammad was a leader of the Black Muslims' Temple of Islam in the 1940s, 1950s, and
1960s.

In my slow, painstaking, ragged handwriting, I copied into my tablet 7
everything printed on that first page, down to the punctuation marks.

I believe it took me a day. Then, aloud, I read back, to myself, every- 8
thing I'd written on the tablet. Over and over, aloud, to myself, I read my own
handwriting.

I woke up the next morning, thinking about those words—immensely 9
proud to realize that not only had I written so much at one time, but I'd
written words that I never knew were in the world. Moreover, with a little
effort, I also could remember what many of these words meant. I reviewed
the words whose meanings I didn't remember. Funny thing, from the dictionary first page right now, that "aardvark" springs to my mind. The dictionary
had a picture of it, a long-tailed, long-eared, burrowing African mammal,
which lives off termites caught by sticking out its tongue as an anteater does
for ants.

I was so fascinated that I went on—I copied the dictionary's next page. 10
And the same experience came when I studied that. With every succeeding
page, I also learned of people and places and events from history. Actually
the dictionary is like a miniature encyclopedia. Finally the dictionary's A
section had filled a whole tablet—and I went on into the B's. That was the
way I started copying what eventually became the entire dictionary. It went
a lot faster after so much practice helped me to pick up handwriting speed.
Between what I wrote in my tablet, and writing letters, during the rest of my
time in prison I would guess I wrote a million words.

I suppose it was inevitable that as my word-base broadened, I could for 11
the first time pick up a book and read and now begin to understand what the
book was saying. Anyone who has read a great deal can imagine the new
world that opened. Let me tell you something: from then until I left that
prison, in every free moment I had, if I was not reading in the library, I was
reading on my bunk. You couldn't have gotten me out of books with a wedge.
Between Mr. Muhammad's teachings, my correspondence, my visitors—usually Ella and Reginald—and my reading of books, months passed without my
even thinking about being imprisoned. In fact, up to then, I never had been
so truly free in my life.

The Norfolk Prison Colony's library was in the school building. A 12
variety of classes was taught there by instructors who came from such places
as Harvard and Boston universities. The weekly debates between inmate
teams were also held in the school building. You would be astonished to
know how worked up convict debaters and audiences would get over subjects
like "Should Babies Be Fed Milk?"

Available on the prison library's shelves were books on just about every 13
general subject. Much of the big private collection that Parkhurst had willed
to the prison was still in crates and boxes in the back of the library—thousands of old books. Some of them looked ancient: covers faded, old-time
parchment-looking binding. Parkhurst, I've mentioned, seemed to have been
principally interested in history and religion. He had the money and the

special interest to have a lot of books that you wouldn't have in general circulation. Any college library would have been lucky to get that collection.

As you can imagine, especially in a prison where there was heavy 14 emphasis on rehabilitation, an inmate was smiled upon if he demonstrated an unusually intense interest in books. There was a sizable number of well-read inmates, especially the popular debaters. Some were said by many to be practically walking encyclopedias. They were almost celebrities. No university would ask any student to devour literature as I did when this new world opened to me, of being able to read and *understand.*

I read more in my room than in the library itself. An inmate who was 15 known to read a lot could check out more than the permitted maximum number of books. I preferred reading in the total isolation of my own room.

When I had progressed to really serious reading, every night at about 16 ten P.M. I would be outraged with the "lights out." It always seemed to catch me right in the middle of something engrossing.

Fortunately, right outside my door was a corridor light that cast a glow 17 into my room. The glow was enough to read by, once my eyes adjusted to it. So when "lights out" came, I would sit on the floor where I could continue reading in that glow.

At one-hour intervals the night guards paced past every room. Each 18 time I heard the approaching footsteps, I jumped into bed and feigned sleep. And as soon as the guard passed, I got back out of bed onto the floor area of that light-glow, where I would read for another fifty-eight minutes—until the guard approached again. That went on until three or four every morning. Three or four hours of sleep a night was enough for me. Often in the years in the streets I had slept less than that.

The teachings of Mr. Muhammad stressed how history had been "whit- 19 ened"—when white men had written history books, the black man simply had been left out. Mr. Muhammad couldn't have said anything that would have struck me much harder. I had never forgotten how when my class, me and all of those whites, had studied seventh-grade United States history back in Mason, the history of the Negro had been covered in one paragraph, and the teacher had gotten a big laugh with his joke, "Negroes' feet are so big that when they walk, they leave a hole in the ground."

This is one reason why Mr. Muhammad's teachings spread so swiftly 20 all over the United States, among *all* Negroes, whether or not they became followers of Mr. Muhammad. The teachings ring true—to every Negro. You can hardly show me a black adult in America—or a white one, for that matter—who knows from the history books anything like the truth about the black man's role. In my own case, once I heard of the "glorious history of the black man," I took special pains to hunt in the library for books that would inform me on details about black history.

I can remember accurately the very first set of books that really im- 21 pressed me. I have since bought that set of books and I have it at home for my children to read as they grow up. It's called *Wonders of the World.* It's full of pictures of archeological finds, statues that depict, usually, non-European people.

I found books like Will Durant's *Story of Civilization.* I read H. G. Wells' Outline of History. Souls of Black Folk by W. E. B. Du Bois gave me a glimpse into the black people's history before they came to this country. Carter G. Woodson's *Negro History* opened my eyes about black empires before the black slave was brought to the United States, and the early Negro struggles for freedom.

J. A. Rogers' three volumes of *Sex and Race* told about race-mixing before Christ's time; about Aesop being a black man who told fables; about Egypt's Pharaohs; about the great Coptic Christian Empires; about Ethiopia, the earth's oldest continuous black civilization, as China is the oldest continuous civilization.

Mr. Muhammad's teaching about how the white man had been created led me to *Findings in Genetics* by Gregor Mendel.* (The dictionary's G section was where I had learned what "genetics" meant.) I really studied this book by the Austrian monk. Reading it over and over, especially certain sections, helped me to understand that if you started with a black man, a white man could be produced; but starting with a white man, you never could produce a black man—because the white chromosome is recessive. And since no one disputes that there was but one Original Man, the conclusion is clear.

During the last year or so, in the *New York Times,* Arnold Toynbee used the word "bleached" in describing the white man. (His words were: "White [i.e. bleached] human beings of North European origin. . . .") Toynbee also referred to the European geographic area as only a peninsula of Asia. He said there is no such thing as Europe. And if you look at the globe, you will see for yourself that America is only an extension of Asia. (But at the same time Toynbee is among those who have helped to bleach history. He has written that Africa was the only continent that produced no history. He won't write that again. Every day now, the truth is coming to light.)

I never will forget how shocked I was when I began reading about slavery's total horror. It made such an impact upon me that it later became one of my favorite subjects when I became a minister of Mr. Muhammad's. The world's most monstrous crime, the sin and the blood on the white man's hands, are almost impossible to believe. Books like the one by Frederick Olmstead opened my eyes to the horrors suffered when the slave was landed in the United States. The European woman, Fannie Kimball, who had married a Southern white slaveowner, described how human beings were degraded. Of course I read *Uncle Tom's Cabin.* In fact, I believe that's the only novel I have ever read since I started serious reading.

Parkhurst's collection also contained some bound pamphlets of the Abolitionist Anti-Slavery Society of New England. I read descriptions of atrocities, saw those illustrations of black slave women tied up and flogged with whips; of black mothers watching their babies being dragged off, never to be seen by their mothers again; of dogs after slaves, and of the fugitive

*Gregor Mendel (1822–1884), Austrian Augustinian monk, father of genetic science.

slave catchers, evil white men with whips and clubs and chains and guns. I
read about the slave preacher Nat Turner, who put the fear of God into the
white slavemaster. Nat Turner wasn't going around preaching pie-in-the-sky
and "non-violent" freedom for the black man. There in Virginia one night
in 1831, Nat and seven other slaves started out at his master's home and
through the night they went from one plantation "big house" to the next,
killing, until by the next morning 57 white people were dead and Nat had
about 70 slaves following him. White people, terrified for their lives, fled from
their homes, locked themselves up in public buildings, hid in the woods, and
some even left the state. A small army of soldiers took two months to catch
and hang Nat Turner. Somewhere I have read where Nat Turner's example
is said to have inspired John Brown to invade Virginia and attack Harper's
Ferry nearly thirty years later, with thirteen white men and five Negroes.

I read Herodotus, "the father of History," or, rather, I read about him. 28
And I read the histories of various nations, which opened my eyes gradually,
then wider and wider, to how the whole world's white men had indeed acted
like devils, pillaging and raping and bleeding and draining the whole world's
non-white people. I remember, for instance, books such as Will Durant's *The
Story of Oriental Civilization,* and Mahatma Gandhi's accounts of the struggle to
drive the British out of India.

Book after book showed me how the white man had brought upon the 29
world's black, brown, red, and yellow peoples every variety of the sufferings
of exploitation. I saw how since the sixteenth century, the so-called "Christian trader" white man began to ply the seas in his lust for Asian and African
empires, and plunder, and power. I read, I saw, how the white man never has
gone among the non-white peoples bearing the Cross in the true manner and
spirit of Christ's teachings—meek, humble, and Christlike.

I perceived, as I read, how the collective white man had been actually 30
nothing but a piratical opportunist who used Faustian machinations to make
his own Christianity his initial wedge in criminal conquests. First, always
"religiously," he branded "heathen" and "pagan" labels upon ancient non-
white cultures and civilizations. The stage thus set, he then turned upon his
non-white victims his weapons of war.

I read how, entering India—half a *billion* deeply religious brown peo- 31
ple—the British white man, by 1759, through promises, trickery and manipu-
lations, controlled much of India through Great Britain's East India Company.
The parasitical British administration kept tentacling out to half of the sub-
continent. In 1857, some of the desperate people of India finally mutinied—
and, excepting the African slave trade, nowhere has history recorded any
more unnecessary bestial and ruthless human carnage than the British suppression of the non-white Indian people.

Over 115 million African blacks—close to the 1930's population of the 32
United States—were murdered or enslaved during the slave trade. And I read
how when the slave market was glutted, the cannibalistic white powers of
Europe next carved up, as their colonies, the richest areas of the black conti-

nent. And Europe's chancelleries for the next century played a chess game of naked exploitation and power from Cape Horn to Cairo.

Ten guards and the warden couldn't have torn me out of those books. 33 Not even Elijah Muhammad could have been more eloquent than those books were in providing indisputable proof that the collective white man had acted like a devil in virtually every contact he had with the world's collective non-white man. I listen today to the radio, and watch television, and read the headlines about the collective white man's fear and tension concerning China. When the white man professes ignorance about why the Chinese hate him so, my mind can't help flashing back to what I read, there in prison, about how the blood forebears of this same white man raped China at a time when China was trusting and helpless. Those original white "Christian traders" sent into China millions of pounds of opium. By 1839, so many of the Chinese were addicts that China's desperate government destroyed twenty thousand chests of opium. The first Opium War was promptly declared by the white man. Imagine! Declaring *war* upon someone who objects to being narcotized! The Chinese were severely beaten, with Chinese-invented gunpowder.

The Treaty of Nanking made China pay the British white man for the 34 destroyed opium; forced open China's major ports to British trade; forced China to abandon Hong Kong; fixed China's import tariffs so low that cheap British articles soon flooded in, maiming China's industrial development.

After a second Opium War, the Tientsin Treaties legalized the ravaging 35 opium trade, legalized a British-French-American control of China's customs. China tried delaying that Treaty's ratification; Peking was looted and burned.

"Kill the foreign white devils!" was the 1901 Chinese war cry in the 36 Boxer Rebellion. Losing again, this time the Chinese were driven from Peking's choicest areas. The vicious, arrogant white man put up the famous signs, "Chinese and dogs not allowed."

Red China after World War II closed its doors to the Western white 37 world. Massive Chinese agricultural, scientific, and industrial efforts are described in a book that *Life* magazine recently published. Some observers inside Red China have reported that the world never has known such a hate-white campaign as is now going on in this non-white country where, present birthrates continuing, in fifty more years Chinese will be half the earth's population. And it seems that some Chinese chickens will soon come home to roost, with China's recent successful nuclear tests.

Let us face reality. We can see in the United Nations a new world order 38 being shaped, along color lines—an alliance among the non-white nations. America's U.N. Ambassador Adlai Stevenson complained not long ago that in the United Nations "a skin game" was being played. He was right. He was facing reality. A "skin game" *is* being played. But Ambassador Stevenson sounded like Jesse James accusing the marshal of carrying a gun. Because who in the world's history ever has played a worse "skin game" than the white man?

Mr. Muhammad, to whom I was writing daily, had no idea of what a 39

new world had opened up to me through my efforts to document his teachings in books.

When I discovered philosophy, I tried to touch all the landmarks of 40
philosophical development. Gradually, I read most of the old philosophers,
Occidental and Oriental. The Oriental philosophers were the ones I came to
prefer; finally, my impression was that most Occidental philosophy had
largely been borrowed from the Oriental thinkers. Socrates, for instance,
traveled in Egypt. Some sources even say that Socrates was initiated into some
of the Egyptian mysteries. Obviously Socrates got some of his wisdom among
the East's wise men.

I have often reflected upon the new vistas that reading opened to me. 41
I knew right there in prison that reading had changed forever the course of
my life. As I see it today, the ability to read awoke inside me some long
dormant craving to be mentally alive. I certainly wasn't seeking any degree,
the way a college confers a status symbol upon its students. My homemade
education gave me, with every additional book that I read, a little bit more
sensitivity to the deafness, dumbness, and blindness that was afflicting the
black race in America. Not long ago, an English writer telephoned me from
London, asking questions. One was, "What's your alma mater?" I told him,
"Books." You will never catch me with a free fifteen minutes in which I'm
not studying something I feel might be able to help the black man.

Yesterday I spoke in London, and both ways on the plane across the 42
Atlantic I was studying a document about how the United Nations proposes
to insure the human rights of the oppressed minorities of the world. The
American black man is the world's most shameful case of minority oppression. What makes the black man think of himself as only an internal United
States issue is just a catch-phrase, two words, "civil rights." How is the black
man going to get "civil rights" before first he wins his *human* rights? If the
American black man will start thinking about his *human* rights, and then start
thinking of himself as part of one of the world's great peoples, he will see he
has a case for the United Nations.

I can't think of a better case! Four hundred years of black blood and 43
sweat invested here in America, and the white man still has the black man
begging for what every immigrant fresh off the ship can take for granted the
minute he walks down the gangplank.

But I'm digressing. I told the Englishman that my alma mater was books, 44
a good library. Every time I catch a plane, I have with me a book that I want
to read—and that's a lot of books these days. If I weren't out here every day
battling the white man, I could spend the rest of my life reading, just satisfying my curiosity—because you can hardly mention anything I'm not curious
about. I don't think anybody ever got more out of going to prison than I did.
In fact, prison enabled me to study far more intensively than I would have
if my life had gone differently and I had attended some college. I imagine that
one of the biggest troubles with colleges is there are too many distractions,
too much panty-raiding, fraternities, and boola-boola and all of that. Where

else but in a prison could I have attacked my ignorance by being able to study intensely sometimes as much as fifteen hours a day?

Questions for Discussion

1. Does it seem to you that the following accusation is metaphorically true, literally true, or simply untrue: "The collective white man had acted like a devil in virtually every contact he had with the world's collective non-white man" (¶33)? What kinds of evidence would be required to prove or disprove such a claim? Can you think of examples that would seem to bear it out or to make it doubtful? Do you think Malcolm X uses his own examples fairly or unfairly?

2. Malcolm X expresses exhilaration at "being able to read and *understand*" (¶14). Is his delight entirely political and racial? Is there a part of him that thrills *as a person* to learning, not just as someone who wants to achieve political or religious goals? What evidence can you point to? Does the distinction between "reading politically" and "reading as a person" seem useful to you?

3. Is Malcolm X's distinction between "civil rights" and "human rights" (¶42) clear to you? How would you explain the difference to someone who had not read the *Autobiography*? Must one precede the other either in time or importance?

4. How would you describe Malcolm X's tone? (*Tone* is a word commonly used to suggest tone of voice, but we shall always use it to suggest the whole range of emotions that authors share with readers.) Does he sound angry, amused, hurt, outraged, friendly, aggressive, confiding, frank? Can you think of other adjectives that come closer to his implied relation with you? What sort of reader does he seem to address? (*Note:* Throughout this text, you will find that asking about tone will be profitable, whether we remind you of it or not.)

5. In his account of Nat Turner (¶27), Malcolm X claims that Turner "put the fear of God into the white slavemaster" by killing 57 white people in one night. Is it clear whether the author approves or disapproves of this event? Would you respond differently, either to the event itself or to Malcolm X's account of it, if you knew whether the 57 murdered people were slaves or slavemasters? Field bosses? Children? Look up the life of Nat Turner in a good encyclopedia. What differences do you find between the account there and Malcolm X's? Are Malcolm X's claims about the biases of white historians relevant here?

6. In the light of what seems to be Malcolm X's purpose, does he make effective use of the Jesse James simile (¶38)? (A *simile* implies an analogy:

A is to *B* as *C* is to *D*. For instance, winter relates to mittens as summer relates to swimsuits.) Can you work out the implied analogy of the Jesse James simile? Is it persuasive?

Suggested Essay Topics

1. Make a list of the possible motives that drove Malcolm X to be such a dedicated and persistent learner: for example, ambition, love of power, greed, desire to be known as a scholar, curiosity, boredom, hope of out-smarting other people, desire to improve the world. Then study the text again to see which ones seem most strongly suggested by what the author says. Write an essay designed to convince your classmates that your view of what drove him is the most likely one.

2. On the basis of Malcolm X's essay and your own experience, define the qualities and behavior of the good student. In an essay directed to fellow students (or, if you prefer, in a letter to your parents), evaluate your own persistence and eagerness in learning, and discuss whether you are a typical or exceptional student. In the course of your discussion, try to explain Malcolm X's assertion that while learning, "months passed without my even thinking about being imprisoned. In fact, up to then, I had never been so truly free in my life" (¶11).

Adrienne Rich

Since the 1960s, women have justified increased involvement in life outside of the home by constructing "gender critiques" of many segments of American life. They have pointed out the "gender gap" in hiring, in salaries, and in promotions; they have demanded maternity leaves and maternity benefits; and they have opened up one professional field after another to which the doors had been traditionally either closed or opened to only a few. In this terse and taut essay, Adrienne Rich (b. 1929)—noted poet, teacher, essayist, and feminist—examines the purpose of a college education from an unabashed gender perspective.

In asserting, however, that women must "claim" an education, not just receive one, Rich advances at least two notions that apply equally well to all students regardless of sex. The first notion says that students must assume personal responsibility for their education by taking themselves seriously as learners; the second says that learning must be active rather than passive. As you read, try to form a clear idea of what active versus passive learning means and what responsibilities both teachers and students must meet to ensure that active learning occurs. Consider the extent to which classes on your own campus stress active learning, and cite concrete examples of occasions or decisions that exemplify Rich's idea of taking personal responsibility for one's own education.

CLAIMING AN EDUCATION

From *On Lies, Secrets, and Silence* (1977).*

For this convocation, I planned to separate my remarks into two parts: some thoughts about you, the women students here, and some thoughts about us who teach in a women's college. But ultimately, those two parts are indivisible. If university education means anything beyond the processing of human beings into expected roles, through credit hours, tests, and grades (and I believe that in a women's college especially it *might* mean much more), it implies an ethical and intellectual contract between teacher and student. This contract must remain intuitive, dynamic, unwritten; but we must turn to it again and again if learning is to be reclaimed from the depersonalizing and cheapening pressures of the present-day academic scene. 1

The first thing I want to say to you who are students, is that you cannot afford to think of being here to *receive* an education; you will do much better to think of yourselves as being here to *claim* one. One of the dictionary definitions of the verb "to claim" is: *to take as the rightful owner; to assert in the face of possible contradiction.* "To receive" is *to come into possession of; to act as receptacle or container for; to accept as authoritative or true.* The difference is that between acting and being acted-upon, and for women it can literally mean the difference between life and death. 2

One of the devastating weaknesses of university learning, of the store of knowledge and opinion that has been handed down through academic training, has been its almost total erasure of women's experience and thought from the curriculum, and its exclusion of women as members of the academic community. Today, with increasing numbers of women students in nearly every branch of higher learning, we still see very few women in the upper levels of faculty and administration in most institutions. Douglass College itself is a women's college in a university administered overwhelmingly by men, who in turn are answerable to the state legislature, again composed predominantly of men. But the most significant fact for you is that what you learn here, the very texts you read, the lectures you hear, the way your studies are divided into categories and fragmented one from the other—all this reflects, to a very large degree, neither objective reality, nor an accurate picture of the past, nor a group of rigorously tested observations about human 3

*This talk was given at the Douglass College Convocation, September 6, 1977, and first printed in *The Common Woman,* a feminist literary magazine founded by Rutgers University women in New Brunswick, New Jersey.

behavior. What you can learn here (and I mean not only at Douglass but any college in any university) is how *men* have perceived and organized their experience, their history, their ideas of social relationships, good and evil, sickness and health, etc. When you read or hear about "great issues," "major texts," "the mainstream of Western thought," you are hearing about what men, above all white men, in their male subjectivity, have decided is important.

Black and other minority peoples have for some time recognized that   4
their racial and ethnic experience was not accounted for in the studies broadly labeled human; and that even the sciences can be racist. For many reasons, it has been more difficult for women to comprehend our exclusion, and to realize that even the sciences can be sexist. For one thing, it is only within the last hundred years that higher education has grudgingly been opened up to women at all, even to white, middle-class women. And many of us have found ourselves poring eagerly over books with titles like: *The Descent of Man; Man and His Symbols; Irrational Man; The Phenomenon of Man; The Future of Man; Man and the Machine; From Man to Man; May Man Prevail?; Man, Science and Society;* or *One-Dimensional Man*—books pretending to describe a "human" reality that does not include over one-half the human species.

Less than a decade ago, with the rebirth of a feminist movement in this   5
country, women students and teachers in a number of universities began to demand and set up women's studies courses—to *claim* a woman-directed education. And, despite the inevitable accusations of "unscholarly," "group therapy," "faddism," etc., despite backlash and budget cuts, women's studies are still growing, offering to more and more women a new intellectual grasp on their lives, new understanding of our history, a fresh vision of the human experience, and also a critical basis for evaluating what they hear and read in other courses, and in the society at large.

But my talk is not really about women's studies, much as I believe in   6
their scholarly, scientific, and human necessity. While I think that any Douglass student has everything to gain by investigating and enrolling in women's studies courses, I want to suggest that there is a more essential experience that you owe yourselves, one which courses in women's studies can greatly enrich, but which finally depends on you, in all your interactions with yourself and your world. This is the experience of *taking responsibility toward yourselves*. Our upbringing as women has so often told us that this should come second to our relationships and responsibilities to other people. We have been offered ethical models of the self-denying wife and mother; intellectual models of the brilliant but slapdash dilettante who never commits herself to anything the whole way, or the intelligent woman who denies her intelligence in order to seem more "feminine," or who sits in passive silence even when she disagrees inwardly with everything that is being said around her.

Responsibility to yourself means refusing to let others do your thinking,   7
talking, and naming for you; it means learning to respect and use your own brains and instincts; hence, grappling with hard work. It means that you do not treat your body as a commodity with which to purchase superficial

intimacy or economic security; for our bodies and minds are inseparable in this life, and when we allow our bodies to be treated as objects, our minds are in mortal danger. It means insisting that those to whom you give your friendship and love are able to respect your mind. It means being able to say, with Charlotte Brontë's *Jane Eyre:* "I have an inward treasure born with me, which can keep me alive if all the extraneous delights should be withheld or offered only at a price I cannot afford to give."

Responsibility to yourself means that you don't fall for shallow and easy solutions—predigested books and ideas, weekend encounters guaranteed to change your life, taking "gut" courses instead of ones you know will challenge you, bluffing at school and life instead of doing solid work, marrying early as an escape from real decisions, getting pregnant as an evasion of already existing problems. It means that you refuse to sell your talents and aspirations short, simply to avoid conflict and confrontation. And this, in turn, means resisting the forces in society which say that women should be nice, play safe, have low professional expectations, drown in love and forget about work, live through others, and stay in the places assigned to us. It means that we insist on a life of meaningful work, insist that work be as meaningful as love and friendship in our lives. It means, therefore, the courage to be "different"; not to be continuously available to others when we need time for ourselves and our work; to be able to demand of others—parents, friends, roommates, teachers, lovers, husbands, children—that they respect our sense of purpose and our integrity as persons. Women everywhere are finding the courage to do this, more and more, and we are finding that courage both in our study of women in the past who possessed it, and in each other as we look to other women for comradeship, community, and challenge. The difference between a life lived actively, and a life of passive drifting and dispersal of energies, is an immense difference. Once we begin to feel committed to our lives, responsible to ourselves, we can never again be satisfied with the old, passive way.

Now comes the second part of the contract. I believe that in a women's college you have the right to expect your faculty to take you seriously. The education of women has been a matter of debate for centuries, and old, negative attitudes about women's role, women's ability to think and take leadership, are still rife both in and outside the university. Many male professors (and I don't mean only at Douglass) still feel that teaching in a women's college is a second-rate career. Many tend to eroticize their women students—to treat them as sexual objects—instead of demanding the best of their minds. (At Yale a legal suit [*Alexander* v. *Yale*] has been brought against the university by a group of women students demanding a stated policy against sexual advances toward female students by male professors.) Many teachers, both men and women, trained in the male-centered tradition, are still handing the ideas and texts of that tradition on to students without teaching them to criticize its antiwoman attitudes, its omission of women as part of the species. Too often, all of us fail to teach the most important thing, which is that clear thinking, active discussion, and excellent writing are all necessary for intellec-

tual freedom, and that these require *hard work.* Sometimes, perhaps in discour-
agement with a culture which is both anti-intellectual and antiwoman, we
may resign ourselves to low expectations for our students before we have
given them half a chance to become more thoughtful, expressive human
beings. We need to take to heart the words of Elizabeth Barrett Browning,
a poet, a thinking woman, and a feminist, who wrote in 1845 of her impatience with studies which cultivate a "passive recipiency" in the mind, and
asserted that "women want to be made to *think actively:* their apprehension is
quicker than that of men, but their defect lies for the most part in the logical
faculty and in the higher mental activities." Note that she implies a defect
which can be remedied by intellectual training; *not* an inborn lack of ability.

I have said that the contract on the student's part involves that you   10
demand to be taken seriously so that you can also go on taking yourself
seriously. This means seeking out criticism, recognizing that the most affirming thing anyone can do for you is demand that you push yourself
further, show you the range of what you *can* do. It means rejecting attitudes
of "take-it-easy," "why-be-so-serious," "why-worry-you'll-probably-get-
married-anyway." It means assuming your share of responsibility for what
happens in the classroom, because that affects the quality of your daily life
here. It means that the student sees herself engaged *with* her teachers in an
active, ongoing struggle for a real education. But for her to do this, her
teachers must be committed to the belief that women's minds and experience
are intrinsically valuable and indispensable to any civilization worthy the
name; that there is no more exhilarating and intellectually fertile place in the
academic world today than a women's college—*if* both students and teachers
in large enough numbers are trying to fulfill this contract. The contract is
really a pledge of mutual seriousness about women, about language, ideas,
methods, and values. It is our shared commitment toward a world in which
the inborn potentialities of so many women's minds will no longer be wasted,
raveled-away, paralyzed, or denied.

Questions for Discussion

1. Discuss with your classmates what Rich means by active and passive
   learning. Give examples of each from both high school and college. Can
   you make a list of advantages and disadvantages of each kind of learning,
   or do all the advantages fall on one side or the other? Are there different
   advantages and disadvantages for students as compared to teachers? Why
   or why not?

2. In paragraph 8 Rich lists many traits that she indirectly ascribes to women
   students in the past, traits that she advises present students to avoid. How
   many of these "traditional" traits do you and your classmates see com-

monly exhibited by the women on your campus? Do the women in your class think that female students today are more willing to take responsibility for their own education than they were in 1977, when Rich wrote her essay? Do you see any differences between men and women on this score? What kind of evidence on either side of this question can you point to?

3. Rich says in paragraph 9 that students "have the right to expect your faculty to take you seriously." Do students in your class think they *are* generally taken seriously by the faculty at your college or university? Is there any feeling among students that women are taken less seriously than men?

4. Is there any feeling among students that women find it more difficult to take *themselves* seriously? If so, what reasons can be offered to explain this phenomenon? What are the clues that a teacher does or does not take students (or students of one sex) seriously?

5. What do students do or not do that *invites* teachers to view them seriously or dismissively? How much responsibility must students accept for setting the tone of their classes? What strategies are open to students who want to influence the tone of their classes?

Suggested Essay Topics

1. In a document addressed to the students and teachers of your college or university, write up a "Contract of Serious Education" in which you (1) define "serious education," (2) state the teachers' responsibilities for making it happen, and (3) state the students' responsibilities for making it happen. Write the contract in plain, direct, forceful language, and focus on terms of such importance that you think every student and teacher in your institution should want to sign it.

2. Choose an idea, theory, concept, interpretation, or problem that you have recently encountered in one of your courses and put yourself in the position of a teacher required to teach it to a class of first-year college students. In your essay (directed to, say, your department head or someone responsible for overseeing your teaching), describe how you would go about teaching the idea or theory so that the students would engage in active rather than passive learning. If this involves asking a series of questions, make the questions part of your essay (along with an explanation of what you hope to achieve by asking them). Finally, explain why the teaching techniques you have chosen will promote active learning.

IDEAS IN DEBATE

Theodore Roosevelt
Alfred North Whitehead

Theodore Roosevelt

Theodore Roosevelt (1858–1919), twenty-sixth president of the United States, headed the government during a period of intense economic expansion and population growth. America was flexing its muscles at home and around the world. Industrialization of the economy was nearly complete, the country was crisscrossed by transcontinental railroad traffic, frontier wilderness was rapidly fading into history, and many Americans felt that expansion and opportunity would continue forever.

Within this context of energetic moneymaking and social mobility, the question of education's role in helping America realize its promise was a natural topic for the president to address. Roosevelt had a distinct theme about American education, a theme in keeping both with his own character as a robust man of action and with the emerging character of a nation that in many ways reflected his own no-nonsense, get-the-job-done temperament. His theme distinguishes "literary" training, by which he means most of what we call the liberal arts, from technical training, by which he means the kinds of skills necessary in an industrial job market. "Literary" training produces "scholars," while technical training produces citizens. As you read, try to determine whether you think this distinction adequately expresses the relationship between citizenship and education, or whether it confuses more than it clarifies. What does Roosevelt oppose to education "of the head," as he calls it? And why does he think of the different forms of education as opposed in the first place? What is the role of book learning in technical and industrial training? Why does he imply that people like workers and farmers can do without intellectual cultivation? If book learning is useful only for scholars, how useful is it really?

Roosevelt's prejudice against what we today call liberal education, the cultivation of knowledge and intellectual power for their own sake, and the corresponding prejudice in favor of what is deemed practical, are deeply rooted in American society. Roosevelt may have reinforced this prejudice, but he did not invent it. We probably have more terms of contempt for intellectuals and academics and for ideas and theory than any other society in Western culture. While "expert" is for us a term of honor, referring to the "know-how" specialist, we save terms like "pointy-headed intellectual," "egghead," "absent-minded professor," and "dry as dust" for people who spend much time in the world of books and ideas. We dismiss an idea as "merely academic" if it seems useless to us, we accuse college professors of having their "heads in the clouds" or of "living in ivory towers," and we constantly distinguish between school on the one hand and the "real world" on the other, as if nothing that happened in school had any bearing on the life that really counts, and as if the world of learning were merely a trivial corridor to something more important.

One of the reasons for reprinting Roosevelt rather than a contemporary writer is to show just how far back in time this prejudice extends and how little it has changed in at least the last eighty years. What has changed are the kinds of occupations that education today is supposed to serve. Roosevelt wanted industrial education for factory workers and farmers; we want pre-professional education for such occupations as business managers, computer experts, and communications consultants. But Roosevelt's prejudice has been handed down to us intact. Many people still view education primarily as a means of getting a head start on the employment and income ladder, not as a cultivation of mind, character, or citizenship. And if that is its purpose, then its content, or so the argument goes, ought to be limited to the skills and information the student will need as a wage-worker (Roosevelt's concern) or as a professional (today's concern). All of Roosevelt's opinions about education could be transferred into today's schools without sounding old-fashioned or out of place as long as we merely changed his "workers" and "farmers" to "professionals," and his "industrial training" to "pre-professional training." The argument about education's ends would remain undisturbed.

As you read Roosevelt, think back to the other arguments about education you have encountered: Cousins arguing that "if the main purpose of a university is job training, then the underlying philosophy of our government has little meaning" (p. 6); and Malcolm X reporting that he was so engrossed in learning that even in prison he "never had been so truly free" (p. 11). These views are quite different from Roosevelt's, though not always antithetical to his. The liberal view of education is always capacious enough to include room for technical and pre-professional education, but it denies that education should be limited to professional ends alone. Those on the other side, however, almost always want to do away with, or at least depreciate the value of, any kind of education not directly related to job skills. As you read, try to determine your own views on this important subject. If you are a freshman, you will spend much money and time obtaining your education during the next four years. Now is the time to make sure that you don't settle for less than the real thing. In the movie Auntie Mame, Mame sneers at people who never stretch their capacities: "Life is a banquet," she says, "and most poor suckers are starving to death." Students have to endure powerful vocational pressures today, but they might do well to consider whether the narrow job-skills view of education will put them in the pitiable position of sitting at the banquet of education and starving their minds because they have uncritically inherited a prejudice in favor of dry toast and weak tea.

THE WELFARE OF THE WAGE-WORKER

From Roosevelt's sixth annual message to Congress, December 3, 1906, and "The Man Who Works with His Hands," an address delivered at the Semicentennial Celebration of the Founding of Agricultural Colleges in the United States, Lansing, Michigan, May 31, 1907.

It would be impossible to overstate (though it is of course difficult quantita- 1
tively to measure) the effect upon a nation's growth to greatness of what may
be called organized patriotism, which necessarily includes the substitution of
a national feeling for mere local pride; with as a resultant a high ambition for
the whole country. No country can develop its full strength so long as the
parts which make up the whole each put a feeling of loyalty to the part above
the feeling of loyalty to the whole. This is true of sections and it is just as
true of classes. The industrial and agricultural classes must work together,
capitalists and wage-workers must work together, if the best work of which
the country is capable is to be done. It is probable that a thoroughly efficient
system of education comes next to the influence of patriotism in bringing
about national success of this kind. Our Federal form of government, so
fruitful of advantage to our people in certain ways, in other ways undoubtedly limits our national effectiveness. It is not possible, for instance, for the
National Government to take the lead in technical industrial education, to see
that the public-school system of this country develops on all its technical,
industrial, scientific, and commercial sides. This must be left primarily to the
several States. Nevertheless, the National Government has control of the
schools of the District of Columbia, and it should see that these schools
promote and encourage the fullest development of the scholars in both commercial and industrial training. The commercial training should in one of its
branches deal with foreign trade. The industrial training is even more important. It should be one of our prime objects as a nation, so far as feasible,
constantly to work toward putting the mechanic, the wage-worker who
works with his hands, on a higher plane of efficiency and reward, so as to
increase his effectiveness in the economic world, and the dignity, the remuneration, and the power of his position in the social world. Unfortunately, at
present the effect of some of the work in the public schools is in the exactly
opposite direction. If boys and girls are trained merely in literary accomplishments, to the total exclusion of industrial, manual, and technical training, the
tendency is to unfit them for industrial work and to make them reluctant to
go into it, or unfitted to do well if they do go into it. This is a tendency which
should be strenuously combated. Our industrial development depends
largely upon technical education, including in this term all industrial education, from that which fits a man to be a good mechanic, a good carpenter, or
blacksmith, to that which fits a man to do the greatest engineering feat. The
skilled mechanic, the skilled workman, can best become such by technical
industrial education. The far-reaching usefulness of institutes of technology

and schools of mines or of engineering is now universally acknowledged, and no less far-reaching is the effect of a good building or mechanical trades-school, a textile, or watchmaking, or engraving school. All such training must develop not only manual dexterity but industrial intelligence. In international rivalry this country does not have to fear the competition of pauper labor as much as it has to fear the educated labor of specially trained competitors; and we should have the education of the hand, eye, and brain which will fit us to meet such competition.

In every possible way we should help the wage-worker who toils with his hands and who must (we hope in a constantly increasing measure) also toil with his brain. Under the Constitution the national legislature can do but little of direct importance for his welfare save where he is engaged in work which permits it to act under the interstate commerce clause of the Constitution; and this is one reason why I so earnestly hope that both the legislative and judicial branches of the government will construe this clause of the Constitution in the broadest possible manner. We can, however, in such a matter as industrial training, in such a matter as child-labor and factory laws, set an example to the States by enacting the most advanced legislation that can wisely be enacted for the District of Columbia.

The only other persons whose welfare is as vital to the welfare of the whole country as is the welfare of the wage-workers, are the tillers of the soil, the farmers. It is a mere truism to say that no growth of cities, no growth of wealth, no industrial development can atone for any falling off in the character and standing of the farming population. During the last few decades this fact has been recognized with ever-increasing clearness. There is no longer any failure to realize that farming, at least in certain branches, must become a technical and scientific profession. This means that there must be open to farmers the chance for technical and scientific training, not theoretical merely but of the most severely practical type. The farmer represents a peculiarly high type of American citizenship, and he must have the same chance to rise and develop as other American citizens have. Moreover, it is exactly as true of the farmer, as it is of the business man and the wage-worker, that the ultimate success of the nation of which he forms a part must be founded not alone on material prosperity but upon high moral, mental, and physical development. This education of the farmer—self-education by preference, but also education from the outside, as with all other men—is peculiarly necessary here in the United States, where the frontier conditions even in the newest States have now nearly vanished, where there must be a substitution of a more intensive system of cultivation for the old wasteful farm management, and where there must be a better business organization among the farmers themselves.

Several factors must co-operate in the improvement of the farmer's condition. He must have the chance to be educated in the widest possible sense—in the sense which keeps ever in view the intimate relationship between the theory of education and the facts of life. In all education we should widen our aims.* It is a good thing to produce a certain number of trained scholars and students; but the education superintended by the State must seek rather to produce a hundred good citizens than merely one scholar, and it must be turned now and then from the class-book to the study of the great book of nature itself. This is especially true of the farmer, as has been pointed out again and again by all observers most competent to pass practical judgment on the problems of our country life. All students now realize that education must seek to train the executive powers of young people and to confer more real significance upon the phrase "dignity of labor," and to prepare the pupils so that, in addition to each developing in the highest degree his individual capacity for work, they may together help create a right public opinion, and show in many ways social and co-operative spirit.

. . .

As a people there is nothing in which we take a juster pride than our   5 educational system. It is our boast that every boy or girl has the chance to get a school training; and we feel it is a prime national duty to furnish this training free, because only thereby can we secure the proper type of citizenship in the average American. Our public schools and our colleges have done their work well, and there is no class of our citizens deserving of heartier praise than the men and women who teach in them.

Nevertheless, for at least a generation we have been waking to the   6 knowledge that there must be additional education beyond that provided in the public school as it is managed to-day. Our school system has hitherto been well-nigh wholly lacking on the side of industrial training, of the training which fits a man for the shop and the farm. This is a most serious lack, for no one can look at the peoples of mankind as they stand at present without realizing that industrial training is one of the most potent factors in national development. We of the United States must develop a system under which each individual citizen shall be trained so as to be effective individually as an economic unit, and fit to be organized with his fellows so that he and they can work in efficient fashion together. This question is vital to our future progress, and public attention should be focussed upon it. Surely it is eminently in accord with the principles of our democratic life that we should furnish the highest average industrial training for the ordinary skilled workman. But it is a curious thing that in industrial training we have tended to devote our energies to producing high-grade men at the top rather than in the ranks. Our engineering schools, for instance, compare favorably with the best in Europe, whereas we have done almost nothing to equip the private soldiers of the industrial army—the mechanic, the metal-worker, the carpenter. Indeed, too often our schools train away from the shop and the forge; and this fact, together with the abandonment of the old apprentice system, has re-

*In talking about education today, we would probably take "widen our aims" to mean more liberal arts courses and fewer programs made up of exclusively technical or pre-professional courses. Roosevelt means exactly the opposite: "widen our aims" means less academic work and more pre-professional and technical training.

sulted in such an absence of facilities for providing trained journeymen that in many of our trades almost all the recruits among the workmen are foreigners. Surely this means that there must be some systematic method provided for training young men in the trades, and that this must be co-ordinated with the public-school system. No industrial school can turn out a finished journeyman; but it can furnish the material out of which a finished journeyman can be made, just as an engineering school furnishes the training which enables its graduates speedily to become engineers. . . .

We have been fond as a nation of speaking of the dignity of labor,   7
meaning thereby manual labor. Personally I don't think that we begin to understand what a high place manual labor should take; and it never can take this high place unless it offers scope for the best type of man. We have tended to regard education as a matter of the head only, and the result is that a great many of our people, themselves the sons of men who worked with their hands, seem to think that they rise in the world if they get into a position where they do no hard manual work whatever; where their hands will grow soft, and their working clothes will be kept clean. Such a conception is both false and mischievous. There are, of course, kinds of labor where the work must be purely mental, and there are other kinds of labor where, under existing conditions, very little demand indeed is made upon the mind, though I am glad to say that I think the proportion of men engaged in this kind of work is diminishing. But in any healthy community, in any community with the great solid qualities which alone make a really great nation, the bulk of the people should do work which makes demands upon both the body and the mind. Progress cannot permanently consist in the abandonment of physical labor, but in the development of physical labor so that it shall represent more and more the work of the trained mind in the trained body. To provide such training, to encourage in every way the production of the men whom it alone can produce is to show that as a nation we have a true conception of the dignity and importance of labor. The calling of the skilled tiller of the soil, the calling of the skilled mechanic, should alike be recognized as professions, just as emphatically as the callings of lawyer, of doctor, of banker, merchant, or clerk. The printer, the electrical worker, the house-painter, the foundryman, should be trained just as carefully as the stenographer or the drug clerk. They should be trained alike in head and in hand. They should get over the idea that to earn twelve dollars a week and call it "salary" is better than to earn twenty-five dollars a week and call it "wages." The young man who has the courage and the ability to refuse to enter the crowded field of the so-called professions and to take to constructive industry is almost sure of an ample reward in earnings, in health, in opportunity to marry early, and to establish a home with reasonable freedom from worry. We need the training, the manual dexterity and industrial intelligence, which can be best given in a good agricultural, or building, or textile, or watchmaking, or engraving, or mechanical school. It should be one of our prime objects to put the mechanic, the wage-worker who works with his hands, and who ought to work in a constantly larger degree with his head, on a higher plane of

efficiency and reward, so as to increase his effectiveness in the economic world, and therefore the dignity, the remuneration, and the power of his position in the social world. To train boys and girls in merely literary accomplishments to the total exclusion of industrial, manual, and technical training, tends to unfit them for industrial work; and in real life most work is industrial.

The problem of furnishing well-trained craftsmen, or rather journey-   8
men fitted in the end to become such, is not simple—few problems are simple in the actual process of their solution—and much care and forethought and practical common sense will be needed, in order to work it out in a fairly satisfactory manner. It should appeal to all our citizens. I am glad that societies have already been formed to promote industrial education, and that their membership includes manufacturers and leaders of labor-unions, educators and publicists, men of all conditions who are interested in education and in industry. It is such co-operation that offers most hope for a satisfactory solution of the question as to what is the best form of industrial school, as to the means by which it may be articulated with the public-school system, and as to the way to secure for the boys trained therein the opportunity to acquire in the industries the practical skill which alone can make them finished journeymen. . . .

Agricultural colleges and farmers' institutes have done much in instruc-   9
tion and inspiration; they have stood for the nobility of labor and the necessity of keeping the muscles and the brain in training for industry. They have developed technical departments of high practical value. They seek to provide for the people on the farms an equipment so broad and thorough as to fit them for the highest requirements of our citizenship; so that they can establish and maintain country homes of the best type, and create and sustain a country civilization more than equal to that of the city. The men they train must be able to meet the strongest business competition, at home or abroad, and they can do this only if they are trained not alone in the various lines of husbandry but in successful economic management. These colleges, like the State experiment stations, should carefully study and make known the needs of each section, and should try to provide remedies for what is wrong.

The education to be obtained in these colleges should create as intimate   10
a relationship as is possible between the theory of learning and the facts of actual life. Educational establishments should produce highly trained scholars, of course; but in a country like ours, where the educational establishments are so numerous, it is folly to think that their main purpose is to produce these highly trained scholars. Without in the least disparaging scholarship and learning—on the contrary, while giving hearty and ungrudging admiration and support to the comparatively few whose primary work should be creative scholarship—it must be remembered that the ordinary graduate of our colleges should be and must be primarily a man and not a scholar. Education should not confine itself to books. It must train executive power, and try to create that right public opinion which is the most potent factor in the proper solution of all political and social questions. Book-

learning is very important, but it is by no means everything; and we shall never get the right idea of education until we definitely understand that a man may be well trained in book-learning and yet, in the proper sense of the word, and for all practical purposes, be utterly uneducated; while a man of comparatively little book-learning may, nevertheless, in essentials, have a good education.

Questions for Discussion

1. If you have ever felt like objecting to what Roosevelt calls "literary" courses—liberal arts courses such as literature, history, philosophy, and languages—on the grounds that they just aren't "useful," go back over the other selections in this chapter, including Whitehead (who follows Roosevelt), and see if you and your classmates can come up with defenses for these kinds of courses, either by using an enlarged notion of usefulness or by arguing that usefulness is not the only relevant criterion.

2. What is revealed about the nature of Roosevelt's prejudices by his curious distinction in paragraph 4 between "trained scholars and students" on the one hand and "good citizens" on the other? "The State," he contends, "must seek rather to produce a hundred good citizens than merely one scholar." What is he supposing about the nature of each that justifies his placing them in opposition like this? Do you think his suppositions are justified? Can you think of good reasons why the trained scholar might be not just a good citizen but potentially a superior one? (He creates another curious distinction in paragraph 10 when he says, "It must be remembered that the ordinary graduate of our colleges should be and must be primarily a man and not a scholar.") Can you state his prejudice against scholars in your own words? Do you hear this same prejudice repeated today?

3. In paragraph 6 Roosevelt takes a tone that suggests that skills training—technical education in general—is the underdog and that he is trying to make more room in the typical curriculum for it against the dominance of "literary" studies. Do the studies that Roosevelt calls literary still dominate education today, or has the trend he points to been reversed? Has education been improved by developments since Roosevelt's day? Has society been well- or ill-served by the decline of liberal education and the dominance of pre-professional education (at the high school and college levels)?

4. If we substitute modern terms for Roosevelt's terms in the last sentence of paragraph 7, do his remarks here sound like comments that you could hear on your campus any day of the week? "Merely literary accomplishments . . . tend to unfit [students] for professional work; and in real life

most work is [professional]." Can you provide any evidence to suggest that this statement is simply not true? And can you find good reasons to object to education's being excluded from the "real world"? Do you object to having your life as a student called unreal simply because you may not yet be a homeowner, taxpayer, or full-time employee? (Of course many of you are all three of these things, and some of you are, in addition, parents, sometimes single parents, and you are pursuing an education as well. You of course know that all these activities are part of the real world.) If student life is not real, what is it and why do you have to pay so much for it?

Suggested Essay Topics

1. If you have ever heard your teachers, counselors, parents, or anyone else use the expression "the real world" in such a way as to imply that students are outside of it, select one such person and write him or her a persuasive letter challenging the use of the expression, the assumptions behind it, and the implications that follow from it. You will want to know, among other things, what the possible criteria for "real" are in this kind of usage, and, since society is urging you on the one hand to get an education, why it takes such a dismissive view of that education on the other.

2. The kind of job-skills education recommended by Roosevelt has pretty nearly become the rule for certain kinds of professional programs such as those in medical schools. Alfred North Whitehead, a prominent philosopher whose essay follows, thinks that this narrow kind of education has become a disaster both for the colleges that give it and the students who take it. After you have read Whitehead's essay, write a dialogue in which you portray Whitehead and Roosevelt debating this point. Give each the best arguments you can, and make clear at the end whether one has won or whether they have come to a draw.

Alfred North Whitehead

An English philosopher and mathematician, instructor of Bertrand Russell and later Russell's co-author on the Principia Mathematica, *and founder of a mode of thought called "process philosophy" (influential on scientists, philosophers, and theologians alike), Alfred North Whitehead (1861–1947) remains one of those figures in our day—like Plato, Aquinas, Kant, or Coleridge in earlier centuries—who seems to have become established as a permanent and almost official instructor of mankind. His technical writings, as in* Process and Reality, *are forbiddingly difficult, but his general writings, as in this piece, combine great depth of thought with a delightful clarity of style. Perhaps no one will ever find*

Whitehead easy to read; as he says in paragraph 11, "If it were easy, the book ought to be burned." But he has the kind of clarity we all seek, and his style is no more difficult than his ideas themselves require.

As you work through his ideas about the aims of education, compare his description of a genuine education with an accurate description of your own education, both past and present, and with the aims of education as presented to you by your parents and high school counselors or teachers. You might use his essay as a source of new ideas about what is happening to you and your fellow students this year.

His main concerns seem to be (1) that whatever we learn should be truly useful (he takes pains to define what useful means to us now, in a present that contains both the past and the future), (2) that all learning should constantly shift back and forth between general and specialized knowledge, and (3) that studying anything merely to pass a standardized exam kills all real learning.

THE AIMS OF EDUCATION

From *"The Aims of Education" and Other Essays* (1929).

Culture is activity of thought, and receptiveness to beauty and humane feeling. Scraps of information have nothing to do with it. A merely well-informed man is the most useless bore on God's earth. What we should aim at producing is men who possess both culture and expert knowledge in some special direction. Their expert knowledge will give them the ground to start from, and their culture will lead them as deep as philosophy and as high as art. We have to remember that the valuable intellectual development is self-development, and that it mostly takes place between the ages of sixteen and thirty. As to training, the most important part is given by mothers before the age of twelve. A saying due to Archbishop Temple illustrates my meaning. Surprise was expressed at the success in after-life of a man, who as a boy at Rugby had been somewhat undistinguished. He answered, "It is not what they are at eighteen, it is what they become afterwards that matters." 1

In training a child to activity of thought, above all things we must beware of what I will call "inert ideas"—that is to say, ideas that are merely received into the mind without being utilized, or tested, or thrown into fresh combinations. 2

In the history of education, the most striking phenomenon is that schools of learning, which at one epoch are alive with a ferment of genius, in a succeeding generation exhibit merely pedantry and routine. The reason is, that they are overladen with inert ideas. Education with inert ideas is not only useless: it is, above all things, harmful—*Corruptio optimi, pessima* [The corruption of the best is the worst]. Except at rare intervals of intellectual ferment, education in the past has been radically infected with inert ideas. That is the reason why uneducated clever women, who have seen much of the world, are in middle life so much the most cultured part of the community. They have been saved from this horrible burden of inert ideas. Every 3 intellectual revolution which has ever stirred humanity into greatness has been a passionate protest against inert ideas. Then, alas, with pathetic ignorance of human psychology, it has proceeded by some educational scheme to bind humanity afresh with inert ideas of its own fashioning.

Let us now ask how in our system of education we are to guard against   4
this mental dryrot. We enunciate two educational commandments, "Do not teach too many subjects," and again, "What you teach, teach thoroughly."

The result of teaching small parts of a large number of subjects is the   5
passive reception of disconnected ideas, not illumined with any spark of vitality. Let the main ideas which are introduced into a child's education be few and important, and let them be thrown into every combination possible. The child should make them his own, and should understand their application here and now in the circumstances of his actual life. From the very beginning of his education, the child should experience the joy of discovery. The discovery which he has to make, is that general ideas give an understanding of that stream of events which pours through his life, which is his life. By understanding I mean more than a mere logical analysis, though that is included. I mean "understanding" in the sense in which it is used in the French proverb, "To understand all, is to forgive all." Pedants sneer at an education which is useful. But if education is not useful, what is it? Is it a talent, to be hidden away in a napkin? Of course, education should be useful, whatever your aim in life. It was useful to Saint Augustine and it was useful to Napoleon. It is useful, because understanding is useful.

I pass lightly over that understanding which should be given by the   6
literary side of education.* Nor do I wish to be supposed to pronounce on the relative merits of a classical or a modern curriculum. I would only remark that the understanding which we want is an understanding of an insistent present. The only use of a knowledge of the past is to equip us for the present. No more deadly harm can be done to young minds than by depreciation of the present. The present contains all that there is. It is holy ground; for it is the past, and it is the future.† At the same time it must be observed that an age is no less past if it existed two hundred years ago than if it existed two thousand years ago. Do not be deceived by the pedantry of dates. The ages of Shakespeare and of Molière are no less past than are the ages of Sophocles and of Virgil. The communion of saints is a great and inspiring assemblage, but it has only one possible hall of meeting, and that is, the present; and the mere lapse of time through which any particular group of saints must travel to reach that meeting-place, makes very little difference.

Passing now to the scientific and logical side of education, we remember   7
that here also ideas which are not utilised are positively harmful. By utilising an idea, I mean relating it to that stream, compounded of sense perceptions,

---

*By passing "lightly" over the "literary side of education," Whitehead is referring to what *we* would call "the humanities," especially literature, philosophy, history, and languages. He largely ignores these and discusses mainly scientific and mathematical examples because, first, he was himself a mathematician and, second, his audience was the Mathematical Association.

†See Karl Popper's treatment of this same idea in "Utopia and Violence," pp. 79–80, ¶34–37.

feelings, hopes, desires, and of mental activities adjusting thought to thought, which forms our life. I can imagine a set of beings which might fortify their souls by passively reviewing disconnected ideas. Humanity is not built that way—except perhaps some editors of newspapers.

In scientific training, the first thing to do with an idea is to prove it. But allow me for one moment to extend the meaning of "prove"; I mean—to prove its worth. Now an idea is not worth much unless the propositions in which it is embodied are true. Accordingly an essential part of the proof of an idea is the proof, either by experiment or by logic, of the truth of the propositions. But it is not essential that this proof of the truth should constitute the first introduction to the idea. After all, its assertion by the authority of respectable teachers is sufficient evidence to begin with. In our first contact with a set of propositions, we commence by appreciating their importance. That is what we all do in after-life. We do not attempt, in the strict sense, to prove or to disprove anything, unless its importance makes it worthy of that honour. These two processes of proof, in the narrow sense, and of appreciation, do not require a rigid separation in time. Both can be proceeded with nearly concurrently. But in so far as either process must have the priority, it should be that of appreciation by use.

Furthermore, we should not endeavour to use propositions in isolation. Emphatically I do not mean, a neat little set of experiments to illustrate Proposition I and then the proof of Proposition I, a neat little set of experiments to illustrate Proposition II and then the proof of Proposition II, and so on to the end of the book. Nothing could be more boring. Interrelated truths are utilised *en bloc,* and the various propositions are employed in any order, and with any reiteration. Choose some important applications of your theoretical subject; and study them concurrently with the systematic theoretical exposition. Keep the theoretical exposition short and simple, but let it be strict and rigid so far as it goes. It should not be too long for it to be easily known with thoroughness and accuracy. The consequences of a plethora of half-digested theoretical knowledge are deplorable.* Also the theory should not be muddled up with the practice. The child should have no doubt when it is proving and when it is utilising. My point is that what is proved should be utilised, and that what is utilised should—so far as is practicable—be proved. I am far from asserting that proof and utilisation are the same thing.

At this point of my discourse, I can most directly carry forward my argument in the outward form of a digression. We are only just realising that the art and science of education require a genius and a study of their own; and that this genius and this science are more than a bare knowledge of some branch of science or of literature. This truth was partially perceived in the past generation; and headmasters, somewhat crudely, were apt to supersede learning in their colleagues by requiring left-hand bowling and a taste for football. But culture is more than cricket, and more than football, and more than extent of knowledge.

*Recall the epigraph from Alexander Pope, "A little learning is a dangerous thing" (p. 3.)

Education is the acquisition of the art of the utilisation of knowledge.   11
This is an art very difficult to impart. Whenever a textbook is written of real
educational worth, you may be quite certain that some reviewer will say that
it will be difficult to teach from it. Of course it will be difficult to teach from
it. If it were easy, the book ought to be burned; for it cannot be educational.
In education, as elsewhere, the broad primrose path leads to a nasty place.
This evil path is represented by a book or a set of lectures which will practically enable the student to learn by heart all the questions likely to be asked
at the next external examination.* And I may say in passing that no educational system is possible unless every question directly asked of a pupil at any
examination is either framed or modified by the actual teacher of that pupil
in that subject. The external assessor may report on the curriculum or on the
performance of the pupils, but never should be allowed to ask the pupil a
question which has not been strictly supervised by the actual teacher, or at
least inspired by a long conference with him. There are a few exceptions to
this rule, but they are exceptions, and could easily be allowed for under the
general rule.

We now return to my previous point, that theoretical ideas should   12
always find important applications within the pupil's curriculum. This is not
an easy doctrine to apply, but a very hard one. It contains within itself the
problem of keeping knowledge alive, of preventing it from becoming inert,
which is the central problem of all education.

The best procedure will depend on several factors, none of which can   13
be neglected, namely, the genius of the teacher, the intellectual type of the
pupils, their prospects in life, the opportunities offered by the immediate
surroundings of the school, and allied factors of this sort. It is for this reason
that the uniform external examination is so deadly. We do not denounce it
because we are cranks, and like denouncing established things. We are not
so childish. Also, of course, such examinations have their use in testing
slackness. Our reason of dislike is very definite and very practical. It kills the
best part of culture. When you analyse in the light of experience the central
task of education, you find that its successful accomplishment depends on a
delicate adjustment of many variable factors. The reason is that we are dealing with human minds, and not with dead matter. The evocation of curiosity,
of judgment, of the power of mastering a complicated tangle of circumstances, the use of theory in giving foresight in special cases—all these powers
are not to be imparted by a set rule embodied in one schedule of examination
subjects.

I appeal to you, as practical teachers. With good discipline, it is always   14
possible to pump into the minds of a class a certain quantity of inert knowledge. You take a text-book and make them learn it. So far, so good. The child
then knows how to solve a quadratic equation. But what is the point of
teaching a child to solve a quadratic equation? There is a traditional answer

*External examinations are standardized tests administered by state employees, school inspec-
tors, who are "external" to the school where they give the tests.

to this question. It runs thus: The mind is an instrument, you first sharpen it, and then use it; the acquisition of the power of solving a quadratic equation is part of the process of sharpening the mind. Now there is just enough truth in this answer to have made it live through the ages. But for all its half-truth, it embodies a radical error which bids fair to stifle the genius of the modern world. I do not know who was first responsible for this analogy of the mind to a dead instrument. For aught I know, it may have been one of the seven wise men of Greece, or a committee of the whole lot of them. Whoever was the originator, there can be no doubt of the authority which it has acquired by the continuous approval bestowed upon it by eminent persons. But whatever its weight of authority, whatever the high approval which it can quote, I have no hesitation in denouncing it as one of the most fatal, erroneous, and dangerous conceptions ever introduced into the theory of education. The mind is never passive; it is a perpetual activity, delicate, receptive, responsive to stimulus. You cannot postpone its life until you have sharpened it. Whatever interest attaches to your subject-matter must be evoked here and now; whatever powers you are strengthening in the pupil, must be exercised here and now; whatever possibilities of mental life your teaching should impart, must be exhibited here and now. That is the golden rule of education, and a very difficult rule to follow.

The difficulty is just this: the apprehension of general ideas, intellectual ¹⁵ habits of mind, and pleasurable interest in mental achievement can be evoked by no form of words, however accurately adjusted. All practical teachers know that education is a patient process of the mastery of details, minute by minute, hour by hour, day by day. There is no royal road to learning through an airy path of brilliant generalisations. There is a proverb about the difficulty of seeing the wood because of the trees. That difficulty is exactly the point which I am enforcing. The problem of education is to make the pupil see the wood by means of the trees.

The solution which I am urging, is to eradicate the fatal disconnection ¹⁶ of subjects which kills the vitality of our modern curriculum. There is only one subject-matter for education, and that is Life in all its manifestations. Instead of this single unity, we offer children—Algebra, from which nothing follows; Geometry, from which nothing follows; Science, from which nothing follows; History, from which nothing follows; a Couple of Languages, never mastered; and lastly, most dreary of all, Literature, represented by plays of Shakespeare, with philological notes and short analyses of plot and character to be in substance committed to memory. Can such a list be said to represent Life, as it is known in the midst of the living of it? The best that can be said of it is, that it is a rapid table of contents which a deity might run over in his mind while he was thinking of creating a world, and has not yet determined how to put it together.

Let us now return to quadratic equations. We still have on hand the ¹⁷ unanswered question. Why should children be taught their solution? Unless quadratic equations fit into a connected curriculum, of course there is no reason to teach anything about them. Furthermore, extensive as should be the place of mathematics in a complete culture, I am a little doubtful whether for many types of boys algebraic solutions of quadratic equations do not lie on the specialist side of mathematics. I may here remind you that as yet I have not said anything of the psychology or the content of the specialism, which is so necessary a part of an ideal education. But all that is an evasion of our real question, and I merely state it in order to avoid being misunderstood in my answer.

Quadratic equations are part of algebra, and algebra is the intellectual 18
instrument which has been created for rendering clear the quantitative aspects of the world. There is no getting out of it. Through and through the world is infected with quantity. To talk sense, is to talk in quantities. It is no use saying that the nation is large,—How large? It is no use saying that radium is scarce,—How scarce? You cannot evade quantity. You may fly to poetry and to music, and quantity and number will face you in your rhythms and your octaves. Elegant intellects which despise the theory of quantity, are but half developed. They are more to be pitied than blamed. The scraps of gibberish, which in their school-days were taught to them in the name of algebra, deserve some contempt.

This question of the degeneration of algebra into gibberish, both in 19
word and in fact, affords a pathetic instance of the uselessness of reforming educational schedules without a clear conception of the attributes which you wish to evoke in the living minds of the children. A few years ago there was an outcry that school algebra was in need of reform, but there was a general agreement that graphs would put everything right. So all sorts of things were extruded, and graphs were introduced. So far as I can see, with no sort of idea behind them, but just graphs. Now every examination paper has one or two questions on graphs. Personally I am an enthusiastic adherent of graphs. But I wonder whether as yet we have gained very much. You cannot put life into any schedule of general education unless you succeed in exhibiting its relation to some essential characteristic of all intelligent or emotional perception. It is a hard saying, but it is true; and I do not see how to make it any easier. In making these little formal alterations you are beaten by the very nature of things. You are pitted against too skilful an adversary, who will see to it that the pea is always under the other thimble.

Reformation must begin at the other end. First, you must make up your 20
mind as to those quantitative aspects of the world which are simple enough to be introduced into general education; then a schedule of algebra should be framed which will find its exemplification in these applications. We need not fear for our pet graphs, they will be there in plenty when we once begin to treat algebra as a serious means of studying the world. Some of the simplest applications will be found in the quantities which occur in the simplest study of society. The curves of history are more vivid and more informing than the dry catalogues of names and dates which comprise the greater part of that arid school study. What purpose is effected by a catalogue of undistinguished kings and queens? Tom, Dick, or Harry, they are all dead. General resurrections are failures, and are better postponed. The quantitative flux of the forces

of modern society is capable of very simple exhibition. Meanwhile, the idea of the variable, of the function, of rate of change, of equations and their solution, of elimination, are being studied as an abstract science for their own sake. Not, of course, in the pompous phrases with which I am alluding to them here, but with that iteration of simple special cases proper to teaching.

If this course be followed, the route from Chaucer to the Black Death, 21 from the Black Death to modern Labour troubles, will connect the tales of the medieval pilgrims with the abstract science of algebra, both yielding diverse aspects of that single theme, Life. I know what most of you are thinking at this point. It is that the exact course which I have sketched out is not the particular one which you would have chosen, or even see how to work. I quite agree. I am not claiming that I could do it myself. But your objection is the precise reason why a common external examination system* is fatal to education. The process of exhibiting the applications of knowledge must, for its success, essentially depend on the character of the pupils and the genius of the teacher. Of course I have left out the easiest applications with which most of us are more at home. I mean the quantitative sides of sciences, such as mechanics and physics.

. . .

I must beg you to remember what I have been insisting on above. In the 22 first place, one train of thought will not suit all groups of children. For example, I should expect that artisan children will want something more concrete and, in a sense, swifter than I have set down here. Perhaps I am wrong, but that is what I should guess. In the second place, I am not contemplating one beautiful lecture stimulating, once and for all, an admiring class. That is not the way in which education proceeds. No; all the time the pupils are hard at work solving examples, drawing graphs, and making experiments, until they have a thorough hold on the whole subject. I am describing the interspersed explanations, the directions which should be given to their thoughts. The pupils have got to be made to feel that they are studying something, and are not merely executing intellectual minuets.

Finally, if you are teaching pupils for some general examination, the 23 problem of sound teaching is greatly complicated. Have you ever noticed the zig-zag moulding round a Norman arch? The ancient work is beautiful, the modern work is hideous. The reason is, that the modern work is done to exact measure, the ancient work is varied according to the idiosyncrasy of the workman. Here it is crowded, and there it is expanded. Now the essence of getting pupils through examinations is to give equal weight to all parts of the schedule. But mankind is naturally specialist. One man sees a whole subject, where another can find only a few detached examples. I know that it seems contradictory to allow for specialism in a curriculum especially designed for a broad culture. Without contradictions the world would be simpler, and

*Common external exams are what Americans call "standardized exams"—tests made out by government employees or professional committees and administered to students on a mass scale ("in common").

perhaps duller. But I am certain that in education wherever you exclude specialism you destroy life.

. . .

Fortunately, the specialist side of education presents an easier problem 24 than does the provision of a general culture. For this there are many reasons. One is that many of the principles of procedure to be observed are the same in both cases, and it is unnecessary to recapitulate. Another reason is that specialist training takes place—or should take place—at a more advanced stage of the pupil's course, and thus there is easier material to work upon. But undoubtedly the chief reason is that the specialist study is normally a study of peculiar interest to the student. He is studying it because, for some reason, he wants to know it. This makes all the difference. The general culture is designed to foster an activity of mind; the specialist course utilises this activity. But it does not do to lay too much stress on these neat antitheses. As we have already seen, in the general course foci of special interest will arise; and similarly in the special study, the external connections of the subject drag thought outwards.

Again, there is not one course of study which merely gives general 25 culture, and another which gives special knowledge. The subjects pursued for the sake of a general education are special subjects specially studied; and, on the other hand, one of the ways of encouraging general mental activity is to foster a special devotion. You may not divide the seamless coat of learning. What education has to impart is an intimate sense for the power of ideas, for the beauty of ideas, and for the structure of ideas, together with a particular body of knowledge which has peculiar reference to the life of the being possessing it.

The appreciation of the structure of ideas is that side of a cultured mind 26 which can only grow under the influence of a special study. I mean that eye for the whole chess-board, for the bearing of one set of ideas on another. Nothing but a special study can give any appreciation for the exact formulation of general ideas, for their relations when formulated, for their service in the comprehension of life. A mind so disciplined should be both more abstract and more concrete. It has been trained in the comprehension of abstract thought and in the analysis of facts.

Finally, there should grow the most austere of all mental qualities; I 27 mean the sense for style. It is an aesthetic sense, based on admiration for the direct attainment of a foreseen end, simply and without waste. Style in art, style in literature, style in science, style in logic, style in practical execution have fundamentally the same aesthetic qualities, namely, attainment and restraint. The love of a subject in itself and for itself, where it is not the sleepy pleasure of pacing a mental quarter-deck, is the love of style as manifested in that study.

Here we are brought back to the position from which we started, the 28 utility of education. Style, in its finest sense, is the last acquirement of the educated mind; it is also the most useful. It pervades the whole being. The administrator with a sense for style hates waste; the engineer with a sense for style economises his material; the artisan with a sense for style prefers good work. Style is the ultimate morality of mind.

But above style, and above knowledge, there is something, a vague 29 shape like fate above the Greek gods. That something is Power. Style is the fashioning of power, the restraining of power. But, after all, the power of attainment of the desired end is fundamental. The first thing is to get there. Do not bother about your style, but solve your problem, justify the ways of God to man, administer your province, or do whatever else is set before you.

Where, then, does style help? In this, with style the end is attained 30 without side issues, without raising undesirable inflammations. With style you attain your end and nothing but your end. With style the effect of your activity is calculable, and foresight is the last gift of gods to men. With style your power is increased, for your mind is not distracted with irrelevancies, and you are more likely to attain your object. Now style is the exclusive privilege of the expert. Whoever heard of the style of an amateur painter, of the style of an amateur poet? Style is always the product of specialist study, the peculiar contribution of specialism to culture.

English education in its present phase suffers from a lack of definite aim, 31 and from an external machinery which kills its vitality. Hitherto in this address I have been considering the aims which should govern education. In this respect England halts between two opinions. It has not decided whether to produce amateurs or experts. The profound change in the world which the nineteenth century has produced is that the growth of knowledge has given foresight. The amateur is essentially a man with appreciation and with immense versatility in mastering a given routine. But he lacks the foresight which comes from special knowledge. The object of this address is to suggest how to produce the expert without loss of the essential virtues of the amateur. The machinery of our secondary education is rigid where it should be yielding, and lax where it should be rigid. Every school is bound on pain of extinction to train its boys for a small set of definite examinations. No headmaster has a free hand to develop his general education or his specialist studies in accordance with the opportunities of his school, which are created by its staff, its environment, its class of boys, and its endowments. I suggest that no system of external tests which aims primarily at examining individual scholars can result in anything but educational waste.

Primarily it is the schools and not the scholars which should be in- 32 spected. Each school should grant its own leaving certificates, based on its own curriculum. The standards of these schools should be sampled and corrected. But the first requisite for educational reform is the school as a unit, with its approved curriculum based on its own needs, and evolved by its own staff. If we fail to secure that, we simply fall from one formalism into another, from one dung-hill of inert ideas into another.

In stating that the school is the true educational unit in any national 33 system for the safeguarding of efficiency, I have conceived the alternative system as being the external examination of the individual scholar. But every Scylla is faced by its Charybdis—or, in more homely language, there is a ditch on both sides of the road. It will be equally fatal to education if we fall into the hands of a supervising department which is under the impression that it can divide all schools into two or three rigid categories, each type being forced to adopt a rigid curriculum. When I say that the school is the educational unit, I mean exactly what I say, no larger unit, no smaller unit. Each school must have the claim to be considered in relation to its special circumstances. The classifying of schools for some purposes is necessary. But no absolutely rigid curriculum, not modified by its own staff, should be permissible. Exactly the same principles apply, with the proper modifications, to universities and to technical colleges.

When one considers in its length and in its breadth the importance of 34 this question of the education of a nation's young, the broken lives, the defeated hopes, the national failures, which result from the frivolous inertia with which it is treated, it is difficult to restrain within oneself a savage rage. In the conditions of modern life the rule is absolute, the race which does not value trained intelligence is doomed. Not all your heroism, not all your social charm, not all your wit, not all your victories on land or at sea, can move back the finger of fate. To-day we maintain ourselves. To-morrow science will have moved forward yet one more step, and there will be no appeal from the judgment which will then be pronounced on the uneducated.

Questions for Discussion

1. What does Whitehead mean by "inert ideas"? What is bad about them? Why does a head full of inert ideas not contain real learning? Is the distinction between inert ideas and real learning one that you think most of your teachers have taken into account? Is your university or college different from high school in its commitment to genuine learning? *Should* there be a difference on this score between high school and college?

2. Do you agree with Whitehead's "two educational commandments" in paragraph 4? How do you decide how many subjects are "too many" (too many for what?), and what is the difference between thorough teaching and superficial teaching? Does the difference between *thorough* and *superficial* apply to students as well as teachers?

3. What does Whitehead mean by saying that "the understanding which we want is an understanding of an insistent present" (¶6)? When read out of context this comment may sound difficult or obscure, but do the examples in the remainder of the paragraph make it clear? How would you capture the meaning of paragraph 6 in your own words?

4. Whitehead insists that the metaphors teachers and students unconsciously work with largely determine what they do. Why does he object so strongly to the metaphor "the mind is an instrument" (¶14)? Can you think of other

metaphors that teachers and students implicitly accept? For example, education as pouring knowledge into pitchers? Education as training (as with animals)? Education as programming (as of computers)? Which of these metaphors do you like the best? Is your preferred metaphor fully adequate, or does it still fall short? What alternative metaphors can you create on your own—metaphors for either the mind or for learning—that accurately capture the most important aims of education?

5. Although Whitehead rejects the metaphor "the mind is an instrument," he uses many others (e.g., in ¶15, ¶29, and ¶30). Do these seem effective? Why? Why would an author choose a metaphor rather than saying something "straight out"?

6. By having "style" Whitehead seems to mean possessing the sophistication in any activity that comes from knowing it so intimately that one can move inside the activity by "feel," not thought. Dancers, scientists, athletes, and musicians may all exhibit style in this sense. Can you cite particular people who exhibit style in this way?

Suggested Essay Topics

1. Whitehead asserts (¶11 and ¶15, for example) that if education is too easy, no real learning takes place. Write a paper in which you argue either (1) that Whitehead is right and that the educational programs you have experienced commit the fatal mistake of both underestimating and underchallenging students or (2) that Whitehead is wrong and that a good education should advance in small increments so that students are never forced to fail or to work so hard that they lose interest.

2. Write a letter to the United States Secretary of Education arguing that our nation's specialists are too narrowly trained or that our generalists are too generally trained. Be sure to say what they are too general or specialized *for,* and give concrete examples from both personal and national experience.

2

REASON AND CRITICAL THINKING

Thinking Critically, Thinking Together

He who knows only his own side of the case, knows little of that.
His reasons may be good, and no one may have
been able to refute them. But if he is equally unable to refute
the reasons on the opposite side; if he does not
so much as know what they are, he has no ground
for preferring either opinion.
John Stuart Mill

If some great Power would agree to make me always think
what is true and do what is right, on condition of being turned into
a sort of clock and wound up every morning
before I got out of bed, I should instantly close with the offer.
Thomas Henry Huxley

Although it might belong to Socrates and other minds
of the like craft to acquire virtue by reason, the human race
would long since have ceased to be, had its preservation depended
only on the reasonings of the individuals composing it.
Rousseau

It is not the feeling sure of a doctrine (be it what it may)
which I call an assumption of infallibility. It is the undertaking
to decide that question *for others,* without allowing
them to hear what can be said on the contrary side.
John Stuart Mill

Elaine Morgan

*In this essay Elaine Morgan (b. 1920),
Welsh author and teacher, criticizes male prejudices revealed in current evolutionary
theory. Her criticism is not that all male biologists and anthropologists are malicious
male chauvinists but that many of them are simply sloppy thinkers. Androcentric
(male-centered) thinking has been around for so long, she argues (¶10), and has seemed
so unquestionably true that few male scientists—despite their commitment, as scientists, to open-mindedness and neutral observation—can break through the crust of
inherited prejudices and look clearly at evolutionary theory's supporting ideas and
data.*

*She supports her own position by re-examining notions that have been long
accepted as adequate accounts of human development. Without indulging in technical
or abstract language, relying simply on careful reasoning and fresh vision, she shows
that if scientists had thought as hard about women as they have about men, the
inadequacy of their accounts would have been revealed long ago.*

*You have undoubtedly been told by your teachers over the years that having
good reasons for your opinions is perhaps more important than having good opinions.
And you may recall occasions on which being forced to support your opinions with
good reasons made you see how few you had or how flimsy they were. The most useful
part of your education is learning how to ask yourself the kind of penetrating questions
that your best teachers have always asked you, learning how to criticize your own ideas
by using the same hard tests they have employed. The purging of error, the straightening of twisted logic, the reformulation of ideas, and the search for new information
in the light of new perspectives—these are the grounds of progress in all thinking.*

*By showing how to ask "Why?" and "How do you know that?" about
"self-evident" opinions, Morgan exemplifies not only the healthy activity of critical
thinking within a discipline but also the kind of critical thinking that education, at
its best, teaches us to do on our own.*

THE MAN-MADE MYTH

Chapter 1 of *The Descent of Woman* (1972).

According to the Book of Genesis, God first created man. Woman was not 1
only an afterthought, but an amenity. For close on two thousand years this
holy scripture was believed to justify her subordination and explain her
inferiority; for even as a copy she was not a very good copy. There were
differences. She was not one of His best efforts.

There is a line in an old folk song that runs: "I called my donkey a horse 2
gone wonky." Throughout most of the literature dealing with the differences
between the sexes there runs a subtle underlying assumption that woman is
a man gone wonky; that woman is a distorted version of the original blueprint; that they are the norm, and we are the deviation.

It might have been expected that when Darwin came along and wrote 3
an entirely different account of *The Descent of Man,* this assumption would have
been eradicated, for Darwin didn't believe she was an afterthought: he believed her origin was at least contemporaneous with man's. It should have led
to some kind of breakthrough in the relationship between the sexes. But it
didn't.

Almost at once men set about the congenial and fascinating task of 4
working out an entirely new set of reasons why woman was manifestly
inferior and irreversibly subordinate, and they have been happily engaged in
this ever since. Instead of theology they use biology, and ethology, and
primatology, but they use them to reach the same conclusions.

They are now prepared to debate the most complex problems of eco- 5
nomic reform not in terms of the will of God, but in terms of the sexual
behavior patterns of the cichlid fish; so that if a woman claims equal pay or
the right to promotion there is usually an authoritative male thinker around
to deliver a brief homily on hormones, and point out that what she secretly
intends by this, and what will inevitably result, is the "psychological castration" of the men in her life.

Now, that may look to us like a stock piece of emotional blackmail—like 6
the woman who whimpers that if Sonny doesn't do as she wants him to do,
then Mother's going to have one of her nasty turns. It is not really surprising
that most women who are concerned to win themselves a new and better
status in society tend to sheer away from the whole subject of biology and
origins, and hope that we can ignore all that and concentrate on ensuring that
in the future things will be different.

I believe this is a mistake. The legend of the jungle heritage and the 7
evolution of man as a hunting carnivore has taken root in man's mind as
firmly as Genesis ever did. He may even genuinely believe that equal pay will
do something terrible to his gonads. He has built a beautiful theoretical
construction, with himself on the top of it, buttressed with a formidable array
of scientifically authenticated facts. We cannot dispute the facts. We should

not attempt to ignore the facts. What I think we can do is to suggest that the currently accepted interpretation of the facts is not the only possible one.

I have considerable admiration for scientists in general, and evolution- 8
ists and ethologists in particular, and though I think they have sometimes gone astray, it has not been purely through prejudice. Partly it is due to sheer semantic accident—the fact that "man" is an ambiguous term. It means the species; it also means the male of the species. If you begin to write a book about man or conceive a theory about man you cannot avoid using this word. You cannot avoid using a pronoun as a substitute for the word, and you will use the pronoun "he" as a simple matter of linguistic convenience. But before you are halfway through the first chapter a mental image of this evolving creature begins to form in your mind. It will be a male image, and he will be the hero of the story: everything and everyone else in the story will relate to him.

All this may sound like a mere linguistic quibble or a piece of feminist 9
petulance. If you stay with me, I hope to convince you it's neither. I believe the deeply rooted semantic confusion between "man" as a male and "man" as a species has been fed back into and vitiated a great deal of the speculation that goes on about the origins, development, and nature of the human race.

A very high proportion of the thinking on these topics is androcentric 10
(male-centered) in the same way as pre-Copernican thinking was geocentric. It's just as hard for man to break the habit of thinking of himself as central to the species as it was to break the habit of thinking of himself as central to the universe. He sees himself quite unconsciously as the main line of evolution, with a female satellite revolving around him as the moon revolves around the earth. This not only causes him to overlook valuable clues to our ancestry, but sometimes leads him into making statements that are arrant and demonstrable nonsense.

The longer I went on reading his own books about himself, the more 11
I longed to find a volume that would begin: "When the first ancestor of the human race descended from the trees, she had not yet developed the mighty brain that was to distinguish her so sharply from all other species. . . ."

Of course, she was no more the first ancestor than he was—but she was 12
no *less* the first ancestor, either. She was there all along, contributing half the genes to each succeeding generation. Most of the books forget about her for most of the time. They drag her onstage rather suddenly for the obligatory chapter on Sex and Reproduction, and then say: "All right, love, you can go now," while they get on with the real meaty stuff about the Mighty Hunter with his lovely new weapons and his lovely new straight legs racing across the Pleistocene plains. Any modifications in her morphology are taken to be imitations of the Hunter's evolution, or else designed solely for his delecta-tion.

Evolutionary thinking has been making great strides lately. Archeolo- 13
gists, ethologists, paleontologists, geologists, chemists, biologists, and physi-cists are closing in from all points of the compass on the central area of

mystery that remains. For despite the frequent triumph dances of researchers coming up with another jawbone or another statistic, some part of the miracle is still unaccounted for. Most of their books include some such phrase as: ". . . the early stages of man's evolutionary progress remain a total mystery." "Man is an accident, the culmination of a series of highly improbable coincidences. . . ." "Man is a product of circumstances special to the point of disbelief." They feel there is still something missing, and they don't know what.

The trouble with specialists is that they tend to think in grooves. From   14
time to time something happens to shake them out of that groove. Robert Ardrey tells how such enlightenment came to Dr. Kenneth Oakley when the first Australopithecus remains had been unearthed in Africa: "The answer flashed without warning in his own large-domed head: 'Of course we believed that the big brain came first! We assumed that the first man was an Englishman!'" Neither he, nor Ardrey in relating the incident, noticed that he was still making an equally unconscious, equally unwarrantable assumption. One of these days an evolutionist is going to strike a palm against his large-domed head and cry: "Of course! We assumed the first human being was a man!"

First, let's have a swift recap of the story as currently related, for despite   15
all the new evidence recently brought to light, the generally accepted picture of human evolution has changed very little.

Smack in the center of it remains the Tarzanlike figure of the prehomi-   16
nid male who came down from the trees, saw a grassland teeming with game, picked up a weapon, and became a Mighty Hunter.

Almost everything about us is held to have derived from this. If we walk   17
erect it was because the Mighty Hunter had to stand tall to scan the distance for his prey. If we lived in caves it was because hunters need a base to come home to. If we learned to speak it was because hunters need to plan the next safari and boast about the last. Desmond Morris, pondering on the shape of a woman's breasts, instantly deduces that they evolved because her mate became a Mighty Hunter, and defends this preposterous proposition with the greatest ingenuity. There's something about the Tarzan figure which has them all mesmerized.

I find the whole yarn pretty incredible. It is riddled with mysteries, and   18
inconsistencies, and unanswered questions. Even more damning than the unanswered questions are the questions that are never even asked, because, as Professor Peter Medawar has pointed out, "scientists tend not to ask themselves questions until they can see the rudiments of an answer in their minds." I shall devote this chapter to pointing out some of these problems before outlining a new version of the Naked Ape story [in following chapters not reprinted here] which will suggest at least possible answers to every one of them, and fifteen or twenty others besides.

The first mystery is, "What happened during the Pliocene?"   19

There is a wide acceptance now of the theory that the human story   20

began in Africa. Twenty million years ago in Kenya, there existed a flourishing population of apes of generalized body structure and of a profusion
of types from the size of a small gibbon up to that of a large gorilla. Dr.
L. S. B. Leakey has dug up their bones by the hundred in the region of Lake
Victoria, and they were clearly doing very well there at the time. It was a
period known as the Miocene. The weather was mild, the rainfall was heavier
than today, and the forests were flourishing. So far, so good.

Then came the Pliocene drought. Robert Ardrey writes of it: "No mind   21
can apprehend in terms of any possible human experience the duration of the
Pliocene. Ten desiccated years were enough, a quarter of a century ago, to
produce in the American Southwest that maelstrom of misery, the dust bowl.
To the inhabitant of the region the ten years must have seemed endless. But
the African Pliocene lasted twelve million."

On the entire African continent no Pliocene fossil bed has ever been   22
found. During this period many promising Miocene ape species were, not
surprisingly, wiped out altogether. A few were trapped in dwindling pockets
of forest and when the Pliocene ended they reappeared as brachiating apes—
specialized for swinging by their arms.

Something astonishing also reappeared—the Australopithecines, first   23
discovered by Professor Raymond Dart in 1925 and since unearthed in considerable numbers by Dr. Leakey and others.

Australopithecus emerged from his horrifying twelve-million-year or-   24
deal much refreshed and improved. The occipital condyles of his skull suggest
a bodily posture approaching that of modern man, and the orbital region,
according to Sir Wilfred le Gros Clark, has "a remarkably human appearance." He was clever, too. His remains have been found in the Olduvai Gorge
in association with crude pebble tools that have been hailed as the earliest
beginning of human culture. Robert Ardrey says: "We entered the [Pliocene]
crucible a generalized creature bearing only the human potential. We emerged
a being lacking only a proper brain and a chin. What happened to us along
the way?" The sixty-four-thousand-dollar question: "What happened to
them? Where did they go?"

Second question: "Why did they stand upright?" The popular versions   25
skim very lightly over this patch of thin ice. Desmond Morris says simply:
"With strong pressure on them to increase their prey-killing prowess, they
became more upright—fast, better runners." Robert Ardrey says equally
simply: "We learned to stand erect in the first place as a necessity of the
hunting life."

But wait a minute. We were quadrupeds. These statements imply that   26
a quadruped suddenly discovered that he could move faster on two legs than
on four. Try to imagine any other quadruped discovering that—a cat? a dog?
a horse?—and you'll see that it's totally nonsensical. Other things being
equal, four legs are bound to run faster than two. The bipedal development
was violently unnatural.

Stoats, gophers, rabbits, chimpanzees, will sit or stand bipedally to gaze 27
into the distance, but when they want speed they have sense enough to use

all the legs they've got. The only quadrupeds I can think of that can move faster on two legs than four are things like kangaroos—and a small lizard called the Texas boomer, and he doesn't keep it up for long. The secret in these cases is a long heavy counterbalancing tail which we certainly never had. You may say it was a natural development for a primate because primates sit erect in trees—but *was* it natural? Baboons and macaques have been largely terrestrial for millions of years without any sign of becoming bipedal.

George A. Bartholomew and Joseph B. Birdsell point out: ". . . the   28 extreme rarity of bipedalism among animals suggests that it is inefficient except under very special circumstances. Even modern man's unique vertical locomotion when compared to that of quadrupedal mammals, is relatively ineffective. . . . A significant nonlocomotor advantage must have resulted."

What was this advantage? The Tarzanists suggest that bipedalism en-   29 abled this ape to race after game while carrying weapons—in the first instance, presumably pebbles. But a chimp running off with a banana (or a pebble), if he can't put it in his mouth, will carry it in one hand and gallop along on the others, because even *three* legs are faster than two. So what was our ancestor supposed to be doing? Shambling along with a rock in each hand? Throwing boulders that took two hands to lift?

No. There must have been a pretty powerful reason why we were   30 constrained over a long period of time to walk about on our hind legs *even though it was slower.* We need to find that reason.

Third question: How did the ape come to be using these weapons,   31 anyway? Again Desmond Morris clears this one lightly, at a bound: "With strong pressure on them to increase their prey-killing prowess . . . their hands became strong efficient weapon-holders." Compared to Morris, Robert Ardrey is obsessed with weapons, which he calls "mankind's most significant cultural endowment." Yet his explanation of how it all started is as cursory as anyone else's: "In the first evolutionary hour of the human emergence we became sufficiently skilled in the use of weapons to render redundant our natural primate daggers" (i.e., the large prehominid canine teeth).

But wait a minute—how? and why? Why did one, and only one, species   32 of those Miocene apes start using weapons? A cornered baboon will fight a leopard; a hungry baboon will kill and eat a chicken. He could theoretically pick up a chunk of flint and forget about his "natural primate daggers," and become a Mighty Hunter. He doesn't do it, though. Why did we? Sarel Eimerl and Irven de Vore point out in their book *The Primates:*

"Actually, it takes quite a lot of explaining. For example, if an animal's   33 normal mode of defense is to flee from a predator, it flees. If its normal method of defense is to fight with its teeth, it fights with its teeth. It does not suddenly adopt a totally new course of action, such as picking up a stick or a rock and throwing it. The idea would simply not occur to it, and even if it did, the animal would have no reason to suppose that it would work."

Now primates do acquire useful tool-deploying habits. A chimpanzee   34 will use a stick to extract insects from their nests, and a crumpled leaf to sop up water. Wolfgang Köhler's apes used sticks to draw fruit toward the bars of their cage, and so on.

But this type of learning depends on three things. There must be leisure   35
for trial-and-error experiment. The tools must be either in unlimited supply (a forest is full of sticks and leaves) or else in *exactly the right place.* (Even Köhler's brilliant Sultan could be stumped if the fruit was in front of him and a new potential tool was behind him—he needed them both in view at the same time.) Thirdly, for the habit to stick, the same effect must result from the same action every time.

Now look at that ape. The timing is wrong—when he's faced with a   36
bristling rival or a charging cat or even an escaping prey, he won't fool around inventing fancy methods. A chimp sometimes brandishes a stick to convey menace to an adversary, but if his enemy keeps coming, he drops the stick and fights with hands and teeth. Even if we postulate a mutant ape cool enough to think, with the adrenalin surging through his veins, "There must be a better way than teeth," he still has to be lucky to notice that right in the middle of the primeval grassland there happens to be a stone of convenient size, precisely between him and his enemy. And when he throws it, he has to score a bull's-eye, first time and every time. Because if he failed to hit a leopard he wouldn't be there to tell his progeny that the trick only needed polishing up a bit; and if he failed to hit a springbok he'd think: "Ah well, that obviously doesn't work. Back to the old drawing board."

No. If it had taken all that much luck to turn man into a killer, we'd all   37
be still living on nut cutlets.

A lot of Tarzanists privately realize that their explanations of bipedal-   38
ism and weapon-wielding won't hold water. They have invented the doctrine of "feedback," which states that though these two theories are separately and individually nonsense, together they will just get by. It is alleged that the ape's bipedal gait, however unsteady, made him a better rock thrower (why?) and his rock throwing, however inaccurate, made him a better biped. (Why?) Eimerl and de Vore again put the awkward question: Since chimps can both walk erect and manipulate simple tools, "why was it only the hominids who benefited from the feed-back?" You may well ask.

Next question: Why did the naked ape become naked?   39

Desmond Morris claims that, unlike more specialized carnivores such as   40
lions and jackals, the ex-vegetarian ape was not physically equipped to "make lightning dashes after his prey." He would "experience considerable overheating during the hunt, and the loss of body hair would be of great value for the supreme moments of the chase."

This is a perfect example of androcentric thinking. There were two sexes   41
around at the time, and I don't believe it's ever been all that easy to part a woman from a fur coat, just to save the old man from getting into a muck-sweat during his supreme moments. What was supposed to be happening to the female during this period of denudation?

Dr. Morris says: "This system would not work, of course, if the climate   42 was too intensely hot, because of damage to the exposed skin." So he is obviously dating the loss of hair later than the Pliocene "inferno." But the next period was the turbulent Pleistocene, punctuated by mammoth African "pluvials," corresponding to the Ice Ages of the north. A pluvial was century after century of torrential rainfall; so we have to picture our maternal ancestor sitting naked in the middle of the plain while the heavens emptied, needing both hands to keep her muddy grip on a slippery, squirming, equally naked infant. This is ludicrous. It's no advantage to the species for the Mighty Hunter to return home safe and cool if he finds his son's been dropped on his head and his wife is dead of hypothermia.

This problem could have been solved by dimorphism—the loss of hair 43 could have gone further in one sex than the other. So it did, of course. But unfortunately for the Tarzanists it was the stay-at-home female who became nakedest, and the overheated hunter who kept the hair on his chest.

Next question: Why has our sex life become so involved and confusing? 44

The given answer, I need hardly say, is that it all began when man 45 became a hunter. He had to travel long distances after his prey and he began worrying about what the little woman might be up to. He was also anxious about other members of the hunting pack, because, Desmond Morris explains, "if the weaker males were going to be expected to cooperate on the hunt, they had to be given more sexual rights. The females would have to be more shared out."

Thus it became necessary, so the story goes, to establish a system of 46 "pair bonding" to ensure that couples remained faithful for life. I quote: "The simplest and most direct method of doing this was to make the shared activities of the pair more complicated and more rewarding. In other words, to make sex sexier."

To this end, the Naked Apes sprouted ear lobes, fleshy nostrils, and 47 everted lips, all allegedly designed to stimulate one another to a frenzy. Mrs. A.'s nipples became highly erogenous, she invented and patented the female orgasm, and she learned to be sexually responsive at all times, even during pregnancy, "because with a one-male–one-female system, it would be dangerous to frustrate the male for too long a period. It might endanger the pair bond." He might go off in a huff, or look for another woman. Or even refuse to cooperate on the hunt.

In addition, they decided to change over to face-to-face sex, instead of 48 the male mounting from behind as previously, because this new method led to "personalized sex." The frontal approach means that "the incoming sexual signals and rewards are kept tightly linked with the identity signals from the partner." In simpler words, you know who you're doing it with.

This landed Mrs. Naked Ape in something of a quandary. Up till then, 49 the fashionable thing to flaunt in sexual approaches had been "a pair of fleshy, hemispherical buttocks." Now all of a sudden they were getting her nowhere. She would come up to her mate making full-frontal identity signals like mad with her nice new earlobes and nostrils, but somehow he just didn't want to know. He missed the fleshy hemispheres, you see. The position was parlous, Dr. Morris urges. "If the female of our species was going to success-fully shift the interest of the male round to the front, evolution would have to do something to make the frontal region more stimulating." Guess what? Right the first time: she invested in a pair of fleshy hemispheres in the thoracic region and we were once more saved by the skin of our teeth.

All this is good stirring stuff, but hard to take seriously. Wolf packs manage to cooperate without all this erotic paraphernalia. Our near relatives the gibbons remain faithful for life without "personalized" frontal sex, with-out elaborate erogenous zones, without perennial female availability. Why couldn't we?

Above all, since when has increased sexiness been a guarantee of in-creased fidelity? If the naked ape could all this added sexual potential in his own mate, how could he fail to see the same thing happening to all the other females around him? What effect was that supposed to have on him, especially in later life when he noticed Mrs. A.'s four hemispheres becoming a little less fleshy than they used to be?

We haven't yet begun on the unasked questions. Before ending this chapter I will mention just two out of many.

First: If female orgasm was evolved in our species for the first time to provide the woman with a "behavioral reward" for increased sexual activity, why in the name of Darwin has the job been so badly bungled that there have been whole tribes and whole generations of women hardly aware of its existence? Even in the sex-conscious U.S.A., according to Dr. Kinsey, it rarely gets into proper working order before the age of about thirty. How could natural selection ever have operated on such a rickety, unreliable, late-devel-oping endowment when in the harsh conditions of prehistory a woman would be lucky to survive more than twenty-nine years, anyway?

Second: Why in our species has sex become so closely linked with aggression? In most of the higher primates sexual activity is the one thing in life which is totally incompatible with hostility. A female primate can imme-diately deflect male wrath by presenting her backside and offering sex. Even a male monkey can calm and appease a furious aggressor by imitating the gesture. Nor is the mechanism confined to mammals. Lorenz tells of an irate lizard charging down upon a female painted with male markings to deceive him. When he got close enough to realize his mistake, the taboo was so immediate and so absolute that his aggression went out like a light, and being too late to stop himself he shot straight up into the air and turned a back somersault.

Female primates admittedly are not among the species that can count on this absolute chivalry at all times. A female monkey may be physically chastised for obstreperous behavior; or a male may (on rare occasions) direct hostility against her when another male is copulating with her; but between the male and female engaged in it, sex is always the friendliest of interactions. There is no more hostility associated with it than with a session of mutual grooming.

How then have sex and aggression, the two irreconcilables of the animal kingdom, become in our species alone so closely interlinked that the words for sexual activity are spat out as insults and expletives? In what evolutionary terms are we to explain the Marquis de Sade, and the subterranean echoes that his name evokes in so many human minds?

Not, I think, in terms of Tarzan. It is time to approach the whole thing 57 again right from the beginning: this time from the distaff side, and along a totally different route.

Questions for Discussion

1. Do you think that Morgan's sharpening of her feminist axe dulls her overall argument? Does she seem more intent on being a feminist thinker than a scientific thinker? Or do you think that her feminist examples are appropriate to her task?

2. Morgan's tone varies greatly from moment to moment. Often she sounds neutral, scientific: "We cannot dispute the facts. We should not attempt to ignore the facts. What I think we can do is to suggest that the currently accepted interpretation of the facts is not the only possible one" (¶7). But often enough she becomes ironic or even sarcastic: "I don't believe it's ever been all that easy to part a woman from a fur coat, just to save the old man from getting into a muck-sweat during his supreme moments" (¶41); Mrs. A. "invented and patented the female orgasm" (¶47); "He may even genuinely believe that equal pay will do something terrible to his gonads" (¶7). Do you find these two styles compatible? Does she mix them effectively? What is the effect of mixing them? Do the passages with ironic zingers in them affect your view of her credibility? Why?

3. In paragraphs 25–30, Morgan discusses the emergence of bipedalism in human beings and argues that the conventional explanation—that walking upright made men faster and better hunters—simply does not hold water. Discuss in detail the objections she raises. Her questions are based on logic, not specialized knowledge. Do they make sense to you? Can you think of arguments that either support or undercut her criticisms?

4. The following "skeleton" outline is intended to reveal the connecting "joints" in Morgan's argument. Choose any essay you have read so far and try to bare the skeletal framework for it as we have done for Morgan's essay.

   I. Paragraphs 1–14: *Introduction:* Morgan lays out the topic, thesis, and general form of her argument.
      A. Paragraphs 1–7: Exposition of *topic,* the relation between evolutionary theory in biology and the status of women in society. The *thesis* statement emerges in the last sentence of paragraph 7: "The currently accepted interpretation of the facts is not the only possible one."

B. Paragraphs 8–14: *General overview of argument* and beginning development. Even scientific thinkers do not think open-mindedly about evolution. She cites three reasons:
  1. Paragraphs 8–9: Language itself reinforces male prejudices.
  2. Paragraphs 10–13: Tradition reinforces male prejudices (brilliant metaphor from astronomy).
  3. Paragraph 14: Narrowness of specialized thinking reinforces male prejudices; specialists tend to think "in grooves."

II. Paragraphs 15–56: *Detailed critique* of "grooved" views in evolutionary theory.
  A. Paragraphs 15–24: Summary of conventional views in current theory.
    1. Paragraphs 15–18: The development of human beings is largely built on the nature of early man as a "Mighty Hunter."
    2. Paragraphs 19–24: The standard problem that must be explained in anthropology.
  B. Paragraphs 25–30: The problem of how to explain the upright walk.
    1. Paragraph 25: The current explanation is based on the Mighty Hunter theory.
    2. Paragraphs 26–30: Critique that shows inadequacy of the current explanation.
  C. Paragraphs 31–38: The problem of how to explain emergence of weapons.
    1. Paragraph 31: The current explanation is based on the Mighty Hunter theory.
    2. Paragraphs 32–38: Critique—the necessities of hunting don't suffice as an explanation.
  D. Paragraphs 39–43: The problem of how to explain loss of hair.
    1. Paragraph 40: Again, the theory is based on the Mighty Hunter explanation.
    2. Paragraphs 41–43: Critique.
  E. Paragraphs 44–51: The problem of how to explain distinctive sexual practices of human beings.
    1. Paragraphs 45–49: Again we are given the conventional Mighty Hunter view.
    2. Paragraphs 50–56: Critique.

III. Paragraph 57: *Conclusion:* Reiteration of the thesis that current theory is inadequate to explain the data.

Suggested Essay Topics

1. In paragraph 10, Morgan compares androcentric thinking to pre-Copernican thinking and develops the comparison in a couple of sentences. In a short paper, begin by quoting the first three sentences of paragraph 10, then continue to develop the comparison. You might go on to compare some early feminist (e.g., Margaret Sanger or Susan B. Anthony) to Copernicus, or compare male chauvinists to Copernicus's contemporaries. The point of this essay is to give you practice in making an extended analogy work for you. Few devices are more powerful than extended analogies for packing meaning and effect into a compressed space. By contrast, nothing will seem less effective than an analogy that strikes a reader as far-fetched or inappropriate.

2. Pick an issue that is accompanied by widely accepted arguments that seem as objectionable to you as androcentric arguments seem to Morgan. Possible topics might include the arms race, space travel, a nuclear freeze, the "first-strike option," or abortion rights; or, if you wish to stick to issues you know firsthand, you might write on open dorm policies, tuition increases, the value of Greek-letter societies, or the money spent on athletics.

   In an essay directed to your fellow students or in a memo or letter addressed to responsible officials, imitate Morgan's style of attack (¶25–30 or ¶31–38 provide a model). Begin with a short statement of the issue, proceed to give the conventional view you find objectionable, and then develop your objections, relying not on special information but on tight reasoning. Like Morgan, you do not have to replace the ideas you criticize with a whole new set; your objective is simply to point out as many flaws as possible in the arguments you are attacking. Try to go for the basic ideas, not trivialities.

William Golding

In this essay the British novelist William Golding (b. 1911), author of The Lord of the Flies, *provides a humorous, yet serious, description of three levels of thinking. He draws his examples of each from his own experience in school, starting with grammar school and ending with the university. As you read, try to determine whether the three levels of schooling he talks about correspond to the three levels of thinking he describes. Consider whether you can verify his categories with examples from your own experience. Can you map his progress from thinking as a "hobby" to thinking as a "professional" (¶47)? Does the kind of thinking you are being taught in college fall within Golding's categories?*

THINKING AS A HOBBY

From *Holiday*, August 1961.

While I was still a boy, I came to the conclusion that there were three grades of thinking; and since I was later to claim thinking as my hobby, I came to an even stranger conclusion—namely, that I myself could not think at all.

I must have been an unsatisfactory child for grownups to deal with. I remember how incomprehensible they appeared to me at first, but not, of course, how I appeared to them. It was the headmaster of my grammar school who first brought the subject of thinking before me—though neither in the way, nor with the result he intended. He had some statuettes in his study.

1

2

They stood on a high cupboard behind his desk. One was a lady wearing nothing but a bath towel. She seemed frozen in an eternal panic lest the bath towel slip down any farther; and since she had no arms, she was in an unfortunate position to pull the towel up again. Next to her, crouched the statuette of a leopard, ready to spring down at the top drawer of a filing cabinet labeled A–AH. My innocence interpreted this as the victim's last, despairing cry. Beyond the leopard was a naked, muscular gentleman, who sat, looking down, with his chin on his fist and his elbow on his knee. He seemed utterly miserable.

Some time later, I learned about these statuettes. The headmaster had placed them where they would face delinquent children, because they symbolized to him the whole of life. The naked lady was the Venus of Milo. She was Love. She was not worried about the towel. She was just busy being beautiful. The leopard was Nature, and he was being natural. The naked, muscular gentleman was not miserable. He was Rodin's Thinker, an image of pure thought. It is easy to buy small plaster models of what you think life is like.

I had better explain that I was a frequent visitor to the headmaster's study, because of the latest thing I had done or left undone. As we now say, I was not integrated. I was, if anything, disintegrated; and I was puzzled. Grownups never made sense. Whenever I found myself in a penal position before the headmaster's desk, with the statuettes glimmering whitely above him, I would sink my head, clasp my hands behind my back and writhe one shoe over the other.

The headmaster would look opaquely at me, through flashing spectacles.

"What are we going to do with you?"

Well, what were they going to do with me? I would writhe my shoe some more and stare down at the worn rug.

"Look up, boy! Can't you look up?"

Then I would look up at the cupboard, where the naked lady was frozen in her panic and the muscular gentleman contemplated the hindquarters of the leopard in endless gloom. I had nothing to say to the headmaster. His spectacles caught the light so that you could see nothing human behind them. There was no possibility of communication.

"Don't you ever think at all?"

No, I didn't think, wasn't thinking, couldn't think—I was simply waiting in anguish for the interview to stop.

"Then you'd better learn—hadn't you?"

On one occasion the headmaster leaped to his feet, reached up and plonked Rodin's masterpiece on the desk before me.

"That's what a man looks like when he's really thinking."

I surveyed the gentleman without interest or comprehension.

"Go back to your class."

Clearly there was something missing in me. Nature had endowed the rest of the human race with a sixth sense and left me out. This must be so, I mused, on my way back to the class, since whether I had broken a window, or failed to remember Boyle's Law, or been late for school, my teachers produced me one, adult answer: "Why can't you think?"

As I saw the case, I had broken the window because I had tried to hit 18 Jack Arney with a cricket ball and missed him; I could not remember Boyle's Law because I had never bothered to learn it; and I was late for school because I preferred looking over the bridge into the river. In fact, I was wicked. Were my teachers, perhaps, so good that they could not understand the depths of my depravity? Were they clear, untormented people who could direct their every action by this mysterious business of thinking? The whole thing was incomprehensible. In my earlier years, I found even the statuette of the Thinker confusing. I did not believe any of my teachers were naked, ever. Like someone born deaf, but bitterly determined to find out about sound, I watched my teachers to find out about thought.

There was Mr. Houghton. He was always telling me to think. With a 19 modest satisfaction, he would tell me that he had thought a bit himself. Then why did he spend so much time drinking? Or was there more sense in drinking than there appeared to be? But if not, and if drinking were in fact ruinous to health—and Mr. Houghton was ruined, there was no doubt about that—why was he always talking about the clean life and the virtues of fresh air? He would spread his arms wide with the action of a man who habitually spent his time striding along mountain ridges.

"Open air does me good, boys—I know it!" 20

Sometimes, exalted by his own oratory, he would leap from his desk and 21 hustle us outside into a hideous wind.

"Now, boys! Deep breaths! Feel it right down inside you—huge 22 draughts of God's good air!"

He would stand before us, rejoicing in his perfect health, an open-air 23 man. He would put his hands on his waist and take a tremendous breath. You could hear the wind, trapped in the cavern of his chest and struggling with all the unnatural impediments. His body would reel with shock and his ruined face go white at the unaccustomed visitation. He would stagger back to his desk and collapse there, useless for the rest of the morning.

Mr. Houghton was given to high-minded monologues about the good 24 life, sexless and full of duty. Yet in the middle of one of these monologues, if a girl passed the window, tapping along on her neat little feet, he would interrupt his discourse, his neck would turn of itself and he would watch her out of sight. In this instance, he seemed to me ruled not by thought but by an invisible and irresistible spring in his nape.

His neck was an object of great interest to me. Normally it bulged a bit 25 over his collar. But Mr. Houghton had fought in the First World War along- side both Americans and French, and had come—by who knows what il- logic?—to a settled detestation of both countries. If either country happened to be prominent in current affairs, no argument could make Mr. Houghton

think well of it. He would bang the desk, his neck would bulge still further
and go red. "You can say what you like," he would cry, "but I've thought
about this—and I know what I think!"

Mr. Houghton thought with his neck.   26

There was Miss Parsons. She assured us that her dearest wish was our   27
welfare, but I knew even then, with the mysterious clairvoyance of childhood, that what she wanted most was the husband she never got. There was
Mr. Hands—and so on.

I have dealt at length with my teachers because this was my introduc-   28
tion to the nature of what is commonly called thought. Through them I
discovered that thought is often full of unconscious prejudice, ignorance and
hypocrisy. It will lecture on disinterested purity while its neck is being remorselessly twisted toward a skirt. Technically, it is about as proficient as
most businessmen's golf, as honest as most politicians' intentions, or—to
come near my own preoccupation—as coherent as most books that get written. It is what I came to call grade-three thinking, though more properly, it
is feeling, rather than thought.

True, often there is a kind of innocence in prejudices, but in those days   29
I viewed grade-three thinking with an intolerant contempt and an incautious
mockery. I delighted to confront a pious lady who hated the Germans with
the proposition that we should love our enemies. She taught me a great truth
in dealing with grade-three thinkers; because of her, I no longer dismiss
lightly a mental process which for nine-tenths of the population is the nearest
they will ever get to thought. They have immense solidarity. We had better
respect them, for we are outnumbered and surrounded. A crowd of grade-
three thinkers, all shouting the same thing, all warming their hands at the fire
of their own prejudices, will not thank you for pointing out the contradictions
in their beliefs. Man is a gregarious animal, and enjoys agreement as cows will
graze all the same way on the side of a hill.

Grade-two thinking is the detection of contradictions. I reached grade   30
two when I trapped the poor, pious lady. Grade-two thinkers do not stam-
pede easily, though often they fall into the other fault and lag behind. Grade-
two thinking is a withdrawal, with eyes and ears open. It became my hobby
and brought satisfaction and loneliness in either hand. For grade-two thinking destroys without having the power to create. It set me watching the
crowds cheering His Majesty the King and asking myself what all the fuss
was about, without giving me anything positive to put in the place of that
heady patriotism. But there were compensations. To hear people justify their
habit of hunting foxes and tearing them to pieces by claiming that the foxes
liked it. To hear our Prime Minister talk about the great benefit we conferred
on India by jailing people like Pandit Nehru and Gandhi. To hear American
politicians talk about peace in one sentence and refuse to join the League of
Nations in the next. Yes, there were moments of delight.

But I was growing toward adolescence and had to admit that Mr.   31
Houghton was not the only one with an irresistible spring in his neck. I, too,

felt the compulsive hand of nature and began to find that pointing out contradiction could be costly as well as fun. There was Ruth, for example, a serious and attractive girl. I was an atheist at the time. Grade-two thinking is a menace to religion and knocks down sects like skittles. I put myself in a position to be converted by her with an hypocrisy worthy of grade three. She was a Methodist—or at least, her parents were, and Ruth had to follow suit. But, alas, instead of relying on the Holy Spirit to convert me, Ruth was foolish enough to open her pretty mouth in argument. She claimed that the Bible (King James Version) was literally inspired. I countered by saying that the Catholics believed in the literal inspiration of Saint Jerome's *Vulgate,* and the two books were different. Argument flagged.

At last she remarked that there were an awful lot of Methodists, and 32 they couldn't be wrong, could they—not all those millions? That was too easy, said I restively (for the nearer you were to Ruth, the nicer she was to be near to) since there were more Roman Catholics than Methodists anyway; and they couldn't be wrong, could they—not all those hundreds of millions? An awful flicker of doubt appeared in her eyes. I slid my arm round her waist and murmured breathlessly that if we were counting heads, the Buddhists were the boys for my money. But Ruth had *really* wanted to do me good, because I was so nice. She fled. The combination of my arm and those countless Buddhists was too much for her.

That night her father visited my father and left, red-cheeked and indig- 33 nant. I was given the third degree to find out what had happened. It was lucky we were both of us only fourteen. I lost Ruth and gained an undeserved reputation as a potential libertine.

So grade-two thinking could be dangerous. It was in this knowledge, at 34 the age of fifteen, that I remember making a comment from the heights of grade two, on the limitations of grade three. One evening I found myself alone in the school hall, preparing it for a party. The door of the headmaster's study was open. I went in. The headmaster had ceased to thump Rodin's Thinker down on the desk as an example to the young. Perhaps he had not found any more candidates, but the statuettes were still there, glimmering and gathering dust on top of the cupboard. I stood on a chair and rearranged them. I stood Venus in her bath towel on the filing cabinet, so that now the top drawer caught its breath in a gasp of sexy excitement. "A-ah!" The portentous Thinker I placed on the edge of the cupboard so that he looked down at the bath towel and waited for it to slip.

Grade-two thinking, though it filled life with fun and excitement, did 35 not make for content. To find out the deficiencies of our elders bolsters the young ego but does not make for personal security. I found that grade two was not only the power to point out contradictions. It took the swimmer some distance from the shore and left him there, out of his depth. I decided that Pontius Pilate was a typical grade-two thinker. "What is truth?" he said, a very common grade-two thought, but one that is used always as the end of an argument instead of the beginning. There is a still higher grade of thought which says, "What is truth?" and sets out to find it.

But these grade-one thinkers were few and far between. They did not 36
visit my grammar school in the flesh though they were there in books. I
aspired to them, partly because I was ambitious and partly because I now saw
my hobby as an unsatisfactory thing if it went no further. If you set out to
climb a mountain, however high you climb, you have failed if you cannot
reach the top.

I *did* meet an undeniably grade-one thinker in my first year at Oxford. 37
I was looking over a small bridge in Magdalen Deer Park, and a tiny mustached and hatted figure came and stood by my side. He was a German who
had just fled from the Nazis to Oxford as a temporary refuge. His name was
Einstein.

But Professor Einstein knew no English at that time and I knew only 38
two words of German. I beamed at him, trying wordlessly to convey by my
bearing all the affection and respect that the English felt for him. It is possible—and I have to make the admission—that I felt here were two grade-one
thinkers standing side by side; yet I doubt if my face conveyed more than a
formless awe. I would have given my Greek and Latin and French and a good
slice of my English for enough German to communicate. But we were divided;
he was as inscrutable as my headmaster. For perhaps five minutes we stood
together on the bridge, undeniable grade-one thinker and breathless aspirant.
With true greatness, Professor Einstein realized that any contact was better
than none. He pointed to a trout wavering in midstream.

He spoke: *"Fisch."* 39

My brain reeled. Here I was, mingling with the great, and yet helpless 40
as the veriest grade-three thinker. Desperately I sought for some sign by
which I might convey that I, too, revered pure reason. I nodded vehemently.
In a brilliant flash I used up half my German vocabulary.

"Fisch. Ja. Ja." 41

For perhaps another five minutes we stood side by side. Then Professor 42
Einstein, his whole figure still conveying good will and amiability, drifted
away out of sight.

I, too, would be a grade-one thinker. I was irreverent at the best of times. 43
Political and religious systems, social customs, loyalties and traditions, they
all came tumbling down like so many rotten apples off a tree. This was a fine
hobby and a sensible substitute for cricket, since you could play it all the year
round. I came up in the end with what must always remain the justification
for grade-one thinking, its sign, seal and charter. I devised a coherent system
for living. It was a moral system, which was wholly logical. Of course, as I
readily admitted, conversion of the world to my way of thinking might be
difficult, since my system did away with a number of trifles, such as big
business, centralized government, armies, marriage. . . .

It was Ruth all over again. I had some very good friends who stood by 44
me, and still do. But my acquaintances vanished, taking the girls with them.
Young women seemed oddly contented with the world as it was. They valued
the meaningless ceremony with a ring. Young men, while willing to concede
the chaining sordidness of marriage, were hesitant about abandoning the

organizations which they hoped would give them a career. A young man on
the first rung of the Royal Navy, while perfectly agreeable to doing away with
big business and marriage, got as red-necked as Mr. Houghton when I proposed a world without any battleships in it.

Had the game gone too far? Was it a game any longer? In those prewar   45
days, I stood to lose a great deal, for the sake of a hobby.

Now you are expecting me to describe how I saw the folly of my ways   46
and came back to the warm nest, where prejudices are so often called loyalties, where pointless actions are hallowed into custom by repetition, where
we are content to say we think when all we do is feel.

But you would be wrong. I dropped my hobby and turned professional.   47

If I were to go back to the headmaster's study and find the dusty   48
statuettes still there, I would arrange them differently. I would dust Venus
and put her aside, for I have come to love her and know her for the fair thing
she is. But I would put the Thinker, sunk in his desperate thought, where
there were shadows before him—and at his back, I would put the leopard,
crouched and ready to spring.

Questions for Discussion

1. What are the distinguishing features of each of Golding's levels of thinking? Do you know people who exemplify each kind? Are there persons in
   your college or university—administrators or professors, perhaps—whose
   wide recognizability make them good examples for the whole class to
   discuss? Are there times or occasions when even grade-three thinking is
   defensible? When? Why? If not, why not?

2. Can you point to details in paragraphs 4–16 that reveal Golding as a master
   storyteller? How do these narratives enhance his essay?

3. In what ways do the three statuettes seem to relate to Golding's three
   categories of thinking? Why does he rearrange the statuettes so that the
   leopard seems about to spring onto the back of the thinker? Does this
   rearrangement imply that Golding has reassessed the difficulty of thinking
   since he attended grammar school or since he gave it up as a hobby and
   turned professional?

4. Thinking as a hobby, as a game, seems to match which of Golding's levels
   of thinking? Does Golding reserve his highest praise for thinking as a
   hobby? If he offers criticism of this kind of thinking, what sort of criticism
   is it and in what paragraphs does he advance it?

5. Do you find that you can identify Golding's three levels of thinking with
   the kind of thinking that characterizes any particular group or organization
   in society? Is it possible to say that politicians, for example—or the clergy,
   business executives, or single-issue proponents—generally fall into one

level of thinking rather than another? Can you point to exceptions within groups?

Suggested Essay Topics

1. In an essay directed to your classmates, draw a verbal portrait of the best "grade-one" thinker you have ever personally known. Provide at least one anecdote about this person's thinking habits. The point of your essay is to define first-rate thinking as vividly as possible.

   As you write, think of the devices and strategies that Golding uses to achieve vividness: construction of little scenarios (¶4–16 and ¶37–42), use of images (Mr. Houghton's neck; people warming their hands at the fire of their own prejudices; the headmaster's opaque, flashing spectacles), and use of irony ("It is easy to buy small plaster models of what you think life is like"; "Were my teachers, perhaps, so good that they could not understand the depths of my depravity?"). Try to incorporate some of these devices into the writing of your own essay.

2. Go back through your memory's catalog of former teachers and, in imitation of Golding, pick out a few who exemplify his three levels of thinking. Write a feature article for a magazine or newspaper giving the traits, mannerisms, or examples from their behavior that illustrate the category you placed them in. Make your descriptions of these teachers your main support in an essay designed to persuade the public of the kind of thinking people should demand from teachers as the molders of each new generation.

IDEAS IN DEBATE

Paul Goodman
Karl R. Popper

Paul Goodman

As you read this essay and the next one, try to ascertain as clearly as possible whether Goodman's and Popper's definitions of utopian overlap perfectly, somewhat, or not at all. Also look for the criteria—the standards—by which each author constructs his judgments of utopian thinking. Although Goodman (1911–1972) recommends utopian thinking and Popper rejects it, they will only be in real disagreement if they are each using the same definition. Is their disagreement only apparent or real?

Your view of other differences between them will depend in large part on how you answer the previous question. For example, Popper is profoundly opposed to violence, whereas Goodman recommends a "new form" of society, "the conflictful community" (¶27), a phrase suggestive, if not of violence, at least of tension and social stress. As you read, try to determine what Goodman means by "conflictful community" and whether it really opposes Popper's "reasonableness" (¶6–8).

Finally, what is each author's overall intention? If the audiences addressed by each writer were completely won over and if they had an accurate understanding of what each author wanted them to believe or do, which opinions and behavior would readers adopt—and which would they abandon?

Asking such questions is not merely an academic exercise, useful only in school. When people who feel hostile and suspicious of each other fail to resolve their differences, it is not always because they are deliberately vicious, implacably pigheaded, or fond of violence. Sometimes people simply fail to understand where their beliefs and values support or contradict each other. Nothing is commoner in politics, for example, than to hear a so-called debate in which nothing gets genuinely debated because the speakers talk right past each other, failing to see that their opinions are not really very far apart. Trying to figure out precisely where Goodman and Popper agree and disagree can serve as a model of the kind of analysis needed to solve some of the world's most serious problems.

UTOPIAN THINKING

From *Utopian Essays and Practical Proposals* (1961).

Let me use ideas of mine as an example, since I am notoriously a "utopian   1
thinker." That is, on problems great and small, I try to think up direct
expedients that do not follow the usual procedures, and they are always
called "impractical" and an "imposition on people by an intellectual." The
question is—and I shall try to pose it fairly—in what sense are such expedients really practical, and in what sense are they really *not* practical? Consider
half a dozen little thumbnail ideas.*

The ceremony at my boy's public school commencement is poor. We   2
ought to commission the neighborhood writers and musicians to design
it. There is talk about aiding the arts, and this is the way to advance them,
for, as Goethe said, "The poetry of public occasions is the highest kind."
It gives a real subject to the poet, and ennobles the occasion.

Similarly, we do not adequately use our best talents. We ought to get   3
our best designers to improve some of the thousands of ugly small towns
and make them unique places to be proud of, rather than delegate such
matters to professionals in bureaucratic agencies, when we attend to them
at all. A few beautiful models would be a great incentive to others.

In our educational system, too much is spent for plant and not enough   4
for teachers. Why not try, as a pilot project, doing without the school
building altogether for a few hundred kids for most of the day? Conceive
of a teacher in charge of a band of ten, using the city itself as the material
for the curriculum and the background for the teaching. Since we are
teaching *for* life, try to get a little closer to it. My guess is that one could
considerably diminish the use of present classrooms and so not have to
increase their number.

The problem with the old ladies in a Home is to keep them from   5
degenerating, so we must provide geriatric "occupational therapy." The
problem with the orphans in their Home is that, for want of individual
attention, they may grow up as cold or "psychopathic personalities." But
the old ladies could serve as grandmothers for the orphans, to their mutual
advantage. The meaning of community is people using one another as
resources.

It is false to say that community is not possible in a great city, for   6
6,000,000 can be regarded as 2,000 neighborhoods of 3,000. These make
up one metropolis and enjoy its central advantages, yet they can have a
variety of particular conditions of life and have different complexes of
community functions locally controlled. E.g., many neighborhoods might
have local control of their small grade-schools, with the city enforcing

*Goodman in fact considers seven ideas.

minimum standards and somewhat equalizing the funds. Political initiative is the means of political education.

In any city, we can appreciably diminish commutation by arranging   7
mutually satisfactory exchanges of residence to be near work. The aim of
planning is to diminish in-between services that are neither production
nor consumption. More generally, if this wasted time of commutation
were considered *economically* as part of the time of labor, there would soon
be better planning and more decentralization.

In New York City, the automobile traffic is not worth the nuisance it   8
causes. It would be advantageous simply to ban all private cars. Nearly
everyone would have faster transportation. Besides, we could then close
off about three-quarters of the streets and use them as a fund of land for
neighborhood planning.

Now, apart from the particular merits or demerits of any of these ideas,   9
what is wrong with this *style* of thinking, which aims at far-reaching social
and cultural advantages by direct and rather dumb-bunny expedients? I think
that we can see very simply why it is "utopian."

It is risky. The writers and musicians designing the commencement   10
ceremony would offend the parents, and the scandal would be politically
ruinous to the principal, the school board, and the mayor. Nobody expects
the ceremonial to be anything but boring, so let sleeping dogs lie. Artists are
conceited anyway and would disdain the commissions. So with the small
towns: the "best designers" would make the local hair stand on end. As for
the thought of children being educated by roaming the streets and blocking
traffic, it is a lulu and the less said the better.

Further, such thinking confuses administrative divisions. Community   11
arrangements are always awkwardly multipurpose. What department is responsible? Who budgets? It is inefficient not to have specialized equipment,
special buildings, and specialists.

Further, community creates conflict, for incompatibles are thrown to-   12
gether. And there is definitely an imposition of values. "Community" is an
imposed value, for many people want to be alone instead of sharing responsibilities or satisfactions; that is why they came to the big city. The notion of
living near work, or of a work-residence community, implies that people like
their work; but most people today don't.

Further, most such proposals are probably illegal; there would never be   13
an end to litigation. They override the usual procedures, so there is no experience of the problems that might arise; one cannot assess consequences or refer
to standard criteria.

Further, they are impracticable. To effect a change in the usual proce-   14
dures generally requires the pressure of some firm that will profit by it; such
things do not happen just because they would be "advantageous"; one can
hardly get the most trivial zoning regulation passed.

Finally, such proposals are impractical if only because they assume that 15
the mass of people have more sense and energy than they in fact have. In
emergencies, people show remarkable fortitude and choose sensible values
and agree to practical expedients because it is inevitable; but not ordinarily.
The quotation from Goethe is typical; it is "true," but not for us.

This is a fair picture of our dilemma. A direct solution of social problems 16
disturbs too many fixed arrangements. Society either does not want such
solutions, or society is not up to them—it comes to the same thing. The
possibility of a higher quality of experience arouses distrust rather than
enthusiasm. People must be educated slowly. On the other hand, the only
way *to* educate them, to change the present tone, is to cut through habits,
especially the character-defense of saying "nothing can be done" and with-
drawing into conformity and privacy. We must prove by experiment that
direct solutions are feasible. To "educate" in the accustomed style only wors-
ens the disease. And if we do *not* improve the standard of our present experience, it will utterly degenerate.

Therefore we must confront the dilemma as our problem. Our present 17
"organized" procedures are simply not good enough to cope with our technological changes. They debase the users of science, they discourage inventive
solutions, they complicate rather than simplify, they drive away some of the
best minds. Yet other procedures rouse anxiety and seem unrealistic and
irresponsible—whether or not they actually are. The question is, what kind
of social science can solve a dilemma of this kind? Let us approach this
question by deviating to a more philosophical consideration.

Let us attempt a list of postulates for a pragmatic social science: 18

1. The fact that the problem is being studied is a factor in the situation. 19
   The experimenter is one of the participants and this already alters the
   locus of the problem, usefully objectifying it.
2. The experimenter cannot know definitely what he is after, he has no 20
   fixed hypothesis to demonstrate, for he hopes that an unthought-of-
   solution will emerge in the process of coping with the problem. It is an
   "open" experiment.
3. The experimenter, like the other participants, is "engaged"; he has a 21
   moral need to come to a solution, and is therefore willing to change his
   own conceptions, and even his own character. As Biddle has said: "A
   hopeful attitude toward man's improvability may become a necessary
   precondition to further research," for otherwise one cannot morally
   engage oneself.
4. Since he does not know the outcome, the experimenter must risk confu- 22
   sion and conflict, and try out untested expedients. The safeguard is to
   stay in close contact with the concrete situation and to be objective and
   accurate in observation and reporting, and rigorous in analysis.

In the context of a pragmatic social science, utopian thinking at once 23
falls into place. Utopian ideas may be practical hypotheses, that is, expedients

for pilot experimentation. Or they may be stimuli for response, so that people get to know what they themselves mean. The fact that such ideas go against the grain of usual thinking is an advantage, for they thereby help to change the locus of the problem, which could not be solved in the usual terms. For instance, they may raise the target of conceivable advantages to a point where certain disadvantages, which were formerly prohibitive, now seem less important. (The assurance of help for an underprivileged child to go to college may make it worthwhile for him not to become delinquent. This has been the point of the "utopian" Higher Horizons program in the New York City schools.) Further, if a utopian expedient seems *prima facie* sensible, directly feasible, and technically practical, and is nevertheless unacceptable, there is a presumption that we are dealing with an "inner conflict," prejudice, the need to believe that nothing can be done, and the need to maintain the status quo.

As an illustration of the several points of this essay, consider utopian 24 planning for increased face-to-face community, people using one another as resources and sharing more functions of life and society. In a recent discussion I had with Herbert Gans of the University of Pennsylvania and other sociologists, it was agreed by all that our present social fragmentation, individual isolation, and family privacy are undesirable. Yet it was also agreed that to throw people together *as they are*—and how else do we have them?—causes inevitable conflicts. Here is our dilemma.

Gans argued that the attempt at community often leads to nothing at 25 all being done, instead of, at least, some useful accommodation. In Levittown, for example, a project in the community school fell through because the middle-class parents wanted a more intensive program to assure their children's "careers" (preparation for "prestige" colleges), whereas the lower-middle-class parents, who had lower status aims, preferred a more "progressive" program. "In such a case," said Gans, "a utopian will give up the program altogether and say that people are stupid."

My view is very different. It is that such a conflict is not an obstacle to 26 community but a golden opportunity, *if the give-and-take can continue, if contact can be maintained.* The continuing conflict cuts through the character-defense of people and *defeats* their stupidity, for stupidity is a character-defense. And the heat of the conflict results in better mutual understanding and fraternity. In Levittown, the job of the sociologist should have been not merely to infer the class conflict, but to bring it out into the open, to risk intensifying it by moving also into concealed snobbery and resentment (and racial feeling?), and to confront these people with the *ad hominem* problem: are such things indeed more important to you than, as neighbors, educating your children together?

In our era, to combat the emptiness of technological life, we have to 27 think of a new form, the conflictful community. Historically, close community has provided warmth and security, but it has been tyrannical, anti-liberal, and static (conformist small towns). We, however, have to do with already thoroughly urbanized individuals with a national culture and a scientific technology. The Israeli kibbutzim offer the closest approximation. Some of them have been fanatically dogmatic according to various ideologies, and often tyrannical; nevertheless, their urban Jewish members, rather well educated on the average, have inevitably run into fundamental conflict. Their atmosphere has therefore been sometimes unhappy but never deadening, and they have produced basic social inventions and new character-types. Is such a model improvable and adaptable to cities and industrial complexes? Can widely differing communities be accommodated in a larger federation? How can they be encouraged in modern societies? These are utopian questions.

Questions for Discussion

1. What passages can you point to that, taken together, constitute an adequate definition of Goodman's "utopian thinking"? Does most of the class agree about which passages to use?

2. Can you and other class members come up with examples of people from contemporary life—intellectuals or politicians, say—who seem to fit Goodman's definition of utopian thinkers? Can you think of examples of what Goodman might call anti-utopians?

3. In paragraphs 19–22 Goodman lists four postulates that describe what he calls "a pragmatic social science." How does this description differ, if at all, from a description you might make of the "hard" sciences: physics, chemistry, geology, and so on? Is social science as Goodman conceives of it really capable of achieving the social ends he wants?

4. Have someone who knows the Israeli kibbutzim do a report that explains what Goodman means when he says the kibbutzim "offer the closest approximation" to "a new form [of society], the conflictful community" (¶27).

Suggested Essay Topics

1. Take any one of Goodman's miniature arguments in paragraphs 2–8 and use it as a thesis statement for a more developed argument that you make yourself. The essay will be easier to write and probably more effective if you choose a specific audience. It is clear in paragraph 8, for example, that the intended audience is residents of New York City, not just anyone. Once you pick your audience, you may want to revise or refine the thesis statement to fit that audience better.

2. This suggestion is a variation on topic 1. Using Goodman's statements in paragraphs 2–8 as a model, construct a thesis of your own that recommends some significant kind of social change or reform; then develop reasons to show why your recommendations are both advantageous and workable.

Karl R. Popper

Philosopher Karl Popper (b. 1902) was born and educated in Vienna, but he taught and wrote at the University of London from 1945 until his retirement in 1969.

We are replacing our usual introduction with another demonstration of "How to Read an Argument." This demonstration is more extended than the one following Norman Cousins's essay (pp. 6–9). Here we offer first some suggestions about how to read an essay like Popper's. Then we follow the essay with an analysis that "walks through" the essay point by point.

How to Read an Argument:
Demonstration II

By now you have seen that arguments reveal a variety of purposes, tones, and shapes: sleek and streamlined, colloquial and chatty, complicated and interlocking, formal and lofty, and so on. The different varieties, moreover, require different kinds of reading skills. Our early demonstration of how to read the kind of argument used by Norman Cousins in "How to Make People Smaller Than They Are" provides only a start, on one kind of essay.

Popper's essay, "Utopia and Violence," is strikingly different from Cousins's in both structure and tone. While Cousins's kind of essay uses simple language and makes broad points unsupported by extended argument, Popper's essay relies on (1) complex thought (the author troubles himself throughout to qualify, define, and explain with precision), (2) formal tone (he uses the vocabulary and sentence structure of someone engaged in a serious task directed at an educated audience), (3) analytical methodology (he elaborately separates his position into parts), and (4) intellectual intent (he primarily addresses his audience's capacity for thoughtful rather than emotional response).

To inexperienced readers such arguments often seem a tangle of briers in which they wander lost and frustrated, annoyed at the teacher for assigning such thorny stuff and increasingly gloomy about the chances of escaping with any dignity or understanding. Unfortunately, there are no secret maps for keeping one's bearings inside such arguments—if there were, none of us would require either practice or intelligence. But there are some guideposts that can help to point us in the right direction. What follows here is a list of questions to ask as one reads essays like Popper's. Trying to fit the answers into a coherent reading of the text will move one toward a genuine "meeting" with a new and challenging author, even when, as is almost always the case, the text still refuses to yield itself up completely.

1. Topic. What is the author's topic—the general area of interest and concern being dealt with?

2. Thesis. What is the author's thesis—that is, what specific proposition or hypothesis concerning the general topic is the author making? The thesis is a proposition that the author wants to persuade the reader to believe.

3. Definitions of Terms. *What words or phrases seem crucial to the author's argument, and what meanings, explicit or implied, does he or she focus on throughout the essay? It is only by thinking hard about definitions that we turn* words *into the* terms *that form the elements of an author's argument.*

4. Evidence: Facts, Examples, Statistics, Analogies, and the Like. *Good readers persistently ask authors, at every step in a given argument, "What's your evidence?" Authors often openly welcome the question, especially those who exhibit great care and formality in their reasoning. And most authors, if their tasks are at all serious, in some way anticipate our habit of questioning the evidence. But the answers will vary greatly from author to author and from subject to subject, both in kind and quality. For some subjects, some authors will ask us to take examples from "real life," or even invented examples, as hard proof. (Much of Einstein's evidence in his early papers consisted of "thought experiments" that could not possibly be carried out in reality.) Other authors will offer us extensive statistical analyses. Others still will depend on analogies; astronomers often have to do so. When used appropriately, examples and analogies count as evidence. They often constitute the only kinds of evidence we can lay our hands on. Thus they are not to be automatically despised or dismissed because they are not scientific or factual. One mark of a liberal education is to know what kinds of evidence are appropriate, or even possible, in a given subject. As Aristotle says, it is foolish to ask for greater precision of proof than a given subject allows.*

The only rule for the reader, then, is to check in every case to discover whether the required kind of evidence has in fact been offered. What an author says *supports a claim must really do so. Controversies in all areas of life often revolve around just this issue, because no one has ever been able to formulate a uniform "code of evidence" applicable to all cases of serious reasoning.*

The most frequently praised kind of evidence these days is probably "the facts." Even people who fiercely dispute their interpretation and significance generally agree that once "facts" are ascertained, they must *be taken into account. To many people, the "harder" or more solid a fact is, the more weight it carries: the height of Mount Everest, the atomic weight of elements, the statistics about lung cancer, the life expectancy of American females, or the size of the gross national product. To others, a sensation, a feeling, a dream, an ambition, or a sense of awe can qualify as a fact.*

Obviously the whole realm of discourse would be a lot easier to manage if facts had an intrinsic, self-announcing quality that set them off into easily recognizable categories—but they do not. No datum simply is *a relevant fact; it* becomes *a fact in an argument as one decides how it can be used to support a conclusion. Nothing is more common than debaters denying the relevance, or even the solidity, of each other's facts. Despite their elusiveness, however, they can be the strongest kind of evidence whenever both parties to a discussion can agree about what they are. To insert them successfully into an argument is like thumping a trump card on an opponent's ace.*

5. Literary Devices. *Literary devices—such as personification, imagery, hyperbole, and irony—are sometimes powerfully persuasive. Metaphors are especially important. Sometimes their effect is local, limited to a particular sentence or paragraph, as when we said that reading some essays is like getting lost in a brier patch. But sometimes they exert a controlling influence over both the meaning and the structure of a whole argument. If we had said, for example, that reading essays is like diving for pearls (you take a deep breath, plunge into alien waters, grab frantically at all of the oysters you can pry loose, and finally pop to the surface hoping you've snagged a pearl somewhere in your take), and if we had tried to make everything else we said about reading consistent with our pearl-diving metaphor,* then *we would have been operating under the influence of a controlling metaphor. Not every author relies on extended metaphors, and not all authors are even conscious of what metaphors they do use. But metaphors are usually present in an essay (some scholars claim they are inescapable), and whenever metaphors occur, they, like all other literary devices, are crucially important.*

6. Assumptions.   All arguments take some things for granted in order to get themselves launched. Even positions that rely, like Popper's, on close reasoning still rest on a foundation of (implied or stated) ideas, principles, or value judgments that the author simply assumes *to be true; demonstrations of their truth are seldom offered, although they may be subject to rational criticism and defense elsewhere.*

In order to make this argument about how to read certain kinds of essays, for example, we unavoidably rest our case on several assumptions. We assume, first, that the essays we read together have coherent meanings that are, on the whole, "public" and not just private. Otherwise we could not talk about ways of drawing out those meanings for general discussion. Second, we assume that it is better to get at an author's meaning by means of a systematic method, analyzing an argument for topic, thesis, definitions, assumptions, and so on. Third, we assume that this method can itself be discussed—it, too, is coherent and can be publicly assessed—and it can be duplicated and applied to any number of arguments. If we were operating on a contrary set of assumptions—that nonreplicable and unsystematic private intuitions were the foundation of all understanding—then we would have no business describing a method *for reading an essay.*

Each of our assumptions, like those behind any argument, might be challenged and in turn defended. But whether we choose to accept or reject an author's assumptions, it is essential to our understanding to identify them.

7. Logical Coherence.   Once an author's assumptions have been uncovered, the reader is ready to ask questions about logical inference. We all feel that catching an author in an illogicality weighs heavily against a conclusion. Whenever authors contradict themselves, claim to have proved something that they have only asserted, cite inappropriate or inconclusive evidence, fail to cite evidence where it is necessary, ignore evidence that undercuts their case, call their opponents names instead of disproving their arguments, and jump over large areas of argumentative terrain that need to be surveyed, they have (at least partially) discredited their position. They may even have discredited themselves personally, giving the impression that they are "up to something" or that they are tackling a task beyond their abilities. In short, we all have a strong sense that the logical relationships within a position are among the most important determiners of its credibility.

The logic of an argument can be assessed by readers in three ways: first, by analyzing the formal relationships between premises and conclusions, an activity that can be done in a highly technical way by logicians and philosophers but can also be done in a less technical way by the general reader (see the section on "logical fallacies" in your rhetoric book or handbook); second, by testing an author's claims against knowledge, experience, and evidence of your own; and third, by testing an author's claims against your intuitions, sometimes even in the absence of hard evidence or reasons, about what makes "good sense."

None of these is an infallible test of an author's logic, but they are all that we have to work with. The places to look for logical connections or illogical jumps are at points of transition, when terms of conclusion such as hence, therefore, *and* finally *appear, and at points where examples and metaphors are offered. These are the places where authors sometimes fail to link the parts of their arguments together tightly. The reader can test the "tightness" by going back to a concluding term and tracing the links that lead up to it or by asking critically whether the example or metaphor really applies in the way that the author claims.*

8. Overall Structure. *All the while you are asking our first seven questions about an essay, you are in fact working to discover the structure of the argument— progressing a long way toward discovering the steps, large and small, that the author is taking. A final way of checking your reconstruction is to look again at all of the "signals of transition" that provide clues about where the author* thinks *the argument has come from and where it is going: transitional paragraphs only one or two sentences long; words like* therefore, then, thus, so, hence, nevertheless, finally; *and designations of series, such as* first, second, what's more. *Though you may have attempted an outline of the essay at earlier points, it may sometimes be only at this final moment of synthesis that you can construct one that satisfies you fully.*

Now, keeping these eight guideposts in mind, read Popper's essay as critically as you can. Although we will offer our analysis of "Utopia and Violence" at the end of the essay, try to construct your own before you read ours. You will then be better able to assess whether we have followed our own guideposts well or badly.

UTOPIA AND VIOLENCE

From *Conjectures and Refutations: The Growth of Scientific Knowledge* (1963; 2d ed. 1965; 3d ed. 1969; we are reprinting from the 2d ed.).

There are many people who hate violence and are convinced that it is one of their foremost and at the same time one of their most hopeful tasks to work for its reduction and, if possible, for its elimination from human life. I am among these hopeful enemies of violence. I not only hate violence, but I firmly believe that the fight against it is not at all hopeless. I realize that the task is difficult. I realize that, only too often in the course of history, it has happened that what appeared at first to be a great success in the fight against violence was followed by defeat. I do not overlook the fact that the new age of violence which was opened by the two world wars is by no means at an end. Nazism and Fascism are thoroughly beaten, but I must admit that their defeat does not mean that barbarism and brutality have been defeated. On the contrary, it is no use closing our eyes to the fact that these hateful ideas achieved something like victory in defeat. I have to admit that Hitler succeeded in degrading the moral standards of our Western world, and that in the world of today there is more violence and brutal force than would have been tolerated even in the decade after the first world war. And we must face the possibility that our civilization may ultimately be destroyed by those new weapons which Hitlerism wished upon us, perhaps even within the first decade* after the second world war; for no doubt the spirit of Hitlerism won its greatest victory over us when, after its defeat, we used the weapons which the threat of Nazism had induced us to develop. But in spite of all this I am today no less hopeful than I have ever been that violence can be defeated. It is our only hope; and long stretches in the history of Western as well as of Eastern civilizations prove that it need not be a vain hope—that violence *can* be reduced, and brought under the control of reason.

This is perhaps why I, like many others, believe in reason; why I call   2
myself a rationalist. I am a rationalist because I see in the attitude of reasonableness the only alternative to violence.

When two men disagree, they do so either because their opinions differ,   3
or because their interests differ, or both. There are many kinds of disagreement in social life which must be decided one way or another. The question may be one which must be settled, because failure to settle it may create new difficulties whose cumulative effects may cause an intolerable strain, such as a state of continual and intense preparation for deciding the issue. (An armaments race is an example.) To reach a decision may be a necessity.

How can a decision be reached? There are, in the main, only two possi-   4
ble ways: argument (including arguments submitted to arbitration, for example to some international court of justice) and violence. Or, if it is interests that clash, the two alternatives are a reasonable compromise or an attempt to destroy the opposing interest.

A rationalist, as I use the word, is a man who attempts to reach decisions   5
by argument and perhaps, in certain cases, by compromise, rather than by violence. He is a man who would rather be unsuccessful in convincing another man by argument than successful in crushing him by force, by intimidation and threats, or even by persuasive propaganda.

We shall understand better what I mean by reasonableness if we con-   6
sider the difference between trying to convince a man by argument and trying to persuade him by propaganda.

---

*This was written in 1947. Today I should alter this passage merely by replacing "first" by "second." [Popper's note.]

The difference does not lie so much in the use of argument. Propaganda   7
often uses argument too. Nor does the difference lie in our conviction that
our arguments are conclusive, and must be admitted to be conclusive by any
reasonable man. It lies rather in an attitude of give and take, in a readiness
not only to convince the other man but also possibly to be convinced by him.
What I call the attitude of reasonableness may be characterized by a remark
like this: "I think I am right, but I may be wrong and you may be right, and
in any case let us discuss it, for in this way we are likely to get nearer to a
true understanding than if we each merely insist that we are right."

It will be realized that what I call the attitude of reasonableness or the   8
rationalistic attitude presupposes a certain amount of intellectual humility.
Perhaps only those can take it up who are aware that they are sometimes
wrong, and who do not habitually forget their mistakes. It is born of the
realization that we are not omniscient, and that we owe most of our knowledge to others. It is an attitude which tries as far as possible to transfer to the
field of opinions in general the two rules of every legal proceeding: first, that
one should always hear both sides, and secondly, that one does not make a
good judge if one is a party to the case.

I believe that we can avoid violence only in so far as we practise this   9
attitude of reasonableness when dealing with one another in social life; and
that any other attitude is likely to produce violence—even a one-sided attempt to deal with others by gentle persuasion, and to convince them by
argument and example of those insights we are proud of possessing, and of
whose truth we are absolutely certain. We all remember how many religious
wars were fought for a religion of love and gentleness; how many bodies were
burned alive with the genuinely kind intention of saving souls from the
eternal fire of hell. Only if we give up our authoritarian attitude in the realm
of opinion, only if we establish the attitude of give and take, of readiness to
learn from other people, can we hope to control acts of violence inspired by
piety and duty.

There are many difficulties impeding the rapid spread of reasonableness.   10
One of the main difficulties is that it always takes two to make a discussion
reasonable. Each of the parties must be ready to learn from the other. You
cannot have a rational discussion with a man who prefers shooting you to
being convinced by you. In other words, there are limits to the attitude of
reasonableness. It is the same with tolerance. You must not, without qualification, accept the principle of tolerating all those who are intolerant; if you
do, you will destroy not only yourself, but also the attitude of tolerance. (All
this is indicated in the remark I made before—that reasonableness must be
an attitude of *give and take.*)

An important consequence of all this is that we must not allow the   11
distinction between attack and defence to become blurred. We must insist
upon this distinction, and support and develop social institutions (national
as well as international) whose function it is to discriminate between aggression and resistance to aggression.

I think I have said enough to make clear what I intend to convey by   12 calling myself a rationalist. My rationalism is not dogmatic. I fully admit that I cannot rationally prove it. I frankly confess that I choose rationalism because I hate violence, and I do not deceive myself into believing that this hatred has any rational grounds. Or to put it another way, my rationalism is not self-contained, but rests on an irrational faith in the attitude of reasonableness. I do not see that we can go beyond this. One could say, perhaps, that my irrational faith in equal and reciprocal rights to convince others and be convinced by them is a faith in human reason; or simply, that I believe in man.

If I say that I believe in man, I mean in man as he is; and I should never 13 dream of saying that he is wholly rational. I do not think that a question such as whether man is more rational than emotional or *vice versa* should be asked: there are no ways of assessing or comparing such things. I admit that I feel inclined to protest against certain exaggerations (arising largely from a vulgarization of psycho-analysis) of the irrationality of man and of human society. But I am aware not only of the power of emotions in human life, but also of their value. I should never demand that the attainment of an attitude of reasonableness should become the one dominant aim of our lives. All I wish to assert is that this attitude can become one that is never wholly absent—not even in relationships which are dominated by great passions, such as love.*

My fundamental attitude towards the problem of reason and violence 14 will by now be understood; and I hope I share it with some of my readers and with many other people everywhere. It is on this basis that I now propose to discuss the problem of Utopianism.

I think we can describe Utopianism as a result of a form of rationalism, 15 and I shall try to show that this is a form of rationalism very different from the form in which I and many others believe. So I shall try to show that there exist at least two forms of rationalism, one of which I believe is right and the other wrong; and that the wrong kind of rationalism is the one which leads to Utopianism.

As far as I can see, Utopianism is the result of a way of reasoning which 16 is accepted by many who would be astonished to hear that this apparently quite inescapable and self-evident way of reasoning leads to Utopian results. This specious reasoning can perhaps be presented in the following manner.

An action, it may be argued, is rational if it makes the best use of the 17 available means in order to achieve a certain end. The end, admittedly, may be incapable of being determined rationally. However this may be, we can judge an action rationally, and describe it as rational or adequate, only relative to some given end. Only if we have an end in mind, and only relative to such an end, can we say that we are acting rationally.

Now let us apply this argument to politics. All politics consists of 18 actions; and these actions will be rational only if they pursue some end. The

*The existentialist Jaspers writes, "This is why love is cruel, ruthless; and why it is believed in, by the genuine lover, only if it is so." This attitude, to my mind, reveals weakness rather than the strength it wishes to show; it is not so much plain barbarism as an hysterical attempt to play the barbarian. (*Cf.* my *Open Society,* 4th edn., vol. II, p. 317.) [Popper's note.]

end of a man's political actions may be the increase of his own power or wealth. Or it may perhaps be the improvement of the laws of the state, a change in the structure of the state.

In the latter case political action will be rational only if we first deter-　19 mine the final ends of the political changes which we intend to bring about. It will be rational only relative to certain ideas of what a state ought to be like. Thus it appears that as a preliminary to any rational political action we must first attempt to become as clear as possible about our ultimate political ends; for example the kind of state which we should consider the best; and only afterwards can we begin to determine the means which may best help us to realize this state, or to move slowly towards it, taking it as the aim of an historical process which we may to some extent influence and steer towards the goal selected.

Now it is precisely this view which I call Utopianism. Any rational and　20 nonselfish political action, on this view, must be preceded by a determination of our ultimate ends, not merely of intermediate or partial aims which are only steps towards our ultimate end, and which therefore should be considered as means rather than as ends; therefore rational political action must be based upon a more or less clear and detailed description or blueprint of our ideal state, and also upon a plan or blueprint of the historical path that leads towards this goal.

I consider what I call Utopianism an attractive and, indeed, an all too　21 attractive theory; for I also consider it dangerous and pernicious. It is, I believe, self-defeating, and it leads to violence.

That it is self-defeating is connected with the fact that it is impossible　22 to determine ends scientifically. There is no scientific way of choosing between two ends. Some people, for example, love and venerate violence. For them a life without violence would be shallow and trivial. Many others, of whom I am one, hate violence. This is a quarrel about ends. It cannot be decided by science. This does not mean that the attempt to argue against violence is necessarily a waste of time. It only means that you may not be able to argue with the admirer of violence. He has a way of answering an argument with a bullet if he is not kept under control by the threat of counter-violence. If he is willing to listen to your arguments without shooting you, then he is at least infected by rationalism, and you may, perhaps, win him over. This is why arguing is no waste of time—as long as people listen to you. But you cannot, by means of argument, make people listen to argument; you cannot, by means of argument, convert those who suspect all argument, and who prefer violent decisions to rational decisions. You cannot prove to them that they are wrong. And this is only a particular case, which can be generalized. No decision about aims can be established by *purely* rational or scientific means. Nevertheless argument may prove extremely helpful in reaching a decision about aims.

Applying all this to the problem of Utopianism, we must first be quite　23 clear that the problem of constructing a Utopian blueprint cannot possibly be solved by science alone. Its aims, at least, must be given before the social scientist can begin to sketch his blueprint. We find the same situation in the natural sciences. No amount of physics will tell a scientist that it is the right thing for him to construct a plough, or an aeroplane, or an atomic bomb. Ends must be adopted by him, or given to him; and what he does *qua* [as] scientist is only to construct means by which these ends can be realized.

In emphasizing the difficulty of deciding, by way of rational argument, 24 between different Utopian ideals, I do not wish to create the impression that there is a realm—such as the realm of ends—which goes altogether beyond the power of rational criticism (even though I certainly wish to say that the realm of ends goes largely beyond the power of *scientific* argument). For I myself try to argue about this realm; and by pointing out the difficulty of deciding between competing Utopian blueprints, I try to argue rationally against choosing ideal ends of this kind. Similarly, my attempt to point out that this difficulty is likely to produce violence is meant as a rational argument, although it will appeal only to those who hate violence.

That the Utopian method, which chooses an ideal state of society as the 25 aim which all our political actions should serve, is likely to produce violence can be shown thus. Since we cannot determine the ultimate ends of political actions scientifically, or by purely rational methods, differences of opinion concerning what the ideal state should be like cannot always be smoothed out by the method of argument. They will at least partly have the character of religious differences. And there can be no tolerance between these different Utopian religions. Utopian aims are designed to serve as a basis for rational political action and discussion, and such action appears to be possible only if the aim is definitely decided upon. Thus the Utopianist must win over, or else crush, his Utopianist competitors who do not share his own Utopian aims and who do not profess his own Utopianist religion.

But he has to do more. He has to be very thorough in eliminating and 26 stamping out all heretical competing views. For the way to the Utopian goal is long. Thus the rationality of his political action demands constancy of aim for a long time ahead; and this can only be achieved if he not merely crushes competing Utopian religions, but as far as possible stamps out all memory of them.

The use of violent methods for the suppression of competing aims 27 becomes even more urgent if we consider that the period of Utopian construction is liable to be one of social change. In such a time ideas are liable to change also. Thus what may have appeared to many as desirable at the time when the Utopian blueprint was decided upon may appear less desirable at a later date. If this is so, the whole approach is in danger of breaking down. For if we change our ultimate political aims while attempting to move towards them we may soon discover that we are moving in circles. The whole method of first establishing an ultimate political aim and then preparing to move towards it must be futile if the aim may be changed during the process of its realization. It may easily turn out that the steps so far taken lead in fact away from the new aim. And if we then change direction in accordance with our new aim we expose ourselves to the same risk. In spite of all the sacrifices which we may have made in order to make sure that we are acting rationally, we may get exactly nowhere—although not exactly to that "nowhere" which is meant by the word "Utopia."

Again, the only way to avoid such changes of our aims seems to be to 28 use violence, which includes propaganda, the suppression of criticism, and the annihilation of all opposition. With it goes the affirmation of the wisdom and foresight of the Utopian planners, of the Utopian engineers who design and execute the Utopian blueprint. The Utopian engineers must in this way become omniscient as well as omnipotent. They become gods. Thou shalt have no other Gods before them.

Utopian rationalism is a self-defeating rationalism. However benevo- 29 lent its ends, it does not bring happiness, but only the familiar misery of being condemned to live under a tyrannical government.

It is important to understand this criticism fully. I do not criticize politi- 30 cal ideals as such, nor do I assert that a political ideal can never be realized. This would not be a valid criticism. Many ideals have been realized which were once dogmatically declared to be unrealizable, for example, the establishment of workable and untyrannical institutions for securing civil peace, that is, for the suppression of crime within the state. Again, I see no reason why an international judicature and an international police force should be less successful in suppressing international crime, that is, national aggression and the ill-treatment of minorities or perhaps majorities. I do not object to the attempt to realize such ideals.

Wherein, then, lies the difference between those benevolent Utopian 31 plans to which I object because they lead to violence, and those other important and far-reaching political reforms which I am inclined to recommend?

If I were to give a simple formula or recipe for distinguishing between 32 what I consider to be admissible plans for social reform and inadmissible Utopian blueprints, I might say:

Work for the elimination of concrete evils rather than for the realization 33 of abstract goods. Do not aim at establishing happiness by political means. Rather aim at the elimination of concrete miseries. Or, in more practical terms: fight for the elimination of poverty by direct means—for example, by making sure that everybody has a minimum income. Or fight against epidemics and disease by erecting hospitals and schools of medicine. Fight illiteracy as you fight criminality. But do all this by direct means. Choose what you consider the most urgent evil of the society in which you live, and try patiently to convince people that we can get rid of it.

But do not try to realize these aims indirectly by designing and working 34 for a distant ideal of a society which is wholly good. However deeply you may feel indebted to its inspiring vision, do not think that you are obliged to work for its realization, or that it is your mission to open the eyes of others to its beauty. Do not allow your dreams of a beautiful world to lure you away from the claims of men who suffer here and now. Our fellow men have a claim to our help; no generation must be sacrificed for the sake of future generations, for the sake of an ideal of happiness that may never be realized.

In brief, it is my thesis that human misery is the most urgent problem of a rational public policy and that happiness is not such a problem. The attainment of happiness should be left to our private endeavours.

It is a fact, and not a very strange fact, that it is not so very difficult to   35
reach agreement by discussion on what are the most intolerable evils of our society, and on what are the most urgent social reforms. Such an agreement can be reached much more easily than an agreement concerning some ideal form of social life. For the evils are with us here and now. They can be experienced, and are being experienced every day, by many people who have been and are being made miserable by poverty, unemployment, national oppression, war and disease. Those of us who do not suffer from these miseries meet every day others who can describe them to us. This is what makes the evils concrete. This is why we can get somewhere in arguing about them; why we can profit here from the attitude of reasonableness. We can learn by listening to concrete claims, by patiently trying to assess them as impartially as we can, and by considering ways of meeting them without creating worse evils.

With ideal goods it is different. These we know only from our dreams   36
and from the dreams of our poets and prophets. They cannot be discussed, only proclaimed from the housetops. They do not call for the rational attitude of the impartial judge, but for the emotional attitude of the impassioned preacher.

The Utopianist attitude, therefore, is opposed to the attitude of reason-   37
ableness. Utopianism, even though it may often appear in a rationalist disguise, cannot be more than a pseudo-rationalism.

What, then, is wrong with the apparently rational argument which I   38
outlined when presenting the Utopianist case? I believe that it is quite true that we can judge the rationality of an action only in relation to some aims or ends. But this does not necessarily mean that the rationality of a political action can be judged only in relation to an *historical* end. And it surely does not mean that we must consider every social or political situation merely from the point of view of some preconceived historical ideal, from the point of view of an alleged ultimate aim of the development of history. On the contrary, if among our aims and ends there is anything conceived in terms of human happiness and misery, then we are bound to judge our actions in terms not only of possible contributions to the happiness of man in a distant future, but also of their more immediate effects. We must not argue that a certain social situation is a mere means to an end on the grounds that it is merely a transient historical situation. For all situations are transient. Similarly we must not argue that the misery of one generation may be considered as a mere means to the end of securing the lasting happiness of some later generation or generations; and this argument is improved neither by a high degree of promised happiness nor by a large number of generations profiting by it. All generations are transient. All have an equal right to be considered, but our immediate duties are undoubtedly to the present generation and to

the next. Besides, we should never attempt to balance anybody's misery against somebody else's happiness.

With this the apparently rational arguments of Utopianism dissolve into 39 nothing. The fascination which the future exerts upon the Utopianist has nothing to do with rational foresight. Considered in this light the violence which Utopianism breeds looks very much like the running amok of an evolutionist metaphysics, of an hysterical philosophy of history, eager to sacrifice the present for the splendours of the future, and unaware that its principle would lead to sacrificing each particular future period for one which comes after it; and likewise unaware of the trivial truth that the ultimate future of man—whatever fate may have in store for him—can be nothing more splendid than his ultimate extinction.

The appeal of Utopianism arises from the failure to realize that we 40 cannot make heaven on earth. What I believe we can do instead is to make life a little less terrible and a little less unjust in each generation. A good deal can be achieved in this way. Much has been achieved in the last hundred years. More could be achieved by our own generation. There are many pressing problems which we might solve, at least partially, such as helping the weak and the sick, and those who suffer under oppression and injustice; stamping out unemployment; equalizing opportunities; and preventing international crime, such as blackmail and war instigated by men like gods, by omnipotent and omniscient leaders. All this we might achieve if only we could give up dreaming about distant ideals and fighting over our Utopian blueprints for a new world and a new man. Those of us who believe in man as he is, and who have therefore not given up the hope of defeating violence and unreason, must demand instead that every man should be given the right to arrange his life himself so far as this is compatible with the equal rights of others.

We can see here that the problem of the true and the false rationalisms 41 is part of a larger problem. Ultimately it is the problem of a sane attitude towards our own existence and its limitations—that very problem of which so much is made now by those who call themselves "Existentialists," the expounders of a new theology without God. There is, I believe, a neurotic and even an hysterical element in this exaggerated emphasis upon the fundamental loneliness of man in a godless world, and upon the resulting tension between the self and the world. I have little doubt that this hysteria is closely akin to Utopian romanticism, and also to the ethic of hero-worship, to an ethic that can comprehend life only in terms of "dominate or prostrate yourself." And I do not doubt that this hysteria is the secret of its strong appeal. That our problem is part of a larger one can be seen from the fact that we can find a clear parallel to the split between true and false rationalism even in a sphere apparently so far removed from rationalism as that of religion. Christian thinkers have interpreted the relationship between man and God in at least two very different ways. The sane one may be expressed by: "Never forget that men are not Gods; but remember that there is a divine spark in them." The other exaggerates the tension between man and God, and the baseness of man as well as the heights to which men may aspire. It introduces the ethic of "dominate or prostrate yourself" into the relationship of man and God. Whether there are always either conscious or unconscious dreams of godlikeness and of omnipotence at the roots of this attitude, I do not know. But I think it is hard to deny that the emphasis on this tension can arise only from an unbalanced attitude towards the problem of power.

This unbalanced (and immature) attitude is obsessed with the problem   42 of power, not only over other men, but also over our natural environment— over the world as a whole. What I might call, by analogy, the "false religion," is obsessed not only by God's power over men but also by His power to create a world; similarly, false rationalism is fascinated by the idea of creating huge machines and Utopian social worlds. Bacon's "knowledge is power" and Plato's "rule of the wise" are different expressions of this attitude which, at bottom, is one of claiming power on the basis of one's superior intellectual gifts. The true rationalist, by contrast, will always know how little he knows, and he will be aware of the simple fact that whatever critical faculty or reason he may possess he owes to intellectual intercourse with others. He will be inclined, therefore, to consider men as fundamentally equal, and human reason as a bond which unites them. Reason for him is the precise opposite of an instrument of power and violence: he sees it as a means whereby these may be tamed.

Analysis of "Utopia and Violence"

If we apply our method for reading an argument to Popper's essay, what does it yield? Let us look systematically at all eight guideposts.

1. Topic.   *Popper begins in paragraph 1 by making three claims: (1) that he along with many other persons hates violence, (2) that the world has become increasingly violent in the aftermath of the two world wars, and (3) that he remains nevertheless convinced that violence can be reduced and "brought under the control of reason." Doing so, he says, "is our only hope." Apparently, then, Popper's topic is the relationship between reason and violence. Notice, however, that this is only a general area of concern. Discovering that Popper is interested in the relationship between reason and violence does not reveal what direction his concern will take or what point about that relationship he wants to make. In other words, we know his topic but not his thesis.*

2. Thesis.   *Notice that paragraph 2 is very short, only two sentences long. Such paragraphs are often transitional. This one sums up the point of paragraph 1, but in doing so Popper manages to indicate clearly his* thesis, *the point he wants to make: "I see in the attitude of reasonableness the only alternative to violence."*

3. Definitions of Terms. *We know from Popper's thesis statement that there are two crucial terms in his argument,* reasonableness *and* violence. *The second of these he does not define in any special way. He seems to take it for granted that we all know what violence is, and, indeed, his incidental allusions to violence are all conventional: people shooting each other, aggression between nations, certain kinds of oppression by political rulers, and so on.*

Reasonableness, however, has for him a very precise, special meaning, and he expends a considerable amount of effort and space clarifying this key term. He begins by saying what it is not. Reasonableness, he contends, is not merely knowing how to use reason in order to make arguments. Propagandists, tyrants, and oppressors of all sorts know how to use reason to make arguments. Rather, reasonableness "lies . . . in an attitude of give and take, in a readiness not only to convince the other man but also possibly to be convinced by him" (¶7).

But what does give-and-take *mean? Primarily it means "humility," "the realization that we are not omniscient, and that we owe most of our knowledge to others" (¶8). (Notice, by the way, that Popper repeats this idea clearly at the end of his essay [¶42]: "The true rationalist . . . will always know . . . that whatever . . . reason he may possess he owes to intellectual intercourse with others." The more times an author repeats an idea in the course of an essay, especially if the repetitions come at key spots such as the beginning and the end, the more you are justified in assuming that the idea possesses central importance.)*

In paragraph 9 we learn that humility is not only the admission that we have learned most of what we know from others, but that even our most precious values, even our certainties, are still susceptible to correction. Good intentions do not automatically produce good effects. In the Middle Ages torture was accepted as a device not only for discovering the truth, but also for making wrongdoers confess so that their souls might be saved even as their bodies perished. And in the modern period every violent revolution has produced mass killings by those whose sole professed aim was to create a better society. The number of victims maimed, tortured, and killed in any period would be much smaller if all certainties had been subject to give-and-take. Popper's point is that no *belief, no matter how noble or true, allows us to assume our own infallibility; even if our opinions are true, we can never* know *them to be true in an absolute sense, and, in any event, inflicting pain, destruction, and violence, even in the interests of true opinions, involves us in an irreconcilable contradiction between the nobility of our aims and the ignobility of our methods.*

Another term that Popper defines with precision (although it takes less effort because it is derived from his term reasonableness) *is the word* rationalist. *A rationalist, as Popper uses the term, is simply a person committed to give-and-take, to tolerance, and to compromise (at least about conflicts of interest, if not about conflicts of opinion) when give-and-take is abandoned by those he is trying to talk to.*

A fourth crucial term, utopianism, *does not show up until paragraph 14. As with the term* reasonableness, *you can form a fairly clear notion of its importance in Popper's argument simply from the amount of discussion he devotes to its clarification. Reasonableness, it turns out, is the hero of his piece; utopianism is the villain. Notice here, by the way, how metaphors exert a controlling influence on one's understanding. The metaphor of "heroes versus villains," which comes from melodramas and westerns, is not used by Popper; we use it in trying to understand him. Notice further that if we were to base our analysis on this metaphor alone, we would trivialize his argument.*

Yet our metaphor is appropriate if we apply it with caution, for Popper really intends not only to reveal the evil consequences of accepting utopianism, but to discredit it so thoroughly that no thinking person could retain faith in it after reading his argument. While avoiding melodramatic metaphors, he nevertheless suggests that this is a showdown, that he has viewed this evil phenomenon long enough to be convinced of its dangerousness, that he has thought out his arguments with care and precision, and that he is determined to leave no chink for utopianism to weasel through.

As he develops his views on utopianism at length (¶15–29), we see that he has two main charges to level against it: "It is, I believe, self-defeating, and it leads to violence" (¶21). If this were self-evident to everyone, merely to say it would be at once to express the argument and to prove it. But it is not self-evident, and that is what justifies drawing out the argument. Far from being obviously evil, utopianism, claims Popper, is "an all too attractive theory" (¶21) "which is accepted by many who would be astonished to hear" that it leads inescapably to violence (¶16). These claims place on Popper two burdens: first, to show how *utopianism leads to violence and, second, to show* why *it is attractive (and, necessarily, why its attractiveness is illusory).*

Utopianism is attractive because, by definition, it is a form of rationalism (although unlike reasonableness), and it may therefore seem a credible mode of thinking to anyone who values rationality (¶15). It looks *rational because it engages in the process of constructing means to achieve already chosen ends (¶20). But, Popper claims, looks are in this case deceptive, for utopianism is "specious reasoning" (¶16), which is to say fair-looking but false.*

The falseness of utopianism lies not so much in looking for means to achieve aims—this is rational enough—but in choosing aims that are so difficult to define and so impossible to achieve that they lead inevitably (or so he claims) to violence among those responsible for achieving them. "Utopianists" move "rationally" toward the ideal state, and that, says Popper, is where the trouble begins. Ideal ends, by definition, exist both so far removed from everyday experience and so far removed into the future that "differences of opinion concerning what the ideal state should be like cannot always be smoothed out by the method of argument. They will at least partly have the character of religious differences. And there can be no tolerance between these different Utopian religions" (¶25). Moreover, goals lying so far removed from experience and so far into the future cannot be kept in focus if competing views and shifts of goals are allowed. Thus, on its way toward the noble aim of creating a perfect society, utopianism always winds up employing means that create not only an imperfect society (presumably what we all begin with anyway) but the most imperfect form of society altogether: a totalitarianism that sacrifices everything in the present—the justice, comfort, security, and peace of the present generation—for the good of the ideal future state.

It should be clear by this point that a full understanding of crucial terms sometimes leads us to the very heart of an author's argument. This is not always true, but you should be alert to the possibility.

4. Evidence: Facts, Examples, Statistics, Analogies, and the Like.

Unlike many a serious thinker, Popper relies on few examples, no statistics, and practically no facts. The force of his essay rests almost wholly on the logical coherence of his arguments. Given his aim, one would expect that historical examples might have been useful, but he grounds the argument in logic alone, not on examples that others (presumably the utopianists) could explain away or quibble about. The only place where examples become telling is his catalog (¶33–35) of concrete ills that we should be trying to rid ourselves of: disease, poverty, crime, and so on. If we did not find these examples appropriate his argument would suffer, but because he sticks generally to the obvious ills that, as he says, everyone already recognizes, he runs little risk of discrediting himself with implausible examples. Insofar as the examples he does use are universally admitted to exist, they have the status of facts in his argument. He makes no appeal to other kinds of facts that are often thought useful, such as statistics, measurements, or polls.

5. Literary Devices.

Popper relies no more on colorful literary devices and metaphors than he does on examples and collections of facts. Like almost all authors, he uses some metaphors, but these are strictly low-key and directly functional rather than "literary." He uses only the kind of metaphors we all use every day—as when he speaks of blueprints for society and moving in circles (¶27)—and their impact is restricted to small passages. None of them determines either his view of his topic or the structure of his essay. Perhaps the most potent metaphor in the whole essay is his allusion in paragraph 28 to "Utopian engineers" who think themselves "omniscient as well as omnipotent"—a metaphor that alludes to the view projected by George Orwell in Nineteen Eighty-Four *and used in a host of science fiction movies. But whether "engineers" is not more of a cliché than a vivid picture is an open question. It is certainly not the most chilling image for political oppressors that he might have picked. The restraint seems deliberate. Even in his final sentence, for example, where he speaks of taming the instruments of power and violence, at the terminal point where many authors would be tempted to pull out all the stops, Popper avoids any striving for a highly charged, triumphant final chord. He seems vigorous but controlled from beginning to end. (Of course one might, as we suggested earlier, claim to see an unspoken master metaphor in the "showdown" or "war" Popper conducts between reason and violence. It is important to think about the implications of unspoken governing metaphors, but this sort of critique is better conducted at a stage following your first thorough analysis of the essay.)*

6. Assumptions.   *Perhaps because he is a philosopher, Popper is unusually clear about his assumptions. This is not the case with all writers; many authors seem guided by assumptions that they are only dimly aware of, and their conclusions and assumptions do not always seem consistent.*

The first assumption without which Popper's argument would be impossible, as he is well aware, is his "faith in human reason": "I believe in man," he says (¶12). Without this faith in the capacity of human beings not only to achieve understanding through reason but also to pattern behavior according to reason's light, writing this article would be a futile, self-contradictory undertaking.

Popper's second important assumption is about the limitations of reason. While he is advocating reasonableness with all the energy he can muster, he is only too aware that not everything can be decided on rational grounds alone, especially ultimate goals: "No decision about aims can be established by purely rational or scientific means" (¶22). For example, he says, "No amount of physics will tell a scientist that it is the right thing for him to construct a plough, or an aeroplane, or an atomic bomb" (¶23). This does not mean that all ends, as value judgments, are irrational impulse or whimsy, nor does it mean that they are incapable of reasoned defense. But it does mean that they are the product of vision, intuitions, and experience that go beyond logical argument.

This assumption plays a crucial role in Popper's argument, for if he assumed that final ends could be rationally determined, he would be undercutting his charge that utopianism's rational goals for the future lead to concrete evils in the present.

Popper's third crucial assumption is his belief that "no generation must be sacrificed for the sake of future generations, for the sake of an ideal of happiness that may never be realized" (¶34). He makes this same assertion another time or two in different words in the same paragraph, and utters it once again toward the end of paragraph 38: "We must not argue that a certain social situation is a mere means to an end on the grounds that it is merely a transient historical situation." The development of this assumption's meaning occupies the whole last section of the essay, from paragraphs 32 to 42.

At this point you may be wanting to say, "It is all very well to point out assumptions, and it is all very helpful when you do, but how do you recognize one in the first place? How did you know that these utterances contained assumptions?" It is a good question, but one to which there is no formulaic answer. The necessary skills are experience at reading arguments like this, experience at thinking about the kinds of ideas they contain, careful observation of the pattern of ideas and expression, and attention to logical connections. This may sound like a tall order for the inexperienced reader, but no one, not even the most inexperienced reader, comes to a piece of writing totally devoid of the powers of observation and logic. And every reader can detect the presence of important generalizations for which no extended argument is offered; they are what is assumed.

When readers who are paying close attention to what Popper is saying come, for example, to paragraph 32, they do not have to be college professors to observe that Popper's offer of "a simple formula or recipe" signals a shift of focus and tone. As the passage proceeds, Popper increasingly abandons neutrality of tone and addresses the reader in a more direct, personal, urgent way: "Do not try," he says, and "do not think," and "do not allow" (¶34). His increasing passion is one of the best clues that you are approaching a nodal point where assumptions lurk. Whenever an author's language becomes prescriptive and personal—"I feel," "I believe," "you must," "you must not"—chances are you are treading on the holy ground of fundamental assumptions.

      7. Logical Coherence. *We saw earlier that Popper has two main charges to level against utopianism: that it is self-defeating and that it inevitably leads to violence. The first of these charges he supports convincingly, but the second seems less well supported. In paragraphs 22–28, for example, he launches into an extended argument about the procedure that turns utopian dreams into totalitarian states, but while he shows clearly that utopian ideals will always outpace achievement and are therefore self-defeating, he does not show that the inevitable consequence of this failure is violence. Even if he were able to show that that is what usually happens* in fact, *he would not have proved its inevitability* in principle.

      Why would Popper neglect to provide proof for such a crucial point, while elsewhere he demonstrates impressive logical rigor? We might be tempted to assign the status of "assumption" to this point, but Popper himself, as we have seen, is careful to separate his fundamental assumptions from assertions he means to support—and he does, it seems, intend to argue for the violent consequences of utopianism.

      In a case like this, where logical coherence inexplicably breaks down, it is useful to search out any other failures or missing steps in the logic and to try to discern a motive *behind the author's neglect. Another place where Popper has omitted steps in his argument is paragraph 38. Suddenly, without explanation, he introduces an element that seems totally unprepared for: "I believe that it is quite true that we can judge the rationality of an action only in relation to some aims or ends. But this does not necessarily mean that the rationality of a political action can be judged only in relation to an* historical *end." The abrupt insertion of a concern about* historical *ends right in the middle of his argument about* ideal *ends, without preparation or explanation, raises questions. There is a jump here in the logic that requires an explanation outside the boundaries of the argument itself.*

      Perhaps the explanation is that Popper, without ever naming Marxist philosophy in his article, is nevertheless constructing an argument against it. Other writings of his show that he is an implacable foe of Marxist political philosophy, that he considers Marxist philosophers the most hopeless of all utopianists, and the Soviet Union the clearest example of how utopian dreams turn into totalitarian nightmares.

      Why, then, does he not mention that it is the Marxists' *historical ends that he objects to? The question is impossible to answer if the only answer lies in Popper's private motives. But the position itself suggests an answer. If he can demonstrate that* all *utopian thinking is equally invalid, then it* must *follow that Marxist thinking also stands condemned. But if he makes his quarrel with Marxism alone, he winds up with a weaker position even if he wins, for combating Marxism without combating utopianism means that he must attack Marxism on the basis of its policies, not its principles. He wants the stronger case that will discredit Marxism* and *its cousins once and for all, and the stronger case requires an attack on Marxism's underlying principles.*

Does this attack on Marxism undermine the logical coherence of Popper's essay? Probably not, since one can easily guess his motive for avoiding a direct attack. But it is surely a weakness of Popper's presentation that one cannot find a sufficient number of references within the essay to make this motive clear. And even putting his presentation aside, one illogicality clearly remains: He has not shown that Marxist utopianism must always produce totalitarian states or, more generally, that utopianism must always lead to violence. It is difficult to say just how much this illogicality weakens his entire position. Here is where one must test the logic of a position with one's intuitions about what makes "good sense" and about the limits of our ability to prove generalizations concerning human possibilities.

8. Overall Structure.   The problem of how to discover a controlling structure in an argument is no different from the problem of how to discover a set of controlling assumptions. You have to pay close attention and then practice on essay after essay. From the beginning of Popper's essay it is apparent that he is concerned about violence and reasonableness, but it is not clear how the expression of that concern is going to be patterned until we come to paragraph 14. The careful reader will at this point observe that Popper explicitly defines what he has been up to for the first 13 paragraphs: "My fundamental attitude towards the problem of reason and violence will by now be understood." Building on this first clear indication of structure, let us see if we can discern the shape of the essay as a whole.

I. Paragraphs 1–14: Introduction of topic, thesis, and definition of reasonableness.
  A. Paragraph 1, like most first paragraphs, is an introduction to the topic, the relationship between reason and violence.
  B. Paragraph 2 sums up paragraph 1 and states Popper's thesis.
  C. Paragraphs 3–9 refine the topic and thesis, mainly by providing a definition of *reasonableness* and by providing some appropriate concrete examples.
  D. Paragraphs 10–13 discuss the proper domain of reason, each paragraph adding a refinement to the idea.
  E. Paragraph 14 is transitional, introducing "the problem of Utopianism."
II. Paragraphs 15–29 express the main body of Popper's objections to utopianism.
  A. Paragraphs 15–21 argue that utopianism gives a rational appearance because it lays out goals and selects means for achieving them. This section ends with one of Popper's typical transitional paragraphs (¶21), just two sentences long, introducing a new direction to the discussion.
  B. Paragraphs 22–28 clarify the danger pointed to in the transitional paragraph.
    1. Paragraphs 22–24 begin to explain the danger.
    2. Paragraphs 25–28 become increasingly practical, culminating in a description of utopian planners as "engineers" who pretend to "become omniscient as well as omnipotent."
  C. Paragraph 29 is another two-sentence transition.
III. Paragraphs 30–40 make Popper's suggestions for how to avoid utopian thinking.

A. Paragraphs 30–32 are a buildup to his catalog of non-utopian remedies.

    1. Paragraph 30 clarifies his critique: He wants the reader to be clear that he does not consider utopian thinking pernicious merely because it spins out ideals.

    2. Paragraph 31 seems to ask (not quite this bluntly), "Well, then, if ideal-oriented thinking isn't the problem, what is?"

    3. Paragraph 32 directly responds: "All right, I'll answer that question, but not by giving more criticisms, which I've already done. I will instead propose concrete remedies."

B. Paragraphs 33–35 provide the concrete remedies. Popper here lists the ills that political planners should be trying to solve: the concrete evils of every-day life, the obvious ones that everybody already agrees about.

C. Paragraphs 36–40 directly answer the question asked in paragraph 31, the answer made clearer now that we know what Popper's remedies are. The answer is that utopianism is not evil merely because it is idealistic; the problem is the *kinds* of ideals it commits itself to. Utopianism always as-sumes a dogmatic character, Popper claims, because it focuses on a future period of perfect happiness, and this seduces utopian-minded planners into thinking that they are justified in sacrificing the quality of present life for an anticipated, hoped-for, perfect, but always equally distant life in the future.

IV. Paragraphs 41–42 conclude Popper's case by positing the relationship between utopianism and general culture.

A. Paragraph 41 argues that utopianism is one small current in a vast tide of anti-rational, hysterical, exaggerated, and immature responses to the prob-lem of power afflicting Western culture in general. The essence of this attitude is that human beings in the modern world are given to thinking of themselves either as gods or worms, and both attitudes tend to give rulers a handy justification for walking over the people beneath them. If rulers are gods, they can do no wrong. If subjects are worms, they can be done no wrong. He sees this attitude also manifested in both religious and philosophical thinking, not just in political thinking.

B. Paragraph 42 makes Popper's final point that this attitude, like the utopian thinking it spawns, always leads to violence. In response to that prospect, Popper ends where he began, by advocating reasonableness—intellectual humility and free give-and-take—as the only possible remedy.

Suggested Essay Topics

1. Write an essay addressed to Popper either commending or criticizing his claim that utopianism inevitably leads to violence. Unless you have fairly strong views about how his idea works on the large scale of political movements, you will do better to relate it to your personal experience of trying to reconcile ideal goals with practical necessities. You might, for example, make use of the popular expression "The perfect is the enemy of the good" and discuss how standards of perfection have sometimes prevented you from doing as well as you could. Or you might make use of opposing popular expressions ("Nothing ventured, nothing gained," "Difficult tasks take time; the impossible takes a little longer") by showing

how striving for perfection has sometimes led to real—though still imperfect—performance.

2. Select some document or text such as the Declaration of Independence, the
   Sermon on the Mount, or Book I of Plato's *Republic*—any document or text
   that makes sweeping recommendations about how people should live,
   especially if those recommendations include strong criticism of the status
   quo—and using either Goodman's or Popper's definitions of utopian
   thinking, show how the document is or is not utopian and whether its
   recommendations, utopian or not, are really practical.

3. You may find it useful to vary topic 2 by turning it into a letter to Popper,
   arguing against his position using arguments derived from Plato, or vice
   versa.

3

LANGUAGE

Reading and Writing,
Words and Experience

Reading is to the mind what exercise is to the body.
Richard Steele

Reading maketh a full man; conference a ready man and writing an exact man.
Sir Francis Bacon

For know you well, my dear Crito, that to
express oneself badly is not only faulty as far as the
language goes, but does some harm to the soul.
Socrates, in Plato's Phaedo

Without precision of meaning we damage not simply language,
but thought. The language we share is beautiful
and alarmingly complex. Try as we may, we are all likely to make
mistakes, and very few among us can claim to know the
English language to perfection. But we can try.
Robert Davies

Inspiration usually comes during work, rather than before it.
Madeline L'Engle

Style in its simplest definition, it seems to me, is sound—the sound
of self. It arises out of the whole concept of the work,
from the very pulsebeat of the writer and all that has gone
to make him, so that it is sometimes difficult to decide definitely where
technique and style have their firm boundary lines.
Eleanor Cameron

Rewriting isn't virtuous. It isn't something that ought to be done.
It is simply something that most writers find
they have to do to discover what they have to say
and how to say it.
Donald M. Murray

Wayne C. Booth and Marshall W. Gregory

CORRECTNESS AND ERRORS

For centuries people have claimed that the English language is in danger of 1
corruption and decay. Hundreds of books and articles have warned against
the "corruption" of English. In 1924, for example, R. W. Chapman, speaking
of "The Decay of Syntax," said that "the morbid state of modern English
prose is generally recognized by competent judges. . . . Any beauty in modern
English prose can be only the beauty of decay." As early as 1712 the great
satirist Jonathan Swift suggested that to combat the threat of change, which
he saw as the threat of decline, an "Academy" should be formed to establish
and preserve the correct forms. Some nations have established such bodies,
and to this day, in France and other nations, such official or semi-official
"academies" issue formal decisions about which words or expressions will be
given a badge of approval.

Nobody has succeeded in establishing such an academy to oversee the 2
development of English. But many have tried, and many others have deplored
the seemingly chaotic way in which new and forbidden expressions make
their way from being outlawed—as "slang" or "foreign" or "vulgar" or "colloquial"—to being used by careful writers.

Many linguists have claimed that these purifying efforts are entirely 3
misguided. Since all languages are constantly changing, and since there is
never any clearly established authority to say which changes are good and
which are bad, our ideas about good English must always shift according to
the usage of whatever group we address.

The "warfare" between the linguists and the purists has often been 4
bitter and confusing. It has been marked by much name-calling, and it reveals
a good deal of puzzlement and anxiety on all sides. (See, for example, the
controversy about *Webster's Third International Dictionary,* as recorded in *Dictionaries and That Dictionary,* edited in 1962 by Wilma Ebbitt and James Sledd.)

Few of us can hope to figure out the rights and wrongs of such an elaborate and prolonged controversy. But we can profit from becoming aware of the issues and thinking about what our own practice will be. Our choices must always be dictated both by our effort to address different readers successfully and by our own knowledge, or lack of knowledge, about what expressions hinder our communication.

We soon learn that "correctness" is at best a mere beginning. Observing correctness in writing is like observing the speed limit while driving: Following the "rules" may have the negative virtue of keeping you out of trouble, but, in and of itself, it cannot produce the positive virtue of good writing. Every beginner soon learns, moreover, that there is no end to the number of "mistakes" teachers can find in an essay; almost all of us have experienced a sense of hopelessness when we've seen our manuscripts marked again and again with corrections that seem endless.

Should teachers and students stop worrying, then, about correctness, as "permissivists" have argued? We all know that if we do so, we will make a lot of trouble for ourselves. Some people will refuse to read what we write if they find it full of "errors," even when linguists point out that many of those very "errors" have been accepted by great authors from Shakespeare's time to the present. But deciding to concentrate on avoiding errors will not work either; we authors can attest to that. As we have worked on this book we have constantly discovered "errors," real or imaginary, in each other's writing, and we know from experience that, even after careful correction by editors at Harper & Row, our readers will discover faults we never dreamed of.

Thus our choices in this matter are complicated. If we wrote, "Neither one of us don't know nothing about grammar," or if we commited many mispellings like these, and if you decided that we didn't know any better, you would probably stop using this book. But if we worried too much about catching every conceivable error, we would have to stop writing. So we all have a problem here—the problem of finding a livable "mean" between an overanxious care that makes writing either painful or impossible, on the one hand, and the carelessness that will leave readers confused or drive them away, on the other.

Like many problems in life, this one cannot be dodged. With every word we utter, we either *meet* those we address or we *fail* to, and our success will depend in part on learning how, in any given situation, to be as "correct" as that situation requires. This in turn means that to learn to write well, we must learn to think hard about different situations. The kind of language accepted as correct English in a college essay may be fatal in a dormitory bull session, and vice versa.

As you struggle to find appropriate language for your various writing tasks, you may at times become almost immobilized for fear of committing errors you never dreamed of. When this happens, you should remind yourself of four points implicit in all of your work this year.

First, you are not alone. Every author in this book has depended on the corrections of other people; most authors show their writing to friends before sending it to the printer, and all of them depend finally on copy editors whose professional task is to improve manuscripts. Our own discussions in this "reader," for example, have been re-written again and again, taking into account the corrections of so many readers, paid and unpaid, that we have lost count. That you need help with your writing is thus no disgrace.

Second, although possible errors in writing may seem infinite in num-   12
ber, the really crippling ones are relatively rare. If you think hard about the *kinds* of errors you find flagged in your papers, you can soon learn to avoid those that give the most trouble. Seldom will a single error ever ruin an essay by itself.

Third, remember that you are learning correct ways of writing even as   13
you read the essays here. Even when you are not thinking about errors at all, you are learning to avoid them simply by paying attention to the texts you are assigned. If you had to memorize a full list of all the possible bad ways of writing, you would have reason to be discouraged. But by engaging with people who write well, you will automatically take in their ways—if you really pay attention.

Finally, don't forget that correctness is only a means to much more   14
important ends. You are learning to *say something worth saying;* and, if you face the challenges offered in this book, your writing will to a surprising degree "clean itself up." Most of the "errors" you now commit you would recognize yourself, if you really paid attention to your words as closely as the authors anthologized in this book have attended to theirs. And by following them in the close attention they practice, you will learn what it means to choose words that do their job.

One last hint: Nothing works quite so well for spotting errors as reading   15
your work aloud, slowly. Your worst errors will jump out at you when you hear yourself saying something that does not make good sense.

Helen Keller

The story of Helen Keller's life (1880–1968) is engrossing for the same reasons that all good memoirs are engrossing. They bring us into contact with an instructive, engaging mind, and they seem to offer us clues about how to face problems in our own lives. By presenting us with emotions that either parallel or differ from our own, memoirs confirm everyone's membership in the human community and simultaneously affirm everyone's individual uniqueness. Beyond this, however, Helen Keller's story offers us insight into a gripping topic larger than her life but on which her life and experience cast real illumination: the topic of how human beings acquire language and how, in acquiring it, they find, or perhaps create, their distinctively human nature.

Helen Keller was born a normal child, but at 19 months she was stricken with a severe disease that left her both blind and deaf. "Gradually," she says, "I got used to the silence and darkness that surrounded me, and forgot that it had ever been different." Despite the silence and darkness, the little girl came to understand a good deal of what was going on around her. She records that at age 5 she learned to fold and put away clean clothes, that she always knew when her mother and aunt were going out, and that she always wanted to accompany them. But without language she had no ideas, no means of living in a world of experience larger than immediate sensations and feelings, no way of holding on to memories or of formulating hopes and desires, no way of organizing the world conceptually, and, most important of all, no way of thinking her own thoughts and sharing them with others.

We are inclined to take language for granted. We live so much inside it that we no more think about it than we think about the beating of our own hearts or the air we breathe. But just as hearts may perform either well or poorly and air may be either pure or polluted, so our language may be used either more or less accurately, more or less sensitively, and more or less masterfully. Helen Keller was human, clearly, despite her immense handicap, but it is also clear that as she acquired language she came into an increasingly fuller ownership of her human birthright, an increasingly fuller experience of her own human nature.

This raises a question, doesn't it? If human nature and language are as intimately connected as Helen Keller's story suggests, and if language ownership is not an all-or-nothing thing but is instead mastered by degrees, does this not suggest that any enhancement or strengthening of our language will also enhance and strengthen our fundamental humanity? Is it possible, in other words, that being human (except in the most minimal biological sense) is not in itself an all-or-nothing thing? Is it possible that developing certain capacities within us may in fact bring us into fuller possession of what it means to be a human being? Helen Keller's story seems to suggest so.

If this suggestion is sound, implications for your own education follow. This view of language would clearly imply, for example, that courses that force you to deal with texts and thus increase your language power by constant exercise—humanities courses such as history, literature, languages, religion, and philosophy, to mention a few— may in fact be among the most useful courses you could take, useful if becoming more fully and powerfully human is useful. As you read, consider whether Helen Keller's story challenges any of your views or expectations about your own education, and whether her experience justifies your re-thinking or even re-tooling any of your educational ambitions.

THE KEY TO LANGUAGE

Our title for Chapters 4 and 6 of *The Story of My Life* (1902).

The most important day I remember in all my life is the one on which my teacher, Anne Mansfield Sullivan, came to me. I am filled with wonder when I consider the immeasurable contrasts between the two lives which it con-

1

nects. It was the third of March, 1887, three months before I was seven years old.

On the afternoon of that eventful day, I stood on the porch, dumb, 2 expectant. I guessed vaguely from my mother's signs and from the hurrying to and fro in the house that something unusual was about to happen, so I went to the door and waited on the steps. The afternoon sun penetrated the mass of honeysuckle that covered the porch, and fell on my upturned face. My fingers lingered almost unconsciously on the familiar leaves and blossoms which had just come forth to greet the sweet southern spring. I did not know what the future held of marvel or surprise for me. Anger and bitterness had preyed upon me continually for weeks and a deep languor had succeeded this passionate struggle.

Have you ever been at sea in a dense fog, when it seemed as if a tangible 3 white darkness shut you in, and the great ship, tense and anxious, groped her way toward the shore with plummet and sounding-line, and you waited with beating heart for something to happen? I was like that ship before my education began, only I was without compass or sounding-line, and had no way of knowing how near the harbour was. "Light! give me light!" was the wordless cry of my soul, and the light of love shone on me in that very hour.

I felt approaching footsteps. I stretched out my hand as I supposed to 4 my mother. Some one took it, and I was caught up and held close in the arms of her who had come to reveal all things to me, and, more than all things else, to love me.

The morning after my teacher came she led me into her room and gave 5 me a doll. The little blind children at the Perkins Institution had sent it and Laura Bridgman had dressed it; but I did not know this until afterward. When I had played with it a little while, Miss Sullivan slowly spelled into my hand the word "d-o-l-l." I was at once interested in this finger play and tried to imitate it. When I finally succeeded in making the letters correctly I was flushed with childish pleasure and pride. Running downstairs to my mother I held up my hand and made the letters for doll. I did not know that I was spelling a word or even that words existed; I was simply making my fingers go in monkey-like imitation. In the days that followed I learned to spell in this uncomprehending way a great many words, among them *pin, hat, cup* and a few verbs like *sit, stand* and *walk*. But my teacher had been with me several weeks before I understood that everything has a name.

One day, while I was playing with my new doll, Miss Sullivan put my 6 big rag doll into my lap also, spelled "d-o-l-l" and tried to make me understand that "d-o-l-l" applied to both. Earlier in the day we had had a tussle over the words "m-u-g" and "w-a-t-e-r." Miss Sullivan had tried to impress it upon me that "m-u-g" is *mug* and that "w-a-t-e-r" is *water,* but I persisted in confounding the two. In despair she had dropped the subject for the time, only to renew it at the first opportunity. I became impatient at her repeated attempts and, seizing the new doll, I dashed it upon the floor. I was keenly delighted when I felt the fragments of the broken doll at my feet. Neither sorrow nor regret followed my passionate outburst. I had not loved the doll.

In the still, dark world in which I lived there was no strong sentiment or tenderness. I felt my teacher sweep the fragments to one side of the hearth, and I had a sense of satisfaction that the cause of my discomfort was removed. She brought me my hat, and I knew I was going out into the warm sunshine. This thought, if a wordless sensation may be called a thought, made me hop and skip with pleasure.

We walked down the path to the well-house, attracted by the fragrance 7 of the honeysuckle with which it was covered. Some one was drawing water and my teacher placed my hand under the spout. As the cool stream gushed over one hand she spelled into the other the word *water,* first slowly, then rapidly. I stood still, my whole attention fixed upon the motions of her fingers. Suddenly I felt a misty consciousness as of something forgotten—a thrill of returning thought; and somehow the mystery of language was revealed to me. I knew then that "w-a-t-e-r" meant the wonderful cool something that was flowing over my hand. That living word awakened my soul, gave it light, hope, joy, set it free! There were barriers still, it is true, but barriers that could in time be swept away.

I left the well-house eager to learn. Everything had a name, and each 8 name gave birth to a new thought. As we returned to the house every object which I touched seemed to quiver with life. That was because I saw everything with the strange, new sight that had come to me. On entering the door I remembered the doll I had broken. I felt my way to the hearth and picked up the pieces. I tried vainly to put them together. Then my eyes filled with tears; for I realized what I had done, and for the first time I felt repentance and sorrow.

I learned a great many new words that day. I do not remember what 9 they all were; but I do know that *mother, father, sister, teacher* were among them—words that were to make the world blossom for me, "like Aaron's rod, with flowers." It would have been difficult to find a happier child than I was as I lay in my crib at the close of that eventful day and lived over the joys it had brought me, and for the first time longed for a new day to come.

. . .

I had now the key to all language, and I was eager to learn to use it. 10 Children who hear acquire language without any particular effort; the words that fall from others' lips they catch on the wing, as it were, delightedly, while the little deaf child must trap them by a slow and often painful process. But whatever the process, the result is wonderful. Gradually from naming an object we advance step by step until we have traversed the vast distance between our first stammered syllable and the sweep of thought in a line of Shakespeare.

At first, when my teacher told me about a new thing I asked very few 11 questions. My ideas were vague, and my vocabulary was inadequate; but as my knowledge of things grew, and I learned more and more words, my field of inquiry broadened, and I would return again and again to the same subject, eager for further information. Sometimes a new word revived an image that some earlier experience had engraved on my brain.

I remember the morning that I first asked the meaning of the word   12
"love." This was before I knew many words. I had found a few early violets
in the garden and brought them to my teacher. She tried to kiss me; but at
that time I did not like to have any one kiss me except my mother. Miss
Sullivan put her arm gently round me and spelled into my hand, "I love
Helen."

"What is love?" I asked.   13

She drew me closer to her and said, "It is here," pointing to my heart,   14
whose beats I was conscious of for the first time. Her words puzzled me very
much because I did not then understand anything unless I touched it.

I smelt the violets in her hand and asked, half in words, half in signs,   15
a question which meant, "Is love the sweetness of flowers?"

"No," said my teacher.   16

Again I thought. The warm sun was shining on us.   17

"Is this not love?" I asked, pointing in the direction from which the heat   18
came, "Is this not love?"

It seemed to me that there could be nothing more beautiful than the sun,   19
whose warmth makes all things grow. But Miss Sullivan shook her head, and
I was greatly puzzled and disappointed. I thought it strange that my teacher
could not show me love.

A day or two afterward I was stringing beads of different sizes in   20
symmetrical groups—two large beads, three small ones, and so on. I had made
many mistakes, and Miss Sullivan had pointed them out again and again with
gentle patience. Finally I noticed a very obvious error in the sequence and for
an instant I concentrated my attention on the lesson and tried to think how
I should have arranged the beads. Miss Sullivan touched my forehead and
spelled with decided emphasis, "Think."

In a flash I knew that the word was the name of the process that was   21
going on in my head. This was my first conscious perception of an abstract
idea.

For a long time I was still—I was not thinking of the beads in my lap,   22
but trying to find a meaning for "love" in the light of this new idea. The sun
had been under a cloud all day, and there had been brief showers; but
suddenly the sun broke forth in all its southern splendour.

Again I asked my teacher, "Is this not love?"   23

"Love is something like the clouds that were in the sky before the sun   24
came out," she replied. Then in simpler words than these, which at that time
I could not have understood, she explained: "You cannot touch the clouds,
you know; but you feel the rain and know how glad the flowers and the
thirsty earth are to have it after a hot day. You cannot touch love either; but
you feel the sweetness that it pours into everything. Without love you would
not be happy or want to play."

The beautiful truth burst upon my mind—I felt that there were invisible   25
lines stretched between my spirit and the spirits of others.

From the beginning of my education Miss Sullivan made it a practice   26
to speak to me as she would speak to any hearing child; the only difference

was that she spelled the sentences into my hand instead of speaking them. If I did not know the words and idioms necessary to express my thoughts she supplied them, even suggesting conversation when I was unable to keep up my end of the dialogue.

This process was continued for several years; for the deaf child does not 27 learn in a month, or even in two or three years, the numberless idioms and expressions used in the simplest daily intercourse. The little hearing child learns these from constant repetition and imitation. The conversation he hears in his home stimulates his mind and suggests topics and calls forth the spontaneous expression of his own thoughts. This natural exchange of ideas is denied to the deaf child. My teacher, realizing this, determined to supply the kinds of stimulus I lacked. This she did by repeating to me as far as possible, verbatim, what she heard, and by showing me how I could take part in the conversation. But it was a long time before I ventured to take the initiative, and still longer before I could find something appropriate to say at the right time.

The deaf and the blind find it very difficult to acquire the amenities of 28 conversation. How much more this difficulty must be augmented in the case of those who are both deaf and blind! They cannot distinguish the tone of the voice or, without assistance, go up and down the gamut of tones that give significance to words; nor can they watch the expression of the speaker's face, and a look is often the very soul of what one says.

[Attached here are two letters from Keller's revered teacher, Anne Mansfield Sullivan, which describe from the teacher's point of view the events that Keller has just narrated. What is interesting here are Sullivan's ideas about how language is learned by anyone, not just deaf children. Her description of young Helen turning more and more human as she acquires language is both moving and instructive.

Anne Sullivan was 14 years older than Helen Keller. Very early in her life she had been struck blind through illness and had entered the Perkins Institution for the blind the same year Helen was born. Later her sight was partially restored. The skills she learned at Perkins qualified her to be Keller's teacher. The letters here are addressed to Mrs. Sophia C. Hopkins, a matron at the Perkins Institution who had been like a mother to Sullivan. It is evident in these letters that Sullivan had a clear idea of what she was doing and was critically analyzing the effectiveness of her means of teaching Keller as she went along.]

April 5, 1887.

I must write you a line this morning because something very important 1 has happened. Helen has taken the second great step in her education. She has learned that *everything has a name, and that the manual alphabet is the key to everything she wants to know.*

In a previous letter I think I wrote you that "mug" and "milk" had given 2 Helen more trouble than all the rest. She confused the nouns with the verb "drink." She didn't know the word for "drink," but went through the pantomime of drinking whenever she spelled "mug" or "milk." This morning, while she was washing, she wanted to know the name for "water." When she wants to know the name of anything, she points to it and pats my hand. I spelled "w-a-t-e-r" and thought no more about it until after breakfast. Then it occurred to me that with the help of this new word I might succeed in straightening out the "mug-milk" difficulty. We went out to the pump-house, and I made Helen hold her mug under the spout while I pumped. As the cold water gushed forth, filling the mug, I spelled "w-a-t-e-r" in Helen's free hand. The word coming so close upon the sensation of cold water rushing over her hand seemed to startle her. She dropped the mug and stood as one transfixed. A new light came into her face. She spelled "water" several times. Then she dropped on the ground and asked for its name and pointed to the pump and the trellis, and suddenly turning round she asked for my name. I spelled "Teacher." Just then the nurse brought Helen's little sister into the pump-house, and Helen spelled "baby" and pointed to the nurse. All the way back to the house she was highly excited, and learned the name of every object she touched, so that in a few hours she had added thirty new words to her vocabulary. Here are some of them: *Door, open, shut, give, go, come,* and a great many more.

P.S.—I didn't finish my letter in time to get it posted last night; so I shall add a line. Helen got up this morning like a radiant fairy. She had flitted from object to object, asking the name of everything and kissing me for very gladness. Last night when I got in bed, she stole into my arms of her own accord and kissed me for the first time, and I thought my heart would burst, so full was it of joy.

                                                        April 10, 1887.

I see an improvement in Helen from day to day, almost from hour to hour. Everything must have a name now. Wherever we go, she asks eagerly for the names of things she has not learned at home. She is anxious for her friends to spell, and eager to teach the letters to every one she meets. She drops the signs and pantomime she used before, as soon as she has words to supply their place, and the acquirement of a new word affords her the liveliest pleasure. And we notice that her face grows more expressive each day.

I have decided not to try to have regular lessons for the present. I am going to treat Helen exactly like a two-year-old child. It occurred to me the other day that it is absurd to require a child to come to a certain place at a certain time and recite certain lessons, when he has not yet acquired a working vocabulary. I sent Helen away and sat down to think. I asked myself, *"How does a normal child learn language?"* The answer was simple, "By imitation." The child comes into the world with the ability to learn, and he learns of himself, provided he is supplied with sufficient outward stimulus. He sees people do things, and he tries to do them. He hears others speak, and he tries to speak. *But long before he utters his first word, he understands what is said to him.* I have been observing Helen's little cousin lately. She is about fifteen months old, and already understands a great deal. In response to questions she points out prettily her nose, mouth, eye, chin, cheek, ear. If I say, "Where is baby's other ear?" she points it out correctly. If I hand her a flower, and say, "Give it to mamma," she takes it to her mother. If I say, "Where is the little rogue?" she hides behind her mother's chair, or covers her face with her hands and peeps out at me with an expression of genuine roguishness. She obeys many commands like these: "Come," "Kiss," "Go to papa," "Shut the door," "Give me the biscuit." But I have not heard her try to say any of these words, although they have been repeated hundreds of times in her hearing, and it is perfectly evident that she understands them. These observations have given me a clue to the method to be followed in teaching Helen language. *I shall talk into her hand as we talk into the baby's ears.* I shall assume that she has the normal child's capacity of assimilation and imitation. *I shall use complete sentences in talking to her,* and fill out the meaning with gestures and her descriptive signs when necessity requires it; but I shall not try to keep her mind fixed on any one thing. I shall do all I can to interest and stimulate it, and wait for results.

Questions for Discussion

1. Keller's story makes clear that even in her pre-language existence she had a life of some feelings and emotions. She could experience anger, frustration, and pleasure. But the absence of language seems to have had a muting effect on even these; of other emotions she seems to have had little knowledge at all, especially emotions of companionship or tenderness. "In the still, dark world in which I lived," she says, "there was no strong sentiment of tenderness" (¶6). Does this surprise you? Would you have thought that language was essential to having a fully developed, mature emotional life? Does Keller's experience on this score corroborate the point we make in our comments about language's being intimately tied to the development of one's human capacities, one's basic human nature? If so, how? If not, why not?

2. The philosopher Alfred North Whitehead said that "the souls of men are the gift from language to mankind." And Helen Keller records her sudden discovery of the word *water* in similar terms: "I knew then that 'w-a-t-e-r' meant the wonderful cool something that was flowing over my hand. That living word awakened my soul, gave it light, hope, joy, set it free!" (¶7). What do you think these two writers mean by the assertion that language liberates or awakens the soul? Is this just gushy talk for an incommunicable emotional experience, or does it mean anything you can pin down in other words? If so, what other words?

3. "Everything had a name, and each name gave birth to a new thought," says Keller (¶7). Can you imagine our language devoid of the names of things? What would a language of all verbs, adverbs, and other parts of speech, but no nouns, be like? How would it alter human perception and experience? If this is too hard to imagine, picture a more limited case: a language with nouns but without proper names. Could we adapt to such a life, such a language? How? How would it alter our perception and experience?

4. In her pre-language stage, Keller reports that "I did not then understand anything unless I touched it" (¶14). We hear a lot of talk these days about rediscovering the kind of knowledge acquired through bodily sensations. The people who engage in this talk frequently assert the value of physical knowledge as an antidote to our tendency in modern society to distance everything with language that is too abstract, too conceptual, too removed from immediate experience. Use Helen Keller's story to help you construct a refutation of this view. Or, if you think this view is basically correct, show how Keller's acquisition of language is different from the kind of language being criticized by the "truth of the body" people.

5. Anne Sullivan reports that after Keller had begun to acquire language, "we notice that her face grows more expressive each day" (¶4). Why would this be the case? If you have ever had the opportunity to observe anyone with an extremely limited ownership of language, can you recall any notable features or absences of expressiveness that would throw light on Sullivan's meaning?

Suggested Essay Topics

1. Write an essay on discussion question 3 directed to your instructor. Or, if that kind of speculation seems too abstract, write a dialogue in which you picture two people—two students having lunch together in the cafeteria, for example—having a conversation in a version of English that includes nouns but no proper names. Address your piece of writing to the kind of general reader who might see it in the creative writing section of a magazine or as a feature essay in a newspaper.

2. Go to the library and look up one of the numerous accounts of feral children—children raised in complete absence from human contact (usually by animals, as the accounts go)—and write an essay in which you compare the indoctrination of these children into human society to Helen Keller's recovery of language. Conclude with appropriate observations about the nature and importance of language to human nature and experience. Direct the essay to your classmates. [One of the best-known accounts of a feral child is *The Wild Boy of Averyon* by Jean-Marc Gaspard Itard, translated by George and Muriel Humphrey (Prentice-Hall, 1962), which served as the inspiration for François Truffaut's film *L'Enfant sauvage (The Wild Child).*]

George Orwell

George Orwell (1903–1950) was a Brit-
ish novelist, journalist, political commentator and satirist. He is most famous as the
author of two satiric fables warning of the dangers and exposing the operations of
tyrannical governments, Animal Farm *(1945) and* Nineteen Eighty-Four
(1949). These works have been translated into most major languages and are studied
by scholars and schoolchildren alike.

"Politics and the English Language" is almost as widely read as Orwell's
fiction. Its title clearly indicates Orwell's central concern: "In our time," he says,
"political speech and writing are largely the defence of the indefensible" (¶13). His
thesis is that there is a direct and traceable relationship between political brutality and
imprecise, vague, evasive, and cliché-ridden English. Immoral politics and bad writing
reinforce each other, each one becoming in turn both a cause and an effect.

Three different groups contribute most directly to the deterioration of political
language: (1) governments that want to find easier ways of masking their "indefensi-
ble" acts of brutality; (2) persons connected with brutal governments who have a vested
interest in disguising their governments' acts; and (3) people who do not want to see
political brutality for what it is because they do not want to take responsibility for
stopping it.

In exposing this problem, Orwell is not completely pessimistic. Things are bad,
he says, and getting worse all the time, but the state of neither politics nor language
is hopeless. Political brutality and bad writing are not natural forces as inevitable as
the seasons; they are instead the product of choices. *Governments are not required*
to murder dissidents—they choose to. No one forces citizens to settle for language that
disguises their government's murder of dissidents—they choose to. And what people
choose at one time to do, they can choose at another time to undo.

Orwell's essay is an attempt to persuade us to undo perversions of politics and
power by forcing us to attend to the language that supports them. The kind of world
we live in, he says, is not just the world that happens to us; it is also the world we
make. He insists that the effects of a hard-headed demand that world governments say
clearly what they are doing and why they are doing it, combined with a hard-headed
diligence from ourselves in demanding clear and vigorous expression, will improve both
political conduct and the use of English.

After studying Orwell's essay, your class may want to subscribe to the Quarterly Review of Doublespeak, *published by the National Council of Teachers of*
English. The review annually announces the "Orwell Award" for the best book
exposing abuse of language, and the "Doublespeak Award," a mock prize for "misuses
of language with pernicious social or political consequences." In 1982 two of the
Doublespeak Awards were given to Lawrence A. Kudlow, chief economist of the Office
of Management and Budget, "for creating the phrase 'revenue enhancement,' which
was used by the Reagan administration instead of the phrase 'tax increase,'" and to
Secretary of the Interior James Watt, "who said, 'I never use the words Republicans
and Democrats. It's liberals and Americans'" (see the January 1983 issue).

POLITICS AND
THE ENGLISH LANGUAGE

From *"Shooting an Elephant" and Other Essays* (1950).

Most people who bother with the matter at all would admit that the English language is in a bad way, but it is generally assumed that we cannot by conscious action do anything about it. Our civilization is decadent and our language—so the argument runs—must inevitably share in the general collapse. It follows that any struggle against the abuse of language is a sentimental archaism, like preferring candles to electric light or hansom cabs to aeroplanes. Underneath this lies the half-conscious belief that language is a natural growth and not an instrument which we shape for our own purposes. 1

Now, it is clear that the decline of a language must ultimately have political and economic causes: it is not due simply to the bad influence of this or that individual writer. But an effect can become a cause, reinforcing the original cause and producing the same effect in an intensified form, and so on indefinitely. A man may take to drink because he feels himself to be a failure, and then fail all the more completely because he drinks. It is rather the same thing that is happening to the English language. It becomes ugly and inaccurate because our thoughts are foolish, but the slovenliness of our language makes it easier for us to have foolish thoughts. The point is that the process is reversible. Modern English, especially written English, is full of bad habits which spread by imitation and which can be avoided if one is willing to take the necessary trouble. If one gets rid of these habits one can think more clearly, and to think clearly is a necessary first step towards political regeneration: so that the fight against bad English is not frivolous and is not the exclusive concern of professional writers. I will come back to this presently, and I hope that by that time the meaning of what I have said here will have become clearer. Meanwhile, here are five specimens of the English language as it is now habitually written. 2

These five passages have not been picked out because they are especially bad—I could have quoted far worse if I had chosen—but because they illustrate various of the mental vices from which we now suffer. They are a little below the average, but are fairly representative samples. I number them so that I can refer back to them when necessary: 3

> (1) I am not, indeed, sure whether it is not true to say that the Milton who once seemed not unlike a seventeenth-century Shelley had not become, out of an experience ever more bitter in each year, more alien [*sic*] to the founder of that Jesuit sect which nothing could induce him to tolerate.—Professor Harold Laski (Essay in *Freedom of Expression*)

> (2) Above all, we cannot play ducks and drakes with a native battery of idioms which prescribes such egregious collocations of vocables as the basic *put up with* for *tolerate* or *put at a loss* for *bewilder*. —Professor Lancelot Hogben (*Interglossa*)

(3) On the one side we have the free personality: by definition it is not neurotic, for it has neither conflict nor dream. Its desires, such as they are, are transparent, for they are just what institutional approval keeps in the forefront of consciousness; another institutional pattern would alter their number and intensity; there is little in them that is natural, irreducible, or culturally dangerous. But *on the other side,* the social bond itself is nothing but the mutual reflection of these self-secure integrities. Recall the definition of love. Is not this the very picture of a small academic? Where is there a place in this hall of mirrors for either personality or fraternity?— Essay on psychology in *Politics* (New York)

(4) All the "best people" from the gentlemen's clubs, and all the frantic fascist captains, united in common hatred of Socialism and bestial horror of the rising tide of the mass revolutionary movement, have turned to acts of provocation, to foul incendiarism, to medieval legends of poisoned wells, to legalize their own destruction of proletarian organizations, and rouse the agitated petty-bourgeoisie to chauvinistic fervor on behalf of the fight against the revolutionary way out of the crisis.—Communist pamphlet

(5) If a new spirit *is* to be infused into this old country, there is one thorny and contentious reform which must be tackled, and that is the humanization and galvanization of the B.B.C. Timidity here will bespeak canker and atrophy of the soul. The heart of Britain may be sound and of strong beat, for instance, but the British lion's roar at present is like that of Bottom in Shakespeare's *Midsummer Night's Dream*—as gentle as any sucking dove. A virile new Britain cannot continue indefinitely to be traduced in the eyes, or rather ears, of the world by the effete languors of Langham Place, brazenly masquerading as "standard English." When the Voice of Britain is heard at nine o'clock, better far and infinitely less ludicrous to hear aitches honestly dropped than the present priggish, inflated, inhibited, school-ma'amish arch braying of blameless bashful mewing maidens!—Letter in *Tribune*

Each of these passages has faults of its own, but, quite apart from avoidable ugliness, two qualities are common to all of them. The first is staleness of imagery; the other is lack of precision. The writer either has a meaning and cannot express it, or he inadvertently says something else, or he is almost indifferent as to whether his words mean anything or not. This mixture of vagueness and sheer incompetence is the most marked characteristic of modern English prose, and especially of any kind of political writing. As soon as certain topics are raised, the concrete melts into the abstract and no one seems able to think of turns of speech that are not hackneyed: prose consists less and less of *words* chosen for the sake of their meaning, and more and more of *phrases* tacked together like the sections of a prefabricated hen-house. I list below, with notes and examples, various of the tricks by means of which the work of prose-construction is habitually dodged:

Dying Metaphors.   A newly invented metaphor assists thought by evok-   5
ing a visual image, while on the other hand a metaphor which is technically
"dead" (e.g. *iron resolution*) has in effect reverted to being an ordinary word and
can generally be used without loss of vividness. But in between these two
classes there is a huge dump of worn-out metaphors which have lost all
evocative power and are merely used because they save people the trouble
of inventing phrases for themselves. Examples are: *Ring the changes on, take up
the cudgels for, toe the line, ride roughshod over, stand shoulder to shoulder with, play into
the hands of, no axe to grind, grist to the mill, fishing in troubled waters, rift within the lute,
on the order of the day, Achilles' heel, swan song, hotbed.* Many of these are used
without knowledge of their meaning (what is a "rift," for instance?), and
incompatible metaphors are frequently mixed, a sure sign that the writer is
not interested in what he is saying. Some metaphors now current have been
twisted out of their original meaning without those who use them even being
aware of the fact. For example, *toe the line* is sometimes written *tow the line.*
Another example is *the hammer and the anvil,* now always used with the implication that the anvil gets the worst of it. In real life it is always the anvil that
breaks the hammer, never the other way about: a writer who stopped to think
what he was saying would be aware of this, and would avoid perverting the
original phrase.

Operators or *Verbal False Limbs.*   These save the trouble of picking out   6
appropriate verbs and nouns, and at the same time pad each sentence with
extra syllables which give it an appearance of symmetry. Characteristic
phrases are *render inoperative, militate against, make contact with, be subjected to, give rise
to, give grounds for, have the effect of, play a leading part (role) in, make itself felt, take effect,
exhibit a tendency to, serve the purpose of, etc., etc.* The keynote is the elimination of
simple verbs. Instead of being a single word, such as *break, stop, spoil, mend, kill,*
a verb becomes a *phrase,* made up of a noun or adjective tacked on to some
general-purposes verb such as *prove, serve, form, play, render.* In addition, the
passive voice is wherever possible used in preference to the active, and noun
constructions are used instead of gerunds (*by examination of* instead of *by examining*). The range of verbs is further cut down by means of the *-ize* and *de-*
formations, and the banal statements are given an appearance of profundity
by means of the *not un-* formation. Simple conjunctions and prepositions are
replaced by such phrases as *with respect to, having regard to, the fact that, by dint of,
in view of, in the interests of, on the hypothesis that;* and the ends of sentences are
saved from anticlimax by such resounding common-places as *greatly to be
desired, cannot be left out of account, a development to be expected in the near future, deserving
of serious consideration, brought to a satisfactory conclusion,* and so on and so forth.

Pretentious Diction.   Words like *phenomenon, element, individual* (as noun),   7
*objective, categorical, effective, virtual, basic, primary, promote, constitute, exhibit, exploit,
utilize, eliminate, liquidate,* are used to dress up simple statements and give an air
of scientific impartiality to biased judgments. Adjectives like *epoch-making, epic,
historic, unforgettable, triumphant, age-old, inevitable, inexorable, veritable,* are used to

dignify the sordid processes of international politics, while writing that aims
at glorifying war usually takes on an archaic color, its characteristic words
being: *realm, throne, chariot, mailed fist, trident, sword, shield, buckler, banner, jackboot,
clarion.* Foreign words and expressions such as *cul de sac, ancien régime, deus ex
machina, mutatis mutandis, status quo, gleichschaltung, weltanschauung,* are used to give
an air of culture and elegance. Except for the useful abbreviations *i.e., e.g.,* and
etc., there is no real need for any of the hundreds of foreign phrases now
current in English. Bad writers, and especially scientific, political and sociological writers, are nearly always haunted by the notion that Latin or Greek
words are grander than Saxon ones, and unnecessary words like *expedite,
ameliorate, predict, extraneous, deracinated, clandestine, subaqueous* and hundreds of
others constantly gain ground from their Anglo-Saxon opposite numbers.*
The jargon peculiar to Marxist writing (*hyena, hangman, cannibal, petty bourgeois,
these gentry, lacquey, flunkey, mad dog, White Guard,* etc.) consists largely of words
and phrases translated from Russian, German or French; but the normal way
of coining a new word is to use a Latin or Greek root with the appropriate
affix and, where necessary, the *-ize* formation. It is often easier to make up
words of this kind (*deregionalize, impermissible, extramarital, non-fragmentary* and so
forth) than to think up the English words that will cover one's meaning. The
result, in general, is an increase in slovenliness and vagueness.

Meaningless Words.   In certain kinds of writing, particularly in art criticism and literary criticism, it is normal to come across long passages which
are almost completely lacking in meaning.† Words like *romantic, plastic, values,
human, dead, sentimental, natural, vitality,* as used in art criticism, are strictly
meaningless, in the sense that they not only do not point to any discoverable
object, but are hardly ever expected to do so by the reader. When one critic
writes, "The outstanding feature of Mr. X's work is its living quality," while
another writes, "The immediately striking thing about Mr. X's work is its
peculiar deadness," the reader accepts this as a simple difference of opinion.
If words like *black* and *white* were involved, instead of the jargon words *dead*
and *living,* he would see at once that language was being used in an improper
way. Many political words are similarly abused. The word *Fascism* has now
no meaning except in so far as it signifies "something not desirable." The
words *democracy, socialism, freedom, patriotic, realistic, justice,* have each of them
several different meanings which cannot be reconciled with one another. In

*An interesting illustration of this is the way in which the English flower names which were in
use till very recently are being ousted by Greek ones, *snapdragon* becoming *antirrhinum, forget-me-not*
becoming *myosotis,* etc. It is hard to see any practical reason for this change of fashion: it is
probably due to an instinctive turning-away from the more homely word and a vague feeling
that the Greek word is scientific. [Orwell's note.]

†Example: "Comfort's catholicity of perception and image, strangely Whitmanesque in range,
almost the exact opposite in aesthetic compulsion, continues to evoke that trembling atmospheric
accumulative hinting at a cruel, an inexorably serene timelessness. . . . Wrey Gardiner scores by
aiming at simple bull's-eyes with precision. Only they are not so simple, and through this
contented sadness runs more than the surface bitter-sweet of resignation." (*Poetry Quarterly*)
[Orwell's note.]

the case of a word like *democracy,* not only is there no agreed definition, but the attempt to make one is resisted from all sides. It is almost universally felt that when we call a country democratic we are praising it: consequently the defenders of every kind of régime claim that it is a democracy, and fear that they might have to stop using the word if it were tied down to any one meaning. Words of this kind are often used in a consciously dishonest way. That is, the person who uses them has his own private definition, but allows his hearer to think he means something quite different. Statements like *Marshal Pétain was a true patriot, The Soviet Press is the freest in the world, The Catholic Church is opposed to persecution,* are almost always made with intent to .deceive. Other words used in variable meanings, in most cases more or less dishonestly, are: *class, totalitarian, science, progressive, reactionary, bourgeois, equality.*

Now that I have made this catalogue of swindles and perversions, let me give another example of the kind of writing that they lead to. This time it must of its nature be an imaginary one. I am going to translate a passage of good English into modern English of the worst sort. Here is a well-known verse from *Ecclesiastes:*

"I returned and saw under the sun, that the race is not to the swift, nor the battle to the strong, neither yet bread to the wise, nor yet riches to men of understanding, nor yet favour to men of skill; but time and chance happeneth to them all."

Here it is in modern English:

"Objective consideration of contemporary phenomena compels the conclusion that success or failure in competitive activities exhibits no tendency to be commensurate with innate capacity, but that a considerable element of the unpredictable must invariably be taken into account."

This is a parody, but not a very gross one. Exhibit (3), above, for instance, contains several patches of the same kind of English. It will be seen that I have not made a full translation. The beginning and ending of the sentence follow the original meaning fairly closely, but in the middle the concrete illustrations—race, battle, bread—dissolve into the vague phrase "success or failure in competitive activities." This had to be so, because no modern writer of the kind I am discussing—no one capable of using phrases like "objective consideration of contemporary phenomena"—would ever tabulate his thoughts in that precise and detailed way. The whole tendency of modern prose is away from concreteness. Now analyse these two sentences a little more closely. The first contains forty-nine words but only sixty syllables, and all its words are those of everyday life. The second contains thirty-eight words of ninety syllables: eighteen of its words are from Latin roots, and one from Greek. The first sentence contains six vivid images, and only one phrase ("time and chance") that could be called vague. The second contains not a single fresh, arresting phrase, and in spite of its ninety syllables it gives only a shortened version of the meaning contained in the first. Yet without a doubt it is the second kind of sentence that is gaining ground in modern English. I do not want to exaggerate. This kind of writing is not yet universal, and outcrops of simplicity will occur here and there in the worst-written page. Still, if you or I were told to write a few lines on the uncertainty of human fortunes, we should probably come much nearer to my imaginary sentence than to the one from *Ecclesiastes.*

As I have tried to show, modern writing at its worst does not consist in picking out words for the sake of their meaning and inventing images in order to make the meaning clearer. It consists in gumming together long strips of words which have already been set in order by someone else, and making the results presentable by sheer humbug. The attraction of this way of writing is that it is easy. It is easier—even quicker, once you have the habit—to say *In my opinion it is not an unjustifiable assumption that* than to say *I think.* If you use ready-made phrases, you not only don't have to hunt about for words; you also don't have to bother with the rhythms of your sentences, since these phrases are generally so arranged as to be more or less euphonious. When you are composing in a hurry—when you are dictating to a stenographer, for instance, or making a public speech—it is natural to fall into a pretentious, Latinized style. Tags like *a consideration which we should do well to bear in mind* or *a conclusion to which all of us would readily assent* will save many a sentence from coming down with a bump. By using stale metaphors, similes and idioms, you save much mental effort, at the cost of leaving your meaning vague, not only for your reader but for yourself. This is the significance of mixed metaphors. The sole aim of a metaphor is to call up a visual image. When these images clash—as in *The Fascist octopus has sung its swan song, the jackboot is thrown into the melting pot*—it can be taken as certain that the writer is not seeing a mental image of the objects he is naming; in other words he is not really thinking. Look again at the examples I gave at the beginning of this essay. Professor Laski (1) uses five negatives in fifty-three words. One of these is superfluous, making nonsense of the whole passage, and in addition there is the slip *alien* for akin, making further nonsense, and several avoidable pieces of clumsiness which increase the general vagueness. Professor Hogben (2) plays ducks and drakes with a battery which is able to write prescriptions, and, while disapproving of the everyday phrase *put up with,* is unwilling to look *egregious* up in the dictionary and see what it means; (3), if one takes an uncharitable attitude towards it, is simply meaningless: probably one could work out its intended meaning by reading the whole of the article in which it occurs. In (4), the writer knows more or less what he wants to say, but an accumulation of stale phrases chokes him like tea leaves blocking a sink. In (5), words and meaning have almost parted company. People who write in this manner usually have a general emotional meaning—they dislike one thing and want to express solidarity with another—but they are not interested in the detail of what they are saying. A scrupulous writer, in every sentence that he writes, will ask himself at least four questions, thus: What am I trying to say? What words will express it? What image or idiom will make it clearer? Is this image fresh enough to have an effect? And he will probably ask himself two more: Could I put it more shortly? Have I said anything that is avoidably ugly? But you are not obliged to go to all this trouble. You can shirk it by simply throwing your mind open and letting the ready-made phrases come crowding in. They

will construct your sentences for you—even think your thoughts for you, to
a certain extent—and at need they will perform the important service of
partially concealing your meaning even from yourself. It is at this point that
the special connection between politics and the debasement of language
becomes clear.

In our time it is broadly true that political writing is bad writing. Where   12
it is not true, it will generally be found that the writer is some kind of rebel,
expressing his private opinions and not a "party line." Orthodoxy, of whatever color, seems to demand a lifeless, imitative style. The political dialects
to be found in pamphlets, leading articles, manifestos, White Papers and the
speeches of under-secretaries do, of course, vary from party to party, but they
are all alike in that one almost never finds in them a fresh, vivid, home-made
turn of speech. When one watches some tired hack on the platform mechanically repeating the familiar phrases—*bestial atrocities, iron heel, bloodstained tyranny,
free peoples of the world, stand shoulder to shoulder*—one often has a curious feeling
that one is not watching a live human being but some kind of dummy: a
feeling which suddenly becomes stronger at moments when the light catches
the speaker's spectacles and turns them into blank discs which seem to have
no eyes behind them. And this is not altogether fanciful. A speaker who uses
that kind of phraseology has gone some distance towards turning himself into
a machine. The appropriate noises are coming out of his larynx, but his brain
is not involved as it would be if he were choosing his words for himself. If
the speech he is making is one that he is accustomed to make over and over
again, he may be almost unconscious of what he is saying, as one is when one
utters the responses in church. And this reduced state of consciousness, if not
indispensable, is at any rate favorable to political conformity.

In our time, political speech and writing are largely the defence of the   13
indefensible. Things like the continuance of British rule in India, the Russian
purges and deportations, the dropping of the atom bombs on Japan, can
indeed be defended, but only by arguments which are too brutal for most
people to face, and which do not square with the professed aims of political
parties. Thus political language has to consist largely of euphemism, ques-
tion-begging and sheer cloudy vagueness. Defenceless villages are bombarded from the air, the inhabitants driven out into the countryside, the cattle
machine-gunned, the huts set on fire with incendiary bullets: this is called
pacification. Millions of peasants are robbed of their farms and sent trudging
along the roads with no more than they can carry: this is called *transfer of
population* or *rectification of frontiers*. People are imprisoned for years without trial,
or shot in the back of the neck or sent to die of scurvy in Arctic lumber camps:
this is called *elimination of unreliable elements*. Such phraseology is needed if one
wants to name things without calling up mental pictures of them. Consider
for instance some comfortable English professor defending Russian totalitarianism. He cannot say outright, "I believe in killing off your opponents when
you can get good results by doing so." Probably, therefore, he will say
something like this:

"While freely conceding that the Soviet régime exhibits certain features   14

Smells ← [handwritten: Small step from being insincere to being dishonest.]

which the humanitarian may be inclined to deplore, we must, I think, agree that a certain curtailment of the right to political opposition is an unavoidable concomitant of transitional periods, and that the rigors which the Russian people have been called upon to undergo have been amply justified in the sphere of concrete achievement."

The inflated style is itself a kind of euphemism. A mass of Latin words   15
falls upon the facts like soft snow, blurring the outlines and covering up all the details. The great enemy of clear language is insincerity. When there is a gap between one's real and one's declared aims, one turns as it were instinctively to long words and exhausted idioms, like a cuttlefish squirting out ink. In our age there is no such thing as "keeping out of politics." All issues are political issues, and politics itself is a mass of lies, evasions, folly, hatred and schizophrenia. When the general atmosphere is bad, language must suffer. I should expect to find—this is a guess which I have not sufficient knowledge to verify—that the German, Russian and Italian languages have all deteriorated in the last ten or fifteen years, as a result of dictatorship.

But if thought corrupts language, language can also corrupt thought. A   16
bad usage can spread by tradition and imitation, even among people who should and do know better. The debased language that I have been discussing is in some ways very convenient. Phrases like *a not unjustifiable assumption, leaves much to be desired, would serve no good purpose, a consideration which we should do well to bear in mind,* are a continuous temptation, a packet of aspirins always at one's elbow. Look back through this essay, and for certain you will find that I have again and again committed the very faults I am protesting against. By this morning's post I have received a pamphlet dealing with conditions in Germany. The author tells me that he "felt impelled" to write it. I open it at random, and here is almost the first sentence that I see: "[The Allies] have an opportunity not only of achieving a radical transformation of Germany's social and political structure in such a way as to avoid a nationalistic reaction in Germany itself, but at the same time of laying the foundations of a co-operative and unified Europe." You see, he "feels impelled" to write—feels, presumably, that he has something new to say—and yet his words, like cavalry horses answering the bugle, group themselves automatically into the familiar dreary pattern. This invasion of one's mind by ready-made phrases (*lay the foundations, achieve a radical transformation*) can only be prevented if one is constantly on guard against them, and every such phrase anaesthetizes a portion of one's brain.

I said earlier that the decadence of our language is probably curable.   17
Those who deny this would argue, if they produced an argument at all, that language merely reflects existing social conditions, and that we cannot influence its development by any direct tinkering with words and constructions. So far as the general tone or spirit of a language goes, this may be true, but it is not true in detail. Silly words and expressions have often disappeared, not through any evolutionary process but owing to the conscious action of a minority. Two recent examples were *explore every avenue* and *leave no stone unturned,* which were killed by the jeers of a few journalists. There is a long

list of flyblown metaphors which could similarly be got rid of if enough
people would interest themselves in the job; and it should also be possible
to laugh the *not un-* formation out of existence,* to reduce the amount of Latin
and Greek in the average sentence, to drive out foreign phrases and strayed
scientific words, and, in general, to make pretentiousness unfashionable. But
all these are minor points. The defence of the English language implies more
than this, and perhaps it is best to start by saying what it does *not* imply.

To begin with it has nothing to do with archaism, with the salvaging   18
of obsolete words and turns of speech, or with the setting up of a "standard
English" which must never be departed from. On the contrary, it is especially concerned with the scrapping of every word or idiom which has out-
worn its usefulness. It has nothing to do with correct grammar and syntax,
which are of no importance so long as one makes one's meaning clear, or
with the avoidance of Americanisms, or with having what is called a "good
prose style." On the other hand it is not concerned with fake simplicity and
the attempt to make written English colloquial. Nor does it even imply in
every case preferring the Saxon word to the Latin one, though it does imply
using the fewest and shortest words that will cover one's meaning. What is
above all needed is to let the meaning choose the word, and not the other
way about. In prose, the worst thing one can do with words is to surrender
to them. When you think of a concrete object, you think wordlessly, and
then, if you want to describe the thing you have been visualizing, you
probably hunt about till you find the exact words that seem to fit it. When
you think of something abstract you are more inclined to use words from
the start, and unless you make a conscious effort to prevent it, the existing
dialect will come rushing in and do the job for you, at the expense of blurring or even changing your meaning. Probably it is better to put off using
words as long as possible and get one's meaning as clear as one can through
pictures or sensations. Afterwards one can choose—not simply *accept*—the
phrases that will best cover the meaning, and then switch round and decide
what impression one's words are likely to make on another person. This last
effort of the mind cuts out all stale or mixed images, all prefabricated
phrases, needless repetitions, and humbug and vagueness generally. But one
can often be in doubt about the effect of a word or a phrase, and one needs
rules that one can rely on when instinct fails. I think the following rules
will cover most cases:

   (i) Never use a metaphor, simile or other figure of speech which you are
      used to seeing in print.
  (ii) Never use a long word where a short one will do.
 (iii) If it is possible to cut a word out, always cut it out.

*One can cure oneself of the *not un-* formation by memorizing this sentence: *A not unblack dog was
chasing a not unsmall rabbit across a not ungreen field.* [Orwell's note.]

(iv) Never use the passive where you can use the active.

(v) Never use a foreign phrase, a scientific word or a jargon word if you can think of an everyday English equivalent.

(vi) Break any of these rules sooner than say anything outright barbarous.

These rules sound elementary, and so they are, but they demand a deep change of attitude in anyone who has grown used to writing in the style now fashionable. One could keep all of them and still write bad English, but one could not write the kind of stuff that I quoted in those five specimens at the beginning of this article.

I have not here been considering the literary use of language, but merely 19 language as an instrument for expressing and not for concealing or preventing thought. Stuart Chase and others have come near to claiming that all abstract words are meaningless, and have used this as a pretext for advocating a kind of political quietism. Since you don't know what Fascism is, how can you struggle against Fascism? One need not swallow such absurdities as this, but one ought to recognize that the present political chaos is connected with the decay of language, and that one can probably bring about some improvement by starting at the verbal end. If you simplify your English, you are freed from the worst follies of orthodoxy. You cannot speak any of the necessary dialects, and when you make a stupid remark its stupidity will be obvious, even to yourself. Political language—and with variations this is true of all political parties, from Conservatives to Anarchists—is designed to make lies sound truthful and murder respectable, and to give an appearance of solidity to pure wind. One cannot change this all in a moment, but one can at least change one's own habits, and from time to time one can even, if one jeers loudly enough, send some worn-out and useless phrase—some *jackboot, Achilles' heel, hotbed, melting pot, acid test, veritable inferno* or other lump of verbal refuse—into the dustbin where it belongs.

make Hot air sound solid!

Imprecise language

Questions for Discussion

1. Orwell begins by claiming that modern English is ugly, slovenly, and in decline. These charges must sound to many readers like highly subjective accusations, difficult if not impossible to document, and they are flatly denied by many scientific linguists. Does his claim seem to you convincing? (Remember that it is much easier to show that many people use language badly than to show that people in general speak and write worse now than they used to.) A second claim is that "the decline of a language must ultimately have political and economic causes" (¶2). How does he argue for this position? Do you accept it? If not, would you say that he

has a serious argument worth thinking about? If you are dubious, where do you think Orwell has gone wrong in his argument?

2. Orwell claims that one of the surest symptoms of a language's abuse is staleness of imagery (figurative language that no longer evokes mental pictures or concrete sensations). Consider the following images by Orwell himself. Are they stale or fresh? Do they evoke effective concrete pictures or feelings?

    a. Modern prose is "tacked together like the sections of a prefabricated hen-house" (¶4).
    b. "Now that I have made this catalogue of swindles and perversions . . ." (¶9).
    c. "The writer knows more or less what he wants to say, but an accumulation of stale phrases chokes him like tea leaves blocking a sink" (¶11).
    d. The typical political speaker often seems "unconscious of what he is saying, as one is when one utters the responses in church" (¶12).
    e. "A mass of Latin words falls upon the facts like soft snow" (¶15).
    f. Insincerity in writing leads "instinctively to long words and exhausted idioms, like a cuttlefish squirting out ink" (¶15).
    g. Stock phrases "are a continuous temptation, a packet of aspirins always at one's elbow" (¶16).
    h. Any stock phrase is a "lump of verbal refuse" that should be sent "into the dustbin [garbage can] where it belongs" (¶19).

    Are all of these images equally effective? Are (f) and (g), for example, as good as (d) and (e)? (How do stock phrases resemble a packet of aspirins?) In general, does Orwell follow his own rule of using images that are fresh and effective?

3. Does the kind of argument Orwell constructs about the passage from Ecclesiastes (¶9–10)—counting the ratio of words to syllables—seem convincing? That is, is it a convincing way to show that writing is flaccid by remarking on its unusually high number of syllables per word? Will the ratio he deplores always produce the same effect? Can you rewrite the passage using many-syllabled words without being abstract and vague?

4. Do Orwell's "rules" for writing good English prose (¶18) sound like the rules you have read in English grammar texts? Do they sound easier or harder to follow? Does his argument convince you that following his rules will help you in your writing?

5. Do you think Orwell overstates his case when he says that writing good English "has nothing to do with correct grammar and syntax, which are of no importance so long as one makes one's meaning clear" (¶18)? Could you really write a business letter that was clear but ungrammatical? Do you find other points that seem to be overstated merely for strong effect?

Suggested Essay Topics

1. Select a document famous in American political history (such as the Declaration of Independence, Abraham Lincoln's Gettysburg Address or Second

Inaugural Address, John F. Kennedy's Inaugural Address of 1960, or Hubert Humphrey's attack on "states' rights" at the Democratic National Convention in 1948). Read the whole speech and then evaluate one or two paragraphs according to Orwell's standards as summarized in paragraph 18 and defended throughout his essay. Direct your essay to your classmates, showing them why the speech you are examining is either a good or bad specimen of English prose, according to Orwell's standards.

2. Examine Orwell's own writing from the standpoint of his "rules" in paragraph 18, and write him a letter either commending or criticizing him for meeting (or not meeting) his own standards. Be sure to show concretely in particular passages how he either succeeds or fails.

IDEAS IN DEBATE

Bruno Bettelheim and Karen Zelan
Richard Wright

Bruno Bettelheim and Karen Zelan

*The psychologist Bruno Bettelheim (b. 1903) has made important contributions in many fields: the study of mental disorders in children (*The Empty Fortress*), the nature of totalitarianism and the experience of the holocaust under the Nazis (*The Informed Heart*), the moral and social effects of different kinds of children's literature (*The Uses of Enchantment*). Karen Zelan (b. 1934) is a research colleague of Bettelheim's and a child psychologist specializing in learning disorders. Together they have recently conducted an extensive study of how children are taught to read and why the teaching so often fails.*

If you think back to when you were learning to read, you will remember that many children—you may even have been one of them—"hated school" and especially hated those moments when the teacher required each child to read a few words aloud. Bettelheim and Zelan argue that although learning to read must always be hard work, it can be work of the kind that leads to love, not hate—if the kind of reading that children do rewards them from the beginning with understanding and enjoyment. They find, however, that too many of today's reading texts cannot give such rewards because they are empty of human meaning. Most children, say Bettelheim and Zelan, will naturally rebel against such books and may, ultimately, learn to "hate reading."

If Bettelheim and Zelan are right, they have discovered one main cause of many of America's educational problems. If you do not love to read, or if you have friends who say that they have never been "readers," the problem may well be traced to the kinds of stories, or non-stories, you were fed in the beginning years.

WHY CHILDREN DON'T LIKE TO READ

Originally published in *The Atlantic Monthly*, November 1981; reprinted as part of *On Learning to Read: The Child's Fascination with Meaning* (1981).

A child's attitude toward reading is of such importance that, more often than not, it determines his scholastic fate. Moreover, his experiences in learning to read may decide how he will feel about learning in general, and even about himself as a person.

Family life has a good deal to do with the development of a child's   2
ability to understand, to use, and to enjoy language. It strongly influences his
impression of the value of reading, and his confidence in his intelligence and
academic abilities. But regardless of what the child brings from home to
school, the most important influence on his ability to read once he is in class
is how his teacher presents reading and literature. If the teacher can make
reading interesting and enjoyable, then the exertions required to learn how
will seem worthwhile.

A child takes great pleasure in becoming able to read some words. But   3
the excitement fades when the texts the child must read force him to reread
the same word endlessly. Word recognition—"decoding" is the term used by
educational theorists—deteriorates into empty rote learning when it does not
lead directly to the reading of meaningful content. The longer it takes the
child to advance from decoding to meaningful reading, the more likely it
becomes that his pleasure in books will evaporate. A child's ability to read
depends unquestionably on his learning pertinent skills. But he will not be
interested in learning basic reading skills if he thinks he is expected to master
them for their own sake. That is why so much depends on what the teacher,
the school, and the textbooks emphasize. From the very beginning, the child
must be convinced that skills are only a means to achieve a goal, and that the
only goal of importance is that he become literate—that is, come to enjoy
literature and benefit from what it has to offer.

A child who is made to read, "Nan had a pad. Nan had a tan pad. Dad   4
ran. Dad ran to the pad," and worse nonsense can have no idea that books
are worth the effort of learning to read. His frustration is increased by the fact
that such a repetitive exercise is passed off as a story to be enjoyed. The worst
effect of such drivel is the impression it makes on a child that sounding out
words on a page—decoding—is what reading is all about. If, on the contrary,
a child were taught new skills as they became necessary to understand a
worthwhile text, the empty achievement "Now I can decode some words"
would give way to the much more satisfying recognition "Now I am reading
something that adds to my life." From the start, reading lessons should
nourish the child's spontaneous desire to read books by himself.

Benjamin S. Bloom, professor of education at the University of Chicago,   5
has found that who will do well in school and who will do poorly is largely
determined by the end of the third grade. Thus, reading instruction during
the first three grades is crucial. Unfortunately, the primers used in most
American schools up to and sometimes through the third grade convey no
sense that there are rewards in store. And since poor readers continue to be
subjected to these primers well past the third grade, their reading can only
get worse as their interests and experience diverge further from the content
of the books.

. . .

For many decades, textbooks have been used as the basis for reading   6
instruction by the vast majority of elementary school teachers, and they are
much worse today than [they were fifty years ago]. According to one study,

first readers published in the 1920s contained an average of 645 new words. By the late 1930s, this number had dropped to about 460 words. In the 1940s and 1950s, vocabulary declined further, to about 350 words. The vocabularies of primers in seven textbook series published between 1960 and 1963 ranged from 113 to 173 new words. More recent primers, compared with the 1920s editions, also have small vocabularies. For example, *Let's See the Animals,* published in 1970 by Bowmar/Noble, introduces 108 new words; *May I Come In?,* published in 1973, by Ginn & Company, introduces 219 new words; *Finding Places,* published by the American Book Company, in 1980, introduces 192 new words. Although in the 1920s few children went to kindergarten and little preschool reading instruction was given, by the 1970s, when many children were attending kindergarten and reading was consistently taught there, the first-grade primers contained only a quarter of the vocabulary presented to first-graders fifty years ago.

When they enter school, most children already know and use 4,000 or   7 more words. Nobody has to make a deliberate effort to teach them these words, with the exception of the first few learned in infancy. Children make words their own because they want to, because they find them pleasing and useful. Even the least verbal group of first-graders has mastered well over 2,000 words, thus invalidating the claim that children of culturally deprived families would be unfairly burdened by primers of larger vocabulary. This condescending assumption ignores the richness of daily life in even the poorest households. By encouraging the adoption of less challenging books, it has helped to deprive most children at school just as poverty deprives many children at home.

· · ·

Research in the teaching of reading, far from justifying the continuous   8 reduction in the number of words used in primers, fails to show any reason for it. It is therefore hard to understand why textbook publishers have pursued this course, and why educators have not rebelled. One possible explanation is that as primers become simpler, children, because they are bored, read them with less and less facility. The publishers, in response, make the books even simpler and, thus, even less effective.

Primers have no authors. Many people help to create the books, and the   9 financial investment required runs into the millions. (The sizable staff of one large publishing house worked for five years to produce a first-grade program alone.) Yet despite such prodigious effort and expense, all basic series are more or less alike. To recoup the large investment in a series, a publishing house must be able to sell it to schools all over the country. It cannot risk controversy.

We can cite two examples from our own experience. One publisher, in   10 an effort to improve a first-grade reader, came up with a story in which children bring a balloon home from a fair, whereupon a cat leaps on it and it bursts. The story would seem harmless enough to most people, but when the book was tested in an Illinois school system, cat-lovers were outraged: the story had maligned their pets, turned children against animals, and so on. The local school superintendent, who was coming up for re-election, decided to withdraw the book, and the publisher, fearing similar setbacks elsewhere, decided to drop the story.

Another publishing house was preparing a new edition of its widely 11 used series. One of us, asked to consult, objected in detail to the blandness of the stories proposed. The company's vice-president in charge of textbooks confessed that he, too, thought the stories would bore young readers, but he was obliged to keep in mind that neither children nor teachers buy textbooks: school boards and superintendents do. And their first concern is that no one mind their choices. Fairy tales, for example, would never do. Some people would complain that the stories insult stepmothers; others would find the punishment of evildoers too cruel.

The result of such constraints is a book full of endlessly repeated words 12 passed off as stories. Many teachers have told us that they don't like such a book, but assume that since a primer has been put together by experts, and approved by experts, it must be appropriate for children even if it is obnoxious to an adult. In the course of our research on the teaching of reading we have talked to children who were not so credulous. Many told us that their teachers must have faked an interest in the stories, or that they must think children are not very smart.

Fourth- and fifth-graders who had left the beginners' books behind 13 described their resentments to us quite clearly. One rather quiet boy, who preferred to read or work by himself and rarely participated in class, spoke up all on his own and with deep feeling. He had felt so ashamed to say the things written in primers that he could not bring himself to do it. And although he now liked reading a lot, he said, he still had a hard time reading aloud.

The first- and second-graders were as unhappy with their books as the 14 older children remembered being. They said they read only because they had to, and that on their own they would never choose such "junk." "It's all impossible," one of them said. When he was asked why, answers came from around the room: "The children aren't real!" "They aren't angry!" When one child exclaimed, "They aren't anything!" all agreed that there was nothing more to be said.

Textbook writers and publishers know that their books are dull, and 15 they have tried to make them more attractive by commissioning many colorful illustrations. For example, the number of pictures in primers of the Scott, Foresman series doubled between 1920 and 1962, from about one picture per one hundred words to nearly two per hundred words. The trouble with pictures is that the printed text becomes even less appealing in comparison. Words seem to be less vivid and to convey less information. Worse, being able to guess from the pictures what the text is about, a child who is reluctant to read has no incentive to learn.

The publishers' advice to teachers reinforces this syndrome. Typically, 16 the elaborate teachers' guides for each book in a series suggest that the class be asked questions about the pictures before reading the story. Yet there is evidence that pictures retard or interfere with learning to read. Consider the following report by a psychologist of reading, Eleanor J. Gibson: "Children in the second term of kindergarten were given practice with three-letter common words ('cat,' 'bed,' 'dog,' etc.) on flash cards. In one group, the word on the card was accompanied by the appropriate picture. In another, it appeared alone. Training trials, in which the experimenter pronounced the word as it was displayed to the child, alternated with test trials [in which] the child was shown the word alone and asked to say what it was. The picture group made significantly more errors and took longer . . . than the group without pictures. The pictorial redundancy appeared to be distracting rather than useful." Yet in most of the preprimers and primers in classrooms today, words are used primarily as labels and captions.

Learning to read is not an entertainment but hard work. Rather than face this directly, publishers seek to distract children with references to play. But allusions to strenuous physical activities make a child want to move, not think. Worse, a first-grader knows from his own experience just how complex a ball game can be. So a weak story about a ball game is most likely to convince the child that reading about a ball game is dull compared with playing in one. 17

In Harper & Row's "Janet and Mark" series (1966), school makes its first appearance in second grade in *All Through the Year*. The last section of the book is titled "Too Much Is Too Much of Anything," and the first story about the things that are too much, "A Feeling in the Air," is about school. "Everyone was waiting. . . . It was the last day of school. A little while, and it would be all over." The children are "daydreaming . . . of baseball and swimming and bicycle rides." In the last picture of the story, we see them streaming out of the school building, joyful to be released. 18

Psychoanalytic studies of the so-called "double bind" have shown that nothing is more confusing and disturbing to a child, or has more detrimental effects, than contradictory messages from an adult about important issues. Almost every preprimer and primer bears such contradictory messages. Tacitly, they say that the educational system, which requires the child to go to school and presents him with a book so that he may learn to read, holds that school and learning are serious business. But the explicit message of the text and pictures is that the child should think—that is, read—only about playing. The idea seems to be that a suggestion of what books are really for—to open new worlds of thought and imagination—would have the most undesirable consequences for the child's reading achievement. 19

From a psychoanalytic perspective, the primers' emphasis on play ensures that the books will be addressed solely to the child's pleasure-seeking ego—the earliest, most basic, but also most primitive motivating force in man. But as the child reaches school age, around age five, he should have learned to exchange (at least to some extent) living by the pleasure principle for making choices in accord with the reality principle. The primers, by presenting him almost exclusively with images of fun, throw the child back to the developmental phase he is trying, with difficulty, to outgrow. Such primers 20 insult the child's intelligence and his sense of worth, and the offense goes far to explain why children reject their reading books as empty. The books talk down to children; they do not take children's aspirations seriously.

In class, children read aloud. For some time to come, even if the child 21 does not voice what he is reading, he will form the words with his lips. Reading aloud feels to a child as if he were speaking to his teacher, or whoever might be listening to him. For that matter, it is not unusual for a child to think that his teacher wrote the book, and has planted messages for him in it. In a conversation, we wish to hold our listener's attention and impress him with what we have to say. But the teacher is oblivious of the child's impression that reading aloud is a sort of conversation; instead, the teacher listens carefully to make sure that the child reads the words as they are printed in the book, and corrects him when he fails. To do so is a teacher's duty, according to the teaching methods favored in this country; it may also be the only way a teacher can remain alert through the near-hypnotic effect of the words. In any case, the child experiences the teacher's interruptions as rejection, which certainly does not make reading more attractive to him.

Furthermore, a child may have good reason to make a mistake. Reading 22 for meaning is anything but passive, even when the content is absorbed exactly as presented. And the more intent a reader is on taking in the meaning, the more active he is in his reading. In order for a child to maintain the minimal interest necessary for reading a story, he may try to correct the story or improve it by misreading it. The barrenness of the text may tempt the child to project meaning where there is none.

The texts of preprimers and primers consist of words that can be readily 23 sounded out. But these words are often combined in sentences that no one would ever say. Such a text is actually harder for the beginner to read. For example, because the child usually learns early to recognize the words "store" and "man," one widely used basal text (*People Read,* one of the Bank Street readers) tells about a "store man" when referring to a salesman. Out of a wish to make learning to read easy, children who know the word that the text of this story means to convey are asked to recognize and use in their reading a phrase that rarely comes up in writing or speech. To compound the irony, the phrase appears in a book whose title by implication promises to tell how everybody reads and what they read. The result is that children may be provoked to errors by the discrepancy between ordinary language and the uncommon language of the book.

We have spent a number of years observing school reading lessons, and 24 have learned that children make mistakes for many reasons, in addition to the obvious one of ignorance. For example, a first-grade boy was reading "Van's Cave," a story in the 1969 J. B. Lippincott series about a hunter and his dog, Spot. The story goes that the hunter shoots five ducks, which the dog retrieves. They then return to the cave, where they live. The man starts a fire on which he plans to roast the ducks. The text says: "Spot must not leave the ducks. He can see a wolf near the cave." This, inexplicably, is accompanied by a picture showing the dog asleep. The boy reversed the meaning of the sentence by reading, instead, "He can't see a wolf near the cave." It is possible that the boy did so because the picture shows the dog asleep. But it is more likely that the boy's knowledge of dog behavior made it seem unreasonable to him that a dog would sleep when it saw a wolf lurking nearby. A first-grader might also wish to believe that his dog would safeguard him. So the misreading of "can't" for "can," seemingly a simple error, reflects on one level the child's attempt to bring what the text says into accord with the picture. On another level, it may register the boy's protest against a dog that sleeps when its master needs protection. Finally, the misreading is a statement correctly describing normal dog behavior.

One first-grade girl complained about a story in McGraw-Hill's Sullivan 25
Storybook series which told of a ball falling into a patch of tar. She thought it should have said that the ball fell into a puddle. The teacher, knowing that this phonics-based text used "patch of tar" in preference to "puddle" because these words are pronounced as printed, while "puddle" is pronounced "pud-del," said that perhaps the author of the story thought children would have difficulty in recognizing "puddle." By this she meant difficulty in decoding and reading the word. But the girl fastened on the exact words the teacher had used. She was indignant, and angrily exclaimed, "I know 'puddle' when I see it." We cannot say for sure that her remark did not simply reflect the fact that the word "puddle" was in her active vocabulary, while the words "patch of tar" were not, but the way she expressed herself suggests a more subtle reason for her sense of insult. She made it clear that she saw puddles in everyday life, not tar patches; and her reaction entailed the wish that teachers and those who write for children show respect for a child's experiences of the world.

Another smart first-grader puzzled his teacher because all year he had 26
balked at reading, despite evidence that he knew how. On the day we observed him, the boy made numerous errors—for example, reading "stick" for "chick." This, the teacher told him, showed he had not mastered word beginnings and endings, and that he should therefore continue with his exercises. The boy refused.

The teacher then suggested that we read with him, upon which the boy 27
strenuously protested that the workbook the teacher had assigned to him was boring. (The book, part of McGraw-Hill's Sullivan Programmed Reading series, is typical of most workbooks, in that the exercises require the student to fill in missing letters.) With our encouragement, the boy made one more attempt; again he read "stick" for "chick." But this time, before anyone had time to react, he corrected himself and angrily blurted out: "Fill in the blanks, that's all I get! Witch, witch, witch . . . ditch, ditch, ditch . . . stick, stick, stick . . . chick, chick, chick!" And that was it. He would not do any more reading with us that day. The boy had made error upon error, in this way giving vent to his negative feelings. But by pairing "witch" with "ditch," and "stick" with "chick," he showed that he understood well the different word beginnings and endings, and that his substitutions were not made in ignorance.

A couple of days later, we again asked the boy to read. He refused the 28

Sullivan series but was willing to try something more interesting. We settled on *The Bear Detectives,* by Stan and Jan Berenstain. The story tells how Papa Bear and his children hunt for a missing pumpkin, using a detective kit. Although the small bears discover various clues to the pumpkin's where-abouts, they can't find it. After reading the story eagerly for some thirty pages, the boy substituted the word "defective" for "detective": "He's in the barn. This is it! Hand me that defective kit." Earlier he had read "detective" correctly, demonstrating that he was well able to read the word—that he knew what it designated and how it fit into the story. It seemed to us that the boy, having read for so many pages that the detective kit was no help in the search for the pumpkin, and carried away by the excited wish of the bears to find it, was once more expressing his frustration with a text.

A few days later, this boy's workbook again required him to read a list 29 of words that, bereft of context, made no sense. He then read "dump" for "jump." Responding to the feelings this misreading suggested, we asked, "Who wants to dump this?" The boy immediately read the correct word, "jump," and then nodded at us. When we asked him why he wanted to dump the workbook, his unhesitating reply was, " 'Cause it's garbage."

Just as children are likely to change the words of a dull story in order 30 to make it more interesting, they are also likely to change the words of an interesting story because they have a personal stake in the meaning. For example, one competent first-grader read a story to us smoothly and with interest and comprehension in her voice. The story was about tigers, and the little girl made only one mistake: she consistently read "tigger" for "tiger." It is easy to understand why this child would shy away from thinking about dangerous tigers in favor of contemplating the harmless character of Tigger in the Pooh books, which were favorites of hers. Her switch in thought seemed to relieve her fear about what the ferocious beast would do next as the story unfolded.

It requires considerable ingenuity on the part of first-graders to make 31 radical alterations in meanings by only the slightest change of letters. In the examples of the boy reading about the dog and the wolf and the girl reading about the tiger, the children retained all the letters of the printed word, adding to them a single letter. By adding a "t," the boy substituted correct animal behavior for an incorrect description of it, and by adding a "g," the girl replaced an animal threatening danger and destruction with one symbol-izing safety and pleasure. In the third example, by substituting one letter for another in a nine-letter word, the child expressed his dissatisfaction with the uselessness of an object that played a central role in the story he was reading.

When a child utters a word entirely different from the one printed in 32 the book, teachers are likely to assume, correctly, that the child's attention has wandered, or that he may have given up on reading a word that is hard for him. When what the child reads is only slightly different from what is printed, teachers are also likely to conclude that the child has a problem—faulty discrimination between letters—even though the error may change the meaning of the sentence radically. They assume this despite the fact that the child has already read most letters as printed, suggesting that he was paying attention to the page and could recognize the letters correctly. But what if a child's substitution of one or a few letters makes good—though altered—sense within the context of a story? Perhaps he has perceived what the printed word signifies, decided that it is unacceptable, and found a solution that suits his purposes.

A teacher's reflex to catch and correct mistakes is but one example of a situation that occurs over and over again in schools, and not only where beginners are taught to read: the educator's faith in abstract theories about how learning must proceed blinds him to the sophistication of the child's mind. The teacher's insistence on accuracy often barely hides the fact that what is involved is also a power play, in which the teacher uses her superior knowledge and her authority to gain her point. The child—consciously or, more often, subconsciously—reacts to being the victim of such a power play, and is antagonistic. Unfortunately, many children manage to defeat the teacher by refusing to learn; their victory robs them of their chance to be educated, and it deprives society of competent citizens.

It is not impossible to teach children to read while respecting their intelligence and dignity. The primers used in Europe are generally far more difficult than those in use in this country. We believe their success is proved by the fact that at the end of the first grade, the average European child has a larger reading vocabulary than that of the average American child. Moreover, reading retardation, the curse of so many young Americans, is much less common among European children and, when it occurs, is rarely as severe.

The most recent series of basic readers published in Switzerland stands as a notable alternative to the American textbooks that we have complained about. The early reading program consists of three preprimers and one primer. The preprimers are loose-leaf booklets, each page (with a single exception) comprising a few short lines of text and an illustration. Since there are no pictures on the covers of the booklets, the child is encouraged to form his own opinion of what each booklet is about by reading.

The first preprimer is entitled *We are all here,* meaning "here to read together." Its first page has only two words: "I am." And on this page there is no picture, no face to rival the child's own. The Swiss child's reading thus begins with the strongest statement of self-assertion imaginable. After sixteen more pages, each with a few words for the child to learn, there follow twenty-eight pages devoted either to snatches of well-known songs or to a few lines from popular fairy tales. In this way, the first preprimer leads easily to the next, *Once upon a time,* which is composed of five fairy tales from Grimm. Though quite simple, these versions are nonetheless faithful in all essentials to the originals.

The third Swiss preprimer, *Edi,* is about a little boy who might be the peer of the children reading about him. The first page shows Edi with his school satchel on his back, standing between his father and mother. The story goes that Edi, who has eaten something that disagrees with him, gets sick and is sent to the country to stay with relatives and get well. We follow Edi's experiences on the farm until the end of the book, when he returns home, his health fully restored. There he finds that while he was away, his mother had a baby; Edi has a sister. Edi's story deals with two of the most critical events in a child's life: sickness and the birth of a sibling.

The primer of the Swiss series, *It's your turn,* meaning "it's your turn to 38 read," begins with counting rhymes and songs typically sung by children as accompaniment to their games. Since Swiss children know all these rhymes and songs, they know how the words they are decoding ought to sound, and so it is likely that at this more difficult level of reading, their attempts will be error-free. Thus the children's confidence in their ability to read this new, thicker, rather scary-looking book is supported, and they are ready for the remaining sections, which are longer and a little harder.

It's your turn has many colorful pictures that embellish the text without 39 giving away its meaning; the child *must* read in order to understand. For example, a poem by Christian Morgenstern, "Winternight," is illustrated by a picture of a town at night, covered with falling snow; the picture conveys the spirit of the poem but permits no conclusion about its substance. In addition to the Morgenstern poem, the book contains a number of other poems and short stories, many by famous German authors. The selection represents all periods of German literature: contemporary, Romantic, classical, and medieval, and legendary folktales, rhymes, and riddles.

This first Swiss reader, like its American counterparts, tries to introduce 40 children to reading by means of attractive and fairly easy material. The chief difference is that none of the pieces in the Swiss reader patronize the child; there is no deviation from ordinary language or ordinary usage. Children have been reciting the counting rhymes to each other for hundreds of years. No words are avoided because they might be difficult (as is done constantly in American primers)—and they prove not to be too hard, because the child who uses them in everyday conversation already knows what they mean, and is thus eager to master whatever technical obstacles they present on the page. In one way or another, all the stories appeal to children of primary age, but in none of them is there even the mention of active play. If anything, the pieces are on the contemplative side, though with a light touch. The most impressive difference between this book and American primers is the literary quality of many of its selections. The Swiss primer manages to introduce the child to literacy at the same time that it teaches him the rudiments of reading.

These primers, used in the German-speaking parts of Switzerland, have 41 a special lesson to teach American educators and publishers. It has been argued that our primers have to employ unnaturally simple words because many minority children speak a different language at home: Spanish, Chinese, "black English," and so on. But the language that *all* children growing up in the German parts of Switzerland speak—a dialect called *Schweizer Deutsch,* or Swiss German—is very different from the High German they must speak and read in school. Although during the first few months of school the children are allowed to speak to the teacher in their dialect, from the start they learn to read only the High German in which their primers are published.

For some reason, Swiss children do not find this enforced bilingualism such a handicap that they fail to become able readers. We believe that their lack of difficulty is explained to a great extent by the fact that they like what they are given to read.

Questions for Discussion

1. Can you summarize the differences between the Swiss basic readers that the authors admire and the American texts they deplore? Is the difference to be found in the method of presentation, in the subject matter, or in both?

2. Compare your earliest memories of learning to read with those of your classmates. Are there strong differences among you about how pleasant or disagreeable it was? Can you remember the first book you really enjoyed? (Gregory remembers *Smoky the Crow,* Booth *The Wizard of Oz,* both from the second grade. Neither of us can remember a single reading from the first grade, except for the Dick and Jane books, which were dismal, dismal.)

3. What kind of people do Bettelheim and Zelan seem to be, judging from the things they say and the way they write? Give evidence for your opinion from their own words. (One result of getting an education should be an expansion of your vocabulary for describing people—their character, their ethos. When you ask, "What kind of person is he?" how many kinds do you have in mind?)

4. Bettelheim and Zelan suggest an analogy (¶7) between the child's learning to talk and learning to read: If children learn to talk "because they want to," obviously they will learn to read if they want to. Do you think that the analogy is sound? In answering, remember that a fitting analogy does not require that *all* details in the comparison match perfectly, only that the directly pertinent elements do.

5. In what paragraphs do the authors provide evidence for their conclusions? Do different kinds of evidence carry different weight here? For example, is the account of Swiss schools and their success more or less persuasive than the quotations from the American primers?

6. In paragraph 21 the authors say that children experience reading aloud as conversation. Is silent reading also experienced as conversation? If you ask a book a question, can it ever be said to "reply"? Do some textbooks make us feel like holding a conversation, while some merely talk *at* us, and still others seem to address someone *behind* us, someone wearing an academic robe and mortarboard? (Most textbooks we authors remember from college had this last tone.) What makes the difference?

Suggested Essay Topics

1. In the children's literature section of the library, find a reading primer and do a careful book review from the point of view of Bettelheim and Zelan. Your basic question is, "Would it be a good book to learn to read from?" Be sure to do some thinking about the kind of reader you are addressing, whether librarians, elementary teachers, parents, or the children themselves.

2. This assignment is somewhat more ambitious. Read all or part of *The Uses of Enchantment* by Bettelheim. Then choose a short section from his defense of fairy tales and discuss whether it seems persuasive and why. Again you should think about whom you are trying to convince. For this assignment you might think of writing a letter to the editor of *The Atlantic Monthly* (where "Why Children Don't Like to Read" originally appeared) praising or condemning the authors for their argument. Or you might imagine yourself writing the authors directly, giving carefully considered reasons why you find their arguments strong or weak.

Richard Wright

In the other "Ideas in Debate" essay, Bruno Bettelheim and Karen Zelan assert that a child "will not be interested in learning basic reading skills if he thinks he is expected to master them for their own sake. . . . The child must be convinced that skills are only a means to achieve a goal." If "for their own sake" means that children are taught reading skills as a dead-end activity, leading to nothing more exciting or illuminating than good or bad grades on reading tests, surely Bettelheim and Zelan are right. But if children are given worthy goals that can be met by learning to read—goals that belong to them as well as to the teacher—then presumably they will be motivated to learn eagerly. At that point there is not much distance between learning reading skills "for their own sake" and learning them to achieve goals. No two poles could be farther apart than the reading goals in today's minimum-achievement classroom, where reading is often taught as a mechanical activity that goes nowhere, and the goals of Richard Wright's (1908–1960) passionate reader in "The Library Card."

"I hungered for books," he says, "[for] new ways of looking and seeing. It was not a matter of believing what I read, but of feeling something new, of being affected by something that made the look of the world different" (¶23). "It would have been impossible for me to have told anyone what I derived from these novels, for it was nothing less than a sense of life itself" (¶28). Clearly, books for this young narrator are doorways into a wider existence than he could ever have experienced on his own, and in his eagerness to reach that wider existence he opened one door after another. What does this experience suggest about the way reading should

be taught to children in school? And what does it suggest about the kinds of reading they ought to do?

As you read, consider whether most of us share the narrator's hunger for a wider existence than our ordinary one. Is it possible to see people's interest in television, movies, plays, and song as different aspects of this hunger to be taken beyond our own lives, to learn how others see, feel, and think? If most of us do share this hunger (and if there are some who do not, why don't they?), why is the satisfying of this hunger not more frequently offered as the goal of learning to read? Six-year-old children may not be ready for a theoretical discussion of the issues, but isn't it true that they will certainly recognize the difference between reading as a narrow mechanical end and reading as a means of learning about the immense world around them? And at the high school and college levels, what is the proportion of reading that is done for sheer pleasure and general learning as compared to the reading that is done to acquire specific information? Does Richard Wright's account of how his world opened up make you wish you could take time to read more in your own life?

THE LIBRARY CARD

Chapter 13 of *Black Boy*.

One morning I arrived early at work and went into the bank lobby where the   1 Negro porter was mopping. I stood at a counter and picked up the Memphis *Commercial Appeal* and began my free reading of the press. I came finally to the editorial page and saw an article dealing with one H. L. Mencken. I knew by hearsay that he was the editor of the *American Mercury,* but aside from that I knew nothing about him. The article was a furious denunciation of Mencken, concluding with one, hot, short sentence: Mencken is a fool.

I wondered what on earth this Mencken had done to call down upon   2 him the scorn of the South. The only people I had ever heard denounced in the South were Negroes, and this man was not a Negro. Then what ideas did Mencken hold that made a newspaper like the *Commercial Appeal* castigate him publicly? Undoubtedly he must be advocating ideas that the South did not like. Were there, then, people other than Negroes who criticized the South? I knew that during the Civil War the South had hated northern whites, but I had not encountered such hate during my life. Knowing no more of Mencken than I did at that moment, I felt a vague sympathy for him. Had not the South, which had assigned me the role of a non-man, cast at him its hardest words?

Now, how could I find out about this Mencken? There was a huge   3 library near the riverfront, but I knew that Negroes were not allowed to patronize its shelves any more than they were the parks and playgrounds of the city. I had gone into the library several times to get books for the white men on the job. Which of them would now help me to get books? And how could I read them without causing concern to the white men with whom I worked? I had so far been successful in hiding my thoughts and feelings from them, but I knew that I would create hostility if I went about the business of reading in a clumsy way.

I weighed the personalities of the men on the job. There was Don, a Jew; but I distrusted him. His position was not much better than mine and I knew that he was uneasy and insecure; he had always treated me in an offhand, bantering way that barely concealed his contempt. I was afraid to ask him to help me get books; his frantic desire to demonstrate a racial solidarity with the whites against Negroes might make him betray me.

Then how about the boss? No, he was a Baptist and I had the suspicion that he would not be quite able to comprehend why a black boy would want to read Mencken. There were other white men on the job whose attitudes showed clearly that they were Kluxers or sympathizers, and they were out of the question.

There remained only one man whose attitude did not fit into an anti-Negro category, for I had heard the white men refer to him as a "Pope lover." He was an Irish Catholic and was hated by the white Southerners. I knew that he read books, because I had got him volumes from the library several times. Since he, too, was an object of hatred, I felt that he might refuse me but would hardly betray me. I hesitated, weighing and balancing the imponderable realities.

One morning I paused before the Catholic fellow's desk.

"I want to ask you a favor," I whispered to him.

"What is it?"

"I want to read. I can't get books from the library. I wonder if you'd let me use your card?"

He looked at me suspiciously.

"My card is full most of the time," he said.

"I see," I said and waited, posing my question silently.

"You're not trying to get me into trouble, are you, boy?" he asked, staring at me.

"Oh, no, sir."

"What book do you want?"

"A book by H. L. Mencken."

"Which one?"

"I don't know. Has he written more than one?"

"He has written several."

"I didn't know that."

"What makes you want to read Mencken?"

"Oh, I just saw his name in the newspaper," I said.

"It's good of you to want to read," he said. "But you ought to read the right things."

I said nothing. Would he want to supervise my reading?

"Let me think," he said. "I'll figure out something."

I turned from him and he called me back. He stared at me quizzically.

"Richard, don't mention this to the other white men," he said.

"I understand," I said. "I won't say a word."

A few days later he called me to him.

"I've got a card in my wife's name," he said. "Here's mine."   10

"Thank you, sir."

"Do you think you can manage it?"

"I'll manage fine," I said.

"If they suspect you, you'll get in trouble," he said.

"I'll write the same kind of notes to the library that you wrote when you sent me for books," I told him. "I'll sign your name."

He laughed.

"Go ahead. Let me see what you get," he said.

That afternoon I addressed myself to forging a note. Now, what were   11
the names of books written by H. L. Mencken? I did not know any of them.
I finally wrote what I thought would be a foolproof note: *Dear Madam: Will you please let this nigger boy*—I used the word "nigger" to make the librarian feel that I could not possibly be the author of the note—*have some books by H. L. Mencken?* I forged the white man's name.

I entered the library as I had always done when on errands for whites,   12
but I felt that I would somehow slip up and betray myself. I doffed my hat, stood a respectful distance from the desk, looked as unbookish as possible, and waited for the white patrons to be taken care of. When the desk was clear of people, I still waited. The white librarian looked at me.

"What do you want, boy?"

As though I did not possess the power of speech, I stepped forward and   13
simply handed her the forged note, not parting my lips.

"What books by Mencken does he want?" she asked.

"I don't know, ma'am," I said, avoiding her eyes.

"Who gave you this card?"

"Mr. Falk," I said.

"Where is he?"

"He's at work, at the M—— Optical Company," I said. "I've been in   14
here for him before."

"I remember," the woman said. "But he never wrote notes like this."

Oh, God, she's suspicious. Perhaps she would not let me have the   15
books? If she had turned her back at that moment, I would have ducked out the door and never gone back. Then I thought of a bold idea.

"You can call him up, ma'am," I said, my heart pounding.   16

"You're not using these books, are you?" she asked pointedly.

"Oh, no, ma'am. I can't read."

"I don't know what he wants by Mencken," she said under her breath.

I knew now that I had won; she was thinking of other things and the   17
race question had gone out of her mind. She went to the shelves. Once or twice she looked over her shoulder at me, as though she was still doubtful. Finally she came forward with two books in her hands.

"I'm sending him two books," she said. "But tell Mr. Falk to come in   18
next time, or send me the names of the books he wants. I don't know what he wants to read."

I said nothing. She stamped the card and handed me the books. Not 19
daring to glance at them, I went out of the library, fearing that that woman
would call me back for further questioning. A block away from the library
I opened one of the books and read a title: *A Book of Prefaces.* I was nearing my
nineteenth birthday and I did not know how to pronounce the word "preface." I thumbed the pages and saw strange words and strange names. I shook
my head, disappointed, looked at the other book; it was called *Prejudices.* I
knew what that word meant; I had heard it all my life. And right off I was
on guard against Mencken's books. Why would a man want to call a book
Prejudices? The word was so stained with all my memories of racial hate that
I could not conceive of anybody using it for a title. Perhaps I had made a
mistake about Mencken? A man who had prejudices must be wrong.

When I showed the books to Mr. Falk, he looked at me and frowned. 20
"That librarian might telephone you," I warned him.

"That's all right," he said. "But when you're through reading those
books, I want you to tell me what you get out of them."

That night in my rented room, while letting the hot water run over my 21
can of pork and beans in the sink, I opened *A Book of Prefaces* and began to read.
I was jarred and shocked by the style, the clear, clean, sweeping sentences.
Why did he write like that? And how did one write like that? I pictured the
man as a raging demon, slashing with his pen, consumed with hate, denouncing everything American, extolling everything European or German, laughing
at the weaknesses of people, mocking God, authority. What was this? I stood
up, trying to realize what reality lay behind the meaning of the words . . .
Yes, this man was fighting, fighting with words. He was using words as a
weapon, using them as one would use a club. Could words be weapons? Well,
yes, for here they were. Then, maybe, perhaps, I could use them as a weapon?
No. It frightened me. I read on and what amazed me was not what he said,
but how on earth anybody had the courage to say it.

Occasionally I glanced up to reassure myself that I was alone in the 22
room. Who were these men about whom Mencken was talking so passionately? Who was Anatole France? Joseph Conrad? Sinclair Lewis, Sherwood
Anderson, Dostoevski, George Moore, Gustave Flaubert, Maupassant, Tol-
stoy, Frank Harris, Mark Twain, Thomas Hardy, Arnold Bennett, Stephen
Crane, Zola, Norris, Gorky, Bergson, Ibsen, Balzac, Bernard Shaw, Dumas,
Poe, Thomas Mann, O. Henry, Dreiser, H. G. Wells, Gogol, T. S. Eliot, Gide,
Baudelaire, Edgar Lee Masters, Stendhal, Turgenev, Huneker, Nietzsche, and
scores of others? Were these men real? Did they exist or had they existed?
And how did one pronounce their names?

I ran across many words whose meanings I did not know, and I either 23
looked them up in a dictionary or, before I had a chance to do that, encountered the word in a context that made its meaning clear. But what strange
world was this? I concluded the book with the conviction that I had somehow
overlooked something terribly important in life. I had once tried to write, had
once reveled in feeling, had let my crude imagination roam, but the impulse
to dream had been slowly beaten out of me by experience. Now it surged up

again and I hungered for books, new ways of looking and seeing. It was not a matter of believing or disbelieving what I read, but of feeling something new, of being affected by something that made the look of the world different.

As dawn broke I ate my pork and beans, feeling dopey, sleepy. I went to work, but the mood of the book would not die; it lingered, coloring everything I saw, heard, did. I now felt that I knew what the white men were feeling. Merely because I had read a book that had spoken of how they lived and thought, I identified myself with that book. I felt vaguely guilty. Would I, filled with bookish notions, act in a manner that would make the whites dislike me? 24

I forged more notes and my trips to the library became frequent. Reading grew into a passion. My first serious novel was Sinclair Lewis's *Main Street.* It made me see my boss, Mr. Gerald, and identify him as an American type. I would smile when I saw him lugging his golf bags into the office. I had always felt a vast distance separating me from the boss, and now I felt closer to him, though still distant. I felt now that I knew him, that I could feel the very limits of his narrow life. And this had happened because I had read a novel about a mythical man called George F. Babbitt. 25

The plots and stories in the novels did not interest me so much as the point of view revealed. I gave myself over to each novel without reserve, without trying to criticize it; it was enough for me to see and feel something different. And for me, everything was something different. Reading was like a drug, a dope. The novels created moods in which I lived for days. But I could not conquer my sense of guilt, my feeling that the white men around me knew that I was changing, that I had begun to regard them differently. 26

Whenever I brought a book to the job, I wrapped it in newspaper—a habit that was to persist for years in other cities and under other circumstances. But some of the white men pried into my packages when I was absent and they questioned me. 27

"Boy, what are you reading those books for?"

"Oh, I don't know, sir."

"That's deep stuff you're reading, boy."

"I'm just killing time, sir."

"You'll addle your brains if you don't watch out."

I read Dreiser's *Jennie Gerhardt* and *Sister Carrie* and they revived in me a vivid sense of my mother's suffering; I was overwhelmed. I grew silent, wondering about the life around me. It would have been impossible for me to have told anyone what I derived from these novels, for it was nothing less than a sense of life itself. All my life had shaped me for the realism, the naturalism of the modern novel, and I could not read enough of them. 28

Steeped in new moods and ideas, I bought a ream of paper and tried to write; but nothing would come, or what did come was flat beyond telling. I discovered that more than desire and feeling were necessary to write and I dropped the idea. Yet I still wondered how it was possible to know people sufficiently to write about them? Could I ever learn about life and people? To me, with my vast ignorance, my Jim Crow station in life, it seemed a task 29 impossible of achievement. I now knew what being a Negro meant. I could endure the hunger. I had learned to live with hate. But to feel that there were feelings denied me, that the very breath of life itself was beyond my reach, that more than anything else hurt, wounded me. I had a new hunger.

In buoying me up, reading also cast me down, made me see what was 30 possible, what I had missed. My tension returned, new, terrible, bitter, surging, almost too great to be contained. I no longer *felt* that the world about me was hostile, killing; I *knew* it. A million times I asked myself what I could do to save myself, and there were no answers. I seemed forever condemned, ringed by walls.

I did not discuss my reading with Mr. Falk, who had lent me his library 31 card; it would have meant talking about myself and that would have been too painful. I smiled each day, fighting desperately to maintain my old behavior, to keep my disposition seemingly sunny. But some of the white men discerned that I had begun to brood.

"Wake up there, boy!" Mr. Olin said one day.   32

"Sir!" I answered for the lack of a better word.

"You act like you've stolen something," he said.

I laughed in the way I knew he expected me to laugh, but I resolved to 33 be more conscious of myself, to watch my every act, to guard and hide the new knowledge that was dawning within me.

If I went north, would it be possible for me to build a new life then? 34 But how could a man build a life upon vague, unformed yearnings? I wanted to write and I did not even know the English language. I bought English grammars and found them dull. I felt that I was getting a better sense of the language from novels than from grammars. I read hard, discarding a writer as soon as I felt that I had grasped his point of view. At night the printed page stood before my eyes in sleep.

Mrs. Moss, my landlady, asked me one Sunday morning: 35

"Son, what is this you keep on reading?"

"Oh, nothing. Just novels."

"What you get out of 'em?"

"I'm just killing time," I said.

"I hope you know your own mind," she said in a tone which implied that she doubted if I had a mind.

I knew of no Negroes who read the books I liked and I wondered if any 36 Negroes ever thought of them. I knew that there were Negro doctors, lawyers, newspapermen, but I never saw any of them. When I read a Negro newspaper I never caught the faintest echo of my preoccupation in its pages. I felt trapped and occasionally, for a few days, I would stop reading. But a vague hunger would come over me for books, books that opened up new avenues of feeling and seeing, and again I would forge another note to the white librarian. Again I would read and wonder as only the naïve and unlettered can read and wonder, feeling that I carried a secret, criminal burden about with me each day.

That winter my mother and brother came and we set up housekeeping, 37 buying furniture on the installment plan, being cheated and yet knowing no way to avoid it. I began to eat warm food and to my surprise found that regular meals enabled me to read faster. I may have lived through many illnesses and survived them, never suspecting that I was ill. My brother obtained a job and we began to save toward the trip north, plotting our time, setting tentative dates for departure. I told none of the white men on the job that I was planning to go north; I knew that the moment they felt I was thinking of the North they would change toward me. It would have made them feel that I did not like the life I was living, and because my life was completely conditioned by what they said or did, it would have been tantamount to challenging them.

I could calculate my chances for life in the South as a Negro fairly clearly now.   38

I could fight the southern whites by organizing with other Negroes, as my grandfather had done. But I knew that I could never win that way; there were many whites and there were but few blacks. They were strong and we were weak. Outright black rebellion could never win. If I fought openly I would die and I did not want to die. News of lynchings were frequent.   39

I could submit and live the life of a genial slave, but that was impossible. All of my life had shaped me to live by my own feelings, and thoughts. I could make up to Bess and marry her and inherit the house. But that, too, would be the life of a slave; if I did that, I would crush to death something within me, and I would hate myself as much as I knew the whites already hated those who had submitted. Neither could I ever willingly present myself to be kicked, as Shorty had done. I would rather have died than do that.   40

I could drain off my restlessness by fighting with Shorty and Harrison. I had seen many Negroes solve the problem of being black by transferring their hatred of themselves to others with a black skin and fighting them. I would have to be cold to do that, and I was not cold and I could never be.   41

I could, of course, forget what I had read, thrust the whites out of my mind, forget them; and find release from anxiety and longing in sex and alcohol. But the memory of how my father had conducted himself made that course repugnant. If I did not want others to violate my life, how could I voluntarily violate it myself?   42

I had no hope whatever of being a professional man. Not only had I been so conditioned that I did not desire it, but the fulfillment of such an ambition was beyond my capabilities. Well-to-do Negroes lived in a world that was almost as alien to me as the world inhabited by whites.   43

What, then, was there? I held my life in my mind, in my consciousness each day, feeling at times that I would stumble and drop it, spill it forever. My reading had created a vast sense of distance between me and the world in which I lived and tried to make a living, and that sense of distance was increasing each day. My days and nights were one long, quiet, continuously contained dream of terror, tension, and anxiety. I wondered how long I could bear it.   44

Questions for Discussion

1. Having been deprived of learning, the young narrator views it as a great privilege. He does not view learning as a way of gaining power in the world or of increasing his income—those thoughts do not seem even to cross his mind—but simply as a way of learning about lives, thoughts, and feelings other than his own. Discuss with your classmates the extent to which you think student apathy about learning derives from its being forced on children as a requirement rather than held out as a privilege. If you were to try to influence students in grade school and high school to become more enthusiastic readers and learners, what changes or tactics would you recommend? What new instructions would you give to teachers and administrators? What changes of behavior or attitude would you recommend to students themselves?

2. What is the social function of "boy" used as a form of address to blacks? Can you suggest why the whites in the story constantly repeat this term?

3. Why does the narrator in paragraphs 24 and 26 say that he felt guilty for the reading he was doing?

4. In trying to learn to write, the narrator says that he "bought English grammars" but "felt that I was getting a better sense of the language from novels than from grammars." Does this ring true to you? Do you think that increasing your reading will automatically improve your grammar? Would a steady reader ever have to study grammar formally in order to use it correctly? As you think about the answer to this question, consider the grammar of pre-school children who have never studied grammar. If they are surrounded by grammatically correct speakers, is their own grammar generally correct? If so, does this fact suggest an answer to the question of whether you can learn grammar from reading as well as by listening?

5. In discussion with your classmates, compare the various English and reading teachers you have had over the years. How many students think their teachers were successful at instilling a love of reading? How many think their teachers were poor? Are there similarities among the good teachers? Among the bad?

Suggested Essay Topics

1. In paragraph 24 the young narrator reports that after an all-night orgy of reading, "I went to work, but the mood of the book would not die; it lingered, coloring everything I saw, heard, did." If you have ever had this kind of experience yourself—the experience of a book's mood, characters, and events occupying your mind so vividly that they colored the world around you—give a specific account of the book's lingering effects. After reading Sinclair Lewis's *Main Street,* for example, the narrator achieves an entirely new understanding of his boss; he learns something about his boss's values and inner life that he could never have learned firsthand. Can you give an account of any similar experience, when a book gave you a fresher perspective or a deeper understanding of some (formerly inscruta-

ble) person or event? Direct your essay to your classmates, with the aim of explaining how the book achieved its effect.

2. Re-read a book that was a favorite of yours when you were a child. Then write an essay explaining how you would present this book to children today if you were a parent or a teacher using it to teach reading. Think back on your own experience with reading teachers, either in school or at home, and explain the strategies you would employ to lift children up to a love of reading. If it seems appropriate, pick a passage or two and discuss your selection in detail.

4

IMAGINATION AND ART

The Nature and Value of Imagination

I am certain of nothing but the holiness of the heart's affections
and the truth of imagination—what the imagination seizes as
beauty must be truth—whether it existed before or not.
John Keats

States have been governed here and there, heaven knows how;
but not by poetry, it is certain. Literature is a seducer;
we had almost said a harlot. She may do to trifle with; but woe to the
state whose statesmen write verses, and whose lawyers
read more in Tom Moore [a poet] than in Brackton [a jurist].
This is a dangerous state of society. . . . The real happiness of man,
of the mass, not of the few, depends on the knowledge
of things, not on that of words.
Westminster Review

Then I asked: "Does a firm persuasion that a thing is so, make it so?"
He replied: "All Poets believe that it does, and in ages
of imagination this firm persuasion removed mountains;
but many are not capable of a firm persuasion of anything."
William Blake

We turn to stories and pictures and music because they show us
who and what and why we are, and what our relationship
is to life and death, what is essential, and what, despite the arbitrariness
of falling beams, will not burn.
Madeline L'Engle

Out of chaos the imagination frames a thing of beauty.
John Livingston Lowes

Jacob Bronowski

Jacob Bronowski (1908–1974), a famous mathematician and philosopher and creator of the highly acclaimed television series The Ascent of Man, *argues here that imagination—the ability "to make images and to move them about inside one's head in new arrangements"—is not only a uniquely human power but also the source of progress and invention in all human activities.*

By pointing out that every new line of inquiry or action in human affairs exists first in the mind as a model of something that might-be-but-is-not-yet, Bronowski discovers one important way that the arts and sciences overlap. Scientists and engineers no less than artists and poets rely on imagination as the seedbed of all flowering ideas. In claiming that the arts and the sciences are not enemies but allies, Bronowski attempts to apply a healing salve to one of the most unfortunate, unnecessary, and potentially disastrous wounds in modern culture: the split between the scientists and the humanists.

THE REACH OF IMAGINATION

From *Proceedings of the American Academy of Arts and Letters and the National Institute of Arts and Letters* 17 (1967) and *The American Scholar* 36 (1967).

For three thousand years, poets have been enchanted and moved and per- 1 plexed by the power of their own imagination. In a short and summary essay I can hope at most to lift one small corner of that mystery; and yet it is a critical corner. I shall ask, What goes on in the mind when we imagine? You will hear from me that one answer to this question is fairly specific: which is to say, that we can describe the working of the imagination. And when we describe it as I shall do, it becomes plain that imagination is a specifically *human* gift. To imagine is the characteristic act, not of the poet's mind, or the painter's, or the scientist's, but of the mind of man.

My stress here on the word *human* implies that there is a clear difference 2
in this between the actions of men and those of other animals. Let me then
start with a classical experiment with animals and children which Walter
Hunter thought out in Chicago about 1910. That was the time when scientists
were agog with the success of Ivan Pavlov in forming and changing the reflex
actions of dogs, which Pavlov had first announced in 1903. Pavlov had been
given a Nobel prize the next year, in 1904; although in fairness I should say
that the award did not cite his work on the conditioned reflex, but on the
digestive glands.

Hunter duly trained some dogs and other animals on Pavlov's lines. 3
They were taught that when a light came on over one of three tunnels out
of their cage, that tunnel would be open; they could escape down it, and were
rewarded with food if they did. But once he had fixed that conditioned reflex,
Hunter added to it a deeper idea: he gave the mechanical experiment a new
dimension, literally—the dimension of time. Now he no longer let the dog go
to the lighted tunnel at once; instead, he put out the light, and then kept the
dog waiting a little while before he let him go. In this way Hunter timed how
long an animal can remember where he has last seen the signal light to his
escape route.

The results were and are staggering. A dog or a rat forgets which one 4
of three tunnels has been lit up within a matter of seconds—in Hunter's
experiment, ten seconds at most. If you want such an animal to do much
better than this, you must make the task much simpler: you must face him
with only two tunnels to choose from. Even so, the best that Hunter could
do was to have a dog remember for five minutes which one of two tunnels
had been lit up.

I am not quoting these times as if they were exact and universal: they 5
surely are not. Hunter's experiment, more than fifty years old now, had many
faults of detail. For example, there were too few animals, they were oddly
picked, and they did not all behave consistently. It may be unfair to test a
dog for what he *saw,* when he commonly follows his nose rather than his eyes.
It may be unfair to test any animal in the unnatural setting of a laboratory
cage. And there are higher animals, such as chimpanzees and other primates,
which certainly have longer memories than the animals that Hunter tried.

Yet when all these provisos have been made (and met, by more modern 6
experiments) the facts are still startling and characteristic. An animal cannot
recall a signal from the past for even a short fraction of the time that a man
can—for even a short fraction of the time that a child can. Hunter made
comparable tests with six-year-old children, and found, of course, that they
were incomparably better than the best of his animals. There is a striking and
basic difference between a man's ability to imagine something that he saw or
experienced, and an animal's failure.

Animals make up for this by other and extraordinary gifts. The salmon 7
and the carrier pigeon can find their way home as we cannot; they have, as
it were, a practical memory that man cannot match. But their actions always
depend on some form of habit: on instinct or on learning, which reproduce

by rote a train of known responses. They do not depend, as human memory does, on calling to mind the recollection of absent things.

Where is it that the animal falls short? We get a clue to the answer, I think, when Hunter tells us how the animals in his experiment tried to fix their recollection. They most often pointed themselves at the light before it went out, as some gun dogs point rigidly at the game they scent—and get the name *pointer* from the posture. The animal makes ready to act by building the signal into its action. There is a primitive imagery in its stance, it seems to me; it is as if the animal were trying to fix the light in its mind by fixing it in its body. And indeed, how else can a dog mark and (as it were) name one of three tunnels, when he has no such words as *left* and *right*, and no such numbers as *one, two, three?* The directed gesture of attention and readiness is perhaps the only symbolic device that the dog commands to hold on to the past, and thereby to guide himself into the future.   8

I used the verb *to imagine* a moment ago, and now I have some ground for giving it a meaning. *To imagine* means to make images and to move them about inside one's head in new arrangements. When you and I recall the past, we imagine it in this direct and homely sense. The tool that puts the human mind ahead of the animal is imagery. For us, memory does not demand the preoccupation that it demands in animals, and it lasts immensely longer, because we fix it in images or other substitute symbols. With the same symbolic vocabulary we spell out the future—not one but many futures, which we weigh one against another.   9

I am using the word *image* in a wide meaning, which does not restrict it to the mind's eye as a visual organ. An image in my usage is what Charles Peirce called a *sign*, without regard for its sensory quality. Peirce distinguished between different forms of signs, but there is no reason to make his distinction here, for the imagination works equally with them all, and that is why I call them all images.   10

Indeed, the most important images for human beings are simply words, which are abstract symbols. Animals do not have words, in our sense: there is no specific center for language in the brain of any animal, as there is in the human brain. In this respect at least we know that the human imagination depends on a configuration in the brain that has only evolved in the last one or two million years. In the same period, evolution has greatly enlarged the front lobes in the human brain, which govern the sense of the past and the future; and it is a fair guess that they are probably the seat of our other images. (Part of the evidence for this guess is that damage to the front lobes in primates reduces them to the state of Hunter's animals.) If the guess turns out to be right, we shall know why man has come to look like a highbrow or an egghead: because otherwise there would not be room in his head for his imagination.   11

The images play out for us events which are not present to our senses, and thereby guard the past and create the future—a future that does not yet exist, and may never come to exist in that form. By contrast, the lack of symbolic ideas, or their rudimentary poverty, cuts off an animal from the past   12 and the future alike, and imprisons him in the present. Of all the distinctions between man and animal, the characteristic gift which makes us human is the power to work with symbolic images: the gift of imagination.

This is really a remarkable finding. When Philip Sidney in 1580 de- 13
fended poets (and all unconventional thinkers) from the Puritan charge that they were liars, he said that a maker must imagine things that are not. Halfway between Sidney and us, William Blake said, "What is now proved was once only imagin'd." About the same time, in 1796, Samuel Taylor Coleridge for the first time distinguished between the passive fancy and the active imagination, "the living Power and prime Agent of all human Percep-tion." Now we see that they were right, and precisely right: the human gift is the gift of imagination—and that is not just a literary phrase.

Nor is it just a literary gift; it is, I repeat, characteristically human. 14
Almost everything that we do that is worth doing is done in the first place in the mind's eye. The richness of human life is that we have many lives; we live the events that do not happen (and some that cannot) as vividly as those that do; and if thereby we die a thousand deaths, that is the price we pay for living a thousand lives. (A cat, of course, has only nine.) Literature is alive to us because we live its images, but so is any play of the mind—so is chess: the lines of play that we foresee and try in our heads and dismiss are as much a part of the game as the moves that we make. John Keats said that the unheard melodies are sweeter, and all chess players sadly recall that the combinations that they planned and which never came to be played were the best.

I make this point to remind you, insistently, that imagination is the 15
manipulation of images in one's head; and that the rational manipulation belongs to that, as well as the literary and artistic manipulation. When a child begins to play games with things that stand for other things, with chairs or chessmen, he enters the gateway to reason and imagination together. For the human reason discovers new relations between things not by deduction, but by that unpredictable blend of speculation and insight that scientists call induction, which—like other forms of imagination—cannot be formalized. We see it at work when Walter Hunter inquires into a child's memory, as much as when Blake and Coleridge do. Only a restless and original mind would have asked Hunter's questions and could have conceived his experi-ments, in a science that was dominated by Pavlov's reflex arcs and was heading toward the behaviorism of John Watson.

Let me find a spectacular example for you from history. What is the 16
most famous experiment that you had described to you as a child? I will hazard that it is the experiment that Galileo is said to have made in Sidney's age, in Pisa about 1590, by dropping two unequal balls from the Leaning Tower. There, we say, is a man in the modern mold, a man after our own hearts: he insisted on questioning the authority of Aristotle and St. Thomas Aquinas, and seeing with his own eyes whether (as they said) the heavy ball would reach the ground before the light one. Seeing is believing.

Yet seeing is also imagining. Galileo did challenge the authority of 17

Aristotle, and he did look hard at his mechanics. But the eye that Galileo used was the mind's eye. He did not drop balls from the Leaning Tower of Pisa—and if he had, he would have got a very doubtful answer. Instead, Galileo made an imaginary experiment in his head, which I will describe as he did years later in the book he wrote after the Holy Office silenced him: the *Discorsi . . . intorno à due nuove scienze,* which was smuggled out to be printed in the Netherlands in 1638.

Suppose, said Galileo, that you drop two unequal balls from the tower   18
at the same time. And suppose that Aristotle is right—suppose that the heavy ball falls faster, so that it steadily gains on the light ball, and hits the ground first. Very well. Now imagine the same experiment done again, with only one difference: this time the two unequal balls are joined by a string between them. The heavy ball will again move ahead, but now the light ball holds it back and acts as a drag or brake. So the light ball will be speeded up and the heavy ball will be slowed down; they must reach the ground together because they are tied together, but they cannot reach the ground as quickly as the heavy ball alone. Yet the string between them has turned the two balls into a single mass which is heavier than either ball—and surely (according to Aristotle) this mass should therefore move faster than either ball? Galileo's imaginary experiment has uncovered a contradiction; he says trenchantly,

> You see how, from your assumption that a heavier body falls more rapidly than a lighter one, I infer that a (still) heavier body falls more slowly.

There is only one way out of the contradiction: the heavy ball and the light ball must fall at the same rate, so that they go on falling at the same rate when they are tied together.

This argument is not conclusive, for nature might be more subtle (when   19
the two balls are joined) than Galileo has allowed. And yet it is something more important: it is suggestive, it is stimulating, it opens a new view—in a word, it is imaginative. It cannot be settled without an actual experiment, because nothing that we imagine can become knowledge until we have translated it into, and backed it by, real experience. The test of imagination is experience. But then, that is as true of literature and the arts as it is of science. In science, the imaginary experiment is tested by confronting it with physical experience; and in literature, the imaginative conception is tested by confronting it with human experience. The superficial speculation in science is dismissed because it is found to falsify nature; and the shallow work of art is discarded because it is found to be untrue to our own nature. So when Ella Wheeler Wilcox died in 1919,* more people were reading her verses than Shakespeare's; yet in a few years her work was dead. It had been buried by its poverty of emotion and its trivialness of thought; which is to say that it

*American journalist and poet (1850–1919) who for many years published a daily poem for a syndicate of newspapers. She published over 20 volumes of verse but is now seldom read.

had been proved to be as false to the nature of man as, say, Jean Baptiste Lamarck* and Trofim Lysenko† were false to the nature of inheritance. The strength of the imagination, its enriching power and excitement, lies in its interplay with reality—physical and emotional.

I doubt if there is much to choose here between science and the arts: the imagination is not much more free, and not much less free, in one than in the other. All great scientists have used their imagination freely, and let it ride them to outrageous conclusions without crying "Halt!" Albert Einstein fiddled with imaginary experiments from boyhood, and was wonderfully ignorant of the facts that they were supposed to bear on. When he wrote the first of his beautiful papers on the random movement of atoms, he did not know that the Brownian motion which it predicted could be seen in any laboratory. He was sixteen when he invented the paradox that he resolved ten years later, in 1905, in the theory of relativity, and it bulked much larger in his mind than the experiment of Albert Michelson and Edward Morley which had upset every other physicist since 1881. All his life Einstein loved to make up teasing puzzles like Galileo's, about falling lifts [elevators] and the detection of gravity; and they carry the nub of the problems of general relativity on which he was working. 20

Indeed, it could not be otherwise. The power that man has over nature and himself, and that a dog lacks, lies in his command of imaginary experience. He alone has the symbols which fix the past and play with the future, possible and impossible. In the Renaissance, the symbolism of memory was thought to be mystical, and devices that were invented as mnemonics (by Giordano Bruno, for example, and by Robert Fludd) were interpreted as magic signs. The symbol is the tool which gives man his power, and it is the same tool whether the symbols are images or words, mathematical signs or mesons. And the symbols have a reach and a roundness that goes beyond their literal and practical meaning. They are the rich concepts under which the mind gathers many particulars into one name, and many instances into one general induction. When a man says *left* and *right,* he is outdistancing the dog not only in looking for a light; he is setting in train all the shifts of meaning, the overtones and the ambiguities, between *gauche* and *adroit* and *dexterous,* between *sinister* and the sense of right. When a man counts *one, two, three,* he is not only doing mathematics; he is on the path to the mysticism of numbers in Pythagoras and Vitruvius and Kepler, to the Trinity and the signs of the Zodiac. 21

I have described imagination as the ability to make images and to move them about inside one's head in new arrangements. This is the faculty that is specifically human, and it is the common root from which science and 22

---

*French naturalist (1744–1829) who held that environmental adaptations could be genetically transmitted.

†Soviet biologist (1898–1976) who developed a doctrine of genetics based partly on the ideas of Lamarck, which denied the existence of genes and plant hormones. His doctrine was eventually discredited, but not before greatly harming Soviet genetic research, agruicultural practices, and scientific education.

literature both spring and grow and flourish together. For they do flourish (and languish) together; the great ages of science are the great ages of all the arts, because in them powerful minds have taken fire from one another, breathless and higgledy-piggledy, without asking too nicely whether they ought to tie their imagination to falling balls or a haunted island. Galileo and Shakespeare, who were born in the same year, grew into greatness in the same age; when Galileo was looking through his telescope at the moon, Shakespeare was writing *The Tempest;* and all Europe was in ferment, from Johannes Kepler to Peter Paul Rubens, and from the first table of logarithms by John Napier to the Authorised Version of the Bible.

Let me end with a last and spirited example of the common inspiration 23 of literature and science, because it is as much alive today as it was three hundred years ago. What I have in mind is man's ageless fantasy, to fly to the moon. I do not display this to you as a high scientific enterprise; on the contrary, I think we have more important discoveries to make here on earth than wait for us, beckoning, at the horned surface of the moon. Yet I cannot belittle the fascination which that ice-blue journey has had for the imagination of men, long before it drew us to our television screens to watch the tumbling of astronauts. Plutarch and Lucian, Ariosto and Ben Jonson wrote about it, before the days of Jules Verne and H. G. Wells and science fiction. The seventeenth century was heady with new dreams and fables about voyages to the moon. Kepler wrote one full of deep scientific ideas, which (alas) simply got his mother accused of witchcraft. In England, Francis Godwin wrote a wild and splendid work, *The Man in the Moone,* and the astronomer John Wilkins wrote a wild and learned one, *The Discovery of a New World.* They did not draw a line between science and fancy; for example, they all tried to guess just where in the journey the earth's gravity would stop. Only Kepler understood that gravity has no boundary, and put a law to it—which happened to be the wrong law.

All this was a few years before Isaac Newton was born, and it was all 24 in his head that day in 1666 when he sat in his mother's garden, a young man of twenty-three, and thought about the reach of gravity. This was how he came to conceive his brilliant image, that the moon is like a ball which has been thrown so hard that it falls exactly as fast as the horizon, all the way round the earth. The image will do for any satellite, and Newton modestly calculated how long therefore an astronaut would take to fall round the earth once. He made it ninety minutes, and we have all seen now that he was right; but Newton had no way to check that. Instead he went on to calculate how long in that case the distant moon would take to round the earth, if indeed it behaves like a thrown ball that falls in the earth's gravity, and if gravity obeyed a law of inverse squares. He found that the answer would be twenty-eight days.

In that telling figure, the imagination that day chimed with nature, and 25 made a harmony. We shall hear an echo of that harmony on the day when we land on the moon, because it will be not a technical but an imaginative triumph, that reaches back to the beginning of modern science and literature both. All great acts of imagination are like this, in the arts and in science, and convince us because they fill out reality with a deeper sense of rightness. We start with the simplest vocabulary of images, with *left* and *right* and *one, two, three,* and before we know how it happened the words and the numbers have conspired to make a match with nature: we catch in them the pattern of mind and matter as one.

Questions for Discussion

1. To test Bronowski's argument, picture yourself unable to forecast any event in your life beyond the completion of this assignment. Does the fact that you have to use your imagination to picture *not* having an imagination show the pervasiveness of imaginative activity?

2. As you look forward to the events of this coming weekend—a date, trip home, movie, or concert—does your foreknowledge exist in your head only as an abstraction, a string of words naming the events? Or does it consist of actual images—pictures—of yourself in the future?

3. Is imagination as Bronowski defines it co-existent with consciousness? As long as you are conscious, does the making of images in your mind ever totally cease? We sometimes talk about our minds being "blank," usually as an exaggerated way of saying we can't remember something, but is your mind ever *really* blank?

4. If one pole of imagination is the recollection of images from the past (memory), then the other pole is the creation of images about the future (forecasting). While our usual forecasts picture only what will or may happen, pictures of what is unlikely or impossible to happen can also come to mind (for example, imagining ourselves invisible, meeting a griffin at lunch, or going to class at the speed of light). Yet imagining impossible things, which is what fantasy and science fiction writers do all the time, can be made to seem plausible, even gripping. The movie *Frankenstein* was made in the 1930s and has become a classic; the television series *Star Trek* is more than two decades old and still going strong. Does all this suggest the importance of imaginative activity for human beings? Does it suggest a distinction between imaginative and imaginary? Try putting this distinction into your own words.

5. What is the relationship between the quality of our lives and the quality of our imaginings? Does repeated exposure to images of brutality and violence on television actually make it easier to imagine doing brutal and violent acts? If they become easier to imagine, do they become easier to do? Are children more susceptible to the implanting of images than older

persons? If so, does this lend weight to Socrates' argument (from *The Republic*, pp. 167–171) that the imaginative fare dished out to children ought to be censored?

Suggested Essay Topics

1. Paragraph 16 begins, "Let me find a spectacular example for you from history." For the next four paragraphs Bronowski not only gives us a spectacular example from history but also gives us a spectacular example of how to use an example. The four paragraphs could almost be lifted out as a miniature essay in themselves.

   Using these paragraphs as a model, develop some idea taken from Bronowski's essay. You might take as your thesis, for example, either of the two sentences at the beginning of paragraph 14: "Almost everything that we do that is worth doing is done in the first place in the mind's eye" or "The richness of human life is that we have many lives; we live the events that do not happen (and some that cannot) as vividly as those that do." Employing either of these sentences as a topic, think back to some experience that you anticipated keenly but that did *not* happen, and turn your account of the discrepancies between what you anticipated and what really happened into an extended example modeled on Bronowski's four paragraphs.

2. Write an account of one of your most vivid imaginative experiences, such as a dream, nightmare, daydream, fantasy, or ambition. After making the account as vivid as possible, describe the importance of this imagined experience to you or the role it plays in your life. Does it serve as motivation? As something you want to work toward? Something you want to avoid? Why do you remember it or keep coming back to it?

Ursula Le Guin

Whereas Bronowski inquires into the relationship between imagination and action, Le Guin (b. 1929) inquires into the relationship between imagination, truth, and maturity. In the course of her essay, which was originally delivered as a talk, Le Guin makes several controversial statements: that Americans disapprove of fantasy out of fear, that the disapproval of fantasy is merely a symptom of a more general disapproval of fiction, that the need for imaginative expression and development is fundamental to maturity, that the daily stock market report is a "masterpiece of total unreality," that the indulgence in formula fictions and pornography reflects a starved imagination looking for nourishment, and that mature adults are not those who have outgrown childhood but those who have carried their childhood with them as they have grown up, *not* out.

These are a great number of controversial statements, especially in so brief an essay, yet Le Guin does not seem to be merely thrashing about or lashing out at vaguely defined "enemies." Although she does not stop to provide a supportive argument for each of her controversial assertions (can you see reasons why she would not argue in more detail in this essay?), she nevertheless seems clearly in charge of her topic and unhesitatingly articulates the value and role of fantasy as she sees it.

Indeed, Le Guin's clarity of mind about the issues she raises—especially in combination with the firm certitude of her tone—challenges the reader to consider the supporting arguments that might be used to bolster her views. At the very least she invites her readers to reconsider the truth of a whole cluster of American commonplaces about "getting ahead," about "outgrowing" childhood, about the synonymity of truth and facts, and about the superior value of "realistic" fiction over fantasy.

WHY ARE AMERICANS AFRAID OF DRAGONS?

This essay originally appeared in *PNLA Quarterly* 38 (Winter 1974).

1   This was to be a talk about fantasy. But I have not been feeling very fanciful lately, and could not decide what to say; so I have been going about picking people's brains for ideas. "What about fantasy? Tell me something about fantasy." And one friend of mine said, "All right, I'll tell you something fantastic. Ten years ago, I went to the children's room of the library of such-and-such a city, and asked for *The Hobbit;** and the librarian told me, 'Oh, we keep that only in the adult collection; we don't feel that escapism is good for children.' "

2   My friend and I had a good laugh and shudder over that, and we agreed that things have changed a great deal in these past ten years. That kind of moralistic censorship of works of fantasy is very uncommon now, in the children's libraries. But the fact that the children's libraries have become oases in the desert doesn't mean that there isn't still a desert. The point of view from which that librarian spoke still exists. She was merely reflecting, in perfect good faith, something that goes very deep in the American character: a moral disapproval of fantasy, a disapproval so intense, and often so aggressive, that I cannot help but see it as arising, fundamentally, from fear.

3   So: Why are Americans afraid of dragons?

4   Before I try to answer my question, let me say that it isn't only Americans who are afraid of dragons. I suspect that almost all very highly technological peoples are more or less antifantasy. There are several national literatures which, like ours, have had no tradition of adult fantasy for the past several hundred years: the French, for instance. But then you have the Germans, who have a good deal; and the English, who have it, and love it, and

*A fantasy novel by J. R. R. Tolkien (1892–1973), who also wrote the trilogy *The Lord of the Rings* and scholarly works on British medieval literature.

do it better than anyone else. So this fear of dragons is not merely a Western, or a technological, phenomenon. But I do not want to get into these vast historical questions; I will speak of modern Americans, the only people I know well enough to talk about.

In wondering why Americans are afraid of dragons, I began to realize   5
that a great many Americans are not only antifantasy, but altogether antifiction. We tend, as a people, to look upon all works of the imagination either as suspect, or as contemptible.

"My wife reads novels. I haven't got the time."   6

"I used to read that science fiction stuff when I was a teenager, but of   7
course I don't now."

"Fairy stories are for kids. I live in the real world."   8

Who speaks so? Who is it that dismisses *War and Peace, The Time Machine,*   9
and *A Midsummer Night's Dream* with this perfect self-assurance? It is, I fear, the man in the street—the hardworking, over-thirty American male—the men who run this country.

Such a rejection of the entire art of fiction is related to several American   10
characteristics: our Puritanism, our work ethic, our profit-mindedness, and even our sexual mores.

To read *War and Peace* or *The Lord of the Rings* plainly is not "work"—you   11
do it for pleasure. And if it cannot be justified as "educational" or as "self-improvement," then, in the Puritan value system, it can only be self-indulgence or escapism. For pleasure is not a value, to the Puritan; on the contrary, it is a sin.

Equally, in the businessman's value system, if an act does not bring in   12
an immediate, tangible profit, it has no justification at all. Thus the only person who has an excuse to read Tolstoy or Tolkien is the English teacher, because he gets paid for it. But our businessman might allow himself to read a best-seller now and then: not because it is a good book, but because it is a best-seller—it is a success, it has made money. To the strangely mystical mind of the money-changer, this justifies its existence; and by reading it he may participate, a little, in the power and mana of its success. If this is not magic, by the way, I don't know what is.

The last element, the sexual one, is more complex. I hope I will not be   13
understood as being sexist if I say that, within our culture, I believe that this antifiction attitude is basically a male one. The American boy and man [are] very commonly forced to define [their] maleness by rejecting certain traits, certain human gifts and potentialities, which our culture defines as "womanish" or "childish." And one of these traits or potentialities is, in cold sober fact, the absolutely essential human faculty of imagination.

Having got this far, I went quickly to the dictionary.   14

The *Shorter Oxford Dictionary* says: "Imagination. 1. The action of imagin-   15
ing, or forming a mental concept of what is not actually present to the senses; 2. The mental consideration of actions or events not yet in existence."

Very well; I certainly can let "absolutely essential human faculty"   16
stand. But I must narrow the definition to fit our present subject. By "imagi-

nation," then I personally mean the free play of the mind, both intellectual and sensory. By "play" I mean recreation, re-creation, the recombination of what is known into what is new. By "free" I mean that the action is done without an immediate object of profit—spontaneously. That does not mean, however, that there may not be a purpose behind the free play of the mind, a goal; and the goal may be a very serious object indeed. Children's imaginative play is clearly a practicing at the acts and emotions of adulthood; a child who did not play would not become mature. As for the free play of an adult mind, its result may be *War and Peace,* or the theory of relativity.

To be free, after all, is not to be undisciplined. I should say that the   17
discipline of the imagination may in fact be the essential method or technique of both art and science. It is our Puritanism, insisting that discipline means repression or punishment, which confuses the subject. To discipline something, in the proper sense of the word, does not mean to repress it, but to train it—to encourage it to grow, and act, and be fruitful, whether it is a peach tree or a human mind.

I think that a great many American men have been taught just the   18
opposite. They have learned to repress their imagination, to reject it as something childish or effeminate, unprofitable, and probably sinful.

They have learned to fear it. But they have never learned to discipline   19
it at all.

Now, I doubt that the imagination can be suppressed. If you truly   20
eradicated it in a child, he would grow up to be an eggplant. Like all our evil propensities, the imagination will out. But if it is rejected and despised, it will grow into wild and weedy shapes; it will be deformed. At its best, it will be mere ego-centered daydreaming; at its worst, it will be wishful thinking, which is a very dangerous occupation when it is taken seriously. Where literature is concerned, in the old, truly Puritan days, the only permitted reading was the Bible. Nowadays, with our secular Puritanism, the man who refuses to read novels because it's unmanly to do so, or because they aren't true, will most likely end up watching bloody detective thrillers on the television, or reading hack Westerns or sports stories, or going in for pornography, from *Playboy* on down. It is his starved imagination, craving nourishment, that forces him to do so. But he can rationalize such entertainment by saying that it is realistic—after all, sex exists, and there are criminals, and there are baseball players, and there used to be cowboys—and also by saying that it is virile, by which he means that it doesn't interest most women.

That all these genres are sterile, hopelessly sterile, is a reassurance to   21
him, rather than a defect. If they were genuinely realistic, which is to say genuinely imagined and imaginative, he would be afraid of them. Fake realism is the escapist literature of our time. And probably the ultimate escapist reading is that masterpiece of total unreality, the daily stock market report.

Now what about our man's wife? She probably wasn't required to   22
squelch her private imagination in order to play her expected role in life, but she hasn't been trained to discipline it, either. She is allowed to read novels, and even fantasies. But, lacking training and encouragement, her fancy is

likely to glom on to very sickly fodder, such things as soap operas, and "true romances," and nursy novels, and historico-sentimental novels, and all the rest of the baloney ground out to replace genuine imaginative works by the artistic sweatshops of a society that is profoundly distrustful of the uses of the imagination.

What, then, are the uses of the imagination? [23]

You see, I think we have a terrible thing here: a hardworking, upright, [24] responsible citizen, a full-grown, educated person, who is afraid of dragons, and afraid of hobbits, and scared to death of fairies. It's funny, but it's also terrible. Something has gone very wrong. I don't know what to do about it but to try and give an honest answer to that person's question, even though he often asks it in an aggressive and contemptuous tone of voice. "What's the good of it all?" he says. "Dragons and hobbits and little green men—what's the *use* of it?"

The truest answer, unfortunately, he won't even listen to. He won't hear [25] it. The truest answer is, "The use of it is to give you pleasure and delight."

"I haven't got the time," he snaps, swallowing a Maalox pill for his ulcer [26] and rushing off to the golf course.

So we try the next-to-truest answer. It probably won't go down much [27] better, but it must be said: "The use of imaginative fiction is to deepen your understanding of your world, and your fellow men, and your own feelings, and your destiny."

To which I fear he will retort, "Look, I got a raise last year, and I'm [28] giving my family the best of everything, we've got two cars and a color TV. I understand enough of the world!"

And he is right, unanswerably right, if that is what he wants, and all [29] he wants.

The kind of thing you learn from reading about the problems of a hobbit [30] who is trying to drop a magic ring into an imaginary volcano has very little to do with your social status, or material success, or income. Indeed, if there is any relationship, it is a negative one. There is an inverse correlation between fantasy and money. That is a law, known to economists as Le Guin's Law. If you want a striking example of Le Guin's Law, just give a lift to one of those people along the roads who own nothing but a backpack, a guitar, a fine head of hair, a smile, and a thumb. Time and again, you will find that these waifs have read *The Lord of the Rings*—some of them can practically recite it. But now take Aristotle Onassis, or J. Paul Getty: could you believe that those men ever had anything to do, at any age, under any circumstances, with a hobbit?

But, to carry my example a little further, and out of the realm of [31] economics, did you ever notice how very gloomy Mr. Onassis and Mr. Getty and all those billionaires look in their photographs? They have this strange, pinched look, as if they were hungry. As if they were hungry for something, as if they had lost something and were trying to think where it could be, or perhaps what it could be, what it was they've lost.

Could it be their childhood? [32]

So I arrive at my personal defense of the uses of the imagination, 33 especially in fiction, and most especially in fairy tale, legend, fantasy, science fiction, and the rest of the lunatic fringe. I believe that maturity is not an outgrowing, but a growing up: that an adult is not a dead child, but a child who survived. I believe that all the best faculties of a mature human being exist in the child, and that if these faculties are encouraged in youth they will act well and wisely in the adult, but if they are repressed and denied in the child they will stunt and cripple the adult personality. And finally, I believe that one of the most deeply human, and humane, of these faculties is the power of imagination: so that it is our pleasant duty, as librarians, or teachers, or parents, or writers, or simply as grownups, to encourage that faculty of imagination in our children, to encourage it to grow freely, to flourish like the green bay tree, by giving it the best, absolutely the best and purest, nourishment that it can absorb. And never, under any circumstances, to squelch it, or sneer at it, or imply that it is childish, or unmanly, or untrue.

For fantasy is true, of course. It isn't factual, but it is true. Children 34 know that. Adults know it too, and that is precisely why many of them are afraid of fantasy. They know that its truth challenges, even threatens, all that is false, all that is phony, unnecessary, and trivial in the life they have let themselves be forced into living. They are afraid of dragons, because they are afraid of freedom.

So I believe that we should trust our children. Normal children do not 35 confuse reality and fantasy—they confuse them much less often than we adults do (as a certain great fantasist pointed out in a story called "The Emperor's New Clothes"). Children know perfectly well that unicorns aren't real, but they also know that books about unicorns, if they are good books, are true books. All too often, that's more than Mummy and Daddy know; for, in denying their childhood, the adults have denied half their knowledge, and are left with the sad, sterile little fact: "Unicorns aren't real." And that fact is one that never got anybody anywhere (except in the story "The Unicorn in the Garden," by another great fantasist, in which it is shown that a devotion to the unreality of unicorns may get you straight into the loony bin). It is by such statements as, "Once upon a time there was a dragon," or "In a hole in the ground there lived a hobbit"—it is by such beautiful non-facts that we fantastic human beings may arrive, in our peculiar fashion, at the truth.

Questions for Discussion

1. How would you explain in your own words Le Guin's implied distinction between escapism and fantasy? Why, in Le Guin's view, are they not the same? Which one is preferable? Why do many Americans confuse them?

2. In paragraphs 12 and 21, Le Guin makes two extremely unconventional references to institutionalized forms of moneymaking. In paragraph 12 she calls the mind of the money-changer "strangely mystical" and refers to his tendency to be interested in stories of great monetary success as "magic." In paragraph 21 she calls the daily stock market report "that masterpiece of total unreality." In neither paragraph does she pause to provide a detailed explanation of what she means. On the basis of your reading of the whole essay, what do you think she means? If you were to fill out this part of her argument as you think she might have done, what would you say?

3. Once you have answered question 2, the obvious follow-up is, do you *agree* with Le Guin's view of the "unrealistic" character of moneymaking and stock investing? Since many people, perhaps most, think of moneymaking as extremely practical, what sense does Le Guin make by referring to it as "unrealistic"?

4. How would you explain in your own words Le Guin's assertion that "fake realism is the escapist literature of our time" (¶21)? What does she seem to mean? Give some appropriate examples to illustrate the kind of thing she is referring to.

5. Do you agree or disagree with Le Guin in paragraph 34 that "fantasy is true, of course. It isn't factual, but it is true"? How would you restate this assertion in your own words? What reasons can you offer for corroborating or contradicting it? Is the converse—that facts can be false—ever true?

Suggested Essay Topics

1. Jump ahead and read Plato's argument from book 2 of *The Republic* (which we have titled "Censorship," pp. 167–171). Then write a dialogue in which you picture Plato and Le Guin arguing the relative advantages and disadvantages of allowing children to read "untrue" stories. Try to make sure, first, that you render each writer's position accurately and, second, that you make each writer truly meet the other's arguments.

2. Choose a particular work of fantasy that you like (you may use movies and TV programs as well as literature) and, in the kind of essay that you might send to a science fiction journal, analyze whether the work lives up to Le Guin's assertion in paragraph 27 that "the use of imaginative fiction is to deepen your understanding of your world, and your fellow men, and your own feelings, and your destiny." If the essay is to be effective, the challenge you must meet is to be concrete and detailed and to focus on specific parts of the work in question (plot, language, characterizations, whatever) *and* on the way they are used to meet the goals set out by Le Guin.

IDEAS IN DEBATE

Maxim Gorky
Plato

Maxim Gorky

In the following excerpts, the great Russian author Maxim Gorky (1868–1936) describes his first entry into the world of literature and its beneficent effects on his character. His views create a stark contrast with those of Plato, whose attacks on literature follow Gorky's praise of it. For Plato, literature is suspect because it is composed of fictions, which Plato views simply as untruths, and because it "feeds and waters the passions" instead of strengthening the intellect. But the features of literature condemned by Plato are precisely the features that Gorky praises. Where Plato sees a fundamental ethical unhealthiness in developing deep feelings and attachments to the inferior objects of this inferior material world, including people, Gorky sees an ethical health in the formation of such sympathies. And he is both vivid and passionate in his description of how books helped him to enlarge and humanize his feelings toward his fellow creatures.

The world of peasants and workers in pre-Revolutionary Russia could be grim and even brutish, just as Gorky describes it. In such a world one could conceivably argue—indeed, many have—that the primary needs of the body must be tended first and that the needs of the spirit as addressed by literature, religion, and art must wait until people are decently fed, housed, and clothed. When reading Gorky's account of the effects of learning to read, thus having access to other, larger worlds of feeling and thought, one cannot help feeling that Gorky would reject the view, no matter how well-intended, that the cultivation of bodily needs should always take precedence over the cultivation of spiritual and intellectual needs. It would be a worthwhile exercise as you read to try to provide the rebuttal that you think Gorky, arguing from his own experience, might want to give to such views.

As you go from Gorky to Plato, try to give each writer's views a full and sympathetic hearing, and then decide which view seems to capture more of the truth. Plato is severe and rigorous, yet lifted to greatness by the greatness of his goal: to establish the groundwork for a truly just society. Gorky is affectionate and engaging, yet he too focuses on a great goal: the moral improvement of the individual. As you read, you might ask yourself whether Plato's severity tends to slide toward the coldness of tyranny and whether Gorky's warmth tends to slide toward the gushiness of sentimentality. Regardless of what judgments you finally make about them, they are among the authors who teach readers as much about themselves as about the subject of their reading.

ON BOOKS

From "How I Studied" (1918) and "On Books" (1925); translated by Julius Katzer.

It was at about the age of fourteen that I first learnt to read intelligently. By that time I was attracted not only by the plot in a book—the more or less interesting development of the events depicted; I was beginning to appreciate the beauty of the descriptions, muse upon the characters of the men and women in the story, vaguely surmise as to the author's aims, and sense with alarm the difference between that which was spoken of in books and that which was prompted by life. [1]

I was having a hard time then, for I was working for dyed-in-the-wool philistines, people for whom plenteous food was the acme of enjoyment, and whose only amusement was going to church, whither they would sally forth gaudily bedecked in the fashion of people setting out for the theatre or a promenade. My work was back-breaking, so that my mind was almost benumbed; weekdays and holidays were equally cluttered up with toil that was petty, meaningless and futile. [2]

The house my employers lived in belonged to a road-contractor, a short, stocky man from somewhere along the River Klyazma. With his pointed beard and grey eyes, he was always ill-tempered, rude and cruel in a cold-blooded sort of way. He had about thirty men working for him, all of them peasants from Vladimir Gubernia, who lived in a gloomy cellar with a cement floor and little windows below ground level. Toil-worn and weary, they would emerge from their cellar in the evening, after a supper of evil-smelling cabbage soup with tripe or salt-beef that reeked of saltpetre, and sprawl about in the filthy yard, for the air in their damp cellar was suffocating and poisoned by the fumes from the huge stove there. [3]

The contractor would appear at the window of his room and start yelling at his men. "So you're in the yard again, you bastards! Lying all over the place like swine! I have respectable folk living in my house! Do you think they enjoy seeing the likes of you out there?" [4]

The workers would obediently return to their cellar. They were all woe-begone people, who spoke and laughed but seldom, and hardly ever sang songs; their clothes besmeared with clay and mud, they seemed to me corpses that had been resuscitated against their will so as to suffer torment for another term of life. [5]

The "respectable folk" were army officers, who drank and gambled, beat their servants black and blue, and thrashed their mistresses, loudly dressed, cigarette-smoking women, who were heavy drinkers, too, and would clout the officers' servants mercilessly. The latter also drank inordinately, and would guzzle themselves blind drunk. [6]

On Sundays the contractor would seat himself on the porch steps, a long 7 narrow ledger in one hand and a pencil stub in the other. The navvies would shuffle up to him one by one, as though they were beggars. They spoke in hushed tones, bowing and scratching their heads, while the contractor would yell for the whole world to hear, "Shut up! A ruble will do! Eh, what's that? Do you want a thick ear? You're getting more than you're worth as it is! Get the hell out of here! Get moving!"

I knew that among the navvies there were quite a few men hailing from 8 the same village as the contractor, and even several relatives of his, but he treated them all in the same harsh, unfeeling manner. The navvies too were harsh and unfeeling towards one another and particularly towards the officers' servants. Bloody free fights would start in the yard every other Sunday, and the air would be blue with the foul language used. The navvies fought without any malice, as though they were performing some irksome duty; battered and bruised, they would creep out of the fray and in silence examine their scratches and injuries, testing loosened teeth with unclean fingers. A smashed face or a black-and-blue eye never evoked the least compassion, but things were different if a shirt proved in shreds; then the regret was general, and the mauled owner of the shirt would sullenly brood over his loss and sometimes shed tears.

Such scenes brought up in me a heavy feeling I cannot describe. I was 9 sorry for these people, but in a way that was cold and aloof. There never arose in me a desire to say a kind word to any of them or help one who had had the worst of it in a fight—at least to bring him some water to wash away the sickeningly thick blood, mixed with mud or dust, that oozed out of cuts and injuries. In fact I disliked these people, was somewhat afraid of them, and spoke the word muzhik in much the same way as my employers, or the officers, the regimental priest, the cook who lived next door, or even the officers' servants; all these spoke of the muzhiks with contempt.

Feeling sorry for people is a distressing business; one always prefers the 10 joy of loving someone, but there was nobody there I could love. It was with all the more ardency that I got to love books.

There was much in my environment that was wicked and savage, and 11 gave birth to a feeling of acute loathing. I shall not dwell on this; you are yourselves aware of the hell of that kind of life, the contumely heaped upon man by man, and that morbid urge to inflict torment which slaves so delight in. It was in such accursed conditions that I first began to read good and serious books by foreign authors.

I shall probably prove unable to express with sufficient vividness and 12 convincingness the measure of my amazement when I felt that almost each book seemed to open up before me a window into a new and unfamiliar world, and told me of people, sentiments, thoughts and relationships that I had never before known or seen. It even seemed to me that the life around me, all the harsh, filthy and cruel things that were taking place around me every day—all these were not real or necessary. What was real and necessary was to be found only in books, where everything was more reasonable,

beautiful and humane. True, books also spoke of human boorishness, stupidity and suffering; they depicted mean and evil men too, but next to these were
others, the like of whom I had never seen or even heard of, men that were
clean and truthful, strong in spirit, and ready to sacrifice their very lives for
the triumph of the truth or the beauty of an exploit.

Intoxicated by the novelty and the spiritual wealth of the world that   13
books had revealed to me, I at first began to consider books finer, more
interesting and akin to me than people were, and was, I think, a little blinded
by looking upon the realities of life through the prism of books. However,
life, that wisest and severest of teachers, soon cured me of that delightful
blindness.

On Sundays, when my employers would go visiting or promenading, I   14
used to climb out through the window of the stifling and greasy-smelling
kitchen on to the roof, where I could read undisturbed. Down below I could
see sleepy or half-drunk navvies lurching about the yard or hear the house-
maids, washerwomen and cooks squeal at the uncouth advances made by the
officers' servants. From my eyrie I looked down upon the yards and magnificently despised the vile, drunken and loose life about me.

One of the navvies was their foreman, an elderly little man named   15
Stepan Lyoshin, angular and ill-knit of figure, lean and sinewy, his eyes like
those of a hungry tom-cat, and his lanky greying beard growing in funny
patches over his brown face, scraggy neck and in his ears. Ragged of dress
and dirtier than all the others, he was the most sociable among them. They
all stood in awe of him, and even the master lowered his strident and angry
voice when addressing him. I often heard the men curse Lyoshin behind his
back as "that stingy bastard, that Judas of a lickspittle."

Old Lyoshin was a brisk man, but not fussy; he had a way of sliding   16
imperceptibly into some corner of the yard wherever two or three of the men
would get together; he would come up to them, with a leer on his face, sniff
through his broad nose, and ask:

"So what, eh?"   17

It seemed to me that he was always on the look-out for something,   18
waiting for some word to be said.

Once, when I was sitting on the roof of the shed, he climbed wheezing   19
up the ladder to where I was, sat down next to me, and, after sniffing the air,
said:

"It smells of hay. . . . This is a fine place you've found, clean and away   20
from people. . . . What's that you are reading?"

He looked at me in a friendly way and I willingly told him what I was   21
reading about.

"Yes," he said, wagging his head. "That's how it is."   22

He fell silent for a while, picking with a grimy finger at a broken toe-nail   23
on his left foot, and suddenly began to talk in a low, sing-song tone, as though
telling a story, squinting at me the while.

"There was a learned gentleman in Vladimir, Sabaneyev by name, a   24
grand gentleman, and he had a son—I think he was called Petrusha or some-

thing like that. I can't quite call his name to mind. Anyway, this Petrusha was reading books all the time and tried to get others interested, but in the end he was copped."

"What for?" I asked.

"Oh, for all that sort of thing! Don't you go in for reading, but if you do, keep mum about it!"

He sniggered, winked to me, and went on:

"I can see what kind of fellow you are—kind of serious and you keep out of mischief. Well, there's no harm in that. . . ."

He sat with me for a short while and then went down into the yard. From that time on I noticed that Lyoshin kept an eye on me. He was always coming up to me with the same question, "So what, eh?"

Once I told him a story that had gripped my imagination, something about the victory of good over evil. He heard me out very attentively, nodded his head, and said, "Such things do happen."

"Do they happen?" I asked in joy.

"Of course they may. All kinds of things happen," the old man asserted. "Here's what I'll tell you. . . ." and he told me a story, quite a good one, about flesh-and-blood people, not people out of books, and in conclusion said impressively:

"You see, you can't understand these things in full, but you've got to understand the chief thing, to wit that there are no end of little things, and the people have got all tangled up in such trifles. They don't know what path they should follow, so they don't know the way to God. People are hemmed in by trifles, if you understand what I mean."

These words seemed to arouse something vivifying in my heart and I seemed to have suddenly emerged into the light. Indeed, the life around me was full of trifles, with its scuffles, its wickedness, petty thievery and foul language, which, I suppose, is so lavish because a man lacks pure and sweet words.

The old man was five times as old as I was and knew a lot, so that if he said that good things really happen in life I had every reason to believe him. I was eager to believe him, for books had already taught me to believe in man. I felt that, after all, books did depict actual life, that they were, so to say, copied from reality, and that therefore there must exist good men, quite unlike that brute of a contractor, or my employers, or the drunken officers, or, for that matter, everybody else I knew.

This discovery was of great joy to me, and I began to take a happier view of life and be more friendly and considerate to people; when I read something that was good or elevated the spirit I tried to tell the navvies and the officers' servants all about it. They were not very good listeners, and, I think, did not believe me very much; Stepan Lyoshin, however, kept on saying, "Such things do happen. All kinds of things happen, my lad."

This brief and wise statement was of a surprisingly intense significance to me. The oftener I heard it, the more it aroused in me a sense of courage and pertinacity, an acute desire to achieve my ends. If indeed "all kinds of things happen," then what I wanted could also come about. I have noticed that it is just when life has given me its hardest knocks, on the bad days, which have been only too numerous in my life, that a sense of courage and pertinacity has always surged up in me and I have been overcome by a youthful and Herculean urge to cleanse the Augean stables of life. This has remained with me to this day when I am fifty; it will remain with me till my dying day. I owe this quality in me to books, which are the gospel of the human spirit and reflect the anguish and the torment of man's growing soul; to science, which is the poetry of the mind, and to art, which is the poetry of the heart.

Books continued to open new vistas before me, two illustrated maga- 38
zines, the *Vsemirnaya Illustratsiya (World Illustrated)* and the *Zhivopisnoye Obozrenie (Pictorial Review),* being of particular value to me. Their depictions of cities, people and events abroad, expanded more and more the world before me, and I felt it growing, huge, enthralling and full of great works.

The temples and palaces, so unlike our churches and houses, the differ- 39
ently clad people, the land that men had adorned in so different a manner, the wondrous machines and the marvellous things they produced—all these evoked in me an unaccountable feeling of exhilaration and a desire to make and build something too.

Everything was different and unfamiliar, but I sensed vaguely that 40
behind it all stood one and the same force—man's creativity, and my feeling of consideration and respect for people mounted.

I was spellbound when I saw in a magazine a portrait of Faraday, the 41
famous scientist, read an article about him, much of which I could not understand, and learnt from it that Faraday had been a simple workman. This fact seemed fairy-like to me, and became imbedded in my mind.

"How can that be?" I asked myself incredulously. "It means that one of 42
these navvies may also become a scientist. Perhaps I, too, may become one."

That was something I could not believe, and I began to make inquiries 43
whether there had been other famous men who had first been working men. I discovered none in the magazines, but a Gymnasium* pupil I knew told me that very many well-known people had first been workers, and named some of them, including Stephenson, but I did not believe him.

The more I read, the closer books bound me to the world and the more 44
vivid and significant life became for me. I saw that there were people whose life was worse and harder than mine. Though I derived some comfort from this, I did not grow reconciled to the outrageous facts of the life about me. I saw too that there were such who were able to live a life of interest and happiness in a way none about me knew how to. From the pages of almost every book sounded a subdued but insistent message that perturbed me, called me into the unknown, and plucked at my heart. All men were suffering in one way or another; all were dissatisfied with life and sought something that was better, and this made them closer and more understandable to me.

*High school.

Books enshrouded the whole world in a mournful aspiration towards better things, and each one of them seemed a soul tacked down to paper by characters and words which came to life the moment my eyes and my mind came into contact with them.

I often wept as I read—so moving were the stories about people, so dear 45 and close did they become to me. Lad as I was, pestered with senseless toil and berated with senseless vituperation, I promised myself in the most solemn of terms that I would help people and render them honest service when I grew up.

Like some wondrous birds out of fairy tales, books sang their songs to 46 me and spoke to me as though communing with one languishing in prison; they sang of the variety and richness of life, of man's audacity in his strivings towards goodness and beauty. The more I read, the more a wholesome and kindly spirit filled my heart, and I grew calmer, my self-confidence developed, my work improved, and I paid ever less heed to the innumerable spurns life was dealing me.

Each book was a rung in my ascent from the brutish to the human, 47 towards an understanding of a better life and a thirst after that life. Replete with all I had read, feeling for all the world like some vessel brimming over with exhilarating drink, I would go to the officers' servants and the navvies and tell them my stories, enacting the scenes in them.

This amused my listeners. 48

"A regular rogue!" they would exclaim. "A real comedian! You should 49 join a travelling show or play at a fair!"

Of course, that was not what I had expected but I was pleased neverthe- 50 less.

However, I was sometimes able, not very frequently of course, to make 51 the Vladimir muzhiks listen to me with bated breath and on more than one occasion aroused some of them to delight and even to tears; such things convinced me all the more that there was a living and stimulating force in books.

One of the men, Vasily Rybakov by name, a morose and silent young 52 fellow of great physical strength, whose favourite prank it was to jostle others and send them flying, once led me aside to a place behind the stable, and said to me:

"Listen here, Alexei, learn me to read books and I'll pay you fifty 53 kopeks, and if you don't I'll bash your head in for you. I swear it!" and he crossed himself sweepingly.

I stood in fear of his gloomy horse-play and began instructing him, my 54 heart in my mouth, but things went well from the very start. Rybakov proved diligent at the unfamiliar work and very quick of understanding. Once, five weeks or so later, on his way back from work, he beckoned to me mysteriously, pulled a crumpled scrap of paper out of his pocket and started muttering in his agitation:

"See here. I tore this off a fence. What's written here, eh? Wait a 55 jiffy—'House for sale'—is that right? 'For sale,' eh?"

"That's what it says." 56

Rybakov's eyes rolled frighteningly, and his forehead became covered 57
with sweat. After a silence he grabbed me by the shoulder, shook me a little
and said in a low tone:

"You see it was like this. When I looked at that there fence something 58
started whispering in me like—'House for sale'. . . . Lordie, lordie. . . . Just
like a whisper in me, 'swelp me! Listen, d'you think I've really gone and learnt
to read?"

"You try and read some more." 59

He bent low over the scrap of paper and began in a whisper, "Two—is 60
that right?—storey . . . brick . . ."

A broad smile spread all over his ugly face. He reared his head, swore 61
an oath and with a laugh started to fold up the paper.

"I'll keep this to remember the day, this being the first like. . . . O Lord 62
. . . don't you see? Just like a whisper. Queer things do happen, my lad! Well,
well!"

I burst out laughing at his crude joy, his childlike perplexity at the 63
mystery revealed to him, the magic of little black characters being able to
unfold before him another's thoughts, ideas, and very soul.

I could say quite a lot regarding the way book-reading—that familiar, 64
everyday but yet mysterious process of man's fusion with the great minds of
all ages and peoples—at times suddenly reveals to man the meaning of life
and his place in it; I know a multitude of such marvellous instances imbued
with an almost magic beauty.

There is one such instance I would like to mention, which refers to a 65
time when I was living in Arzamas under police surveillance. My next-door
neighbour, the chief of the local agricultural board,* who had developed such
an intense dislike of my person that he even instructed his housemaid to
avoid talking to my cook in the evening after working hours, had a policeman
stationed right under my windows. Whenever the latter thought it fit, he
would peer into my rooms with naïve incivility. This had the effect of in-
timidating the townspeople, and for quite a long time none of them ventured
to call on me.

One day—it was a church holiday—a one-eyed man came to see me. 66
He had a bundle under one arm and said he had a pair of boots to sell. I told
him I did not need any boots, at which the man, after looking suspiciously
into the next room, addressed me in an undertone.

"The boots are only an excuse for coming to see you. What I really want 67
is to ask you whether you could let me have a good book to read."

The expression of his solitary eye was so sincere and intelligent that it 68
allayed suspicion, and his reply to my question as to what kind of book he
wanted clinched the matter for me. Looking around as he spoke, he said in
a deliberate if timid tone:

---

*In Russian, _Zemsky nachalnik_—prior to the Revolution, head of an authority with court and
administrative powers over the local peasantry. [Translator's note]

"I'd like something about the laws of life, Mr. Writer, that's to say, 69
about the laws of the world. I can't make them out, I mean the way one
should live and that kind of thing. There's a professor of mathematics from
Kazan, who lives close by and he teaches me some mathematics. You see, he
does that because I do his shoe repairs and take care of his garden—I'm a
gardener too. Well, mathematics don't help me with the questions that interest me, and he is a man of few words. . . ."

I gave him a poorish book by Dreyfus entitled *World and Social Evolution*, 70
the only book on the subject that I could lay my hands on at the moment.

"Thank you kindly," said the one-eyed man, carefully concealing the 71
book in his boot top. "May I come to you for a talk when I have read the
book? . . . Only I'll come on the pretext of pruning the raspberry bushes in
your garden, because, you see, the police are keeping an eye on you, and in
general, it's awkward for me. . . ."

When he came again five days later, in a white apron, equipped with 72
bass and a pair of shears, I was much surprised by his jaunty air. There was
a merry gleam in his eye and his voice rang loud and strong. The first thing
he did was to bring an open palm emphatically down on the book I had given
him, and state hurriedly:

"May I draw the conclusion from this here book that there is no God?" 73

I am no believer in hasty "conclusions," so I began to question him in 74
a cautious sort of way as to what had led him to just that "conclusion."

"For me that is the chief thing!" he said fervently but quietly. "I argue 75
in the way many like me do: if the Almighty does really exist and everything
depends on His will, then I must live in humble submission to His commandments. I've read a lot of divine literature—the Bible and a host of theological
works, but what I want to know is whether I'm responsible for myself and
my life, or not? Scripture says no, you must live according to God's will, for
science will get you nowhere. That means that astronomy is all sham and
invention; so's mathematics and everything else. Of course, you don't stand
for blind obedience yourself, do you?"

"No, I don't," I said. 76

"Then why should I agree to it? You have been sent out here to be under 77
observation by the police because you're a dissenter. That means that you've
risen up against the Gospel, because, as I see it, all dissent must be directed
against Holy Scripture. All the laws of submission come from the Scriptures,
while the laws of freedom all come from science, that's to say, from the mind
of man. Let's argue farther: if God exists, I have no say in the matter, but if
there's no God then I'm personally responsible for everything—for myself
and for all other folks. I want to be responsible, after the example set by the
holy fathers of the Church, but only in a different way—not through submission to the evil of life but by resistance to it!"

His palm again came down on the book, and he went on with a convic- 78
tion that sounded inflexible.

"All submission is evil because it goes to strengthen evil. You must 79
forgive me, but this is a book I believe in. To me it's like a path through a

thick forest. I've made up my mind for myself—I am personally responsible
for everything!"

Our friendly talk continued late into the night, and I saw that a medio- 80
cre little book had tipped the balance: it had turned his rebellious searchings
into a fervent conviction, into joyous worship of the beauty and might of
World Reason.

This fine, intelligent man did, in fact, wage a struggle against the evil 81
of life, and perished courageously in 1907.

Just as they had done to the morose Rybakov, books whispered in my 82
ear of the existence of another life, one that was more worthy of man than
that which I was living; just as they had done to the one-eyed shoemaker,
they showed me my place in life. By inspiring the mind and the heart, books
helped me to extricate myself from the foul morass that would have engulfed
me in its stupidity and boorishness. By expanding the limits of my world,
books told me of the majesty and beauty of man's strivings towards a better
life, of how much he had achieved in the world and what fearful sufferings
this had cost him.

In my soul there mounted a regard for man, for any man, whatever he 83
might be; there burgeoned in me respect for his labour and love of his restless
spirit. Life was becoming easier and more joyous, replete with a new and
profound meaning.

Just as with the one-eyed shoemaker, books bred in me a sense of 84
personal responsibility for all the evil in life and evoked in me a reverence
for the human mind's creativity.

It is with profound belief in the truth of my conviction that I say to all: 85
Love books; they will make your life easier, render you friendly service in
finding your way through the motley and tumultuous confusion of ideas,
emotions and happenings, teach you to respect yourselves and others, and fill
the mind and the heart with love for the world and man.

Even if hostile to your beliefs, any book that has been written in 86
honesty, out of love of people, out of good will, is admirable.

Any kind of knowledge is useful, as is knowledge of the mind's fallacies 87
and of mistaken emotions.

Love books, which are a source of knowledge; only knowledge is salu- 88
tary, and knowledge alone can make you spiritually strong, honest and intelligent people, capable of cherishing a sincere love of man, respect for his
labour and a warm admiration for the splendid fruits of his ceaseless and high
endeavour.

Everything man has done, every single thing that exists, contains some 89
particle of man's soul. This pure and noble soul is contained in science and
in art in greater degree than in anything else, and speaks with the greatest
eloquence and clarity through the medium and agency of books.

. . .

It is to books that I owe everything that is good in me. Even in my youth 90
I realized that art is more generous than people are. I am a book-lover; each
one of them seems a miracle to me, and the author a magician. I am unable

to speak of books otherwise than with the deepest emotion and a joyous enthusiasm. That may seem ridiculous but it is the truth. It will probably be said that this is the enthusiasm of a barbarian; let people say what they will—I am beyond cure.

When I hold a new book in my hand, something made at a printing- 91 house by a type-setter, a hero in his way, with the aid of a machine invented by another hero, I get a feeling that something living, wonderful and able to speak to me has entered my life—a new testament, written by man about himself, about a being more complex than anything else in the world, the most mysterious and the most worthy of love, a being whose labour and imagination have created everything in the world that is instinct with grandeur and beauty.

Books guide me through life, which I know fairly well, but they always 92 have a way of telling me something new which I did not previously know or notice in man. In a whole book you may find nothing but a single telling sentence, but it is that very sentence that draws you closer to man and reveals a new smile or a new grimace.

The majesty of the stellar world, the harmonious mechanism of the 93 Universe, and all that astronomy and cosmology speak of with such eloquence do not move me or evoke enthusiasm in me. My impression is that the Universe is not at all as amazing as the astronomers would have us think and that in the birth and death of worlds there is immeasurably more meaningless chaos than divine harmony.

Somewhere in the infinity of the Milky Way a sun has become extinct 94 and the planets about it are plunged into eternal night; that, however, is something that will not move me at all, but the death of Camille Flammarion, a man with a superb imagination, gave me deep sorrow.

Everything that we find fair and beautiful has been devised or narrated 95 by man. It is to be regretted that he has often had to create suffering too, and heighten it, as has been done by Dostoyevsky, Baudelaire and the like. Even in this I see a desire to embellish and alleviate that which is drab and hateful in life.

There is no beauty in the Nature that surrounds us and is so hostile to 96 us; beauty is something that man himself creates out of the depth of his soul. Thus, the Finn transfigures his bogs, forests and rusty-coloured granite, with its scanty and dwarfish vegetation, into scenes of beauty, and the Arab convinces himself that the desert is fair. Beauty is born of man's striving to contemplate it. I take delight not in chaotic and serrated mountain masses, but in the splendour man has endowed them with. I stand in admiration at the ease and magnanimity with which man is transforming Nature, a magnanimity which is all the more astonishing for the Earth's being, if one gives the matter closer thought, a far from cosy place to live in. Think of earthquakes, hurricanes, snowstorms, floods, extremes of heat and cold, noxious insects and microbes and a thousand and one other things that would make our life quite intolerable were man less of a hero than he is.

Our existence has always and everywhere been tragic, but man has 97 converted these numberless tragedies into works of art. I know of nothing more astonishing or more wonderful than this transformation. That is why in a little volume of Pushkin's poems or in a novel by Flaubert I find more wisdom and living beauty than in the cold twinkling of the stars, the mechanical rhythm of the oceans, the rustling of forests, or the silence of the wilderness.

The silence of the wilderness? It has been forcefully conveyed by the   98
Russian composer Borodin in one of his works. The *aurora borealis?* I give preference to Whistler's pictures. It was a profound truth that John Ruskin pronounced when he said that English sunsets had become more beautiful after Turner's pictures.

I would love our sky far more if the stars were larger, brighter and closer   99
to us. They have, indeed, become more beautiful since astronomers have been telling us more about them.

The world I live in is a world of little Hamlets and Othellos, a world   100
of Romeos and Goriots, Karamazovs and Mr. Dombey, of David Copperfield, Madame Bovary, Manon Lescaut, Anna Karenina, a world of little Don Quixotes and Don Juans.

Out of such insignificant creatures, out of the like of us, poets have   101
created majestic images and made them undying.

We live in a world in which it is impossible to understand man unless   102
we read books written about him by men of science and men of letters. Flaubert's *Un coeur simple* is precious to me as a gospel; Knut Hamsun's *Landstrykere (Growth of the Soil)* amazes me in the same way as the *Odyssey* does. I am sure that my grandchildren will read Romain Rolland's *Jean Christophe* and revere the author's greatness of heart and mind, his unquenchable love of mankind.

I am well aware that this kind of love is thought out of fashion today,   103
but what of it? It lives on without waning, and we go on living its joys and sorrows.

I even think that this love is growing ever stronger and more conscious.   104
Whilst this tends to lend a certain restraint and pragmatism to its manifestations, it in no wise diminishes the irrationality of this sentiment in our time, when the struggle for life has become so bitter.

I have no desire to know anything but man, to approach whom books   105
are friendly and generous guides; there is in me an ever deeper respect for the unassuming heroes who have created everything that is beautiful and grand in the world.

Questions for Discussion

1. Gorky's assertion that his first serious reading produced the feeling "that almost each book seemed to open up before me a window into a new and

unfamiliar world" (¶12) sounds remarkably similar to the narrator in Richard Wright's story "The Library Card." Both young men fasten passionately on books as a mode of vicarious experience quite different from the dreary, oppressive world of their everyday lives, and both feel that their emotional and spiritual capacities are enlarged by reading. If these views ring true to you, what arguments can you infer from them to answer people who say that required literature courses in college are a waste of time?

2. Aristotle says that literature is a form of learning and that human beings' instinctive love of learning is one of the causes of our powerful attachment to literature. But Plato says that we can't learn the highest truth from literature because it is composed of made-up stories—fictions (or, as he would have it, lies). Which of these two views coincides more closely with Gorky's, and which paragraphs can you point to as evidence for your answer?

3. In paragraph 46 Gorky says, "The more I read, the more a wholesome and kindly spirit filled my heart, and I grew calmer, my self-confidence developed, my work improved, and I paid ever less heed to the innumerable spurns life was dealing me." Later on he says, "Love books; they will . . . teach you to respect yourselves and others, and fill the mind and the heart with love for the world and man" (¶85). These passages describe a highly interesting consequence of reading, but Gorky provides no account of the *mechanism* of it. That is, he doesn't say *how* literature achieves such large and beneficial effects. In discussion with your classmates, can you fill in this part of Gorky's position? Assume for the sake of the argument that he is right, that literature can actually achieve such happy results, and attempt to construct an explanation—it may be purely hypothetical or based on personal experience—of the process, or practice, or whatever it is that might be the *cause* of such effects.

4. Now turn to the other side and assume that Gorky is wrong, that literature cannot in itself produce such deep improvement in the character of a reader, and look for arguments and examples that refute his position.

5. Having now argued both sides of the position, get behind the one that seems to you more true, and attempt to discuss additional arguments and better examples to support it.

6. In paragraph 102 Gorky asserts that "it is impossible to understand man unless we read books written about him by men of science and men of letters." Do you believe this is true? Can you imagine for a moment what would happen to your understanding of other human beings if everything you had ever read about them in works of literature and science were suddenly erased from your memory? Could you have gained all that knowledge of others by firsthand, personal observation? If not, does this provide you with more grounds for arguing that college students ought to read as much literature as possible?

Suggested Essay Topics

1. Write a letter to the author of your favorite novel or poem, explaining to the writer the work's effects, if any, on your beliefs, views, and character. One way to test for such effects is to ask yourself how your views and beliefs might be different if you had never read that particular work. There are many accounts of people whose lives have been dramatically changed by their reading of a single book that gave them a whole new way of understanding themselves or the world around them. The effects you are invited to describe here may not be that dramatic, but most of us have been strongly influenced by at least a few books or poems at some point in our lives. Your letter will give you an opportunity to think about this influence in some detail and to explain to the author how that influence has operated in your life.

2. After you have read the following Plato selection, use Plato as one of your sources in constructing an argument that refutes Gorky's optimistic opinion that books will "fill the mind and the heart with love for the world and man" (¶85). You may concede to Gorky that this effect may occur if the *right* books are read, but this concession will not prevent you from arguing that quite contrary effects may result if readers read the *wrong* books. Choose some book that in your opinion would have a pernicious influence on the character of a reader who succumbed to it—a book, say, that invites the reader to find a real thrill in violence against other people, invites the reader to take a dismissive view of women or minorities, or invites a view of sex as manipulative, self-serving, masochistic, or sadistic. Argue in specific terms, referring to passages and events in the book, showing how the story invites these effects and why they would be ethically bad for any of us to experience.

Plato

In The Republic, *Plato (c. 427–347 B.C.) constructs a series of long conversations between Socrates and some of his fellow citizens. The time is about 450 B.C.; the place is Athens, center of Greek culture; and the topic they are discussing is "justice" and how they would go about constructing the best sort of society to achieve it. They are discussing, in other words, what an ideal society would look like—how it would educate its citizens to live just and beautiful lives, keep itself solvent, protect itself, administer its laws, and worship its gods. They try to consider everything, in short, that the creators of a state would have to make decisions about if they were to build it from the ground up.*

The state they talk about is "ideal" not in the sense that it is sheer fantasy or so outlandish that it bears no resemblance to the society everyone already knows.

Instead, their state is ideal in the sense that its creators are imagining themselves free to make it without having to solve all the practical problems that would hit them if they were to cast off their old state and start over. They do not have to deal, for example, with people's resistance to change, people's fears of the unknown, or the disruptions that would occur if established ways of doing things were suddenly abandoned.

One of the most important questions they discuss is how they should educate the state's rulers—"guardians"—in their youth. In addressing this problem Socrates pictures a committee of older guardians, all philosophers—that is, lovers of truth, not professionals—setting out a curriculum for the younger guardians who will actually conduct the day-to-day business of the state when they grow up. Socrates bases his educational ideas on the assumption that the kind of training a society gives its youth determines the kind of adults that society gets. This was not a novel idea even then, but few thinkers have pursued its implications as thoroughly and vigorously as Socrates.

It seems obvious to him that if education feeds both the mind and the character of a society's youth, then only first-rate fare should be proffered to them. In trying to decide what is first-rate, Socrates picks a quarrel with literature. Stories, he claims, feed youth with lies that teach them to disrespect the gods and imitate the immoral behavior of heroes in myths, legends, and poems. He recommends protecting youth from corrupt literature by state censorship. Judges are to decide on the acceptability of stories and poems before they are given to children to read.

Our selection opens where Socrates is just beginning to bare the heart of his argument.

CENSORSHIP

Our title for this portion of *The Republic,* book 2.

Then he who is to be a really good and noble guardian of the State will require to unite in himself philosophy and spirit and swiftness and strength? 1

Undoubtedly.

Then we have found the desired natures; and now that we have found them, how are they to be reared and educated? Is not this an inquiry which may be expected to throw light on the greater inquiry which is our final end—How do justice and injustice grow up in States? For we do not want either to omit what is to the point or to draw out the argument to an inconvenient length.

Adeimantus thought that the inquiry would be of great service to us. 2

Then, I said, my dear friend, the task must not be given up, even if somewhat long.

Certainly not.

Come then, and let us pass a leisure hour in story-telling, and our story shall be the education of our heroes.

By all means.

And what shall be their education? It would be hard, I think, to find a better than the traditional system, which has two divisions, gymnastic for the body, and music for the soul.

True.

Presumably we shall begin education with music, before gymnastic can   3
begin.

By all means.

And when you speak of music, do you include literature or not?

I do.

And literature may be either true or false?

Yes.

Both have a part to play in education, but we must begin with the false?

I do not understand your meaning, he said.

You know, I said, that we begin by telling children stories which, though not wholly destitute of truth, are in the main fictitious; and these stories are told them when they are not of an age for gymnastics.

Very true.

That was my meaning when I said that we must teach music before gymnastics.

Quite right, he said.

You know also that the beginning is the most important part of any   4
work, especially in the case of a young and tender thing; for that is the time at which the character is being formed and the desired impression is more readily taken.

Quite true.

And shall we just carelessly allow children to hear any casual tales which may be devised by casual persons, and to receive into their minds ideas for the most part the very opposite of those which we shall wish them to have when they are grown up?

We cannot.

Then the first thing will be to establish a censorship of the writers of   5
fiction, and let the censors receive any tale of fiction which is good, and reject the bad; and we will persuade mothers and nurses to tell their children the authorized ones only. Let them fashion the mind with such tales, even more fondly than they mould the body with their hands; but most of those which are now in use must be discarded.

Of what tales are you speaking? he said.

You may find a model of the lesser in the greater, I said; for they must both be of the same type, and the same spirit ought to be found in both of them.

Very likely, he replied; but I do not as yet know what you would term   6
the greater.

Those, I said, which are narrated by Homer and Hesiod, and the rest of the poets, who have ever been the great story-tellers of mankind.

But which stories do you mean, he said; and what fault do you find with them?

A fault which is fundamental and most serious, I said; the fault of saying what is false, and doing so for no good purpose.

But when is this fault committed?

Whenever an erroneous representation is made of the nature of gods and heroes,—as when a painter paints a picture not having the shadow of a likeness to his subject.

Yes, he said, that sort of thing is certainly very blameable; but what are the stories which you mean?

First of all, I said, there was that greatest of all falsehoods on great subjects, which the misguided poet told about Uranus,—I mean what Hesiod says that Uranus did, and how Cronus retaliated on him.* The doings of Cronus, and the sufferings which in turn his son inflicted upon him, even if they were true, ought certainly not to be lightly told to young and thoughtless persons; if possible, they had better be buried in silence. But if there is an absolute necessity for their mention, a chosen few might hear them in a mystery, and they should sacrifice not a common pig, but some huge and unprocurable victim, so that the number of the hearers may be very few indeed.

Why, yes, said he, those stories are extremely objectionable.

Yes, Adeimantus, they are stories not to be repeated in our State; the young man should not be told that in committing the worst of crimes he is far from doing anything outrageous; and that even if he chastises in savage fashion his father when he does wrong, he will only be following the example of the first and greatest among the gods.

I entirely agree with you, he said; in my opinion those stories are quite unfit to be repeated.

Neither, if we mean our future guardians to regard the habit of lightly quarrelling among themselves as of all things the basest, should any word be said to them of the wars in heaven, and of the plots and fightings of the gods against one another, for they are not true. No, we shall never mention the battles of the giants, or let them be embroidered on garments; and we shall be silent about the innumerable other quarrels of gods and heroes with their friends and relatives. If we intend to persuade them that quarrelling is unholy, and that never up to this time has there been any hatred between citizens, then the stories which old men and old women tell them as children should be in this strain; and when they grow up, the poets also should be obliged to compose for them in a similar spirit. But the narrative of Hephaestus binding Hera his mother, or how on another occasion his father sent him flying for taking her part when she was being beaten, and all the battles of the gods in Homer—these tales must not be admitted into our State, whether they are supposed to have an allegorical meaning or not. For a young person cannot judge what is allegorical and what is literal; anything that he receives into his mind at that age is likely to become indelible and unalterable; and

*Uranus, the first lord of the universe, is depicted as having thrown his children into Tartarus, a dark pit under the earth. He was eventually attacked and defeated by Cronus, his youngest but strongest son, who drove Uranus away with a sickle made by Uranus's wife, Gaea. Cronus was in turn eventually dethroned by his son Zeus.

therefore it is most important that the tales which the young first hear should
be models of virtuous thoughts.

There you are right, he replied; but if anyone asks where are such   9
models to be found and of what tales are you speaking—how shall we answer
him?

I said to him, You and I, Adeimantus, at this moment are not poets, but
founders of a State: now the founders of a State ought to know the general
forms in which poets should cast their tales, and the limits which must be
observed by them, but to make the tales is not their business.

Very true, he said; but what are these forms of theology which you   10
mean?

Something of this kind, I replied:—God* is always to be represented as
he truly is, whatever be the sort of poetry, epic, lyric or tragic, in which the
representation is given.

Right.

And is he not truly good? And must he not be represented as such?

Certainly.

And no good thing is hurtful?

No, indeed.

And that which is not hurtful hurts not?

Certainly not.

And that which hurts not does no evil?

No.

And can that which does no evil be a cause of evil?

Impossible.

And the good is advantageous?

Yes.

And therefore the cause of well-being?

Yes.

It follows therefore that the good is not the cause of all things, but of
those which are as they should be; and it is not to be blamed for evil.

Assuredly.

Then God, if he be good, is not the author of all things, as the many   11
assert, but he is the cause of a few things only, and not of most things that
occur to men. For few are the goods of human life, and many are the evils,
and the good is to be attributed to God alone; of the evils the causes are to
be sought elsewhere, and not in him.

That appears to me to be most true, he said.

Then we must not listen to Homer or to any other poet who is guilty
of the folly of saying that

  Two casks lie at the threshold of Zeus, full of lots, one of good, the
  other of evil lots;

*See discussion question 4 on page 172.

and that he to whom Zeus gives a mixture of the two

> Sometimes meets with evil fortune, at other times with good;

but that he to whom is given the cup of unmingled ill,

> Him wild hunger drives o'er the beauteous earth.

And again—

> Zeus, who is the dispenser of good and evil to us.

And if anyone asserts that the violation of oaths and treaties, which was really the work of Pandarus, was brought about by Athena and Zeus, or that the strife and competition between the gods was instigated by Themis and Zeus, he shall not have our approval; neither will we allow our young men to hear the words of Aeschylus, that

> God plants guilt among men when he desires utterly to destroy a house.

And if a poet writes of the sufferings of Niobe—the subject of the tragedy in which these iambic verses occur—or of the house of Pelops, or of the Trojan war or on any similar theme, either we must not permit him to say that these are the works of God, or if they are of God, he must devise some explanation of them such as we are seeking: he must say that God did what was just and right, and they were the better for being punished. But that those who are punished are miserable, and that God is the author of their misery—the poet is not to be permitted to say; though he may say that the wicked were miserable because they required to be punished, and were benefited by receiving punishment from God; but that God being good is the author of evil to anyone is to be denied. We shall insist that it is not said or sung or heard in verse or prose by anyone whether old or young in any well-ordered commonwealth. Such a fiction would be impious, disastrous to us, and inconsistent with itself.

I agree with you, he replied, and am ready to give my assent to the law.

Questions for Discussion

1. In the poems and legends Socrates refers to in paragraphs 6–8, Greek heroes and gods are often shown behaving out of greed, spite, envy, jealousy, disrespect, and pride—almost the whole range of human vices.

Do you think Socrates is right in saying that young people will more likely commit vices themselves if they have "seen" them committed by gods and heroes in stories?

2. Socrates advances his argument about literature and character by means of an analogy with food and health. (For references to analogy, see the Rhetorical Index.) Can you state the analogy? Do you agree with it? Are feminists and minority representatives using this same analogy when they object to the moral effects of stories in which women, say, or blacks are depicted in demeaning ways? Do *you* object to such stories? On what grounds? Can you provide examples for class discussion?

3. If you accept Socrates' analogy and thus accept his definition of the problem, do you also accept his solution? Do you think that censorship is (1) a desirable solution or (2) a workable solution? In thinking about censorship, consider these questions:

   a. What is the possibility that the apparatus of censorship (committees, police, courts, suits, countersuits, and so on) might threaten the health of the state more than bad literature?

   b. Who is going to keep the censors pure? What happens if they need censoring? Who decides?

   c. How can a society be sure that its censors will never make a mistake?

   d. How does a society blend all of the competing standards for purity into one workable set of guidelines?

   e. Does free discussion disappear in a censored society?

   f. What happens to artistic expression in a censored society? (What about art in Nazi Germany or the Soviet Union? If no one in your class knows anything about such art, you might elect a committee to look into it and prepare a report for the rest of the class.)

4. In Benjamin Jowett's translation of Plato, from which we have excerpted the selections by Plato in this book, you will notice that both the terms *God* and *the gods* are used. Such terms cause problems in all translations, not only because of their inherent ambiguities but because they carry so many different meanings for modern readers. We should therefore be alert to probe *possible* meanings rather than settling on some one meaning that the words have had for us in other contexts. The warning may be especially important in reading Plato. Francis Cornford, in his preface to his translation of *The Republic,* says, "Some authors can be translated almost word for word. . . . This method cannot do justice to the matter and the manner of Plato's discourse. . . . Many key-words, such as 'music,' 'gymnastic,' 'virtue,' 'philosophy,' have shifted their meaning or acquired false associations for English ears." Cornford tells us that Plato "uses the singular 'god' and the plural 'the gods' with an indifference startling to the modern monotheist," and in his translation he avoids the form *God* entirely, in the belief that there is no notion in Plato quite like what is suggested to most modern readers by the term.

If no one in your class knows ancient Greek to assist in discussing the possible meanings of *God* and *the gods* in this selection, some students might be given the special assignment of consulting two or three other standard translations—the Paul Shorey translation in the Loeb Classical Library series, for example, or the Cornford translation. They could then photocopy the passages about *God* and *the gods,* or other troublesome passages, and bring them to class.

You may be shocked by the differences you find. Are they so great that they make reading the translations useless? What sorts of advice can you give yourself about reading other translations, on the basis of what you have found in comparing these translations?

Suggested Essay Topics

1. Clearly, Socrates is concerned about the moral influence of models that children meet in the stories they read. If children see Greek gods and heroes misbehaving, they will bend, like pliant plants, in those directions without realizing what is happening to them.

   Write an essay directed to a group of parents warning them that some of the models held out to children today are objectionable on the grounds given by Socrates. (You might watch some kids' programs, such as Saturday morning cartoons, in order to make your argument concrete and detailed.) Your purpose is to make a case, with illustrative examples, that the visual models children see on television are "bad" for them. You will, of course, have to say what you mean by *bad* and explain how important the problem is for society as a whole.

2. Read through a group of children's books in the library. Do you find material that you object to? Are there demeaning or stereotypical portrayals of minority groups, women, children, immigrants, or others? Try to find some old books from the late 1940s or early 1950s. Do you notice any difference between the depictions of stereotyped groups in older books as compared to more recent ones?

   If you find offensive material, choose an appropriate audience (your parents, the books' publishers, a grade-school teacher, etc.) and write an essay showing why the books you name are not good reading fare for young children. Be specific: Indicate why you find the material objectionable; indicate the ages you think make sensible cutoff points for parental or school supervision of youngsters' reading; say whether you think supervision ought to include actual censorship; and, if so, say why you accept censoring children's reading but not that of adults.

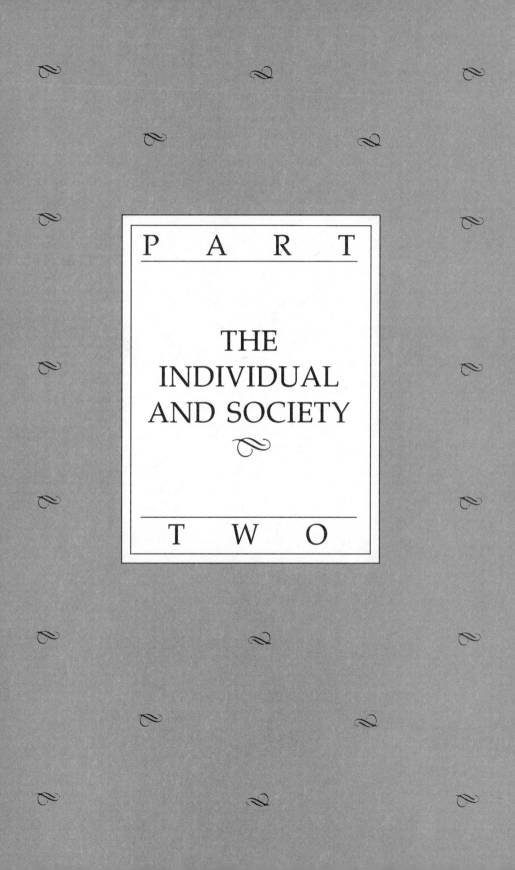

PART

THE
INDIVIDUAL
AND SOCIETY

TWO

⁓5⁓

PERSONAL GOALS

What Should I Become?

Sow an act, and you reap a habit. Sow a habit, and you reap
a character. Sow a character, and you reap a destiny.
Charles Reade

Do not ask for success; success is for swine.
Anonymous

The only infallible criterion of wisdom to vulgar judgments—success.
Edmund Burke

To burn always with this hard, gemlike flame, to maintain
this ecstasy, is success in life.
Walter Pater

What is the chief end of man? To glorify God
and to enjoy him forever.
Shorter Catechism

He that can apprehend and consider vice with all her baits
and seeming pleasures, and yet abstain, and yet distinguish, and yet prefer
that which is truly better, he is the true wayfaring Christian.
I cannot praise a fugitive and cloistered virtue,
unexercised and unbreathed, that never sallies out and
sees her adversary, but slinks out of the race, where that immortal garland
is to be run for, not without dust and heat.
Assuredly we bring not innocence into the world, we bring
impurity much rather: that which purifies us is trial,
and trial is by what is contrary.
John Milton

That action is best, which procures the greatest happiness for
the greatest number.
Francis Hutcheson
(followed by many later utilitarians)

Phyllis Rose

This chapter focuses on personal goals: not simply on what we want out of life, but on what we want to make out of ourselves. We are all prone to carry on internal conversations such as, "If I do X, which I already know is the right thing to do, how will others see me? Will they understand me? How will they judge me? If I don't do X because I fear being misunderstood or disliked, how will I live with myself? What kind of person will I have become then?"

Asking such questions can underscore for us all just how vulnerable the self can sometimes feel. Don't we all share a certain shrinking when we anticipate criticism or rejection? Don't we all know that sweet flow of energy and jubilation when we have just received assurance that we, our precious selves, are indeed admired or loved? In an insightful essay, Phyllis Rose (b. 1942) takes note of these two poles and describes a typical human movement: the pendulum swing we all make between self-love and self-loathing or, in the jargon of the day, between being "up" about ourselves and being "down" about ourselves.

In the best tradition of the comic essay that makes a serious point while being funny, Rose shows that she knows us, that she knows how we all go up and down in our self-esteem. But of course she could know such a private thing about us only if in fact it is both private and universal. Rose knows us because in this respect she is us. She knows that we are all heirs to the human capacity for despair and hope, joy and sorrow.

So what do we make of our swings? Is this simply the way it is? Does self-consciousness doom us to eternal pendulum swings of feeling? Perhaps, but are we really helpless? Wouldn't things be better if we were more in control? Wouldn't life have been better even for the successful George Eliot referred to in Rose's essay if she hadn't had to spend so much emotion worrying about whether she was a noodle? Wouldn't Rose like to give up those days when she feels like an impostor? And wouldn't we all like to turn our paralyzing fears into liberating energies?

Rose's examples offer us suggestions—no recipes, but suggestions—for liberating ourselves. That the successful people of the world share our fears about achievement and self-worth suggests that we may be wrong to take it all so seriously, to take every occasion of self-loathing as if it were The End. Can we infer from Rose's examples that we take ourselves too seriously most of the time, whether we're feeling up or down? If so, those life-or-death dramas when we feel like failures or frauds may be nothing but our own emotional hype. Knowing this might lower some of our soaring highs, but it might also take some of the depths out of our sagging lows. We might just discover that life doesn't have to be a constant switch between Ferris wheel heights and roller coaster plunges. In any event, Rose's fine essay invites us to take a hard look at the various selves we create inside.

HEROIC FANTASIES, NERVOUS DOUBTS

From the *New York Times* "Hers" column (March 22, 1984).

1 Recently a young man presented a bouquet to the secretary of the English department. She was astounded. "But I don't even know you!" she said. He quickly explained that he was just the florist's messenger; the card would tell her who had sent the flowers. They came, as it happened, from a grateful professor. But what strikes me is that for a split second she thought a complete stranger was offering her flowers, and although this surprised her it was not inconceivable.

2 Why should it be? Don't we all harbor fantasies of a brass band's arriving at our door one day to play in our honor? Of Warren Beatty's standing on our front step with a red ribbon around his neck? I know I do. Like gold coins in a garbage dump, sprinkled here and there in the midst of our self-distrust are these glittering visions of our worth and importance. We may suspect during many waking hours that we have no worth or importance and at the same time hope that the world, perhaps in the form of a young man bearing flowers, will one day pay them tribute.

3 Such fantasies seem to me entirely healthy, as bankable as my metaphorical gold coins. Sometimes they are linked to myths we hold about our lives. Everyone, for example, has a story about his or her birth. I have always been told and believed that I was born in Doctors Hospital with the fleet massing in the East River beneath my mother's window for the invasion of North Africa. Was the fleet really massing in the East River for the invasion of North Africa? An easy question to answer for certain, but I never will, for the facts in this case, as in many others, are less important to me than their significance, the myth.

4 Some part of me thinks—has always thought—that the invasion of North Africa was an elegant pretext, a cover story, an excuse. World War II or no, the fleet would have been there festively "massing"—I imagine this to consist of a lot of nuzzling between ships and blowing of horns—in honor of my birth. The fleet massed for me the way the fairies gathered for the birth

of Sleeping Beauty. The fleet bestowed blessings on me and wished me well in life. On successive birthdays I have waited for the fleet, in some form, to return. It never does. Nevertheless, whatever is strong in my ego may be said to be strong because I believe that the fleet massed below my mother's window on the day of my birth.

The expectation that the world will congratulate us for living tends to focus on birthdays, and usually what happens on birthdays is nothing. I'm speaking of adults. Indeed, that's one way you can tell when you're grown up: nothing happens on your birthday. I knew I was grown up when I turned 38 and even my mother forgot my birthday. I was so depressed after looking through the mail that I went back to bed. My son, then 8, found me there, the shades drawn on a bright Saturday afternoon. I disclosed the problem. "Don't move," he said. "I'll be right back." Half an hour later he returned and thrust something large at me in a brown paper bag. "You don't have to use these," he said, "but I want you to have them." He had grabbed all his capital—$2—had gone to the nearest store and had bought the biggest thing he could get for his money: a five-pound bag of potatoes. Now I have a special place in my heart for potatoes. Still, it's not the fleet or a brass band or Warren Beatty.

The average person's mixture of arrogance and self-loathing, of daring and fear, never ceases to amaze me. We want to bring down the house. We want the house to stand, protecting us. We want to be invulnerable through strength. We want to be invulnerable because there's nothing there to hurt. We want to be everything and nothing. I sometimes believe I am the prize package my kindly parents always told me I was. But just as often getting out of bed in the morning seems a plucky thing to do. (At such moments of existential panic,* I find enormously helpful the phrase "another day, another dollar," which takes this risky business of getting out of bed away from metaphysics and into the realm of the practical, where it belongs.)

Often I think I'm the only person for the job, whatever the job may be: cooking pasta al pesto, planning a trip, writing a certain biography. But often I feel like an impostor as writer, teacher, human being. I like attention but I suffer from stage fright. If I had to say what it is I'm afraid of, I guess it's that my self won't be there when I need it. I'm afraid people will see through me and find there's nothing there.

I once appeared on a TV talk show with Joey Skaggs, the artist who specializes in putting things over on people. For example, he will announce that he intends to windsurf from Hawaii to California or that, as king of the gypsies, he is calling for a work stoppage of gypsies to protest the term gypsy moth. People believe him, and that constitutes the work of art. He is a media artist, a public-relations artist. I like his work and envy his talent. Before the

*The existential philosophers who were influential in the post–World War II period were given to insisting that human beings had to *assert* their personal worth in the face of a meaningless universe. Rose is joking on how panicky that act of self-assertion can make her.

TV show we chatted. He showed me his clippings, an enormous scrapbook full of them. Worried that I would be found invisible when I appeared on TV, I could not bring myself to look at this massive evidence of Joey Skaggs's reality. I guess he thought I was bored by it or contemptuous. "It's hard to take in all at once," he said. I told him that wasn't the problem. "It makes me feel like nothing by comparison," I said. Joey, a nice man, conned me into comfort. "Believe me," he said, waving his hand to take in the studio and his clipping book, "it's all this that's nothing."

I used to think these problems of self-esteem were peculiarly female. 9
Now I'm not sure. When I began teaching 14 years ago I was convinced that establishing authority in the classroom was more of a problem for me than for my male colleagues. Before the start of each semester I had terrible anxiety dreams: I would go to composition class prepared to teach Shakespeare or vice versa, I would suddenly be called upon to lecture on the history of Japanese theater or to announce the Harvard-Yale game, I would forget to show up for the first class or I would show up naked. That dream in particular seemed to me a woman's dream. Women are not bred to authority, I thought. If I set myself up as an authority, people will see I'm a fraud.

At this time, the early 70's, I found myself at a New Haven dinner party 10
seated next to a Yale geologist who was about to retire after a long and distinguished teaching career. Professor Flint told me that there were many things he would miss about teaching but one thing he would not miss: the nightmares he had at the start of every semester in which he presented himself at the podium for the first lecture and discovered he was naked.

Perhaps we should all have tapes of loved ones telling us the stories of 11
our lives in mythic form—how the fleet massed and so on—just as Olympic athletes have think-positive tapes prescribed by their sports psychologists. Few of us need tapes to remind us how insignificant we are. The anxieties speak for themselves. There was a Roman emperor who had a slave at his side all the time to remind him he was mortal. But probably more of us are like George Eliot,* who, according to her companion, needed a slave at her side constantly whispering, "You are not a noodle."

Questions for Discussion

1. Most people have both anxiety dreams and wish-fulfillment dreams. Without getting embarrassingly personal, can you and your classmates share some of these dreams? Is there a great deal of similarity among them?

*George Eliot, the pseudonym of Mary Ann Evans (1819–1880), one of the most successful and critically acclaimed novelists of the nineteenth century. Her novels include *Adam Bede* (1859) and *Middlemarch* (1871–1872).

If not, does this suggest that we are more different in this respect than the introduction and Rose's essay suggests? If they are similar, does this corroborate the suggestion than we are all pretty much alike in this respect regardless of past successes?

2. In how many places and in how many different forms do you find the swing from self-love to self-loathing recorded? Do the lyrics to some songs, for example, express the former, while the lyrics to others express inner doubts and fears? Can you give examples? What about characters on TV programs and in the movies? What about characters in drama? Hamlet, for example—if we take his soliloquies to express private thought—goes up and down in his own self-estimation much more than anyone else in the play knows. Do you find Hamlet's pattern repeated in other characters in other plays? At a quite different literary level, what about cartoons? Garfield the cat seems the epitome of arrogant self-confidence, but when he gets down on himself about his weight, he becomes another cat altogether. What other instances of our preoccupation with how we feel about ourselves can you cite from the culture around you?

3. How many people do you know who do not seem ever to need the slave whispering, "You are not a noodle," but who in fact could sometimes use another slave to whisper, "You are overbearing, egotistical, and obnoxious"? Do you think these people have their own moments of barren self-confidence, or are there a few of us who never lose our grip on who we want to be? If the latter, what we have said so far is wrong; self-doubt is only widespread but not really universal. What is your opinion? Can you support it with examples?

Suggested Essay Topics

1. St. Paul's definition of love (p. 201) suggests that the self finds its most complete fulfillment not in taking in assurance and affection but in passing these on to others. If you have ever been the recipient of a gift of love when you felt that you needed it most, when you were feeling like a barren thing, your own worst self, give an account of the experience—why you needed it, how the gift was given, the effects it worked—addressed to your classmates as an example of the kind of help we may be to one another in times of stress or trouble.

2. If you have ever given such a gift as described in topic 1, give an account of what motivated you, how you knew the gift was needed, what it cost you, and the effects it had—not to pat yourself on the back as a good person but to record what you learned or how you grew.

Margaret Sanger

       Margaret Sanger (1883–1966) was the earliest influential advocate for the spread of birth control information in America. In 1921, working against intense opposition, she organized the first American birth control conference, and she continued to write books and publish magazines on the subject over several decades. In this essay Sanger recounts the episodes that led up to the crucial moment when she made her lifelong commitment to the cause of birth control education.

       As Sanger makes her way steadily toward the greatest decision of her life, she makes the reader aware of all that she will have to fight against in forging an unconventional path, especially difficult for a woman in her era. She will have to fight to reduce her own ignorance, fight the taboo against speaking out on sexual matters, fight against religious opposition, and, finally, fight against those who would dismiss her as an unfeminine radical at best, a meddling crackpot at worst.

       Notice how the issue that was to dominate Sanger's life does not gain sharp focus until she becomes acquainted with the poor, who suffered most from excessive childbearing. Once she starts working among them, she learns to see them not as statistics or generalized "unfortunates" but as individuals (¶15). We can almost always endure reports of the catastrophes of anonymous masses with less discomfort than we can the minor troubles of people whom we know as individuals. Our sympathies are always more quickly awakened and brought into play by concrete images than by vague abstractions. Sanger is presumably aware of this tendency in her readers as she works to portray the suffering poor as vividly as possible without lapsing into lurid or implausible melodrama.

THE TURBID EBB AND FLOW OF MISERY

Chapter 7 of *An Autobiography* (1938). Sanger has taken her chapter title from a line in Matthew Arnold's poem "Dover Beach."

> Every night and every morn
> Some to misery are born.
> Every morn and every night
> Some are born to sweet delight.
> Some are born to sweet delight,
> Some are born to endless night.
>   WILLIAM BLAKE

During these years [about 1912] in New York trained nurses were in great demand. Few people wanted to enter hospitals; they were afraid they might be "practiced" upon, and consented to go only in desperate emergencies. Sentiment was especially vehement in the matter of having babies. A woman's own bedroom, no matter how inconveniently arranged, was the usual place for her lying-in. I was not sufficiently free from domestic duties to be a general nurse, but I could ordinarily manage obstetrical cases because I was notified far enough ahead to plan my schedule. And after serving my two weeks I could get home again.

Sometimes I was summoned to small apartments occupied by young clerks, insurance salesmen, or lawyers, just starting out, most of them under thirty and whose wives were having their first or second baby. They were always eager to know the best and latest method in infant care and feeding. In particular, Jewish patients, whose lives centered around the family, welcomed advice and followed it implicitly.

But more and more my calls began to come from the Lower East Side, as though I were being magnetically drawn there by some force outside my control. I hated the wretchedness and hopelessness of the poor, and never experienced that satisfaction in working among them that so many noble women have found. My concern for my patients was now quite different from my earlier hospital attitude. I could see that much was wrong with them which did not appear in the physiological or medical diagnosis. A woman in childbirth was not merely a woman in childbirth. My expanded outlook included a view of her background, her potentialities as a human being, the kind of children she was bearing, and what was going to happen to them.

The wives of small shopkeepers were my most frequent cases, but I had carpenters, truck drivers, dishwashers, and pushcart vendors. I admired intensely the consideration most of these people had for their own. Money to pay doctor and nurse had been carefully saved months in advance—parents-in-law, grandfathers, grandmothers, all contributing.

As soon as the neighbors learned that a nurse was in the building they came in a friendly way to visit, often carrying fruit, jellies, or gefüllter fish made after a cherished recipe. It was infinitely pathetic to me that they, so poor themselves, should bring me food. Later they drifted in again with the excuse of getting the plate, and sat down for a nice talk; there was no hurry. Always back of the little gift was the question, "I am pregnant (or my daughter, or my sister is). Tell me something to keep from having another baby. We cannot afford another yet."

I tried to explain the only two methods I had ever heard of among the middle classes, both of which were invariably brushed aside as unacceptable. They were of no certain avail to the wife because they placed the burden of responsibility solely upon the husband—a burden which he seldom assumed. What she was seeking was self-protection she could herself use, and there was none.

Below this stratum of society was one in truly desperate circumstances. The men were sullen and unskilled, picking up odd jobs now and then, but more often unemployed, lounging in and out of the house at all hours of the day and night. The women seemed to slink on their way to market and were without neighborliness.

These submerged, untouched classes were beyond the scope of organized charity or religion. No labor union, no church, not even the Salvation

Army reached them. They were apprehensive of everyone and rejected help of any kind, ordering all intruders to keep out; both birth and death they considered their own business. Social agents, who were just beginning to appear, were profoundly mistrusted because they pried into homes and lives, asking questions about wages, how many were in the family, had any of them ever been in jail. Often two or three had been there or were now under suspicion of prostitution, shoplifting, purse snatching, petty thievery, and, in consequence, passed furtively by the big blue uniforms on the corner.

The utmost depression came over me as I approached this surreptitious region. Below Fourteenth Street I seemed to be breathing a different air, to be in another world and country where the people had habits and customs alien to anything I had ever heard about.

There were then approximately ten thousand apartments in New York into which no sun ray penetrated directly; such windows as they had opened only on a narrow court from which rose fetid odors. It was seldom cleaned, though garbage and refuse often went down into it. All these dwellings were pervaded by the foul breath of poverty, that moldy, indefinable, indescribable smell which cannot be fumigated out, sickening to me but apparently unnoticed by those who lived there. When I set to work with antiseptics, their pungent sting, at least temporarily, obscured the stench.

I remember one confinement case to which I was called by the doctor of an insurance company. I climbed up the five flights and entered the airless rooms, but the baby had come with too great speed. A boy of ten had been the only assistant. Five flights was a long way; he had wrapped the placenta in a piece of newspaper and dropped it out the window into the court.

Many families took in "boarders," as they were termed, whose small contributions paid the rent. These derelicts, wanderers, alternately working and drinking, were crowded in with the children; a single room sometimes held as many as six sleepers. Little girls were accustomed to dressing and undressing in front of the men, and were often violated, occasionally by their own fathers or brothers, before they reached the age of puberty.

Pregnancy was a chronic condition among the women of this class. Suggestions as to what to do for a girl who was "in trouble" or a married woman who was "caught" passed from mouth to mouth—herb teas, turpentine, steaming, rolling downstairs, inserting slippery elm, knitting needles, shoe-hooks. When they had word of a new remedy they hurried to the drugstore, and if the clerk were inclined to be friendly he might say, "Oh, that won't help you, but here's something that may." The younger druggists usually refused to give advice because, if it were to be known, they would come under the law; midwives were even more fearful. The doomed women implored me to reveal the "secret" rich people had, offering to pay me extra to tell them; many really believed I was holding back information for money. They asked everybody and tried anything, but nothing did them any good. On Saturday nights I have seen groups of from fifty to one hundred with their shawls over their heads waiting outside the office of a five-dollar abortionist.

Each time I returned to this district, which was becoming a recurrent nightmare, I used to hear that Mrs. Cohen "had been carried to a hospital, but had never come back," or that Mrs. Kelly "had sent the children to a neighbor and had put her head into the gas oven." Day after day such tales were poured into my ears—a baby born dead, great relief—the death of an older child, sorrow but again relief of a sort—the story told a thousand times of death from abortion and children going into institutions. I shuddered with horror as I listened to the details and studied the reasons back of them— destitution linked with excessive childbearing. The waste of life seemed utterly senseless. One by one worried, sad, pensive, and aging faces mar- shaled themselves before me in my dreams, sometimes appealingly, some- times accusingly.

These were not merely "unfortunate conditions among the poor" such 15 as we read about. I knew the women personally. They were living, breathing, human beings, with hopes, fears, and aspirations like my own, yet their weary, misshapen bodies, "always ailing, never failing," were destined to be thrown on the scrap heap before they were thirty-five. I could not escape from the facts of their wretchedness; neither was I able to see any way out. My own cozy and comfortable family existence was becoming a reproach to me.

Then one stifling mid-July day of 1912 I was summoned to a Grand 16 Street tenement. My patient was a small, slight Russian Jewess, about twenty-eight years old, of the special cast of feature to which suffering lends a madonna-like expression. The cramped three-room apartment was in a sorry state of turmoil. Jake Sachs, a truck driver scarcely older than his wife, had come home to find the three children crying and her unconscious from the effects of a self-induced abortion. He had called the nearest doctor, who in turn had sent for me. Jake's earnings were trifling, and most of them had gone to keep the none-too-strong children clean and properly fed. But his wife's ingenuity had helped them to save a little, and this he was glad to spend on a nurse rather than have her go to a hospital.

The doctor and I settled ourselves to the task of fighting the septicemia. 17 Never had I worked so fast, never so concentratedly. The sultry days and nights were melted into a torpid inferno. It did not seem possible there could be such heat, and every bit of food, ice, and drugs had to be carried up three flights of stairs.

Jake was more kind and thoughtful than many of the husbands I had 18 encountered. He loved his children, and had always helped his wife wash and dress them. He had brought water up and carried garbage down before he left in the morning, and did as much as he could for me while he anxiously watched her progress.

After a fortnight Mrs. Sachs' recovery was in sight. Neighbors, ordi- 19 narily fatalistic as to the results of abortion, were genuinely pleased that she had survived. She smiled wanly at all who came to see her and thanked them gently, but she could not respond to their hearty congratulations. She ap- peared to be more despondent and anxious than she should have been, and spent too much time in meditation.

At the end of three weeks, as I was preparing to leave the fragile patient   20
to take up her difficult life once more, she finally voiced her fears, "Another
baby will finish me, I suppose?"

"It's too early to talk about that," I temporized.   21

But when the doctor came to make his last call, I drew him aside. "Mrs.   22
Sachs is terribly worried about having another baby."

"She well may be," replied the doctor, and then he stood before her and   23
said, "Any more such capers, young woman, and there'll be no need to send
for me."

"I know, doctor," she replied timidly, "but," and she hesitated as   24
though it took all her courage to say it, "what can I do to prevent it?"

The doctor was a kindly man, and he had worked hard to save her, but   25
such incidents had become so familiar to him that he had long since lost
whatever delicacy he might once have had. He laughed good-naturedly. "You
want to have your cake and eat it too, do you? Well, it can't be done."

Then picking up his hat and bag to depart he said, "Tell Jake to sleep   26
on the roof."

I glanced quickly at Mrs. Sachs. Even through my sudden tears I could   27
see stamped on her face an expression of absolute despair. We simply looked
at each other, saying no word until the door had closed behind the doctor.
Then she lifted her thin, blue-veined hands and clasped them beseechingly.
"He can't understand. He's only a man. But you do, don't you? Please tell me
the secret, and I'll never breathe it to a soul. *Please!*"

What was I to do? I could not speak the conventionally comforting   28
phrases which would be of no comfort. Instead, I made her as physically easy
as I could and promised to come back in a few days to talk with her again.
A little later, when she slept, I tiptoed away.

Night after night the wistful image of Mrs. Sachs appeared before me.   29
I made all sorts of excuses to myself for not going back. I was busy on other
cases; I really did not know what to say to her or how to convince her of my
own ignorance; I was helpless to avert such monstrous atrocities. Time rolled
by and I did nothing.

The telephone rang one evening three months later, and Jake Sachs'   30
agitated voice begged me to come at once; his wife was sick again and from
the same cause. For a wild moment I thought of sending someone else, but
actually, of course, I hurried into my uniform, caught up my bag, and started
out. All the way I longed for a subway wreck, an explosion, anything to keep
me from having to enter that home again. But nothing happened, even to
delay me. I turned into the dingy doorway and climbed the familiar stairs
once more. The children were there, young little things.

Mrs. Sachs was in a coma and died within ten minutes. I folded her still   31
hands across her breast, remembering how they had pleaded with me, begging so humbly for the knowledge which was her right. I drew a sheet over
her pallid face. Jake was sobbing, running his hands through his hair and
pulling it out like an insane person. Over and over again he wailed, "My God!
My God! My God!"

I left him pacing desperately back and forth, and for hours I myself   32
walked and walked and walked through the hushed streets. When I finally
arrived home and let myself quietly in, all the household was sleeping. I
looked out my window and down upon the dimly lighted city. Its pains and
griefs crowded in upon me, a moving picture rolled before my eyes with
photographic clearness: women writhing in travail to bring forth little babies;
the babies themselves naked and hungry, wrapped in newspapers to keep
them from the cold; six-year-old children with pinched, pale, wrinkled faces,
old in concentrated wretchedness, pushed into gray and fetid cellars, crouching on stone floors, their small scrawny hands scuttling through rags, making
lamp shades, artificial flowers; white coffins, black coffins, coffins, coffins
interminably passing in never-ending succession. The scenes piled one upon
another on another. I could bear it no longer.

As I stood there the darkness faded. The sun came up and threw its   33
reflection over the house tops. It was the dawn of a new day in my life also.
The doubt and questioning, the experimenting and trying, were now to be
put behind me. I knew I could not go back merely to keeping people alive.

I went to bed, knowing that no matter what it might cost, I was finished   34
with palliatives and superficial cures; I was resolved to seek out the root of
evil, to do something to change the destiny of mothers whose miseries were
vast as the sky.

Questions for Discussion

1. In paragraphs 1–8, Sanger refers to three distinct social levels. What are
   they? What characterizes each one? How do they differ?
2. Compare Sanger's organization with the cinematographic device of the
   panorama. Paragraphs 1–15 begin as if from far above the city and the
   crowd; subsequent paragraphs begin to focus on things in more detail, and
   they continue to do so with increasing vividness until the Sachses' story
   begins in paragraph 16. Can you trace the progress of this organization in
   more detail? What are its effects?
3. In paragraph 25, Sanger gives the doctor on the Sachs case credit for being
   "a kindly man." Does his response to Mrs. Sachs's plea justify this credit?
   Can you defend his comments in paragraphs 25–26 in any way?

Suggested Essay Topics

1. Select a moment or an episode in your own life that you now see was
   decisive in giving you a sense of direction about something specific—for
   example, whether or not to go to college, to get engaged, to register for the
   draft, or to stand up for an unpopular cause. In an essay addressed to your

fellow students, recount that moment or episode as Sanger does, giving your readers a vivid picture of the buildup of feelings and ideas that led to your decision. (Naturally, you will have to pick a decision that was dramatic and trying for you, not one that you made casually or that someone else made for you.)

2. In an essay directed to the (real or imaginary) school board in your hometown, make an argument recommending or opposing classes on sex education that would include information on contraceptives. Like Sanger, you should use concrete illustrations to buttress your argument (you may make them up, if necessary, but write about them as if they were firsthand observations). You should also make clear, as she does, the principle you are defending or the goal you are pursuing.

Lorraine Hansberry

Although she only lived to age 34, Lorraine Hansberry (1930–1965) wrote at least one classic play, A Raisin in the Sun, *four other plays that she did not live to see produced, and many occasional pieces, some of which are only now being collected and published. When she was 29,* Raisin *won the Best Play of the Year award from the New York Drama Critics. Hansberry was the first black playwright to receive this honor.*

We have placed "In Defense of the Equality of Men*" here, rather than in the chapter called "Men and Women," because the argument, while undeniably about the relationship between the sexes, focuses more on personal goals than on sex-specific roles. Hansberry is concerned with the difficulty facing* anyone *who wants to become a whole person in a society that imposes stereotypes on both men* and *women. Thus Hansberry's topic focuses less on how men and women treat each other than on how society tells them they* should *treat each other and on the resulting strains, indignities, and impoverishments that afflict both sexes when they try to meet society's demands.*

In answer to the question that forms the subtitle of this chapter—"What Should I Become?"—Hansberry asserts that neither men nor women can be free to discover, or create, the best version of themselves when they are reared in traditions that impose on men the necessity of always pretending to be superior and strong and impose on women the necessity of always propping up men and massaging their egos as if they were children too weak to face the truth about their own defects. Such impositions, Hansberry asserts, not only insult both men and women but also retard all progress in society.

In response to worriers who fear that women's liberation will produce unsexed or masculine women, Hansberry asserts that what will emerge instead is more interesting women and more completely developed men. She further assumes that most men and women will welcome such changes and that those who do fear change and thus attempt to block it are not preserving a golden past but preventing the emergence of a more lustrous future.

The somewhat breezy colloquial style of this piece is a function of its having been written (and published) originally not as a scholarly essay but as a feature article intended for a popular magazine. As a professional writer, Hansberry was master of a variety of styles for a variety of occasions.

IN DEFENSE OF THE EQUALITY OF *MEN*

This essay, probably written in 1961, was intended for publication in a popular magazine to be called *The Fair Sex*. The magazine never appeared.

There is currently mushrooming in the land a voluminous body of opinion 1 in which scores of magazine writers, television panelists, and conference speakers with weighted eyebrows and ominous sentences allude to a peril in the Republic such as might herald a second coming of the British. Book, speech, and dissertation titles make the matter explicit: "Modern Woman— The Lost Sex";* "Trousered Mothers and Dishwashing Dads"; "American Man in a Woman's World"; etc.

Women, it is said, have ceased being, of all things, *women*. The conclu- 2 sion has now been drawn in many circles that womanhood's historical insistance on ever-increasing measures of equality has resulted in women becoming "the imitations of men"—and, it is sometimes added, with something of a Calvinist shout: "Very bad imitations!"

The total theme of the alarm is that the "roles of the sexes are disappear- 3 ing," and according to one analyst: "We are drifting toward a social structure made up of he-women and she-men." Which, all will admit, if it is true, is pretty scary business!

To aid in the terror, some contemporary schools of psychoanalytical 4 thought have been right in there giving leadership, guiding the worried along paths of "explanation" which have to do with their own preoccupations with "phallus envy," "castration complexes," and the rest of it: the inevitable result being that large numbers of people are now inclined to speak of the hardly new quest for universal equality as a neurotic disorder! "A disorder," we are informed, which seems to be sweeping other modern civilizations as well. For what else could be at the root, for example, of the "trouble in Australia," where a study reveals that sixty percent of the husbands in Melbourne reported that they help their wives with the dishes and yet another twenty-two percent get breakfast for the family in the mornings?

It appears that the horrified commentators have taken note of some very 5 real disorders in modern life and deduced, rather automatically, that the

---

*Title of an influential book (1947) by Marynia Farnham and Ferdinand Lundberg.

causes must lie in the disintegration of our most entrenched traditions. Yet few of these seers, remarkably enough, seem to have seriously considered the alternative: that the problems might in fact lie in the lingering *life* of certain of our traditions.

There are, to be sure, other observers—a counter force holding their 6 own—who suggest that, at best, the alarm is rooted in archaic concepts and, at worst, is in itself presumptious as the dickens! Striking a note of rationality, they argue that what we are dealing with is the oldest phenomenon of the planet: *change*. The implication being that, contrary to negative legends, the human race possesses an incredible capacity to adapt itself, physically and psychologically, to its own ever-improving technological condition. Thus, modern man—modern urban man in particular—has begun to lose his *reasons* for the retention of formerly rigid notions of occupational, avocational, or even psychic categorizations which were apparently essential to his forebears in their more primitive social systems.

Affairs behind executive or professorial desks have tended to make 7 "brute strength" irrelevant; World War II showed that virtually the same thing was true for the assembly line. And even if there were wild boars and such things still to be hunted for survival, the force required on the trigger of an automatic weapon is hardly the same once needed to pummel some-thing with a stone axe. Increasingly, it is a human being's thinking capacity, not his bulk, which most equips him for modern life; whatever there once was of a realistic reason for physique determining labor is rapidly disappearing. In that light it is not extraordinary to behold the human attitude also chang-ing. If modern trade unionism, white-collar labor, and the eight-hour day have contrived to diminish the laboring hours of the husband, it is to his credit that he has begun of his own volition to apply his new and hard-won leisure to sharing some part of his wife's still often twelve-to-fourteen-hour workday. It suggests that more than being a question for concern, it is one for celebration inasmuch as for the first time in history the family may now be growing toward a circumstantial reality which will allow it to become the truly harmonized, cooperative unit the human dream has always longed for it to be.

The current aspiration for the retention of ancient polarized concepts of 8 strict divisions of labor reflects a social order which has effectively kept womanhood in her well-known second-class situation, but which is less often criticized for imposing *upon males* the most unreasonable and unneces-sary burdens of "superiority" and "authority," which, in fact, work only to insult their humanness and *deny the reality of their civilized state.*

Most apologists for a male supremacist culture do not dream that they 9 savagely downgrade *men* in their efforts to provide them with a socially guaranteed place of privilege on the human scale. Yet, it was not romanticism alone, but also shimmering human practicality, which led the great humanist thinkers and artists of history to postulate, in poetry and prose, the ideas that, for instance, the rich must be inevitably degraded, in *human* terms, in a world where so many starve; that the educated remain, in large measure, untested for their wisdom when so few can read or write. And, certainly, in our own time, in the United States, it has become increasingly clear that white Americans are among the most compromised people on the face of the earth, because of their steady demonstration of their fear of running a non-handicapped race with their black countrymen.

If modern males are suffering from high percentages of ulcer, heart 10 ailment, and a thousand-and-one nervous disorders, this might well be the burden imposed on their nervous systems from subjecting the reality of present-day life to the totems and taboos* of the primeval, medieval, and Victorian past. As in all questions where nonconformity carries heavy penalties, great numbers of males are naturally reticent to articulate their dissent from the "favors" heaped upon them. But, occasionally, usually in the more acceptable guise of "explaining" to women how to give artificially contrived sustenance to the male ego, the plea can be discerned. John Kord Lagemann provides an excellent example in an article in *Redbook* entitled "The Male Sex": "The average male would be happy to drop the he-man pose if he didn't feel it would mean losing face as a man. It isn't because of his male instinct that he shies away from washing dishes, changing diapers, working under a woman boss or enjoying string quartets and modern art. It's because he suspects that other people, including his wife—despite their protestations to the contrary—still look on these chores and pastimes as 'unnatural' for a man."

We have all become so preoccupied with the "usurpation of the male's 11 authority by the female" that we have neglected to analyze the vestigial presumption of that self-awarded authority; in so doing, we have also neglected to be outraged and shocked by the equally widespread assumption that men are in reality inferior human beings who have to be "propped up." The institutional acceptance of woman as a second-class human being carries its own dynamic which inadvertantly must, of necessity, present men as flagrantly unintelligent and somewhat dehumanized creatures. In "Making Marriage Work," featured in a widely read woman's magazine, the professor-analyst author tackled what might seem, to the excessively civilized, a resolved question: *"Should a Husband Strike His Wife?"* Bending to enlightenment, the writer opined, "It is impossible to condone such behavior." He then went on, however, to modify that bit of radical abandon by advising his readers that the "provocation" by wives was undoubtedly far greater than they realized. He offered the following directions to wives as to how best avoid their partially deserved beatings: "Gauge his mood; avoid arguments; indulge his whims; help him relax; share his burdens; keep love alive."

Now it must be clear that any group of human beings who *could* impose 12 such saintly behavior on themselves at will, presumably after their own fairly exhausting and temper-rousing workdays, would be a superior lot indeed. But rather more outrageous is the assumption that men must be placated, outwitted, humored, and patronized like the family pet of whom we do not expect rationality and emotional control. One wonders how the writer sup-

---

*An allusion to Sigmund Freud's (1856–1939) *Totem and Taboo* (1913).

poses the criminal charge of "assault" ever found its way to the law books (evolved as it was by *male* representatives of social authority who could not apparently find within *themselves* justification for such behavior regardless of the sex of the victim).

Many men have cast wary eyes at the false crutches handed their sex: 13
Shakespeare toyed freely with pompous assumptions of masculine superiority in several of his works; Mark Twain in his witticisms; Zola in his novels; Frederick Douglass from the antislavery podium; August Bebel in his great studies; John Stuart Mill in his essays; Whitman in his poetry; William Godwin in the stuff of his life and his writings; Karl Marx in the development of his economic theories; and, of course, in our own time, George Bernard Shaw in almost every wise and irreverent word he wrote. None of these figures found themselves diminished by an impending "threat" of the equality of women; most of them took the position that its accomplishment bode but another aspect of the liberation of *men,* in all senses of that mighty word.

It required, in fact, the industrial revolution and the winds of *égalité* from   14
the American and French revolutions before history could thrust forward a woman to set down the case for the "Rights of Woman" in 1792. That the brilliant Jacobin Englishwoman Mary Wollstonecraft did so raised all the stormy outrage that the conservative thinkers of her time, male and female, could muster.* That the outrage has lingered and all but obscured her name and her book is a revealing indicator of the unfinished character of what is sometimes called, improperly, the "sexual revolution."

It is worth the digression to remark that whole generations have come   15
to maturity believing that "feminists," upper- or lowercase, were strident, ludicrous creatures in incongruous costumes of feathered hats and oversized bloomers, who marched about, mainly through the saloons of the land, conking poor, peaceful, beer-guzzling males over the head. The image successfully erases a truer and more cogent picture. In deed and oratory, in their recognition of direct political action as opposed to parlor and bedroom wheedling of husbands and fathers as the true key to social transformation, American Feminist leaders, in particular, set a path that a grateful society will undoubtedly, in time, celebrate. The scope of their understanding of the evils of their times is summed up magnificently in a portion of a speech by Susan B. Anthony as she addressed the court where she was being sentenced to jail for voting in the state of New York in 1879: "Your denial of my right to vote is the denial of my right of consent as one of the governed, the denial of my right of representation as one of the taxed, the denial of my right to a trial by a jury of my peers. . . . But, yesterday, the same man-made forms of law declared it a crime punishable with a $1,000 fine and six months' imprisonment, for you, or me, or any of us, to give a cup of cold water, a crust of bread, or a night's shelter to a panting fugitive as he was tracking his way to Canada. And every man or woman in whose veins coursed a drop of human sympathy violated that wicked law, reckless of consequences, and was justified in doing

*A reference to Mary Wollstonecraft's (1759–1797) *Vindication of the Rights of Woman* (1792), a powerful attack on sexist conventions and assumptions.

so. As then, the slaves who got their freedom must yet take it over, or under, or through the unjust forms of law, precisely so now must women, to get their right to a voice in this Government, take it; I have taken mine, and mean to take it at every possible opportunity."

This thrilling American patriot, not less than the Franklin radicals or the   16
Jeffersonian democrats—and like scores of other Feminists—put her comfort, and in some brutal instances her very life, upon the line in order to do no more and certainly no less than enlarge the Constitutional promises of the American Republic to include the largest numbers of its people of both sexes. As is apparent from the text of her speech she and the other leaders of the Feminist movement (Lucretia Mott, Elizabeth Cady Stanton, Sojourner Truth, and Harriet Tubman, among many*) gave equally of their energies to the greatest issue of their time, the antislavery struggle, as their spiritual descendants were to give theirs, in another period, to prison reform, the eradication of illiteracy, conservation, and the crowning achievement of the abolition of child labor. We might well long for the day when the knowledge of the debt all society owes to organized womanhood in bringing the human race closer together, not pushing it farther apart, will still the laughter in the throats of the now uninformed.

Nonetheless, the lingering infamy in which "feminism" is generally   17
held helps to explain the mystery of the widespread notion that the emancipation of the modern American woman is an accomplished fact, despite all evidence that she does not universally get "equal pay for equal work," that she is discouraged flatly in many occupations and government posts, and that her advance into executive positions is held stringently in check. It also helps to explain the eager mythology of the "tyranny of women" who allegedly rule over the home and even the wealth of the nation. In his book *America as a Civilization,* Max Lerner replies to the myth thusly: "The catch is that women hold their purchasing power largely as wives and have acquired their wealth mainly as widows; economically they are disbursing agents, not principals. . . . The real control of the wealth is in the hands of male trustees, lawyers and bankers. Few women are directors of big corporations, just as there are few who form government policies. . . . The minority of women who are powerful in their ownership of wealth are functionless with respect to their wealth, because they lack strategic control of it."

As for the "tyranny of Mom," Mom has been effectively toppled from   18
her pedestal without society taking a second look to discover, if all those dreadful things are really true about her, *how* she got that way. Our culture has been slow to assume responsibility for ordinary women who have been told, starting with the cradle, that home and husband and children will be the sources of all reward in life, the foundations of all true happiness; it has had almost nothing to say about what she should do with herself when the children are grown and her husband is exhausted and bored with excessive

*Lucretia Mott (1793–1880), feminist and reformer; Elizabeth Cady Stanton (1815–1902), feminist and co-worker with Anthony (see above); Sojourner Truth (c. 1797–1883), former slave and feminist (see above); Harriet Tubman (1820?–1913), fugitive slave and rescuer of slaves.

attention, preoccupied as he is with other aspects of the world. Mah-jongg and matinees in the city seem to her to lack purpose, and, whether we like it or not, that is the thing that human beings tend to crave: purpose.

The glaring fact is that Mom's life needs liberation as much as everyone   19
else's. To say so is to be thought of as attacking the "bedrock of our way of life" and all of that, but it must be said. Mom must be allowed to think of herself, as Simone de Beauvoir has insisted brilliantly,* as a human being first and a mother second. Housewives insist on identifying themselves, to the frustration of the experts, as *"only* housewives" because, apparently, they perceive that housework and care of the family is but humankind's necessity of function: things requisite to existence; essentials which should permit us to . . . something else. We do not live to wash our faces and eat our meals, we wash our faces and eat our meals in order to participate in the world: in the classroom, in the factory, in the office, in the shop, in the national and international halls of government, in the scientific laboratory and in the studios where the arts are created. *The Feminists did not create the housewife's dissatisfaction with her lot—the Feminists came from out of the only place they could have come—the housewives of the world!* Satisfaction for the housewife, then, lies not in a new program of propaganda to exalt what remains, and always will remain, drudgery; but in the continued effort to reduce it to a hardly perceptible (if ever necessary) interruption in the pursuit of productive labors and creative expression. Satisfaction lies in allowing and encouraging men to freely assume more and more equal relationship with their children and their wives. The argument against this is difficult to understand since the more interesting the lives of the parents (both parents), the more interesting we have every right to expect future generations to be.

One area of the national life where the estate of woman is certainly   20
never debated, and may be passed over quickly, is in the newest crop of "For Men Only" magazines where the whole thing has been resolved by reducing the entire relationship between men and women to a long and rather boring (not to add mechanical) tableaux of simple-minded and degrading animal essences. There, Woman the Child, Woman the Animal, Woman Upside-down-and-naked, Woman the Harem Fantasy—is replete with no conflict and no aspiration, the sex-object of men who cannot fathom the nature of their own delusions. The symptomatic fumes of Romanesque decay which exude from the same pages, where some of the world's most established writers are obliged, like musicians in a whorehouse, to appear between "play-mates," is stultifying. To say so, however, is not to long for a new wave of "banning": that unfortunate practice always ends up by lynching the brave new thoughts in the world and merely covering up our social filth. It is to long for a deeper appraisal of what we really want for ourselves and our children; to long for a cultural climate where Mrs. Roosevelt's† image will be projected

*In *The Second Sex* (1949).
†Eleanor Roosevelt (1884–1962), widow of President Franklin D. Roosevelt, was the first U.S. delegate to the United Nations (1945) and one of the authors of the Universal Declaration of Human Rights (1948).

to our young men and women with more regularity than the current courtesans.

It is, finally, a longing that another generation of girls will not have to 21 grow up under a certain pragmatism which insists that men do not like "brainy" women. That notion is a terrible cheat to all, and one of the most belittling indictments of men. Girls are better taught to "reach for the stars" even in the matter of seeking or accepting a mate. The grim possibility is that she who "hides her brains" will, more than likely, end up with a mate who is only equal to a woman with "hidden brains" or none at all. That hardly gives the children of such a union a robust start in life. To hide one's mental capacity is a personality disfigurement which is even more grotesque than to flaunt it—which, at least, boasts *pride.*

There *are* men who find love affairs of stature enough. Men who neither 22 desire nor tolerate affected vacuity: who wish mutuality and stimulation. In this writer's experience *those* are the exciting men; they exist. A woman who is willing to be herself and pursue her own potentials—it is time it was said—runs not so much the risk of loneliness as the challenge of exposure to more interesting men—and people in general.

There are, it is true, perhaps larger numbers of men who have mis- 23 taken WOMAN herself for the antagonism between the sexes. And, heaven knows, women passionately, often hysterically, feed the delusion. But it *is* a delusion: it is the codified barriers *between* the sexes that cause the trouble. Accordingly, some men are overwhelmed by the pressures upon their "masculinity" as they understand it, and move through life in perpetual states of agitation because, they are certain, of their persecution by women. Some of them, a few, become pathological woman-haters and proceed to hate all women: those in their "place" at home; and those "out of it." They have hatred of the women who will not sleep with them and hatred for those who will. Their hostility should not be met with hostility: they are frightened and pathetic human beings, as much caught in a social trap as their feminine counterparts who, it is true, get more and uglier attention in popular conversation and literature. These people are the most extreme victims of the *inequality* between the sexes; the rest of us are victims in other ways. In their situation, a member of the opposite sex does not have to open his or her mouth, they just have to *be* and they have offended. The weight is put upon our shoulders when we are hardly out of the womb, *all* of us, and it is more than a little tragic, this exaggerated sense of alienation from one another that we are taught. Having paid such terrible prices for it, need we despair for its passing?

With the barriers should go many of the arbitrary definitions struc- 24 tured into our very language from out of the past: the classification of occupations, activities, roles by gender; the built-in assumption of maleness in certain words; the adjectives which still confuse and confine us in our thinking and make it possible for serious sociologists and psychologists to draw conclusions from "masculine-feminine" charts which are based on nothing other than conditioned concepts of what is "natural" (for whom?). Within that scale, male journalists, firemen and policemen have scored "less masculine" than other men, such as laborers, because of their occupational interest in "womanish" concerns like the human condition and saving lives! Among women, domestic servants score the highest "femininity" ratings of all—because of their demonstrated "interest" in cleaning house!

At the heart of this incredible mish-mosh of nonsense is the time-honored but perfectly silly habit of attributing to a given set of universally human capacities a qualification which implies that they are unique to one sex, race, or culture. (It is by that outrage that the people of Europe and their descendants in North America innocently go on speaking of objective adjectives such as "modern" or even "progressive" as if they were virtually synonymous with the geographical noun "the West"—to the wonder (and fury) of at least two-thirds of the world. Modern ideas, one notes, function elsewhere and, in some instances, these days especially, with greater acceleration. It was not "the West," after all, that first punctured space* and it is the women of Ghana who vote and the women of Switzerland who do not.) Thus, women who seek objective fulfillment as people are not trying to be "men" (or good or bad "imitations" of them)—they are trying to be successful human beings.

Finally, it is not to be doubted that our clinging to the habits of the past gives all of us some comfort in this thus-far-unexplained universe: it is always reassuring to think that our ancestors "did it" the same way. But in medicine the price of dogged superstition has too often been death, and in all human affairs there comes a time—to let go. With regard to the sexual connotations of words, can we all not think of what a dream will be realized for the race when the noun "soldier," for example, ceases to conjure up romantic notions of masculinity, but will instead have been unsexed and (at long last) put in its true place in history by the more accurate associations it recalls: "tragedy . . . the organized waste of human life and potential"?

None of this, we can rest easy, will dissipate the *true* distinction between the sexes: that will not happen because nobody *desires* for it to happen. The French have remarked on that matter for all time†—to which one need only add another *"Vive!"*

*The Russians launched *Sputnik,* the first rocket-fueled satellite, in 1957.

†A reference to the French adage *Vive la différence*—"Long live the difference" (between men and women).

Questions for Discussion

1. Although a feminist essay, "In Defense of the Equality of *Men*" discusses men more than it discusses women. Is the title merely ironic? Is it ironic at all? If so, what is ironic about it? If it is ironic, who or what is being attacked? If Hansberry seriously desires the equality of men, what reasons does she offer and what social or psychological forces does she think oppose it?

2. As a dramatist, Hansberry captures the rhythms of spoken speech so masterfully that she manages to make even a prose essay sound like an extended monologue delivered by a lively, intelligent, and passionate speaker. This essay does not sound like an academically sanitized meditation. Demonstrate Hansberry's grasp of vernacular by reading paragraphs aloud in class, noting that Hansberry frequently uses sentence fragments where they would be used in spoken speech and even relies on a few slangy colloqualisms. Does this colloquial tone work throughout the essay, or does the author at times diminish the seriousness of her argument by lapsing too far into an unserious tone?

3. When Hansberry wrote this essay in 1961, she thought it accurate to refer to "the lingering infamy in which 'feminism' is generally held" (¶17). Do you think this description is still accurate, or do you think that society has come to accept feminism as socially and intellectually respectable? How many men and women in your class would not object to being identified in the campus newspaper—during an interview, say—as a "feminist"? How many men would object (or would not object) to dating a woman who called herself a feminist? Do the tallies produced by these questions surprise you? If so, can you identify the source of your mistaken predictions?

4. Ask each person in your class to write a one-word definition of "feminism," and then have each person read the definition aloud. If there is little agreement, are there at least any *patterns* of meaning, and can the class agree on an operational definition to use for the remainder of the discussion?

5. In paragraph 21 Hansberry refers to the often-repeated belief that men do not like "brainy women." What is the response to this assertion among the men and women in your class? Can any of the women recount the personal experience of feeling social pressure to disguise their intelligence or to remain silent about their superior grasp of information so as not to perform better than boys in school? Can any of the men contradict or corroborate the assertion on the basis of their personal experience? If some men in class admit to not liking "brainy women," what reasons do they offer?

Suggested Essay Topics

1. By using such reference works as the *Social Sciences and Humanities Index* and the *Readers' Guide to Periodical Literature,* find some anti-feminist essays from

roughly the same period as Hansberry's essay and compare one of the best-written of them with Hansberry's, pointing out to your audience (your own classmates) the opposing theses and the quality of the supporting arguments that each author uses.

2. Keeping the subtitle of this chapter—"What Should I Become?"—in mind, direct an essay to your classmates in which you discuss how the messages about sexuality and sex roles that you have heard all your life from family, relatives, and community (school, church, friends, and so on) have affected your sense of the possibilities of what you may or may not become. Note the strengths or anxieties that have been programmed into you by these messages, and give a concrete picture of the person you hope to become, focusing specifically on the role you expect to play as a man or woman relating to members of the opposite sex as mates, co-workers, and friends.

IDEAS IN DEBATE

St. Paul
Bertrand Russell
Shirley Jackson

St. Paul

Of all the parts of the New Testament, the thirteenth chapter of First Corinthians is probably better known than any except the stories about Christ's birth. It is quoted so often that readers may rush through the familiar words with the impression that they are easy to understand. But everyone who studies them carefully will find that the chapter can yield more than one meaning. Part of our difficulty is that translators do not agree on the best English equivalent for the Greek word agape, *here translated as* love. *The translators who wrote the King James Version of the Bible, nearly four centuries ago, chose* charity. *Both of these English terms are deeply ambiguous, even more ambiguous, scholars tell us, than* agape, *which was distinguished by the Greeks from the term for sexual love (*eros*) and the term for loving friendship (*philia*).*

Obviously, some of the meanings that we associate with either English term cannot possibly fit what Paul claims to be the most important of all human spiritual qualities: Agape *has nothing to do with such phrases as "to* love *sport" or "to give generously to a* charity.*" But the difficulties we find here in determining meaning run far deeper than simply explaining the Greek words that lie behind the English. Paul is attempting to describe a condition of the soul that is essentially beyond literal definition; no words for that condition could ever be freed of all vagueness. Whatever Paul means by* love *or* charity, *it is not something that could be pinned down once and for all. In talking of such matters, he cannot avoid a tone that is oblique, suggestive, oracular, or even a bit gnomic. It is as if he had just come down from a mountaintop with a message from God. (See discussion questions 4–8 for "I Owe Nothing to My Brothers" by Ayn Rand, pp. 256–257.)*

We suggest that you read the passage several times, aloud and silently, first in the modern translation that we reprint from the New English Bible and then in a copy of the King James Version. You will probably find, like many another student of the chapter, that even after studying it for an hour or so you are still puzzled about many words and phrases. You may also find, like many readers before you, that the puzzlement is part of the power the words contain. Though all guides to good writing tell us to be "as clear as possible," some of the world's greatest writing is about matters that can never be reduced to clear and simple propositions.

Of course some statements that offer multiple suggestions and meanings may appear *to be rich when they are not; they may be merely confused or even badly written. Unfortunately, there is no infallible test in reading prose for separating real gold from fool's gold. Readers are forced to rely on the same powers of judgment and discrimination in reading prose as they use when "reading" people. We meet phonies both in person and in prose, but by keeping a sharp eye for details and a sharp ear for tone we can separate truly rich writing from the merely muddled.*

What we can certainly become clear about is the source of our problems. As you prepare for class discussion, try to determine the sources both of what hostile critics would call vagueness and of what friendly readers might call spiritual richness. Can you see why such a passage would have become one of the most frequently quoted religious pronouncements of all time?

Note that we print the traditional verse numbers as well as our usual paragraph numbers.

I CORINTHIANS 13

And now I will show you the best way of all. 1

¹I may speak in tongues of men or of angels, but if I am without love, 2
I am a sounding gong or a clanging cymbal. ²I may have the gift of prophecy, and know every hidden truth; I may have faith strong enough to move mountains; but if I have no love, I am nothing. ³I may dole out all I possess, or even give my body to be burnt, but if I have no love, I am none the better.

⁴Love is patient; love is kind and envies no one. Love is never boastful, ⁵nor conceited, nor rude; never selfish, not quick to take offence. Love keeps 3
no score of wrongs; ⁶does not gloat over other men's sins, but delights in the truth. ⁷There is nothing love cannot face; there is no limit to its faith, its hope, and its endurance.

⁸Love will never come to an end. Are there prophets? their work will 4
be over. Are there tongues of ecstasy? they will cease. Is there knowledge? it will vanish away; ⁹for our knowledge and our prophecy alike are partial, ¹⁰and the partial vanishes when wholeness comes. ¹¹When I was a child, my speech, my outlook, and my thoughts were all childish. When I grew up, I had finished with childish things. ¹²Now we see only puzzling reflections in a mirror, but then we shall see face to face. My knowledge now is partial; then it will be whole, like God's knowledge of me. ¹³In a word, there are three things that last for ever: faith, hope, and love; but the greatest of them all is love.

Questions for Discussion

1. As we have suggested, guides to good writing often tell us that if a passage is written well, the reader should be able to summarize its meaning in one sentence. Can you summarize Paul's meaning in a sentence? In a paragraph? If so, can you get all other members of the class to accept your summary? If your class cannot agree on a summary, does this show the passage to be bad writing?

2. How would you state the purpose of the passage? Does it seem to be different from the meaning? Can you see anything in the purpose you have described that would force an author to be vague in meaning? Can you see any way in which an author could write with simple clarity about such matters?

3. How is the chapter organized? Do all of the sentences in each paragraph contribute to the same general point, as your own sentences are often expected to do? (Note that the paragraphing has been provided by modern translators; only the verse divisions appear in earlier printings.) What is the effect of the passage's organization?

4. We could describe verses 4–7 as Paul's effort to define an indefinable word by giving examples of what love *is,* while verses 1–3 give examples of what love *is not.* Do you see anything in either set of examples that would explain why modern translators would find the word *love* to be clearer than the word *charity?*

Suggested Essay Topics

1. Make a short list of words that might carry some of the meaning that Paul gives to *agape;* for example, *generosity, fellow feeling, compassion, sympathy,* or *large-mindedness.* Then write a brief paper (no more than one page) defending or rejecting the one that seems most nearly adequate or most inadequate for its job in Paul's chapter.

2. Choose some general quality or trait that you admire in other people; if possible, find one that you admire more than any other. Don't worry about whether it is one that everyone else would value to the same degree; after all, Paul must have known that many of his readers would disagree with his praise of love/charity/*agape,* or he would not have troubled to write his "praise poem." Write a passage praising the quality you have chosen; "imitate" Paul as much as you like, but try to find language that you think will appeal not only to your classmates but to all the world.

Bertrand Russell

Bertrand Russell (1872–1970) was a mathematician, social activist, controversialist, and philosopher, unquestionably one of the most influential of twentieth-century authors. In scores of books, he expressed strong opinions about a great many subjects, including education, sexual behavior, Christianity (see pp. 478–487), and the stockpiling of nuclear weapons. He particularly detested the last two.

Whatever his topic, he always expresses himself in an enviably straightforward, vigorous prose, the kind that looks easy to write—until one tries to duplicate its combination of relaxed ease and taut muscularity. His critics have called his prose "slick," but everyone acknowledges its power.

In The Conquest of Happiness, *Russell examines happiness as a human objective and argues that its acquisition is neither as difficult nor as elusive as most people think. In the selection reprinted here he focuses on two variables, one working against happiness and the other for it. Avoiding the first, sickly self-absorption, will prevent us from straying from the main road to happiness. Achieving the second, robust zest, will carry us toward our destination in the straightest possible line.*

As you read, try to decide whether Russell gives you adequate or clear advice about how to be happy and whether he himself sounds genuinely happy or merely resigned to a disappointing world.

HAPPINESS

From chapter 1, "What Makes People Unhappy?"; chapter 10, "Is Happiness Still Possible?"; and chapter 11, "Zest," of *The Conquest of Happiness* (1930). The title is ours.

Perhaps the best introduction to the philosophy [of happiness] which I wish to advocate will be a few words of autobiography. I was not born happy. As a child, my favorite hymn was: "Weary of earth and laden with my sin." At the age of five, I reflected that, if I should live to be seventy, I had only endured, so far, a fourteenth part of my whole life, and I felt the long-spread-out boredom ahead of me to be almost unendurable. In adolescence, I hated life and was continually on the verge of suicide, from which, however, I was restrained by the desire to know more mathematics. Now, on the contrary, I enjoy life; I might almost say that with every year that passes I enjoy it more. This is due partly to having discovered what were the things that I most desired, and having gradually acquired many of these things. Partly it is due to having successfully dismissed certain objects of desire—such as the acquisition of indubitable knowledge about something or other—as essentially unattainable. But very largely it is due to a diminishing preoccupation with myself. Like others who had a Puritan education, I had the habit of meditating on my sins, follies, and shortcomings. I seemed to myself—no doubt justly—a miserable specimen. Gradually I learned to be indifferent to myself and my deficiencies; I came to center my attention increasingly upon external

1

objects: the state of the world, various branches of knowledge, individuals for whom I felt affection. External interests, it is true, bring each its own possibility of pain: the world may be plunged in war, knowledge in some direction may be hard to achieve, friends may die. But pains of these kinds do not destroy the essential quality of life, as do those that spring from disgust with self. And every external interest inspires some activity which, so long as the interest remains alive, is a complete preventive of *ennui* [boredom]. Interest in oneself, on the contrary, leads to no activity of a progressive kind. It may lead to the keeping of a diary, to getting psychoanalyzed, or perhaps to becoming a monk. But the monk will not be happy until the routine of the monastery has made him forget his own soul. The happiness which he attributes to religion he could have obtained from becoming a crossing-sweeper, provided he were compelled to remain one. External discipline is the only road to happiness for those unfortunates whose self-absorption is too profound to be cured in any other way.

. . .

Happiness is of two sorts, though, of course, there are intermediate degrees. The two sorts I mean might be distinguished as plain and fancy, or animal and spiritual, or of the heart and of the head. The designation to be chosen among these alternatives depends, of course, upon the thesis to be proved. I am at the moment not concerned to prove any thesis, but merely to describe. Perhaps the simplest way to describe the difference between the two sorts of happiness is to say that one sort is open to any human being, and the other only to those who can read and write. When I was a boy I knew a man bursting with happiness whose business was digging wells. He was of enormous height and of incredible muscles; he could neither read nor write, and when in the year 1885 he got a vote for Parliament,* he learnt for the first time that such an institution existed. His happiness did not depend upon intellectual sources; it was not based upon belief in natural law, or the perfectibility of the species, or the public ownership of public utilities, or the ultimate triumph of the Seventh Day Adventists, or any of the other creeds which intellectuals consider necessary to their enjoyment of life. It was based upon physical vigor, a sufficiency of work, and the overcoming of not insuperable obstacles in the shape of rock. The happiness of my gardener is of the same species; he wages a perennial war against rabbits, of which he speaks exactly as Scotland Yard† speaks of Bolsheviks;‡ he considers them dark, designing and ferocious, and is of opinion that they can only be met by means of a cunning equal to their own. Like the heroes of Valhalla§ who spent every day hunting a certain wild boar, which they killed every evening but which miraculously came to life again in the morning, my gardener can slay his

*1884 was the year that the right to vote was extended to all men (not women) in England.
†British counterpart of the FBI.
‡The revolutionary wing of the Russian Social Democratic party that seized supreme power in Russia during the Revolution (1917–1920).
§In Norse mythology, the eternal home of slain warriors.

Zest → Keen Enjoyment or gusto

enemy one day without any fear that the enemy will have disappeared the next day. Although well over seventy, he works all day and bicycles sixteen hilly miles to and from his work, but the fount of joy is inexhaustible, and it is "they rabbits" that supply it.

. . .

Thesis The secret of happiness is this: let your interests be as wide as possible, (3) and let your reactions to the things and persons that interest you be as far as possible friendly rather than hostile.

. . .

I [now] propose to deal with what seems to me the most universal and   4 distinctive mark of happy men, namely, zest, —*Stipulative def.*

Perhaps the best way to understand what is meant by zest will be to   5 consider the different ways in which men behave when they sit down to a meal. There are those to whom a meal is merely a bore; no matter how excellent the food may be, they feel that it is uninteresting. They have had excellent food before, probably at almost every meal they have eaten. They have never known what it was to go without a meal until hunger became a raging passion, but have come to regard meals as merely conventional occurrences, dictated by the fashions of the society in which they live. Like everything else, meals are tiresome, but it is no use to make a fuss, because nothing else will be less tiresome. Then there are the invalids who eat from a sense of duty, because the doctor has told them that it is necessary to take a little nourishment in order to keep up their strength. Then there are the epicures, who start hopefully, but find that nothing has been quite so well cooked as it ought to have been. Then there are the gormandizers, who fall upon their food with eager rapacity, eat too much, and grow plethoric and stertorous. Finally there are those who begin with sound appetite are glad of their food, eat until they have had enough, and then stop. Those who are set down before the feast of life have similar attitudes towards the good things which it offers. The happy man corresponds to the last of our eaters. What hunger is in relation to food, zest is in relation to life. The man who is bored with his meals corresponds to the victim of Byronic unhappiness. The invalid who eats from a sense of duty corresponds to the ascetic, the gormandizer to the voluptuary. The epicure corresponds to the fastidious person who condemns half the pleasures of life as unaesthetic. Oddly enough all these types, with the possible exception of the gormandizer, despise the man of healthy appetite and consider themselves his superiors. It seems to them vulgar to enjoy food because you are hungry or to enjoy life because it offers a variety of interesting spectacles and surprising experiences. From the height of their disillusionment they look down upon those whom they despise as simple souls. For my part, I have no sympathy with this outlook. All disenchantment is to me a malady, which, it is true, certain circumstances may render inevitable, but which none the less, when it occurs, is to be cured as soon as possible, not to be regarded as a higher form of wisdom. Suppose one man likes strawberries and another does not; in what respect is the latter superior? There is no abstract and impersonal proof either that strawberries are good or that they are not good. To the man who likes them they are good, to the man who dislikes them they are not. But the man who likes them has a pleasure which the other does not have; to that extent his life is more enjoyable and he is better adapted to the world in which both must live. What is true in this trivial instance is equally true in more important matters. The man who enjoys watching football is to that extent superior to the man who does not. The man who enjoys reading is still more superior to the man who does not, since opportunities for reading are more frequent than opportunities for watching football. The more things a man is interested in, the more opportunities of happiness he has and the less he is at the mercy of fate, since if he loses one thing he can fall back upon another. Life is too short to be interested in everything, but it is good to be interested in as many things as are necessary to fill our days. We are all prone to the malady of the introvert, who, with the manifold spectacle of the world spread out before him, turns away and gazes only upon the emptiness within. But let us not imagine that there is anything grand about the introvert's unhappiness.

There were once upon a time two sausage machines, exquisitely constructed for the purpose of turning pig into the most delicious sausages. One of these retained his zest for pig and produced sausages innumerable, the other said: "What is pig to me? My own works are far more interesting and wonderful than any pig." He refused pig and set to work to study his inside. When bereft of its natural food, his inside ceased to function, and the more he studied it, the more empty and foolish it seemed to him to be. All the exquisite apparatus by which the delicious transformation had hitherto been made stood still, and he was at a loss to guess what it was capable of doing. This second sausage machine was like the man who has lost his zest, while the first was like the man who has retained it. The mind is a strange machine which can combine the materials offered to it in the most astonishing ways, but without materials from the external world it is powerless, and unlike the sausage machine it must seize its materials for itself, since events only become experiences through the interest that we take in them: if they do not interest us, we are making nothing of them. The man, therefore, whose attention is turned within finds nothing worthy of his notice, whereas the man whose attention is turned outward can find within, in those rare moments when he examines his soul, the most varied and interesting assortment of ingredients being dissected and recombined into beautiful or instructive patterns.

The forms of zest are innumerable. Sherlock Holmes, it may be remembered, picked up a hat which he happened to find lying in the street. After looking at it for a moment he remarked that its owner had come down in the world as the result of drink and that his wife was no longer so fond of him as she used to be. Life could never be boring to a man to whom casual objects offered such a wealth of interest. Think of the different things that may be noticed in the course of a country walk. One man may be interested in the birds, another in the vegetation, another in the geology, yet another in the agriculture, and so on. Any one of these things is interesting if it interests you, and, other things being equal, the man who is interested in any one of them is a man better adapted to the world than the man who is not interested.

How extraordinarily different, again, are the attitudes of different people to their fellow men! One man, in the course of a long train journey, will fail entirely to observe any of his fellow travelers, while another will have summed them all up, analyzed their characters, made a shrewd guess at their circumstances, and perhaps even ascertained the most secret histories of several of them. People differ just as much in what they feel towards others as in what they ascertain about them. Some men find almost everybody boring, others quickly and easily develop a friendly feeling towards those with whom they are brought in contact, unless there is some definite reason for feeling otherwise. Take again such a matter as travel; some men will travel through many countries, going always to the best hotels, eating exactly the same food as they would eat at home, meeting the same idle rich whom they would meet at home, conversing on the same topics upon which they converse at their own dinner table. When they return, their only feeling is one of relief at having done with the boredom of expensive locomotion. Other men wherever they go see what is characteristic, make the acquaintance of people who typify the locality, observe whatever is of interest either historically or socially, eat the food of the country, learn its manners and its language, and come home with a new stock of pleasant thoughts for winter evenings.

In all these different situations the man who has the zest for life has the advantage over the man who has none. Even unpleasant experiences have their uses to him. I am glad to have smelt a Chinese crowd and a Sicilian village, though I cannot pretend that my pleasure was very great at the moment. Adventurous men enjoy shipwrecks, mutinies, earthquakes, conflagrations, and all kinds of unpleasant experiences, provided they do not go so far as to impair health. They say to themselves in an earthquake, for example, "So that is what an earthquake is like," and it gives them pleasure to have their knowledge of the world increased by this new item. It would not be true to say that such men are not at the mercy of fate, for if they should lose their health they would be very likely to lose their zest at the same time, though this is by no means certain. I have known men die at the end of years of slow torture, and yet retain their zest almost till the last moment. Some forms of ill health destroy zest, others do not. I do not know whether the biochemists are able as yet to distinguish between these kinds. Perhaps when biochemistry has made further advances we shall all be able to take tablets that will ensure our feeling an interest in everything, but until that day comes we are compelled to depend upon common-sense observation of life to judge what are the causes that enable some men to take an interest in everything, while compelling others to take an interest in nothing.

Zest is sometimes general, sometimes specialized. It may be very spe-   10
cialized indeed. Readers of Borrow* may remember a character who occurs
in "Lavengro." He had lost his wife, to whom he was devoted, and felt for
a time that life had grown utterly barren. But by profession he was a tea
merchant, and in order to endure life he taught himself unaided to read the
Chinese inscriptions on the tea chests that passed through his hands. In the
end this gave him a new interest in life, and he began to study with avidity
everything that concerned China. I have known men who were entirely
absorbed in the endeavor to find out all about the Gnostic heresy, and other
men whose principal interest lay in collating the manuscripts and early editions of Hobbes.† It is quite impossible to guess in advance what will interest
a man, but most men are capable of a keen interest in something or other, and
when once such an interest has been aroused their life becomes free from
tedium. Very specialized interests are, however, a less satisfactory source of
happiness than a general zest for life, since they can hardly fill the whole of
a man's time, and there is always the danger that he may come to know all
there is to know about the particular matter that has become his hobby.

It will be remembered that among our different types at the banquet we   11
included the gormandizer, whom we were not prepared to praise. The reader
may think that the man with zest whom we have been praising does not differ
in any definable way from the gormandizer. The time has come when we
must try to make the distinction between the two types more definite.

The ancients [i.e., the ancient Greeks], as every one knows, regarded   12
moderation as one of the essential virtues. Under the influence of romanticism and the French Revolution this view was abandoned by many, and
overmastering passions were admired, even if, like those of Byron's heroes,
they were of a destructive and antisocial kind. The ancients, however, were
clearly in the right. In the good life there must be a balance between different
activities, and no one of them must be carried so far as to make the others
impossible. The gormandizer sacrifices all other pleasures to that of eating,
and by so doing diminishes the total happiness of his life. Many other
passions besides eating may be carried to a like excess. The Empress Josephine
was a gormandizer in regard to clothes. At first Napoleon used to pay her
dressmaker's bills, though with continually increasing protest. At last he told
her that she really must learn moderation, and that in future he would only
pay her bills when the amount seemed reasonable. When her next dressmaker's bill came in, she was for a moment at her wit's end, but presently
she bethought herself of a scheme. She went to the War Minister and demanded that he should pay her bill out of the funds provided for the war.
Since he knew that she had the power to get him dismissed, he did so, and
the French lost Genoa in consequence. So at least some books say, though I
am not prepared to vouch for the exact truth of the story. For our purpose
it is equally apt whether true or an exaggeration, since it serves to show how

---

*George Henry Borrow (1803–1881), English author and linguist.
†Thomas Hobbes (1588–1679), English philosopher.

far the passion for clothes may carry a woman who has the opportunity to indulge it. Dipsomaniacs and nymphomaniacs are obvious examples of the same kind of thing. The principle in these matters is fairly obvious. All our separate tastes and desires have to fit into the general framework of life. If they are to be a source of happiness they must be compatible with health, with the affection of those whom we love, and with the respect of the society in which we live. Some passions can be indulged to almost any extent without passing beyond these limits, others cannot. The man, let us say, who loves chess, if he happens to be a bachelor with independent means, need not restrict his passion in any degree, whereas if he has a wife and children and no independent means, he will have to restrict it very severely. The dipsomaniac and the gormandizer, even if they have no social ties, are unwise from a self-regarding point of view, since their indulgence interferes with health, and gives them hours of misery in return for minutes of pleasure. Certain things form a framework within which any separate passion must live if it is not to become a source of misery. Such things are health, the general possession of one's faculties, a sufficient income to provide for necessaries, and the most essential social duties, such as those towards wife and children. The man who sacrifices these things for chess is essentially as bad as the dipsomaniac. The only reason we do not condemn him so severely is that he is much less common and that only a man of somewhat rare abilities is likely to be carried away by absorption in so intellectual a game. The Greek formula of moderation practically covers these cases. The man who likes chess sufficiently to look forward throughout his working day to the game that he will play in the evening is fortunate, but the man who gives up work in order to play chess all day has lost the virtue of moderation. It is recorded that Tolstoy, in his younger and unregenerate days, was awarded the military cross for valor in the field, but when the time came for him to be presented with it, he was so absorbed in a game of chess that he decided not to go. We can hardly find fault with Tolstoy on this account, since to him it might well be a matter of indifference whether he won military decorations or not; but in a lesser man such an act would have been one of folly.

As a limitation upon the doctrine that has just been set forth, it ought 13 to be admitted that some performances are considered so essentially noble as to justify the sacrifice of everything else on their behalf. The man who loses his life in the defense of his country is not blamed if thereby his wife and children are left penniless. The man who is engaged in experiments with a view to some great scientific discovery or invention is not blamed afterwards for the poverty that he has made his family endure, provided that his efforts are crowned with ultimate success. If, however, he never succeeds in making the discovery or the invention that he was attempting, public opinion condemns him as a crank, which seems unfair, since no one in such an enterprise can be sure of success in advance. During the first millennium of the Christian era a man who abandoned his family for a saintly life was praised, though nowadays it would be held that he ought to make some provision for them.

I think there is always some deep-seated psychological difference be- 14 tween the gormandizer and the man of healthy appetite. The man in whom one desire runs to excess at the expense of all others is usually a man with some deep-seated trouble, who is seeking escape from a specter. In the case of the dipsomaniac this is obvious: men drink in order to forget. If they had no specters in their lives, they would not find drunkenness more agreeable than sobriety. As the legendary Chinaman said: "Me no drinkee for drinkee, me drinkee for drunkee." This is typical of all excessive and one-sided passions. It is not pleasure in the object itself that is sought, but oblivion. There is, however, a very great difference according as oblivion is sought in a sottish manner or by the exercise of faculties in themselves desirable. Borrow's friend who taught himself Chinese in order to be able to endure the loss of his wife was seeking oblivion, but he sought it in an activity that had no harmful effects, but on the contrary improved his intelligence and his knowledge. Against such forms of escape there is nothing to be said. It is otherwise with the man who seeks oblivion in drinking or gambling or any other form of unprofitable excitement. There are, it is true, border-line cases. What should we say of the man who runs mad risks in aëroplanes or on mountain tops, because life has become irksome to him? If his risks serve any public object, we may admire him, but if not, we shall have to place him only slightly above the gambler and drunkard.

Genuine zest, not the sort that is really a search for oblivion, is part of 15 the natural make-up of human beings except in so far as it has been destroyed by unfortunate circumstances. Young children are interested in almost everything that they see and hear; the world is full of surprises to them, and they are perpetually engaged with ardor in the pursuit of knowledge, not, of course, of scholastic knowledge,* but of the sort that consists in acquiring familiarity with the objects that attract their attention. Animals, even when adult, retain their zest provided they are in health. A cat in an unfamiliar room will not sit down until it has sniffed at every corner on the off chance that there may be a smell of mouse somewhere. The man who has never been fundamentally thwarted will retain his natural interest in the external world, and so long as he retains it he will find life pleasant unless his liberty is unduly curtailed. Loss of zest in civilized society is very largely due to the restrictions upon liberty which are essential to our way of life. The savage hunts when he is hungry, and in so doing is obeying a direct impulse. The man who goes to his work every morning at a certain hour is actuated fundamentally by the same impulse, namely the need to secure a living, but in his case the impulse does not operate directly and at the moment when it is felt; it operates indirectly through abstractions, beliefs and volitions. At the moment when the man starts off to his work he is not feeling hungry, since he has just had his breakfast. He merely knows that hunger will recur, and that going to his work is a means of satisfying future hunger. Impulses are irregular, whereas habits, in a civilized society, have to be regular. Among savages, even collective enterprises, in so far as they exist, are spontaneous and impulsive. When

---

*Knowledge considered useless, irrelevant, and dull.

the tribe is going to war the tom-tom rouses military ardor, and herd excitement inspires each individual to the necessary activity. Modern enterprises cannot be managed in this way. When a train has to be started at a given moment it is impossible to inspire the porters, the engine driver and the signalman by means of barbaric music. Each of them must do his job merely because it has to be done. Their motive, that is to say, is indirect: they have no impulse towards the activity, but only towards the ultimate reward of the activity. A great deal of social life has the same defect. People converse with each other, not from any wish to do so, but because of some ultimate benefit that they hope to derive from cooperation. At every moment of life the civilized man is hedged about by restrictions of impulse: if he happens to feel cheerful he must not sing or dance in the street, while if he happens to feel sad he must not sit on the pavement and weep, for fear of obstructing pedestrian traffic. In youth his liberty is restricted at school, in adult life it is restricted throughout his working hours. All this makes zest more difficult to retain, for the continual restraint tends to produce weariness and boredom. Nevertheless, a civilized society is impossible without a very considerable degree of restraint upon spontaneous impulse, since spontaneous impulse will only produce the simplest forms of social cooperation, not those highly complex forms which modern economic organization demands. In order to rise above these obstacles to zest a man needs health and superabundant energy, or else, if he has that good fortune, work that he finds interesting on its own account. Health, so far as statistics can show, has been steadily improving in all civilized countries during the last hundred years, but energy is more difficult to measure, and I am doubtful whether physical vigor in moments of health is as great as it was formerly. The problem here is to a great extent a social problem, and as such I do not propose to discuss it in the present volume. The problem has, however, a personal and psychological aspect which we have already discussed in connection with fatigue. Some men retain their zest in spite of the handicaps of civilized life, and many men could do so if they were free from the inner psychological conflicts upon which a great part of their energy is expended. Zest demands energy more than sufficient for the necessary work, and this in turn demands the smooth working of the psychological machine. Of the causes promoting the smooth working I shall have more to say in later chapters. ●

Questions for Discussion

1. Russell begins by expressing an obvious contempt for self-absorption. "Interest in oneself," he says, ". . . leads to no activity of a progressive kind" (¶1). There has been an increasing emphasis in recent years on "learning to like your *self*," "learning to know the real *you*," "being in touch with your feelings"—phrases that suggest that we should constantly be

asking ourselves whether we are happy. Self-help therapies, counseling groups, human development seminars, and other group efforts designed to help people "work through their problems" have become everyday features of our social landscape. (The 1970s, for example, were labeled the "me" generation, and popular songs with titles like "[I Did It] My Way" and "I've Got To Be Me" expressed a general current during this decade.) Does Russell make a convincing argument against this sort of "interiorism"? Do you know many people who are preoccupied with their inner feelings? Are these people generally more or less sensitive to the feelings of others? More or less happy than others?

2. Is Russell's description of what he calls "plain" happiness, the sort that is "open to any human being" (¶2), something you know about from experience? Can you describe it in your own words based on your own knowledge? The distinction between happiness "of the heart and of the head" (¶2) is not a subtle one, but is it useful to Russell's purpose? What *is* Russell's purpose?

3. How many different types of eaters does Russell characterize in paragraph 5? Can you describe each of them clearly? What different attitudes toward life does each represent?

4. Do you agree with the analogy "What hunger is in relation to food, zest is in relation to life" (¶5)? Do you agree that zest (as Russell defines it) is an essential ingredient in happiness?

5. Is the analogy of the sausage-making machines (¶6) an effective device for showing the unhealthiness of too much introspection? Does it help make his point persuasive and forceful?

6. People of zest, as Russell describes them, are apparently a sort of ideal (although Russell does not explicitly say so), with perfect balance, all normal appetites, no excesses, no quirks, no self-absorptions, no self-induced miseries, and no nonsense about wanting more than is good for them. Do you know anyone like this? If not, does that make you doubt the validity of the characterization? Or can you accept it as a useful ideal even if you have never met its complete realization in life? Do you know various people whom you can plot along a continuum from less to more zestful?

7. Do you agree that the constraints of civilized living in complex societies tend to cut off spontaneity and thus thwart zest (¶15)? Does Russell's description of people who are unable to break into song when they feel happy (because modern society pressures us to be conventional) strike a sympathetic chord in you? Have you ever felt your own zest blocked by such pressure?

Suggested Essay Topics

1. Do you know people who fail to practice moderation—who "breathe, eat, and sleep" sports or music, for example—and seem happy doing so? If so,

address an argument to Russell himself, considering whether such immoderation is "good" for a person and whether the happiness one then feels is real or mistaken.

2. A recent survey has shown that people in their late teens and early twenties report themselves to be much less happy than people in their sixties do. Assuming that you have heard no more about the survey than that, write a thoughtful letter to the newspaper that reported the results, either explaining why people are happier after 60 than before 25 or arguing that the survey must have been oversimplified, confusing things like comfort or sleepiness or self-complacency with happiness, and things like restlessness, dissatisfaction, and insecurity with unhappiness.

Shirley Jackson

The subtitle of this chapter—"What Should I Become?"—asks a question about character. It does not ask who we want to be, as if all we had to do were to choose and then have the matter forever settled. It asks instead who we want to become, implying that character is not a static thing, that it is in constant formation as a consequence of the choices we make in everyday living. Earlier in this chapter, St. Paul provided us with one of our culture's most influential and long-lasting definitions of the goals of character. St. Paul states clearly that the goal of character is love: "In a word, there are three things that last forever: faith, hope, and love; but the greatest of them all is love" (p. 201).

Over the centuries this brief statement has seemed to many people to express a fundamental criterion of good character. Viewed as St. Paul seems to view it, the power to give and to receive love is the greatest source of good within and among individuals. With it one may be open to change and generous to others, for love unstops the ears and stirs the heart to charity. Those who can love may sometimes be weak and sometimes make mistakes, but they do not fall willingly into malice. Accepting love creates self-respect, and giving love creates fellow-feeling. Both are the enemy of malice. People who lack this power, however, may be led to malice through their own emptiness. They will be victims of whatever social forces get to them first. They will have no motives for generosity beyond their training in good manners or the promptings of self-interest and nothing to prop up their self-esteem but the goodwill of their neighbors, which must be purchased at the price of conforming to community conventions and accepted truths. People who cannot love can seldom afford to point out their neighbors' inadequacies, for they have no internal strength to fall back on if their neighbors reject them. They must thus pay the price of conformity even if the community's accepted truths are really cruel falsehoods.

In Shirley Jackson's (1919–1965) "Flower Garden" we see this principle illustrated and dramatized. A woman is jarred out of her ordinary habits and faced with a crisis: whether to challenge or to accept her community's racism. She is called upon to love another person, not romantically but charitably. She is called upon to be fair, decent, and just. Both her fundamental sympathies and her conscience stir her to answer this call with courage and justice. But to do so she must face the real possibility of losing her place in a small community where place is almost everything. She even faces the possibility, more remote but still real, of losing her home and family. In the midst of this dilemma her character hangs in the balance. Will she have enough courage? Does she love justice more than social position? She cannot dodge these issues. She must choose, and the choice she makes will constitute a decision about character, about who she is to become.

The narrator allows us to see that up to the present, Mrs. Winning has lived in a state of silent, resentful, incipient rebellion against the cold self-importance of her husband's family. She has longed for a life of independence symbolized by the cottage, and of passion and warmth symbolized by the flower garden. But when the opportunity of allying herself with another person who shares her longing for independence and warmth, and who is thus a natural friend and companion, brings her into conflict with her family's and community's disapproval, she cannot face her potential losses. We see her at the story's end turning away from new possibilities—new possibilities for herself, literally her "self," and her community—and turning toward conformity, toward sameness, and toward a falsehood that wounds both victim and victimizer.

As you read, compare Mrs. Winning's shaping of her character with that of Margaret Sanger (pp. 183–189), who also faced a crisis of character. Does St. Paul's formulation about love give you a way of explaining the differences between these two people? Would it be helpful to augment the religious perspective with theories of personality from psychology or sociology? Finally, regardless of what theories we appeal to, one fundamental question remains: What would each of us have done in Mrs. Winning's place? Surely we can see that to have chosen other than she did would have been costly. Who among us would have had the necessary strength to give and receive the needed love? There are no easy answers.

FLOWER GARDEN

From *The Lottery* (1948).

After living in an old Vermont manor house together for almost eleven years, the two Mrs. Winnings, mother and daughter-in-law, had grown to look a good deal alike, as women will who live intimately together, and work in the same kitchen and get things done around the house in the same manner. Although young Mrs. Winning had been a Talbot, and had dark hair which she wore cut short, she was now officially a Winning, a member of the oldest family in town, and her hair was beginning to grey where her mother-in-law's hair had greyed first, at the temples; they both had thin sharp-featured faces and eloquent hands, and sometimes when they were washing dishes or shelling peas or polishing silverware together, their hands, moving so quickly and similarly, communicated more easily and sympathetically than their minds ever could. Young Mrs. Winning thought sometimes, when she sat at the breakfast table next to her mother-in-law, with her baby girl in the high-chair close by, that they must resemble some stylized block print for a New England wallpaper; mother, daughter, and granddaughter, with perhaps Plymouth Rock or Concord Bridge in the background.

On this, as on other cold mornings, they lingered over their coffee,   2
unwilling to leave the big kitchen with the coal stove and the pleasant atmosphere of food and cleanliness, and they sat together silently sometimes until the baby had long finished her breakfast and was playing quietly in the special baby corner, where uncounted Winning children had played with almost identical toys from the same heavy wooden box.

"It seems as though spring would never come," young Mrs. Winning   3
said. "I get so tired of the cold."

"Got to be cold some of the time," her mother-in-law said. She began   4
to move suddenly and quickly, stacking plates, indicating that the time for sitting was over and the time for working had begun. Young Mrs. Winning, rising immediately to help, thought for the thousandth time that her mother-in-law would never relinquish the position of authority in her own house until she was too old to move before anyone else.

"And I wish someone would move into the old cottage," young Mrs.   5
Winning added. She stopped halfway to the pantry with the table napkins and said longingly, "If only *someone* would move in before spring." Young Mrs. Winning had wanted, long ago, to buy the cottage herself, for her husband to make with his own hands into a home where they could live with their children, but now, accustomed as she was to the big old house at the top of the hill where her husband's family had lived for generations, she had only a great kindness left toward the little cottage, and a wistful anxiety to see some happy young people living there. When she heard it was sold, as all the old houses were being sold in these days when no one could seem to find a newer place to live, she had allowed herself to watch daily for a sign that someone new was coming; every morning she glanced down from the back porch to see if there was smoke coming out of the cottage chimney, and every day going down the hill on her way to the store she hesitated past the cottage, watching carefully for the least movement within. The cottage had been sold in January and now, nearly two months later, even though it seemed prettier and less worn with the snow gently covering the overgrown garden and icicles in front of the blank windows, it was still forlorn and empty, despised since the day long ago when Mrs. Winning had given up all hope of ever living there.

Mrs. Winning deposited the napkins in the pantry and turned to tear   6
the leaf off the kitchen calendar before selecting a dish towel and joining her mother-in-law at the sink. "March already," she said despondently.

"They *did* tell me down at the store yesterday," her mother-in-law said,   7
"that they were going to start painting the cottage this week."

"Then that *must* mean someone's coming!"   8

"Can't take more than a couple of weeks to paint inside that little   9
house," old Mrs. Winning said.

It was almost April, however, before the new people moved in. The   10
snow had almost melted and was running down the street in icy, half-solid
rivers. The ground was slushy and miserable to walk on, the skies grey and
dull. In another month the first amazing green would start in the trees and
on the ground, but for the better part of April there would be cold rain and
perhaps more snow. The cottage had been painted inside, and new paper put
on the walls. The front steps had been repaired and new glass put into the
broken windows. In spite of the grey sky and the patches of dirty snow the
cottage looked neater and firmer, and the painters were coming back to do
the outside when the weather cleared. Mrs. Winning, standing at the foot of
the cottage walk, tried to picture the cottage as it stood now, against the
picture of the cottage she had made years ago, when she had hoped to live
there herself. She had wanted roses by the porch; that could be done, and the
neat colorful garden she had planned. She would have painted the outside
white, and that too might still be done. Since the cottage had been sold she
had not gone inside, but she remembered the little rooms, with the windows
over the garden that could be so bright with gay curtains and window boxes,
the small kitchen she would have painted yellow, the two bedrooms upstairs
with slanting ceilings under the eaves. Mrs. Winning looked at the cottage
for a long time, standing on the wet walk, and then went slowly on down
to the store.

The first news she had of the new people came, at last, from the grocer   11
a few days later. As he was tying the string around the three pounds of
hamburger the large Winning family would consume in one meal, he asked
cheerfully, "Seen your new neighbors yet?"

"Have they moved in?" Mrs. Winning asked. "The people in the cot-   12
tage?"

"Lady in here this morning," the grocer said. "Lady and a little boy,   13
seem like nice people. They say her husband's dead. Nice-looking lady."

Mrs. Winning had been born in the town and the grocer's father had   14
given her jawbreakers and licorice in the grocery store while the present
grocer was still in high school. For a while, when she was twelve and the
grocer's son was twenty, Mrs. Winning had hoped secretly that he would
want to marry her. He was fleshy now, and middle-aged, and although he
still called her Helen and she still called him Tom, she belonged now to the
Winning family and had to speak critically to him, no matter how unwill-
ingly, if the meat were tough or the butter price too high. She knew that
when he spoke of the new neighbor as a "lady" he meant something different than if he had spoken of her as a "woman" or a "person." Mrs. Winning knew that he spoke of the two Mrs. Winnings to his other customers

as "ladies." She hesitated and then asked, "Have they really moved in to stay?"

"She'll have to stay for a while," the grocer said drily. "Bought a week's 15 worth of groceries."

Going back up the hill with her package Mrs. Winning watched all the 16 way to detect some sign of the new people in the cottage. When she reached the cottage walk she slowed down and tried to watch not too obviously. There was no smoke coming from the chimney, and no sign of furniture near the house, as there might have been if people were still moving in, but there was a middle-aged car parked in the street before the cottage and Mrs. Winning thought she could see figures moving past the windows. On a sudden irresistible impulse she turned and went up the walk to the front porch, and then, after debating for a moment, on up the steps to the door. She knocked, holding her bag of groceries in one arm, and then the door opened and she looked down on a little boy, about the same age, she thought happily, as her own son.

"Hello," Mrs. Winning said.   17

"Hello," the boy said. He regarded her soberly.   18

"Is your mother here?" Mrs. Winning asked. "I came to see if I could 19 help her move in."

"We're all moved in," the boy said. He was about to close the door, but 20 a woman's voice said from somewhere in the house, "Davey? Are you talking to someone?"

"That's my mommy," the little boy said. The woman came up behind 21 him and opened the door a little wider. "Yes?" she said.

Mrs. Winning said, "I'm Helen Winning. I live about three houses up 22 the street, and I thought perhaps I might be able to help you."

"Thank you," the woman said doubtfully. She's younger than I am, 23 Mrs. Winning thought, she's about thirty. And pretty. For a clear minute Mrs. Winning saw why the grocer had called her a lady.

"It's so nice to have someone living in this house," Mrs. Winning said 24 shyly. Past the other woman's head she could see the small hallway, with the larger living-room beyond and the door on the left going into the kitchen, the stairs on the right, with the delicate stair-rail newly painted; they had done the hall in light green, and Mrs. Winning smiled with friendship at the woman in the doorway, thinking, She *has* done it right; this is the way it should look after all, she knows about pretty houses.

After a minute the other woman smiled back, and said, "Will you come 25 in?"

As she stepped back to let Mrs. Winning in, Mrs. Winning wondered 26 with a suddenly stricken conscience if perhaps she had not been too forward, almost pushing herself in. . . . "I hope I'm not making a nuisance of myself," she said unexpectedly, turning to the other woman. "It's just that I've been wanting to live here myself for so long." Why did I say that, she wondered;

it had been a very long time since young Mrs. Winning had said the first thing that came into her head.

"Come see *my* room," the little boy said urgently, and Mrs. Winning 27 smiled down at him.

"I have a little boy just about your age," she said. "What's your name?" 28

"Davey," the little boy said, moving closer to his mother. "Davey Wil- 29 liam MacLane."

"My little boy," Mrs. Winning said soberly, "is named Howard Talbot 30 Winning."

The little boy looked up at his mother uncertainly, and Mrs. Winning, 31 who felt ill at ease and awkward in this little house she so longed for, said, "How old are you? My little boy is five."

"I'm five," the little boy said, as though realizing it for the first time. 32 He looked again at his mother and she said graciously, "Will you come in and see what we've done to the house?"

Mrs. Winning put her bag of groceries down on the slim-legged table 33 in the green hall, and followed Mrs. MacLane into the living-room, which was L-shaped and had the windows Mrs. Winning would have fitted with gay curtains and flower-boxes. As she stepped into the room, Mrs. Winning realized, with a quick wonderful relief, that it was really going to be all right, after all. Everything, from the andirons in the fireplace to the books on the table, was exactly as Mrs. Winning might have done if she were eleven years younger; a little more informal, perhaps, nothing of quite such good quality as young Mrs. Winning might have chosen, but still richly, undeniably right. There was a picture of Davey on the mantel, flanked by a picture which Mrs. Winning supposed was Davey's father; there was a glorious blue bowl on the low coffee table, and around the corner of the L stood a row of orange plates on a shelf, and a polished maple table and chairs.

"It's lovely," Mrs. Winning said. This could have been mine, she was 34 thinking, and she stood in the doorway and said again, "It's perfectly lovely."

Mrs. MacLane crossed over to the low armchair by the fireplace and 35 picked up the soft blue material that lay across the arm. "I'm making curtains," she said, and touched the blue bowl with the tip of one finger. "Somehow I always make my blue bowl the center of the room," she said. "I'm having the curtains the same blue, and my rug—when it comes!—will have the same blue in the design."

"It matches Davey's eyes," Mrs. Winning said, and when Mrs. MacLane 36 smiled again she saw that it matched Mrs. MacLane's eyes too. Helpless before so much that was magic to her, Mrs. Winning said, "*Have* you painted the kitchen yellow?"

"Yes," Mrs. MacLane said, surprised. "Come and see." She led the way 37 through the L, around past the orange plates to the kitchen, which caught the late morning sun and shone with clean paint and bright aluminum; Mrs. Winning noticed the electric coffeepot, the waffle iron, the toaster, and thought, *She* couldn't have much trouble cooking, not with just the two of them.

"When I have a garden," Mrs. MacLane said, "we'll be able to see it 38 from almost all the windows." She gestured to the broad kitchen windows, and added, "I love gardens. I imagine I'll spend most of my time working in this one, as soon as the weather is nice."

"It's a good house for a garden," Mrs. Winning said. "I've heard that 39 it used to be one of the prettiest gardens on the block."

"I thought so too," Mrs. MacLane said. "I'm going to have flowers on 40 all four sides of the house. With a cottage like this you can, you know."

Oh, I know, I know, Mrs. Winning thought wistfully, remembering the 41 neat charming garden she could have had, instead of the row of nasturtiums along the side of the Winning house, which she tended so carefully; no flowers would grow well around the Winning house, because of the heavy old maple trees which shaded all the yard and which had been tall when the house was built.

Mrs. MacLane had had the bathroom upstairs done in yellow, too, and 42 the two small bedrooms with overhanging eaves were painted green and rose. "All garden colors," she told Mrs. Winning gaily, and Mrs. Winning, thinking of the oddly matched, austere bedrooms in the big Winning house, sighed and admitted that it would be wonderful to have window seats under the eaved windows. Davey's bedroom was the green one, and his small bed was close to the window. "This morning," he told Mrs. Winning solemnly, "I looked out and there were four icicles hanging by my bed."

Mrs. Winning stayed in the cottage longer than she should have; she felt 43 certain, although Mrs. MacLane was pleasant and cordial, that her visit was extended past courtesy and into curiosity. Even so, it was only her sudden guilt about the three pounds of hamburger and dinner for the Winning men that drove her away. When she left, waving good-bye to Mrs. MacLane and Davey as they stood in the cottage doorway, she had invited Davey up to play with Howard, Mrs. MacLane up for tea, both of them to come for lunch some day, and all without the permission of her mother-in-law.

Reluctantly she came to the big house and turned past the bolted front 44 door to go up the walk to the back door, which all the family used in the winter. Her mother-in-law looked up as she came into the kitchen and said irritably, "I called the store and Tom said you left an hour ago."

"I stopped off at the old cottage," Mrs. Winning said. She put the 45 package of groceries down on the table and began to take things out quickly, to get the doughnuts on to a plate and the hamburger into the pan before too much time was lost. With her coat still on and her scarf over her head she moved as fast as she could while her mother-in-law, slicing bread at the kitchen table, watched her silently.

"Take your coat off," her mother-in-law said finally. "Your husband 46 will be home in a minute."

By twelve o'clock the house was noisy and full of mud tracked across 47 the kitchen floor. The oldest Howard, Mrs. Winning's father-in-law, came in from the farm and went silently to hang his hat and coat in the dark hall before speaking to his wife and daughter-in-law; the younger Howard, Mrs.

Winning's husband, came in from the barn after putting the truck away and nodded to his wife and kissed his mother; and the youngest Howard, Mrs. Winning's son, crashed into the kitchen, home from kindergarten, shouting, "Where's dinner?"

The baby, anticipating food, banged on her high-chair with the silver   48 cup which had first been used by the oldest Howard Winning's mother. Mrs. Winning and her mother-in-law put plates down on the table swiftly, knowing after many years the exact pause between the latest arrival and the serving of food, and with a minimum of time three generations of the Winning family were eating silently and efficiently, all anxious to be back about their work: the farm, the mill, the electric train; the dishes, the sewing, the nap. Mrs. Winning, feeding the baby, trying to anticipate her mother-in-law's gestures of serving, thought, today more poignantly than ever before, that she had at least given them another Howard, with the Winning eyes and mouth, in exchange for her food and her bed.

After dinner, after the men had gone back to work and the children were   49 in bed, the baby for her nap and Howard resting with crayons and coloring book, Mrs. Winning sat down with her mother-in-law over their sewing and tried to describe the cottage.

"It's just perfect," she said helplessly. "Everything is so pretty. She   50 invited us to come down some day and see it when it's all finished, the curtains and everything."

"I was talking to Mrs. Blake," the elder Mrs. Winning said, as though   51 in agreement. "She says the husband was killed in an automobile accident. *She* had some money in her own name and I guess she decided to settle down in the country for the boy's health. Mrs. Blake said he looked peakish."

"She loves gardens," Mrs. Winning said, her needle still in her hand for   52 a moment. "She's going to have a big garden all around the house."

"She'll need help," the elder woman said humorlessly, "that's a mighty   53 big garden she'll have."

"She has the *most* beautiful blue bowl, Mother Winning. You'd love it,   54 it's almost like silver."

"Probably," the elder Mrs. Winning said after a pause, "probably her   55 people came from around here a ways back, and *that's* why she's settled in these parts."

The next day Mrs. Winning walked slowly past the cottage, and slowly   56 the next, and the day after, and the day after that. On the second day she saw Mrs. MacLane at the window, and waved, and on the third day she met Davey on the sidewalk. "When are you coming to visit my little boy?" she asked him, and he stared at her solemnly and said, "Tomorrow."

Mrs. Burton, next-door to the MacLanes, ran over on the third day they   57 were there with a fresh apple pie, and then told all the neighbors about the yellow kitchen and the bright electric utensils. Another neighbor, whose husband had helped Mrs. MacLane start her furnace, explained that Mrs.

MacLane was only very recently widowed. One or another of the townspeople called on the MacLanes almost daily, and frequently, as young Mrs.
Winning passed, she saw familiar faces at the windows, measuring the blue
curtains with Mrs. MacLane, or she waved to acquaintances who stood chat-
ting with Mrs. MacLane on the now firm front steps. After the MacLanes had
been in the cottage for about a week Mrs. Winning met them one day in the
grocery and they walked up the hill together, and talked about putting Davey
into the kindergarten. Mrs. MacLane wanted to keep him home as long as
possible, and Mrs. Winning asked her, "Don't you feel terribly tied down,
having him with you all the time?"

"I like it," Mrs. MacLane said cheerfully, "we keep each other company," and Mrs. Winning felt clumsy and ill-mannered, remembering Mrs.
MacLane's widowhood.

As the weather grew warmer and the first signs of green showed on the
trees and on the wet ground, Mrs. Winning and Mrs. MacLane became better
friends. They met almost daily at the grocery and walked up the hill together,
and twice Davey came up to play with Howard's electric train, and once Mrs.
MacLane came up to get him and stayed for a cup of coffee in the great
kitchen while the boys raced round and round the table and Mrs. Winning's
mother-in-law was visiting a neighbor.

"It's such an old house," Mrs. MacLane said, looking up at the dark
ceiling. "I love old houses; they feel so secure and warm, as though lots of
people had been perfectly satisfied with them and they *knew* how useful they
were. You don't get that feeling with a new house."

"This dreary old place," Mrs. Winning said. Mrs. MacLane, with a
rose-colored sweater and her bright soft hair, was a spot of color in the
kitchen that Mrs. Winning knew she could never duplicate. "I'd give anything in the world to live in your house," Mrs. Winning said.

"*I* love it," Mrs. MacLane said. "I don't think I've ever been so happy.
Everyone around here is so nice, and the house is so pretty, and I planted a
lot of bulbs yesterday." She laughed. "I used to sit in that apartment in New
York and dream about planting bulbs again."

Mrs. Winning looked at the boys, thinking how Howard was half-a-
head taller, and stronger, and how Davey was small and weak and loved his
mother adoringly. "It's been good for Davey already," she said. "There's color
in his cheeks."

"Davey loves it," Mrs. MacLane agreed. Hearing his name Davey came
over and put his head in her lap and she touched his hair, bright like her own.
"We'd better be getting home, Davey boy," she said.

"Maybe our flowers have grown some since yesterday," said Davey.

Gradually the days became miraculously long and warm, and Mrs.
MacLane's garden began to show colors and became an ordered thing, still
very young and unsure, but promising rich brilliance for the end of the
summer, and the next summer, and summers ten years from now.

"It's even better than I hoped," Mrs. MacLane said to Mrs. Winning, 67
standing at the garden gate. "Things grow so much better here than almost
anywhere else."

Davey and Howard played daily after the school was out for the sum- 68
mer, and Howard was free all day. Sometimes Howard stayed at Davey's
house for lunch, and they planted a vegetable patch together in the MacLane
back yard. Mrs. Winning stopped for Mrs. MacLane on her way to the store
in the mornings and Davey and Howard frolicked ahead of them down the
street. They picked up their mail together and read it walking back up the
hill, and Mrs. Winning went more cheerfully back to the big Winning house
after walking most of the way home with Mrs. MacLane.

One afternoon Mrs. Winning put the baby in Howard's wagon and with 69
the two boys they went for a long walk in the country. Mrs. MacLane picked
Queen Anne's lace and put it into the wagon with the baby; and the boys
found a garter snake and tried to bring it home. On the way up the hill Mrs.
MacLane helped pull the wagon with the baby and the Queen Anne's lace,
and they stopped halfway to rest and Mrs. MacLane said, "Look, I believe
you can see my garden all the way from here."

It was a spot of color almost at the top of the hill and they stood looking 70
at it while the baby threw the Queen Anne's lace out of the wagon. Mrs.
MacLane said, "I always want to stop here to look at it," and then, "Who is
that *beautiful* child?"

Mrs. Winning looked, and then laughed. "He *is* attractive, isn't he," she 71
said. "It's Billy Jones." She looked at him herself, carefully, trying to see him
as Mrs. MacLane would. He was a boy about twelve, sitting quietly on a wall
across the street, with his chin in his hands, silently watching Davey and
Howard.

"He's like a young statue," Mrs. MacLane said. "So brown, and will you 72
look at that face?" She started to walk again to see him more clearly, and Mrs.
Winning followed her. "Do I know his mother and fath—?"

"The Jones children are half-Negro," Mrs. Winning said hastily. "But 73
they're all beautiful children; you should see the girl. They live just outside
town."

Howard's voice reached them clearly across the summer air. "Nigger," 74
he was saying, "nigger, nigger boy."

"Nigger," Davey repeated, giggling. 75

Mrs. MacLane gasped, and then said, *"Davey,"* in a voice that made 76
Davey turn his head apprehensively. Mrs. Winning had never heard her
friend use such a voice, and she too watched Mrs. MacLane.

"Davey," Mrs. MacLane said again, and Davey approached slowly. 77
"What did I hear you say?"

"Howard," Mrs. Winning said, "leave Billy alone." 78

"Go tell that boy you're sorry," Mrs. MacLane said. "Go at once and 79
tell him you're sorry."

Davey blinked tearfully at his mother and then went to the curb and 80
called across the street, "I'm sorry."

Howard and Mrs. Winning waited uneasily, and Billy Jones across the 81
street raised his head from his hands and looked at Davey and then, for a long
time, at Mrs. MacLane. Then he put his chin on his hands again.

Suddenly Mrs. MacLane called, "Young man—Will you come here a 82
minute, please?"

Mrs. Winning was surprised, and stared at Mrs. MacLane, but when the 83
boy across the street did not move, Mrs. Winning said sharply, "Billy! Billy
Jones! Come here at once!"

The boy raised his head and looked at them, and then slid slowly down 84
from the wall and started across the street. When he was across the street and
about five feet from them he stopped, waiting.

"Hello," Mrs. MacLane said gently, "what's your name?" 85

The boy looked at her for a minute and then at Mrs. Winning, and Mrs. 86
Winning said, "He's Billy Jones. Answer when you're spoken to, Billy."

"Billy," Mrs. MacLane said. "I'm sorry my little boy called you a name, 87
but he's very little and he doesn't always know what he's saying. But he's
sorry, too."

"Okay," Billy said, still watching Mrs. Winning. He was wearing an old 88
pair of blue jeans and a torn white shirt, and he was barefoot. His skin and
hair were the same color, the golden shade of a very heavy tan, and his hair
curled lightly; he had the look of a garden statue.

"Billy," Mrs. MacLane said, "how would you like to come and work for 89
me? Earn some money?"

"Sure," Billy said. 90

"Do you like gardening?" Mrs. MacLane asked. Billy nodded soberly. 91
"Because," Mrs. MacLane went on enthusiastically, "I've been needing some-
one to help me with my garden, and it would be just the thing for you to do."
She waited a minute and then said, "Do you know where I live?"

"Sure," Billy said. He turned his eyes away from Mrs. Winning and for 92
a minute looked at Mrs. MacLane, his brown eyes expressionless. Then he
looked back at Mrs. Winning, who was watching Howard up the street.

"Fine," Mrs. MacLane said. "Will you come tomorrow?" 93

"Sure," Billy said. He waited for a minute, looking from Mrs. MacLane 94
to Mrs. Winning, and then ran back across the street and vaulted over the
wall where he had been sitting. Mrs. MacLane watched him admiringly. Then
she smiled at Mrs. Winning and gave the wagon a tug to start it up the hill
again. They were nearly at the MacLane cottage before Mrs. MacLane finally
spoke. "I just can't stand that," she said, "to hear children attacking people
for things they can't help."

"They're strange people, the Joneses," Mrs. Winning said readily. "The 95
father works around as a handyman; maybe you've seen him. You see—" she
dropped her voice—"the mother was white, a girl from around here. A local
girl," she said again, to make it more clear to a foreigner. "She left the whole
litter of them when Billy was about two, and went off with a white man."

"Poor children," Mrs. MacLane said. 96

"They're all right," Mrs. Winning said. "The church takes care of them, 97

of course, and people are always giving them things. The girl's old enough
to work now, too. She's sixteen, but. . . ."

"But what?" Mrs. MacLane said, when Mrs. Winning hesitated.   98

"Well, people talk about her a lot, you know," Mrs. Winning said.   99
"Think of her mother, after all. And there's another boy, couple of years older
than Billy."

They stopped in front of the MacLane cottage and Mrs. MacLane   100
touched Davey's hair. "Poor unfortunate child," she said.

"Children *will* call names," Mrs. Winning said. "There's not much you 101
can do."

"Well . . ." Mrs. MacLane said. "Poor child."   102

The next day, after the dinner dishes were washed, and while Mrs.   103
Winning and her mother-in-law were putting them away, the elder Mrs.
Winning said casually, "Mrs. Blake tells me your friend Mrs. MacLane was
asking around the neighbors how to get hold of the Jones boy."

"She wants someone to help in the garden, I think," Mrs. Winning said 104
weakly. "She needs help in that big garden."

"Not *that* kind of help," the elder Mrs. Winning said. "You tell her 105
about them?"

"She seemed to feel sorry for them," Mrs. Winning said, from the   106
depths of the pantry. She took a long time settling the plates in even stacks
in order to neaten her mind. She *shouldn't* have done it, she was thinking, but
her mind refused to tell her why. She should have asked me first, though, she
thought finally.

The next day Mrs. Winning stopped off at the cottage with Mrs. Mac- 107
Lane after coming up the hill from the store. They sat in the yellow kitchen
and drank coffee, while the boys played in the back yard. While they were
discussing the possibilities of hammocks between the apple trees there was
a knock at the kitchen door and when Mrs. MacLane opened it she found a
man standing there, so that she said, "Yes?" politely, and waited.

"Good morning," the man said. He took off his hat and nodded his head 108
at Mrs. MacLane. "Billy told me you was looking for someone to work your
garden," he said.

"Why . . ." Mrs. MacLane began, glancing sideways uneasily at Mrs.   109
Winning.

"I'm Billy's father," the man said. He nodded his head toward the back 110
yard and Mrs. MacLane saw Billy Jones sitting under one of the apple trees,
his arms folded in front of him, his eyes on the grass at his feet.

"How do you do," Mrs. MacLane said inadequately.   111

"Billy told me you said for him to come work your garden," the man   112
said. "Well, now, I think maybe a summer job's too much for a boy his age,
he ought to be out playing in the good weather. And that's the kind of work
I do anyway, so's I thought I'd just come over and see if you found anyone
yet."

He was a big man, very much like Billy, except that where Billy's hair 113 curled only a little, his father's hair curled tightly, with a line around his head where his hat stayed constantly, and where Billy's skin was a golden tan, his father's skin was darker, almost bronze. When he moved, it was gracefully, like Billy, and his eyes were the same fathomless brown. "Like to work this garden," Mr. Jones said, looking around. "Could be a mighty nice place."

"You were very nice to come," Mrs. MacLane said. "I certainly do need 114 help."

Mrs. Winning sat silently, not wanting to speak in front of Mr. Jones. 115 She was thinking, I wish she'd ask me first, this is impossible . . . and Mr. Jones stood silently, listening courteously, with his dark eyes on Mrs. Mac-Lane while she spoke. "I guess a lot of the work would be too much for a boy like Billy," she said. "There are a lot of things I can't even do myself, and I was sort of hoping I could get someone to give me a hand."

"That's fine, then," Mr. Jones said. "Guess I can manage most of it," he 116 said, and smiled.

"Well," Mrs. MacLane said, "I guess that's all settled, then. When do 117 you want to start?"

"How about right now?" he said. 118

"Grand," Mrs. MacLane said enthusiastically, and then, "Excuse me for 119 a minute," to Mrs. Winning over her shoulder. She took down her gardening gloves and wide straw hat from the shelf by the door. "Isn't it a lovely day?" she asked Mr. Jones as she stepped out into the garden while he stood back to let her pass.

"You go along home now, Bill," Mr. Jones called as they went toward 120 the side of the house.

"Oh, why not let him stay?" Mrs. MacLane said. Mrs. Winning heard 121 her voice going on as they went out of sight. "He can play around the garden, and he'd probably enjoy . . ."

For a minute Mrs. Winning sat looking at the garden, at the corner 122 around which Mr. Jones had followed Mrs. MacLane, and then Howard's face appeared around the side of the door and he said, "Hi, is it nearly time to eat?"

"Howard," Mrs. Winning said quietly, and he came in through the door 123 and came over to her. "It's time for you to run along home," Mrs. Winning said. "I'll be along in a minute."

Howard started to protest, but she added, "I want you to go right away. 124 Take my bag of groceries if you think you can carry it."

Howard was impressed by her conception of his strength, and he lifted 125 down the bag of groceries; his shoulders, already broad out of proportion, like his father's and his grandfather's, strained under the weight, and then he steadied on his feet. "Aren't I strong?" he asked exultantly.

"*Very* strong," Mrs. Winning said. "Tell Grandma I'll be right up. I'll just 126 say good-bye to Mrs. MacLane."

Howard disappeared through the house; Mrs. Winning heard him walk- 127 ing heavily under the groceries, out through the open front door and down the steps. Mrs. Winning rose and was standing by the kitchen door when Mrs. MacLane came back.

"You're not ready to go?" Mrs. MacLane exclaimed when she saw Mrs. 128
Winning with her jacket on. "Without finishing your coffee?"

"I'd better catch Howard," Mrs. Winning said. "He ran along ahead." 129

"I'm sorry I left you like that," Mrs. MacLane said. She stood in the 130
doorway beside Mrs. Winning, looking out into the garden. "How *wonderful*
it all is," she said, and laughed happily.

They walked together through the house; the blue curtains were up by 131
now, and the rug with the touch of blue in the design was on the floor.

"Good-bye," Mrs. Winning said on the front steps. 132

Mrs. MacLane was smiling, and following her look Mrs. Winning 133
turned and saw Mr. Jones, his shirt off and his strong back shining in the sun
as he bent with a scythe over the long grass at the side of the house. Billy
lay nearby, under the shade of the bushes; he was playing with a grey kitten.
"I'm going to have the finest garden in town," Mrs. MacLane said proudly.

"You won't have him working here past today, will you?" Mrs. Win- 134
ning asked. "Of course you won't have him any longer than just today?"

"But surely—" Mrs. MacLane began, with a tolerant smile, and Mrs. 135
Winning, after looking at her for an incredulous minute, turned and started,
indignant and embarrassed, up the hill.

Howard had brought the groceries safely home and her mother-in-law 136
was already setting the table.

"Howard says you sent him home from MacLane's," her mother-in-law 137
said, and Mrs. Winning answered briefly, "I thought it was getting late."

The next morning when Mrs. Winning reached the cottage on her way 138
down to the store she saw Mr. Jones swinging the scythe expertly against the
side of the house, and Billy Jones and Davey sitting on the front steps
watching him. "Good morning, Davey," Mrs. Winning called, "is your
mother ready to go downstreet?"

"Where's Howard?" Davey asked, not moving. 139

"He stayed home with his grandma today," Mrs. Winning said brightly. 140
"Is your mother ready?"

"She's making lemonade for Billy and me," Davey said. "We're going 141
to have it in the garden."

"Then tell her," Mrs. Winning said quickly, "tell her that I said I was 142
in a hurry and that I had to go on ahead. I'll see her later." She hurried on
down the hill.

In the store she met Mrs. Harris, a lady whose mother had worked for 143
the elder Mrs. Winning nearly forty years before. "Helen," Mrs. Harris said,
"you get greyer every year. You ought to stop all this running around."

Mrs. Winning, in the store without Mrs. MacLane for the first time in 144
weeks, smiled shyly and said that she guessed she needed a vacation.

"Vacation!" Mrs. Harris said. "Let that husband of yours do the 145
housework for a change. He doesn't have nuthin' else to do."

She laughed richly, and shook her head. "Nuthin' else to do," she said. 146
"The Winnings!"

Before Mrs. Winning could step away Mrs. Harris added, her laughter 147
penetrated by a sudden sharp curiosity: "Where's that dressed-up friend of
yours get to? Usually downstreet together, ain't you?"

Mrs. Winning smiled courteously, and Mrs. Harris said, laughing again, 148
"Just couldn't believe those shoes of hers, first time I seen them. Them shoes!"

While she was laughing again Mrs. Winning escaped to the meat 149
counter and began to discuss the potentialities of pork shoulder earnestly
with the grocer. Mrs. Harris only says what everyone else says, she was
thinking, are they talking like that about Mrs. MacLane? Are they laughing
at her? When she thought of Mrs. MacLane she thought of the quiet house,
the soft colors, the mother and son in the garden; Mrs. MacLane's shoes were
green and yellow platform sandals, odd-looking certainly next to Mrs. Winning's solid white oxfords, but so inevitably right for Mrs. MacLane's house,
and her garden. . . . Mrs. Harris came up behind her and said, laughing again,
"What's she got, that Jones fellow working for her now?"

When Mrs. Winning reached home, after hurrying up the hill past the 150
cottage, where she saw no one, her mother-in-law was waiting for her in front
of the house, watching her come the last few yards. "Early enough today,"
her mother-in-law said. "MacLane out of town?"

Resentful, Mrs. Winning said only, "Mrs. Harris nearly drove me out 151
of the store, with her jokes."

"Nothing wrong with Lucy Harris getting away from that man of hers 152
wouldn't cure," the elder Mrs. Winning said. Together, they began to walk
around the house to the back door. Mrs. Winning, as they walked, noticed
that the grass under the trees had greened up nicely, and that the nasturtiums
beside the house were bright.

"I've got something to say to you, Helen," the elder Mrs. Winning said 153
finally.

"Yes?" her daughter-in-law said. 154

"It's the MacLane girl, about her, I mean. You know her so well, you 155
ought to talk to her about that colored man working there."

"I suppose so," Mrs. Winning said. 156

"You *sure* you told her? You told her about those people?" 157

"I told her," Mrs. Winning said. 158

"He's there every blessed day," her mother-in-law said. "And working 159
out there without his shirt on. He goes in the house."

And that evening Mr. Burton, next-door neighbor to Mrs. MacLane, 160
dropped in to see the Howard Winnings about getting a new lot of shingles
at the mill; he turned, suddenly, to Mrs. Winning, who was sitting sewing
next to her mother-in-law at the table in the front room, and raised his voice
a little when he said, "Helen, I wish you'd tell your friend Mrs. MacLane to
keep that kid of hers out of my vegetables."

"Davey?" Mrs. Winning said involuntarily. 161

"No," Mr. Burton said, while all the Winnings looked at the younger 162
Mrs. Winning, "no, the other one, the colored boy. He's been running loose
through our back yard. Makes me sort of mad, that kid coming in spoiling

other people's property. You know," he added, turning to the Howard Winnings, "you know, that does make a person mad." There was a silence, and
then Mr. Burton added, rising heavily, "Guess I'll say good-night to you
people."

They all attended him to the door and came back to their work in   163
silence. I've got to do something, Mrs. Winning was thinking, pretty soon
they'll stop coming to me first, they'll tell someone else to speak to *me*. She
looked up, found her mother-in-law looking at her, and they both looked
down quickly.

Consequently Mrs. Winning went to the store the next morning earlier   164
than usual, and she and Howard crossed the street just above the MacLane
house, and went down the hill on the other side.

"Aren't we going to see Davey?" Howard asked once, and Mrs. Win-   165
ning said carelessly, "Not today, Howard. Maybe your father will take you
out to the mill this afternoon."

She avoided looking across the street at the MacLane house, and hurried   166
to keep up with Howard.

Mrs. Winning met Mrs. MacLane occasionally after that at the store or   167
the post office, and they spoke pleasantly. When Mrs. Winning passed the
cottage after the first week or so, she was no longer embarrassed about going
by, and even looked at it frankly once or twice. The garden was going
beautifully; Mr. Jones's broad back was usually visible through the bushes,
and Billy Jones sat on the steps or lay on the grass with Davey.

One morning on her way down the hill Mrs. Winning heard a conversa-   168
tion between Davey MacLane and Billy Jones; they were in the bushes
together and she heard Davey's high familiar voice saying, "Billy, you want
to build a house with me today?"

"Okay," Billy said. Mrs. Winning slowed her steps a little to hear.   169

"We'll build a big house out of branches," Davey said excitedly, "and   170
when it's finished we'll ask my mommy if we can have lunch out there."

"You can't build a house just out of branches," Billy said. "You ought   171
to have wood, and boards."

"And chairs and tables and dishes," Davey agreed. "And walls."   172

"Ask your mommy can we have two chairs out here," Billy said. "Then   173
we can pretend the whole garden is our house."

"And I'll get us some cookies, too," Davey said. "And we'll ask my   174
mommy and your daddy to come in our house." Mrs. Winning heard them
shouting as she went down along the sidewalk.

You have to admit, she told herself as though she were being strictly   175
just, you have to admit that he's doing a lot with that garden; it's the prettiest
garden on the street. And Billy acts as though he had as much right there as
Davey.

As the summer wore on into long hot days undistinguishable one from   176
another, so that it was impossible to tell with any real accuracy whether the
light shower had been yesterday or the day before, the Winnings moved out

into their yard to sit after supper, and in the warm darkness. Mrs. Winning sometimes found an opportunity of sitting next to her husband so that she could touch his arm; she was never able to teach Howard to run to her and put his head in her lap, or inspire him with other than the perfunctory Winning affection, but she consoled herself with the thought that at least they were a family, a solid respectable thing.

The hot weather kept up, and Mrs. Winning began to spend more time 177 in the store, postponing the long aching walk up the hill in the sun. She stopped and chatted with the grocer, with other young mothers in the town, with older friends of her mother-in-law's, talking about the weather, the reluctance of the town to put in a decent swimming pool, the work that had to be done before school started in the fall, chickenpox, the P.T.A. One morning she met Mrs. Burton in the store, and they spoke of their husbands, the heat, and the hot-weather occupations of their children before Mrs. Burton said: "By the way, Johnny will be six on Saturday and he's having a birthday party; can Howard come?"

"Wonderful," Mrs. Winning said, thinking. His good white shorts, the 178 dark blue shirt, a carefully wrapped present.

"Just about eight children," Mrs. Burton said, with the loving careless- 179 ness mothers use in planning the birthday parties of their children. "They'll stay for supper, of course—send Howard down about three-thirty."

"That sounds so nice," Mrs. Winning said. "He'll be delighted when I 180 tell him."

"I thought I'd have them all play outdoors most of the time," Mrs. 181 Burton said. "In this weather. And then perhaps a few games indoors, and supper. Keep it simple—*you* know." She hesitated, running her finger around and around the top rim of a can of coffee. "Look," she said, "I hope you won't mind me asking, but would it be all right with you if I didn't invite the MacLane boy?"

Mrs. Winning felt sick for a minute, and had to wait for her voice to 182 even out before she said lightly, "It's all right with me if it's all right with *you*; why do you have to ask *me*?"

Mrs. Burton laughed. "I just thought you might mind if he didn't 183 come."

Mrs. Winning was thinking, Something bad has happened, somehow 184 people think they know something about me that they won't say, they all pretend it's nothing, but this never happened to me before; I live with the Winnings, don't I? "Really," she said, putting the weight of the old Winning house into her voice, "why in the *world* would it bother me?" Did I take it too seriously, she was wondering, did I seem too anxious, should I have let it go?

Mrs. Burton was embarrassed, and she set the can of coffee down on 185 the shelf and began to examine the other shelves studiously. "I'm sorry I mentioned it at all," she said.

Mrs. Winning felt that she had to say something further, something to 186 state her position with finality, so that no longer would Mrs. Burton, at least, dare to use such a tone to a Winning, presume to preface a question with "I hope you don't mind me asking." "After all," Mrs. Winning said carefully, weighing the words, "she's like a second mother to Billy."

Mrs. Burton, turning to look at Mrs. Winning for confirmation, grimaced and said, "Good Lord, Helen!"   187

Mrs. Winning shrugged and then smiled and Mrs. Burton smiled and then Mrs. Winning said, "I do feel so sorry for the little boy, though."   188

Mrs. Burton said, "Such a sweet little thing, too."   189

Mrs. Winning had just said, "He and Billy are together *all* the time now," when she looked up and saw Mrs. MacLane regarding her from the end of the aisle of shelves; it was impossible to tell whether she had heard them or not. For a minute Mrs. Winning looked steadily back at Mrs. MacLane, and then she said, with just the right note of cordiality, "Good morning, Mrs. MacLane. Where is your little boy this morning?"   190

"Good morning, Mrs. Winning," Mrs. MacLane said, and moved on past the aisle of shelves, and Mrs. Burton caught Mrs. Winning's arm and made a desperate gesture of hiding her face and, unable to help themselves, both she and Mrs. Winning began to laugh.   191

Soon after that, although the grass in the Winning yard under the maple trees stayed smooth and green, Mrs. Winning began to notice in her daily trips past the cottage that Mrs. MacLane's garden was suffering from the heat. The flowers wilted under the morning sun, and no longer stood up fresh and bright; the grass was browning slightly and the rose bushes Mrs. MacLane had put in so optimistically were noticeably dying. Mr. Jones seemed always cool, working steadily; sometimes bent down with his hands in the earth, sometimes tall against the side of the house, setting up a trellis or pruning a tree, but the blue curtains hung lifelessly at the windows. Mrs. MacLane still smiled at Mrs. Winning in the store, and then one day they met at the gate of Mrs. MacLane's garden and, after hesitating for a minute, Mrs. MacLane said, "Can you come in for a few minutes? I'd like to have a talk, if you have time."   192

"Surely," Mrs. Winning said courteously, and followed Mrs. MacLane up the walk, still luxuriously bordered with flowering bushes, but somehow disenchanted, as though the summer heat had baked away the vivacity from the ground. In the familiar living-room Mrs. Winning sat down on a straight chair, holding herself politely stiff, while Mrs. MacLane sat as usual in her armchair.   193

"How is Davey?" Mrs. Winning asked finally, since Mrs. MacLane did not seem disposed to start any conversation.   194

"He's very well," Mrs. MacLane said, and smiled as she always did when speaking of Davey. "He's out back with Billy."   195

There was a quiet minute, and then Mrs. MacLane said, staring at the blue bowl on the coffee table, "What I wanted to ask you is, what on earth is gone wrong?"   196

Mrs. Winning had been holding herself stiff in readiness for some such   197

question, and when she said, "I don't know what you mean," she thought,
I sound exactly like Mother Winning, and realized, I'm enjoying this, just as
she would; and no matter what she thought of herself she was unable to keep
from adding, "*Is* something wrong?"

"Of course," Mrs. MacLane said. She stared at the blue bowl, and said   198
slowly, "When I first came, everyone was so nice, and they seemed to like
Davey and me and want to help us."

That's wrong, Mrs. Winning was thinking, you mustn't ever talk about   199
whether people like you, that's bad taste.

"And the garden was going so well," Mrs. MacLane said helplessly.   200
"And now, no one ever does more than just speak to us—I used to say 'Good
morning' over the fence to Mrs. Burton, and she'd come to the fence and we'd
talk about the garden, and now she just says 'Morning' and goes in the
house—and no one ever smiles, or anything."

This is dreadful, Mrs. Winning thought, this is childish, this is com-   201
plaining. People treat you as you treat them, she thought; she wanted desperately to go over and take Mrs. MacLane's hand and ask her to come back and
be one of the nice people again; but she only sat straighter in the chair and
said, "I'm sure you must be mistaken. I've never heard anyone speak of it."

"*Are* you sure?" Mrs. MacLane turned and looked at her. "Are you sure   202
it isn't because of Mr. Jones working here?"

Mrs. Winning lifted her chin a little higher and said, "Why on earth   203
would anyone around here be rude to you because of Jones?"

Mrs. MacLane came with her to the door, both of them planning vigor-   204
ously for the days some time next week when they would all go swimming,
when they would have a picnic, and Mrs. Winning went down the hill
thinking, The nerve of her, trying to blame the colored folks.

Toward the end of the summer there was a bad thunderstorm, breaking   205
up the prolonged hot spell. It raged with heavy wind and rain over the town
all night, sweeping without pity through the trees, pulling up young bushes
and flowers ruthlessly; a barn was struck on one side of town, the wires pulled
down on another. In the morning Mrs. Winning opened the back door to find
the Winning yard littered with small branches from the maples, the grass bent
almost flat to the ground.

Her mother-in-law came to the door behind her. "Quite a storm," she   206
said, "did it wake you?"

"I woke up once and went to look at the children," Mrs. Winning said.   207
"It must have been about three o'clock."

"I was up later," her mother-in-law said. "I looked at the children too;   208
they were both asleep."

They turned together and went in to start breakfast.   209

Later in the day Mrs. Winning started down to the store; she had almost   210
reached the MacLane cottage when she saw Mrs. MacLane standing in the
front garden with Mr. Jones standing beside her and Billy Jones with Davey
in the shadows of the front porch. They were all looking silently at a great

branch from one of the Burtons' trees that lay across the center of the garden, crushing most of the flowering bushes and pinning down what was to have been a glorious tulip bed. As Mrs. Winning stopped, watching, Mrs. Burton came out on to her front porch to survey the storm damage, and Mrs. Mac-Lane called to her, "Good morning, Mrs. Burton, it looks like we have part of your tree over here."

"Looks so," Mrs. Burton said, and she went back into her house and   211
closed the door flatly.

Mrs. Winning watched while Mrs. MacLane stood quietly for a minute.   212
Then she looked up at Mr. Jones almost hopefully and she and Mr. Jones looked at one another for a long time. Then Mrs. MacLane said, her clear voice carrying lightly across the air washed clean by the storm: "Do you think I ought to give it up, Mr. Jones? Go back to the city where I'll never have to see another garden?"

Mr. Jones shook his head despondently, and Mrs. MacLane, her shoul-   213
ders tired, went slowly over and sat on her front steps and Davey came and sat next to her. Mr. Jones took hold of the great branch angrily and tried to move it, shaking it and pulling until his shoulders tensed with the strength he was bringing to bear, but the branch only gave slightly and stayed, clinging to the garden.

"Leave it alone, Mr. Jones," Mrs. MacLane said finally. "Leave it for the   214
next people to move!"

But still Mr. Jones pulled against the branch, and then suddenly Davey   215
stood up and cried out, "There's Mrs. Winning! Hi, Mrs. Winning!"

Mrs. MacLane and Mr. Jones both turned, and Mrs. MacLane waved   216
and called out, "Hello!"

Mrs. Winning swung around without speaking and started, with great   217
dignity, back up the hill toward the old Winning house.

Questions for Discussion

1. In paragraph 10 Mrs. Winning thinks back on her earlier dreams of living in the cottage. What do her specific dreams of decorating and colors suggest about her inner life? About her distance from the other Winnings? About how happy she is?

2. What does the fact that the same people see each other every day—at the grocery store, at the post office, and on the single main street—suggest about the closeness of community standards? How is the size of a town a force for conformity?

3. How do the names of the Winnings, especially the men's names, suggest the view that the Winnings take of their own importance? How does the location of the Winning house reinforce this view?

4. What is the significance for Mrs. Winning's inner life that "no flowers would grow well around the Winning house, because of the heavy old maple trees which shaded all the yard and which had been tall when the house was built" (¶41)?

5. What is the significance for Mrs. Winning's inner life that when her husband comes in from the farm for the noon meal, he "nodded to his wife and kissed his mother" (¶47)?

6. What does Mrs. Winning's explanation of the name-calling episode (¶101) suggest about her character? What can we "read" in her joining Mrs. Burton's laughter in paragraph 191? Above all, what is suggested by her realization in paragraph 197 that she *enjoys* sounding just like Mother Winning?

7. What features in the Winning family make you sympathize with Mrs. Winning's position? What is suggested about the function and status of women in the Winning family by Mrs. Winning's silent thought that "she had at least given them another Howard, with the Winning eyes and mouth, in exchange for her food and bed" (¶48)?

Suggested Essay Topics

1. Write an essay to your class in which, speaking as Mrs. Winning, you explain your actions as they must have appeared to you. Allow Mrs. Winning to make the best case in her own defense that you can imagine, allowing her, perhaps, to predict the consequences if she had taken a different tack; in short, allow her to construct her own standards. After you have given her her say, conclude with a page of response in which you determine which parts of her justification are valid and which are not.

2. Write a dialogue or conversation in which you picture Mrs. MacLane and Mrs. Winning meeting years later and discussing the events recorded in Jackson's story. The conversation could go in many different directions; you will have to choose one direction and stick with it. There could be recriminations and counteraccusations. You could invent any number of evil consequences for either or both women. Or you could have them arrive at an understanding of each other, seeing each other's limitations but also the pressure they were under at the time, and being willing to forgive. Or you could imagine a host of other kinds of confrontations. Try to keep in mind, however, that the story is fundamentally about possibilities of character and that your conversation should both express and illuminate the character of the women involved.

THE INDIVIDUAL
AND COMMUNITY

*The Life of Citizenship,
the Role of Friendship*

Power tends to corrupt; absolute power corrupts absolutely.
Lord Acton

Liberty means responsibility. That is why most men dread it.
George Bernard Shaw

Authority and power are two different things: *Power* is the force
by means of which you can oblige others to obey you.
Authority is the *right* to direct and comment, to be listened to or obeyed
by others. Authority requests power. Power without authority
is tyranny.
Jacques Maritain

If all mankind minus one were of one opinion,
and only one person were of the contrary opinion,
mankind would be no more justified in
silencing that one person, than he, if he had the power,
would be justified in silencing mankind.
John Stuart Mill

For discipline is the channel in which our acts run strong
and deep; where there is no direction, the deeds of men run shallow
and wander and are wasted.
Ursula K. Le Guin

The tree of liberty must be refreshed from time to time with
the blood of patriots and tyrants. It is its natural manure.
Thomas Jefferson

Strange it is, that men should admit the validity of the arguments
for free discussion, but object to their being "pushed to an extreme";
not seeing that unless the reasons are good
for an extreme case, they are not good for any case.
John Stuart Mill

W. H. Auden

One of the most widely admired English poets of the twentieth century was W. H. Auden (1907–1973). Few poets in any language have ever written about more widely diverse subjects or mastered more contrasting poetic styles. Because many of his poems express controversial ideas, he was sometimes dismissed as "not a true poet" by critics who thought that poetry should not be used to advance arguments. Some other critics dismissed him because they hated his ideas—politically radical in his youth, Christian after his conversion in the late 1930s. But in the years since his death, almost everyone has acknowledged that he was a great master of the art of making ideas live by testing them in verse.

"The Unknown Citizen" is one of Auden's many satirical poems presented in the form of mock biography. You might begin by reading it aloud. Do you find that some of the lines simply cannot be read in a tone of straightforward praise? Now read through the poem, pencil in hand, underlining all the suggestions that something has certainly "been wrong" about this life. In doing so, you will find yourself contradicting the views of the official speaker of the poem, who is not Auden but a character who can give this kind of praise without being ironic. By determining that the poem is a satire against the speaker and his kind, you are thus simultaneously deciphering Auden's irony. (Satire and irony are often confused, and you may find it useful to look them up in your dictionary.)

Such satirical poems can deceive us if we fail to see that they contain much more than a paraphrased summary of their meanings. Suppose we concluded, for example, "The poem says that happiness is not to be found in conformity" or "People who merely conform to public standards destroy themselves." Obviously if that is all that the poem says, Auden could have said it just like that. In reading poems that are worth reading at all, we find that the deeper our experience goes, the less we are satisfied with such summaries. They can be useful as entries into poems and as stimulation for our own further writing, but since this is a poem, the pursuit of such meanings is only the

beginning of our pleasure. As you read and re-read the poem, then, ask yourself what
it offers that could not have been achieved in any prose statement.

THE UNKNOWN CITIZEN

Completed in March 1939.

> *(To JS/07/M/378*
> *This Marble Monument*
> *Is Erected by the State)*

He was found by the Bureau of Statistics to be   1
One against whom there was no official complaint,
And all the reports on his conduct agree
That, in the modern sense of an old-fashioned word, he was a saint,
For in everything he did he served the Greater Community.   5
Except for the War till the day he retired
He worked in a factory and never got fired,
But satisfied his employers, Fudge Motors Inc.
Yet he wasn't a scab or odd in his views,
For his Union reports that he paid his dues,   10
(Our report on his Union shows it was sound)
And our Social Psychology workers found
That he was popular with his mates and liked a drink.
The Press are convinced that he bought a paper every day
And that his reactions to advertisements were normal in every way.   15
Policies taken out in his name prove that he was fully insured,
And his Health-card shows he was once in hospital but left it cured.
Both Producers Research and High-Grade Living declare
He was fully sensible to the advantages of the Instalment Plan
And had everything necessary to the Modern Man,   20
A phonograph, a radio, a car and a frigidaire.
Our researchers into Public Opinion are content
That he held the proper opinions for the time of year;
When there was peace, he was for peace; when there was war, he went.
He was married and added five children to the population,   25
Which our Eugenist says was the right number for a parent of his generation,
And our teachers report that he never interfered with their education.
Was he free? Was he happy? The question is absurd:
Had anything been wrong, we should certainly have heard.

Questions for Discussion

1. Can you and other members of your class agree about the main "message" of this poem? Why or why not?

2. One obvious difference between the poem and a paraphrase of it is that the line endings rhyme. Do all of them rhyme precisely? What would you say to someone who, in reading the poem aloud, pronounced *Inc.* as "Incorporated"? What do you make of the irregularity of the rhymes? Try reading aloud the little epigraph about the monument. How does the buried trick with rhyme help prepare the reader for the kind of reading required in the rest of the poem?

3. In finding both regularities and irregularities in the poem, you have no doubt noticed that you cannot read the lines aloud in any simple ta-túm-ty-túm-ty rhythm. If you count the number of syllables in each line, you find few with the same number—another irregularity. If you assume that Auden is not simply careless or unable to make regular rhymes, meter, and rhythm, can you think of any good reasons for his being what we might call "half-regular." Do his irregularities-within-regularity reinforce or even transform something about the "message"?

Suggested Essay Topics

1. Write a brief portrait of an extremely "happy, well-adjusted" person you know who, contrary to appearances, leads an empty life. Feel free to imitate any of Auden's methods, including verse if that seems tempting. Think of your reader not as your teacher but as someone coming across your work in a "reader" like this one.

2. Write a short magazine article delivering a straightforward attack on the oppressiveness and conformity that Auden attacks indirectly with his ironic portrait. (Decide in advance what kind of magazine your piece is designed for.) You might then want to add a paragraph, addressed to your teacher, describing the differences between Auden's account and yours, or perhaps even explaining why yours doesn't work as well or what gave you special difficulties.

Mary McCarthy

Mary McCarthy's (b. 1912) "Artists in Uniform," first published in 1953, raises several important issues about the individual in relationship to the community. Part of the drama inside the story derives from the drama that was occurring outside of the story. In the early 1950s the cold war—the period of Soviet-American antagonism and military feinting that began at the end of World War II and led to the Cuban missile crisis of 1963—was in full swing and America was in the throes of a "red scare." Grade-school children were regularly drilled on how to climb dutifully under their desks in the event of a nuclear attack, people dug bomb shelters in their back yards, the signing of "loyalty oaths" was proposed as a prerequisite to some kinds of employment, and a series of books, articles, movies, and TV programs all fed the fear that communists were infiltrating every level of American society. Senator Joseph McCarthy (no relation to Mary McCarthy) was reinforcing that fear with his notorious Senate "hearings," in which artists, intellectuals, academics, and other political liberals were harassed, bullied, humiliated, and defamed in front of the whole country. Television, in its infancy as a mass commodity, seized on the hearings as one of its early "media events."

McCarthy's "hearings" did not succeed in unearthing any proven communists or conspiracies during the entire period of its operations. But they did succeed in scaring into silence most politicians who wanted to speak up in favor of civil liberties, and they fostered a climate of fear and suspicion in which political liberals might at any time or place—even in a passenger train winding its way across Indiana in a heat wave—find themselves the targets of insinuations or accusations that their patriotism was weak, that their loyalty was suspect, or that they were "soft on communism."

In a police state, such social pressures can be an effective mechanism for strangling dissent, criticism, or innovative thinking before the words ever get uttered. In a democracy, such pressure threatens to cut off democratic processes at the root. Conformity becomes enforced not by the secret police at the door but by the fear of majority opinion. But the narrator in "Artists in Uniform" does not feel comfortable. Discovering with shock that her sophisticated clothing has revealed her to the men in the club car as not just an artist but an artist of an intellectual, "liberal" stamp—as if she were in uniform—she immediately feels vulnerable to potential attacks on her political beliefs. Yet her contempt for the cliché-ridden, knee-jerk mentality of her car companions spurs her to go on the attack herself, to attempt to overturn their vague accusations about communism among academics and Jews. The trouble is, she does not really possess any more facts about communism among these groups than do her opponents, and in the attempt to speak for pure reason and a liberal, unprejudiced mentality, she finds herself committing every intellectual sin she detests in the others.

Although McCarthy records elsewhere that the primary events of this story really happened to her, we should be leery of assuming that every detail of speech, thought, and action is a biographical fact. Regardless of how much the biography and the fiction overlap (or fail to), McCarthy portrays a character caught up in issues of importance for us all. As you read, consider the possibility that McCarthy writes this story not as an exposé of the Colonel—his prejudice is of the garden variety: common, rank, easily recognizable—but as an exposé of herself (or of people generally like her): the intellectual who sets up her own fall through excessive pride. Notice her smugness as she says, "It seemed to me that the writer or intellectual had a certain missionary usefulness in just such accidental gatherings as this, if he spoke not as an intellectual but as a normal member of the public" (¶3)—as if the "normal public" were too stupid to form sound opinions without guidance from intellectuals such as she, who will of course avoid condescending to their inferiors by pretending to be normal themselves. Here is condescension with a vengeance, not merely committing the sin of pride but pretending to be noble.

Consider, however, whether the story may contain a larger object of attack than either of the main characters. Is it possible that the story's larger target is a society that fosters extremist positions, that permits conformity to be a cover for non-thinkers like the Colonel while forcing intellectuals like McCarthy's narrator into defensive positions that short-circuit clear thinking? McCarthy invites us to consider seriously the uniforms we ourselves may wear and how we react to the perceived uniforms of others.

ARTISTS IN UNIFORM

From *On the Contrary* (1953).

> The Colonel went out sailing,
> He spoke with Turk and Jew . . .

"Pour it on Colonel," cried the young man in the Dacron suit excitedly, making his first sortie into the club-car conversation. His face was white as Roquefort and of a glistening, cheese-like texture; he had a shock of tow-colored hair, badly cut and greasy, and a snub nose with large gray pores. Under his darting eyes were two black craters. He appeared to be under some intense nervous strain and had sat the night before in the club car drinking bourbon with beer chasers and leafing magazines which he frowningly tossed aside, like cards into a discard heap. This morning he had come in late, with a hangdog, hangover look, and had been sitting tensely forward on a settee, smoking cigarettes and following the conversation with little twitches of the nose and quivers of the body, as a dog follows a human conversation, veering its mistrustful eyeballs from one speaker to another and raising its head eagerly at its master's voice. The Colonel's voice, rich and light and plausible, had in fact abruptly risen and swollen, as he pronounced his last sentence. "I can tell you one thing," he said harshly. "They weren't named Ryan or Murphy!"

A sort of sigh, as of consummation, ran through the club car. "Pour it on, Colonel, give it to them, Colonel, that's right, Colonel," urged the young man in a transport of admiration. The Colonel fingered his collar and modestly smiled. He was a thin, hawklike, black-haired handsome man with a bright blue bloodshot eye and a well-pressed, well-tailored uniform that did not show the effects of the heat—the train, westbound for St. Louis, was passing through Indiana, and, as usual in a heat-wave, the air-conditioning had not met the test. He wore the Air Force insignia, and there was something in his light-boned, spruce figure and keen, knifelike profile that suggested a classic image of the aviator, ready to cut, piercing, into space. In base fact, however, the Colonel was in procurement,* as we heard him tell the mining engineer who had just bought him a drink. From several silken hints that parachuted into the talk, it was patent to us that the Colonel was a man who knew how to enjoy this earth and its pleasures: he led, he gave us to think, a bachelor's life of abstemious dissipation and well-rounded sensuality. He had accepted the engineer's drink with a mere nod of the glass in acknowledgment, like a genial Mars quaffing a libation; there was clearly no prospect of his buying a second in return, not if the train were to travel from here to the Mojave Desert. In the same way, an understanding had arisen that I, the only woman in the club car, had become the Colonel's perquisite; it was taken for granted, without an invitation's being issued, that I was to lunch with him in St. Louis, where we each had a wait between trains—my plans for seeing the city in a taxicab were dished.

From the beginning, as we eyed each other over my volume of Dickens   3
("*The Christmas Carol?*" suggested the Colonel, opening relations), I had guessed that the Colonel was of Irish stock, and this, I felt, gave me an advantage, for he did not suspect the same of me; strangely so, for I am supposed to have the map of Ireland written on my features. In fact, he had just wagered, with a jaunty, sidelong grin at the mining engineer, that my people "came from Boston from way back," and that I—narrowed glance, running, like steel measuring-tape, up and down my form—was a professional sculptress. I might have laughed this off, as a crudely bad guess like his *Christmas Carol,* if I had not seen the engineer nodding gravely, like an idol, and the peculiar young man bobbing his head up and down in mute applause and agreement. I was wearing a bright apple-green raw silk blouse and a dark-green rather full raw silk skirt, plus a pair of pink glass earrings; my hair was done up in a bun. It came to me, for the first time, with a sort of dawning horror, that I had begun, in the course of years, without ever guessing it, to look irrevocably Bohemian.† Refracted from the three men's eyes was a strange vision of myself as an artist, through and through, stained with my occupation like the dyer's hand. All I lacked, apparently, was a pair of sandals. My sick heart sank to my Ferragamo shoes; I had always particularly preened myself on being an artist in disguise. And it was not only a question of personal vanity—it seemed to me that the writer or intellectual had a certain missionary usefulness in just such accidental gatherings as this, if he spoke not as an intellectual but as a normal member of the public. Now, thanks to the Colonel, I slowly became aware that my contributions to the club-car conversation were being watched and assessed as coming from *a certain quarter.* My costume, it seemed, carefully assembled as it had been at an expensive shop, was to these observers simply a uniform that blazoned a caste and

---

*Procurement is a clerking, not a combat, function. The procurement clerk edits purchase requests, invites bids from suppliers, and makes out orders for procurement of materials—in this case for the Air Force.

†Unconventional, anti-establishment, scornful of middle-class values.

allegiance just as plainly as the Colonel's khaki and eagles. *"Gardez,"* [take care] I said to myself. But, as the conversation grew tenser and I endeavored to keep cool, I began to writhe within myself, and every time I looked down, my contrasting greens seemed to be growing more and more lurid and taking on an almost menacing light, like leaves just before a storm that lift their bright undersides as the air becomes darker. We had been speaking, of course, of Russia,* and I had mentioned a study that had been made at Harvard of political attitudes among Iron Curtain refugees. Suddenly, the Colonel had smiled. "They're pretty Red at Harvard, I'm given to understand," he observed in a comfortable tone, while the young man twitched and quivered urgently. The eyes of all the men settled on me and waited. I flushed as I saw myself reflected. The woodland greens of my dress were turning to their complementary red, like a color-experiment in psychology or a traffic light changing. Down at the other end of the club car, a man looked up from his paper. I pulled myself together. "Set your mind at rest, Colonel," I remarked dryly. "I know Harvard very well and they're conservative to the point of dullness. The only thing crimson is the football team." This disparagement had its effect. "So . . . ?" queried the Colonel. "I thought there was some professor. . . ." I shook my head. "Absolutely not. There used to be a few fellow-travelers, but they're very quiet these days, when they haven't absolutely recanted. The general atmosphere is more anti-Communist than the Vatican." The Colonel and the mining engineer exchanged a thoughtful stare and seemed to agree that the Delphic oracle that had just pronounced knew whereof it spoke. "Glad to hear it," said the Colonel. The engineer frowned and shook his fat wattles; he was a stately, gray-haired, plump man with small hands and feet and the pampered, finical tidiness of a small-town widow. "There's so much hearsay these days," he exclaimed vexedly. "You don't know *what* to believe."

I reopened my book with an air of having closed the subject and read   4
a paragraph three times over. I exulted to think that I had made a modest contribution to sanity in our times, and I imagined my words pyramiding like a chain letter—the Colonel telling a fellow-officer on the veranda of a club in Texas, the engineer halting a works-superintendent in a Colorado mine shaft: "I met a woman on the train who claims . . . Yes, absolutely. . . ." Of course, I did not know Harvard as thoroughly as I pretended, but I forgave myself by thinking it was the convention of such club-car symposia in our positivistic country to speak from the horse's mouth.

Meanwhile, across the aisle, the engineer and the Colonel continued   5
their talk in slightly lowered voices. From time to time, the Colonel's polished index-fingernail scratched his burnished black head and his knowing blue eye forayed occasionally toward me. I saw that still I was a doubtful quantity to them, a movement in the bushes, a noise, a flicker, that was figuring in their crenelated thought as "she." The subject of Reds in our colleges had not, alas,

*In the early 1950s, at the height of the cold war, talk of Soviet-American antagonisms was common enough to be referred to by an "of course."

been finished; they were speaking now of another university and a woman faculty-member who had been issuing Communist statements. This story somehow, I thought angrily, had managed to appear in the newspapers without my knowledge, while these men were conversant with it; I recognized a big chink in the armor of my authority. Looking up from my book, I began to question them sharply, as though they were reporting some unheard-of natural phenomenon. "When?" I demanded. "Where did you see it? What was her name?" This request for the professor's name was a headlong attempt on my part to buttress my position, the implication being that the identities of all university professors were known to me and that if I were but given the name I could promptly clarify the matter. To admit that there was a single Communist in our academic system whose activities were hidden from me imperiled, I instinctively felt, all the small good I had done here. Moreover, in the back of my mind, I had a supreme confidence that these men were wrong: the story, I supposed, was some tattered piece of misinformation they had picked up from a gossip column. Pride, as usual, preceded my fall. To the Colonel, the demand for the name was not specific but generic: what *kind* of name was the question he presumed me to be asking. "Oh," he said slowly with a luxurious yawn, "Finkelstein or Fishbein or Feinstein."* He lolled back in his seat with a side glance at the engineer, who deeply nodded. There was a voluptuary pause, as the implication sank in. I bit my lip, regarding this as a mere diversionary tactic. "Please!" I said impatiently. "Can't you remember exactly?" The Colonel shook his head and then his spare cheekbones suddenly reddened and he looked directly at me. "I can tell you one thing," he exclaimed irefully. "They weren't named Ryan or Murphy."

The Colonel went no further; it was quite unnecessary. In an instant, the young man was at his side, yapping excitedly and actually picking at the military sleeve. The poor thing was transformed, like some creature in a fairy tale whom a magic word releases from silence. "That's right, Colonel," he happily repeated. "I know them. *I* was at Harvard in the business school, studying accountancy. I left. I couldn't take it." He threw a poisonous glance at me, and the Colonel, who had been regarding him somewhat doubtfully, now put on an alert expression and inclined an ear for his confidences. The man at the other end of the car folded his newspaper solemnly and took a seat by the young man's side. "They're all Reds, Colonel," said the young man. "They teach it in the classroom. I came back here to Missouri. It made me sick to listen to the stuff they handed out. If you didn't hand it back, they flunked you. Don't let anybody tell you different." "You are wrong," I said coldly and closed my book and rose. The young man was still talking eagerly, and the three men were leaning forward to catch his every gasping word, like three astute detectives over a dying informer, when I reached the door and cast a last look over my shoulder at them. For an instant, the Colonel's eye met mine, and I felt his scrutiny processing my green back as I tugged open

*Jewish-sounding names—which makes the Colonel's comment an anti-Semitic slur.

the door and met a blast of hot air, blowing my full skirt wide. Behind me, in my fancy, I saw four sets of shrugging brows.

In my own car, I sat down, opposite two fat nuns, and tried to assemble   7
my thoughts. I ought to have spoken, I felt, and yet what could I have said? It occurred to me that the four men had perhaps not realized why I had left the club car with such abruptness: was it possible that they thought I was a Communist, who feared to be unmasked? I spurned this possibility, and yet it made me uneasy. For some reason, it troubled my *amour-propre* * to think of my anti-Communist self living on, so to speak, green in their collective memory as a Communist or fellow-traveler. In fact, though I did not give a fig for the men, I hated the idea, while a few years ago I should have counted it a great joke. This, it seemed to me, was a measure of the change in the social climate. I had always scoffed at the notion of liberals "living in fear" of political demagoguery in America, but now I had to admit that if I was not fearful, I was at least uncomfortable in the supposition that anybody, anybody whatever, could think of me, precious me, as a Communist.† A remoter possibility was, of course, that back there my departure was being ascribed to Jewishness, and this too annoyed me. I am in fact a quarter Jewish, and though I did not "hate" the idea of being taken for a Jew, I did not precisely like it, particularly under these circumstances. I wished it to be clear that I had left the club car for intellectual and principled reasons; I wanted those men to know that it was not I, but my principles, that had been offended. To let them conjecture that I had left because I was Jewish would imply that only a Jew could be affronted by an anti-Semitic outburst: a terrible idea. Aside from anything else, it voided the whole concept of transcendence, which was very close to my heart, the concept that man is more than his circumstances, more even than himself.

However you looked at the episode, I said to myself nervously, I had   8
not acquitted myself well. I ought to have done or said something concrete and unmistakable. From this, I slid glassily to the thought that those men ought to be punished, the Colonel, in particular, who occupied a responsible position. In a minute, I was framing a businesslike letter to the Chief of Staff, deploring the Colonel's conduct as unbecoming to an officer and identifying him by rank and post, since unfortunately I did not know his name. Earlier in the conversation, he had passed some comments on "Harry"‡ that bordered positively on treason, I said to myself triumphantly. A vivid image of the proceedings against him presented itself to my imagination: the long military tribunal with a row of stern soldierly faces glaring down at the

---

*Self-pride.

†This was the period in which Senator Joseph McCarthy was holding his notorious "hearings," in which he frequently accused artists and intellectuals of being communists. Such accusations, which could not be rebutted in a Senate hearing as they could have been in a court of law, ruined several careers and cost others both heavy loss of income and great personal anguish.

‡Harry Truman, president of the United States from 1945 to 1953.

Colonel. I myself occupied only an inconspicuous corner of this tableau, for, to tell the truth, I did not relish the role of the witness. Perhaps it would be wiser to let the matter drop . . . ? We were nearing St. Louis now; the Colonel had come back into my car, and the young accountant had followed him, still talking feverishly. I pretended not to see them and turned to the two nuns, as if for sanctuary from this world and its hatreds and revenges. Out of the corner of my eye, I watched the Colonel, who now looked wry and restless; he shrank against the window as the young man made a place for himself amid the Colonel's smart luggage and continued to express his views in a pale breathless voice. I smiled to think that the Colonel was paying the piper. For the Colonel, anti-Semitism was simply an aspect of urbanity, like a knowledge of hotels or women. This frantic psychopath of an accountant was serving him as a nemesis, just as the German people had been served by their psychopath, Hitler. Colonel, I adjured him, you have chosen, between him and me; measure the depth of your error and make the best of it! No intervention on my part was now necessary; justice had been meted out. Nevertheless, my heart was still throbbing violently, as if I were on the verge of some dangerous action. What was I to do, I kept asking myself, as I chatted with the nuns, if the Colonel were to hold me to that lunch? And I slowly and apprehensively revolved this question, just as though it were a matter of the most serious import. It seemed to me that if I did not lunch with him—and I had no intention of doing so—I had the dreadful obligation of telling him why.

He was waiting for me as I descended the car steps. "Aren't you coming to lunch with me?" he called out and moved up to take my elbow. I began to tremble with audacity. "No," I said firmly, picking up my suitcase and draping an olive-green linen duster over my arm. "I can't lunch with you." He quirked a wiry black eyebrow. "Why not?" he said. "I understood it was all arranged." He reached for my suitcase. "No," I said, holding on to the suitcase. "I can't." I took a deep breath. "I have to tell you. I think you should be *ashamed* of yourself, Colonel, for what you said in the club car." The Colonel stared; I mechanically waved for a red-cap, who took my bag and coat and went off. The Colonel and I stood facing each other on the emptying platform. "What do you mean?" he inquired in a low, almost clandestine tone. "Those anti-Semitic remarks," I muttered, resolutely. "You ought to be *ashamed.*" The Colonel gave a quick, relieved laugh. "Oh, come now," he protested. "I'm sorry," I said. "I can't have lunch with anybody who feels that way about the Jews." The Colonel put down his attaché case and scratched the back of his lean neck. "Oh, come now," he repeated, with a look of amusement. "You're not Jewish, are you?" "No," I said quickly. "Well, then . . ." said the Colonel, spreading his hands in a gesture of bafflement. I saw that he was truly surprised and slightly hurt by my criticism, and this made me feel wretchedly embarrassed and even apologetic, on my side, as though I had called attention to some physical defect in him, of which he himself was unconscious. "But I might have been," I stammered. "You had no way of knowing. You oughtn't to talk like that." I recognized, too late, that I was strangely reducing the whole matter to a question of etiquette: "Don't start anti-Semitic talk before making sure there are no Jews present." "Oh, hell," said the Colonel, easily. "I can tell a Jew." "No, you can't," I retorted, thinking of my Jewish grandmother, for by Nazi criteria I was Jewish. "Of course I can," he insisted. "So can you." We had begun to walk down the platform side by side, disputing with a restrained passion that isolated us like a pair of lovers. All at once, the Colonel halted, as though struck with a thought. "What *are* you, anyway?" he said meditatively, regarding my dark hair, green blouse, and pink earrings. Inside myself, I began to laugh. "Oh," I said gaily, playing out the trump I had been saving, "I'm Irish, like you, Colonel." "How did you know?" he said amazedly. I laughed aloud. "I can tell an Irishman," I taunted. The Colonel frowned. "What's your family name?" he said brusquely. "McCarthy." He lifted an eyebrow, in defeat, and then quickly took note of my wedding ring. "That your maiden name?" I nodded. Under this peremptory questioning, I had the peculiar sensation that I get when I am lying; I began to feel that "McCarthy" was a nom de plume,* a coinage of my artistic personality. But the Colonel appeared to be satisfied. "Hell," he said, "come on to lunch, then. With a fine name like that, you and I should be friends." I still shook my head, though by this time we were pacing outside the station restaurant; my baggage had been checked in a locker; sweat was running down my face and I felt exhausted and hungry. I knew that I was weakening and I wanted only an excuse to yield and go inside with him. The Colonel seemed to sense this. "Hell," he conceded. "You've got me wrong. I've got nothing against the Jews. Back there in the club car, I was just stating a simple fact: you won't find an Irishman sounding off for the Commies. You can't deny that, can you?"

His voice rose persuasively; he took my arm. In the heat, I wilted and   10
we went into the air-conditioned cocktail lounge. The Colonel ordered two old-fashioneds. The room was dark as a cave and produced, in the midst of the hot midday, a hallucinated feeling, as though time had ceased, with the weather, and we were in eternity together. As the Colonel prepared to relax, I made a tremendous effort to guide the conversation along rational, purposive lines; my only justification for being here would be to convert the Colonel. "There *have* been Irishmen associated with the Communist party," I said suddenly, when the drinks came. "I can think of two." "Oh, hell," said the Colonel, "every race and nation has its traitors. What I mean is, you won't find them in numbers. You've got to admit that the Communists in this country are 90 per cent Jewish." "But the Jews in this country aren't 90 per cent Communist," I retorted.

As he stirred his drink, restively, I began to try to show him the reasons   11
why the Communist movement in America had attracted such a large number, relatively, of Jews: how the Communists had been anti-Nazi when no-

*Assumed name, pen name.

body else seemed to care what happened to the Jews in Germany; how the
Communists still capitalized on a Jewish fear of fascism; how many Jews had
become, after Buchenwald,* traumatized by this fear. . . .

But the Colonel was scarcely listening. An impatient frown rested on   12
his jaunty features. "I don't get it," he said slowly. "Why should you be for
them, with a name like yours?" "I'm *not* for the Communists," I cried. "I'm
just trying to explain to you—" "For the Jews," the Colonel interrupted,
irritable now himself. "I've heard of such people but I never met one before."
"I'm not 'for' them," I protested. "You don't understand. I'm not for *any* race
or nation. I'm against those who are against them." This word, *them,* with a
sort of slurring circle drawn round it, was beginning to sound ugly to me.
Automatically, in arguing with him, I seemed to have slipped into the Colonel's style of thought. It occurred to me that defense of the Jews could be a
subtle and safe form of anti-Semitism, an exercise of patronage: as a rational
Gentile, one could feel superior both to the Jews and the anti-Semites. There
could be no doubt that the Jewish question evoked a curious stealthy lust or
concupiscence. I could feel it now vibrating between us over the dark table.
If I had been a good person, I should unquestionably have got up and left.

"I don't get it," repeated the Colonel. "How were you brought up? Were   13
your people this way too?" It was manifest that an odd reversal had taken
place; each of us regarded the other as "abnormal" and was attempting to
understand the etiology of a disease. "Many of my people think just as you
do," I said, smiling coldly. "It seems to be a sickness to which the Irish are
prone. Perhaps it's due to the potato diet," I said sweetly, having divined that
the Colonel came from a social stratum somewhat lower than my own.

But the Colonel's hide was tough. "You've got me wrong," he reiterated,   14
with an almost plaintive laugh. "I don't dislike the Jews. I've got a lot of
Jewish friends. Among themselves, they think just as I do, mark my words.
I tell you what it is," he added ruminatively, with a thoughtful prod of his
muddler, "I draw a distinction between a kike and a Jew." I groaned. "Colonel, I've never heard an anti-Semite who didn't draw that distinction. You
know what Otto Kahn† said? 'A kike is a Jewish gentleman who has just left
the room.' " The Colonel did not laugh. "I don't hold it against some of
them," he persisted, in a tone of pensive justice. "It's not their fault if they
were born that way. That's what I tell them, and they respect me for my
honesty. I've had a lot of discussions; in procurement, you have to do business
with them, and the Jews are the first to admit that you'll find more chiselers
among their race than among the rest of mankind." "It's not a race," I inter-
jected wearily, but the Colonel pressed on. "If I deal with a Jewish manufacturer, I can't bank on his word. I've seen it again and again, every damned
time. When I deal with a Gentile, I can trust him to make delivery as prom-

*A Nazi extermination camp.
†American banker and philanthropist (1867–1934), born in Germany (naturalized in 1917),
president (1918–1931) of the Metropolitan Opera Company; perhaps the greatest patron of the
arts in U.S. history.

ised. That's the difference between the two races. They're just a different breed. They don't have standards of honesty, even among each other." I sighed, feeling unequal to arguing the Colonel's personal experience.

"Look," I said, "you may be dealing with an industry where the Jewish 15 manufacturers are the most recent comers and feel they have to cut corners to compete with the established firms. I've heard that said about Jewish cattle-dealers, who are supposed to be extra sharp. But what I think, really, is that you notice it when a Jewish firm fails to meet an agreement and don't notice it when it's a Yankee." "Hah," said the Colonel. "They'll tell you what I'm telling you themselves, if you get to know them and go into their homes. You won't believe it, but some of my best friends are Jews," he said, simply and thoughtfully, with an air of originality. "They may be *your* best friends, Colonel," I retorted, "but you are not theirs. I defy you to tell me that you talk to them as you're talking now." "Sure," said the Colonel, easily. "More or less." "They must be very queer Jews you know," I observed tartly, and I began to wonder whether there indeed existed a peculiar class of Jews whose function in life was to be "friends" with such people as the Colonel. It was difficult to think that all the anti-Semites who made the Colonel's assertion were the victims of a cruel self-deception.

A dispirited silence followed. I was not one of those liberals who be- 16 lieved that the Jews, alone among peoples, possessed no characteristics whatever of a distinguishing nature—this would mean they had no history and no culture, a charge which should be leveled against them only by an anti-Semite. Certainly, types of Jews could be noted and patterns of Jewish thought and feeling: Jewish humor, Jewish rationality, and so on, not that every Jew reflected every attribute of Jewish life or history. But somehow, with the Colonel, I dared not concede that there was such a thing as a Jew: I saw the sad meaning of the assertion that a Jew was a person whom other people thought was Jewish.

Hopeless, however, to convey this to the Colonel. The desolate truth 17 was that the Colonel was extremely stupid, and it came to me, as we sat there, glumly ordering lunch, that for extremely stupid people anti-Semitism was a form of intellectuality, the sole form of intellectuality of which they were capable. It represented, in a rudimentary way, the ability to make categories, to generalize. Hence a thing I had noted before but never understood: the fact that anti-Semitic statements were generally delivered in an atmosphere of profundity. Furrowed brows attended these speculative distinctions between a kike and a Jew, these little empirical laws that you can't know one without knowing them all. To arrive, indeed, at the idea of a Jew was, for these grouping minds, an exercise in Platonic thought, a discovery of essence,* and to be able to add the great corollary, "Some of my best friends are Jews," was to find the philosopher's cleft between essence and existence. From this, it

---

*For Plato, every object in *this* world—the world perceivable by the physical senses—is merely a shadow of its *essential* identity, a non-material version of itself existing on a spiritual plane. Thus to discover the "essence" of a thing is to discover the ultimate truth about it.

would seem, followed the querulous obstinacy with which the anti-Semite clung to his concept; to be deprived of this intellectual tool by missionaries of tolerance would be, for persons like the Colonel, the equivalent of Western man's losing the syllogism: a lapse into animal darkness. In the club car, we had just witnessed an example: the Colonel with his anti-Semitic observation had come to the mute young man like the paraclete, bearing the gift of tongues.

Here in the bar, it grew plainer and plainer that the Colonel did not 18 regard himself as an anti-Semite but merely as a heavy thinker. The idea that I considered him anti-Semitic sincerely outraged his feelings. "Prejudice" was the last trait he could have imputed to himself. He looked on me, almost respectfully, as a "Jew lover," a kind of being he had heard of but never actually encountered, like a centaur or a Siamese twin, and the interest of relating this prodigy to the natural state of mankind overrode any personal distaste. There I sat, the exception which was "proving" or testing the rule, and he kept pressing me for details of my history that might explain my deviation in terms of the norm. On my side, of course, I had become fiercely resolved that he would learn nothing from me that would make it possible for him to dismiss my anti-anti-Semitism as the product of special circumstances: I was stubbornly sitting on the fact of my Jewish grandmother like a hen on a golden egg. I was bent on making *him* see himself as a monster, a deviation, a heretic from Church and State. Unfortunately, the Colonel, owing perhaps to his military training, had not the glimmering of an idea of what democracy meant; to him, it was simply a slogan that was sometimes useful in war. The notion of an ordained inequality was to him "scientific."

"Honestly," he was saying in lowered tones, as our drinks were taken 19 away and the waitress set down my sandwich and his corned-beef hash, "don't you, brought up the way you were, feel about them the way I do? Just between ourselves, isn't there a sort of inborn feeling of horror that the very word, Jew, suggests?" I shook my head, roundly. The idea of an *innate* anti-Semitism was in keeping with the rest of the Colonel's thought, yet it shocked me more than anything he had yet said. "No," I sharply replied. "It doesn't evoke any feeling one way or the other." "Honest Injun?" said the Colonel. "Think back; when you were a kid, didn't the word, Jew, make you feel sick?"* There was a dreadful sincerity about this that made me answer in an almost kindly tone. "No, truthfully, I assure you. When we were children, we learned to call the old-clothes man a sheeny, but that was just a dirty word to us, like 'Hun' that we used to call after workmen we thought were Germans."

"I don't get it," pondered the Colonel, eating a pickle. "There must be 20 something wrong with you. Everybody is born with that feeling. It's natural; it's part of nature." "On the contrary," I said. "It's something very unnatural that you must have been taught as a child." "It's not something you're *taught*,"

---

*Compare the similarity of the Colonel's views with the views of Hitler in *Mein Kampf* (pp. 307–314).

he protested. "You must have been," I said. "You simply don't remember it. In any case, you're a man now; you must rid yourself of that feeling. It's psychopathic, like that horrible young man on the train." "You thought he was crazy?" mused the Colonel, in an idle, dreamy tone. I shrugged my shoulders. "Of course. Think of his color. He was probably just out of a mental institution. People don't get that tattletale gray except in prison or mental hospitals." The Colonel suddenly grinned. "You might be right," he said. "He was quite a case." He chuckled.

    I leaned forward. "You know, Colonel," I said quickly, "anti-Semitism 21 is contrary to the Church's teaching. God will make you do penance for hating the Jews. Ask your priest; he'll tell you I'm right. You'll have a long spell in Purgatory, if you don't rid yourself of this sin. It's a deliberate violation of Christ's commandment, 'Love thy neighbor.' The Church holds that the Jews have a sacred place in God's design. Mary was a Jew and Christ was a Jew. The Jews are under God's special protection. The Church teaches that the millennium can't come until the conversion of the Jews; therefore, the Jews must be preserved that the Divine Will may be accomplished. Woe to them that harm them, for they controvert God's Will!" In the course of speaking, I had swept myself away with the solemnity of the doctrine. The Great Reconciliation between God and His chosen people, as envisioned by the Evangelist, had for me at that moment a piercing, majestic beauty, like some awesome Tintoretto. I saw a noble spectacle of blue sky, thronged with gray clouds, and a vast white desert, across which God and Israel advanced to meet each other, while below in hell the demons of disunion shrieked and gnashed their teeth.

    "Hell," said the Colonel, jovially. "I don't believe in all that. I lost my 22 faith when I was a kid. I saw that all this God stuff was a lot of bushwa." I gazed at him in stupefaction. His confidence had completely returned. The blue eyes glittered debonairly; the eagles glittered; the narrow polished head cocked and listened to itself like a trilling bird. I was up against an air man with a bird's-eye view, a man who believed in nothing but the law of kind: the epitome of godless materialism. "You still don't hold with that bunk?" the Colonel inquired in an undertone, with an expression of stealthy curiosity. "No," I confessed, sad to admit to a meeting of minds. "You know what got me?" exclaimed the Colonel. "That birth-control stuff. Didn't it kill you?" I made a neutral sound. "I was beginning to play around," said the Colonel, with a significant beam of the eye, "and I just couldn't take that guff. When I saw through the birth-control talk, I saw through the whole thing. They claimed it was against nature, but I claim, if that's so, an operation's against nature. I told my old man that when he was having his kidney stones out. You ought to have heard him yell!" A rich, reminiscent satisfaction dwelt in the Colonel's face.

    This period of his life, in which he had thrown off the claims of the 23 spiritual and adopted a practical approach, was evidently one of those "turning points" to which a man looks back with pride. He lingered over the story of his break with church and parents with a curious sort of heat, as though

the flames of old sexual conquests stirred within his body at the memory of
those old quarrels. The looks he rested on me, as a sharer of that experience,
grew more and more lickerish and assaying. "What got *you* down?" he finally
inquired, settling back in his chair and pushing his coffee cup aside. "Oh,"
I said wearily, "it's a long story. You can read it when it's published." "You're
an author?" cried the Colonel, who was really very slow-witted. I nodded,
and the Colonel regarded me afresh. "What do you write? Love stories?" He
gave a half-wink. "No," I said. "Various things. Articles. Books. Highbrowish
stories." A suspicion darkened in the Colonel's sharp face. "That McCarthy,"
he said. "Is that your pen name?" "Yes," I said, "but it's my real name too.
It's the name I write under *and* my maiden name." The Colonel digested this
thought. "Oh," he concluded.

A new idea seemed to visit him. Quite cruelly, I watched it take posses- 24
sion. He was thinking of the power of the press and the indiscretions of other
military figures, who had been rewarded with demotion. The consciousness
of the uniform he wore appeared to seep uneasily into his body. He straight-
ened his shoulders and called thoughtfully for the check. We paid in silence,
the Colonel making no effort to forestall my dive into my pocketbook. I
should not have let him pay in any case, but it startled me that he did not
try to do so, if only for reasons of vanity. The whole business of paying,
apparently, was painful to him; I watched his facial muscles contract as he
pocketed the change and slipped two dimes for the waitress onto the table,
not daring quite to hide them under the coffee cup—he had short-changed
me on the bill and the tip, and we both knew it. We walked out into the
steaming station and I took my baggage out of the checking locker. The
Colonel carried my suitcase and we strolled along without speaking. Again,
I felt horribly embarrassed for him. He was meditative, and I supposed that
he too was mortified by his meanness about the tip.

"Don't get me wrong," he said suddenly, setting the suitcase down and 25
turning squarely to face me, as though he had taken a big decision. "I may
have said a few things back there about the Jews getting what they deserved
in Germany." I looked at him in surprise; actually, he had not said that to me.
Perhaps he had let it drop in the club car. "But that doesn't mean I approve
of Hitler." "I should hope not," I said. "What I mean is," said the Colonel,
"that they probably gave the Germans a lot of provocation, but that doesn't
excuse what Hitler did." "No," I said, somewhat ironically, but the Colonel
was unaware of anything satiric in the air. His face was grave and determined;
he was sorting out his philosophy for the record. "I mean, I don't approve of
his methods," he finally stated. "No," I agreed. "You mean, you don't approve of the gas chamber." The Colonel shook his head very severely. "Absolutely not! That was terrible." He shuddered and drew out a handkerchief and
slowly wiped his brow. "For God's sake," he said, "don't get me wrong. I
think they're human beings." "Yes," I assented, and we walked along to my
track. The Colonel's spirits lifted, as though, having stated his credo, he had
both got himself in line with public policy and achieved an autonomous

thought. "I mean," he resumed, "you may not care for them, but that's not the same as killing them, in cold blood, like that." "No, Colonel," I said.

He swung my bag onto the car's platform and I climbed up behind it. 26 He stood below, smiling, with upturned face. "I'll look for your article," he cried, as the train whistle blew. I nodded, and the Colonel waved, and I could not stop myself from waving back at him and even giving him the corner of a smile. After all, I said to myself, looking down at him, the Colonel was "a human being." There followed one of those inane intervals in which one prays for the train to leave. We both glanced at our watches. "See you some time," he called. "What's your married name?" "Broadwater," I called back. The whistle blew again. "Brodwater?" shouted the Colonel, with a dazed look of unbelief and growing enlightenment; he was not the first person to hear it as a Jewish name, on the model of Goldwater. "B-r-o-a-d," I began, automatically, but then I stopped. I disdained to spell it out for him; the victory was his. "One of the chosen, eh?" his brief grimace commiserated. For the last time, and in the final fullness of understanding, the hawk eye patrolled the green dress, the duster, and the earrings; the narrow flue of his nostril contracted as he curtly turned away. The train commenced to move.

Questions for Discussion

1. Why is McCarthy's narrator so upset in paragraph 3 to realize that she has been discovered as an artist: "I had always particularly preened myself on being an artist in disguise"? What criticism or support can you offer for her desire to stay unknown as an artist among strangers?

2. What quality in the central figure's character is revealed when she says, "I exulted to think that I had made a modest contribution to sanity in our times, and I imagined my words pyramiding like a chain letter" (¶4)?

3. The reader gradually realizes that the narrator, in conversing with the Colonel, is not only deceiving herself about her own motives but is also being dishonest in her mode of arguing (attacking the Colonel, for example, with Church doctrines that she herself does not believe). Later, however, in writing it all down as a story, she seems completely honest and judgmental about her faults. To what degree does her subsequent honesty redeem her character in the reader's eyes? Are there any who dislike her as a person at the end of the story? For what reasons?

4. What does the narrator mean at the end of paragragh 12 when she says, "If I had been a good person, I should unquestionably have got up and left"? Why does she make this judgment? Do you agree with it? What do you think you would have done in her place?

5. Why does the narrator say at the end, "I disdained to spell it out for him;

the victory was his"? What victory? Why does she not tell him that Broadwater is not a Jewish name? She has argued so hard and spent so much energy trying to convert the Colonel, why does she let him walk away thinking that he now knows why she objected to his anti-Semitism?

Suggested Essay Topics

1. If you have ever felt unfair pressure to conform to majority opinion, write an essay in which you give an account of the experience, explaining how you felt and analyzing, as McCarthy does, the source of the pressure. Finally, evaluate your behavior in the face of it. Address your essay to a sympathetic friend to whom you want to give as complete an account of the experience as possible.

2. Most of us would probably agree with the old aphorism "The majority should rule." But where is the line that, when crossed, turns "majority rule" into "suppression of dissent"? And where is the line that, when crossed, turns the individual rights of the few into tyranny of the underdog? Choose some particular case that interests you and analyze it, attempting to uphold the rights of the individual (or the minority) against the will of the majority or, if the case warrants it, the rights of the majority against the will of the individual (or the minority). You might consider, for example, the justice of upholding minority quotas for job openings or for admission into schools, especially when the quotas seem to force the hiring or admission of minority candidates less qualified than others. Or you might discuss the right of men's and women's private clubs to ban members of the opposite sex, the prohibition of girls from Little League baseball, or some similar matter.

IDEAS IN DEBATE

Ayn Rand
Martin Luther King, Jr.
e. e. cummings

Ayn Rand

Ayn Rand (1905–1982) was born and educated in Russia, where as a young woman she experienced the Bolshevik Revolution and the extreme restrictions of individual freedom that Soviet collectivization imposed. A naturalized American citizen, she published a series of novels and essays urging the pursuit of freedom through a total individualism. The Fountainhead *(1943), probably her best-known novel, portrays a great architect as a model of the achievements possible for a creative and uninhibited individual. Her credo is perhaps best summarized in the oath sworn by the citizens of an imaginary community described in* Atlas Shrugged *(1957): "I will never live for the sake of another man, nor ask any other man to live for mine."*

The following excerpt is from Anthem, *a novelette portraying the fate of a courageous dissenter in a totalitarian state. The excerpt is a hymn of praise sung by the hero to his god—himself. As you read, you might think of similar attitudes expressed in your time—though in a different style (for example, in the 1970s best-seller* Looking Out for No. 1 *by Robert J. Ringer).*

I OWE NOTHING TO MY BROTHERS

Our title for chapter 11 of *Anthem* (1938).

I AM. I THINK. I WILL.

1

My hands . . . My spirit . . . My sky . . . My forest . . . This earth of mine. . . .

2

What must I say besides? These are the words. This is the answer.

3

I stand here on the summit of the mountain. I lift my head and I spread my arms. This, my body and spirit, this is the end of the quest. I wished to

4

know the meaning of things. I am the meaning. I wished to find a warrant for being. I need no warrant for being, and no word of sanction upon my being. I am the warrant and the sanction.

It is my eyes which see, and the sight of my eyes grants beauty to the 5 earth. It is my ears which hear, and the hearing of my ears gives its song to the world. It is my mind which thinks, and the judgment of my mind is the only searchlight that can find the truth. It is my will which chooses, and the choice of my will is the only edict I must respect.

Many words have been granted me, and some are wise, and some are 6 false, but only three are holy: "I will it!"

Whatever road I take, the guiding star is within me; the guiding star and 7 the loadstone which point the way. They point in but one direction. They point to me.

I know not if this earth on which I stand is the core of the universe or 8 if it is but a speck of dust lost in eternity. I know not and I care not. For I know what happiness is possible to me on earth. And my happiness needs no higher aim to vindicate it. My happiness is not the means to any end. It is the end. It is its own goal. It is its own purpose.

Neither am I the means to any end others may wish to accomplish. I am 9 not a tool for their use. I am not a servant of their needs. I am not a bandage for their wounds. I am not a sacrifice on their altars.

I am a man. This miracle of me is mine to own and keep, and mine to 10 guard, and mine to use, and mine to kneel before!

I do not surrender my treasures, nor do I share them. The fortune of my 11 spirit is not to be blown into coins of brass and flung to the winds as alms for the poor of the spirit. I guard my treasures: my thought, my will, my freedom. And the greatest of these is freedom.

I owe nothing to my brothers, nor do I gather debts from them. I ask 12 none to live for me, nor do I live for any others. I covet no man's soul, nor is my soul theirs to covet.

I am neither foe nor friend to my brothers, but such as each of them shall 13 deserve of me. And to earn my love, my brothers must do more than to have been born. I do not grant my love without reason, nor to any chance passer-by who may wish to claim it. I honor men with my love. But honor is a thing to be earned.

I shall choose friends among men, but neither slaves nor masters. And   14
I shall choose only such as please me, and them I shall love and respect, but
neither command nor obey. And we shall join our hands when we wish, or
walk alone when we so desire. For in the temple of his spirit, each man is
alone. Let each man keep his temple untouched and undefiled. Then let him
join hands with others if he wishes, but only beyond his holy threshold.

For the word "We" must never be spoken, save by one's choice and as   15
a second thought. This word must never be placed first within man's soul, else
it becomes a monster, the root of all the evils on earth, the root of man's
torture by men, and of an unspeakable lie.

The word "We" is as lime poured over men, which sets and hardens to   16
stone, and crushes all beneath it, and that which is white and that which is
black are lost equally in the grey of it. It is the word by which the depraved
steal the virtue of the good, by which the weak steal the might of the strong,
by which the fools steal the wisdom of the sages.

What is my joy if all hands, even the unclean, can reach into it? What   17
is my wisdom, if even the fools can dictate to me? What is my freedom, if
all creatures, even the botched and the impotent, are my masters? What is my
life, if I am but to bow, to agree and to obey?

But I am done with this creed of corruption.   18

I am done with the monster of "We," the word of serfdom, of plunder,   19
of misery, falsehood and shame.

And now I see the face of god, and I raise this god over the earth, this   20
god whom men have sought since men came into being, this god who will
grant them joy and peace and pride.

This god, this one word: 21

"I."   22

Questions for Discussion

1. People who like to think in slogans call the 1970s and 1980s "the me
   decades." *Anthem* was written in the 1930s, sometimes called "the decade
   of social responsibility." Does the position expressed in "I Owe Nothing

to My Brothers" seem to resemble or to contrast with the basic beliefs that have been fashionable since you became aware of "beliefs" at all?

2. The doctrine proclaimed in this excerpt from *Anthem* is in one sense deliberately "anti-social." Does it seem to you finally dangerous to society? Give your reasons. What do you think Rand would reply to anyone who claimed that she cared only about the welfare of the selfish and powerful?

3. Phrases like "the me decade," "the decade of social responsibility," "the apathetic decade" (the 1950s), and "the decade of protest" (the 1960s) at best cover only a limited number of the trends and topics of a given period. People pick them up as a way of talking easily about the past, but when we press our memories or do research we usually find more exceptions than illustrations. Ayn Rand might say that our tendency to use these catchphrases in our thinking is just one more example of our being too dependent on other people. Yet she inevitably depends, as we all do, on earlier thinkers (Nietzsche, perhaps, for the glorification of the independent "I"; Thomas Jefferson, for the inalienable right to the pursuit of happiness; Aristotle, for the relentless pursuit of rationality). Thus her ideas, like those of every other thinker, can almost all be traced to predecessors. Does this unavoidable kinship with earlier thinkers seriously undermine Rand's notion that each individual should attempt to worship and serve only the "I"? How does her "I" relate to the "we" who have thought similar thoughts?

4. Although Ayn Rand often advocates reliance on reason as the ultimate test of truth, the tone of this chapter from *Anthem* is "oracular"; it resembles what we might call the "prophetic" tone of I Corinthians 13 (pp. 200–201). Compare, for example, Rand's paragraph 18 with St. Paul's verse 11. The voice in "I Owe Nothing to My Brothers" is that of an "oracle," one who speaks to us from the "summit of the mountain" (like Moses at Mt. Sinai), uttering truths that seem to have come from a higher source than is available to ordinary mortals. Conclusions are pronounced without the usual kinds of supporting evidence, and each assertion is loaded with an unusually strong emotional commitment. Indeed, the whole utterance is couched in the language of scripture ("guiding star," ¶7; "miracle," ¶10; "fortune of my spirit," ¶11; "covet," ¶12; "temple" and "holy," ¶14; and so on). Read the passage slowly and list all the other "scriptural" devices used by the speaker—not just those that explicitly echo the Bible but any device or turn of phrase suggesting that "these utterances are not to be tested by the usual tests. Do not question my word; it comes from on high."

5. When two oracles seem to contradict each other, as do St. Paul and Rand, how are we to deal with them? One simple way would be to dismiss *all* such writing and speaking as absurd because it cannot be tested with rational tests. Another way would be to listen to one of the two voices uncritically: *My* prophet is simply right and yours self-evidently wrong. Can you think of other possibilities?

6. One possible answer to question 5 would be this: When oracles conflict, there may be *some* truth in each, and the way to find out how much is to slow down and think about the *consequences,* both intellectual and practical, of taking the oracles seriously. Oracles do not, in themselves, usually talk about consequences; their tone suggests that life would be simple if we would only give up every reservation and follow the true doctrine. But as readers who want to learn from them, provided that they really have anything worthwhile to teach, we can step back a bit and ask what their message would mean to our effort to build livable worlds for ourselves. First, what do you think would be the consequences, for you, if you decided to put into practice the values expressed by Rand? Second, what would be the consequences for *you* if everyone you know decided to live by these values?

7. Another way to test an oracle is to ask whether the utterance is consistent within itself. Do you detect any internal inconsistencies in Rand's message? In St. Paul's?

8. The past decade has seen a remarkable growth in the popularity and influence of TV evangelists, claiming to offer us a saving truth. One good question to ask of these oracles, a question surprisingly often neglected by people who jump and join, is this: "What is there in it for *you*—the prophet?" Does the question yield different results when asked of St. Paul and when asked of Rand or of the TV evangelists?

Note: The executor of Miss Ayn Rand's estate, Mr. Leonard Peikoff, responding to our request to reprint this selection from *Anthem,* suggested that some of our discussion questions seriously misrepresent Ayn Rand's thought.

Miss Rand repudiates all forms of mysticism and religion; she advocates exclusive reliance on reason as a means of cognition, and she has written an entire book defining her conception of "reason" (*Introduction to Objectivist Epistemology*). To liken her method or approach, therefore, to that of St. Paul, and to describe her viewpoint as "oracular," is unacceptable in point of accuracy and scholarship. *Anthem* is, of course, a novelette, not a philosophical treatise; as such each sentence does not come equipped with lengthy exegesis or geometric demonstration. But this does not mean that the viewpoint is "oracular." Within its own context, the reasons *are* advanced: the events of the preceding story give the rationale for the summarizing conclusion which you wish to quote. For a full proof of Ayn Rand's ethical viewpoint, including a discussion of the meta-ethical problems of validation involved, I would refer you to her book *The Virtue of Selfishness*.

Suggested Essay Topics

1. "I owe nothing to my brothers, nor do I gather debts from them" (¶10). Imagine a friend of yours who, after reading Rand's chapter from *Anthem,*

has decided that her celebration of "I" as against "We" is sound guidance for life. Write *one* of the following letters:

a. A letter arguing against the decision, concentrating on why this one statement seems factually doubtful.
b. A letter arguing in support of her views, concentrating on why this statement seems sound to you.
c. A letter debating the pros and cons of the position, describing as many reasons as you can for and against saying that you "owe" something to your brothers (and sisters).

2. Most of your essays will attempt to give more supporting evidence for your claims than is appropriate in "prophetic" writing. But this topic is your chance to climb onto your own mountaintop and shout whatever truths you would like the whole world to believe. Choose your favorite cause—some behavior or set of beliefs you'd like the whole world to adopt—and let yourself go. (One possibility: a hymn to the god "We," in answer to Rand's celebration of the great god "I.")

Martin Luther King, Jr.

Martin Luther King, Jr. (1929–1968), a leader of the civil rights movement, first achieved national prominence during the late 1950s and early 1960s. The scope of his social vision, the moral integrity of his commitment to nonviolence, the authority of his voice, and the generous, incandescent passion of his love for an America not yet realized marked King early as a force larger than any local or particular movement pushing for social change. In 1964 he was awarded the Nobel Peace Prize. In 1968 he was assassinated while on a visit to Memphis, Tennessee, lending support to a strike for higher wages by the garbage workers of that city.

Like Socrates, who persistently reminded his fellow Athenians that they cared more for custom, comfort, and security than for the pursuit of truth or the cultivation of their souls, King reminded his fellow Americans that they cared more for the color of their fellow citizens' skins than for compassion, dignity, or justice. Also like Socrates, who chose to accept execution as a subversive rather than live in exile from his beloved Athens, King always made it clear that he attacked the practices of his country out of love, not hatred. Socrates could be unmerciful in flogging his friends' inconsistencies, hypocrisies, and deceptions and still show that he preferred their company to all others—that he needled them only because he loved them. In the same way, King could express annoyance, disappointment, frustration, and anger at his fellow Americans' foot-dragging on the issue of social justice (especially the foot-dragging of the self-styled "moderate liberal") and still show that what he wanted was for this country to live up to the dream of its best self.

The title of the piece reprinted here is factual; King wrote this letter while he was indeed in prison. The immediate circumstances and local history of the conflict are partially explained in the letter itself. But of course the significance of such matters shifts for us depending on our perspective. For Booth, who was 42 years old when the letter was written, to re-read it now is to experience again the excitement and admiration he felt at the time. For Gregory, who in 1963 was freshly graduated from an isolated, predominantly white college in central Indiana and who had never before faced seriously the problem of racial injustice, the movement King championed produced what he now considers a major awakening, a transformation of conscience and consciousness. But for most of you who read this book, the events took place before you were born and probably seem to you part of the distant past.

For all of us the meaning of those events shifts as we learn more and more about what they led to. What does not shift, as our memories dim and we become more and more dependent on historical accounts, is our picture of the grandeur of King's achievement. King's letter, addressing the conscience of a nation and testing its moral resolve, embraces far more than Birmingham, Alabama, 1963, as it speaks to people of any time and any place who care about justice.

LETTER FROM BIRMINGHAM JAIL*

From *Why We Can't Wait* (1964).

April 16, 1963

My Dear Fellow Clergymen:

While confined here in the Birmingham city jail, I came across your **1** recent statement calling my present activities "unwise and untimely." Seldom do I pause to answer criticism of my work and ideas. If I sought to answer all the criticisms that cross my desk, my secretaries would have little time for anything other than such correspondence in the course of the day, and I would have no time for constructive work. But since I feel that you are men of genuine good will and that your criticisms are sincerely set forth, I want to try to answer your statement in what I hope will be patient and reasonable terms.

I think I should indicate why I am here in Birmingham, since you have **2** been influenced by the view which argues against "outsiders coming in." I have the honor of serving as president of the Southern Christian Leadership Conference, an organization operating in every southern state, with head-

---

*This response to a published statement by eight fellow clergymen from Alabama (Bishop C. C. J. Carpenter, Bishop Joseph A. Durick, Rabbi Hilton L. Grafman, Bishop Paul Hardin, Bishop Holan B. Harmon, the Reverend George M. Murray, the Reverend Edward V. Ramage and the Reverend Earl Stallings) was composed under somewhat constricting circumstances. Begun on the margins of the newspaper in which the statement appeared while I was in jail, the letter was continued on scraps of writing paper supplied by a friendly Negro trusty, and concluded on a pad my attorneys were eventually permitted to leave me. Although the text remains in substance unaltered, I have indulged in the author's prerogative of polishing it for publication. [King's note]

quarters in Atlanta, Georgia. We have some eighty-five affiliated organizations across the South, and one of them is the Alabama Christian Movement for Human Rights. Frequently we share staff, educational and financial resources with our affiliates. Several months ago the affiliate here in Birmingham asked us to be on call to engage in a nonviolent direct-action program if such were deemed necessary. We readily consented, and when the hour came we lived up to our promise. So I, along with several members of my staff, am here because I was invited here. I am here because I have organizational ties here.

But more basically, I am in Birmingham because injustice is here. Just as the prophets of the eighth century B.C. left their villages and carried their "thus saith the Lord" far beyond the boundaries of their home towns, and just as the Apostle Paul left his village of Tarsus and carried the gospel of Jesus Christ to the far corners of the Greco-Roman world, so am I compelled to carry the gospel of freedom beyond my own home town. Like Paul, I must constantly respond to the Macedonian call for aid.

Moreover, I am cognizant of the interrelatedness of all communities and states. I cannot sit idly by in Atlanta and not be concerned about what happens in Birmingham. Injustice anywhere is a threat to justice everywhere. We are caught in an inescapable network of mutuality, tied in a single garment of destiny. Whatever affects one directly, affects all indirectly. Never again can we afford to live with the narrow, provincial "outside agitator" idea. Anyone who lives inside the United States can never be considered an outsider anywhere within its bounds.

You deplore the demonstrations taking place in Birmingham. But your statement, I am sorry to say, fails to express a similar concern for the conditions that brought about the demonstrations. I am sure that none of you would want to rest content with the superficial kind of social analysis that deals merely with effects and does not grapple with underlying causes. It is unfortunate that demonstrations are taking place in Birmingham, but it is even more unfortunate that the city's white power structure left the Negro community with no alternative.

In any nonviolent campaign there are four basic steps: collection of the facts to determine whether injustices exist; negotiation; self-purification; and direct action. We have gone through all these steps in Birmingham. There can be no gainsaying the fact that racial injustice engulfs this community. Birmingham is probably the most thoroughly segregated city in the United States. Its ugly record of brutality is widely known. Negroes have experienced grossly unjust treatment in the courts. There have been more unsolved bombings of Negro homes and churches in Birmingham than in any other city in the nation. These are the hard, brutal facts of the case. On the basis of these conditions, Negro leaders sought to negotiate with the city fathers. But the latter consistently refused to engage in good-faith negotiation.

Then, last September, came the opportunity to talk with leaders of Birmingham's economic community. In the course of the negotiations, certain promises were made by the merchants—for example, to remove the stores' humiliating racial signs. On the basis of these promises, the Reverend Fred Shuttlesworth and the leaders of the Alabama Christian Movement for Human Rights agreed to a moratorium on all demonstrations. As the weeks and months went by, we realized that we were the victims of a broken promise. A few signs, briefly removed, returned; the others remained.

As in so many past experiences, our hopes had been blasted, and the   8 shadow of deep disappointment settled upon us. We had no alternative except to prepare for direct action, whereby we would present our very bodies as a means of laying our case before the conscience of the local and the national community. Mindful of the difficulties involved, we decided to undertake a process of self-purification. We began a series of workshops on nonviolence, and we repeatedly asked ourselves: "Are you able to accept blows without retaliating?" "Are you able to endure the ordeal of jail?" We decided to schedule our direct-action program for the Easter season, realizing that except for Christmas, this is the main shopping period of the year. Knowing that a strong economic-withdrawal program would be the by-product of direct action, we felt that this would be the best time to bring pressure to bear on the merchants for the needed change.

Then it occurred to us that Birmingham's mayoral election was coming   9 up in March, and we speedily decided to postpone action until after election day. When we discovered that the Commissioner of Public Safety, Eugene "Bull" Connor, had piled up enough votes to be in the run-off, we decided again to postpone action until the day after the run-off so that the demonstrations could not be used to cloud the issues. Like many others, we waited to see Mr. Connor defeated, and to this end we endured postponement after postponement. Having aided in this community need, we felt that our direct-action program could be delayed no longer.

You may well ask: "Why direct action? Why sit-ins, marches and so   10 forth? Isn't negotiation a better path?" You are quite right in calling for negotiation. Indeed, this is the very purpose of direct action. Nonviolent direct action seeks to create such a crisis and foster such a tension that a community which has constantly refused to negotiate is forced to confront the issue. It seeks so to dramatize the issue that it can no longer be ignored. My citing the creation of tension as part of the work of the nonviolent-resister may sound rather shocking. But I must confess that I am not afraid of the word "tension." I have earnestly opposed violent tension, but there is a type of constructive, nonviolent tension which is necessary for growth. Just as Socrates felt that it was necessary to create a tension in the mind so that individuals could rise from the bondage of myths and half-truths to the unfettered realm of creative analysis and objective appraisal, so must we see the need for nonviolent gadflies to create the kind of tension in society that will help men rise from the dark depths of prejudice and racism to the majestic heights of understanding and brotherhood.

The purpose of our direct-action program is to create a situation so   11 crisis-packed that it will inevitably open the door to negotiation. I therefore concur with you in your call for negotiation. Too long has our beloved

Southland been bogged down in a tragic effort to live in monologue rather than dialogue.

One of the basic points in your statement is that the action that I and   12
my associates have taken in Birmingham is untimely. Some have asked: "Why didn't you give the new city administration time to act?" The only answer that I can give to this query is that the new Birmingham administration must be prodded about as much as the outgoing one, before it will act. We are sadly mistaken if we feel that the election of Albert Boutwell as mayor will bring the millennium to Birmingham. While Mr. Boutwell is a much more gentle person than Mr. Connor, they are both segregationists, dedicated to maintenance of the status quo. I have hope that Mr. Boutwell will be reasonable enough to see the futility of massive resistance to desegregation. But he will not see this without pressure from devotees of civil rights. My friends, I must say to you that we have not made a single gain in civil rights without determined legal and nonviolent pressure. Lamentably, it is an historical fact that privileged groups seldom give up their privileges voluntarily. Individuals may see the moral light and voluntarily give up their unjust posture; but, as Reinhold Niebuhr* has reminded us, groups tend to be more immoral than individuals.

We know through painful experience that freedom is never voluntarily   13
given by the oppressor; it must be demanded by the oppressed. Frankly, I have yet to engage in a direct-action campaign that was "well timed" in the view of those who have not suffered unduly from the disease of segregation. For years now I have heard the word "Wait!" It rings in the ear of every Negro with piercing familiarity. This "Wait" has almost always meant "Never." We must come to see, with one of our distinguished jurists, that "justice too long delayed is justice denied."

We have waited for more than 340 years for our constitutional and   14
God-given rights. The nations of Asia and Africa are moving with jetlike speed toward gaining political independence, but we still creep at horse-and-buggy pace toward gaining a cup of coffee at a lunch counter. Perhaps it is easy for those who have never felt the stinging darts of segregation to say, "Wait." But when you have seen vicious mobs lynch your mothers and fathers at will and drown your sisters and brothers at whim; when you have seen hate-filled policemen curse, kick and even kill your black brothers and sisters; when you see the vast majority of your twenty million Negro brothers smothering in an airtight cage of poverty in the midst of an affluent society; when you suddenly find your tongue twisted and your speech stammering as you seek to explain to your six-year-old daughter why she can't go to the public amusement park that has just been advertised on television, and see tears welling up in her eyes when she is told that Funtown is closed to colored children, and see ominous clouds of inferiority beginning to form in her little mental sky, and see her beginning to distort her personality by developing

*American clergyman and theologian (1892–1971). The book King refers to is *Moral Man and Immoral Society* (1932).

an unconscious bitterness toward white people; when you have to concoct an answer for a five-year-old son who is asking: "Daddy, why do white people treat colored people so mean?"; when you take a cross-country drive and find it necessary to sleep night after night in the uncomfortable corners of your automobile because no motel will accept you; when you are humiliated day in and day out by nagging signs reading "white" and "colored"; when your first name becomes "nigger," your middle name becomes "boy" (however old you are) and your last name becomes "John," and your wife and mother are never given the respected title "Mrs."; when you are harried by day and haunted by night by the fact that you are a Negro, living constantly at tiptoe stance, never quite knowing what to expect next, and are plagued with inner fears and outer resentments; when you are forever fighting a degenerating sense of "nobodiness"—then you will understand why we find it difficult to wait. There comes a time when the cup of endurance runs over, and men are no longer willing to be plunged into the abyss of despair. I hope, sirs, you can understand our legitimate and unavoidable impatience.

You express a great deal of anxiety over our willingness to break laws. 15 This is certainly a legitimate concern. Since we so diligently urge people to obey the Supreme Court's decision of 1954 outlawing segregation in the public schools, at first glance it may seem rather paradoxical for us consciously to break laws. One may well ask: "How can you advocate breaking some laws and obeying others?" The answer lies in the fact that there are two types of laws: just and unjust. I would be the first to advocate obeying just laws. One has not only a legal but a moral responsibility to obey just laws. Conversely, one has a moral responsibility to disobey unjust laws. I would agree with St. Augustine that "an unjust law is no law at all."

Now, what is the difference between the two? How does one determine 16 whether a law is just or unjust? A just law is a man-made code that squares with the moral law or the law of God. An unjust law is a code that is out of harmony with the moral law. To put it in the terms of St. Thomas Aquinas: An unjust law is a human law that is not rooted in eternal law and natural law. Any law that uplifts human personality is just. Any law that degrades human personality is unjust. All segregation statutes are unjust because segregation distorts the soul and damages the personality. It gives the segregator a false sense of superiority and the segregated a false sense of inferiority. Segregation, to use the terminology of the Jewish philosopher Martin Buber, substitutes an "I-it" relationship for an "I-thou" relationship and ends up relegating persons to the status of things. Hence segregation is not only politically, economically and sociologically unsound, it is morally wrong and sinful. Paul Tillich has said that sin is separation. Is not segregation an existential expression of man's tragic separation, his awful estrangement, his terrible sinfulness? Thus it is that I can urge men to obey the 1954 decision of the Supreme Court, for it is morally right; and I can urge them to disobey segregation ordinances, for they are morally wrong.

Let us consider a more concrete example of just and unjust laws. An 17 unjust law is a code that a numerical or power majority group compels a minority group to obey but does not make binding on itself. This is *difference* made legal. By the same token, a just law is a code that a majority compels a minority to follow and that it is willing to follow itself. This is *sameness* made legal.

Let me give another explanation. A law is unjust if it is inflicted on a   18 minority that, as a result of being denied the right to vote, had no part in enacting or devising the law. Who can say that the legislature of Alabama which set up that state's segregation laws was democratically elected? Throughout Alabama all sorts of devious methods are used to prevent Negroes from becoming registered voters, and there are some counties in which, even though Negroes constitute a majority of the population, not a single Negro is registered. Can any law enacted under such circumstances be considered democratically structured?

Sometimes a law is just on its face and unjust in its application. For   19 instance, I have been arrested on a charge of parading without a permit. Now, there is nothing wrong in having an ordinance which requires a permit for a parade. But such an ordinance becomes unjust when it is used to maintain segregation and to deny citizens the First-Amendment privilege of peaceful assembly and protest.

I hope you are able to see the distinction I am trying to point out. In   20 no sense do I advocate evading or defying the law, as would the rabid segregationist. That would lead to anarchy. One who breaks an unjust law must do so openly, lovingly, and with a willingness to accept the penalty. I submit that an individual who breaks a law that conscience tells him is unjust, and who willingly accepts the penalty of imprisonment in order to arouse the conscience of the community over its injustice, is in reality expressing the highest respect for law.

Of course, there is nothing new about this kind of civil disobedience.   21 It was evidenced sublimely in the refusal of Shadrach, Meshach and Abed-nego to obey the laws of Nebuchadnezzar, on the ground that a higher moral law was at stake. It was practiced superbly by the early Christians, who were willing to face hungry lions and the excruciating pain of chopping blocks rather than submit to certain unjust laws of the Roman Empire. To a degree, academic freedom is a reality today because Socrates practiced civil disobedience. In our own nation, the Boston Tea Party represented a massive act of civil disobedience.

We should never forget that everything Adolf Hitler did in Germany   22 was "legal" and everything the Hungarian freedom fighters did in Hungary was "illegal." It was "illegal" to aid and comfort a Jew in Hitler's Germany. Even so, I am sure that, had I lived in Germany at the time, I would have aided and comforted my Jewish brothers. If today I lived in a Communist country where certain principles dear to the Christian faith are suppressed, I would openly advocate disobeying that country's antireligious laws.

I must make two honest confessions to you, my Christian and Jewish   23 brothers. First, I must confess that over the past few years I have been gravely disappointed with the white moderate. I have almost reached the regrettable

conclusion that the Negro's great stumbling block in his stride toward freedom is not the White Citizen's Counciler or the Ku Klux Klanner, but the
white moderate, who is more devoted to "order" than to justice; who prefers
a negative peace which is the absence of tension to a positive peace which
is the presence of justice; who constantly says: "I agree with you in the goal
you seek, but I cannot agree with your methods of direct action"; who
paternalistically believes he can set the timetable for another man's freedom;
who lives by a mythical concept of time and who constantly advises the
Negro to wait for a "more convenient season." Shallow understanding from
people of good will is more frustrating than absolute misunderstanding from
people of ill will. Lukewarm acceptance is much more bewildering than
outright rejection.

24 I had hoped that the white moderate would understand that law and
order exist for the purpose of establishing justice and that when they fail in
this purpose they become the dangerously structured dams that block the
flow of social progress. I had hoped that the white moderate would understand that the present tension in the South is a necessary phase of the
transition from an obnoxious negative peace, in which the Negro passively
accepted his unjust plight, to a substantive and positive peace, in which all
men will respect the dignity and worth of human personality. Actually, we
who engage in nonviolent direct action are not the creators of tension. We
merely bring to the surface the hidden tension that is already alive. We bring
it out in the open, where it can be seen and dealt with. Like a boil that can
never be cured so long as it is covered up but must be opened with all its
ugliness to the natural medicines of air and light, injustice must be exposed,
with all the tension its exposure creates, to the light of human conscience and
the air of national opinion before it can be cured.

25 In your statement you assert that our actions, even though peaceful,
must be condemned because they precipitate violence. But is this a logical
assertion? Isn't this like condemning a robbed man because his possession of
money precipitated the evil act of robbery? Isn't this like condemning Socrates because his unswerving commitment to truth and his philosophical inquiries precipitated the act by the misguided populace in which they made him
drink hemlock? Isn't this like condemning Jesus because his unique God-
consciousness and never-ceasing devotion to God's will precipitated the evil
act of crucifixion? We must come to see that, as the federal courts have
consistently affirmed, it is wrong to urge an individual to cease his efforts to
gain his basic constitutional rights because the quest may precipitate violence.
Society must protect the robbed and punish the robber.

26 I had also hoped that the white moderate would reject the myth concerning time in relation to the struggle for freedom. I have just received a
letter from a white brother in Texas. He writes: "All Christians know that the
colored people will receive equal rights eventually, but it is possible that you
are in too great a religious hurry. It has taken Christianity almost two thousand years to accomplish what it has. The teachings of Christ take time to
come to earth." Such an attitude stems from a tragic misconception of time,

from the strangely irrational notion that there is something in the very flow of time that will inevitably cure all ills. Actually, time itself is neutral; it can be used either destructively or constructively. More and more I feel that the people of ill will have used time much more effectively than have the people of good will. We will have to repent in this generation not merely for the hateful words and actions of the bad people but for the appalling silence of the good people. Human progress never rolls in on wheels of inevitability; it comes through the tireless efforts of men willing to be co-workers with God, and without this hard work, time itself becomes an ally of the forces of social stagnation. We must use time creatively, in the knowledge that the time is always ripe to do right. Now is the time to make real the promise of democracy and transform our pending national elegy into a creative psalm of brotherhood. Now is the time to lift our national policy from the quicksand of racial injustice to the solid rock of human dignity.

You speak of our activity in Birmingham as extreme. At first I was rather   27 disappointed that fellow clergymen would see my nonviolent efforts as those of an extremist. I began thinking about the fact that I stand in the middle of two opposing forces in the Negro community. One is a force of complacency, made up in part of Negroes who, as a result of long years of oppression, are so drained of self-respect and a sense of "somebodiness" that they have adjusted to segregation; and in part of a few middle-class Negroes who, because of a degree of academic and economic security and because in some ways they profit by segregation, have become insensitive to the problems of the masses. The other force is one of bitterness and hatred, and it comes perilously close to advocating violence. It is expressed in the various black nationalist groups that are springing up across the nation, the largest and best-known being Elijah Muhammad's Muslim movement. Nourished by the Negro's frustration over the continued existence of racial discrimination, this movement is made up of people who have lost faith in America, who have absolutely repudiated Christianity, and who have concluded that the white man is an incorrigible "devil."

I have tried to stand between these two forces, saying that we need   28 emulate neither the "do-nothingism" of the complacent nor the hatred and despair of the black nationalist. For there is the more excellent way of love and nonviolent protest. I am grateful to God that, through the influence of the Negro church, the way of nonviolence became an integral part of our struggle.

If this philosophy had not emerged, by now many streets of the South   29 would, I am convinced, be flowing with blood. And I am further convinced that if our white brothers dismiss as "rabble-rousers" and "outside agitators" those of us who employ nonviolent direct action, and if they refuse to support our nonviolent efforts, millions of Negroes will, out of frustration and despair, seek solace and security in black-nationalist ideologies—a development that would inevitably lead to a frightening racial nightmare.

Oppressed people cannot remain oppressed forever. The yearning for   30 freedom eventually manifests itself, and that is what has happened to the

American Negro. Something within has reminded him of his birthright of freedom, and something without has reminded him that it can be gained. Consciously or unconsciously, he has been caught up by the *Zeitgeist,* and with his black brothers of Africa and his brown and yellow brothers of Asia, South America and the Caribbean, the United States Negro is moving with a sense of great urgency toward the promised land of racial justice. If one recognizes this vital urge that has engulfed the Negro community, one should readily understand why public demonstrations are taking place. The Negro has many pent-up resentments and latent frustrations, and he must release them. So let him march; let him make prayer pilgrimages to the city hall; let him go on freedom rides—and try to understand why he must do so. If his repressed emotions are not released in nonviolent ways, they will seek expression through violence; this is not a threat but a fact of history. So I have not said to my people: "Get rid of your discontent." Rather, I have tried to say that this normal and healthy discontent can be channeled into the creative outlet of nonviolent direct action. And now this approach is being termed extremist.

But though I was initially disappointed at being categorized as an ex- 31 tremist, as I continued to think about the matter I gradually gained a measure of satisfaction from the label. Was not Jesus an extremist for love: "Love your enemies, bless them that curse you, do good to them that hate you, and pray for them which despitefully use you, and persecute you." Was not Amos an extremist for justice: "Let justice roll down like waters and righteousness like an ever-flowing stream." Was not Paul an extremist for the Christian gospel: "I bear in my body the marks of the Lord Jesus." Was not Martin Luther an extremist: "Here I stand; I cannot do otherwise, so help me God." And John Bunyan: "I will stay in jail to the end of my days before I make a butchery of my conscience." And Abraham Lincoln: "This nation cannot survive half slave and half free." And Thomas Jefferson: "We hold these truths to be self-evident, that all men are created equal . . ." So the question is not whether we will be extremists, but what kind of extremists we will be. Will we be extremists for hate or for love? Will we be extremists for the preservation of injustice or for the extension of justice? In that dramatic scene on Calvary's hill three men were crucified. We must never forget that all three were crucified for the same crime—the crime of extremism. Two were extremists for immorality, and thus fell below their environment. The other, Jesus Christ, was an extremist for love, truth and goodness, and thereby rose above his environment. Perhaps the South, the nation and the world are in dire need of creative extremists.

I had hoped that the white moderate would see this need. Perhaps I was 32 too optimistic; perhaps I expected too much. I suppose I should have realized that few members of the oppressor race can understand the deep groans and passionate yearnings of the oppressed race, and still fewer have the vision to see that injustice must be rooted out by strong, persistent and determined action. I am thankful, however, that some of our white brothers in the South have grasped the meaning of this social revolution and committed themselves to it. They are still all too few in quantity, but they are big in quality.

Some—such as Ralph McGill, Lillian Smith, Harry Golden, James McBride Dabbs, Ann Braden and Sarah Patton Boyle—have written about our struggle in eloquent and prophetic terms. Others have marched with us down nameless streets of the South. They have languished in filthy, roach-infested jails, suffering the abuse and brutality of policemen who view them as "dirty nigger-lovers." Unlike so many of their moderate brothers and sisters, they have recognized the urgency of the moment and sensed the need for powerful "action" antidotes to combat the disease of segregation.

Let me take note of my other major disappointment. I have been so 33 greatly disappointed with the white church and its leadership. Of course, there are some notable exceptions. I am not unmindful of the fact that each of you has taken some significant stands on this issue. I commend you, Reverend Stallings, for your Christian stand on this past Sunday, in welcoming Negroes to your worship service on a nonsegregated basis. I commend the Catholic leaders of this state for integrating Spring Hill College several years ago.

But despite these notable exceptions, I must honestly reiterate that I 34 have been disappointed with the church. I do not say this as one of those negative critics who can always find something wrong with the church. I say this as a minister of the gospel, who loves the church; who was nurtured in its bosom; who has been sustained by its spiritual blessings and who will remain true to it as long as the cord of life shall lengthen.

When I was suddenly catapulted into the leadership of the bus protest 35 in Montgomery, Alabama, a few years ago, I felt we would be supported by the white church. I felt that the white ministers, priests and rabbis of the South would be among our strongest allies. Instead, some have been outright opponents, refusing to understand the freedom movement and misrepresenting its leaders; all too many others have been more cautious than courageous and have remained silent behind the anesthetizing security of stained-glass windows.

In spite of my shattered dreams, I came to Birmingham with the hope 36 that the white religious leadership of this community would see the justice of our cause and, with deep moral concern, would serve as the channel through which our just grievances could reach the power structure. I had hoped that each of you would understand. But again I have been disappointed.

I have heard numerous southern religious leaders admonish their wor- 37 shipers to comply with a desegregation decision because it is the law, but I have longed to hear white ministers declare: "Follow this decree because integration is morally right and because the Negro is your brother." In the midst of blatant injustices inflicted upon the Negro, I have watched white churchmen stand on the sideline and mouth pious irrelevancies and sanctimonious trivialities. In the midst of a mighty struggle to rid our nation of racial and economic injustice, I have heard many ministers say: "Those are social issues, with which the gospel has no real concern." And I have watched many churches commit themselves to a completely otherworldly religion which makes a strange, un-Biblical distinction between body and soul, between the sacred and the secular.

I have traveled the length and breadth of Alabama, Mississippi and all 38
the other southern states. On sweltering summer days and crisp autumn mornings I have looked at the South's beautiful churches with their lofty spires pointing heavenward. I have beheld the impressive outlines of her massive religious-education buildings. Over and over I have found myself asking: "What kind of people worship here? Who is their God? Where were their voices when the lips of Governor Barnett dripped with words of interposition and nullification? Where were they when Governor Wallace gave a clarion call for defiance and hatred? Where were their voices of support when bruised and weary Negro men and women decided to rise from the dark dungeons of complacency to the bright hills of creative protest?"

Yes, these questions are still in my mind. In deep disappointment I have 39
wept over the laxity of the church. But be assured that my tears have been tears of love. There can be no deep disappointment where there is not deep love. Yes, I love the church. How could I do otherwise? I am in the rather unique position of being the son, the grandson and the great-grandson of preachers. Yes, I see the church as the body of Christ. But, oh! How we have blemished and scarred that body through social neglect and through fear of being nonconformists.

There was a time when the church was very powerful—in the time 40
when the early Christians rejoiced at being deemed worthy to suffer for what they believed. In those days the church was not merely a thermometer that recorded the ideas and principles of popular opinion; it was a thermostat that transformed the mores of society. Whenever the early Christians entered a town, the people in power became disturbed and immediately sought to convict the Christians for being "disturbers of the peace" and "outside agitators." But the Christians pressed on, in the conviction that they were "a colony of heaven," called to obey God rather than man. Small in number, they were big in commitment. They were too God-intoxicated to be "astronomically intimidated." By their effort and example they brought an end to such ancient evils as infanticide and gladiatorial contests.

Things are different now. So often the contemporary church is a weak, 41
ineffectual voice with an uncertain sound. So often it is an archdefender of the status quo. Far from being disturbed by the presence of the church, the power structure of the average community is consoled by the church's silent—and often even vocal—sanction of things as they are.

But the judgment of God is upon the church as never before. If today's 42
church does not recapture the sacrificial spirit of the early church, it will lose its authenticity, forfeit the loyalty of millions, and be dismissed as an irrelevant social club with no meaning for the twentieth century. Every day I meet young people whose disappointment with the church has turned into outright disgust.

Perhaps I have once again been too optimistic. Is organized religion too 43
inextricably bound to the status quo to save our nation and the world?

Perhaps I must turn my faith to the inner spiritual church, the church within the church, as the true *ekklesia* and the hope of the world. But again I am thankful to God that some noble souls from the ranks of organized religion have broken loose from the paralyzing chains of conformity and joined us as active partners in the struggle for freedom. They have left their secure congregations and walked the streets of Albany, Georgia, with us. They have gone down the highways of the South on tortuous rides for freedom. Yes, they have gone to jail with us. Some have been dismissed from their churches, have lost the support of their bishops and fellow ministers. But they have acted in the faith that right defeated is stronger than evil triumphant. Their witness has been the spiritual salt that has preserved the true meaning of the gospel in these troubled times. They have carved a tunnel of hope through the dark mountain of disappointment.

I hope the church as a whole will meet the challenge of this decisive   44 hour. But even if the church does not come to the aid of justice, I have no despair about the future. I have no fear about the outcome of our struggle in Birmingham, even if our motives are at present misunderstood. We will reach the goal of freedom in Birmingham and all over the nation, because the goal of America is freedom. Abused and scorned though we may be, our destiny is tied up with America's destiny. Before the pilgrims landed at Plymouth, we were here. Before the pen of Jefferson etched the majestic words of the Declaration of Independence across the pages of history, we were here. For more than two centuries our forebears labored in this country without wages; they made cotton king; they built the homes of their masters while suffering gross injustice and shameful humiliation—and yet out of a bottomless vitality they continued to thrive and develop. If the inexpressible cruelties of slavery could not stop us, the opposition we now face will surely fail. We will win our freedom because the sacred heritage of our nation and the eternal will of God are embodied in our echoing demands.

Before closing I feel impelled to mention one other point in your state-   45 ment that has troubled me profoundly. You warmly commended the Birmingham police force for keeping "order" and "preventing violence." I doubt that you would have so warmly commended the police force if you had seen its dogs sinking their teeth into unarmed, nonviolent Negroes. I doubt that you would so quickly commend the policemen if you were to observe their ugly and inhumane treatment of Negroes here in the city jail; if you were to watch them push and curse old Negro women and young Negro girls; if you were to see them slap and kick old Negro men and young boys; if you were to observe them, as they did on two occasions, refuse to give us food because we wanted to sing our grace together. I cannot join you in your praise of the Birmingham police department.

It is true that the police have exercised a degree of discipline in handling   46 the demonstrators. In this sense they have conducted themselves rather "nonviolently" in public. But for what purpose? To preserve the evil system of segregation. Over the past few years I have consistently preached that nonviolence demands that the means we use must be as pure as the ends we seek. I have tried to make clear that it is wrong to use immoral means to attain moral ends. But now I must affirm that it is just as wrong, or perhaps even more so, to use moral means to preserve immoral ends. Perhaps Mr. Connor and his policemen have been rather nonviolent in public, as was Chief Pritchett in Albany, Georgia, but they have used the moral means of nonviolence to maintain the immoral end of racial injustice. As T. S. Eliot has said: "The last temptation is the greatest treason: To do the right deed for the wrong reason."

I wish you had commended the Negro sit-inners and demonstrators of 47 Birmingham for their sublime courage, their willingness to suffer and their amazing discipline in the midst of great provocation. One day the South will recognize its real heroes. They will be the James Merediths, with the noble sense of purpose that enables them to face jeering and hostile mobs, and with the agonizing loneliness that characterizes the life of the pioneer. They will be old, oppressed, battered Negro women, symbolized in a seventy-two-year-old woman in Montgomery, Alabama, who rose up with a sense of dignity and with her people decided not to ride segregated buses, and who responded with ungrammatical profundity to one who inquired about her weariness: "My feets is tired, but my soul is at rest." They will be the young high school and college students, the young ministers of the gospel and a host of their elders, courageously and nonviolently sitting in at lunch counters and willingly going to jail for conscience' sake. One day the South will know that when these disinherited children of God sat down at lunch counters, they were in reality standing up for what is best in the American dream and for the most sacred values in our Judaeo-Christian heritage, thereby bringing our nation back to those great wells of democracy which were dug deep by the founding fathers in their formulation of the Constitution and the Declaration of Independence.

Never before have I written so long a letter. I'm afraid it is much too 48 long to take your precious time. I can assure you that it would have been much shorter if I had been writing from a comfortable desk, but what else can one do when he is alone in a narrow jail cell, other than write long letters, think long thoughts and pray long prayers?

If I have said anything in this letter that overstates the truth and indi- 49 cates an unreasonable impatience, I beg you to forgive me. If I have said anything that understates the truth and indicates my having a patience that allows me to settle for anything less than brotherhood, I beg God to forgive me.

I hope this letter finds you strong in the faith. I also hope that circum- 50 stances will soon make it possible for me to meet each of you, not as an integrationist or a civil-rights leader but as a fellow clergyman and a Christian brother. Let us all hope that the dark clouds of racial prejudice will soon pass away and the deep fog of misunderstanding will be lifted from our fear-drenched communities, and in some not too distant tomorrow the radiant stars of love and brotherhood will shine over our great nation with all their scintillating beauty.

Yours for the cause of Peace and Brotherhood,
MARTIN LUTHER KING, JR.

Questions for Discussion

1. What reasons does King give for taking time to answer the critics whose letter provoked this reply when he ignores most of his other critics?

2. Do you agree that "anyone who lives inside the United States can never be considered an outsider anywhere within its bounds" (¶4)? Have you heard arguments to the contrary? Do you find King convincing on this question?

3. Can you give an explanation and a justification for the four steps in any nonviolent campaign that King lays out in paragraph 6? Can you explain and justify the order of the steps?

4. How does "direct action" differ from violence (¶8, 10, and 11)?

5. Stylistically, King is master of certain devices that are particularly effective in oral delivery. Identify the device used in paragraph 14, and comment on its effectiveness. What happens to the rhetorical power of the paragraph if you alter the wording to destroy the device—even if you retain the meaning?

6. Can you explain in your own words King's distinction between a "just" and an "unjust" law? Does he support the distinction with convincing argument? Why is it important for him to spend so much space (¶15–22) supporting the validity of this distinction?

7. Why does King find the "white moderate" more objectionable (in some ways) than the outspoken segregationist? Do you think he is justified in his feeling?

8. What is King's criticism of the church with respect to social justice? Do you think the church in America has become less silent and evasive since King criticized it in 1963?

Suggested Essay Topics

1. Powerful metaphors abound in King's letter in almost every paragraph. Pick several that strike you as most impressive and analyze the power they impart to King's prose. One clear way of doing this is to replace each metaphor with a literal statement—the best you can write—and see what happens to the power of the statement. (It may strengthen your analysis if you consider which of the five senses each metaphor appeals to.) Address your paper either to your instructor or to someone you know whose

writing seems to suffer from a poverty of metaphor. Remember that your own tone should vary somewhat, depending on which kind of reader you are trying to convince.

2. Choose some injustice that you have experienced firsthand or know something about, and write two contrasting arguments about it. Address the first one to a sympathetic judge who has asked for a *factual* or *skeletal* account of your argument. Make it as lean, as undoctored, as unliterary as you can. Then write a second account of the same issue, but this time use as much of the kind of stylistic heightening that King uses as you possibly can. Don't worry about being too flowery; treat the assignment as an experiment in packing in rather than cutting out—a chance to try out all kinds of appeals that can reinforce the skeleton of an argument.

e. e. cummings

The poet e. e. cummings (1894–1962) was one of a group of avant-garde poets and novelists who became famous, shortly after World War I, for their experimentation with "shocking" styles. Many of these writers were quickly forgotten, because their tricky rejections of literary convention—with coined words, twisted grammar, "impossible" metaphors, wild or nonexistent punctuation, and strange verse forms and antiforms—soon lost their sense of originality and no longer conveyed the interest even of shock. Those who have endured are those who, like cummings, brought a strong personal passion or vision with their surface innovations. In cummings's best poems one discovers a lyrical or satirical voice that would speak with power even if the surface surprises were removed.

Though many of cummings's effects depend in part on our seeing the printed poem—he liked typographical innovations such as printing his name in all lowercase letters—most of his effects must be heard to be fully enjoyed. The poem we print here, numbered simply "LIV" in Roman numerals (that is, "Poem Number 54," though there is probably a pun on "Live!" as a command), should be read aloud several times before you even try to ask, "What does it mean?" Don't be embarrassed about chanting it like a kind of vigorous drumbeat, leaving as much time for some of the "slow" syllables (e.g., skip and up) as you allow for three or four "fast" ones (e.g., ev-ery-thing and a-round a-gain). Try chanting the lines like this, the way we render lines 14–17, giving an equal amount of time to what happens between the syllables in capital letters:

one's
ANYthing
OLD being
EVerything
NEW with a

WHAT (rest)
WHICH (rest) a-
ROUND we come
WHO

 Written in wartime and published in 1944 in the volume 1×1, *"LIV"*
celebrates the mysterious act of multiplication that love achieves: One times one equals
a new one who is a "we" and not two "I's." When "I love you and you love me"
and when everything that is a "your" becomes a "my," we can celebrate a new world
with a song like this one.

LIV

if everything happens that can't be done
(and anything's righter
than books
could plan)
the stupidest teacher will almost guess   5
(with a run
skip
around we go yes)
there's nothing as something as one

one hasn't a why or because or although 10
(and buds know better
than books
don't grow)
one's anything old being everything new
(with a what   15
which
around we come who)
one's everyanything so

so world is a leaf so tree is a bough
(and birds sing sweeter   20
than books
tell how)
so here is away and so your is a my
(with a down
up   25
around again fly)
forever was never till now

now i love you and you love me
(and books are shuter

than books   30
can be)
and deep in the high that does nothing but fall
(with a shout
each
around we go all)   35
there's somebody calling who's we

we're anything brighter than even the sun
(we're everything greater
than books
might mean)   40
we're everyanything more than believe
(with a spin
leap
alive we're alive)
we're wonderful one times one   45

Questions for Discussion

1. You may at first have been puzzled by some of the non-sentences the poem offers, with their forced joining of terms ordinarily kept separate: "one hasn't a why," "buds know better than books don't grow," "deep in the high," and so on. But after reading the poem a few times you have no doubt begun to see that there is a pattern to these "meaningless" expressions. Try "translating" (paraphrasing) some of the statements that are not strictly grammatical into ordinary English. (For example, for lines 11–13, "Flowers convey to us a knowledge even the wisest books cannot convey," or, for line 9, "Nothing in the world is as fully real, as fully alive, as discovering the 'oneness' of love.") What do your paraphrases lose, if anything, that cummings's words achieve?

2. You will find other authors both in this book and elsewhere making points similar to those you have written as you paraphrased cummings: men and women find their happiness only in working with and for others; individualism is a dangerous thing; and so on. Discuss the different effects that can be achieved when the same idea is treated in poetry and in prose. What, if anything, is lost or gained by conveying an idea through poetry rather than arguing the same idea at length in discursive prose?

Suggested Essay Topics

1. Write an essay comparing what seem to be the assumptions and conclusions of this poem with those of Ayn Rand in the preceding selection.

2. Picture a critic asserting: "In order to praise love, cummings unfortunately finds it necessary to mock books and knowledge and teachers. It is a silly romantic notion to see an opposition between being fully alive in love and learning how to discover what 'books might mean.' " Write an essay either refuting or supporting this criticism. If you support it, direct your essay to cummings himself; if you refute it, direct your essay to the "insensitive" critic who simply fails to see how right cummings really is.

⚬ 7 ⚬

SOCIAL JUSTICE

Minorities and Majorities

To me, anti-Semitism is now the most shocking of all things.
It is destroying much more than the Jews; it is assailing the human mind
at its source, and inviting it to create false categories
before exercising judgment. I am sure we shall win through.
But it will take a long time. . . . For the moment
all we can do is to dig in our heels, and prevent silliness
from sliding into insanity.
E. M. Forster

The Negro wanted to feel pride in his race? With tokenism,
the solution was simple. If all twenty million Negroes would keep looking
at Ralph Bunche [former ambassador to the United Nations],
the one man in so exalted a post would
generate such a volume of pride that it could be cut into
portions and served to everyone.
Martin Luther King, Jr.

In giving freedom to the slave, we assure freedom
to the free—honorable alike in what we give and what we preserve.
Abraham Lincoln

There is no subject on earth so easily understood as that of
the American Indian. Each summer, work camps
disgorge teen-agers on various reservations.
Within one month's time the youngsters acquire a knowledge
of Indians that would astound a college professor.
Vine Deloria, Jr.

None can love freedom heartily, but good men; the rest love
not freedom, but licence.
John Milton

Chief Red Jacket and the Missionary

The story of injustices inflicted upon racial and ethnic minorities in American society, past and present, has been widely documented with case histories and statistics and explained with countless theories. These are useful and informative, but the whole issue has perhaps never been summed up with such simple and powerful eloquence as in the rejection by the Indians (in this episode) of the white man's religion, patronizingly pushed at them by a missionary whose every word reveals his intolerance toward everything Indian. The Indians say that they will accept the white man's religion when they see that it makes whites treat Indians more fairly. By this simple test they at once summarize and condemn the whole tradition of white hypocrisy and greed.

Why should the Indians accept a religion that has allowed the white man to justify the theft of Indian lands and the murder of Indian people? They have learned that listening to the white man always leads to being cheated. Their "smiling" acceptance of the missionary's refusal to shake their hands after they have rejected his religion shows that they clearly see through his professed intention to do them good and perceive his real intention, which is to add the robbery of their religion to the robbery of their lands and way of life.

The narrative that introduces and comments on the speeches is by the anonymous editor of the 1809 edition.

A NATIVE AMERICAN
EPISODE

SPEECHES BY CHIEF RED JACKET AND
THE REVEREND MR. CRAM

From *Indian Speeches; Delivered by Farmer's Brother and Red Jacket, Two Seneca Chiefs* (1809). The title is ours.

[In the summer of 1805, a number of the principal Chiefs and Warriors of the Six Nations, principally Senecas, assembled at Buffalo Creek, in the state of New York, at the particular request of Rev. Mr. Cram, a Missionary from the state of Massachusetts. The Missionary being furnished with an Interpreter, and accompanied by the Agent of the United States for Indian affairs, met the Indians in Council, when the following talk took place.]   1

FIRST, BY THE AGENT. "*Brothers of the Six Nations;* I rejoice to meet you at this time, and thank the Great Spirit, that he has preserved you in health, and given me another opportunity of taking you by the hand.   2

"*Brothers;* The person who sits by me, is a friend who has come a great distance to hold a talk with you. He will inform you what his business is, and it is my request that you would listen with attention to his words."   3

MISSIONARY. "*My Friends;* I am thankful for the opportunity afforded us of uniting together at this time. I had a great desire to see you, and inquire into your state and welfare; for this purpose I have travelled a great distance, being sent by your old friends, the Boston Missionary Society. You will recollect they formerly sent missionaries among you, to instruct you in religion, and labor for your good. Although they have not heard from you for a long time, yet they have not forgotten their brothers the Six Nations, and are still anxious to do you good.   4

"*Brothers;* I have not come to get your lands or your money, but to enlighten your minds, and to instruct you how to worship the Great Spirit agreeably to his mind and will, and to preach to you the gospel of his son Jesus Christ. There is but one religion, and but one way to serve God, and if you do not embrace the right way, you cannot be happy hereafter. You have never worshipped the Great Spirit in a manner acceptable to him; but have, all your lives, been in great errors and darkness. To endeavor to remove these errors, and open your eyes, so that you might see clearly, is my business with you.   5

"*Brothers;* I wish to talk with you as one friend talks with another; and, if you have any objections to receive the religion which I preach, I wish you to state them; and I will endeavor to satisfy your minds, and remove the objections.   6

"*Brothers;* I want you to speak your minds freely; for I wish to reason with you on the subject, and, if possible, remove all doubts, if there be any on your minds. The subject is an important one, and it is of consequence that you give it an early attention while the offer is made you. Your friends, the Boston Missionary Society, will continue to send you good and faithful   7 ministers, to instruct and strengthen you in religion, if, on your part, you are willing to receive them.

"*Brothers;* Since I have been in this part of the country, I have visited   8
some of your small villages, and talked with your people. They appear willing to receive instruction, but, as they look up to you as their older brothers in council, they want first to know your opinion on the subject.

"You have now heard what I have to propose at present. I hope you will   9
take it into consideration, and give me an answer before we part."

[After about two hours consultation among themselves, the Chief, com-   10
monly called by the white people, Red Jacket (whose Indian name is Sagu-yu-what-hah, which interpreted is *Keeper awake*) rose and spoke as follows:]

"*Friend and Brother;* It was the will of the Great Spirit that we should meet   11
together this day. HE orders all things, and has given us a fine day for our Council. HE has taken his garment from before the sun, and caused it to shine with brightness upon us. Our eyes are opened, that we see clearly; our ears are unstopped, that we have been able to hear distinctly the words you have spoken. For all these favors we thank the Great Spirit; and HIM *only.*

"*Brother;* This council fire was kindled by you. It was at your request that   12
we came together at this time. We have listened with attention to what you have said. You requested us to speak our minds freely. This gives us great joy; for we now consider that we stand upright before you, and can speak what we think. All have heard your voice, and all speak to you now as one man. Our minds are agreed.

"*Brother;* You say you want an answer to your talk before you leave this   13
place. It is right you should have one, as you are a great distance from home, and we do not wish to detain you. But we will first look back a little, and tell you what our fathers have told us, and what we have heard from the white people.

"*Brother;* Listen to what we say.   14

"There was a time when our forefathers owned this great island. Their seats extended from the rising to the setting sun. The Great Spirit had made it for the use of Indians. HE had created the buffalo, the deer, and other animals for food. HE had made the bear and the beaver. Their skins served us for clothing. HE had scattered them over the country, and taught us how to take them. HE had caused the earth to produce corn for bread. All this HE had done for his red children, because HE loved them. If we had some disputes about our hunting ground, they were generally settled without the shedding of much blood. But an evil day came upon us. Your forefathers crossed the great water, and landed on this island. Their numbers were small. They found friends and not enemies. They told us they had fled from their country for fear of wicked men, and had come here to enjoy their religion. They asked for a small seat. We took pity on them, granted their request; and they sat down amongst us. We gave them corn and meat, they gave us poison [alluding, it is supposed, to ardent spirits] in return.

"The white people had now found our country. Tidings were carried   15
back, and more came amongst us. Yet we did not fear them. We took them

to be friends. They called us brothers. We believed them, and gave them a larger seat. At length their numbers had greatly increased. They wanted more land; they wanted our country. Our eyes were opened, and our minds became uneasy. Wars took place. Indians were hired to fight against Indians, and many of our people were destroyed. They also brought strong liquor amongst us. It was strong and powerful, and has slain thousands.

"*Brother;* Our seats were once large and yours were small. You have now 16 become a great people, and we have scarcely a place left to spread our blankets. You have got our country, but are not satisfied; you want to force your religion upon us.

"*Brother;* Continue to listen. 17

"You say that you are sent to instruct us how to worship the Great Spirit agreeably to his mind, and, if we do not take hold of the religion which you white people teach, we shall be unhappy hereafter. You say that you are right and we are lost. How do we know this to be true? We understand that your religion is written in a book. If it was intended for us as well as you, why has not the Great Spirit given to us, and not only to us, but why did he not give to our forefathers, the knowledge of that book, with the means of understanding it rightly? We only know what you tell us about it. How shall we know when to believe, being so often deceived by the white people?

"*Brother;* You say there is but one way to worship and serve the Great 18 Spirit. If there is but one religion; why do you white people differ so much about it? Why not all agreed, as you can all read the book?

"*Brother;* We do not understand these things. 19

"We are told that your religion was given to your forefathers, and has been handed down from father to son. We also have a religion, which was given to our forefathers, and has been handed down to us their children. We worship in that way. It teaches us to be thankful for all the favors we receive; to love each other, and to be united. We never quarrel about religion.

"*Brother;* The Great Spirit has made us all, but he has made a great 20 difference between his white and red children. He has given us different complexions and different customs. To you He has given the arts. To these He has not opened our eyes. We know these things to be true. Since He has made so great a difference between us in other things; why may we not conclude that He has given us a different religion according to our understanding? The Great Spirit does right. He knows what is best for his children; we are satisfied.

"*Brother;* We do not wish to destroy your religion, or take it from you. 21 We only want to enjoy our own.

"*Brother;* We are told that you have been preaching to the white people 22 in this place. These people are our neighbors. We are acquainted with them. We will wait a little while, and see what effect your preaching has upon them. If we find it does them good, makes them honest and less disposed to cheat Indians; we will then consider again of what you have said.

"*Brother;* You have now heard our answer to your talk, and this is all we 23 have to say at present.

"As we are going to part, we will come and take you by the hand, and   24
hope the Great Spirit will protect you on your journey, and return you safe
to your friends."

[As the Indians began to approach the missionary, he rose hastily from   25
his seat and replied, that he could not take them by the hand; that there was
no fellowship between the religion of God and the works of the devil.

This being interpreted to the Indians, they smiled, and retired in a   26
peaceable manner.

It being afterwards suggested to the missionary that his reply to the   27
Indians was rather indiscreet; he observed, that he supposed the ceremony of
shaking hands would be received by them as a token that he assented to what
they had said. Being otherwise informed, he said he was sorry for the expressions.]

Questions for Discussion

1. What words and actions can you point to that reveal the unconscious
   bigotry of the missionary?

2. In light of the patronizing tone adopted by the missionary, how do you
   account for the mildness and friendliness of the Indians' reply? Clearly,
   this picture squares badly with the image of the "savage redskin" in novels
   and movies. What reasons can you offer for the persistence of this popular
   but degrading image? Which of those reasons is connected to the attitudes
   exhibited by the missionary?

3. What kind of research, and what kind of thinking about evidence, would
   be required to get a clear picture of what the Senecas were like at the time
   this speech was given? Do you think that any one account, whether from
   the perspective of Indians, of white Americans, or of some "neutral"
   historian from another nation, could capture the full story that lies behind
   Red Jacket's speech?

4. Do you think that the account of Indian history *from the Indians' point of view*
   (¶14–16) is generally accepted today by most white people? If it is, why
   do you think that more has not been done to right the obvious wrongs
   exposed in this history? If you think most white people reject the Indians'
   view, what other views do you think they hold?

Suggested Essay Topics

1. Write another answer to the missionary for the Indians, taking a tone of
   indignation, outrage, or bitterness. You may use the same content or add
   to it from your own store of information; the point is to alter the tone so
   that you change the effect of the message.

2. Write a speech that might serve as a reply to Red Jacket, made by someone who has *really listened* to his arguments. In planning your speech, you should think through the possible lines of argument and the possible tones you might take: humbly apologetic (moving toward explanation); firmly indignant about having been misunderstood and maligned; rational and unemotional, mustering anecdotes and other evidence to show that Indians after all *have* committed cruel acts; and so on. Then choose the tone (implying a character for yourself) that you think will be most likely to be taken as sympathetic, so that the Indians will be most likely to hear your side of the story.

Ralph Ellison

Ralph Ellison (b. 1914) became famous almost overnight with the publication in 1952 of his novel Invisible Man, *the story of a young black man's trek toward self-identity. In a society that tells him he has no right to an identity except that given to him by whites, almost all of whom treat him with contempt, a trek toward identity meets almost impossible conditions. Most of us feel that we have a right not only to our own sense of selfhood but also to be surrounded by people who give us affection, encouragement, guidance, and hope.*

Through the use of symbol and metaphor, "Battle Royal" implies an argument about the position of blacks in a white-dominated power structure. Simply put, blacks must do battle in order to survive, but they must lose their naïveté if they are to battle successfully. As long as they allow whites to set the terms and conditions of battle, as long as they allow whites to set blacks battling against other blacks, and as long as they allow whites to reward them with cheap and phony payoffs that only underscore their inferior status, they will be duped into thinking they are winning a skirmish here and there (a scholarship to an all-black college, for example), but they will lose the royal battle, the battle for dignity, freedom, and self-esteem.

One of the most evocative symbols in the story is the naked dancer. As you read, try to determine how Ellison uses this symbol. Does "the small American flag tattooed upon her belly" (¶7) make her a symbol? If so, of what? Of all the false seductions that whites have held out to blacks who are eager to embrace America's noble slogans about freedom and equality but who are never allowed to join in the dance? The message to blacks has historically been one of "desire but don't possess," "admire but don't touch." And the callous way the white men toss the dancer in the air, defiling her out of sheer lust or greed, seems to highlight their profound ignorance of the grounds of their own freedom and to provide a sad commentary on their profound corruption.

The realization "that I am nobody but myself" (¶1) sounds simple, but to realize what this means in the only way that counts—to be in possession of one's own conscience, one's own sense of worth, and one's own sense of dignity, and to be able to hold to these in spite of social pressure, failure, or disappointment—this is not so simple. When family or society gives us double messages or lies, the realization can be made even harder. As you read, consider in what ways your own experience, whether you are a member of a minority or not, parallels and diverges from the central character's. Perhaps each of us has to fight a battle royal of some kind on the road to self-knowledge. The young man in the story has to identify the real enemy before he can begin to fight effectively, before he can even choose the right battle. How does he do this? What, or who, is his real enemy? His story invites us all to identify the battles that are most necessary or meaningful for us personally.

BATTLE ROYAL

From *Invisible Man* (1952).

It goes a long way back, some twenty years. All my life I had been looking for something, and everywhere I turned someone tried to tell me what it was. I accepted their answers too, though they were often in contradiction and even self-contradictory. I was naïve. I was looking for myself and asking everyone except myself questions which I, and only I, could answer. It took me a long time and much painful boomeranging of my expectations to achieve a realization everyone else appears to have been born with: That I am nobody but myself. But first I had to discover that I am an invisible man!

And yet I am no freak of nature, nor of history. I was in the cards, other things having been equal (or unequal) eighty-five years ago. I am not ashamed of my grandparents for having been slaves. I am only ashamed of myself for having at one time been ashamed. About eighty-five years ago they were told that they were free, united with others of our country in everything pertaining to the common good, and, in everything social, separate like the fingers of the hand. And they believed it. They exulted in it. They stayed in their place, worked hard, and brought up my father to do the same. But my grandfather is the one. He was an odd old guy, my grandfather, and I am told I take after him. It was he who caused the trouble. On his deathbed he called my father to him and said, "Son, after I'm gone I want you to keep up the fight. I never told you, but our life is a war and I have been a traitor all my born days, a spy in the enemy's country ever since I give up my gun back in the Reconstruction. Live with your head in the lion's mouth. I want you to overcome 'em with yeses, undermine 'em with grins, agree 'em to death and destruction, let 'em swoller you till they vomit or bust wide open." They thought the old man had gone out of his mind. He had been the meekest of men. The younger children were rushed from the room, the shades drawn and the flame of the lamp turned so low that it sputtered on the wick like the old man's breathing. "Learn it to the younguns," he whispered fiercely; then he died.

But my folks were more alarmed over his last words than over his dying. It was as though he had not died at all, his words caused so much anxiety. I was warned emphatically to forget what he had said and, indeed, this is the first time it has been mentioned outside the family circle. It had a tremendous effect upon me, however. I could never be sure of what he meant. Grandfather had been a quiet old man who never made any trouble, yet on his deathbed he had called himself a traitor and a spy, and he had spoken of his meekness as a dangerous activity. It became a constant puzzle which lay unanswered in the back of my mind. And whenever things went well for me I remembered my grandfather and felt guilty and uncomfortable. It was as though I was carrying out his advice in spite of myself. And to make it worse, everyone loved me for it. I was praised by the most lily-white men of the town. I was considered an example of desirable conduct—just as my grandfather had been. And what puzzled me was that the old man had defined it as *treachery*. When I was praised for my conduct I felt a guilt that in some way I was doing something that was really against the wishes of the white folks, that if they had understood they would have desired me to act just the opposite, that I should have been sulky and mean, and that that really would have been what they wanted, even though they were fooled and thought they wanted me to act as I did. It made me afraid that some day they would look upon me as a traitor and I would be lost. Still I was more afraid to act any other way because they didn't like that at all. The old man's words were like a curse. On my graduation day I delivered an oration in which I showed that humility was the secret, indeed, the very essence of progress. (Not that I believed this—how could I, remembering my grandfather?—I only believed that it worked.) It was a great success. Everyone praised me and I was invited to give the speech at a gathering of the town's leading white citizens. It was a triumph for our whole community.

It was in the main ballroom of the leading hotel. When I got there I discovered that it was on the occasion of a smoker, and I was told that since I was to be there anyway I might as well take part in the battle royal to be fought by some of my schoolmates as part of the entertainment. The battle royal came first.   4

All of the town's big shots were there in their tuxedos, wolfing down the buffet foods, drinking beer and whiskey and smoking black cigars. It was a large room with a high ceiling. Chairs were arranged in neat rows around three sides of a portable boxing ring. The fourth side was clear, revealing a gleaming space of polished floor. I had some misgivings over the battle royal, by the way. Not from a distaste for fighting, but because I didn't care too much for the other fellows who were to take part. They were tough guys who seemed to have no grandfather's curse worrying their minds. No one could mistake their toughness. And besides, I suspected that fighting a battle royal might detract from the dignity of my speech. In those pre-invisible days I visualized myself as a potential Booker T. Washington.* But the other fellows didn't care too much for me either, and there were nine of them. I felt superior to them in my way, and I didn't like the manner in which we were all crowded together into the servants' elevator. Nor did they like my being there. In fact,   5

*Black American teacher and leader (1856–1915).

as the warmly lighted floors flashed past the elevator we had words over the fact that I, by taking part in the fight, had knocked one of their friends out of a night's work.

We were led out of the elevator through a rococo hall into an anteroom   6
and told to get into our fighting togs. Each of us was issued a pair of boxing gloves and ushered out into the big mirrored hall, which we entered looking cautiously about us and whispering, lest we might accidentally be heard above the noise of the room. It was foggy with cigar smoke. And already the whiskey was taking effect. I was shocked to see some of the most important men of the town quite tipsy. They were all there—bankers, lawyers, judges, doctors, fire chiefs, teachers, merchants. Even one of the more fashionable pastors. Something we could not see was going on up front. A clarinet was vibrating sensuously and the men were standing up and moving eagerly forward. We were a small tight group, clustered together, our bare upper bodies touching and shining with anticipatory sweat; while up front the big shots were becoming increasingly excited over something we still could not see. Suddenly I heard the school superintendent, who had told me to come, yell, "Bring up the shines, gentlemen! Bring up the little shines!"

We were rushed up to the front of the ballroom, where it smelled even   7
more strongly of tobacco and whiskey. Then we were pushed into place. I almost wet my pants. A sea of faces, some hostile, some amused, ringed around us, and in the center, facing us, stood a magnificent blonde—stark naked. There was a dead silence. I felt a blast of cold air chill me. I tried to back away, but they were behind me and around me. Some of the boys stood with lowered heads, trembling. I felt a wave of irrational guilt and fear. My teeth chattered, my skin turned to goose flesh, my knees knocked. Yet I was strongly attracted and looked in spite of myself. Had the price of looking been blindness, I would have looked. The hair was yellow like that of a circus kewpie doll, the face heavily powdered and rouged, as though to form an abstract mask, the eyes hollow and smeared a cool blue, the color of a baboon's butt. I felt a desire to spit upon her as my eyes brushed slowly over her body. Her breasts were firm and round as the domes of East Indian temples, and I stood so close as to see the fine skin texture and beads of pearly perspiration glistening like dew around the pink and erected buds of her nipples. I wanted at one and the same time to run from the room, to sink through the floor, or go to her and cover her from my eyes and the eyes of the others with my body; to feel the soft thighs, to caress her and destroy her, to love her and murder her, to hide from her, and yet to stroke where below the small American flag tattooed upon her belly her thighs formed a capital V. I had a notion that of all in the room she saw only me with her impersonal eyes.

And then she began to dance, a slow sensuous movement; the smoke   8
of a hundred cigars clinging to her like the thinnest of veils. She seemed like a fair bird-girl girdled in veils calling to me from the angry surface of some gray and threatening sea. I was transported. Then I became aware of the clarinet playing and the big shots yelling at us. Some threatened us if we looked and others if we did not. On my right I saw one boy faint. And now

a man grabbed a silver pitcher from a table and stepped close as he dashed
ice water upon him and stood him up and forced two of us to support him
as his head hung and moans issued from his thick bluish lips. Another boy
began to plead to go home. He was the largest of the group, wearing dark red
fighting trunks much too small to conceal the erection which projected from
him as though in answer to the insinuating low-registered moaning of the
clarinet. He tried to hide himself with his boxing gloves.

And all the while the blonde continued dancing, smiling faintly at the   9
big shots who watched her with fascination, and faintly smiling at our fear.
I noticed a certain merchant who followed her hungrily, his lips loose and
drooling. He was a large man who wore diamond studs in a shirtfront which
swelled with the ample paunch underneath, and each time the blonde swayed
her undulating hips he ran his hand through the thin hair of his bald head
and, with his arms upheld, his posture clumsy like that of an intoxicated
panda, wound his belly in a slow and obscene grind. This creature was
completely hypnotized. The music had quickened. As the dancer flung herself
about with a detached expression on her face, the men began reaching out
to touch her. I could see their beefy fingers sink into the soft flesh. Some of
the others tried to stop them and she began to move around the floor in
graceful circles, as they gave chase, slipping and sliding over the polished
floor. It was mad. Chairs went crashing, drinks were spilt, as they ran laughing and howling after her. They caught her just as she reached a door, raised
her from the floor, and tossed her as college boys are tossed at a hazing, and
above her red, fixed-smiling lips I saw the terror and disgust in her eyes,
almost like my own terror and that which I saw in some of the other boys.
As I watched, they tossed her twice and her soft breasts seemed to flatten
against the air and her legs flung wildly as she spun. Some of the more sober
ones helped her to escape. And I started off the floor, heading for the anteroom with the rest of the boys.

Some were still crying and in hysteria. But as we tried to leave we were   10
stopped and ordered to get into the ring. There was nothing to do but what
we were told. All ten of us climbed under the ropes and allowed ourselves
to be blindfolded with broad bands of white cloth. One of the men seemed
to feel a bit sympathetic and tried to cheer us up as we stood with our backs
against the ropes. Some of us tried to grin. "See that boy over there?" one
of the men said. "I want you to run across at the bell and give it to him right
in the belly. If you don't get him, I'm going to get you. I don't like his looks."
Each of us was told the same. The blindfolds were put on. Yet even then I
had been going over my speech. In my mind each word was as bright as flame.
I felt the cloth pressed into place, and frowned so that it would be loosened
when I relaxed.

But now I felt a sudden fit of blind terror. I was unused to darkness. It   11
was as though I had suddenly found myself in a dark room filled with
poisonous cottonmouths. I could hear the bleary voices yelling insistently for
the battle royal to begin.

"Get going in there!"

                                                                         12

"Let me at the big nigger!" 13

I strained to pick up the school superintendent's voice, as though to 14
squeeze some security out of that slightly more familiar sound.

"Let me at those black sonsabitches!" someone yelled. 15

"No, Jackson, no!" another voice yelled. "Here, somebody, help me hold 16
Jack."

"I want to get at that ginger-colored nigger. Tear him limb from limb," 17
the first voice yelled.

I stood against the ropes trembling. For in those days I was what they 18
called ginger-colored, and he sounded as though he might crunch me between
his teeth like a crisp ginger cookie.

Quite a struggle was going on. Chairs were being kicked about and I 19
could hear voices grunting as with a terrific effort. I wanted to see, to see more
desperately than ever before. But the blindfold was as tight as a thick skin-
puckering scab and when I raised my gloved hands to push the layers of white
aside a voice yelled, "Oh, no you don't, black bastard! Leave that alone!"

"Ring the bell before Jackson kills him a coon!" someone boomed in the 20
sudden silence. And I heard the bell clang and the sound of feet scuffling
forward.

A glove smacked against my head. I pivoted, striking out stiffly as 21
someone went past, and felt the jar ripple along the length of my arm to my
shoulder. Then it seemed as though all nine of the boys had turned upon me
at once. Blows pounded me from all sides while I struck out as best I could.
So many blows landed upon me that I wondered if I were not the only
blindfolded fighter in the ring, or if the man called Jackson hadn't succeeded
in getting me after all.

Blindfolded, I could no longer control my motions. I had no dignity. I 22
stumbled about like a baby or a drunken man. The smoke had become thicker
and with each new blow it seemed to sear and further restrict my lungs. My
saliva became like hot bitter glue. A glove connected with my head, filling
my mouth with warm blood. It was everywhere. I could not tell if the
moisture I felt upon my body was sweat or blood. A blow landed hard against
the nape of my neck. I felt myself going over, my head hitting the floor.
Streaks of blue light filled the black world behind the blindfold. I lay prone,
pretending that I was knocked out, but felt myself seized by hands and
yanked to my feet. "Get going, black boy! Mix it up!" My arms were like lead,
my head smarting from blows. I managed to feel my way to the ropes and
held on, trying to catch my breath. A glove landed in my midsection and I
went over again, feeling as though the smoke had become a knife jabbed into
my guts. Pushed this way and that by the legs milling around me, I finally
pulled erect and discovered that I could see the black, sweat-washed forms
weaving in the smoky-blue atmosphere like drunken dancers weaving to the
rapid drumlike thuds of blows.

Everyone fought hysterically. It was complete anarchy. Everybody 23
fought everybody else. No group fought together for long. Two, three, four,
fought one, then turned to fight each other, were themselves attacked. Blows

landed below the belt and in the kidney, with the gloves open as well as closed, and with my eye partly opened now there was not so much terror. I moved carefully, avoiding blows, although not too many to attract attention, fighting from group to group. The boys groped about like blind, cautious crabs crouching to protect their mid-sections, their heads pulled in short against their shoulders, their arms stretched nervously before them, with their fists testing the smoke-filled air like the knobbed feelers of hypersensitive snails. In the corner I glimpsed a boy violently punching the air and heard him scream in pain as he smashed his hand against a ring post. For a second I saw him bent over holding his hand, then going down as a blow caught his unprotected head. I played one group against the other, slipping in and throwing a punch then stepping out of range while pushing the others into the melee to take the blows blindly aimed at me. The smoke was agonizing and there were no rounds, no bells at three minute intervals to relieve our exhaustion. The room spun around me, a swirl of lights, smoke, sweating bodies surrounded by tense white faces. I bled from both nose and mouth, the blood spattering upon my chest.

The men kept yelling, "Slug him, black boy! Knock his guts out!"   24
"Uppercut him! Kill him! Kill that big boy!"   25

Taking a fake fall, I saw a boy going down heavily beside me as though   26 we were felled by a single blow, saw a sneaker-clad foot shoot into his groin as the two who had knocked him down stumbled upon him. I rolled out of range, feeling a twinge of nausea.

The harder we fought the more threatening the men became. And yet,   27 I had begun to worry about my speech again. How would it go? Would they recognize my ability? What would they give me?

I was fighting automatically when suddenly I noticed that one after   28 another of the boys was leaving the ring. I was surprised, filled with panic, as though I had been left alone with an unknown danger. Then I understood. The boys had arranged it among themselves. It was custom for the two men left in the ring to slug it out for the winner's prize. I discovered this too late. When the bell sounded two men in tuxedos leaped into the ring and removed the blindfold. I found myself facing Tatlock, the biggest of the gang. I felt sick at my stomach. Hardly had the bell stopped ringing in my ears than it clanged again and I saw him moving swiftly toward me. Thinking of nothing else to do I hit him smash on the nose. He kept coming, bringing the rank sharp violence of stale sweat. His face was a black blank of a face, only his eyes alive—with hate of me and aglow with a feverish terror from what had happened to us all. I became anxious. I wanted to deliver my speech and he came at me as though he meant to beat it out of me. I smashed him again and again, taking his blows as they came. Then on a sudden impulse I struck him lightly and as we clinched, I whispered, "Fake like I knocked you out, you can have the prize."

"I'll break your behind," he whispered hoarsely.   29
"For *them*?"   30
"For *me*, sonofabitch."   31

They were yelling for us to break it up and Tatlock spun me half around 32
with a blow, and as a joggled camera sweeps in a reeling scene, I saw the
howling red faces crouching tense beneath the cloud of blue-gray smoke. For
a moment the world wavered, unraveled, flowed, then my head cleared and
Tatlock bounced before me. The fluttering shadow before my eyes was his
jabbing left hand. Then falling forward, my head against his damp shoulder,
I whispered.

"I'll make it five dollars more." 33

"Go to hell!" 34

But his muscles relaxed a trifle beneath my pressure and I breathed, 35
"Seven?"

"Give it to your ma," he said, ripping me beneath the heart. 36

And while I still held him I butted him and moved away. I felt myself 37
bombarded with punches. I fought back with hopeless desperation. I wanted
to deliver my speech more than anything else in the world, because I felt only
these men could judge truly my ability, and now this stupid clown was
ruining my chances. I began fighting carefully now, moving in to punch him
and out again with my greater speed. A lucky blow to his chin and I had him
going too—until I heard a loud voice yell, "I got my money on the big boy."

Hearing this, I almost dropped my guard. I was confused: Should I try 38
to win against the voice out there? Would not this go against my speech, and
was not this a moment for humility, for nonresistance? A blow to my head
as I danced about sent my right eye popping like a jack-in-the-box and settled
my dilemma. The room went red as I fell. It was a dream fall, my body languid
and fastidious as to where to land, until the floor became impatient and
smashed up to meet me. A moment later I came to. An hypnotic voice said
FIVE emphatically. And I lay there, hazily watching a dark red spot of my
own blood shaping itself into a butterfly, glistening and soaking into the
soiled gray world of the canvas.

When the voice drawled TEN I was lifted up and dragged to a chair. I 39
sat dazed. My eye pained and swelled with each throb of my pounding heart
and I wondered if now I would be allowed to speak. I was wringing wet, my
mouth still bleeding. We were grouped along the wall now. The other boys
ignored me as they congratulated Tatlock and speculated as to how much
they would be paid. One boy whimpered over his smashed hand. Looking up
front, I saw attendants in white jackets rolling the portable ring away and
placing a small square rug in the vacant space surrounded by chairs. Perhaps,
I thought, I will stand on the rug to deliver my speech.

Then the M.C. called to us, "Come on up here boys and get your 40
money."

We ran forward to where the men laughed and talked in their chairs, 41
waiting. Everyone seemed friendly now.

"There it is on the rug," the man said. I saw the rug covered with coins 42
of all dimensions and a few crumpled bills. But what excited me, scattered
here and there, were the gold pieces.

"Boys, it's all yours," the man said. "You get all you grab." 43

"That's right, Sambo," a blond man said, winking at me confidentially. 44

I trembled with excitement, forgetting my pain. I would get the gold and 45
the bills, I thought. I would use both hands. I would throw my body against
the boys nearest me to block them from the gold.

"Get down around the rug now," the man commanded, "and don't 46
anyone touch it until I give the signal."

"This ought to be good," I heard. 47

As told, we got around the square rug on our knees. Slowly the man 48
raised his freckled hand as we followed it upward with our eyes.

I heard, "These niggers look like they're about to pray!" 49

Then, "Ready," the man said. "Go!" 50

I lunged for a yellow coin lying on the blue design on the carpet, 51
touching it and sending a surprised shriek to join those rising around me. I
tried frantically to remove my hand but could not let go. A hot, violent force
tore through my body, shaking me like a wet rat. The rug was electrified. The
hair bristled up on my head as I shook myself free. My muscles jumped, my
nerves jangled, writhed. But I saw that this was not stopping the other boys.
Laughing in fear and embarrassment, some were holding back and scooping
up the coins knocked off by the painful contortions of the others. The men
roared above us as we struggled.

"Pick it up, goddamnit, pick it up!" someone called like a bass-voiced 52
parrot. "Go on, get it!"

I crawled rapidly around the floor, picking up the coins, trying to avoid 53
the coppers and to get greenbacks and the gold. Ignoring the shock by laughing, as I brushed the coins off quickly, I discovered that I could contain the
electricity—a contradiction, but it works. Then the men began to push us
onto the rug. Laughing embarrassedly, we struggled out of their hands and
kept after the coins. We were all wet and slippery and hard to hold. Suddenly
I saw a boy lifted into the air, glistening with sweat like a circus seal, and
dropped, his wet back landing flush upon the charged rug, heard him yell and
saw him literally dance upon his back, his elbows beating a frenzied tattoo
upon the floor, his muscles twitching like the flesh of a horse stung by many
flies. When he finally rolled off, his face was gray and no one stopped him
when he ran from the floor amid booming laughter.

"Get the money," the M.C. called. "That's good hard American cash!" 54

And we snatched and grabbed, snatched and grabbed. I was careful not 55
to come too close to the rug now, and when I felt the hot whiskey breath
descend upon me like a cloud of foul air I reached out and grabbed the leg
of a chair. It was occupied and I held on desperately.

"Leggo nigger! Leggo!" 56

The huge face wavered down to mine as he tried to push me free. But 57
my body was slippery and he was too drunk. It was Mr. Colcord, who owned
a chain of movie houses and "entertainment palaces." Each time he grabbed
me I slipped out of his hands. It became a real struggle. I feared the rug more
than I did the drunk, so I held on, surprising myself for a moment by trying
to topple *him* upon the rug. It was such an enormous idea that I found myself

actually carrying it out. I tried not to be obvious, yet when I grabbed his leg, trying to tumble him out of the chair, he raised up roaring with laughter, and, looking at me with soberness dead in the eye, kicked me viciously in the chest. The chair leg flew out of my hand and I felt myself going and rolled. It was as though I had rolled through a bed of hot coals. It seemed a whole century would pass before I would roll free, a century in which I was seared through the deepest levels of my body to the fearful breath within me and the breath seared and heated to the point of explosion. It'll all be over in a flash, I thought as I rolled clear. It'll all be over in a flash.

But not yet, the men on the other side were waiting, red faces swollen 58 as though from apoplexy as they bent forward in their chairs. Seeing their fingers coming toward me I rolled away as a fumbled football rolls off the receiver's fingertips, back into the coals. That time I luckily sent the rug sliding out of place and heard the coins ringing against the floor and the boys scuffling to pick them up and the M.C. calling, "All right, boys, that's all. Go get dressed and get your money."

I was limp as a dish rag. My back felt as though it had been beaten with 59 wires.

When we had dressed the M.C. came in and gave us each five dollars, 60 except Tatlock, who got ten for being last in the ring. Then he told us to leave. I was not to get a chance to deliver my speech, I thought. I was going out into the dim alley in despair when I was stopped and told to go back. I returned to the ballroom, where the men were pushing back their chairs and gathering in groups to talk.

The M.C. knocked on a table for quiet. "Gentlemen," he said, "we 61 almost forgot an important part of the program. A most serious part, gentlemen. This boy was brought here to deliver a speech which he made at his graduation yesterday . . ."

"Bravo!" 62

"I'm told that he is the smartest boy we've got out there in Greenwood. 63 I'm told that he knows more big words than a pocket-sized dictionary."

Much applause and laughter. 64

"So now, gentlemen, I want you to give him your attention." 65

There was still laughter as I faced them, my mouth dry, my eye throb- 66 bing. I began slowly, but evidently my throat was tense, because they began shouting, "Louder! Louder!"

"We of the younger generation extol the wisdom of that great leader 67 and educator," I shouted, "who first spoke these flaming words of wisdom. 'A ship lost at sea for many days suddenly sighted a friendly vessel. From the mast of the unfortunate vessel was seen a signal: "Water, water; we die of thirst!" The answer from the friendly vessel came back: "Cast down your bucket where you are." The captain of the distressed vessel, at last heeding the injunction, cast down his bucket, and it came up full of fresh sparkling water from the mouth of the Amazon River.' And like him I say, and in his words, 'To those of my race who depend upon bettering their condition in a foreign land, or who underestimate the importance of cultivating friendly relations with the Southern white man, who is his next-door neighbor, I would say: "Cast down your bucket where you are"—cast it down in making friends in every manly way of the people of all races by whom we are surrounded. . . .' "

I spoke automatically and with such fervor that I did not realize that the 68 men were still talking and laughing until my dry mouth, filling up with blood from the cut, almost strangled me. I coughed, wanting to stop and go to one of the tall brass, sand-filled spittoons to relieve myself, but a few of the men, especially the superintendent, were listening and I was afraid. So I gulped it down, blood, saliva, and all, and continued. (What powers of endurance I had during those days! What enthusiasm! What a belief in the rightness of things!) I spoke even louder in spite of the pain. But still they talked and still they laughed, as though deaf with cotton in dirty ears. So I spoke with greater emotional emphasis. I closed my ears and swallowed blood until I was nauseated. The speech seemed a hundred times as long as before, but I could not leave out a single word. All had to be said, each memorized nuance considered, rendered. Nor was that all. Whenever I uttered a word of three or more syllables a group of voices would yell for me to repeat it. I used the phrase "social responsibility" and they yelled:

"What's that word you say, boy?" 69
"Social responsibility," I said. 70
"What?" 71
"Social . . ." 72
"Louder." 73
". . . responsibility." 74
"More!" 75
"Respon—" 76
"Repeat!" 77
"—sibility." 78

The room filled with the uproar of laughter until, no doubt, distracted 79 by having to gulp down my blood, I made a mistake and yelled a phrase I had often seen denounced with newspaper editorials, heard debated in private.

"Social . . ." 80
"What?" they yelled. 81
". . . equality—" 82

The laughter hung smokelike in the sudden stillness. I opened my eyes, 83 puzzled. Sounds of displeasure filled the room. The M.C. rushed forward. They shouted hostile phrases at me. But I did not understand.

A small dry mustached man in the front row blared out, "Say that 84 slowly, son!"
"What sir?" 85
"Social responsibility, sir," I said. 86
"You weren't being smart, were you, boy?" he said, not unkindly. 87
"No, sir!" 88
"You sure that about 'equality' was a mistake?" 89

"Oh, yes, sir," I said. "I was swallowing blood." 90

"Well, you had better speak more slowly so we can understand. We 91 mean to do right by you, but you've got to know your place at all times. All right, now, go on with your speech."

I was afraid. I wanted to leave but I wanted also to speak and I was afraid 92 they'd snatch me down.

"Thank you, sir," I said, beginning where I had left off, and having them 93 ignore me as before.

Yet when I finished there was a thunderous applause. I was surprised 94 to see the superintendent come forth with a package wrapped in white tissue paper, and, gesturing for quiet, address the men.

"Gentlemen, you see that I did not overpraise this boy. He makes a good 95 speech and some day he'll lead his people in the proper paths. And I don't have to tell you that that is important in these days and times. This is a good, smart boy, and so to encourage him in the right direction, in the name of the Board of Education I wish to present him a prize in the form of this . . ."

He paused, removing the tissue paper and revealing a gleaming calfskin 96 brief case.

". . . in the form of this first-class article from Shad Whitmore's shop." 97

"Boy," he said, addressing me, "take this prize and keep it well. Con- 98 sider it a badge of office. Prize it. Keep developing as you are and some day it will be filled with important papers that will help shape the destiny of your people."

I was so moved that I could hardly express my thanks. A rope of bloody 99 saliva forming a shape like an undiscovered continent drooled upon the leather and I wiped it quickly away. I felt an importance that I had never dreamed.

"Open it and see what's inside," I was told. 100

My fingers a-tremble, I complied, smelling the fresh leather and finding 101 an official-looking document inside. It was a scholarship to the state college for Negroes. My eyes filled with tears and I ran awkwardly off the floor.

I was so overjoyed; I did not even mind when I discovered that the gold 102 pieces I had scrambled for were brass pocket tokens advertising a certain make of automobile.

When I reached home everyone was excited. Next day the neighbors 103 came to congratulate me. I even felt safe from grandfather, whose deathbed curse usually spoiled my triumphs. I stood beneath his photograph with my brief case in hand and smiled triumphantly into his stolid black peasant's face. It was a face that fascinated me. The eyes seemed to follow everywhere I went.

That night I dreamed I was at a circus with him and that he refused to 104 laugh at the clowns no matter what they did. Then later he told me to open my brief case and read what was inside and I did, finding an official envelope stamped with the state seal; and inside the envelope I found another and another, endlessly, and I thought I would fall of weariness. "Them's years," he said. "Now open that one." And I did and in it I found an engraved document containing a short message in letters of gold. "Read it," my grandfather said. "Out loud."

"To Whom It May Concern," I intoned. "Keep This Nigger-Boy Running."   105

I awoke with the old man's laughter ringing in my ears.   106

(It was a dream I was to remember and dream again for many years after.   107
But at that time I had no insight into its meaning. First I had to attend college.)

Questions for Discussion

1. What is your own interpretation of the grandfather's message in paragraph 2? What does he mean when he says, "Our life is a war and I have been a traitor all my born days"?

2. What is meant (in the young man's dream) by the official document inscribed, "To Whom It May Concern, Keep This Nigger-Boy Running" (¶105)? What is the significance of this document's being contained in "an official envelope stamped with the state seal"? How does "running" tie in with the young man's willingness to fight and his gratitude over the scholarship to college?

3. Why is it significant that the smoker is attended by "the most important men of the town . . . bankers, lawyers, judges, doctors, fire chiefs, teachers, merchants. Even one of the more fashionable pastors" (¶6)? What do these men represent in the story?

4. In what sense might it be true to say that the young man, who thinks he sees how the game of progress and social advancement must be played, begins to see more clearly the *real* truth of his situation when he is placed in the blindfold (¶11)?

5. Why is it ironic that the young man "attempts to squeeze some security" out of the school superintendent's voice as the fight begins (¶14)? What does this say about his naïveté?

6. A corrupt system corrupts not just the victimizers but the victims as well. How is the truth of this statement corroborated by the young man's question "What would they give me?" in paragraph 27?

7. What does the young man mean when he says that before he could discover "that I am nobody but myself . . . I had to [experience] much painful boomeranging of my expectations" (¶1)?

Suggested Essay Topics

1. Have you ever felt invisible in Ellison's narrator's sense of the term—felt that some persons, no matter what you do or say to them, will always fail to see you for what you are, will always insist on seeing instead some

image of you or of "your kind" that they have already formed in their own heads? If you have ever experienced this feeling, give an account of it in an essay directed to your fellow students. Use Ellison's analysis to help you explain what it feels like to be treated this way and how you dealt (or are dealing) with it. Your purpose is to try to define the condition of invisibility as *you* have experienced it (with appropriate examples) so that your readers will know not only what the condition has been like but what it has meant (or means) in your life.

2. After thinking about topic 1, write an editorial or a letter to the editor of your campus newspaper, arguing that everyone should wake up and *look* at the *individuals* on campus, instead of making them invisible by lumping them into groups and types. Identify the group stereotypes that make individuals invisible (dumb jocks, dizzy blonds, stupid administrators, and so on), and make your editorial or letter a ringing assertion of these people's right to be viewed and judged as individuals, not as predictable representatives of groups.

Jonathan Swift

Jonathan Swift (1667–1745) was born and educated in Dublin, Ireland, was ordained as an Anglican priest, and from 1713 on held the post of dean of St. Patrick's in Dublin. He wrote on church doctrine, social matters, and politics (especially on the relations between Ireland and England). The latter two topics gave him great scope for his immense gifts as a satirist. He wielded his pen like a scalpel and dissected the objects of his ridicule with deadly accuracy, energy, and finesse. What sets Swift above many other brilliant satirists is the scope and depth of his moral vision. He does not just satirize absurdities, as comedians on late-night television do, jabbing the needle quickly and then running to the next topic. His ridicule goes far beyond merely accurate observation and enters the realm of informed vision. He shows us not simply that human stupidity, greed, or self-deception exists but also how things might be better. It is important to remember that Swift is a satirist, not a cynic: While he thinks many people bad, he does not think all people hopeless. Even as he flays his targets, hanging up the pelts of their hypocrisies and absurdities to swing in the wind of public scrutiny, he points out possible remedies for the evils he attacks.

The main satiric device in "A Modest Proposal" is irony: saying one thing and meaning the opposite. (Irony is a much more sophisticated device than this rough definition implies, but we have insufficient space here for a thorough discussion.) Even this simple definition, however, makes one thing clear: The reader somehow has to know that a meaning beyond the surface meaning must be decoded. Any reader who does not recognize a piece as satire will simply take the surface meaning at face value—and, in the case of "A Modest Proposal," will make a horrible mistake.

As you read, try to spot places where Swift lets you know that a deep decoding is necessary. What are the clues? He cannot use any of the visual or auditory signals that satirists often rely on, such as inflection, body language, gesture, or facial expression. Yet by the third sentence of paragraph 4, far in advance of the outrageous proposal in paragraph 9, you know you are in the presence of a satiric voice. How is the satiric intent conveyed? Are there any sections in which the satire is dropped in favor of straightforward recommendations? If so, where? If not, how do you decide whether his essay includes any positive proposals and where they are stated? Try to decipher not only the satire but the means by which the satire is accomplished.

A MODEST PROPOSAL

First published as "A Modest Proposal for Preventing the Children of Poor People from Being a Burden to Their Parents or the Country" (1729).

It is a melancholy object to those who walk through this great town* or travel in the country, when they see the streets, the roads, and cabin doors, crowded with beggars of the female sex, followed by three, four, or six children, all in rags and importuning every passenger for an alms. These mothers, instead of being able to work for their honest livelihood, are forced to employ all their time in strolling to beg sustenance for their helpless infants, who, as they grow up, either turn thieves for want of work, or leave their dear native country to fight for the Pretender in Spain, or sell themselves to the Barbadoes.†   **1**

I think it is agreed by all parties that this prodigious number of children in the arms, or on the backs, or at the heels of their mothers, and frequently of their fathers, is in the present deplorable state of the kingdom a very great additional grievance; and therefore whoever could find out a fair, cheap, and easy method of making these children sound, useful members of the commonwealth would deserve so well of the public as to have his statue set up for a preserver of the nation.   **2**

Sarcasm

But my intention is very far from being confined to provide only for the children of professed beggars; it is of a much greater extent, and shall take in the whole number of infants at a certain age who are born of parents in effect as little able to support them as those who demand our charity in the streets.   **3**

As to my own part, having turned my thoughts for many years upon this important subject, and maturely weighed the several schemes of other projectors, I have always found them grossly mistaken in their computation.   **4**

*Dublin, capital city of Ireland.

†The pretender to the throne of England was James Stuart (1688–1766), son of the deposed James II. Barbados is an island in the West Indies.

It is true, a child just dropped from its dam may be supported by her milk for a solar year, with little other nourishment; at most not above the value of two shillings,* which the mother may certainly get, or the value in scraps, by her lawful occupation of begging; and it is exactly at one year old that I propose to provide for them in such a manner as instead of being a charge upon their parents or the parish, or wanting food and raiment for the rest of their lives, they shall on the contrary contribute to the feeding, and partly to the clothing, of many thousands.

There is likewise another great advantage in my scheme, that it will prevent those voluntary abortions, and that horrid practice of women murdering their bastard children, alas, too frequent among us, sacrificing the poor innocent babes, I doubt, more to avoid the expense than the shame, which would move tears and pity in the most savage and inhuman breast. 5

The number of souls in this kingdom being usually reckoned one million and a half, of these I calculate there may be about two hundred thousand couple whose wives are breeders; from which number I subtract thirty thousand couples who are able to maintain their own children, although I apprehend there cannot be so many under the present distress of the kingdom; but this being granted, there will remain an hundred and seventy thousand breeders. I again subtract fifty thousand for those women who miscarry, or whose children die by accident or disease within the year. There only remain an hundred and twenty thousand children of poor parents annually born. The question therefore is, how this number shall be reared and provided for, which, as I have already said, under the present situation of affairs, is utterly impossible by all the methods hitherto proposed. For we can neither employ them in handicraft or agriculture; we neither build houses (I mean in the country) nor cultivate land. They can very seldom pick up a livelihood by stealing till they arrive at six years old, except where they are of towardly parts;† although I confess they learn the rudiments much earlier, during which time they can however be looked upon only as probationers, as I have been informed by a principal gentleman in the county of Cavan, who protested to me that he never knew above one or two instances under the age of six, even in a part of the kingdom so renowned for the quickest proficiency in that art. 6

I am assured by our merchants that a boy or a girl before twelve years old is no salable commodity; and even when they come to this age they will not yield above three pounds, or three pounds and half a crown at most on the Exchange; which cannot turn to account either to the parents or the kingdom, the charge of nutriment and rags having been at least four times that value. 7

I shall now therefore humbly propose my own thoughts, which I hope will not be liable to the least objection. 8

I have been assured by a very knowing American of my acquaintance 9

*The British pound sterling was made up of twenty shillings; five shillings made a crown.
†*Towardly* means "advanced"; *parts* refers to abilities or talents.

in London, that a young healthy child well nursed is at a year old a most delicious, nourishing, and wholesome food, whether stewed, roasted, baked, or boiled; and I make no doubt that it will equally serve in a fricassee or a ragout.

I do therefore humbly offer it to public consideration that of the hundred and twenty thousand children, already computed, twenty thousand may be reserved for breed, whereof only one fourth part to be males, which is more than we allow to sheep, black cattle, or swine; and my reason is that these children are seldom the fruits of marriage, a circumstance not much regarded by our savages, therefore one male will be sufficient to serve four females. That the remaining hundred thousand may at a year old be offered in sale to the persons of quality and fortune through the kingdom, always advising the mother to let them suck plentifully in the last month, so as to render them plump and fat for a good table. A child will make two dishes at an entertainment for friends; and when the family dines alone, the fore or hind quarter will make a reasonable dish, and seasoned with a little pepper or salt will be very good boiled on the fourth day, especially in winter.

I have reckoned upon a medium that a child just born will weigh twelve pounds, and in a solar year if tolerably nursed increaseth to twenty-eight pounds.

I grant this food will be somewhat dear, and therefore very proper for landlords, who, as they have already devoured most of the parents, seem to have the best title to the children.

Infant's flesh will be in season throughout the year, but more plentiful in March, and a little before and after. For we are told by a grave author, an eminent French physician,* that fish being a prolific diet, there are more children born in Roman Catholic countries about nine months after Lent than at any other season; therefore, reckoning a year after Lent, the markets will be more glutted than usual, because the number of popish infants is at least three to one in this kingdom; and therefore it will have one other collateral advantage, by lessening the number of Papists among us.

I have already computed the charge of nursing a beggar's child (in which list I reckon all cottagers, laborers, and four fifths of the farmers) to be about two shillings per annum, rags included; and I believe no gentleman would repine to give ten shillings for the carcass of a good fat child, which, as I have said, will make four dishes of excellent nutritive meat, when he hath only some particular friend or his own family to dine with him. Thus the squire will learn to be a good landlord, and grow popular among the tenants; the mother will have eight shillings net profit, and be fit for work till she produces another child.

Those who are more thrifty (as I must confess the times require) may flay the carcass; the skin of which artificially† dressed will make admirable gloves for ladies, and summer boots for fine gentlemen.

---

*François Rabelais (1494?–1553), French satirist, author of *Pantagruel* (1532) and *Gargantua* (1534).
†Skillfully, artistically.

As to our city of Dublin, shambles* may be appointed for this purpose 16 in the most convenient parts of it, and butchers we may be assured will not be wanting; although I rather recommend buying the children alive, and dressing them hot from the knife as we do roasting pigs.

A very worthy person, a true lover of his country, and whose virtues 17 I highly esteem, was lately pleased in discoursing on this matter to offer a refinement upon my scheme. He said that many gentlemen of this kingdom, having of late destroyed their deer, he conceived that the want of venison might be well supplied by the bodies of young lads and maidens, not exceeding fourteen years of age nor under twelve, so great a number of both sexes in every country being now ready to starve for want of work and service; and these to be disposed of by their parents, if alive, or otherwise by their nearest relations. But with due deference to so excellent a friend and so deserving a patriot, I cannot be altogether in his sentiments; for as to the males, my American acquaintance assured me from frequent experience that their flesh was generally tough and lean, like that of our schoolboys, by continual exercise, and their taste disagreeable; and to fatten them would not answer the charge. Then as to the females, it would, I think with humble submission, be a loss to the public, because they soon would become breeders themselves: and besides, it is not improbable that some scrupulous people might be apt to censure such a practice (although indeed very unjustly) as a little bordering upon cruelty; which, I confess, hath always been with me the strongest objection against any project, how well soever intended.

But in order to justify my friend, he confessed that this expedient was 18 put into his head by the famous Psalmanazar, a native of the island Formosa, who came from thence to London above twenty years ago, and in conversation told my friend that in his country when any young person happened to be put to death, the executioner sold the carcass to persons of quality as a prime dainty; and that in his time the body of a plump girl of fifteen, who was crucified for an attempt to poison the emperor, was sold to his Imperial Majesty's prime minister of state, and other great mandarins of the court, in joints from the gibbet, at four hundred crowns. Neither indeed can I deny that if the same use were made of several plump young girls in this town, who without one single groat to their fortunes cannot stir abroad without a chair,† and appear at the playhouse and assemblies in foreign fineries which they never will pay for, the kingdom would not be the worse.

Some persons of a desponding spirit are in great concern about that vast 19 number of poor people who are aged, diseased, or maimed, and I have been desired to employ my thoughts what course may be taken to ease the nation of so grievous an encumbrance. But I am not in the least pain upon that matter, because it is very well known that they are every day dying and rotting by cold and famine, and filth and vermin, as fast as can be reasonably

*Slaughterhouses.
†Sedan chair, an enclosed chair set on horizontal poles, in which the occupant could be conveyed from place to place by two carriers, one in front and one in back.

expected. And as to the younger laborers, they are now in almost as hopeful a condition. They cannot get work, and consequently pine away for want of nourishment to a degree that if at any time they are accidentally hired to common labor, they have not strength to perform it; and thus the country and themselves are happily delivered from the evils to come.

I have too long digressed, and therefore shall return to my subject. I think the advantages by the proposal which I have made are obvious and many, as well as of the highest importance.

For first, as I have already observed, it would greatly lessen the number of Papists, with whom we are yearly overrun, being the principal breeders of the nation as well as our most dangerous enemies; and who stay at home on purpose to deliver the kingdom to the Pretender, hoping to take their advantage by the absence of so many good Protestants, who have chosen rather to leave their country than stay at home and pay tithes against their conscience to an Episcopal curate.*

Secondly, the poorer tenants will have something valuable of their own, which by law may be made liable to distress, and help to pay their landlord's rent, their corn and cattle being already seized and money a thing unknown.

Thirdly, whereas the maintenance of an hundred thousand children, from two years old and upward, cannot be computed at less than ten shillings a piece per annum, the nation's stock will be thereby increased fifty thousand pounds per annum, besides the profit of a new dish introduced to the tables of all gentlemen of fortune in the kingdom who have any refinement in taste. And the money will circulate among ourselves,† the goods being entirely of our own growth and manufacture.

Fourthly, the constant breeders, besides the gain of eight shillings sterling per annum by the sale of their children, will be rid of the charge of maintaining them after the first year.

Fifthly, this food would likewise bring great custom to taverns, where the vintners will certainly be so prudent as to procure the best receipts for dressing it to perfection, and consequently have their houses frequented by all the fine gentlemen, who justly value themselves upon their knowledge in good eating; and a skillful cook, who understands how to oblige his guests, will contrive to make it as expensive as they please.

Sixthly, this would be a great inducement to marriage, which all wise nations have either encouraged by rewards or enforced by laws and penalties. It would increase the care and tenderness of mothers toward their children, when they were sure of a settlement for life to the poor babes, provided in some sort by the public, to their annual profit instead of expense. We should see an honest emulation among the married women, which of them could bring the fattest child to the market. Men would become as fond of their wifes during the time of their pregnancy as they are now of their mares in

*Swift blamed much of Ireland's poverty on large Protestant landowners who, not wanting to pay Anglican (Episcopal) Church tithes (taxes), lived abroad and thus spent their Irish-made money abroad, depriving the Irish economy of their income.
†That is, among the Irish themselves.

foal, their cows in calf, or sows when they are ready to farrow; nor offer to beat or kick them (as is too frequent a practice) for fear of a miscarriage.

Many other advantages might be enumerated. For instance, the addition 27 of some thousand carcasses in our exportation of barreled beef, the propagation of swine's flesh, and improvement in the art of making good bacon, so much wanted among us by the great destruction of pigs, too frequent at our tables, which are no way comparable in taste or magnificence to a well-grown, fat, yearling child, which roasted whole will make a considerable figure at a lord mayor's feast or any other public entertainment. But this and many others I omit, being studious of brevity.

Supposing that one thousand families in this city would be constant 28 customers for infants' flesh, besides others who might have it at merry meetings, particularly weddings and christenings, I compute that Dublin would take off annually about twenty thousand carcasses, and the rest of the kingdom (where probably they will be sold somewhat cheaper) the remaining eighty thousand.

I can think of no one objection that will possibly be raised against this 29 proposal, unless it should be urged that the number of people will be thereby much lessened in the kingdom. This I freely own, and it was indeed one principal design in offering it to the world. I desire the reader will observe, that I calculate my remedy for this one individual kingdom of Ireland and for no other that ever was, is, or I think ever can be upon earth. Therefore let no man talk to me of other expedients: of taxing our absentees at five shillings a pound: of using neither clothes nor household furniture except what is of our own growth and manufacture: of utterly rejecting the materials and instruments that promote foreign luxury: of curing the expensiveness of pride, vanity, idleness, and gaming* in our women: of introducing a vein of parsimony, prudence, and temperance: of learning to love our country, in the want of which we differ even from Laplanders and the inhabitants of Topinamboo: of quitting our animosities and factions, nor acting any longer like the Jews, who were murdering one another at the very moment their city† was taken: of being a little cautious not to sell our country and conscience for nothing: of teaching landlords to have at least one degree of mercy toward their tenants: lastly, of putting a spirit of honesty, industry, and skill into our shopkeepers; who, if a resolution could now be taken to buy only our native goods, would immediately unite to cheat and exact upon us in the price, the measure, and the goodness, nor could ever yet be brought to make one fair proposal of just dealing, though often and earnestly invited to it.

Therefore I repeat, let no man talk to me of these and the like expedi- 30 ents, till he hath at least some glimpse of hope that there will ever be some hearty and sincere attempt to put them in practice.

But as to myself, having been wearied out for many years with offering 31 vain, idle, visionary thoughts, and at length utterly despairing of success, I

---

*Gambling.
†Jerusalem, sacked by the Romans in A.D. 70.

fortunately fell upon this proposal, which, as it is wholly new, so it hath something solid and real, of no expense and little trouble, full in our own power, and whereby we can incur no danger in disobliging England. For this kind of commodity will not bear exportation, the flesh being of too tender a consistence to admit a long continuance in salt, although perhaps I could name a country* which would be glad to eat up our whole nation without it.

After all, I am not so violently bent upon my own opinion as to reject 32 any offer proposed by wise men, which shall be found equally innocent, cheap, easy, and effectual. But before something of that kind shall be advanced in contradiction to my scheme, and offering a better, I desire the author or authors will be pleased maturely to consider two points. First, as things now stand, how they will be able to find food and raiment for an hundred thousand useless mouths and backs. And secondly, there being a round million of creatures in human figure throughout this kingdom, whose sole subsistence put into a common stock would leave them in debt two millions of pounds sterling, adding those who are beggars by profession to the bulk of farmers, cottagers, and laborers, with their wives and children who are beggars in effect; I desire those politicians who dislike my overture, and may perhaps be so bold to attempt an answer, that they will first ask the parents of these mortals whether they would not at this day think it a great happiness to have been sold for food at a year old in the manner I prescribe, and thereby have avoided such a perpetual scene of misfortunes as they have since gone through by the oppression of landlords, the impossibility of paying rent without money or trade, the want of common sustenance, with neither house nor clothes to cover them from the inclemencies of the weather, and the most inevitable prospect of entailing the like or greater miseries upon their breed forever.

I profess, in the sincerity of my heart, that I have not the least personal 33 interest in endeavoring to promote this necessary work, having no other motive than the public good of my country, by advancing our trade, providing for infants, relieving the poor, and giving some pleasure to the rich. I have no children by which I can propose to get a single penny; the youngest being nine years old, and my wife past childbearing.

Questions for Discussion

1. If the satirist Swift is delivering a message that has to be decoded, not the message that is stated, who is delivering the surface message? What does Swift achieve by not speaking "straight," in his own voice? How can you determine the amount of distance between the persona and Swift himself?

*England, of course, against whose occupation of Ireland many Irish are still resentful.

2. In the original edition of Swift's essay, most of paragraph 29 is italicized. Can you think of any rhetorical reasons—purpose, tone, arguments, style, and so on—that would justify Swift's use of italics as a visual signal here? What is the purpose of paragraph 29? Does the purpose differ from that of Swift's other paragraphs? How does paragraph 29 fit into the rest of the essay?

3. Does it matter for Swift's satire whether his persona's statistics are accurate or not? Do you think they are bogus or real? Regardless of the answer to this question, what *rhetorical* effect do they serve? What kind of *character* do they help establish for the persona? How do they fit into Swift's overall satire?

4. Who receives the strongest attack from Swift: the British landlords, the Irish leaders, or the Irish people in general? How do you know?

5. What would the "proposal" gain or lose if the final paragraph were dropped? Does it provide a fitting conclusion for the satire? If so, how? If not, why not?

6. How does the animal imagery—dam, breeder, carcass, and so on—contribute to the satire? Can you think of any other terms that would serve Swift's purpose as well? If not, what does this suggest about the artistry of the satire?

Suggested Essay Topics

1. Write your own satire making fun of some group, person, institution, or human trait. Address it not to your target but to people that you would like to join you in contempt or ridicule of the target.

2. Write two different versions of the same attack, one in a satirical voice, the other as a straightforward denunciation. In a satire you can say you "love" something, and, if the satire is working, the reader will know that you hate it. In a straightforward denunciation you simply say that you hate what you hate. Satire's greater relative complexity does not mean that it is always better for all purposes. After you have written your two versions, write a final paragraph or two evaluating which version works better.

Stephen Spender

Most of the readings in this chapter deal with different versions of racial or ethnic discrimination, but there is one form of discrimination in modern life that embraces all races, ages, and sexes: the discrimination against the urban poor—not those who are struggling to stay economically afloat, and not those whose lives are scrimped and scraped by insufficient income, but those who have no income, those who have gone under: the bag ladies, the hobos, and the winos who beg on the streets, live in the alleys, and sleep on the warm-air gratings of every large American city. They are the unemployed and, in many cases, the unemployable; they are homeless, hopeless, and habituated to neglect. Many of us stop noticing these degraded and unaided folk after a while; we don't wish to see what we cannot understand or help.

Fortunately, however, others not only look but see and in the intensity of their gaze make us look again. They invite us to see what we were too embarrassed or hurried to notice the first time. Spender's (b. 1909) poem captures a moment of intense seeing of these urban poor. He looks at them without sentimentality and insists that we do the same. He admonishes us to "paint here no draped despairs" (l. 12) but to look on wounds that are raw, ugly, and personal, not statistical.

IN RAILWAY HALLS, ON PAVEMENTS NEAR THE TRAFFIC

From *Collected Poems* (1934).

> In railway halls, on pavements near the traffic,
> They beg, their eyes made big by empty staring
> And only measuring Time, like the blank clock.
>
> No, I shall wave no tracery of pen-ornament
> To make them birds upon my singing-tree: 5
> Time merely drives these lives which do not live
> As tides push rotten stuff along the shore.
>
> —There is no consolation, no, none,
> In the curving beauty of that line
> Traced on our graphs through History, where the oppressor   10
>   Starves and deprives the poor.
>
> Paint here no draped despairs, no saddening clouds
> Where the soul rests, proclaims eternity.
> But let the wrong cry out as raw as wounds
> This time forgets and never heals, far less transcends.   15

                                                    1933

Questions for Discussion

1. Why is the clock in line 3 described as "blank"? In what sense is Spender using *blank*?

2. To what do "tracery of pen-ornament" (l. 4) and "singing-tree" (l. 5) refer? Are these appropriate metaphors? How do they aid the poem's effectiveness?

3. Graph lines may have a "curving beauty" (l. 9), but why does Spender find them so sinister? Why is he angry?

4. What is his final judgment about "this time" (l. 15) and its treatment of the poor he is describing?

Suggested Essay Topic

1. Choose some discriminated-against group that is generally as invisible to most of us as the urban poor, and write an indignant letter to the editor of the city newspaper in which you attempt to make this group really visible and awaken the conscience of your fellow citizens about the plight of the real people in the group.

2. Try writing a "social protest" poem of your own, focusing on any groups and taking any tone you choose. Direct the poem toward the kind of general reader who might see it as a published piece in your campus literary magazine.

IDEAS IN DEBATE

Adolf Hitler
Malcolm Hay

Adolf Hitler

*I*nto Mein Kampf *(My Struggle), Adolf Hitler (1889–1945) poured all of the weird fantasies, twisted logic, and racial hatred of a person who seems never to have loved or to have been loved by anyone. (The idolatry he received as Führer was another kind of thing.) His father was a shoemaker, and his mother, who was his father's third wife, had been a maid in the first wife's home. The father died when Hitler was 13; the mother died two years later.*

At age 15, then, Hitler found himself alone in the world and made his way to Vienna, Austria, where he hoped to study art. He lived in Vienna for about nine years, until 1912, existing in miserable poverty, failing his entrance exam into the art academy, and finding himself unable to take up architecture, a second ambition, because he had never completed his secondary education. He squeezed out a barren existence as a building construction worker and also tried painting postcards and selling pictures. But these efforts brought in only pennies. In 1912 Hitler moved to Munich, where he continued to make a scanty living as a commercial artist. He served as a soldier in the German army, 1914–1918, and was wounded in 1916. After the war he became more and more absorbed in political activity, joining the German Workers' party in 1919 and discovering that he was a speaker. He began to gather around him a group of misfits and thugs who with him participated in the "Beer Hall Putsch" of November 8–9, 1923, when Hitler was 34. With the failure of the putsch, he was sentenced to prison on the charge of treason, and while there he began writing Mein Kampf at the suggestion of Rudolf Hess. He was pardoned the next year by a government that was habitually lenient toward right-wing agitators.

In Hitler's account of his Vienna years in Mein Kampf we get a clear picture of his emerging hatred of Jews. At them he directs all the pent-up rage and the psychopathological fury of a man who, small in every sense, had lived a life unloved, unexciting, unrewarded, unsuccessful, and unpromising. This rage was later to transform itself into the calculated murder of more than 6 million Jews.

However, as Malcolm Hay makes clear in the next selection, "The Persecution of Jews," Hitler's choice of the Jews as a scapegoat for his frustrations was not random, idiosyncratic, or accidental. Hatred of Jews was an ancient tradition in Europe, both within the Christian church and outside of it. Anti-Semitism was thus a "safe" outlet for the expression of hatreds that Hitler during his Vienna years had neither the

*imagination nor the influence to vent on other, more powerful groups. The Jews were
traditional targets.*

*We pick up Hitler's story at the point where he tells of coming under the
influence of the mayor of Vienna, Karl Lueger, whose newspaper,* Volksblatt,
*was rabidly anti-Semitic. He begins by saying that when he first came to Vienna
he disliked both Lueger and his anti-Semitic bias. As the account progresses he
records how he gradually came to see anti-Semitism as, for him, an inevitable
position.*

IS THIS A JEW?

From *Mein Kampf.* We are reprinting from the translation by Ralph Manheim. *Mein Kampf* was
originally published in 1925. The title is ours.

These occasions slowly made me acquainted with the man and the move-   1
ment, which in those days guided Vienna's destinies: Dr. Karl Lueger* and
the Christian Social Party.

When I arrived in Vienna, I was hostile to both of them.   2

The man and the movement seemed 'reactionary' in my eyes.   3

My common sense of justice, however, forced me to change this judg-   4
ment in proportion as I had occasion to become acquainted with the man and
his work; and slowly my fair judgment turned to unconcealed admiration.
Today, more than ever, I regard this man as the greatest German mayor of
all times.

How many of my basic principles were upset by this change in my   5
attitude toward the Christian Social movement!

My views with regard to anti-Semitism thus succumbed to the passage   6
of time, and this was my greatest transformation of all.

It cost me the greatest inner soul struggles, and only after months of   7
battle between my reason and my sentiments did my reason begin to emerge
victorious. Two years later, my sentiment had followed my reason, and from
then on became its most loyal guardian and sentinel.

At the time of this bitter struggle between spiritual education and cold   8
reason, the visual instruction of the Vienna streets had performed invaluable
services. There came a time when I no longer, as in the first days, wandered
blindly through the mighty city; now with open eyes I saw not only the
buildings but also the people.

Once, as I was strolling through the Inner City, I suddenly encountered   9
an apparition in a black caftan† and black hair locks. Is this a Jew? was my
first thought.

*Karl Lueger (1844–1910). In 1897, as a member of the anti-Semitic Christian Social Party, he
became mayor of Vienna and kept the post until his death. He also edited the violently anti-
Semitic newspaper *Volksblatt,* which influenced Hitler's views about race, nation, and patriotism.
At first opposed by the Court for his radical nationalism and anti-Semitism, toward the end of
Lueger's career he became more moderate and was reconciled with the Emperor.

†An ankle-length coat-like garment, often striped, with very long sleeves and a sash.

For, to be sure, they had not looked like that in Linz. I observed the man 10 furtively and cautiously, but the longer I stared at this foreign face, scrutinizing feature for feature, the more my first question assumed a new form:

Is this a German? 11

As always in such cases, I now began to try to relieve my doubts by 12 books. For a few hellers I bought the first anti-Semitic pamphlets of my life. Unfortunately, they all proceeded from the supposition that in principle the reader knew or even understood the Jewish question to a certain degree. Besides, the tone for the most part was such that doubts again arose in me, due in part to the dull and amazingly unscientific arguments favoring the thesis.

I relapsed for weeks at a time, once even for months. 13

The whole thing seemed to me so monstrous, the accusations so bound- 14 less, that, tormented by the fear of doing injustice, I again became anxious and uncertain.

● Yet I could no longer very well doubt that the objects of my study were 15 not Germans of a special religion, but a people in themselves; for since I had begun to concern myself with this question and to take cognizance of the Jews, Vienna appeared to me in a different light than before. Wherever I went, I began to see Jews, and the more I saw, the more sharply they became distinguished in my eyes from the rest of humanity. Particularly the Inner City and the districts north of the Danube Canal swarmed with a people which even outwardly had lost all resemblance to Germans.

And whatever doubts I may still have nourished were finally dispelled 16 by the attitude of a portion of the Jews themselves.

Among them there was a great movement, quite extensive in Vienna, 17 which came out sharply in confirmation of the national character of the Jews: this was the *Zionists*. *

It looked, to be sure, as though only a part of the Jews approved this 18 viewpoint, while the great majority condemned and inwardly rejected such a formulation. But when examined more closely, this appearance dissolved itself into an unsavory vapor of pretexts advanced for mere reasons of expedience, not to say lies. For the so-called liberal Jews did not reject the Zionists as non-Jews, but only as Jews with an impractical, perhaps even dangerous, way of publicly avowing their Jewishness.

Intrinsically they remained unalterably of one piece. 19

In a short time this apparent struggle between Zionistic and liberal Jews 20 disgusted me; for it was false through and through, founded on lies and scarcely in keeping with the moral elevation and purity always claimed by this people.

The cleanliness of this people, moral and otherwise, I must say, is a 21 point in itself. By their very exterior you could tell that these were no lovers of water, and, to your distress, you often knew it with your eyes closed. Later

---

*Those Jews who believed that Judaism not only was a religion but conferred a *national* status as well. Zionists thus believe in a Jewish state, not just a Jewish faith.

I often grew sick to my stomach from the smell of these caftan-wearers. Added to this, there was their unclean dress and their generally unheroic appearance.

All this could scarcely be called very attractive; but it became positively 22 repulsive when, in addition to their physical uncleanliness, you discovered the moral stains on this 'chosen people.'

In a short time I was made more thoughtful than ever by my slowly 23 rising insight into the type of activity carried on by the Jews in certain fields.

Was there any form of filth or profligacy, particularly in cultural life, 24 without at least one Jew involved in it?

If you cut even cautiously into such an abscess, you found, like a maggot 25 in a rotting body, often dazzled by the sudden light—a kike!

What had to be reckoned heavily against the Jews in my eyes was 26 when I became acquainted with their activity in the press, art, literature, and the theater.* All the unctuous reassurances helped little or nothing. It sufficed to look at a billboard, to study the names of the men behind the horrible trash they advertised, to make you hard for a long time to come. This was pestilence, spiritual pestilence, worse than the Black Death of olden times, and the people was being infected with it! It goes without saying that the lower the intellectual level of one of these art manufacturers, the more unlimited his fertility will be, and the scoundrel ends up like a garbage separator, splashing his filth in the face of humanity. And bear in mind that there is no limit to their number; bear in mind that for one Goethe Nature easily can foist on the world ten thousand of these scribblers who poison men's souls like germ-carriers of the worse sort, on their fellow men.

It was terrible, but not to be overlooked, that precisely the Jew, in 27 tremendous numbers, seemed chosen by Nature for this shameful calling.

Is this why the Jews are called the 'chosen people'?   28

I now began to examine carefully the names of all the creators of 29 unclean products in public artistic life. The result was less and less favorable for my previous attitude toward the Jews. Regardless how my sentiment might resist, my reason was forced to draw its conclusions.

The fact that nine tenths of all literary filth, artistic trash, and theatrical 30 idiocy can be set to the account of a people, constituting hardly one hundredth of all the country's inhabitants, could simply not be talked away; it was the plain truth.

And I now began to examine my beloved 'world press' from this point 31 of view.

And the deeper I probed, the more the object of my former admiration 32 shriveled. The style became more and more unbearable; I could not help rejecting the content as inwardly shallow and banal; the objectivity of exposi-

*There is not much evidence that Hitler really knew the art, literature, and theatre of his day. These criticisms seem to be parrotings of *Volksblatt* editorials. It was attitudes such as these that eventually led to the Nazi burning of books and the denunciation of writings by "racially inferior" authors.

tion now seemed to me more akin to lies than honest truth; and the writers were—Jews.

A thousand things which I had hardly seen before now struck my 33 notice, and others, which had previously given me food for thought, I now learned to grasp and understand.

I now saw the liberal attitude of this press in a different light; the lofty 34 tone in which it answered attacks and its method of killing them with silence now revealed itself to me as a trick as clever as it was treacherous; the transfigured raptures of their theatrical critics were always directed at Jewish writers, and their disapproval never struck anyone but Germans. The gentle pinpricks against William II revealed its methods by their persistency, and so did its commendation of French culture and civilization. The trashy content of the short story now appeared to me as outright indecency, and in the language I detected the accents of a foreign people; the sense of the whole thing was so obviously hostile to Germanism that this could only have been intentional.

But who had an interest in this? 35

Was all this a mere accident? 36

Gradually I became uncertain. 37

The development was accelerated by insights which I gained into a 38 number of other matters. I am referring to the general view of ethics and morals which was quite openly exhibited by a large part of the Jews, and the practical application of which could be seen.

Here again the streets provided an object lesson of a sort which was 39 sometimes positively evil.

The relation of the Jews to prostitution and, even more, to the white- 40 slave traffic, could be studied in Vienna as perhaps in no other city of Western Europe, with the possible exception of the southern French ports. If you walked at night through the streets and alleys of Leopoldstadt,* at every step you witnessed proceedings which remained concealed from the majority of the German people until the War gave the soldiers on the eastern front occasion to see similar things, or, better expressed, forced them to see them.

When thus for the first time I recognized the Jew as the cold-hearted, 41 shameless, and calculating director of this revolting vice traffic in the scum of the big city, a cold shudder ran down my back.

But then a flame flared up within me. I no longer avoided discussion of 42 the Jewish question; no, now I sought it. And when I learned to look for the Jew in all branches of cultural and artistic life and its various manifestations, I suddenly encountered him in a place where I would least have expected to find him.

When I recognized the Jew as the leader of the Social Democracy,† the 43 scales dropped from my eyes. A long soul struggle had reached its conclusion.

---

*Second District of Vienna, separated from the main part of the city by the Danube Canal. Formerly the ghetto, it still has a predominantly Jewish population. [Original editor's note]
†Socialism, the political theory at the opposite end of the political spectrum from the fascism which Hitler later brought to Germany.

Even in my daily relations with my fellow workers, I observed the 44
amazing adaptability with which they adopted different positions on the
same question, sometimes within an interval of a few days, sometimes in only
a few hours. It was hard for me to understand how people who, when spoken
to alone, possessed some sensible opinions, suddenly lost them as soon as
they came under the influence of the masses. It was often enough to make
one despair. When, after hours of argument, I was convinced that now at last
I had broken the ice or cleared up some absurdity, and was beginning to
rejoice at my success, on the next day to my disgust I had to begin all over
again; it had all been in vain. Like an eternal pendulum their opinions seemed
to swing back again and again to the old madness.

All this I could understand: that they were dissatisfied with their lot and 45
cursed the Fate which often struck them so harshly; that they hated the
employers who seemed to them the heartless bailiffs of Fate; that they cursed
the authorities who in their eyes were without feeling for their situation; that
they demonstrated against food prices and carried their demands into the
streets: this much could be understood without recourse to reason. But what
inevitably remained incomprehensible was the boundless hatred they heaped
upon their own nationality, despising its greatness, besmirching its history,
and dragging its great men into the gutter.

This struggle against their own species, their own clan, their own home- 46
land, was as senseless as it was incomprehensible. It was unnatural.

It was possible to cure them temporarily of this vice, but only for days 47
or at most weeks. If later you met the man you thought you had converted,
he was just the same as before.

His old unnatural state had regained full possession of him. 48

. . .

I gradually became aware that the Social Democratic press was directed 49
predominantly by Jews; yet I did not attribute any special significance to this
circumstance, since conditions were exactly the same in the other papers. Yet
one fact seemed conspicuous: there was not one paper with Jews working on
it which could have been regarded as truly national, according to my education and way of thinking.

I swallowed my disgust and tried to read this type of Marxist press 50
production, but my revulsion became so unlimited in so doing that I endeavored to become more closely acquainted with the men who manufactured
these compendiums of knavery.

From the publisher down, they were all Jews. 51

I took all the Social Democratic pamphlets I could lay hands on and 52
sought the names of their authors: Jews.* I noted the names of the leaders; by far the greatest part were likewise members of the 'chosen people,'
whether they were representatives in the Reichsrat or trade-union secretaries, the heads of organizations or street agitators. It was always the

*The facts do not support this assertion that the leadership of Austrian Social Democracy
was primarily Jewish.

same gruesome picture. The names of the Austerlitzes, Davids, Adlers, Ellenbogens, etc., will remain forever graven in my memory. One thing had grown clear to me: the party with whose petty representatives I had been carrying on the most violent struggle for months was, as to leadership, almost exclusively in the hands of a foreign people; for, to my deep and joyful satisfaction, I had at last come to the conclusion that the Jew was no German.

Only now did I become thoroughly acquainted with the seducer of our people. 53

A single year of my sojourn in Vienna had sufficed to imbue me with the conviction that no worker could be so stubborn that he would not in the end succumb to better knowledge and better explanations. Slowly I had become an expert in their own doctrine and used it as a weapon in the struggle for my own profound conviction. 54

Success almost always favored my side. 55

The great masses could be saved, if only with the gravest sacrifice in time and patience. 56

But a Jew could never be parted from his opinions. 57

At that time I was still childish enough to try to make the madness of their doctrine clear to them; in my little circle I talked my tongue sore and my throat hoarse, thinking I would inevitably succeed in convincing them how ruinous their Marxist madness was; but what I accomplished was often the opposite. It seemed as though their increased understanding of the destructive effects of Social Democratic theories and their results only reinforced their determination. 58

The more I argued with them, the better I came to know their dialectic. First they counted on the stupidity of their adversary, and then, when there was no other way out, they themselves simply played stupid. If all this didn't help, they pretended not to understand, or, if challenged, they changed the subject in a hurry, quoted platitudes which, if you accepted them, they immediately related to entirely different matters, and then, if again attacked, gave ground and pretended not to know exactly what you were talking about. Whenever you tried to attack one of these apostles, your hand closed on a jelly-like slime which divided up and poured through your fingers, but in the next moment collected again. But if you really struck one of these fellows so telling a blow that, observed by the audience, he couldn't help but agree, and if you believed that this had taken you at least one step forward, your amazement was great the next day. The Jew had not the slightest recollection of the day before, he rattled off his same old nonsense as though nothing at all had happened, and, if indignantly challenged, affected amazement; he couldn't remember a thing, except that he had proved the correctness of his assertions the previous day. 59

Sometimes I stood there thunderstruck. 60

I didn't know what to be more amazed at: the agility of their tongues or their virtuosity at lying. 61

Gradually I began to hate them. 62

All this had but one good side: that in proportion as the real leaders or 63
at least the disseminators of Social Democracy came within my vision, my
love for my people inevitably grew. For who, in view of the diabolical craftiness of these seducers, could damn the luckless victims? How hard it was,
even for me, to get the better of this race of dialectical liars! And how futile
was such success in dealing with people who twist the truth in your mouth,
who without so much as a blush disavow the word they have just spoken,
and in the very next minute take credit for it after all.

No. The better acquainted I became with the Jew, the more forgiving 64
I inevitably became toward the worker.

Questions for Discussion

1. If you have ever talked to a fanatical bigot of any kind, compare the
   "reasoning" you encountered then with that in *Mein Kampf.* What seems
   to be the real root of the hatred that emerges in this kind of bigotry? Is
   it a common root, or does it vary unpredictably from person to person?
   This is too big a question to answer factually, of course. But it may be
   useful to share impressions and speculations with your classmates.

2. Notice the self-conscious abandonment of reason in favor of feeling in
   paragraph 7. What would have been the effect of this move on Hitler's
   emerging racial hatred?

3. What is the intended rhetorical effect of the imagery that Hitler employs
   in paragraphs 25, 26, 53, and 59?

4. Discuss the similarities of opinion about Jews in *Mein Kampf,* paragraphs
   21–25, with the opinions of the Colonel in "Artists in Uniform" (p. 248,
   ¶19).

5. It is sometimes said that everyone views the members of *some* groups
   more favorably than others, which is to say that everyone is prejudiced
   to some degree, if by prejudice we mean the expectation that individual
   members of certain groups will behave less admirably than the members
   of our own group. Do you think that this is so? Is it true of you? If it is,
   are you "bigoted"? If you think that you are not but still admit that you
   allow preconceptions about *groups* to affect your judgment of *individuals,*
   how would you define *bigotry* and *prejudice* as distinct from your behavior?

6. It is sometimes said that America is experiencing a new increase in acts
   of bigotry: attacks on individuals merely because they belong to this or
   that group; mailing of anonymous hate mail to members of minority
   groups; publication of journals that include incitement to bigotry. Have
   you noted any such behavior on your own campus? If so, what do you
   think might be an effective way to combat it?

Suggested Essay Topics

1. In "Artists in Uniform" (pp. 247–248), Mary McCarthy's narrator, talking with the anti-Semitic Colonel, says:

> It came to me . . . that for extremely stupid people anti-Semitism was a form of intellectuality, the sole form of intellectuality of which they were capable. It represented, in a rudimentary way, the ability to make categories, to generalize. Hence a thing I had noted before but never understood: the fact that anti-Semitic statements were generally delivered in an atmosphere of profundity. . . . To arrive, indeed, at the idea of a Jew was, for these grouping minds, an exercise in Platonic thought, a discovery of essence. . . . From this, it would seem, followed the querulous obstinacy with which the anti-Semite clung to his concept; to be deprived of this intellectual tool by missionaries of tolerance would be, for persons like the Colonel, the equivalent of Western man's losing the syllogism: a lapse into animal darkness. (¶17)

If you agree that this analysis accurately lays bare the cause of much bigotry in general and is not limited to anti-Semitism, write an essay that analyzes some example of bigotry that you know firsthand, and base your analysis on the perspective provided by McCarthy in the quoted passage.

2. A variation of topic 1: Use McCarthy's perspective as the basis of your analysis of some example of bigotry found in a work of fiction.

Malcolm Hay

In the book from which this excerpt is taken, Europe and the Jews: The Pressure of Christendom on the People of Israel for 1900 Years, *Malcolm Hay (1881–1962) addresses one of the most troublesome of all human questions: Why do the members of one human group hate other groups so much that they are eager to exterminate them? His form of the question—Who is to blame for a given historical crime?—presents one of the most difficult of all writing tasks. To support any conclusions about such broad and elusive questions requires an immense amount of careful research, and to grapple with such emotion-charged matters requires great courage and tact. The author is sure to offend many readers, especially those groups that he blames for crimes they have accused others of committing.*

Through more than 300 pages packed with carefully chosen quotations, Hay argues three main points. First, it is a mistake to blame only Hitler and the Germans for the killing of millions of Jews during World War II; if we in the nations that opposed Hitler had responded with concrete aid as reports of extermination camps filtered into the Allied countries, hundreds of thousands, perhaps millions, of Jews might have been saved. Second, the reason for our indifference to the fate of innocent millions was that we had been taught, by one major "Christian" tradition, that Jews deserved to die because they had killed Christ. Third, the Jews did not kill Christ; Christ was killed, as three of the four Gospels make clear, by Roman soldiers. The Jews who connived in Christ's death were a small group who had to plot secretly with the Romans for fear of resistance from the main body of Jews.

As a Christian himself, Hay is in a better position for making these points than if he were Jewish. Some people would be more tempted to question his objectivity if he clearly had a personal stake in making his case. But in arguing about such complex matters, it is never enough to have a good, seemingly "objective" platform to stand on; final success depends on the quality of our reasoning and the evidence we offer.

As you read this selection (less than one-tenth of Hay's argument), it is important to avoid making up your mind with final assurance. After all, it would take months, perhaps years, of study to check out the reliability of his hundreds of quotations (we have omitted his references to save space) and to reach a point of confident personal understanding of the issues he raises. What we all can do, however, is enlarge our grasp of the issues and our sense of the possible ways of thinking about them. As you read, you may want to question yourself about your own prejudices and your justified beliefs and about possible ways of removing the prejudices and deepening and refining the convictions.

THE PERSECUTION OF JEWS
A CHRISTIAN SCANDAL

Our title for chapter 1, "The Golden Mouth," of *Europe and the Jews: The Pressure of Christendom on the People of Israel for 1900 Years* (1950).

> Suffer no man and no cause to escape the undying penalty which history has the power to inflict on wrong.—Lord Acton

> So I considered again all the oppressions that are done under the sun;
> And beheld the tears of such as were oppressed, and they had no com-
>   forter;
> And on the side of the oppressors there was power,
> But they had no comforter.

> Wherefore I praised the dead that are already dead
> More than the living that are yet alive;
> But better than they both is he that hath not yet been,
> Who hath not seen the evil that is done under the sun.
>   Ecclesiastes IV: 1–3

Men are not born with hatred in their blood. The infection is usually acquired   1
by contact; it may be injected deliberately or even unconsciously, by parents,
or by teachers. Adults, unless protected by the vigor of their intelligence, or
by a rare quality of goodness, seldom escape contagion. The disease may
spread throughout the land like the plague, so that a class, a religion, a nation,

will become the victim of popular hatred without anyone knowing exactly how it all began; and people will disagree, and even quarrel among themselves, about the real reason for its existence; and no one foresees the inevitable consequences.

For hatred dealeth perversely, as St. Paul might have said were he writing to the Corinthians at the present time, and is puffed up with pride; rejoiceth in iniquity; regardeth not the truth. These three things, therefore, corrupt the world: disbelief, despair, and hatred—and of these, the most dangerous of all is hatred.

In the spring of 1945, three trucks loaded with eight to nine tons of human ashes, from the Sachsenhausen concentration camp, were dumped into a canal in order to conceal the high rate of Jewish executions. When a German general was asked at Nuremberg how such things could happen, he replied: "I am of the opinion that when for years, for decades, the doctrine is preached that Jews are not even human, such an outcome is inevitable." This explanation, which gets to the root of the matter, is, however, incomplete. The doctrine which made such deeds inevitable had been preached, not merely for years or for decades, but for many centuries; more than once during the Middle Ages it threatened to destroy the Jewish people. "The Jews," wrote Léon Bloy, "are the most faithful witnesses, the most authentic remainders, of the candid Middle Ages which hated them for the love of God, and so often wanted to exterminate them." In those days the excuse given for killing them was often that they were "not human," and that, in the modern German sense, they were "nonadaptable"; they did not fit into the mediaeval conception of a World State.

The German crime of genocide—the murder of a race—has its logical roots in the mediaeval theory that the Jews were outcasts, condemned by God to a life of perpetual servitude, and it is not, therefore, a phenomenon completely disconnected from previous history. Moreover, responsibility for the nearly achieved success of the German plan to destroy a whole group of human beings ought not to be restricted to Hitler and his gangsters, or to the German people. The plan nearly succeeded because it was allowed to develop without interference.

"It was an excellent saying of Solon's," wrote Richard Bentley, "who when he was asked what would rid the world of injuries, replied: 'If the bystanders would have the same resentment with those that suffer wrong.'" The responsibility of bystanders who remained inactive while the German plan proceeded was recognized by one European statesman, by the least guilty of them all, Jan Masaryk, who had helped to rescue many thousands from the German chambers of death. Masaryk said:

I am not an expert on the Near East and know practically nothing about pipe-lines. But one pipe-line I have watched with horror all my life; it is the pipe-line through which, for centuries, Jewish blood has flowed sporadically, and with horrible, incessant streams from 1933 to 1945. I will not, I cannot, forget this unbelievable fact, and I bow my head in shame as one of those who permitted this greatest of wholesale murders to happen, instead of standing up with courage and decision against its perpetrators before it was too late.

Even after the Nuremberg Laws of 1935, every frontier remained closed   6
against Jews fleeing from German terror, although a few were sometimes allowed in by a back door. Bystanders from thirty-two countries attended a conference at Evian, in 1938, to discuss the refugee problem; they formed a Permanent Intergovernmental Department in London to make arrangements for the admission of Jewish immigrants from Germany. The question of saving Jewish children by sending them to Palestine was not on the agenda of the Committee for assistance to refugees. "Up to August, 1939, the Committee had not succeeded in discovering new opportunities of immigration, though negotiations were proceeding with San Domingo, Northern Rhodesia, the Philippines and British Guiana."

An American writer asked in 1938:   7

> What is to be done with these people, with the millions who are clawing like frantic beasts at the dark walls of the suffocating chambers where they are imprisoned? The Christian world has practically abandoned them, and sits by with hardly an observable twinge of conscience in the midst of this terrible catastrophe. The Western Jews, still potent and powerful, rotate in their smug self-satisfied orbits, and confine themselves to genteel charity.

Until Germany obtained control of the greater part of Western Europe   8
her policy had been directed mainly to compulsory Jewish emigration. But victories in 1940 had opened up new possibilities; and the Jews were therefore driven into ghettos in Poland and neighboring areas, where arrangements were being made for the "final solution," which was proclaimed in 1942, and put into action throughout all Germany and German-occupied territories. "What should be done with them," asked Hans Frank, governor general of occupied Poland, on December 16th, 1941. The German answer was no longer a secret. "I must ask you, gentlemen," said the governor, "to arm yourselves against all feelings of pity. We must annihilate the Jews wherever we find them."

Hitler, in 1941, was still waiting to see what the Christian world was   9
going to do. Had the Allies opened their doors wide, even then, at least a million people, including hundreds of thousands of children, could have been saved. But no doors anywhere were widely opened. Few hearts anywhere were deeply moved. In Palestine, in the corner secured to Jews by the decision of the League of Nations, the entries by land and by sea were guarded by British soldiers and British sailors. Great numbers, especially in Poland, would have fled from the impending terror: *"If only they could,"* wrote Jacques Maritain in 1938, "if only other countries would open their frontiers." The German government at that time, and even after, was not always unwilling,

and in 1939 and 1940, was still prepared to let them go on certain conditions. "The Allies were told that if the Jews of Germany were to receive certificates to Palestine, or visas for any other country, they could be saved. Although for Jews to remain in Germany meant certain death, the pieces of paper needed to save human lives were not granted."

These pieces of paper were not provided, even to save the lives of children. In April, 1943, the Swedish government agreed to ask the German government to permit twenty thousand children to leave Germany for Sweden, provided that Sweden should be relieved of responsibility for them after the war. These children would have been saved had the British government given them certificates for Palestine. But even to save twenty thousand children from being slaughtered by the Germans, "it was not possible," said a British minister in the House of Commons, "for His Majesty's Government to go beyond the terms of policy approved by Parliament."

About the same time, in 1943, the Germans were considering an offer by the Red Cross and the British to evacuate seventy thousand children from Rumania to Palestine. Negotiations dragged on with the usual lack of vigor. And the Germans were persuaded by the Mufti of Jerusalem and Raschid Ali Gailani, prime minister of Iraq, who at the time were living, at German expense, in Berlin, to reject the plan. So the seventy thousand children were sent to the gas chambers.

More than a million children, including uncounted thousands of newborn infants, were killed by the Germans; most of them could have been saved had the countries of the world been determined to save them. But the doors remained closed. The children were taken away from their parents and sent, crowded in the death trains, and alone, to the crematoria of Auschwitz and Treblinka, or to the mass graves of Poland and Western Russia.

The German method of burying people in communal pits was a great improvement on the old system, once considered to be inhuman, of making each condemned man dig his own grave. The shooting of about two million people, whose bodies could not be left lying about, presented a difficult problem owing to the shortage of labor. Jewish women and children, weakened by torture and by long internment in concentration camps, were physically incapable of digging; and the men, when put on the list for "special treatment," were, as a rule, reduced to such a condition by hard labor on meager rations that they could hardly walk. The mass grave was an obvious necessity; but the German stroke of genius was the idea of making their victims get into the grave before they were shot, thus saving the labor of lifting two million dead bodies and throwing them in. Many hundreds of these death pits were dug in Central Europe until the Germans began to apply to extermination their well-known scientific efficiency. One of the largest pits, at Kerch, was examined in 1942 by officials of the Russian army:

It was discovered that this trench, one kilometer in length, four meters wide, and two meters deep, was filled to overflowing with bodies of

women, children, old men, and boys and girls in their teens. Near the
trench were frozen pools of blood. Children's caps, toys, ribbons, torn off
buttons, gloves, milkbottles, and rubber comforters, small shoes,
galoshes, together with torn off hands and feet, and other parts of human
bodies, were lying nearby. Everything was spattered with blood and
brains.

What happened at Dulmo, in the Ukraine, reported by a German 14
witness, Hermann Graebe, is one of the grimmest short stories that has
ever been told in the bloody record of inhuman history. Graebe was man-
ager of a building contractor's business at Dulmo. On October 5, 1942, he
went as usual to his office and there was told by his foreman of terrible
doings in the neighborhood. All the Jews in the district, about five thousand of them, were being liquidated. About fifteen hundred were shot
every day, out in the open air, at a place nearby where three large pits had
been dug, thirty meters long and three meters deep. Graebe and his foreman, who was intensely agitated, got into a car and drove off to the place.
They saw a great mound of earth, twice the length of a cricket pitch and
more than six feet high—a good shooting range. Near the mound were
several trucks packed with people. Guards with whips drove the people off
the trucks. The victims all had yellow patches sewn onto their garments,
back and front—the Jewish badge. From behind the earth mound came the
sound of rifle shots in quick succession. The people from the lorries, men,
women and children of all ages, were herded together near the mound by
an SS man armed with a dog whip. They were ordered to strip. They were
told to put down their clothes in tidy order, boots and shoes, top clothing
and underclothing.

Already there were great piles of this clothing, and a heap of eight 15
hundred to a thousand pairs of boots and shoes. The people undressed. The
mothers undressed the little children, "without screaming or weeping," reported Graebe, five years after. They had reached the point of human suffering where tears no longer flow and all hope has long been abandoned. "They
stood around in family groups, kissed each other, said farewells, and waited."
They were waiting for a signal from the SS man with a whip, who was
standing by the pit. They stood there waiting for a quarter of an hour, waiting
for their turn to come, while on the other side of the earth mound, now that
the shots were no longer heard, the dead and dying were being packed into
the pit. Graebe said:

> I heard no complaints, no appeal for mercy. I watched a family of about
> eight persons, a man and a woman both about fifty, with their grown up
> children, about twenty to twenty-four. An old woman with snow-white
> hair was holding a little baby in her arms, singing to it and tickling it. The
> baby was cooing with delight. The couple were looking at each other
> with tears in their eyes. The father was holding the hand of a boy about
> ten years old and speaking to him softly; the boy was fighting his
> tears . . .

Then suddenly came a shout from the SS man at the pit. They were   16
ready to deal with the next batch. Twenty people were counted off, including
the family of eight. They were marched away behind the earth mound.
Graebe and his foreman followed them. They walked round the mound and
saw the tremendous grave, nearly a hundred feet long and nine feet deep.
"People were closely wedged together and lying on top of each other so that
only their heads were visible. Nearly all had blood running over their shoulders from their heads." They had been shot, in the usual German way, in the
back of the neck. "Some of the shot people were still moving. Some were
lifting their arms and turning their heads to show that they were still alive."

The pit was already nearly full; it contained about a thousand bodies.   17
The SS man who did the shooting was sitting on the edge of the pit, smoking
a cigarette, with a tommy gun on his knee. The new batch of twenty people,
the family of eight and the baby carried in the arms of the woman with
snow-white hair, all completely naked, were directed down steps cut in the
clay wall of the pit, and clambered over the heads of the dead and the dying.
They lay down among them. "Some caressed those who were still alive and
spoke to them in a low voice." Then came the shots from the SS man, who
had thrown away his cigarette. Graebe looked into the pit "and saw the
bodies were twitching, and some heads lying already motionless on top of the
dead bodies that lay under them."

The Jews who died in this manner at Dulmo were the most fortunate   18
ones. They were spared torture in laboratory tests carried out by German
doctors in order to find out how much agony the human body can endure
before it dies; they were spared the choking terror of death in the gas chamber
where hundreds of people at a time, squeezed together as tightly as the room
could hold them, waited for the stream of poison to be turned on, while
members of the German prison staff stood listening for ten or fifteen minutes
until the screaming ceased, until all sounds had ceased, and they could safely
open the door to the dead. And when the door was opened, the torture was
not yet over. Four young Jews, whose turn would come perhaps with the next
batch, dressed in a special sanitary uniform, with high rubber boots and long
leather gauntlets, and provided with grappling irons, were compelled to drag
out the pale dead bodies; and another group of young men was waiting to
load the bodies onto a cart and drive them to the crematorium; and they knew
that their turn, too, would soon come.

Responsibility for these deeds which have dishonored humanity does   19
not rest solely with Hitler and the men who sat in the dock at Nuremberg.
Another tribunal will judge the bystanders, some of them in England, who
watched the murderous beginnings, and then looked away and in their hearts
secretly approved. "The Jewish blood shed by the Nazis," writes J.-P. Sartre,
"is upon the heads of all of us."

As Maxim Gorky said more than thirty years ago, one of the greatest   20
crimes of which men are guilty is indifference to the fate of their fellow men.
This responsibility of the indifferent was recognized by Jacques Maritain a
few years before the final act of the tragedy. "There seems to be a spirit," he

said in 1938, "which, without endorsing excesses committed against Jews
. . . and without professing anti-Semitism, regards the Jewish drama with the
indifference of the rational man who goes coldly along his way." It was this
spirit of indifference, this cold aloofness of the bystanders, which made it
possible for Hitler to turn Europe into a Jewish cemetery. Christian responsibility has, however, been recognized by one English bystander who for many
years had never failed "to have the same resentment with those that suffer
wrong": "In our own day, and within our own civilization," writes Dr. James
Parkes, "more than six million deliberate murders are the consequence of the
teachings about Jews for which the Christian Church is ultimately responsible, and of an attitude to Judaism which is not only maintained by all the
Christian Churches, but has its ultimate resting place in the teaching of the
New Testament itself."

Repressing the instinct to make excuses, read the following words writ- (21)
ten by a survivor of Auschwitz:

> German responsibility for these crimes, however overwhelming it may
> be, is only a secondary responsibility, which has grafted itself, like a
> hideous parasite, upon a secular tradition, which is a Christian tradition.
> How can one forget that Christianity, chiefly from the eleventh century,
> has employed against Jews a policy of degradation and of pogroms, which
> has been extended—among certain Christian people—into contemporary
> history, which can be observed still alive to-day in most Catholic Poland,
> and of which the Hitlerian system has been only a copy, atrociously
> perfected.

Even in countries where pogroms are unknown, it was the coldness, the (22)
indifference of the average man which made the Jewish drama in Europe
possible. "I am convinced," wrote Pierre van Paassen, "that Hitler neither
could nor would have done to the Jewish people what he has done . . . if we
had not actively prepared the way for him by our own unfriendly attitude
to the Jews, by our selfishness and by the anti-Semitic teaching in our
churches and schools."

The way was prepared by a hatred which has a long history. The (23)
inoculation of the poison began long ago in the nurseries of Christendom.

Millions of children heard about Jews for the first time when they
were told the story of how Christ was killed by wicked men; killed by the
Jews; crucified by the Jews. And the next thing they learned was that God
had punished these wicked men and had cursed the whole of their nation
for all time, so that they had become outcasts and were unfit to associate
with Christians. When these children grew up, some of them quarreled
among themselves about the meaning of the word of Christ and about the
story of his life, death and resurrection; and others were Christians only in
name; but most of them retained enough Christianity to continue hating
the perfidious people, the Christ-killers, the deicide [i.e., god-murdering]
race.

Although the popular tradition that "the Jews" crucified Christ goes 24
back to the beginnings of the Christian Church, no justification for it can be
found in the New Testament. St. Matthew, St. Mark and St. Luke all took
special care to impress upon their readers the fact that the Jewish people, their
own people, were not responsible for, and were for the most part ignorant of,
the events which led up to the apprehension, the trial and the condemnation
of Christ. St. Matthew's account of what happened does not provide any
opportunity for people to differ about his meaning. He states quite clearly in
his twenty-sixth chapter that "the Jews" had nothing to do with the plot
against Christ. He explains who the conspirators were, and why they had to
do their work in secret. "Then were gathered together the Chief Priests and
the Ancients of the people into the court of the High Priest who is called
Caiphas. And they consulted together that by subtlety they might apprehend
Jesus and put him to death." Secrecy was essential to the plans of the plotters
because they "feared the multitude" (Matthew XXI:46). They were afraid
that "the Jews" might find out what was brewing and start a riot.

The plot which ended on Calvary began to take shape for the first time 25
at that gathering in the court of Caiphas. These men were engaged upon an
enterprise which they knew would not meet with public approval. They had
no mandate from the Jewish people for what they were about to do. They
did not represent the two or three million Jews who at that time lived in
Palestine, or another million who lived in Egypt, or the millions more who
were scattered all over the Roman Empire. At least three-quarters of all these
people lived and died without ever hearing the name of Christ.

The conspirators did not even represent the wishes of the Jewish popu- 26
lation in and around Jerusalem. They were afraid, explained Matthew, of
arresting Jesus "on the festival day, lest there should be a tumult among the
people."

They had to act promptly; they had to avoid publicity. They employed 27
the crowd of idlers and ruffians which can be always collected for an evil
purpose, to provide a democratic covering for what they proposed to do. This
crowd formed a majority of the people present at the trial; these were the men
who, when Pilate, the pioneer of appeasement, tried to save Christ from their
fury, replied with the fateful words which Matthew recorded in the twenty-
seventh chapter of his Gospel: "And the whole people answering said: 'His
blood be upon us and upon our children.' " Although "the whole people," as
Matthew explained, meant only the people present "who had been persuaded
by the High Priest and the Ancients" (XXVII:20), his text has been used for
centuries by countless Christian preachers as a stimulant to hate and an
excuse for anti-Jewish pogroms. "O cursed race!" thundered Bossuet from his
pulpit, "your prayer will be answered only too effectively; that blood will
pursue you even unto your remotest descendants, until the Lord, weary at last
of vengeance, will be mindful, at the end of time, of your miserable remnant."

St. Mark, also, records that the Jewish people had nothing to do with 28
the plot and that if they had known about it they would have expressed
violent disapproval. "The Chief Priests and the Pharisees sought how they

might destroy him. For they feared him because the whole multitude was in admiration of his doctrine" (XI:18). "They sought to lay hands upon him, but they feared the people" (XII:12). They sought to lay hold on him and kill him, but they said, "not on the festival day, lest there should be a tumult among the people" (XIV:2).

St. Luke tells the same story with the same emphasis. "And the Chief Priests and the Scribes, and the rulers of the people, sought to destroy him. And they found not what to do to him; for all the people were very attentive to hear him" (XIX:47, 48). "The Chief Priests and the Scribes sought to lay hands on him . . . but they feared the people" (XX:19). "And the Chief Priests and the Scribes sought how they might put Jesus to death; but they feared the people" (XXII:2).

This Christian tradition, which made "the Jews" responsible for the death of Christ, first took shape in the Fourth Gospel. St. John deals with the historical beginnings of the Christian Church even more fully than with the ending of the era which preceded the foundation of Christianity. Unlike the other evangelists, he wrote as one outside the Jewish world, as one hostile to it. He was already disassimilated. His Gospel contains the first hint of hostility, the first suggestion of a religious Judaeophobia. He almost invariably employs the phrase "the Jews" when the context shows, and the other evangelists confirm, that he is referring to the action or to the opinions of the High Priests and the Ancients.

Whereas Matthew, Mark and Luke all wrote as if they had foreseen, and were trying to refute in advance, the accusation which would be brought against their fellow-countrymen, John, by his repeated use of the phrase "the Jews," puts into the mind of his readers the idea that they were all guilty. Although Matthew, for instance, says that when Jesus healed the man with a withered hand on the Sabbath, "the Pharisees made a consultation how they might destroy him," John, reporting a similar incident, indicts, not the Pharisees, but "the Jews": "*The Jews* therefore said to him that was healed: it is not lawful for thee to take up thy bed . . . therefore did *the Jews* persecute Jesus because he did these things on the Sabbath" (V:10, 16).

When John tells the story of the blind man, he begins by relating what the Pharisees said, but after the man received his sight his parents are reported to have "feared *the Jews*," although it is obvious from the context that they feared the Pharisees. In the same chapter, John wrote that "*the Jews* had agreed among themselves that if any man should confess him to be the Christ, he should be put out of the synagogue." This agreement had been reached, not by the Jews, but by the Chief Priests and the Ancients. In the tenth chapter, which deals with the action and behavior of this political group, we read that

> a dissension rose again among *the Jews* . . . and many of them said: He hath a devil and is mad . . . In Solomon's Porch *the Jews* therefore came to him and said to him . . . If thou be the Christ tell us plainly . . . *The Jews* then took up stones to stone him . . . *The Jews* answered him—For a good work we stone thee not, but for blasphemy.

John was more careful in his choice of words when he described the 33
details of the crucifixion. He laid special emphasis on the fact that Christ was
crucified, not by the Jews, but by Roman soldiers. "The soldiers therefore,
when they had crucified him, took his garments . . . and also his coat . . . they
said to one another: Let us not cut it, but let us cast lots for it . . . and the
soldiers indeed did these things" (XIX:23, 24). Nevertheless, in John's story
of the apprehension, trial and death of Christ, responsibility is laid, as much
as inference can lay it, on the whole Jewish people; a prominence is given to
the action of "the Jews" which the events as recorded by the other evangelists
do not justify.

Père Lagrange suggested that John made use of the phrase "the Jews" 34
as a literary device to save constant repetition of the words "High Priests and
Pharisees." It is a pity that this interpretation of John's meaning did not occur
to any of the early Fathers. When Origen wrote at the beginning of the fourth
century that "the Jews . . . nailed Christ to the cross," he also may have meant
something different from what he said—but for many centuries his words
were taken as literally true by all Christendom. And consequently, as an
English historian in our own time has admitted, "The crime of a handful of
priests and elders in Jerusalem was visited by the Christian Churches upon
the whole Jewish race."

This tradition has been handed on without much respect for the actual 35
facts as related in the Gospels. Thus, in the thirteenth century, a pious monk,
Jacques de Vitry, went to the Holy Land, visited the site of Calvary and sat
in meditation, as he recorded in his Chronicle, "on the very spot where *the
Jews* divided the garments of Christ, and for his tunic cast lots."

. . .

Margery Kempe, a slightly later visionary . . . , in her description of the 36
Passion [i.e., the suffering and crucifixion], which she imagined she had
actually witnessed, followed the common conviction that Jews had nailed
Christ to the cross. "Sche beheld how the cruel Jewys leydyn his precyows
body to the Crosse and sithyn tokyn a long nayle . . . and wyth gret vilnes
and cruelnes thei dreuyn it thorw hys hande" [She beheld how the cruel Jews
laid his precious body to the Cross and then took a long nail . . . and with
great villainy and cruelty they drove it through his hand]. Pictures of Jews
hammering in the nails helped to encourage both hatred and piety. A writer
at the beginning of the sixteenth century mentions "a Church where there
was placed a Jew, of wood, before the Saviour, grasping a hammer."

Pious ingenuity reached a new peak in Spain where, in the first quarter 37
of the eighteenth century, two hundred years after all the Jews had been
expelled, hatred continued to flourish alongside Christian faith and Christian
superstition. A collection of the fables popular in the Middle Ages, printed
in 1728, entitled *Centinela Contra Judios,* revived the belief that certain Jews, who
were "born with worms in their mouth . . . were descended from a Jewess who
ordered the locksmith who made the nails to crucify Christ to make the points
blunt so that the pain of crucifixion would be greater." In the seventeenth
century a zealous Catholic who was trying to convert Spinoza asked him to

remember "the terrible and unspeakably severe punishments by which the Jews were reduced to the last stages of misery and calamity because they were the authors of Christ's crucifixion."

In order to fortify these traditions, Christian commentators tended in- 38 creasingly to ignore the obvious meaning of the Gospel texts and sometimes substituted the phrase "the Jews" where John himself had written "the High Priests and the Pharisees."

. . .

In Russia popular Christianity produced a pattern of hate similar to that 39 of Western Europe. When the Czarina Elizabeth (1741–1761) was asked to admit Jews into the country for economic reasons, she replied: "I do not wish to obtain any benefits from the enemies of Christ." More than a hundred years later, in 1890, when Alexander III was shown the draft of an official report recommending some relaxation of the oppression from which the Jews of his empire were suffering, he noted in the margin: "But we must not forget that the Jews crucified Christ."

. . .

From the earliest times to the present day, readers of the Fourth Gospel, 40 with rare exceptions, have taken the phrase "the Jews" in its literal sense without any shading of meaning. Consequently the whole literature of Christendom has contributed throughout the centuries to consolidate a tradition not sanctioned by the text of the Synoptic Gospels—one that has brought immeasurable suffering upon countless numbers of innocent human beings: the tradition that "the Jewish nation condemned Christ to be crucified." Joseph Klausner writes:

> The Jews, *as a nation,* were far less guilty of the death of Jesus than the Greeks, as a nation, were guilty of the death of Socrates; but who now would think of avenging the blood of Socrates the Greek upon his countrymen, the present Greek race? Yet these nineteen hundred years past, the world has gone on avenging the blood of Jesus the Jew upon his countrymen, the Jews, who have already paid the penalty, and still go on paying the penalty, in rivers and torrents of blood.

The extent of Jewish responsibility for the apprehension, trial and death 41 of Christ was defined by the highest authority of the Christian Church, St. Peter, whose judgment corrects the bias shown, a generation later, in the Fourth Gospel. The first papal pronouncement on this question was addressed by St. Peter to "Ye men of Israel," a gathering which had assembled in "the Porch which is called Solomon's"; it was addressed to those men only, in that place, and at that time. St. Peter did not acquit these men of guilt; he knew that they had taken some active part in the plot and at the trial; they were, he told them, accessories to the crime. But the final words he used have often been ignored: "And now, brethren, I know you did it through ignorance; as did also your rulers."

Ignorance, defined by Maimonides as "the want of knowledge respect- 42 ing things the knowledge of which can be obtained," is acceptable as an excuse only when it is not culpable. Abelard, in the twelfth century, may have extended too widely the proposition that where there is ignorance there can be no sin, when he said that the rulers of Israel acted "out of zeal for their law," and should therefore be absolved from all guilt. Christian tradition, especially in the early centuries, practically ignored St. Peter's statement that the "rulers" acted through ignorance. St. John Chrysostom, indeed, flatly contradicted St. Peter when he wrote that "the Jews . . . erred not ignorantly but with full knowledge." Whatever degree of guilt the "rulers" may have incurred, there is surely no justification for excluding them from the benefit of the petition and the judgment of Christ—"Father, forgive them for they know not what they do" (Luke XXIII:34). In the Gospel text these words refer quite clearly to the Roman soldiers, and not to the Jews.

The belief current in the Middle Ages which Abelard attacked and St. 43 Bernard defended was that "the Jews" were all guilty; that they had acted with deliberate malice; that their guilt was shared by the whole Jewish people, for all time, and that they, and their children's children to the last generation, were condemned to live in slavery as the servants of Christian princes. That was not the doctrine of St. Peter. If Christians had always remembered his words, the history of the Jews in their long exile would perhaps have been very different, and the civilization of the West might not have witnessed the degradation of humanity which was achieved by the Germans in their death camps and gas chambers.

In spite of St. Peter's judgment the popular Christian doctrine has al- 44 ways been that anyone, whether pagan or Christian, who has at any time persecuted, tortured or massacred Jews has acted as an instrument of Divine wrath. A chronicler, writing in the early years of the thirteenth century, admired the patience of God, who "after the Jews had crucified Our Lord, waited for forty-eight years before chastising them." According to Fleury, who wrote, in the first quarter of the eighteenth century, an enormous and still useful ecclesiastical history, God began to take reprisals against the Jews in the year 38 of the Christian era. In that year, anti-Jewish riots broke out in Alexandria. The rioters were secretly encouraged by Flaccus, the Roman commissioner in Egypt, who took no effective measures to prevent the mob from burning down synagogues, breaking into Jewish shops, and scattering the merchandise into the streets of the city. Flaccus showed his "neutrality" by attempting to disarm, not the rioters, but their victims. "He had searches made in the houses of the Jews on the pretext of disarming the nation, and several women were taken away and tormented when they refused to eat swine's flesh." A great number of Jews were murdered, and their bodies dragged through the streets. "In this manner," wrote Fleury in 1732, "divine vengeance began to be manifested against the Jews."

The sacking of Jerusalem and the destruction of the Temple, in the year 45 70, when more than a million people were massacred with a brutality to which the world has once again become accustomed, were regarded by many pious Christians as part of God's plan of revenge. "The Jews," wrote Sulpicius

Severus, "were thus punished and exiled throughout the whole world, for no other account than for the impious hands they laid upon Christ." This interpretation of the event has been repeated for centuries.

. . .

There are therefore still some people who believe that the Jews were 46 cursed out of Palestine because they had behaved in a manner displeasing to God. If nations were liable to be dispossessed for such a reason, very few of them would enjoy security of tenure. "The Curse," as J.-P. Sartre has recently pointed out, was "geographical."

. . .

To justify the persecution of Jews, two excuses . . . were available to 47 Christians: either the Christians were acting in self-defense, or they were carrying out the will of God. The teaching of the early Fathers made the second excuse plausible. There was no direct incitement to violence. Athanasius did not tell the people to go out and beat up Jews. But he told them that "the Jews were no longer the people of God, but rulers of Sodom and Gomorrah"; and he asked the ominous question: "What is left unfulfilled, that they should now be allowed to disbelieve with impunity?"

When St. Ambrose told his congregations that the Jewish synagogue 48 was "a house of impiety, a receptacle of folly, which God himself has condemned," no one was surprised when the people went off and set fire to one. St. Ambrose accepted responsibility for the outrage. "I declare that I set fire to the synagogue, or at least that I ordered those who did it, that there might not be a place where Christ was denied. If it be objected to me that I did not set the synagogue on fire here, I answer it began to be burnt by the judgment of God." He told the Emperor that people who burnt a synagogue ought not to be punished, such action being a just reprisal because Jews, in the reign of the Emperor Julian, had burnt down Christian churches. In any case, he added, since the synagogues contained nothing of any value, "what could the Jews lose by the fire?" When they complained to the Emperor, he was indignant at their impertinence. They had no place in a court of law, he declared, because nothing they said could ever be believed. "Into what calumnies will they not break out, who, by false witness, calumniated even Christ!"

The Emperor, however, who did not approve of fire-raising propaganda, 49 endeavored to protect the synagogues from the fury of the mob. He received a letter, from an unexpected quarter, asking him to revoke the orders he had given for punishing the offenders, a letter dispatched from the top of a pillar by St. Simeon Stylites. This ascetic, who achieved distinction by living for thirty-six years on top of a pillar fifty feet high, had given up, as G. F. Abbott remarked, "all worldly luxuries except Jew-hatred." He is not the only saint who was unable to renounce the consolations of anti-Semitism.

In the fourth century the natural goodness of men, and even saintliness, 50 did not always operate for the benefit of Jews. St. Gregory of Nyssa, with the eloquence for which he was famous, composed against them a comprehensive indictment:

Slayers of the Lord, murderers of the prophets, adversaries of God, haters of God, men who show contempt for the law, foes of grace, enemies of their father's faith, advocates of the devil, brood of vipers, slanderers, scoffers, men whose minds are in darkness, leaven of the Pharisees, assembly of demons, sinners, wicked men, stoners, and haters of righteousness.

Such exaggeration may have been an offense against charity, but it is 51 not so harmful to the soul as the modern hypocrisy which pretends that the early Christian Fathers were invariably models of proper Christian behavior. "Our duty," wrote Basnage in the seventeenth century, "is to excuse the Fathers in their Extravagance, instead of justifying them, lest such forcible Examples should authorize Modern Divines, and confirm the Hatred and Revenge of writers."

St. John Chrysostom, the Golden-Mouthed, one of the greatest of the 52 Church Fathers, spent his life, in and out of the pulpit, trying to reform the world. Christian writers, of varying shades of belief, have agreed in admiring his fervent love for all mankind, in spite of the fact that he was undoubtedly a socialist. "Chrysostom," said a Protestant divine, "was one of the most eloquent of the preachers who, ever since apostolic times, have brought to men the Divine tidings of truth and love." "A bright cheerful gentle soul," wrote Cardinal Newman, "a sensitive heart, a temperament open to emotion and impulse; and all this elevated, refined, transformed by the touch of heaven,—such was St. John Chrysostom."

Yet in this kindly gentle soul of the preacher who brought to men the 53 tidings of truth and love, was hidden a hard core of hatred. "It must be admitted," wrote an honest French hagiographer, "that, in his homilies against the Jews, he allowed himself to be unduly carried away by an occasional access of passion."

A great deal more than this must be admitted.

The violence of the language used by St. John Chrysostom in his homi- 54 lies against the Jews has never been exceeded by any preacher whose sermons have been recorded. Allowances must, no doubt, be made for the custom of the times, for passionate zeal, and for the fear that some tender shoots of Christian faith might be chilled by too much contact with Jews. But no amount of allowance can alter the fact that these homilies filled the minds of Christian congregations with a hatred which was transmitted to their children, and to their children's children, for many generations. These homilies, moreover, were used for centuries, in schools and in seminaries where priests were taught to preach, with St. John Chrysostom as their model— where priests were taught to hate, with St. John Chrysostom as their model.

There was no "touch of heaven" in the language used by St. John 55 Chrysostom when he was preaching about Jewish synagogues. "The synagogue," he said, "is worse than a brothel . . . it is the den of scoundrels and the repair of wild beasts . . . the temple of demons devoted to idolatrous cults . . . the refuge of brigands and debauchees, and the cavern of devils."

The synagogue, he told his congregations in another sermon, was "a   56
criminal assembly of Jews . . . a place of meeting for the assassins of Christ
. . . a house worse than a drinking shop . . . a den of thieves; a house of ill
fame, a dwelling of iniquity, the refuge of devils, a gulf and abyss of perdi-
tion." And he concluded, exhausted at length by his eloquence: "Whatever
name even more horrible could be found, will never be worse than the
synagogue deserves."

These sermons have not been forgotten; nor has contempt for Judaism   57
diminished among the Christian congregations since they were first preached
more than fifteen hundred years ago.

. . .

In reply to some Christians who had maintained that Jewish synagogues   58
might be entitled to respect because in them were kept the writings of Moses
and the prophets, St. John Chrysostom answered: Not at all! This was a reason
for hating them more, because they use these books, but willfully misunderstand their meaning. "As for me, I hate the synagogue. . . . I hate the Jews
for the same reason."

It is not difficult to imagine the effect such sermons must have had upon   59
congregations of excitable Orientals. Not only every synagogue, Chrysostom
told them, but every Jew, was a temple of the devil. "I would say the same
things about their souls." And he said a great deal more. It was unfit, he
proclaimed, for Christians to associate with a people who had fallen into a
condition lower than the vilest animals. "Debauchery and drunkenness had
brought them to the level of the lusty goat and the pig. They know only one
thing, to satisfy their stomachs, to get drunk, to kill and beat each other up
like stage villains and coachmen."

. . .

When the usual allowances have been made for the manners of the time,   60
pious zeal, oriental imagery, and for any context, setting, or background
which might be urged in mitigation, these are words difficult to justify. This
condemnation of the people of Israel, in the name of God, was not forgotten.
It helped to strengthen the tradition of hate handed on through the Dark Ages
and welcomed by mediaeval Christendom, a tradition which has disfigured
the whole history of Western Europe.

For many centuries the Jews listened to the echo of those three words   61
of St. John Chrysostom, the Golden-Mouthed: "God hates you."

Questions for Discussion

1. There are some passages in the chapter that might be misunderstood
   because Hay speaks with "tongue in cheek," using irony: for example,
   "The German method of burying people in communal pits was a great
   improvement on the old system" (¶13) or "Most of them retained enough

Christianity to continue hating the perfidious people, the Christ-killers" (¶23). What is Hay really saying with these words? What does he gain by seeming to say something else? How many other ironic passages can you find?

2. Occasionally Hay addresses his reader in direct form (for example, the opening phrase of ¶21). Who *is* this reader? Why do you think Hay breaks the conventions of most scholarly writing to become personal in this way?

3. People are sure to respond to this kind of writing in diverse ways, depending on their prior beliefs. Christians are challenged directly to reappraise their traditions. In a sense all other readers are bystanders or eavesdroppers, watching Christians debate about a great wrong that Hay accuses them of having committed. Jewish readers, in contrast, may find the piece too painful to read because of the gruesome details about the Holocaust. Those who are neither Jewish nor Christian may initially feel less concerned—until they examine their own prejudices and reconsider the history of other atrocities that have been committed by groups they are affiliated with. It is important in discussing matters of this kind to recognize that we are *all* implicated in human prejudice, past and present. A college classroom is a rare place where we can discuss such matters without fearing reprisal from authorities or rival gangs, and we should be willing to risk talking frankly with each other.

   With these difficulties and opportunities in mind, see now whether you and your classmates can discuss your deepest prejudices about groups without falling into a pointless or angry shouting match. Do you assume, with or without what you consider to be good evidence, that people of any one group are going to be on "the level of the lusty goat and the pig," that they will "know only one thing, to satisfy their stomachs, to get drunk, to kill and beat each other up like stage villains" (¶59)?

4. If in discussing question 3 you have found strong hostility between two or more groups represented in the class, organize a discussion by assigning contrary roles—for example, have a Christian defend the case for Jews, a Jew speak for American blacks or Indians, a person of French descent defend the English, and so on. Your task, if you take one of these roles, is to show why the prejudice against "your" group is absurd or cruel or mistaken. Try to make your argument as free of name-calling as possible, depending instead on whatever evidence and reasons seem compelling.

5. Some classes have tried the experiment of "practicing" discrimination against a given group for a day or two—a prejudicial treatment invented for the occasion: "No one with blue eyes will be allowed to speak until Friday," "Everyone taller than 5 feet 10 inches must arrive 10 minutes early," and so on. If you are by now fairly easy with each other in class discussion, try inventing such a group (for example, people not from a given part of the country or state, people from a certain kind of school, or people who intend to be science or English majors). Then "give them the treatment." Make the kinds of jokes about them (or about you, if

you're one of the victims) that people make about minority groups. Seat them at the back of the room or in specially created "ghettos," "reservations," or "barrios." Require them to address the rest of the class as "ma'am" and "sir." Do this as long as the victims can stand it and then discuss how it felt, to both the oppressors and the oppressed.

Suggested Essay Topics

1. If you have ever been the victim of injustice based on someone's seeing you as a member of a condemned group, write an account of how it happened and how it felt. (Decide in advance whether you are addressing readers who are already sympathetic to your cause or readers who may share the feelings of your persecutors.) You will have noticed that Hay achieves some of his most powerful effects by using vivid stories. Don't hesitate to be just as vivid in your use of the details of your story.

2. If you have ever committed what you now consider to be an injustice against someone as a result of seeing that person as a member of a given group rather than as an individual, write an account of the event describing how it felt both at the time and when you later decided that you had been unjust. Before you write, study topic 1.

𝟾

WOMEN AND MEN

From Sexism to Feminism

EPIGRAPHS FROM
THE SEXIST TRADITION

There is a good principle which created order, light and man,
and an evil principle which created chaos, darkness and woman.
Pythagoras

Women, then, are only children of a larger growth:
they have an entertaining tattle, and sometimes wit;
but for solid reasoning good-sense, I never knew
in my life one that had it, or who reasoned or acted consequentially
for four and twenty hours together.
Lord Chesterfield

Man is the only male animal who beats his female.
He is therefore the most brutal of all males—unless woman is the most
unbearable of all females, which, after all, is quite plausible.
Georges Courteline

Beat thy wife every morning; if thou know not why, she doth.
Arab saying

Frailty, thy name is woman!
Shakespeare (spoken by Hamlet, about his mother)

The world is full of care, much like unto a bubble;
Women and care, and care and women, and women and care
and trouble.
Reverend Nathaniel Ward
(attributed to a lady at the court of the Queen of Bohemia)

Ever hear of a woman loving a poor man?
Pagnol

EPIGRAPHS FROM
THE FEMINIST TRADITION

All that has been written by men about women must be suspect,
for they are both judge and interested party.
Poulain La Barre

So the image of woman [in advertising] appears plastered on every surface
imaginable, smiling interminably. An apple pie evokes
a glance of tender beatitude, a washing machine causes hilarity,
a cheap box of chocolates brings forth meltingly
joyous gratitude, a Coke is the cause of a rictus of
unutterable brilliance, even a new stick-on bandage
is saluted by a smirk of satisfaction.
Germaine Greer

Total masculinity is an ideal of the frustrated, not a fact of biology.
Harold Rosenberg

It is impossible for a sex or a class to have economic freedom
until everybody has it, and until economic freedom is attained
for everybody, there can be no real freedom for anybody.
Suzanne LaFollette

I long to hear that you have declared an independancy
[for the thirteen colonies]—and by the way in the new Code of
Laws which I suppose it will be necessary for you
to make I desire you would Remember the Ladies, and be more
generous and favorable to them than your ancestors. Do not put
such unlimited power into the hands of the Husbands.
Remember all Men would be tyrants if they could. If
perticuliar care and attention is not paid to the Laidies we are determined
to foment a Rebelion, and will not hold ourselves bound by
any Laws in which we have no voice, or Representation.
Letter from Abigail Adams to John Adams

Yes, ye lordly, ye haughty sex, our souls are by nature *equal* to
yours; the same breath of God animates, enlivens, and invigorates us.
Judith Sargent Murray

I believe that our future salvation lies in a movement
away from sexual polarization and the prison of gender
toward a world in which individual roles
and the modes of personal behavior can be freely chosen.
Carolyn Heilbrun

IDEAS IN DEBATE

Wayne C. Booth and Marshall W. Gregory
St. Thomas Aquinas
Friedrich Nietzsche
Sigmund Freud

Wayne C. Booth and Marshall W. Gregory

THE TRADITIONAL
ABASEMENT OF WOMEN

Until fairly recently, almost all discussions of men and women were by men, and almost all assumed the inferiority, if not the downright viciousness, of women. Occasionally a philosopher like Plato might speculate about what would happen if women were ever given education and rights genuinely equal to those of men, and a few wrote about women as ideal, angelic creatures, far above their wicked menfolk. But whole libraries have been written "proving" that women's intrinsic inferiority justifies social servitude.

One of the most frequently quoted documents in this tradition was Aristotle's argument, in *On the Generation of Animals,* that a woman is a "misbegotten male." In the conception of a child, the "male principle" provides, he said, a form or shape, while the "female principle" provides the matter on which the shape is imposed by the semen. If the imposition of form is successful, a male child is born. If it is a partial failure, a female child—a botched male—results. The male thus provides the "active" role, the female the "passive." According to this view, a highly convenient one for males, nature invites and justifies whatever subordination a given culture chooses to impose on women.

Aristotle was quoted by almost all theorists for about 2000 years. Jewish, Christian, and Islamic theologians borrowed and extended his arguments to buttress their teachings about how a male God founded the universe and how females, from the beginning, were either responsible for or at least symbolic of its instabilities and limitations. His influence can be seen clearly in the brief passage we quote here from Thomas Aquinas (c. 1225–1274), which itself achieved wide influence as a standard Christian way of explaining the story of Adam and Eve. The passages by Nietzsche (1844–1900) and Freud (1856–1939) show that the downgrading of women has hardly been confined to religious theorists; many a secular author has heaped abuse on women, some of it (like that of Schopenhauer, the philosopher, and Strindberg, the playwright) even more aggressively woman-hating (or *misogynistic*) than the passages we quote.

In one respect we are clearly being unjust to such wide-ranging thinkers and prolific writers as Nietzsche and Freud by quoting only snippets from them. All writers can be made to look silly, thoughtless, or incoherent by editing that disembowels their positions. Knowing this, our readers need to understand that we are not trying to take cheap shots at the writers included here. The more creative sides of their thinking are passed over. Our point is not primarily about these specific thinkers at all. We quote from Aquinas, Nietzsche, and Freud not to pillory them but to illustrate some of the content of a centuries-long tradition that precedes them, includes them, and extends far beyond them. They did not create this tradition, but they are symptomatic of it. Thus, while it may be unfair to the wider range and substance of their thought to reprint them so briefly, they help us to make a valid point about hostility to women in Western culture. When feminists argue in favor of fairness and equality for women, their opponent is not one writer or a few male chauvinists but rather a whole set of misogynistic attitudes that thinkers like those reprinted here have helped energize and perpetuate.

Feminist writers of recent times, both male and female, have had to write under the immense pressure of this tradition of contempt, and they have often shown a sense of frustration in trying to deal with it. How does one find arguments to combat opinions that seem so wrongheaded yet deepseated? How does one argue with dogmas uttered by authors who otherwise seem fair-minded and sane? It is no wonder that some writers find it impossible to remain cool and dispassionate in the face of past and present abuses.

The truth may be that there are no decisive arguments that could prove either natural inferiority or natural equality. Like arguments about religious belief, discussion of such matters depends on our deepest assumptions about life and on our experience. Such arguments are never settled once and for all; experience is too rich and diverse for that. But we need no resolution of debate to tell us how important is the quest in modern times for a new way of thinking and talking that will no longer debase or ignore one half of humanity.

St. Thomas Aquinas

THE PRODUCTION OF WOMAN

Whether Woman Should Have Been Made
in the First Production of Things

"Question 92" from the *Summa Theologica* (1265–1272). There are four "articles" in the Question, of which we reprint part of the first.

We proceed thus to the First Article:—

Objection 1. It would seem that woman should not have been made in the first production of things. For the Philosopher [Aristotle] says that the *female is a misbegotten male.* But nothing misbegotten or defective should have been in the first production of things. Therefore woman should not have been made at that first production.

Obj. 2. Further, subjection and limitation were a result of sin, for to the woman was it said after sin (Genesis iii. 16): *Thou shalt be under the man's power;* and Gregory says that, *Where there is no sin, there is no inequality.* But woman is naturally of less strength and dignity than man, *for the agent is always more honorable than the patient,* as Augustine says. Therefore woman should not have been made in the first production of things before sin.

Obj. 3. Further, occasions of sin should be cut off. But God foresaw that woman would be an occasion of sin to man. Therefore He should not have made woman.

On the contrary, It is written (Genesis ii. 18): *It is not good for man to be alone; let us make him a helper like to himself.*

I answer that, It was necessary for woman to be made, as the Scripture says, as *a helper* to man; not, indeed, as a helpmate in other works, as some say, since man can be more efficiently helped by another man in other works; but as a helper in the work of generation. This can be made clear if we observe the mode of generation carried out in various living things. Some living things do not possess in themselves the power of generation, but are generated by an agent of another species; and such are those plants and animals which are generated, without seed, from suitable matter through the active power of the heavenly bodies. Others possess the active and passive generative power together, as we see in plants which are generated from seed. For the noblest vital function in plants is generation, and so we observe that in these the active power of generation invariably accompanies the passive power. Among perfect animals, the active power of generation belongs to the male sex, and the passive power to the female. And as among animals there is a vital operation nobler than generation, to which their life is principally directed, so it happens that the male sex is not found in continual union with the female in perfect animals, but only at the time of coition; so that we may consider that by coition the male and female are one, as in plants they are always united, even though in some cases one of them preponderates, and in some the other. But man is further ordered to a still nobler work of life, and that is intellectual operation.

Therefore there was greater reason for the distinction of these two powers in man; so that the female should be produced separately from the male, and yet that they should be carnally united for generation. Therefore directly after the formation of woman, it was said: _And they shall be two in one flesh_ (Genesis ii. 24).

Reply Obj. 1. As regards the individual nature, woman is defective and 6
misbegotten, for the active power in the male seed tends to the production of a perfect likeness according to the masculine sex; while the production of woman comes from defect in the active power, or from some material indisposition, or even from some external influence, such as that of a south wind, which is moist, as the Philosopher observes. On the other hand, as regards universal human nature, woman is not misbegotten, but is included in nature's intention as directed to the work of generation. Now the universal intention of nature depends on God, Who is the universal Author of nature. Therefore, in producing nature, God formed not only the male but also the female.

Reply Obj. 2. Subjection is twofold. One is servile, by virtue of which a 7
superior makes use of a subject for his own benefit; and this kind of subjection began after sin. There is another kind of subjection, which is called economic or civil, whereby the superior makes use of his subjects for their own benefit and good; and this kind of subjection existed even before sin. For the good of order would have been wanting in the human family if some were not governed by others wiser than themselves. So by such a kind of subjection woman is naturally subject to man, because in man the discernment of reason predominates.

Friedrich Nietzsche

THE UGLINESS OF WOMAN

Our title for part 7, "Our Virtues," aphorism 232, of _Beyond Good and Evil_ (1886).

Woman wants to become self-reliant—and for that reason she is beginning to 1
enlighten men about "woman as such": _this_ is one of the worst developments of the general _uglification_ of Europe. For what must these clumsy attempts of women at scientific self-exposure bring to light! Woman has much reason for shame; so much pedantry, superficiality, schoolmarmishness, petty presumption, petty licentiousness and immodesty lies concealed in woman—one only needs to study her behavior with children!—and so far all this was at bottom best repressed and kept under control by _fear_ of man. Woe when "the eternally boring in woman"*—she is rich in that!—is permitted to venture forth! When

*Allusion to "the Eternal-Feminine" in the penultimate line of Goethe's _Faust._

she begins to unlearn thoroughly and on principle her prudence and art—of grace, of play, of chasing away worries, of lightening burdens and taking things lightly—and her subtle aptitude for agreeable desires!

Even now female voices are heard which—holy Aristophanes!—are 2 frightening: they threaten with medical explicitness what woman *wants* from man, first and last. Is it not in the worst taste when woman sets about becoming scientific that way? So far enlightenment of this sort was fortunately man's affair, man's lot—we remained "among ourselves" in this; and whatever women write about "woman," we may in the end reserve a healthy suspicion whether woman really *wants* enlightenment about herself—whether she *can* will it—

Unless a woman seeks a new adornment for herself that way—I do 3 think adorning herself is part of the Eternal-Feminine—she surely wants to inspire fear of herself—perhaps she seeks mastery. But she does not *want* truth: what is truth to woman? From the beginning, nothing has been more alien, repugnant, and hostile to woman than truth—her great art is the lie, her highest concern is mere appearance and beauty. Let us men confess it: we honor and love precisely *this* art and *this* instinct in woman—we who have a hard time and for our relief like to associate with beings under whose hands, eyes, and tender follies our seriousness, our gravity and profundity almost appear to us like folly.

Finally I pose the question: has ever a woman conceded profundity to 4 a woman's head, or justice to a woman's heart? And is it not true that on the whole "woman" has so far been despised most by woman herself—and by no means by us?

We men wish that woman should not go on compromising herself 5 through enlightenment—just as it was man's thoughtfulness and consideration for woman that found expression in the church decree: *mulier taceat in ecclesia* [woman should be silent in church]! It was for woman's good when Napoleon gave the all too eloquent Madame de Staël to understand: *mulier taceat in politicis* [woman should be silent in politics]! And I think it is a real friend of women that counsels them today: *mulier taceat de muliere* [woman should be silent about woman]!

Sigmund Freud

FEMININITY

From lecture 33 of *New Introductory Lectures on Psycho-analysis* (1933).

As you hear, then, we ascribe a castration complex to women as well. And 1 for good reasons, though its content cannot be the same as with boys. In the latter the castration complex arises after they have learnt from the sight of the female genitals that the organ which they value so highly need not necessarily accompany the body. At this the boy recalls to mind the threats he brought on himself by his doings with that organ, he begins to give credence to them and falls under the influence of fear of castration, which will be the most powerful motive force in his subsequent development. The castration complex of girls is also started by the sight of the genitals of the other sex. They at once notice the difference and, it must be admitted, its significance too. They feel seriously wronged, often declare that they want to "have something like it too," and fall a victim to "envy for the penis," which will leave ineradicable traces on their development and the formation of their character and which will not be surmounted in even the most favourable cases without a severe expenditure of psychical energy. The girl's recognition of the fact of her being without a penis does not by any means imply that she submits to the fact easily. On the contrary, she continues to hold on for a long time to the wish to get something like it herself and she believes in that possibility for improbably long years; and analysis can show that, at a period when knowledge of reality has long since rejected the fulfilment of the wish as unattainable, it persists in the unconscious and retains a considerable cathexis of energy. The wish to get the longed-for penis eventually in spite of everything may contribute to the motives that drive a mature woman to analysis, and what she may reasonably expect from analysis—a capacity, for instance, to carry on an intellectual profession—may often be recognized as a sublimated modification of this repressed wish.

One cannot very well doubt the importance of envy for the penis. You may take it as an instance of male injustice if I assert that envy and jealousy play an even greater part in the mental life of women than of men. It is not that I think these characteristics are absent in men or that I think they have no other roots in women than envy for the penis; but I am inclined to attribute their greater amount in women to this latter influence.

. . .

The discovery that she is castrated is a turning-point in a girl's growth. Three possible lines of development start from it: one leads to sexual inhibition or to neurosis, the second to change of character in the sense of a masculinity complex, the third, finally, to normal femininity. We have learnt a fair amount, though not everything, about all three.

The essential content of the first is as follows: the little girl has hitherto lived in a masculine way, has been able to get pleasure by the excitation of her clitoris and has brought this activity into relation with her sexual wishes directed towards her mother, which are often active ones; now, owing to the influence of her penis-envy, she loses her enjoyment in her phallic sexuality. Her self-love is mortified by the comparison with the boy's far superior equipment and in consequence she renounces her masturbatory satisfaction from her clitoris, repudiates her love for her mother and at the same time not infrequently represses a good part of her sexual trends in general. No doubt her turning away from her mother does not occur all at once, for to begin with the girl regards her castration as an individual misfortune, and only gradually extends it to other females and finally to her mother as well. Her love was directed to her *phallic* mother; with the discovery that her mother is castrated it becomes possible to drop her as an object, so that the motives for hostility, which have long been accumulating, gain the upper hand. This means, therefore, that as a result of the discovery of women's lack of a penis they are debased in value for girls just as they are for boys and later perhaps for men.

Questions for Discussion

1. Restate Aristotle's position about the biological inferiority of women in your own words. Do you know people who take the view that men are "naturally" superior in some ways to women? What traits or abilities do these people ascribe to men and women? Do any of the assumptions about innate masculine and feminine traits match your own experience and observation? If so, which ones? If not, how do you react when you find yourself placed within categories that don't fit?

2. Is Nietzsche's denigration of women foreign to you, or is it the same denigration you hear nowadays, only less antagonistically and abrasively stated? In paragraph 4, for example, Nietzsche claims that " 'woman' has so far been despised most by woman herself." While this is strong language, is its content any different from that of the commonly bandied cliché that women are catty about other women? Can Nietzsche's other insults be restated in contemporary terms? If so, what does this say about contemporary views of women?

3. Ask the teacher to appoint three or four members of the class to ask various members of the psychology department whether they think Freud's notion of "penis envy" is taken seriously today by psychoanalysts and what they themselves think of the notion. Have them report back to the class.

4. Have two or three members of the class examine the wording of the Catholic marriage ceremony (or different versions of it) to see whether any traces of Aquinas's views about the relationship between men and women are reflected in it. Compare the Catholic ceremony to a few Protestant versions. Are there any interesing differences with respect to the roles of men and women?

Suggested Essay Topics

1. Read chapters 3 and 4 ("Biological Facts and Social Consequences" and "Who Said 'The Inferior Sex'?") of *The Natural Superiority of Women* by Ashley Montagu (Macmillan, 1952). Using Montagu as a starting point,

but not limiting yourself to him if you have other scholars or scientists to cite (Montagu offers an annotated bibliography at the end of his book), construct your own rebuttal to Aristotle's views of the natural inferiority of women.

2. In a small notebook that you should carry around with you until this assignment is completed, record for a two-week period all the instances in which you hear people expressing belief in "natural" differences between men and women. Whether the remarks you overhear are insulting or not, comment on the extent to which you think they are inaccurate, misleading, or limiting for either sex, and address your essay to people whose (perhaps unseen) prejudices you would like to make visible.

Francine Frank and Frank Ashen

The struggle to rid society of various kinds of oppression requires analysis on many fronts: political, historical, theological, ethical, and so on. The analysis given to us here by Francine Frank and Frank Ashen is linguistic. The oppression they object to is the unfair and destructive denigration of women as a group; the mechanism of oppression they are attempting to expose is buried so deep within our consciousness that it takes a deliberate and energetic effort at self-examination to see how it operates. It is the mechanism of language itself. Because language lies so deep within us, some of us may be more hostile and defensive when asked to change our linguistic habits than we would be if we were asked to change anything else. The common words by which we refer to everyday objects and experience are more than just useful tools to us; they seem a natural extension of reality itself. Words thus carry an emotional charge, an aura, a mystique that native speakers decode in sophisticated ways without having to think consciously about how they do it.

So it is with words that deprecate, condescend, or depreciate: words that put people down, rob them of their dignity, or diminish their worth as human beings. "Boy"—a generic term of address—could at one time be used by any white person to refer to any black male, regardless of the black man's age, merits, or social standing. The subtle difference between "I know the woman who lives in that house" and "I know the lady who lives in that house" will be picked up by any reasonably educated speaker of English. Frank and Ashen give us many examples of the way English may be used to keep women in an inferior social position, to keep them feeling inferior, useless, incompetent, or powerless. No native speaker has to take a course to learn the use of such language; rather, one almost has to take a course in order to unlearn it, to become aware enough to avoid it. The sexist bias runs deeper than most of us ever recognize until we are challenged to see it by the research and criticism of those who, like Frank and Ashen, spend much more time thinking about these issues than most people.

As you read, try to think of examples from your own experience or reading that support or even extend the authors' arguments. You might also consider to what extent the authors' linguistic examples of sexist language are mirrored in nonverbal aspects of life. Clearly, we have a great many verbal ways of expressing bias against people of despised religions, ethnic origins, and skin color. We have all heard the ugly terms. What about other ways of identifying who is "in" and who is "out" in certain social groups—at school, in the dorm, in the fraternity or sorority house, on the job, in the neighborhood, and in other areas? Can Frank and Ashen's argument help explain such nonverbal modes of differentiation? But when we are talking about language, Frank and Ashen invite us to think more critically about (and listen more carefully to) the uses of language that help create our social and emotional environment.

OF GIRLS AND CHICKS

Chapter 4 of *Language and the Sexes* (1983).

English is a sexist language! Angry women have often been driven to make   1
such a statement. But is it accurate? Can we really label some languages as more sexist than others? In a recent movie, a rather obnoxious adolescent described his favorite pastime as "cruising chicks." If the adolescent had been female, she would not have had a parallel term to refer to finding boys. This asymmetry in vocabulary is a linguistic reflection of sexism in our society.

One of the more intriguing and controversial hypotheses of modern   2
linguistics is the idea that the grammatical structure of a language may influence the thought processes of speakers of that language. Regardless of the truth of that idea, known among linguists as the Sapir-Whorf hypothesis, it seems clear that we can gain insights into the culture and attitudes of a group by examining the language of that group. Eskimos live in an environment in which the condition of snow is vital to survival, and they therefore have a large number of distinct words for different kinds of snow. Most Hindi speakers live in areas of India where it does not snow and, as a result, Hindi has only a single word equivalent to the two English words *snow* and *ice*. In Modern English, the plethora of words such as *road, avenue, freeway, highway, boulevard, street, turnpike, expressway, parkway, lane,* and *interstate* might lead one to conclude that automobiles are very important to Americans, while the relative scarcity of words for various types of kinfolk would suggest that extended familial relationships are not very important to Americans. (We do not, for example, have separate words for our mother's brother and our father's brother.) In this chapter, we will look at the linguistic treatment of women in English for clues to the attitudes towards women held by speakers of English.

First let us consider what the last members of the following groups have   3
in common: Jack and Jill, Romeo and Juliet, Adam and Eve, Peter, Paul and Mary, Hansel and Gretel, Roy Rogers and Dale Evans, Tristan and Isolde, Guys and Dolls, Abelard and Heloise, man and wife, Dick and Jane, Burns

and Allen, Anthony and Cleopatra, Sonny and Cher, Fibber Magee and Molly,* Ferdinand and Isabella, Samson and Delilah, and Stiller and Meara. That's right, it is a group of women who have been put in their place. Not that women must always come last: Snow White gets to precede all seven of the dwarfs, Fran may follow Kukla, but she comes before Ollie,† Anna preceded the King of Siam, although it must be noted that, as colonialism waned, she was thrust to the rear of the billing in "The King and I."‡ Women with guns are also able to command top billing, as in Frankie and Johnny, and Bonnie and Clyde. The moral is clear: a woman who wants precedence in our society should either hang around with dwarfs or dragons, or shoot somebody. "Women and children first" may apply on sinking ships, but it clearly doesn't apply in the English language.

Not only are women put off, they are also put down, numerically and otherwise. In the real world, women slightly outnumber men. But the world created for American schoolchildren presents a different picture. In an article describing the preparation of a dictionary for schoolchildren, Alma Graham recounts the imbalance discovered in schoolbooks in all subjects in use in the early 1970s. A computer analysis of five million words in context revealed many subtle and not-so-subtle clues to the status of women in American society. The numbers alone tell us a lot: men outnumber women seven to one, boys outnumber girls two to one; girls are even in the minority in home economics books, where masculine pronouns outnumber feminine ones two to one. In general, the pronouns *he, him,* and *his* outnumber *she, her,* and *hers* by a ratio of four to one.

When the linguistic context of the above pronouns was analyzed to see if they were generics, referring to people regardless of sex, it was found that of 940 examples, almost eighty percent clearly referred to male human beings; next came references to male animals, to persons such as sailors and farmers, who were assumed to be male, and only thirty-two pronouns were true generics. In another set of words, we do find more women: mothers outnumber fathers, and wives appear three times as often as husbands. However, children are usually labelled by referring to a male parent (Jim's son rather than Betty's son), most mothers have sons rather than daughters, and so do most fathers. There are twice as many uncles as aunts and every firstborn child is a son. It is not altogether clear from all this how the race reproduces itself without dying out in a few generations. Notice further that, although the word *wife* is more frequent, expressions like *the farmer's wife, pioneers and their wives,* etc., indicate that the main characters are male.

Consider now another area of our language. English has a large number of nouns which appear to be neutral with regard to sex, but actually are covertly masculine. Although the dictionary may define *poet* as one who

---

*Popular radio entertainers in the 1930s and 1940s.

†*Kukla, Fran, and Ollie* was a popular TV show in the 1950s. Fran was a human who interacted with the puppets Kukla and Ollie.

‡The 1950s Broadway musical *The King and I* was based on a book titled *Anna and the King of Siam.*

writes poetry, a woman who writes poetry appears so anomalous or threatening to some, that they use the special term *poetess* to refer to her. There is no corresponding term to call attention to the sex of a man who writes poetry, but then we find nothing remarkable in the fact that poetry is written by men. Of course, if a woman is sufficiently meritorious, we may forgive her her sex and refer to her as a poet after all, or, wishing to keep the important fact of her sex in our consciousness, we may call her a *woman poet.* However, to balance the possible reward of having her sex overlooked, there remains the possibility of more extreme punishment; we may judge her work so harshly that she will be labelled a *lady poet.* Once again, the moral is clear: people who write poetry are assumed to be men until proven otherwise, and people identified as women who write poetry are assumed to be less competent than sexually unidentified (i.e., presumably male) people who write poetry.

If the phenomenon we have been discussing were limited to poetry, we 7 might not regard it as very significant; after all, our society tends to regard poets as somewhat odd anyway. But, in fact, it is widespread in the language. There is a general tendency to label the exception, which in most cases turns out to be women. Many words with feminine suffixes, such as *farmerette, authoress,* and *aviatrix,* have such a clear trivializing effect, that there has been a trend away from their use and a preference for *woman author* and the like. The feminines of many ethnic terms, such as *Negress* and *Jewess,* are considered particularly objectionable. Other words, such as *actress* and *waitress,* seem to have escaped the negative connotations and remain in use. However, we note that waiters often work in more expensive establishments than do waitresses, that actresses belong to "Actor's Equity," and that women participants in theatrical groups have begun to refer to themselves as "actors." On rare occasions, this presumption of maleness in terms which should be sexually neutral, works to women's advantage. If someone is called a *bastard,* either as a general term of abuse, or as a statement of the lack of legal marital ties between that person's parents, we assume that person is a male. While an illegitimate child may be of either sex, only men are bastards in common usage. Although the dictionary seems to regard this as a sex-neutral term, a recent dictionary of slang gives the term *bastarda* as a "female bastard/law, Black."[1]

Sometimes the feminine member of a pair of words has a meaning 8 which is not only inferior to the masculine one, but also different from it. Compare, for instance, a *governor* with a *governess* or a *major* with a *majorette.* Ella Grasso was the governor of Connecticut, and a high ranking woman in the U.S. Army would certainly not be a majorette. In a large number of cases, the supposed feminine form does not even exist to refer to a woman occupying a "male" position. Women, for example, may be United States Senators, but there is no such thing as a *Senatress.* Often, where the feminine noun does exist, it will acquire sexual overtones not found in the original: compare a *mistress* with a *master.*

The last effect even spills over to adjectives applied to the two sexes. 9 A *virtuous* man may be patriotic or charitable or exhibit any one of a number of other admirable traits; a *virtuous* woman is chaste. (The word *virtue* is, itself, derived from the Latin word for *man.*) Similarly, consider Robin Lakoff's example[2] of the different implications involved in saying *He is a professional* versus *She is a professional.* * Although adjectives also may come in seemingly equivalent pairs like *handsome* and *pretty,* they prove not to be equivalent in practice; it is a compliment to call a woman *handsome* and an insult to call a man *pretty.* In other cases, where pairs of adjectives exist, one term covers both sexes and the other one tends to refer only to one sex, usually females. So, members of both sexes may be *small,* but only women seem to be *petite;* both boys and girls may have a *lively* personality, but when did you last meet a *vivacious* boy?

In addition to this use of certain adjectives almost exclusively to refer   10
to women, descriptions of women typically include more adjectives and expressions referring to physical appearance than do descriptions of men. The media clearly reflect this tendency; a report on an interview with a well-known woman rarely fails to mention that she is *attractive* or *stylish,* or to say something about her clothes or the color of her hair or eyes, even if the context is a serious one like politics or economics, where such details have no importance. Readers are also likely to be informed of the number and ages of her children. Men are not treated in a parallel fashion.

Verbs turn out to be sex-differentiated also. Prominent among such   11
verbs are those which refer to women's linguistic behavior and reflect some of the stereotypes discussed in an earlier chapter. Women, for example, may *shriek* and *scream,* while men may *bellow.* Women and children (girls?) hold a virtual monopoly on *giggling,* and it seems that men rarely *gossip* or *scold.* There are also a large number of sex-marked verbs which refer to sexual intercourse. In their article, "Sex-marked Predicates in English," Julia P. Stanley and Susan W. Robbins note the abundance of terms which describe the male role in sexual intercourse, and the lack of parallel terms for women's role.[3] Women are thus assigned a passive role in sex by our language.

Another set of words which are presumably sex-neutral are the ones   12
that end in *-man.* This suffix, which is pronounced with a different vowel from the one in the word *man,* supposedly indicates a person of either sex. It is commonly found in words designating professions—*salesman, postman, congressman,* for example—and in some other expressions such as *chairman* and *freshman.* However, the very fact that there exist female counterparts for many of these words, such as *chairwoman* and *congresswoman,* indicates that they are thought of as typically male and, as in the case of poets, when a woman is referred to, her sex must be clearly indicated. In the case of *salesman,* there are a variety of feminine forms: *saleswoman, saleslady,* and *salesgirl.* Although they appear to be synonymous, they convey significant social distinctions; someone referred to as a *saleslady* or a *salesgirl* probably works in a retail establishment such as a department store or a variety store. A woman who sells

---

*Traditionally, the word *professional,* applied to a woman, has been used as a euphemism for *prostitute.*

mainframe computers to large corporations would be called a *saleswoman,* or even a *salesman.* The more important the position, the less likely it is to be held by a *-girl* or a *-lady,* and the more likely it is to be the responsibility of a *-man.*

If speakers of English often have a choice of using separate words for men and women, of pretending that a single word with a male marker like *chairman* refers to both sexes, or of using a truly sex-neutral term like *chairperson* or *chair,* speakers of some other languages do not enjoy such freedom. They are constrained by the grammar of their languages to classify the nouns they use according to something called gender. Grammatical gender is a feature of most European languages and of many others as well. Depending on the language, nouns may be classified according to whether they are animate or inanimate, human or non-human, male or female, or, in the case of inanimate objects, the class may depend on shape or some other characteristic. In some languages, meaning plays little part in determining noun class or gender; it may be predictable from the phonetic shape of the words, or it may be completely arbitrary. In the European tradition, genders are labelled *masculine* and *feminine* and, if there is a third noun class, *neuter.* This is in spite of the fact that most words included in all three of these classes represent inanimate objects like *tables* and *doors,* abstract concepts like *freedom,* or body parts like *head, toe, nose,* etc. Some of us English speakers may begin to wonder about the strange world view of speakers of languages which classify books as masculine and tables as feminine, especially when we notice that the word for nose is feminine in Spanish, but masculine in French and Italian. It turns out, however, that they are not following some animistic practice whereby inanimate objects are thought of as having sexual attributes; in the modern European languages at least, grammatical gender is, for most nouns, a purely arbitrary classification, often the result of linguistic tradition and of a number of historical accidents. The labels come from the fact that most nouns referring to males belong to one class and most nouns referring to females belong to another class and, following the human practice of classifying everything in terms of ourselves, we extend the distinguishing labels to all nouns. There are, not surprisingly, exceptions to this prevalent mode of classification, which lead to the oddity of such words as the French *sentinelle,* 'guard', being grammatically feminine, although most guards are men, while two German words for 'young woman', *Fräulein* and *Mädchen,* are grammatically neuter.

Are speakers of languages with grammatical gender completely strait-jacketed by their grammar and forced to be sexist? We will return to this question in the final chapter. For now, we note that in these languages, the masculine forms usually serve as generics and are considered the general forms, in much the same way as the *-man* words are in English. Just as there are often alternatives to these masculine words in English, other languages also have many words that are potentially neutral and can belong to either gender, depending on the sex of the person referred to—French *poète* and Spanish *poeta* are examples, despite the dictionaries' classification of them as masculine. Yet speakers often insist on signalling the sex of women poets by

adding suffixes parallel to the English -ess, poétesse and poetisa being the French
and Spanish equivalents, or by tacking on the word for woman, as in femme
médecin, one term for a 'woman doctor' in French.

Although it is true that the masculine forms serve as the unmarked or   15
neutral terms in many languages, this does not seem to be a universal feature
of human languages, as some have claimed. Iroquoian languages use feminine
nouns as unmarked or generic terms; however, in the case of Iroquoian
occupational terms, which are composed of a pronoun and a verb (literally
translated as 'she cooks' or 'he cooks'), the sex-typing of the job determines
whether the masculine or feminine pronoun is used. In Modern Standard
Arabic many nouns switch to the feminine gender when they are pluralized.
In many European languages, abstract nouns are predominantly in the feminine gender.

English nouns no longer exhibit grammatical gender, but the language   16
does have a large number of words that refer to members of one sex only.
In addition, when we do not know the sex of the person referred to by a noun
such as writer or student, the choice of the pronoun will, as in Iroquois, often
depend on culturally defined sex roles. Teacher, therefore, is usually she, while
professor, doctor, and priest usually go with he. This brings us to the question of
the "generic" use of he and the word man.

In the case of the word man, as in Man is a primate, it has been argued   17
that this usage is independent of sex, that it refers to all members of the
species, and that it is just an etymological coincidence that the form for the
species is the same as that for the male members of the species. Certainly,
using the same form for the entire species and for half the species creates the
possibility of confusion, as those colonial women discovered who rashly
thought that the word man in the sentence "All men are created equal"
included them. More confusion may come about when we use phrases like
early man. Although this presumably refers to the species, notice how easy it
is to use expressions like early man and his wife and how hard it is to say things
like man is the only animal that menstruates or even early woman and her husband. As
with the poetical examples discussed earlier, the common theme running
through these last examples is that the male is taken as the normal, that
masculine forms refer both to the sex and the species, while women are the
exception, usually absorbed by the masculine, but needing special terms
when they become noticeable.

If the above examples have not convinced you that man as a generic is   18
at best ambiguous, consider the following quote from Alma Graham:

> If a woman is swept off a ship into the water, the cry is "Man over-
> board!" If she is killed by a hit-and-run driver, the charge is "manslaugh-
> ter." If she is injured on the job, the coverage is "workmen's compensa-
> tion." But if she arrives at a threshold marked "Men Only," she knows
> the admonition is not intended to bar animals or plants or inanimate
> objects. It is meant for her.[4]

Historically, *man* did start out as a general term for human beings, but 19
Old English also had separate sex-specific terms: *wif* for women and *wer* or
carl for men. The compound term *wifman* (female person) is the source for
today's *woman,* but the terms for males were lost as *man* came to take on its
sex-specific meaning, thus creating the confusion we have been discussing.
For an authoritative opinion on the modern meaning of this word, we could
turn to the *Oxford English Dictionary,* which notes that the generic use of *man*
is obsolete: "In modern apprehension *man* as thus used primarily denotes the
male sex, though by implication referring also to women." We note that the
"modern apprehension" referred to was the late nineteenth century. If anything, the situation is even clearer today.

An even shorter word which is supposed to include women but often 20
excludes them is the pronoun *he.* Observers have long pointed out the incon-
venience of the ambiguity of this form and the advantages of having a true
generic singular pronoun, which would be sex-neutral. In the absence of such
a sex-neutral pronoun, speakers of English have been expected to utter sentences such as *Everybody should bring his book tomorrow,* where the *everybody* referred
to includes forty women and just one man. For centuries, speakers and writers
of English have been happily getting around this obstacle by using *they* in
such situations, yielding sentences such as *Everybody should bring their book tomorrow.* Unfortunately, since the middle of the eighteenth century, prescriptive
grammarians have been prescribing the use of *he* in these situations and
attacking the use of *they,* by arguing that the use of *they* is a violation of the
rule for pronoun agreement, i.e., a singular noun such as *everybody* should not
take a plural pronoun such as *they.*

Although the prescriptive grammarians have not explained why it is all 21
right for a female person such as *Mary* to be referred to by a masculine
pronoun such as *he,* they have managed to make many people feel guilty
about breaking the law when they use *they* in such sentences. As a result,
many of us consciously avoid the use of *they* in these contexts, and some of
us avoid the use of such sentences at all. Ann Bodine quotes a writer of a
grammatical handbook advocating the latter course when faced with the need
to formulate the sentence, "Everyone in the class worried about the midyear
history exam, but he all passed."[5] In 1850, an actual law was passed on the
subject when the British Parliament, in an attempt to shorten the language
in its legislation, declared: "In all acts words importing the masculine gender
shall be deemed and taken to include females. . ."[6] The importance of short-
ening the language of legislation can clearly be seen by Parliament's use of
"deemed and taken." Statements similar to Parliament's are found in leases
and other legal contracts today, but, as Casey Miller and Kate Swift point out
in *The Handbook of Nonsexist Writing for Writers, Editors and Speakers,* "it was often
conveniently ignored. In 1879, for example, a move to admit female physi-
cians to the all-male Massachusetts Medical Society was effectively blocked
on the grounds that the society's by-laws describing membership used the
pronoun *he.* "[7] Julia Stanley is one of a number of writers who have discred-

ited the "myth of generics" in English. Her essay contains many examples of ambiguous and "pseudo-generic" usages.[8]

Rather than rely on authority or opinion, some scholars have conducted   22
experiments to determine whether or not today's speakers of English perceive the forms *man* and *he* as generic. In one study, Joseph Schneider and Sally Hacker asked some students to find appropriate illustrations for an anthropology book with chapter headings like "Man and His Environment" and "Man and His Family"; another group of students was given titles like "Family Life" and "Urban Life." The students who were assigned titles with the word *man* chose more illustrations of men only, while the second group chose more pictures showing men, women, and children. Other studies have confirmed our tendency to interpret *he* and *man* as masculine unless the context clearly indicates they are meant generically, the contrary of what is usually claimed. One experiment, conducted by Wendy Martyna, that tested the usage and meaning of these words among young people, found that women and men may be using the terms quite differently. The men's usage appears to be based on sex-specific (male) imagery, while the women's usage is based instead on the prescription that *he* should be used when the sex of the person is not specified. Things can now run smoothly with women believing that they are included while men know otherwise.

Being treated as a trivial exception, being made to go to the rear linguis-   23
tically, or even being made to disappear, are not the worst things that happen to women in the English language. Our lopsided lexicon is well supplied with unpleasant labels for women. Many, although by no means all of these, are slang words. The editor of the 1960 edition of the *Dictionary of American Slang* writes that "most American slang is created and used by males." This observation may be prejudiced by the fact that most collectors of American slang are males, but in any case, the words referring to women should give us an idea of the attitudes of American men towards women. The dictionaries reveal an unpleasant picture indeed.

Disregarding the obscene terms, and that is quite a task, since the list   24
of obscene words for women is long, if monotonous, we still find term after term referring to women in a sexually derogatory way. Consider the following small sample: *chick, hussy, tart, broad, dame,* and *bimbo.* In one study, "The Semantic Derogation of Women," Muriel Schulz found over one thousand words and phrases which put women in their place in this way.[9] She analyzes a long series of words which started out as harmless terms or had a positive meaning, and gradually acquired negative connotations. It would seem that men find it difficult to talk about women without insulting them. The opposite is not true—few of the words have masculine counterparts. After going through the lists compiled by Schulz and other writers, one may begin to wonder about the popular belief that men talk about more serious topics than do women. Unless, of course, sexual jokes and insults constitute a serious topic, men should scarcely need so many derogatory terms. An interesting, if depressing, party game is to try to think of positive labels which are used for women.

Let's examine a few examples of words for women, their meanings and 25 their histories. The woman of the house, or *housewife*, became a *hussy* with the passage of time, and eventually the word had to be reinvented with its original meaning. So much for the dignity of housewives. *Madam* and *mistress* did not change in form, but they took on new sex-related meanings, while *Sir* and *master* participate in no double entendres. Many of the most insulting words began life as terms of endearment and evolved into sexual slurs. *Tart*, originally a term of endearment like *sweetie-pie*, came to mean a sexually desirable woman and then a prostitute, while *broad* originally meant a young woman. *Girl* started out meaning a child of either sex, then took on the following meanings at various stages: a female child, a servant, a prostitute, and a mistress. The process then seemed to reverse itself and *girl* has gone back to meaning a female child most of the time, although some of the other meanings remain. *Whore*, which has the same root as Latin *carus*, 'dear', referred at first to a lover of either sex, then only to females, and finally came to mean prostitute. Almost all the words for female relatives—*mother, aunt, daughter*, and the like—have at one time or another been euphemisms for prostitute. Stanley analyzes 220 terms used to describe sexually promiscuous women.[10] This is just a sample of a much larger group, although there are relatively few words to describe sexually promiscuous men. Even though most of the derogatory terms for women originated as positive words, some of them did not: *shrew*, for example, never had a favorable connotation.

There are many animal metaphors used to insult both men and women, 26 *dog* being an example. However, here too, there seem to be more terms of abuse for women: *chick* is one example, another is *cow*, which has been "a rude term for a woman" since the mid-1600s according to one recent dictionary of slang. Side by side with *dog*, which can be used for both sexes, we find *bitch*, limited to women. We know of no animal terms of abuse which are limited to men. In another semantic area, there is the large group of terms used both to label and to address women as objects to be consumed: *tomato, honey, cookie, sweetie-pie*, and *peach* are but a few examples. These are not necessarily derogatory and some of them, like *honey*, can be used by women to address men, but most refer largely or exclusively to women, and there is no parallel set used to refer to men. The food terms have not escaped the process of pejoration which commonly afflicts words for women, as is shown by the example of *tart*, which was included in our discussion of derogatory words.

In an earlier chapter we discussed some of the similarities between 27 stereotypes about the way women speak and beliefs about the speech of other powerless groups. Not surprisingly, there are also many derogatory labels for such groups in the form of ethnic and racial slurs and, like women, they are the butt of many jokes. Once again we find that Black women are doubly insulted. In the words of Patricia Bell Scott, "The English language has dealt a 'low-blow' to the self-esteem of developing Black womanhood."[11] After consulting the 1960 *American Thesaurus of Slang*, Scott states: "From a glance at the synonyms used to describe a Black person, especially a Black woman, one readily senses that there is something inherently negative about 'being Black' and specifically about being a Black woman. The words listed under the heading 'Negress,' in itself an offensive term, have largely negative and sexual connotations."[12] Some of the milder terms listed include *Black doll, femmoke,* and *nigger gal.* Black women do not seem to be treated much better by Black English. Scott also examined handbooks of Black language and found "a preoccupation with physical attractiveness, sex appeal, and skin color, with the light-skinned Black women receiving connotations of positiveness." She concludes that "much of Black English has also dealt Black Womanhood a 'low-blow.' "[13]

At the beginning of this chapter we asserted that one can determine a 28 great deal about the attitudes of a group of speakers by examining their linguistic usage. At the end of this chapter we must conclude that the attitudes towards women reflected in the usage of English speakers are depressing indeed. They have sometimes been belittled and treated as *girls;* at other times, they have been excluded or ignored by the pretense of "generic" terms; they have frequently been defined as sex objects or insulted as prostitutes, or, on the contrary, placed on a pedestal, desexed, and treated with deference, as *ladies.* It is no wonder that many women have rebelled against being the object of such language and have become creators and advocates of new usages designed to bring equity to the English language. . . .

REFERENCES

All references are Frank and Ashen's.

1. Richard A. Spears, *Slang and Euphemism* (Middle Village, N.Y.: Jonathan David, 1981), p. 21.

2. Robin Lakoff, *Language and Woman's Place* (New York: Harper & Row, 1975), p. 30.

3. Julia P. Stanley and Susan W. Robbins, "Sex-marked Predicates in English," *Papers in Linguistics* 11 (1978): 494.

4. Alma Graham, "The Making of a Nonsexist Dictionary," in *Language and Sex,* ed. Barrie Thorn and Nancy Henley (New York: Newbury House, 1975), p. 62.

5. Ann Bodine, "Androcentrism in Prescriptive Grammar: Singular 'They,' Sex-indefinite 'He' and 'He and She,' " *Language in Society* 4 (1975): 140.

6. Ibid., 136.

7. Casey Miller and Kate Swift, *The Handbook of Nonsexist Writing for Writers, Editors and Speakers* (New York: Lippincott & Crowell, 1980), p. 37.

8. Julia P. Stanley, "Gender-Marking in American English: Usage and Reference," in *Sexism and Language,* ed. Alleen Pace Nilsen, Haig Bosmajian, H. Lee Gershuny, and Julia P. Stanley (Urbana, Ill.: National Council of Teachers of English, 1977), pp. 43–74.

9. Muriel Schulz, "The Semantic Derogation of Women," in *Language and Sex,* ed. Barrie Thorn and Nancy Henley (Cambridge, Mass.: Newbury House, 1975), pp. 64–75.

10. Julia P. Stanley, "Paradigmatic Woman: The Prostitute," in *Papers in Language Variation,* ed. David L. Shores and Carol P. Hines (University, Ala.: University of Alabama Press, 1977).

11. Patricia Bell Scott, "The English Language and Black Womanhood: A Low Blow at Self-esteem," *Journal of Afro-American Issues* 2 (1974): 220.

12. Ibid.

13. Ibid., 220–221.

Questions for Discussion

1. Here are some words that refer to women or to activities attributed mainly to women. Following each word are earlier meanings. Comment on political, social, linguistic, and sexual implications. Do you see a sexist pattern in the way the meanings of these words have changed over the years? What are some possible ways of accounting for the pattern?

   a. *shrew:* a malicious, evil, cunning man
   b. *termagant:* a male Saracen idol
   c. *harlot:* a young, base fellow
   d. *scold:* from Old Norse, a poet or lampooner
   e. *baggage:* a worthless fellow
   f. *frump:* a derisive snort > a jeer > ill humor > a cross, dowdy man or woman
   g. *witch:* originally either male or female
   h. *gossip: godsib,* "god-relative" > a familiar acquaintance
   i. *mistress:* feminine of *master*
   j. *madam:* "my lady"

2. Here are some other insulting terms for women: *broad, chippy, drab, floozy, slattern, slut, strumpet, trollop, troll, trot, doxy, hag, harridan, crone, biddy, harpy, vamp, nag, whore, bitch, piece, lay, tail, hen, old maid, wallflower, unladylike, unfeminine, snit, chit, tart, hussy.* What aspects of female reference do most of these words focus on? How many masculine counterparts to these words can you come up with? If there are many fewer insulting terms for men, what does this suggest about the relative differences between men and women, historically, in education, political clout, and social dominance?

3. Consider the way animal terms and animal imagery are employed to make value judgments, to praise, or to insult. Here is a list of animal images, many of them similes, that we use in everyday conversation. Discuss which of them refer mainly to women, which refer mainly to men, and which may refer to either sex. Note which are insulting. Is there a higher percentage of insulting images among the terms that refer mainly to women? If so, why?

   a. eats like a bird, pecks at food
   b. acts like a minx
   c. a real fox, real foxy
   d. talks catty
   e. leads a dog's life, works like a dog
   f. stubborn as a mule
   g. works like a horse
   h. looks fishy
   i. fishing for compliments
   j. gullible as a fish
   k. bull-headed
   l. to cry crocodile tears
   m. dumb as an ox
   n. act like a goose

o. old bat
p. feel sheepish
q. quarrelsome as a shrew
r. busy as a beaver
s. mild as a lamb
t. filthy as a pig, eat like a pig
u. feel squirrelly
v. graceful as a swan
w. playful as a kitten
x. act like a jackass
y. timid as a mouse, quiet as a mouse
z. bull in a china shop

Suggested Essay Topics

1. For 3 weeks conduct an experiment of your own. Buy yourself a small notebook, such as a 3-by-5-inch spiral pad, and carry it with you at all times. In it jot down all the terms of insult that you hear used in reference to men and women. After you have recorded a phrase or term once, make a mark after it for every repeated use that you hear. Also for each term jot down the social context in which it was used (formal, informal, in class, etc.), and record the sex of the speaker. Finally, record whether the sex of the audience was single or mixed. After 3 weeks of keeping records, organize your material and present it in an essay directed to your classmates, drawing whatever implications and conclusions you think are warranted about the way men and women talk about one another on your campus. You might consider making this a feature article or letter to the editor in the campus newspaper. Finally, although this is not part of the essay assignment as such, discuss in class any strong differences that show up in the records of men and women. See if you can determine, for example, whether women talking together without men use more, fewer, or about the same number of insulting terms for men as men use when they are talking together without women.

2. Referring to the reference notes after the Frank and Ashen essay, select three of the following five sources to read more fully: Robin Lakoff, *Language and Woman's Place;* Alma Graham, "The Making of a Nonsexist Dictionary"; Muriel Schulz, "The Semantic Derogation of Women"; Julia P. Stanley, "Paradigmatic Woman: The Prostitute"; Patricia Bell Scott, "The English Language and Black Womanhood: A Low Blow at Self-esteem." After reading three of these sources, write an article for the campus newspaper in which you make the best arguments you can against sexist language usage, providing appropriate examples of its occurrence in the language and analyzing the pernicious social, political, and psychological effects it has on both users and referents.

Betty Roszak

Betty Roszak (b. 1933) is a writer, feminist, and co-editor with her husband, Theodore Roszak, of Masculine/Feminine, *the anthology in which the following essay first appeared.*

The temptation to misread is always strongest when we read essays that include, or seem to include, opinions that we find powerfully appealing or powerfully repulsive. We are more likely to notice statements with a high emotional charge, and more likely to remember them later on, forgetting the original supporting arguments. No doubt you have noticed how newspapers often emphasize a startling event or stirring statement so strongly that they sacrifice accuracy. Even when extracted sentences are quoted accurately, and they often are not, extraction itself always produces some distortion. By quoting out of context, reporters even directly reverse an author's meaning because they fail, for example, to recognize or acknowledge that a passage was written ironically or that it in fact describes a position that the author was attempting to refute.

The danger seems especially strong in an essay like this one. No matter where we stand on the issues Roszak raises, they are charged with emotion, and we are thus even more tempted than usual to notice only the charged moments and overlook how they work within the whole piece.

Any speedy reader can quickly discover here, for example, that Roszak is a feminist and that, like all feminists, she seeks to change things. She "favors abortion" and is convinced that men have on the whole been unjust to women. Whether we like these opinions or not, we are likely to let them overshadow her main points unless we discipline ourselves to the kind of reading that cares more about understanding others than feeding our prejudices or pet ideas. In short, to label the essay or the author with loose, general terms like pro-abortionist *or* radical *is to commit the fault that many good thinkers, including Roszak, warn us about: the fault of polarizing opinions on every issue into two, and often only two, positions and thus artificially simplifying what is actually rich and many-sided.*

As you read, then, resist deciding what the author's main point is until you have not only read through the whole piece once or twice but thought about how it is all put together—and why. Can you prepare a summary that would lead the author to say, "Yes, that was my main point; you have understood"?

By now you've learned not to expect any simple rules for grasping an author's true intention before deciding whether you agree or not. But there are two obvious questions by which you can test your command of an author's intention, both of them useful in reading Roszak. Ask yourself, "If I were writing this piece, trying to say what I think she is saying, would I begin or end it the way she does?" Then ask, "If this essay were my own, would I introduce what I take to be her thesis with the title she uses?" Whenever the answer is "no" to one or both of these questions, either the author has chosen badly or you should try out another possible view of the author's intention.

THE HUMAN CONTINUUM

From *Masculine/Feminine: Readings in Sexual Mythology and the Liberation of Women,* edited by Betty Roszak and Theodore Roszak (1969).

Recent years have seen a resurgence of feminism that has taken mainstream   1
America by surprise. It began with the discontent of lonely middle-class
suburban housewives, whose malady was given a name by Betty Friedan in
her immensely influential book, *The Feminine Mystique.* But it didn't become
what we know as a "women's liberation movement" until the growth of the
New Left from the civil rights and peace movements of the early 1960's. It
wasn't until then that hundreds of young women, many of whom were
seasoned veterans of antiwar and antisegregationist activities, began to realize
the anomaly of their situation. Here they were, radical women involved in
a struggle for human equality and an end to oppression, willing to dedicate
years of effort to effecting political change, and what were they being allowed
to do? Typing, mimeographing, addressing envelopes, sweeping, providing
coffee and sexual diversion for the vigorous young men who were making all
the decisions. Far from going forward together to change the world, men and
women were once more stuck (and this time with a vengeance) with their
time-honored roles: the men to think and act; the women to serve and drudge.
The last equality—that between women and men—was never even mentioned. In fact, movement women found that they were even worse off than
apolitical women, because they were aware of and extremely sensitive to the
hypocrisies of their male colleagues who talked idealistically of equality, but
who acted scornful of women in their everyday lives. The rhetoric of equality
was directed at black, brown, and Third World *men* only. The New Left of
the late sixties had begun to take on a tough, aggressively male tone, born
of the idolization of Ché Guevara, guerrilla warfare, and admiration for the
exaggerated, overcompensating manliness of the Black Panthers. As nonviolence, exemplified by Martin Luther King, Jr., became discredited by revolutionary and black militancy, so the tough style became a political requirement. In deference to this new brutalism men found it easy to take the
necessary traditional he-man attitude toward women, the attitude of dominance and power. This left women in a bewildering dilemma. Were they to
remain in a movement which allowed them to exist only as lackeys and
silently submissive bedmates, or would they refuse to accept a subordinate
status?

As this dilemma is being resolved today, there sounds in the back-   2
ground the laughter of contemptuous radical men: "Crazy feminist bitches!"
The words merely echo a shared male ridicule that knows no class lines.
Women find themselves of necessity beginning to re-examine the traditions
of misogyny that even radical men have unknowingly inherited.

In our cultural past "Woman" was the symbol of sex; and sex, though   3
necessary, was at the same time known to be an abhorrent evil, a degrading
passion. In the Middle Ages, the masculine world view of the church dared

not make light of women. Church authorities of the fifteenth century, ever on the alert for the malevolence of the devil, used a popular handbook on the identification and treatment of witches, the *Malleus Maleficarum*, in searching out evil in the form of women. "What else is woman," says this medieval antisubversive activities manual, "but a foe to friendship, an unescapable punishment, a necessary evil, a natural temptation, a desirable calamity, a domestic danger, a delectable detriment, an evil of nature painted with fair colors?" By the eighteenth century, Rousseau, one of France's most prolific proponents of democratic equality, could write with impunity, "Women have in general no love of any art; they have no proper knowledge of any; and they have no genius," thus curtly dismissing half of humanity to a status of hopeless inferiority. By mid-nineteenth century, the "evil of nature" had turned into an object of scorn, and Schopenhauer's indictment of women as "that undersized, narrow-shouldered, broad-hipped, and short-legged race," denied women even their beauty, their "fair colors," along with their intellectual capacity.

Today's predominantly male society no longer sees women as evil, at   4
least on the surface. The ambivalent fear and attraction of the Middle Ages has changed along with the prevailing attitude toward sex. Now that sexuality has lost its mystery, the once dangerous and seductive female can be safely ignored and denied her power. The fear has turned to ridicule. One cannot ignore evil, but one can pretend that the ridiculous does not exist. Men irritably ask the rhetorical question (echoing Freud) "What do women want?" meaning, of course, that anything women want is absurd. The question is asked not of individual women but of the world, and in an exasperated tone, as if women were dumb and couldn't answer. The false barrier continues to be built: "We" cannot understand "Them." Why are "They" so restive? Further communication between the sexes seems useless. Always it is men talking to men about women.

The fact of ridicule is constantly with us. When it was proposed in 1969   5
in the British House of Commons that attention be paid to developing a contraceptive pill for men, "the idea provoked hearty laughter," according to Paul Vaughan in the London *Observer*. Moreover, he tells us, the British government has rejected outright any allocation of funds for research on a pill for men. When the question was under discussion in the House of Lords, one Labour peer advised the government to ignore " 'these do-gooders who take all the fun out of life' (laughter)." Researchers explain their reluctance to tamper with the male germ cells. Yet the same researchers have not hesitated to tamper with the female germ cells in developing the pill for women. Nor have unpleasant side effects or hazards to women's health deterred them, while they quickly stopped research on a substance being tested on men because it was noted that when men drank alcohol while taking it, their eyes became reddened! Doctors have been known to laugh at the mention of labor pains during childbirth and in the not too distant past have been willing to stand by, calmly withholding anesthetics while women underwent great agonies in labor. So, too, male legislators have laughed at the idea of the

legalization of abortion, hinting at unprecedented promiscuity (on the part of women, not men) if such a thing were allowed. Meanwhile, thousands of desperate women die each year as the direct result of male laws making abortion illegal.

Women are learning the meaning of this male laughter and indifference 6 in the face of the most hazardous and serious biological enterprise women undertake, willingly or not. And in cultural enterprises, whenever women attempt to enter any of the male-dominated professions (who ever heard of a woman chairman of the board, a woman orchestra conductor, a woman Chief Justice, a woman President or a woman getting equal pay for equal work?), we again hear the familiar laughter of male ridicule. If we look at the image of woman men present to us in novels, drama, or advertising, we see a scatterbrained, helpless flunky, or a comical sex-pot, or a dumb beast of burden. Is this what they mean when they exhort us in popular song to "enjoy being a girl"? But women are beginning to relearn the old lesson: in this male-dominated world, it is a misfortune to be born female.

From the very moment of birth a higher value is placed by his society 7 on the male infant, a value which accumulates and accelerates into his adult life. By the time the female infant has grown into adulthood, however, if she has learned society's lessons well, she will have come to acquiesce in her second-class status—to accept unconsciously the burden of her inferiority. No matter what honors she wins, what her exploits, what her achievements or talents, she will always be considered a woman first, and thus inferior to the least honored, talented and worthy male of that society—foremost a sexual being, still fair game for his aggressive sexual fantasies. As Albert Memmi puts it, ". . . every man, no matter how low he may be, holds women in contempt and judges masculinity to be an inestimable good."

Male society's disparagement of women has all the force of an uncon- 8 scious conspiracy. It is even more subtle than the racist and colonial oppressions to which it is so closely allied, because it is softened and hidden by the silken padding of eroticism. We women grow to think that because we are wanted as lovers, wives, and mothers, it might be because we are wanted as human beings. But if by chance or natural inclination we attempt to move outside these male-defined and male-dependent roles, we find that they are, in reality, barriers.

For many women this is the first inkling of the fact of oppression. 9 Pressed from birth into the mold of an exclusively sexual being, the growing girl soon develops what Sartre calls the "phantom personality"; she comes to feel that she is what "they" tell her she is. This other self envelops her like a second skin. When she begins to experience a natural sense of constriction (which is growth), her real feelings clash with what "they" say she should feel. The more forceful and vital she is, the more she will have to repress her real feelings, because girls are to be passive and manipulatable. She becomes frightened, suspicious, anxious about herself. A sense of malaise overcomes her. She must obey the social prohibitions which force her back into the mold of the sexual being. She is not to desire or act, but to *be* desired and acted upon. Many women give up the struggle right there and dully force themselves to remain stunted human beings. The butterfly must not be allowed to come forth from its chrysalis: her vitality is only allowed guilty expression in certain private moments or is turned into sullen resentment which smolders during all her unfulfilled life.

Family and home, which look like a refuge and a sanctuary, turn out to 10 be the same kind of trap. Beyond the marriage ghetto there is outright rejection and exclusion. In the work world there are lower wages, union and employer discrimination, the prohibitive cost of child care. In the professions mere tokenism takes the place of acceptance and equality. The same is true in government and political activity. The single woman knows only too well the psychological exclusionism practiced by male society. She is suspect, or comic, if over a certain age. All men assume she would be married if she could—there must be something psychologically wrong with her if she isn't. And single women have the added burden of not being socially acceptable without an "escort"—a man, any man.

Further, women are the nonexistent people in the very life of the nation 11 itself—now more so even than the blacks who have at last forced themselves into the nation's consciousness. The invisible man has become the invisible *woman*. William James called it a "fiendish punishment" that "one should be turned loose on society and remain absolutely unnoticed by all the members thereof." Yet that is the treatment male society metes out to those women who wish to escape from the male-defined erotic roles. Left out of the history books, not credited with a past worth mentioning in the masculine chronicles of state, women of today remain ignorant of women's movements of the past and the important role individual women have played in the history of the human race. Male historical scholarship sees the suffragists and feminists of the nineteenth century as figures of fun, worthy of only a paragraph here and there, as footnotes on the by-ways of social customs, far from the main roads of masculine endeavor: the wars, political intrigues, and diplomatic maneuverings which make up the history of power.

With the blacks and other oppressed minorities, women can say, "How 12 can we hope to shape the future without some knowledge of our past?" If the historic heroines of feminism are ignored or treated trivially, today's women are hindered from dealing with their own repression. This undermining of self-confidence is common to all oppressed peoples, along with the doubts of the reality of one's own perceptions. Women's self-rejection as worthwhile human beings thus becomes an inevitable extension of the cycle of oppression.

But radical women have begun to rebel against the false, exclusively 13 sexual image men have created for them. And in rebelling, many women are seeing the need for bypassing the marriage ghetto altogether. They are recognizing the true nature of the institution of marriage as an economic bargain glossed over by misty sentimentalizing. Wash off the romantic love ideal, and underneath we see the true face of the marriage contract. It is grimly epitomized by the immortal slogan found chalked on innumerable honeymoon

getaway cars: "She got him today; he'll get her tonight." Or, as put more
sophisticatedly by Robert Briffault, "Whether she aims at freedom or a home
a woman is thrown back on the defense of her own interests; she must defend
herself against man's attempt to bind her, or sell herself to advantage. Woman
is to man a sexual prey; man is to woman an economic prey." And this kind
of oppression cuts across all economic class lines, even though there may be
social differences between streetwalker Jane X, housewife Joan Y, and debu-
tante Jacqueline Z. One may sell her body for a few dollars to the likeliest
passerby; one for a four-bedroomed house in the suburbs; and one for rubies
and yachts. But all must sell their bodies in order to participate in the bargain.
Yet if women were to refuse to enter into the sexual bargain, they not only
would refute the masculine idea of women as property, but they also would
make it possible to free men from the equally self-destructive role of sole
breadwinner. Thus there would be a chance to break the predatory cycle.

Beyond marriage and the old, outmoded roles, radical women are seek- 14
ing new ways of dealing with the oppressive institutions of society. No longer
will they acquiesce in the pattern of dominance and submission. They are
beginning to take control of their own lives, building new relationships,
developing new modes of work, political activity, child rearing and education.
Rejection of male exploitation must start with psychic as well as economic
independence. The new female consciousness is going to develop cooperative
forms of child care; women's centers as sanctuaries for talk, planning, and
action; all-female communes where women can escape for a while from the
all-pervading male influence; the sharing of domestic drudgery with men in
cooperative living arrangements; the building up of competence and self-
confidence in such previously male-dependent endeavors as general mechanical repair work, carpentry, and construction.

By rejecting the false self for so long imposed upon us and in which we 15
have participated unwittingly, we women can forge the self-respect necessary
in order to discover our own true values. Only when we refuse to be made
use of by those who despise and ridicule us, can we throw off our heavy
burden of resentment. We must take our lives in our own hands. This is what
liberation means. Out of a common oppression women can break the stereotypes of masculine-feminine and enter once more into the freedom of the
human continuum.

Women's liberation will thus inevitably bring with it, as a concomitant, 16
men's liberation. Men, no less than women, are imprisoned by the heavy
carapace of their sexual stereotype. The fact that they gain more advantages
and privileges from women's oppression has blinded them to their own
bondage which is the bondage of an artificial duality. This is the male problem: the positing of a difference, the establishment of a dichotomy emphasizing oppositeness. Men are to behave in this way; women in that; women do
this; men do the other. And it just so happens that the way men behave and
act is important and valuable, while what women do is unimportant and
trivial. Instead of identifying both the sexes as part of humanity, there is a

false separation which is to the advantage of men. Masculine society has insisted on seeing in sexuality that same sense of conflict and competition that it has imposed upon its relation to the planet as a whole. From the bedroom to the board room to the international conference table, separateness, differentiation, opposition, exclusion, antithesis have been the cause and goal of the male politics of power. Human characteristics belonging to the entire species have been crystallized out of the living flow of human experience and made into either/or categories. This male habit of setting up boundary lines between imagined polarities has been the impetus for untold hatred and destruction. Masculine/feminine is just one of such polarities among many, including body/mind, organism/environment, plant/animal, good/evil, black/white, feeling/intellect, passive/active, sane/insane, living/ dead. Such language hardens what is in reality a continuum and a unity into separate mental images always in opposition to one another.

If we think of ourselves as "a woman" or "a man," we are already 17 participating in a fantasy of language. People become preoccupied with images of one another—surely the deepest and most desperate alienation there is. The very process of conceptualization warps our primary, unitary feelings of what we are. Mental images take the place of the primary stimuli of sex which involve the entire organism. Instead of a sense of identification, we have pornographic sex with its restrictive emphasis on genital stimulation. This "short circuiting between genitals and cortex" as William E. Galt calls it (in a brilliant article, "The Male-Female Dichotomy," in *Psychiatry,* 1943) is a peculiarly modern distortion of the original, instinctual nature of sex. We are suffering from D. H. Lawrence's "sex in the head." In childhood we know sexuality as a generalized body response; the body is an erotic organ of sensation. To this Freud gave the nasty name of polymorphous perversity. But it is actually the restriction to localized genitality of the so-called "normal" adult that is perverted, in the sense of a twisting away from the original and primary body eroticism. Biological evidence indicates that the sex response is a primitive, gross sensory stimulation—diffused and nonlocalizable. Phallic man, however, wishes to assert the primacy of his aggressive organ. The ego of phallic man divides him off from the rest of the world, and in this symbolic division he maintains the deep-seated tradition of man *against* woman, wresting his sexual pleasure *from* her, like the spoils of war. The total body response must be repressed in order to satisfy the sharpness of his genital cravings.

But in the primary sexual response of the body, there is no differentia- 18 tion between man or woman; there is no "man," there is no "woman" (mental images), just a shared organism responding to touch, smell, taste, sound. The sexual response can then be seen as one part of the species' total response to, and participation in, the environment. We sense the world with our sensitive bodies as an ever-changing flow of relationships in which we move and partake. Phallic man sees the world as a collection of things from which he is sharply differentiated. If we consider the phenomenon of the orgasm in this light, we can see that its basic qualities are the same for male and female.

There can be no real distinction between the feminine and masculine *self-abandonment* in a sexual climax. The self, or controlling power, simply vanishes. All talk of masculine or feminine orgasm misses this point entirely, because this is a surrender which goes beyond masculine or feminine. Yet how many men are there who are willing to see their own sexual vitality as exactly this self-surrender?

When men want desperately to preserve that which they deem mascu- 19 line—the controlling power—then they insist on the necessity of the feminine as that which must be controlled and mastered. Men force themselves into the role of phallic man and seek always to be hard, to be tough, to be competitive, to assert their "manhood." Alan Watts wisely sees this masculine striving for rigidity as "nothing more than an emotional paralysis" which causes men to misunderstand the bisexuality of their own nature, to force a necessarily unsatisfactory sexual response, and to be exploitative in their relations with women and the world.

According to Plato's myth, the ancients thought of men and women as 20 originally a single being cut asunder into male and female by an angry god. There is a good biological basis to this myth; although the sexes are externally differentiated, they are still structurally homologous. Psychologically, too, the speculations of George Groddeck are apt:

> Personal sex cuts right across the fundamental qualities of human nature; the very word suggests the violent splitting asunder of humanity into male and female. *Sexus* is derived from *secare,* to cut, from which we also get *segmentum,* a part cut from a circle. It conveys the idea that man and woman once formed a unity, that together they make a complete whole, the perfect circle of the individuum, and that both sections share the properties of this individuum. These suggestions are of course in harmony with the ancient Hebrew legend, which told how God first created a human being who was both male and female, Adam-Lilith, and later sawed this asunder.[1]

The dichotomizing of human qualities can thus be seen as a basic error in men's understanding of nature. Biologically, both sexes are always present in each. Perhaps with the overcoming of women's oppression, the woman in man will be allowed to emerge. If, as Coleridge said, great minds are androgynous, there can be no feminine or masculine ideal, but only, as the poet realizes,

> . . . what is true is human,
> homosexuality, heterosexuality
> There is something more important:
>
> to be human
> in which kind
> is kind.[2]

REFERENCES

1. *The World of Man* (New York: Vision Press, 1951).
2. Clayton Eshleman, "Holding Duncan's Hand."

Questions for Discussion

1. What is the *main* thesis of Roszak's essay? Does your answer fit her choice of a title and a conclusion? (See again our questions at the end of the introduction, p. 355.)

2. Did any part of this essay make you feel angry or uncomfortable? Elated or supported? If not, what emotions did you feel? Can you explain the basis of your reaction?

3. Discuss with your classmates whether men and women respond differently to Roszak's essay. Do the men find in it a different thesis than the women do? Do the men react to it with different emotions?

4. Conduct a poll of your classmates on the question "Does Roszak argue her case persuasively, providing adequate evidence at each step for the beliefs she wants us to accept?" Those who answer "no" should be asked to find unsupported assertions, and those who answer "yes" should be asked to explain why no further evidence is needed. After discussion, conduct the poll again. Are there any changes of vote? How do you account for the results of your experiment?

5. In paragraph 6, we find a parenthetical question that might be answered as follows: "Well, actually, we *have* heard by now of women who head boards, conduct symphony orchestras, and get equal pay for equal work. We now have a woman Justice of the Supreme Court—not quite the same as Chief Justice or President, perhaps, but we're moving fast." Do you think that such a reply weakens Roszak's case? Why or why not?

6. When you hear terms like *radical, pro-abortionist, feminist,* and *militant* thrown about, do you think that the people who use these terms recognize that there may be different *kinds* of each one of them? Or does the use of such general terms almost automatically erase differences of kind? Through open discussion try to determine whether the class members who use any of these labels to describe themselves really belong to homogeneous groups or whether they retain individual differences despite the labels they accept.

Suggested Essay Topics

1. Roszak generalizes freely about the typical experience of males and females in our society. Your own experience, presumably, either matches or fails to match her generalizations. Write an autobiographical essay (or,

if you prefer, a personal letter to Roszak) in which you describe as precisely as you can how you developed your picture of what it means to be
male or female in our society. Don't try to describe any present inhibitions
or anxieties. Your task is to dramatize how you first learned that "what
a *man* does (or is like) is so-and-so, while what a *woman* does (or is like)
is such-and-such." Then write a concluding paragraph or so appraising
whether Roszak's picture fits your experience. (Note: Do not try to develop
a general thesis about sex or sexual relations in American society or try to
refute or support Roszak's whole position. Limit yourself to comparing
your memories with her claims about what men and women are taught
about themselves "from the very moment of birth" [¶6].)

2. In paragraph 18 Roszak talks about the necessity for men to learn "self-
surrender" as an enlargement of sexual response. She also argues that the
false distinction between male orgasm and female orgasm intensifies alienation between men and women. Write an essay directed to Roszak describing the earliest encounters you can remember with sexual images in fiction
(novels, plays, movies, TV)—images that formed your first expectations
about sex in general and about your role as a male or female partner.
Looking at these images from Roszak's point of view, assess whether they
were "good" for you or not. Be as clear as possible about the reasons for
your judgment.

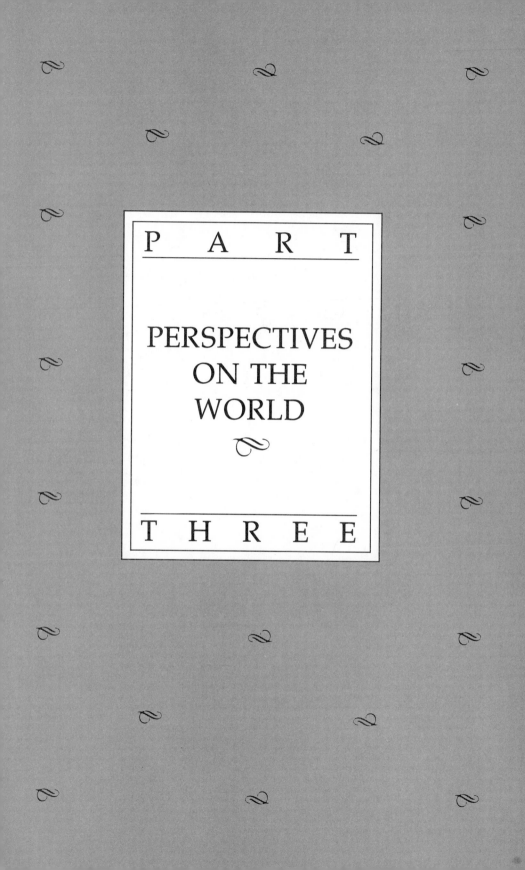

PART

PERSPECTIVES
ON THE
WORLD

THREE

9

HISTORICAL
PERSPECTIVES

Understanding the Present by Learning About the Past

Of the three dimensions of time, only the past is "real" in the absolute sense
that it has occurred, the future is only a concept,
and the present is that fateful split second in which all action takes place.
One of the most disturbing habits of the human mind
is its willful and destructive forgetting of what in its past
does not flatter or confirm its present point of view.
Katherine Anne Porter

Those who do not learn from history are doomed to repeat it.
Karl Marx

If men could learn from history, what lessons it might teach us!
But passion and party blind our eyes, and the light which experience gives
is a lantern on the stern, which shines only on the waves behind us!
Samuel Taylor Coleridge

History is bunk.
Henry Ford

History is philosophy teaching by examples.
Dionysius of Halicarnassus

History is the pack of tricks that the living play on the dead.
Voltaire

What is history but a fable agreed on?
Napoleon

No great man lives in vain. The history of the world is but
the biography of great men.
Thomas Carlyle

Genesis 1–2:3

Obviously history must somehow have begun "in the beginning," "when God began to create the heaven and the earth." Yet no one has ever observed our beginnings, and the anthropologists and cosmologists who try to account today for what happened "then" usually hedge their statements with apologies about guesswork. Ancient authors were less cautious. Most cultures have stories that begin as confidently as the following account from Genesis, the opening story of what Christians call the Old Testament and Jews call the Torah. (Both Jews and Christians use the term Pentateuch to refer to the first five books of the Bible, the books that Moses is said to have received from God.) The authors of the world's many creation stories always know what happened "in the beginning," and the accounts usually explain, as only a story can, how and why things started and how and why they led to the way things are now.

The creation story in the Bible does not even bow in the direction of trying to explain where God came from. Other traditions, such as that of the ancient Greeks, developed much more elaborate accounts of how the beginning could be found behind other beginnings and of how mysterious and amorphous early gods begat later gods who in turn created this or that part of the world. But Genesis begins with a supreme creator unchallenged in his orders and finding it "all," at the end of the creative week, unambiguously "good."

We reprint two translations of Genesis 1–2:3, the first from the King James or "Authorized" Version of the Bible (1611) and the second from a modern translation of the Torah by the Jewish Publication Society of America (1962). The words you will now read constitute perhaps the most-discussed text in Western history. Innumerable books have been written about them, and scholars often disagree over their interpretation. Perhaps you have read or heard them so often that you see no reason to study them further. Or you may have come to accept a history about beginnings that you think makes this one obsolete—something like "In the beginning was a Big Bang, an explosion of an incredibly dense blob of mass or energy that expanded into the still-expanding universe we know today." Or you may believe that the words in Genesis recount a literal history that was written by Moses as one of five books given him by the Lord.

Whatever your view of when and where we began, you can recreate the wonder of this text, with its confident assertions, by asking simply, "What could lead anyone to tell this *kind of history in* this *way to account for our beginnings?"*

Note that we print the traditional verse numbers instead of our usual paragraph numbers. The verses in the King James Version correspond to those in the Torah.

GENESIS 1–2:3

From the King James Version

1.

¹In the beginning God created the heaven and the earth. ²And the earth was without form, and void; and darkness was upon the face of the deep. And the Spirit of God moved upon the face of the waters. ³And God said, Let there be light: and there was light. ⁴And God saw the light, that it was good: and God divided the light from the darkness. ⁵And God called the light Day, and the darkness he called Night. And the evening and the morning were the first day.

⁶And God said, Let there be a firmament in the midst of the waters, and let it divide the waters from the waters. ⁷And God made the firmament, and divided the waters which were under the firmament from the waters which were above the firmament: and it was so. ⁸And God called the firmament Heaven. And the evening and the morning were the second day.

⁹And God said, Let the waters under the heaven be gathered together unto one place, and let the dry land appear: and it was so. ¹⁰And God called the dry land Earth; and the gathering together of the waters called he Seas: and God saw that it was good. ¹¹And God said, Let the earth bring forth grass, the herb yielding seed, and the fruit tree yielding fruit after his kind, whose seed is in itself, upon the earth: and it was so. ¹²And the earth brought forth grass, and herb yielding seed after his kind, and the tree yielding fruit, whose seed was in itself, after his kind: and God saw that it was good. ¹³And the evening and the morning were the third day.

¹⁴And God said, Let there be lights in the firmament of the heaven to divide the day from the night; and let them be for signs, and for seasons, and for days, and years: ¹⁵And let them be for lights in the firmament of the heaven to give light upon the earth: and it was so. ¹⁶And God made two great lights; the greater light to rule the day, and the lesser light to rule the night: he made the stars also. ¹⁷And God set them in the firmament of the heaven to give light upon the earth, ¹⁸and to rule over the day and over the night, and to divide the light from the darkness: and God saw that it was good. ¹⁹And the evening and the morning were the fourth day. ²⁰And God said, Let the waters bring forth abundantly the moving creature that hath life, and

fowl that may fly above the earth in the open firmament of heaven. [21]And God created great whales, and every living creature that moveth, which the waters brought forth abundantly, after their kind, and every winged fowl after his kind: and God saw that it was good. [22]And God blessed them, saying, Be fruitful, and multiply, and fill the waters in the seas, and let fowl multiply in the earth. [23]And the evening and the morning were the fifth day.

[24]And God said, Let the earth bring forth the living creature after his kind, cattle, and creeping thing, and beast of the earth after his kind: and it was so. [25]And God made the beast of the earth after his kind, and cattle after their kind, and every thing that creepeth upon the earth after his kind: and God saw that it was good.

[26]And God said, Let us make man in our image, after our likeness: and let them have dominion over the fish of the sea, and over the fowl of the air, and over the cattle, and over all the earth, and over every creeping thing that creepeth upon the earth. [27]So God created man in his own image, in the image of God created he him; male and female created he them. [28]And God blessed them, and God said unto them, Be fruitful, and multiply, and replenish the earth, and subdue it: and have dominion over the fish of the sea, and over the fowl of the air, and over every living thing that moveth upon the earth.

[29]And God said, Behold, I have given you every herb bearing seed, which is upon the face of all the earth, and every tree, in the which is the fruit of a tree yielding seed; to you it shall be for meat. [30]And to every beast of the earth, and to every fowl of the air, and to every thing that creepeth upon the earth, wherein there is life, I have given every green herb for meat: and it was so. [31]And God saw every thing that he had made, and, behold, it was very good. And the evening and the morning were the sixth day.

2.

[1]Thus the heavens and the earth were finished, and all the host of them. [2]And on the seventh day God ended his work which he had made; and he rested on the seventh day from all his work which he had made. [3]And God blessed the seventh day, and sanctified it: because that in it he had rested from all his work which God created and made.

GENESIS 1–2:3

From the Torah

1.

[1]When God began to create the heaven and the earth—[2]the earth being unformed and void, with darkness over the surface of the deep and a wind from God sweeping over the water—[3]God said, "Let there be light"; and there

was light. [4]God saw that the light was good, and God separated the light from the darkness. [5]God called the light Day, and the darkness He called Night. And there was evening and there was morning, a first day.

[6]God said, "Let there be an expanse in the midst of the water, that it may separate water from water." [7]God made the expanse, and it separated the water which was below the expanse from the water which was above the expanse. And it was so. [8]God called the expanse Sky. And there was evening and there was morning, a second day.

[9]God said, "Let the water below the sky be gathered into one area, that the dry land may appear." And it was so. [10]God called the dry land Earth, and the gathering of waters He called Seas. And God saw that this was good. [11]And God said, "Let the earth sprout vegetation: seed-bearing plants, fruit trees of every kind on earth that bear fruit with the seed in it." And it was so. [12]The earth brought forth vegetation: seed-bearing plants of every kind, and trees of every kind bearing fruit with the seed in it. And God saw that this was good. [13]And there was evening and there was morning, a third day.

[14]God said, "Let there be lights in the expanse of the sky to separate day from night; they shall serve as signs for the set times—the days and the years; [15]and they shall serve as lights in the expanse of the sky to shine upon the earth." And it was so. [16]God made the two great lights, the greater light to dominate the day and the lesser light to dominate the night, and the stars. [17]And God set them in the expanse of the sky to shine upon the earth, [18]to dominate the day and the night, and to separate light from darkness. And God saw that this was good. [19]And there was evening and there was morning, a fourth day.

[20]God said, "Let the waters bring forth swarms of living creatures, and birds that fly above the earth across the expanse of the sky." [21]God created the great sea monsters, and all the living creatures of every kind that creep, which the waters brought forth in swarms; and all the winged birds of every kind. And God saw that this was good. [22]God blessed them, saying, "Be fertile and increase, fill the waters in the seas, and let the birds increase on the earth." [23]And there was evening and there was morning, a fifth day.

[24]God said, "Let the earth bring forth every kind of living creature: cattle, creeping things, and wild beasts of every kind." And it was so. [25]God made wild beasts of every kind and cattle of every kind, and all kinds of creeping things of the earth. And God saw that this was good. [26]And God said, "Let us make man in our image, after our likeness. They shall rule the fish of the sea, the birds of the sky, the cattle, the whole earth, and all the creeping things that creep on earth." [27]And God created man in His image, in the image of God He created him; male and female He created them. [28]God blessed them and God said to them, "Be fertile and increase, fill the earth and master it; and rule the fish of the sea, the birds of the sky, and all the living things that creep on earth."

[29]God said, "See, I give you every seed-bearing plant that is upon all the earth, and every tree that has seed-bearing fruit; they shall be yours for food. [30]And to all the animals on land, to all the birds of the sky, and to everything

that creeps on earth, in which there is the breath of life, [I give] all the green plants for food." And it was so. [31]And God saw all that He had made, and found it very good. And there was evening and there was morning, the sixth day.

2.

[1]The heaven and the earth were finished, and all their array. [2]On the seventh day God finished the work which He had been doing, and He ceased on the seventh day from all the work which He had done. [3]And God blessed the seventh day and declared it holy, because on it God ceased from all the work of creation which He had done.

Questions for Discussion

1. If anyone in the class knows Hebrew well enough to read the original, ask him or her to bring the Torah and talk about other possible translations of passages that seem puzzling.

2. Do you see any logical order in the sequence of what God creates? How would that sequence compare with what you have been told in your biology classes?

3. If you believe that Genesis is completely "mythical," discuss what might be meant by that belief. Is the account fictional in the sense that a novel is? If so, why should so many people have treated it as sacred?

4. Read the next three chapters in either the Old Testament or the Torah. If you were to imagine that they were written in our own time, by a single author who was trying to account for "how things began," what problem or problems about the nature of our world would you say he or she was trying to solve?

5. In many regions of America today there are heated battles between "creationists" and "evolutionists." Usually such battles, whether in courtrooms, popular magazines, or scholarly journals, reveal that neither side fully appreciates the case made by the opponents. What is considered evidence by one side is dismissed as irrelevant or false by the other. If there are proponents and opponents of these views in your class, discuss the kinds of reasons that might be counted as evidence by *both* groups.

Suggested Essay Topics

1. Read in an encyclopedia about the history of translations of the Bible. Then compare our two translations in detail, remembering that ultimately they come from the same Hebrew original. If you discern any patterns of difference in emphasis or meaning, write an essay attempting to account for them. Don't think that you must speak as a biblical scholar. Your task

is not to provide a comparative linguistic or historical account but a rhetorical account. That is, analyze what seem to be different *effects* that different wordings in each translation aim at, and try to reconstruct a picture of the kind of audience that the translators must have had in mind.

2. Write an essay directed to anyone you are fairly sure will initially disagree with you, defending your view of the creation story in Genesis. Whether you view it as literal truth, as poetic myth, as allegory, or as primitive intuition, explain why you think your view is credible, and try to make it as convincing as possible to someone with an opposing view.

Edith Hamilton

Edith Hamilton (1867–1963) was one of the world's leading authorities on Greco-Roman civilization. In a life that spanned nearly a century, she did not publish her first book, The Greek Way, *until she was 63. When she was 90, in a ceremony conducted in the amphitheater of Herodes Atticus at the foot of the Athenian Acropolis, she was made an honorary citizen of Greece, in recognition of her contribution and devotion to classical studies.*

In this essay Hamilton defends the position that even in the modern world, which seems on the surface to be so far removed from the world of classical antiquity, we need not only to be educated about the Greeks but also to be educated by them. Like us, they valued freedom, and their freedom, like ours, was threatened by forces pressing from within and without.

We can be educated by *the Greeks if we study the spirit, the values, and the attitudes that motivated them to create and preserve a free society in the first place. By educating ourselves* about *the Greeks, about their failures and eventual fall from greatness, we can gain some insight into the causes that may cause us also to lose strength and purpose.*

In Hamilton's view, one of the most important things the Greeks can teach us is what kind of education fosters and preserves a free society. Our education differs markedly from the Greeks', and the contrast gives us much to think about. The Greeks understood, Hamilton argues, that a free society depends on a free spirit among its people, among individuals. Thus they directed education toward the cultivation of certain qualities and powers in individuals, *on the assumption that individuals are of intrinsic worth in and of themselves. Greek education did not merely attempt to provide job skills, for the Greeks knew that no amount of professional skill could compensate for a lack of independent spirit and flexible intelligence. Every citizen was educated, says Pericles (the ruler who led Athens at the height of its glory), not to become a cog in the social machine and not to increase the gross national product but "to meet life's chances and changes with the utmost versatility and grace" (¶23).*

Almost all historians believe that a knowledge of the past can enable us to face the problems of the present with deeper understanding, heightened sensitivity, and clearer heads. As you consider the contrasts and similarities that Hamilton lays out between our society and that of the Greeks, between their education and your own, consider also whether the knowledge you thus acquire about the past suggests to you any concrete recommendations for curing the ills of the present, whether in education or in society generally.

THE EVER-PRESENT PAST

First appeared in *The Saturday Evening Post* in 1958 as "The Lessons of the Past"; reprinted under the present title in *The Ever-Present Past* (1964).

Is there an ever-present past? Are there permanent truths which are forever   1
important for the present? Today we are facing a future more strange and
untried than any other generation has faced. The new world Columbus
opened seems small indeed beside the illimitable distances of space before us,
and the possibilities of destruction are immeasurably greater than ever. In
such a position can we afford to spend time on the past? That is the question
I am often asked. Am I urging the study of the Greeks and Romans and their
civilizations for the atomic age?

Yes; that is just what I am doing. I urge it without qualifications. We   2
have a great civilization to save—or to lose. The greatest civilization before
ours was the Greek. They challenge us and we need the challenge. They, too,
lived in a dangerous world. They were a little, highly civilized people, the
only civilized people in the west, surrounded by barbarous tribes and with
the greatest Asiatic power, Persia, always threatening them. In the end they
succumbed, but the reason they did was not that the enemies outside were
so strong, but that their own strength, their spiritual strength, had given way.
While they had it they kept Greece unconquered and they left behind a
record in art and thought which in all the centuries of human effort since has
not been surpassed.

The point which I want to make is not that their taste was superior to   3
ours, not that the Parthenon was their idea of church architecture nor that
Sophocles was the great drawing card in the theaters, nor any of the familiar
comparisons between fifth-century Athens and twentieth-century America,
but that Socrates found on every street corner and in every Athenian equivalent of the baseball field people who were caught up by his questions into
the world of thought. To be able to be caught up into the world of thought—
that is to be educated.

How is that great aim to be reached? For years we have eagerly dis-   4
cussed ways and means of education, and the discussion still goes on. William
James once said that there were two subjects which if mentioned made other
conversation stop and directed all eyes to the speaker. Religion was one and
education the other. Today Russia seems to come first, but education is still
emphatically the second. In spite of all the articles we read and all the

speeches we listen to about it, we want to know more; we feel deeply its importance.

There is today a clearly visible trend toward making it the aim of   5
education to defeat the Russians. That would be a sure way to defeat education. Genuine education is possible only when people realize that it has to do with persons, not with movements.

When I read educational articles it often seems to me that this important   6
side of the matter, the purely personal side, is not emphasized enough; the fact that it is so much more agreeable and interesting to be an educated person than not. The sheer pleasure of being educated does not seem to be stressed. Once long ago I was talking with Prof. Basil L. Gildersleeve of Johns Hopkins University, the greatest Greek scholar our country has produced. He was an old man and he had been honored everywhere, in Europe as well as in America. He was just back from a celebration held for him in Oxford. I asked him what compliment received in his long life had pleased him most. The question amused him and he laughed over it, but he thought too. Finally he said, "I believe it was when one of my students said, 'Professor, you have so much fun with your own mind.' " Robert Louis Stevenson said that a man ought to be able to spend two or three hours waiting for a train at a little country station when he was all alone and had nothing to read, and not be bored for a moment.

What is the education which can do this? What is the furniture which   7
makes the only place belonging absolutely to each one of us, the world within, a place where we like to go? I wish I could answer that question. I wish I could produce a perfect decorator's design warranted to make any interior lovely and interesting and stimulating; but, even if I could, sooner or later we would certainly try different designs. My point is only that while we must and should change the furniture, we ought to throw away old furniture very cautiously. It may turn out to be irreplaceable. A great deal was thrown away in the last generation or so, long enough ago to show some of the results. Furniture which had for centuries been foremost, we lightly, in a few years, discarded. The classics almost vanished from our field of education. That was a great change. Along with it came another. There is a marked difference between the writers of the past and the writers of today who have been educated without benefit of Greek and Latin. Is this a matter of cause and effect? People will decide for themselves, but I do not think anyone will question the statement that clear thinking is not the characteristic which distinguishes our literature today. We are more and more caught up by the unintelligible. People like it. This argues an inability to think, or, almost as bad, a disinclination to think.

Neither disposition marked the Greeks. They had a passion for thinking   8
things out, and they loved unclouded clarity of statement as well as of thought. The Romans did, too, in their degree. They were able to put an idea into an astonishingly small number of words without losing a particle of intelligibility. It is only of late, with a generation which has never had to deal with a Latin sentence, that we are being submerged in a flood of words,

words, words. It has been said that Lincoln at Gettysburg today would have begun in some such fashion as this: "Eight and seven-tenths decades ago the pioneer workers in this continental area implemented a new group based on an ideology of free boundaries and initial equality," and might easily have ended, "That political supervision of the integrated units, for the integrated units, by the integrated units, shall not become null and void on the superficial area of this planet." Along with the banishment of the classics, gobbledegook has come upon us—and the appalling size of the Congressional Record, and the overburdened mail service.

Just what the teaching in the schools was which laid the foundation of the Greek civilization we do not know in detail; the result we do know. Greek children were taught, Plato said, to "love what is beautiful and hate what is ugly." When they grew up their very pots and pans had to be pleasant to look at. It was part of their training to hate clumsiness and awkwardness; they loved grace and practiced it. "Our children," Plato said, "will be influenced for good by every sight and sound of beauty, breathing in, as it were, a pure breeze blowing to them from a good land."

All the same, the Athenians were not, as they showed Socrates when he talked to them, preoccupied with enjoying lovely things. The children were taught to think. Plato demanded a stiff examination, especially in mathematics, for entrance to his Academy. The Athenians were a thinking people. Today the scientists are bearing away the prize for thought. Well, a Greek said that the earth went around the sun, sixteen centuries before Copernicus thought of it. A Greek said if you sailed out of Spain and kept to one latitude, you would come at last to land, seventeen hundred years before Columbus did it. Darwin said, "We are mere schoolboys in scientific thinking compared to old Aristotle." And the Greeks did not have a great legacy from the past as our scientists have; they thought science out from the beginning.

The same is true of politics. They thought that out, too, from the beginning, and they gave all the boys a training to fit them to be thinking citizens of a free state that had come into being through thought.

Basic to all the Greek achievement was freedom. The Athenians were the only free people in the world. In the great empires of antiquity—Egypt, Babylon, Assyria, Persia—splendid though they were, with riches beyond reckoning and immense power, freedom was unknown. The idea of it never dawned in any of them. It was born in Greece, a poor little country, but with it able to remain unconquered no matter what manpower and what wealth were arrayed against her. At Marathon and at Salamis overwhelming numbers of Persians had been defeated by small Greek forces. It had been proved that one free man was superior to many submissively obedient subjects of a tyrant. Athens was the leader in that amazing victory, and to the Athenians freedom was their dearest possession. Demosthenes said that they would not think it worth their while to live if they could not do so as free men, and years later a great teacher said, "Athenians, if you deprive them of their liberty, will die."

Athens was not only the first democracy in the world, it was also at its   13
height an almost perfect democracy—that is, for men. There was no part in
it for women or foreigners or slaves, but as far as the men were concerned
it was more democratic than we are. The governing body was the Assembly,
of which all citizens over eighteen were members. The Council of Five Hundred, which prepared business for the Assembly and, if requested, carried out
what had been decided there, was made up of citizens who were chosen by
lot. The same was true of the juries. Minor officials also were chosen by lot.
The chief magistrates and the highest officers in the army were elected by the
Assembly. Pericles was a general, very popular, who acted for a long time as
if he were head of the state, but he had to be elected every year. Freedom of
speech was the right the Athenians prized most and there has never been
another state as free in that respect. When toward the end of the terrible
Peloponnesian War the victorious Spartans were advancing upon Athens,
Aristophanes caricatured in the theater the leading Athenian generals and
showed them up as cowards, and even then as the Assembly opened, the
herald asked, "Does anyone wish to speak?"

There was complete political equality. It was a government of the peo-   14
ple, by the people, for the people. An unregenerate old aristocrat in the early
fourth century, B.C., writes: "If you *must* have a democracy, Athens is the
perfect example. I object to it because it is based on the welfare of the lower,
not the better, classes. In Athens the people who row the vessels and do the
work have the advantage. It is their prosperity that is important." All the
same, making the city beautiful was important too, as were also the great
performances in the theater. If, as Plato says, the Assembly was chiefly made
up of cobblers and carpenters and smiths and farmers and retail-business
men, they approved the construction of the Parthenon and the other buildings on the Acropolis, and they crowded the theater when the great tragedies
were played. Not only did all free men share in the government; the love of
the beautiful and the desire to have a part in creating it were shared by the
many, not by a mere chosen few. That has happened in no state except
Athens.

But those free Greeks owned slaves. What kind of freedom was that?   15
The question would have been incomprehensible to the ancient world. There
had always been slaves; they were a first necessity. The way of life everywhere was based upon them. They were taken for granted; no one ever gave
them a thought. The very best Greek minds, the thinkers who discovered
freedom and the solar system, had never an idea that slavery was evil. It is
true that the greatest thinker of them all, Plato, was made uncomfortable by
it. He said that slaves were often good, trustworthy, doing more for a man
than his own family would, but he did not follow his thought through. The
glory of being the first one to condemn it belongs to a man of the generation
before Plato, the poet Euripides. He called it "that thing of evil," and in
several of his tragedies showed its evil for all to see. A few centuries later the
great Greek school of the Stoics denounced it. Greece first saw it for what it

is. But the world went on in the same way. The Bible accepts it without comment. Two thousand years after the Stoics, less than a hundred years ago, the American Republic accepted it.

Athens treated her slaves well. A visitor to the city in the early fourth 16 century, B.C., wrote: "It is illegal here to deal a slave a blow. In the street he won't step aside to let you pass. Indeed you can't tell a slave by his dress; he looks like all the rest. They can go to the theater too. Really, the Athenians have established a kind of equality between slaves and free men." They were never a possible source of danger to the state as they were in Rome. There were no terrible slave wars and uprisings in Athens. In Rome, crucifixion was called "the slave's punishment." The Athenians did not practice crucifixion, and had no so-called slave's punishment. They were not afraid of their slaves.

In Athens' great prime Athenians were free. No one told them what 17 they must do or what they should think—no church or political party or powerful private interests or labor unions. Greek schools had no donors of endowments they must pay attention to, no government financial backing which must be made secure by acting as the government wanted. To be sure, the result was that they had to take full responsibility, but that is always the price for full freedom. The Athenians were a strong people; they could pay the price. They were a thinking people; they knew what freedom means. They knew—not that they were free because their country was free, but that their country was free because they were free.

A reflective Roman traveling in Greece in the second century, A.D., said, 18 "None ever throve under democracy save the Athenians; *they* had sane self-control and were law-abiding." He spoke truly. That is what Athenian education aimed at, to produce men who would be able to maintain a self-governed state because they were themselves self-governed, self-controlled, self-reliant. Plato speaks of "the education in excellence which makes men long to be perfect citizens, knowing both how to rule and be ruled." "We are a free democracy," Pericles said. "We do not allow absorption in our own affairs to interfere with participation in the city's; we yield to none in independence of spirit and complete self-reliance, but we regard him who holds aloof from public affairs as useless." They called the useless man a "private" citizen, *idiotes*, from which our word "idiot" comes.

They had risen to freedom and to ennoblement from what Gilbert 19 Murray calls "effortless barbarism"; they saw it all around them; they hated its filth and fierceness; nothing effortless was among the good things they wanted. Plato said, "Hard is the good," and a poet hundreds of years before Plato said,

> Before the gates of Excellence the high gods have placed sweat.
> Long is the road thereto and steep and rough at the first,
> But when the height is won, then is there ease.

When or why the Greeks set themselves to travel on that road we do 20 not know, but it led them away from habits and customs accepted everywhere that kept men down to barbaric filth and fierceness. It led them far. One example is enough to show the way they took. It was the custom— during how many millenniums, who can say?—for a victor to erect a trophy, a monument of his victory. In Egypt, where stone was plentiful, it would be a slab engraved with his glories. Farther east, where the sand took over, it might be a great heap of severed heads, quite permanent objects; bones last a long time. But in Greece, though a man could erect a trophy, it must be made of wood and it could never be repaired. Even as the victor set it up he would see in his mind how soon it would decay and sink into ruin, and there it must be left. The Greeks in their onward pressing along the steep and rough road had learned a great deal. They knew the victor might be the vanquished next time. There should be no permanent records of the manifestly impermanent. They had learned a great deal.

An old Greek inscription states that the aim of mankind should be "to 21 tame the savageness of man and make gentle the life of the world." Aristotle said that the city was built first for safety, but then that men might discover the good life and lead it. So the Athenians did according to Pericles. Pericles said that Athens stood for freedom and for thought and for beauty, but in the Greek way, within limits, without exaggeration. The Athenians loved beauty, he said, but with simplicity; they did not like the extravagances of luxury. They loved the things of the mind, but they did not shrink from hardship. Thought did not cause them to hesitate; it clarified the road to action. If they had riches they did not make a show of them, and no one was ashamed of being poor if he was useful. They were free because of willing obedience to law, not only the written, but still more the unwritten, kindness and compassion and unselfishness and the many qualities which cannot be enforced, which depend on a man's free choice, but without which men cannot live together.

If ever there is to be a truly good and great and enduring republic it must 22 be along these lines. We need the challenge of the city that thought them out, wherein for centuries one genius after another grew up. Geniuses are not produced by spending money. We need the challenge of the way the Greeks were educated. They fixed their eyes on the individual. We contemplate millions. What we have undertaken in this matter of education has dawned upon us only lately. We are trying to do what has never been attempted before, never in the history of the world—educate all the young in a nation of 170 millions; a magnificent idea, but we are beginning to realize what are the problems and what may be the results of mass production of education. So far, we do not seem appalled at the prospect of exactly the same kind of education being applied to all the school children from the Atlantic to the Pacific, but there is an uneasiness in the air, a realization that the individual is growing less easy to find; an idea, perhaps, of what standardization might become when the units are not machines, but human beings.

Here is where we can go back to the Greeks with profit. The Athenians 23 in their dangerous world needed to be a nation of independent men who could take responsibility, and they taught their children accordingly. They thought about every boy. Someday he would be a citizen of Athens, responsible for her safety and her glory, "each one," Pericles said, "fitted to meet life's chances and changes with the utmost versatility and grace." To them education was by its very nature an individual matter. To be properly educated a boy had to be taught music; he learned to play a musical instrument. He had to learn poetry, a great deal of it, and recite it—and there were a number of musical instruments and many poets; though, to be sure, Homer was the great textbook.

That kind of education is not geared to mass production. It does not 24 produce people who instinctively go the same way. That is how Athenian children lived and learned while our millions learn the same lessons and spend hours before television sets looking at exactly the same thing at exactly the same time. For one reason and another we are more and more ignoring differences, if not trying to obliterate them. We seem headed toward a standardization of the mind, what Goethe called "the deadly commonplace that fetters us all." That was not the Greek way.

The picture of the Age of Pericles drawn by the historian Thucydides, 25 one of the greatest historians the world has known, is of a state made up of people who are self-reliant individuals, not echoes or copies, who want to be let alone to do their own work, but who are also closely bound together by a great aim, the commonweal, each one so in love with his country—Pericles' own words—that he wants most of all to use himself in her service. Only an ideal? Ideals have enormous power. They stamp an age. They lift life up when they are lofty; they drag down and make decadent when they are low—and then, by that strange fact, the survival of the fittest, those that are low fade away and are forgotten. The Greek ideals have had a power of persistent life for twenty-five hundred years.

Is it rational that now when the young people may have to face prob- 26 lems harder than we face, is it reasonable that with the atomic age before them, at this time we are giving up the study of how the Greeks and Romans prevailed magnificently in a barbaric world; the study, too, of how that triumph ended, how a slackness and softness finally came over them to their ruin? In the end, more than they wanted freedom, they wanted security, a comfortable life, and they lost all—security and comfort and freedom.

Is not that a challenge to us? Is it not true that into our education have 27 come a slackness and softness? Is hard effort prominent? The world of thought can be entered in no other way. Are we not growing slack and soft in our political life? When the Athenians finally wanted not to give to the state, but the state to give to them, when the freedom they wished most for was freedom from responsibility, then Athens ceased to be free and was never free again. Is not that a challenge?

Cicero said, "To be ignorant of the past is to remain a child." Santayana 28 said, "A nation that does not know history is fated to repeat it." The Greeks can help us, help us as no other people can, to see how freedom is won and how it is lost. Above all, to see in clearest light what freedom is. The first nation in the world to be free sends a ringing call down through the centuries to all who would be free. Greece rose to the very height, not because she was big, she was very small; not because she was rich, she was very poor; not even because she was wonderfully gifted. So doubtless were others in the great empires of the ancient world who have gone their way leaving little for us. She rose because there was in the Greeks the greatest spirit that moves in humanity, the spirit that sets men free.

Plato put into words what that spirit is. "Freedom" he says, "is no 29 matter of laws and constitutions; only he is free who realizes the divine order within himself, the true standard by which a man can steer and measure himself." True standards, ideals that lift life up, marked the way of the Greeks. Therefore their light has never been extinguished.

"The time for extracting a lesson from history is ever at hand for them 30 who are wise." Demosthenes.

Questions for Discussion

1. Hamilton defines being educated as being "able to be caught up into the world of thought" (¶3). What do you think she means by being "caught up"? How does her meaning compare with Whitehead's definition in "The Aims of Education" that "education is the acquisition of the art of the utilization of knowledge" (p. 36, ¶11)?

2. According to Hamilton, the use of one's mind should be a pleasure in itself; she alludes to Robert Louis Stevenson's remark that "a man ought to be able to spend two or three hours waiting for a train at a little country station when he was all alone and had nothing to read, and not be bored for a moment" (¶6). How often do you sit down to think about something, not to daydream or lapse into random thoughts but to concentrate on an issue, topic, or idea? Do you know people who do this? Do you know anyone who seems afraid of the silence that invites thought, who requires the sound of records, television, radio, or friends to fill up the space that might otherwise be threatened by thinking?

3. Is your education enlarging your capacity for sustained thought? Are you being given both things to think *about* and methods to think *by*? Do you find yourself mulling over the ideas from your classes—or, better yet, discussing them with friends—as if they had applications and importance outside of the requirements for the course? If not, do you think this is what you *should be* getting? What are the obstacles preventing it?

4. When Athenian democracy was strong, Hamilton argues, it was strong because citizens generally—both rich and poor, noble and common—*took responsibility* for preserving it (¶17–18). Can you find examples in American society that suggest what happens to democracy when freedom *without* responsibility becomes the aim? Is it your impression that Americans

generally are willing to be responsible for making democracy work? If you think they are not willing, what do you think might account for their unwillingness?

Suggested Essay Topics

1. "In the end, more than they [the Greeks] wanted freedom, they wanted security, a comfortable life, and they lost all—security and comfort and freedom" (¶26). When college students are asked today why they go to college, they frequently cite comfort and security—a good job and a comfortable life—as their reasons for attending college. They seldom say that they want an education in order to make their contribution to freedom and democracy. In an essay or letter directed to Edith Hamilton, defend the goals of today's college students. Counter her claim that an education should be directed toward the cultivation of general powers rather than specific skills, and, since you are rejecting her claim that education helps preserve freedom, make clear what you think does help preserve it and what kind of responsibility that preservation places on individual citizens.

2. Take the opposite position from that of topic 1: In an essay directed to students you know who are bent on education for security and comfort, extend Hamilton's argument that today's education is slack and soft (¶27) and makes no real contribution to freedom in our society. Illustrate her argument with examples from trends in education generally, but especially with examples from your own education (both now and in the past). Contrast the aims of the education you have been given with the aims that Hamilton says guided Greek education—the cultivation of a sense of beauty, proportion, personal grace, excellence, and independent thought— and point out in detail where you think your education has been slack and soft. Make any recommendations you think appropriate.

IDEAS IN DEBATE

Pieter Geyl and Arnold J. Toynbee

Pieter Geyl and Arnold J. Toynbee

*F*ew scholarly works have produced as much debate as Arnold J. Toynbee's Study of History. *Toynbee's massive comparative study of the world's civilizations continues to engage scholars in lively discussions like the one we reprint here, between historian Pieter Geyl and Toynbee himself. And in its time the* Study *provoked unusual debate among general readers. Despite its bulk—the first volume was published in 1934 and the twelfth volume completed the work in 1961—the* Study *was a steady best-seller in the years following World War II.*

Two theses in particular provoked debate among Toynbee's readers. First, Toynbee claimed that all 21 of what he considered the world's major past civilizations (each of which he studied in great detail) exhibited a common pattern in their rise and fall. Each of them began, he said, when some great threat or challenge produced a grand unified response. Working together to overcome apparently insuperable problems, men and women managed, at least 21 times in world history, to create great civilizations. But then, in every case, the spiritual center decayed, social forms fell apart, and the civilization collapsed. Though many readers were exhilarated by the offer of such a unified view of human history, many others (like Pieter Geyl in the exchange that follows) were skeptical about any effort to discern a pattern shared by all civilizations in all periods.

Even more controversial was Toynbee's second claim, that Western civilization has for a long time been on the "falling" side of the curve. Some readers saw Toynbee as saying that we have lost our spiritual center and that individuals can therefore do nothing to prevent the final collapse of our civilization. As you will see in the discussion reprinted here, Toynbee explicitly denied that his view was finally pessimistic; through a spiritual rebirth we might still have a chance to reverse the downward spiral.

The debate we print here is part of a report on a conference, held about midway through Toynbee's prolonged labors, to discuss his first six volumes. In his prepared paper for the conference, Pieter Geyl said,

> I can . . . have little confidence . . . that Professor Toynbee, when later on he undertakes a set examination of our civilization and its prospects, will prove able to enlighten our perplexities; or should I not rather say that we need not let ourselves be frightened by his darkness? We need not accept his view that the whole of modern history from the sixteenth century on has been nothing but a downward course, following the path of rout and rally. We need not let ourselves

*be shaken in our confidence that the future lies open before us, that in the midst
of misery and confusion such as have so frequently occurred in history, we still
dispose of forces no less valuable than those by which earlier generations have
managed to struggle through their troubles.*

*What we print here is a record of the more informal debate that followed the
formal papers. We have no way of knowing how much revision Professors Toynbee
and Geyl gave to their spoken words, but they have clearly kept a tone of spoken
interchange. You may have noticed that most people who debate in public "talk past"
each other most of the time, changing their opponents' points, deliberately or unconsciously, to points that are more easily crushed or dismissed. As you read this debate,
try to determine whether Toynbee and Geyl commit this kind of distortion or manage
really to understand each other. Are Geyl's points the ones that Toynbee answers?
If you had the words of only one of the speakers, would you be able to give a fair account
of the other speaker's views? To answer that question you will of course need to attend
not only to both speakers' conclusions but to the supporting reasons they offer as well.*

CAN WE KNOW THE PATTERN OF THE PAST?

*A Discussion Between Pieter Geyl
and Arnold J. Toynbee*

From Pieter Geyl, Arnold J. Toynbee, and Pitirim Sorokin, *The Pattern of the Past: Can We Determine
It?* (1949).

PROFESSOR GEYL

The six volumes of Toynbee's *Study of History* appeared before the war, but it   1
is since the war that the book and the author have become famous. A generation only just recovering from the terrible experiences of the war and already
anxious about the future, is reading the work in the hope of finding in its
pages the answer to its perplexities. It is indeed the author's claim to discover
for us, in the at first sight chaotic and confusing spectacle of human history,
a pattern, a rhythm. . . .

I must come straight to the main features of the system. Has Toynbee   2
proved that the histories of civilizations fall into these sharply marked stages
of growth and disintegration, separated by breakdown? Has he proved that
the work of the creative minds, or of the creative minorities, can be successful
only in the first stage and that in the second it is doomed to remain so much
fruitless effort?

In my opinion he has not. How do I know that the difference is caused   3
by the triumphant creator acting in a growing society, and the hopelessly
struggling one in a society in disintegration? I have not been convinced of the
essential difference between the phases of civilization. There are evil tendencies and there are good tendencies simultaneously present at every stage of

human history, and the human intellect is not sufficiently comprehensive to weigh them off against each other and to tell, before the event, which is to have the upper hand. As for the theory that the individual leader, or the leading minority, is capable of creative achievement in a growing society only and doomed to disappointment in one that is in disintegration—that theory lapses automatically when the distinction is not admitted in the absolute form in which our author propounds it.

I am glad that you are present here, Toynbee, and going to reply. For this is surely a point of great practical importance. *A Study of History* does not definitely announce ruin as did Spengler's book* by its very title. But in more than one passage you give us to understand that Western civilization broke down as long ago as the sixteenth century, as a result of the wars of religion. The last four centuries of our history would thus, according to your system, be one long process of disintegration, with collapse as the inevitable end— except for the miracle of a reconversion to the faith of our fathers. 4

There is no doubt, when we look around us, a great deal to induce gloom. But I do not see any reason why history should be read so as to deepen our sense of uneasiness into a mood of hopelessness. Earlier generations have also had their troubles and have managed to struggle through. There is nothing in history to shake our confidence that the future lies open before us. 5

PROFESSOR TOYNBEE

The fate of the world—the destiny of mankind—*is* involved in the issue between us about the nature of history. 6

In replying to Professor Geyl now, I am going to concentrate on what, to my mind, are his two main lines of attack. One of his general criticisms is: "Toynbee's view of history induces gloom." The other is: "Toynbee has set himself to do something impossible. He is trying to make sense of human history, and that is beyond the capacity of the human mind." I will pay most attention to this second point, because it is, I am sure, by far the more important of the two. 7

Let me try to dispose of the "gloom" point first. Suppose my view of history did point to a gloomy conclusion, what of it? "Gloomy" and "cheerful" are one thing, "true" and "false" quite another. 8

Professor Geyl has interpreted me rightly in telling you that I have pretty serious misgivings about the state of the world today. Don't you feel the same misgivings? Doesn't Professor Geyl feel them? That surely goes without saying. But what doesn't go without saying is what we are going to do about it; and here Professor Geyl has been handsome to me in telling you where I stand. He has told you that I disbelieve in predestination and am at 9

Der Untergang des Abendlandes, 2 vols. (1918–1922); translated as *The Decline of the West* (1926–1928). Oswald Spengler (1880–1936) made himself internationally famous with a thesis in some ways similar to Toynbee's, but by the time Toynbee was writing, most professional historians were inclined to dismiss Spengler's claim about the *inevitable* decline of the Western world as what Toynbee calls "dogmatic determinism" (¶28).

the opposite pole, on that supremely important question, from the famous
German philosopher Spengler. He has told you that my outlook is the reverse
of historical materialism; that, in my view, the process of civilization is one
of vanquishing the material problems to grapple with the spiritual ones; that
I am a believer in free will; in man's freedom to respond with all his heart
and soul and mind when life presents him with a challenge. Well, that is what
I do believe. But how, I ask you, can one lift up one's heart and apply one's
mind unless one does one's best to find out the relevant facts and to look them
in the face?—the formidable facts as well as the encouraging ones.

In the state of the world today, the two really formidable facts, as I see   10
them, are that the other civilizations that we know of have all broken down,
and that in our recent history one sees some of those tendencies which, in the
histories of the broken-down civilizations, have been the obvious symptoms
of breakdown. But what's the moral? Surely not to shy at the facts. Professor
Geyl himself admits them. And also, surely, not to be daunted by the "sense of
uneasiness" which these formidable facts are bound to give us. "I don't see any
reason," said Professor Geyl just now, "why history should be read so as to
deepen our sense of uneasiness into a mood of hopelessness." That is a telling
criticism of Spengler, who does diagnose that our civilization is doomed, and
who has nothing better to suggest than that we should fold our hands and
await the inevitable blow of the axe. But that ball doesn't take my wicket, for
in my view, as Geyl has told you, uneasiness is a challenging call to action, and
not a death sentence to paralyze our wills. Thank goodness we do know the
fates of the other civilizations; such knowledge is a chart that warns us of the
reefs ahead. Knowledge can be power and salvation if we have the spirit to use
it. There is a famous Greek epigram which runs: "I am the tomb of a ship-
wrecked sailor, but don't let that frighten off you, brother mariner, from
setting sail; because, when we went down, the other ships kept afloat."

"There is nothing in history," said Professor Geyl in his closing sen-   11
tence, "to shake our confidence that the future lies open before us." Those
might have been my own words, but I don't quite see what warrant Professor
Geyl has for using them. The best comfort Professor Geyl can give us is: "If
we take care not to unnerve ourselves by trying to chart the seas, we may be
lucky enough to get by without hitting the rocks." No, I haven't painted him
quite black enough, for his view is still gloomier than that. "To make a chart
of history," he says, "is a sheer impossibility." Professor Geyl's own chart,
you see, is the "perfect and absolute blank" of Lewis Carroll's bellman who
hunted the snark. Geyl, too, has a chart, like Spengler and me. We all of us
have one, whether we own up to it or not, and no chart is more than one man's
shot at the truth. But surely, of those three, the blank is the most useless and
the most dangerous.

Professor Geyl thinks I am a pessimist because I see a way of escape in   12
a reconversion to the faith of our fathers. "This," says Professor Geyl, "is an
unnecessarily gloomy view of our situation"—like the old lady who was
advised to leave it to Providence and exclaimed: "Oh dear, has it come to
that?"

What was our fathers' chart of history? As they saw it, it was a tale told by God, unfolding itself from the Creation through the Fall and the Redemption to the Last Judgment. As Professor Geyl says he sees it, it seems like a tale told by an idiot, signifying nothing. You may not agree with our fathers' view that history is a revelation of God's providence; but it is a poor exchange, isn't it, to swap their faith for the view that history makes no sense. [13]

Of course, Professor Geyl is no more singular in his view than I am in mine. What one may call the nonsense view of history has been fashionable among Western historians for the last few generations. The odd thing is that some of the holders of this view—I don't know whether I could count Professor Geyl among the number—defend it principally on the ground that it is scientific. Of course, it is only human that historians should have wanted to be scientific in an age when science has been enjoying such prestige. I am, myself, a historian who believes that science has an awful lot to teach us. But how strange to suppose that one is being scientific by despairing of making sense! For what is science? It is only another name for the careful and scrupulous use of the human mind. And, if men despair of reason, they are lost. Nature hasn't given us wings, fur, claws, antennae or elephant's trunks; but she has given us the human intellect—the most effective of all implements, if we are not too timid to use it. And what does this scientific intellect do? It looks at the facts, but it doesn't stop there. It looks at the facts and it tries to make sense of them. It does, you see, the very thing that Professor Geyl takes me to task for trying to do with the facts of history. [14]

Is history really too hard a nut for science to crack? When the human intellect has wrested her secret from physical nature, are we going to sit down under an *ex cathedra* dictum that the ambition to discover the secret of human history will always be bound to end in disappointment? We don't need to be told that Man is a harder—a very much harder—nut than the atom. We have discovered how to split the atom and are in danger of splitting it to our own destruction. By comparison with the science of physics, the science of man is so difficult that our discoveries in the two fields have gone forward at an uneven pace till they have got quite out of step with each other. It is partly this that has got us into our present fix. Is science to shirk trying to do anything about it? "The proper study of mankind is man," says Pope. "The human intellect," sighs Geyl, "is not sufficiently comprehensive." [15]

I say: We can't afford such defeatism; it is unworthy of the greatness of man's mind; and it is refuted by the human mind's past achievements. The mind has won all its great victories by well-judged boldness. And today, before our eyes, science is launching a characteristically bold offensive in what is now the key area of the mental battlefield. Why, she has got her nutcrackers round this nut, this human nut, already. One arm of the pincers is the exciting young science of psychology, which is opening out entirely new mental horizons for us, in the very direction in which we are most in need of longer vistas. The other is the forbidding yet rewarding discipline of statistics. Science has set herself now in good earnest to comprehend human nature, and, through understanding, to show it how to master itself and [16] thereby to set itself free. Science, so long preoccupied with the riddles of non-human nature, has now joined in the quests of philosophy and religion, and this diversion of her energies has been timely. There is, indeed, no time to be lost. We are in for a life-and-death struggle. And, at this critical hour, is science to get no support from our professedly scientific historians?

Well, in this "mental fight," I have deliberately risked my neck by   17 putting my own reading of the facts of history on the table. I should never dream of claiming that my particular interpretation is the only one possible. There are, I am sure, many different alternative ways of analyzing history, each of which is true in itself and illuminating as far as it goes, just as, in dissecting an organism, you can throw light on its nature by laying bare either the skeleton or the muscles or the nerves or the circulation of the blood. No single one of these dissections tells the whole truth, but each of them reveals a genuine facet of it. I should be well content if it turned out that I had laid bare one genuine facet of history, and even then, I should measure my success by the speed with which my own work in my own line was put out of date by further work by other people in the same field. In the short span of one lifetime, the personal contribution of the individual scholar to the great and growing stream of knowledge can't be more than a tiny pailful. But if he could inspire—or provoke—other scholars to pour in their pailfuls too, well, then he could feel that he had really done his job. And this job of making sense of history is one of the crying needs of our day—I beg of you, believe me.

PROFESSOR GEYL

Well I must say, Toynbee, that I felt some anxiety while you were pouring   18 out over me this torrent of eloquence, wit and burning conviction, but that was of course what I had to expect from you. And now that it is over I'm relieved to feel that I'm still there, and my position untouched.

Professor Toynbee pictures me as one of those men who mistake the   19 courage to see evils for gloom, and who when others sound the call for action take refuge from the dangers of our time in an illusionist optimism. But have I been saying that we are not in danger? And that no action is required? What I have said is that Toynbee's system induces the wrong kind of gloom because it tends to make action seem useless. "But I am a believer in man's free will," Toynbee replies. I know. But nevertheless, his system lays it down that the civilization which has been overtaken by a breakdown is doomed. Now Toynbee has repeatedly suggested that our Western civilization did suffer a breakdown as long ago as the sixteenth century, and that consequently, try as we may, we cannot avoid disaster. Except in one way, except in case we allow ourselves to be reconverted to the faith of our fathers. And here Toynbee exclaims: "You see, I'm not so gloomy after all." Perhaps not. But if one happens to hold a different opinion both of the efficacy and of the likelihood of application of his particular remedy, one cannot help thinking that Toynbee is but offering us cold comfort. He talks as if we cannot advance matters by "so hotly canvassing and loudly advertising," as he contemptuously puts it, "our political and economic maladies." It is the loss of religious faith that is the deadly danger. To most of us this is indeed condemning all our efforts to futility.

Of course, Toynbee, it is only your picturesque way of putting things when you describe me as one of those historians who cling to the nonsense view of history. Because I cannot accept either your methods or your system it does not follow that to my mind history has no meaning. I do not believe that at any time it will be possible to reduce the past to so rigid a pattern as to enable us to forecast the future—granted. Yet to me, as to you, the greatest function of the historian is to interpret the past—to find sense in it, although at the same time it is the least scientific, the most inevitably subjective of his functions.

I am surprised that you class me with those historians who believe that their view of history rests securely on scientific foundations. In fact it is you who claim to be proceeding on the lines of empiricism towards laws of universal validity, while I have been suggesting that these and other scientific terms which you are fond of using have no real meaning in a historical argument. Even just now, didn't you deduce from the conquest of the mystery of the atom the certainty that man's mind will be able to conquer the mystery of the historical process as well? In my opinion these are fundamentally different propositions.

Let me remind you especially of what I have been saying about the uncertain nature of historical events, and the difficulty of detaching them from their contexts. And also of my contention that the cases and instances strewn over your pages have been arbitrarily selected from an infinite number and haven't therefore that value as evidence which you attach to them.

PROFESSOR TOYNBEE

There can be no doubt that you look upon this last point as an important one. . . . I see what you're getting at. I set out to deal with history in terms of civilizations, of which there are, of course, very few specimens, but in the illustrations I give, and the points I make, I don't confine myself to these rare big fellows, I hop about all over the place, bringing up as illustrations of my points events on a much smaller scale, which to you seem to be chosen arbitrarily, because they're just a few taken out of a large number. They also, as you point out, lend themselves to more interpretations than one. Yes, I think that's fair criticism, and quite telling. In answer I'd say two things. I think, as I said a minute or two ago, the same historical event often can be analyzed legitimately in a number of different ways, each of which brings out some aspect of historical truth which is true as far as it goes, though not the whole truth. I have myself sometimes made the same historical event do double or treble duty in this way, and I don't think this is a misleading way of using facts. As I've said before, several different dissections can all be correct, each in its own line.

My second point is that I bring in these illustrations taken from the small change of history, not for their own sake but to throw indirect light on the big units, which I call civilizations, which are my main concern. I helped myself out in this way because, in the very early stage in human history in which our generation happens to be living, the number of civilizations that have come into existence up to date, is still so small—not more than about twenty, as I make it out.

To take up the case of your own country, Holland, now, which I have 25 used to throw light on the rise of the Egyptian and Sumerian civilizations: you challenged my account of Holland's rise to greatness. I found my explanation of it in the stimulus of a hard country. The people of Holland had to wrest the country from the sea and they rose to the occasion. Your criticism is that I've arbitrarily isolated one fact out of several. The Dutch, you say, didn't do it by themselves, they were helped at the start by efficient outsiders, and then the country, when it had been reclaimed, turned out to have a rich soil, as well as a good situation for commerce.

Yes, of course, those are also facts of Dutch history, but my answer is 26 that they're not the key facts. If the outsiders that you have in mind are the Romans, well, the benefits of Roman efficiency were not enjoyed by Holland alone; Belgium, France and England enjoyed them as well. So Holland's Roman apprenticeship won't account for achievements that are special to Holland and that distinguish her from her neighbors. Then the fertile soil and good location: these aren't causes of Holland's great feat of fighting and beating the North Sea, they're effects and rewards of it. It is a case of "to him that hath, shall be given." What the Dutch had, before these other things were given them, was the strength of will to raise their country out of the waters. The terrific challenge of the sea to a country below sea level is surely the unique and distinguishing feature of Dutch history. With all deference to you, Geyl, as a Netherlander and a historian, I still think I'm right in picking out the response of the people of Holland to this challenge as being the key to the greatness of your country. I do also think that the case of Holland throws valuable light on the cases of Egypt and Babylonia, two other places where people have had to fight swamp and sea in order to reclaim land, and where this struggle between man and nature has brought to life two out of the twenty or so civilizations known to us.

Of course if one could lay hands on some more civilizations, one might 27 be able to study history on that scale without having to bother about little bits and pieces like Holland and England. I wish I were in that happy position, and if you now, Geyl, would help me by taking up your archeological spade and unearthing a few more forgotten civilizations for me, I should be vastly obliged to you. But even if you proved yourself a Layard, Schliemann and Arthur Evans rolled into one, you could only raise my present figure of twenty-one known civilizations to twenty-four, and that of course wouldn't help me to reduce my margin of error appreciably.

To turn for a moment to a different point, I want to correct an impression 28 that I think our listeners may have got, of something else that you were saying just now. Anyway, I got the impression myself that you still thought I claimed to be able to foretell the future from the past, that I'd laid it down that our own civilization was doomed. This is a very important point and I want to make my position on it clear beyond all possibility of mistake. So let me repeat: I don't set up to be a prophet, I don't believe history can be used for telling the world's fortune, I think history can perhaps sometimes show one possibilities or even probabilities, but never certainties. With the awful warning of Spengler's dogmatic determinism before my eyes, I always have been and shall be mighty careful, for my part, to treat the future of our own civilization as an open question—not at all because I'm afraid of committing myself, but because I believe as strongly as you do, Geyl, that it *is* an open question.

PROFESSOR GEYL

Well I'm glad, Toynbee, that you've taken so seriously the objections I've 29 made to the profusion of illustrations from national histories. As to the case of Holland, let me just say that I was not thinking of the Romans only and not even of foreigners primarily. What I meant was that Netherlands civilization did not have its origin or earliest development in the region which was exposed to the struggle with the water, but, on the contrary, this region could be described as a backward part of the Netherlands area as a whole. And as regards the future, in one place of your book you are very near to drawing—as you put it—"the horoscope of our civilization" from the fates of other civilizations, and you suggest repeatedly that we have got into the disintegration stage, which you picture to us so elaborately in your book as leading inevitably to catastrophe. I'm glad to hear now that you did not in fact mean to pass an absolute sentence of death over us.

PROFESSOR TOYNBEE

No, I think we simply don't know. I suppose I must be the last judge of what 30 my own beliefs are.

But now, Geyl, here is a ball I'd like for a change to bowl at you. You've 31 given me an opening by the fair-mindedness and frankness you've shown all through our debate. You've done justice to my contention that while historical facts are in some respects unique, there are other respects in which they belong to a class and are therefore comparable. There is truth, you say, in this, otherwise no general ideas about history could ever be formed, but isolating the comparable elements is ticklish work. It certainly is ticklish work. I speak with feeling from long experience in trying to do precisely that job. But may there not be a moral in this for you and every other historian as well as for me? May not it mean that we ought all of us to give far more time and far more serious and strenuous thought than many of us have ever given to this job of forming one's general ideas? And there is a previous and, to my mind, more important job to be done before that.

We've first to bring into consciousness our existing ideas and to put 32 these trump cards of ours face upwards on the table. All historians are bound, you see, to have general ideas about history. On this point, every stitch of work they do is so much evidence against them. Without ideas, they couldn't think a thought, speak a sentence or write a line on their subjects. Ideas are the machine tools of the mind, and, wherever you see a thought being thrown out, you may be certain that there is an idea at the back of it. This is so obvious that I find it hard to have patience with historians who boast, as some modern Western historians do, that they keep entirely to the facts of history and don't go in for theories. Why, every so-called fact that they present to you had some pattern of theory behind it. Historians who genuinely believe they have no general ideas about history are, I would suggest to them, simply ignorant of the workings of their own minds, and such wilful ignorance is, isn't it, really unpardonable. The intellectual worker who refuses to let himself become aware of the working ideas with which he is operating seems to me to be about as great a criminal as the motorist who first closes his eyes and then steps on the gas. To leave oneself and one's public at the mercy of any fool ideas, if they happen to have taken possession of one's unconscious, is surely the height of intellectual irresponsibility.

I believe our listeners would be very much interested to hear what you 33 say about that.

PROFESSOR GEYL

This is very simple. I agree with you entirely about the impossibility of 34 allowing, as it used to be put, the facts to speak for themselves, and the historian who imagines that he can rule out theory or, let us say, his own individual mind, his personal view of things in general, seems to me a very uninteresting being, or in the majority of cases, when he is obviously only deluding himself and covering his particular partiality with the great word of objectivity and historical science, a very naïve person, and perhaps a very dangerous one.

As a matter of fact this is the spirit in which I have tackled you. When 35 you said that I was an adherent of the nonsense view of history, you were mistaking my position altogether. In my own fashion, when I reject your methods and your conclusions, I am also trying to establish general views about history. Without such views, I know that the records of the past would become utterly chaotic and senseless, and I think I should rather be an astronomer than devote my life to so hopeless and futile a study.

But, to me, one of the great things to realize about history is its infinite 36 complexity, and, when I say infinite, I do mean that not only the number of the phenomena and incidents but their often shadowy and changing nature is such that the attempt to reduce them to a fixed relationship and to a scheme of absolute validity can never lead to anything but disappointment. It is when you present your system in so hard and fast a manner as to seem, at any rate to me, to dictate to the future, that I feel bound to protest, on behalf both of history and of the civilization whose crisis we are both witnessing.

You have twitted me for inviting the world to sail on an uncharted 37 course. Yet I believe that the sense of history is absolutely indispensable for the life of mankind. I believe with Burckhardt that there is wisdom to be gained from the study of the past, but no definite lessons for the actual problems of the present.

PROFESSOR TOYNBEE

Well there! It looks as if, on this question anyway, our two different ap- 38 proaches have brought us on to something like common ground. If I am right in this, I think it is rather encouraging, for this last issue we were discussing is, I am sure, a fundamental one.

PROFESSOR GEYL

Well I see, Toynbee, that our time is up. There are just a few seconds left for 39 me to pay tribute to the courage with which you, as you expressed it yourself, have risked your neck; not by facing me here at the microphone, but by composing that gigantic and impressive scheme of civilizations, which was bound to rouse the skeptics and to be subjected to their criticism. Now I am not such a skeptic as to doubt the rightness of my own position in our debate, but I am one compared with you. Perhaps you will value the assurance from such a one that he himself has found your great work immensely stimulating and that, generally speaking, in the vast enterprise in which we historians are engaged together, daring and imaginative spirits like yourself have an essential function to fulfill.

Questions for Discussion

1. Why does Geyl think that his differences with Toynbee have not just theoretical but great *practical* importance (¶4)?
2. Some historical questions are fairly easy to answer: for example, In what year did you enter high school? Others are more difficult, but not beyond meaningful speculation and argument: for example, What were your *real* reasons for going to college or for choosing this college? And some questions seem clearly beyond human capacity to answer: for example, What were Brutus' feelings as he stabbed Caesar? Does it seem to you that the question "Why do civilizations rise and fall?" is by its nature merely difficult to debate or is finally impossible to debate?
3. Clearly Toynbee and Geyl are convinced that question 2 could be addressed rationally, but few of us will ever know enough about the 21 civilizations to judge or even to debate in any detail about Geyl's and

Toynbee's positions. It is not beyond us, however, to ask which of the two opponents is more convincing, given their arguments as presented. After reading the debate two or three times, choose a paragraph that seems highly persuasive, and list all the reasons you can find to explain why it carries weight for you.

4. The debate contains a good deal of comment by each speaker about the character of the other (for example, ¶18, the beginning of ¶19, and most of ¶39). Each speaker praises the other, and neither one says anything openly nasty about the other. Make two lists of characteristics, favorable and unfavorable, that Geyl attributes to Toynbee and two lists of Geyl's favorable and unfavorable qualities as stated or implied by Toynbee. (Don't list only the openly stated qualities, like the "courage" that Geyl talks about in sentence 2 of ¶39, but also the qualities that are merely implied, like Geyl's suggestion that Toynbee's work is careless and arrogant.) Does Geyl's characterization of Toynbee seem to fit what you can infer about Toynbee from his own words? Does Toynbee's Geyl fit the Geyl who speaks?

5. Study paragraph 18 carefully. What do you think Geyl is trying to accomplish with it? Would you advise Geyl to cut it if he were preparing another printing? Why or why not?

6. In paragraph 19 Geyl suggests (especially in sentences 2–4) that Toynbee has misreported his claims. Is he justified in the claim?

7. Both men seem to agree that "facts do not speak for themselves but must be interpreted" (see, for example, ¶34). Can you state clearly the difference between them about how we should work in interpreting historical facts and making use of them in the present? Support your answer by citing passages.

Suggested Essay Topics

1. Your life has a "history" just as each civilization does, and though that history may seem less complex, it still has consisted of so many details, from the time of your birth until now, that no one could ever list them all (see Geyl's talk about "infinite complexity" in ¶36). Your picture of your past is thus not a report of raw facts but an interpretation that in *some* ways resembles Toynbee's interpretation of civilizations. Choose some important turning point or event from your life, one that depended on your making a conscious choice. Write a history of the choice, your reasons for it, and the consequences, good or bad. You may find it helpful to address your account as a letter to your parents, correcting what you take to be their false view of the event's "history."

2. Write a two-page "history" of what happened to you yesterday. Include an appraisal of whether the day showed signs of moving you upward or downward in your life's "curve."

✎ 10 ✎

SCIENTIFIC PERSPECTIVES

Science, Knowledge, and Morality

If science would discover rather than apply—if, in other words,
men were more interested in knowledge than
in power—mankind would be in a far safer position.
E. M. Forster

[Science] is the distinctive achievement of our history, and . . . nothing less
momentous than the preservation of our culture
hangs on understanding its growth and bearing. But the
influence of science is not simply comfortable. For neither
in public nor in private life can science establish an ethic. It tells
what we can do, never what we should. Its absolute incompetence
in the realm of values is a necessary consequence of the objective posture.
Charles Coulston Gillispie

Science is much closer to myth than a scientific philosophy
is prepared to admit. It is one of the many forms of thought that have been
developed by man, and not necessarily the best.
Paul Feyerabend

I believe that the scientific method, although slow
and never claiming to lead to complete truth, is the only method
which in the long run will give satisfactory foundation for beliefs.
Julian Huxley

The separation of science and non-science is not only artificial
but also detrimental to the advancement of knowledge.
If we want to understand nature, if we want to master our physical
surroundings, then we must use *all* ideas, *all* methods,
and not just a small selection of them. The assertion, however, that there
is no knowledge outside science—*extra scientiam nulla salus*—is
nothing but another and most convenient fairy-tale.
Paul Feyerabend

Lewis Thomas

Lewis Thomas writes of science not as a repellent realm of formulas and figures but as an activity at once important, accessible, and interesting. He does this by refusing to flaunt his expertise, striving instead to communicate his own enthusiasm for ideas.

In this essay, Thomas takes a critical look at science education. He argues that it consistently errs by presenting scientific knowledge to students the way supermarkets present food to their customers—as canned goods already processed by experts and intended to be swallowed whole by the consumer. He thinks that science students should do less indiscriminate swallowing and more critical thinking and that they should learn about areas where science has more questions than answers.

Thomas states his thesis boldly: Science education should expose students to the big controversies as well as the canned goods. He then supports it with a simple plan of organization: In support of his thesis he presents the best examples of interesting controversies he knows about, with some commentary on why they are important. This pattern of organization—thesis followed by illustrative examples—is perhaps the simplest and most often used pattern in all expository writing. It is simple, direct, and clear, and Thomas employs it with a skill that any of us might emulate. His tone also presents a laudable model for this kind of essay: articulate but not pretentious, deeply involved in his subject but not self-absorbed, expert but not pedantic, and friendly but not pushy or chummy.

DEBATING THE UNKNOWABLE

From *The Atlantic Monthly*, July 1981.

The greatest of all the accomplishments of twentieth-century science has been the discovery of human ignorance. We live, as never before, in puzzlement about nature, the universe, and ourselves most of all. It is a new experience for the species. A century ago, after the turbulence caused by Darwin and Wallace had subsided and the central idea of natural selection had been grasped and accepted, we thought we knew everything essential about evolution. In the eighteenth century there were no huge puzzles; human reason was all you needed in order to figure out the universe. And for most of the earlier centuries, the Church provided both the questions and the answers, neatly packaged. Now, for the first time in human history, we are catching glimpses of our incomprehension. We can still make up stories to explain the world, as we always have, but now the stories have to be confirmed and reconfirmed by experiment. This is the scientific method, and once started on this line we cannot turn back. We are obliged to grow up in skepticism, requiring proofs for every assertion about nature, and there is no way out except to move ahead and plug away, hoping for comprehension in the future but living in a condition of intellectual instability for the long time.

It is the admission of ignorance that leads to progress, not so much because the solving of a particular puzzle leads directly to a new piece of understanding but because the puzzle—if it interests enough scientists—leads to *work*. There is a similar phenomenon in entomology known as stigmergy, a term invented by Grassé, which means "to incite to work." When three or four termites are collected together in a chamber they wander about aimlessly, but when more termites are added, they begin to build. It is the presence of other termites, in sufficient numbers at close quarters, that produces the work: they pick up each other's fecal pellets and stack them in neat columns, and when the columns are precisely the right height, the termites reach across and turn the perfect arches that form the foundation of the termitarium. No single termite knows how to do any of this, but as soon as there are enough termites gathered together they become flawless architects, sensing their distances from each other although blind, building an immensely complicated structure with its own air-conditioning and humidity control. They work their lives away in this ecosystem built by themselves. The nearest thing to a termitarium that I can think of in human behavior is the making of language, which we do by keeping *at* each other all our lives, generation after generation, changing the structure by some sort of instinct.

Very little is understood about this kind of collective behavior. It is out of fashion these days to talk of "superorganisms," but there simply aren't enough reductionist details in hand to explain away the phenomenon of termites and other social insects: some very good guesses can be made about their chemical signaling systems, but the plain fact that they exhibit something like a collective intelligence is a mystery, or anyway an unsolved problem, that might contain important implications for social life in general. This mystery is the best introduction I can think of to biological science in college. It should be taught for its strangeness, and for the ambiguity of its meaning. It should be taught to premedical students, who need lessons early in their careers about the uncertainties in science.

College students, and for that matter high school students, should be exposed very early, perhaps at the outset, to the big arguments currently going on among scientists. Big arguments stimulate their interest, and with luck engage their absorbed attention. Few things in life are as engrossing as a good fight between highly trained and skilled adversaries. But the young students are told very little about the major disagreements of the day; they may be taught something about the arguments between Darwinians and their opponents a century ago, but they do not realize that similar disputes about other matters, many of them touching profound issues for our understanding of nature, are still going on and, indeed, are an essential feature of the scientific process. There is, I fear, a reluctance on the part of science teachers to talk about such things, based on the belief that before students can appreciate what the arguments are about they must learn and master the "fundamentals." I would be willing to see some experiments along this line, and I have in mind several examples of contemporary doctrinal dispute in which the drift of the argument can be readily perceived without deep or elaborate knowledge of the subject.

There is, for one, the problem of animal awareness. One school of ethologists devoted to the study of animal behavior has it that human beings are unique in the possession of consciousness, differing from all other creatures in being able to think things over, capitalize on past experience, and hazard informed guesses at the future. Other, "lower," animals (with possible exceptions made for chimpanzees, whales, and dolphins) cannot do such things with their minds; they live from moment to moment with brains that are programmed to respond, automatically or by conditioning, to contingencies in the environment. Behavioral psychologists believe that this automatic or conditioned response accounts for human mental activity as well, although they dislike that word "mental." On the other side are some ethologists who seem to be more generous-minded, who see no compelling reasons to doubt that animals in general are quite capable of real thinking and do quite a lot of it—thinking that isn't as dense as human thinking, that is sparser because of the lack of language and the resultant lack of metaphors to help the thought along, but thinking nonetheless.

The point about this argument is not that one side or the other is in possession of a more powerful array of convincing facts; quite the opposite. There are not enough facts to sustain a genuine debate of any length; the question of animal awareness is an unsettled one. In the circumstance, I put forward the following notion about a small beetle, the mimosa girdler, which undertakes three pieces of linked, sequential behavior: finding a mimosa tree

and climbing up the trunk and out to the end of a branch; cutting a longitudi-
nal slit and laying within it five or six eggs; and crawling back on the limb
and girdling it neatly down into the cambium. The third step is an eight-to-
ten-hour task of hard labor, from which the beetle gains no food for itself—
only the certainty that the branch will promptly die and fall to the ground
in the next brisk wind, thus enabling the larvae to hatch and grow in an
abundance of dead wood. I propose, in total confidence that even though I
am probably wrong nobody today can prove that I am wrong, that the beetle
is not doing these three things out of blind instinct, like a little machine, but
is thinking its way along, just as we would think. The difference is that we
possess enormous brains, crowded all the time with an infinite number of
long thoughts, while the beetle's brain is only a few strings of neurons
connected in a modest network, capable therefore of only three *tiny* thoughts,
coming into consciousness one after the other: find the right tree; get up there
and lay eggs in a slit; back up and spend the day killing the branch so the
eggs can hatch. End of message. I would not go so far as to anthropomorphize
the mimosa tree, for I really do not believe plants have minds, but something
has to be said about the tree's role in this arrangement as a beneficiary:
mimosas grow for twenty-five to thirty years and then die, unless they are
vigorously pruned annually, in which case they can live to be a hundred. The
beetle is a piece of good luck for the tree, but nothing more: one example of
pure chance working at its best in nature—what you might even wish to call
good nature.

This brings me to the second example of unsettlement in biology, cur- 7
rently being rather delicately discussed but not yet argued over, for there is
still only one orthodoxy and almost no opposition, yet. This is the matter of
chance itself, and the role played by blind chance in the arrangement of living
things on the planet. It is, in the orthodox view, pure luck that evolution
brought us to our present condition, and things might just as well have turned
out any number of other, different ways, and might go in any unpredictable
way for the future. There is, of course, nothing chancy about natural selection
itself: it is an accepted fact that selection will always favor the advantaged
individuals whose genes succeed best in propagating themselves within a
changing environment. But the creatures acted upon by natural selection are
themselves there as the result of chance: mutations (probably of much more
importance during the long period of exclusively microbial life starting nearly
4 billion years ago and continuing until about one billion years ago); the
endless sorting and re-sorting of genes within chromosomes during replica-
tion; perhaps recombination of genes across species lines at one time or
another; and almost certainly the carrying of genes by viruses from one
creature to another.

The argument comes when one contemplates the whole biosphere, the 8
conjoined life of the earth. How could it have turned out to possess such
stability and coherence, resembling as it does a sort of enormous developing
embryo, with nothing but chance events to determine its emergence? Lovelock and Margulis, facing this problem, have proposed the Gaia Hypothesis,

which is, in brief, that the earth is itself a form of life, "a complex entity involving the Earth's biosphere, atmosphere, oceans and soil; the totality constituting a feedback or cybernetic system which seeks an optimal physical and chemical environment for life on this planet." Lovelock postulates, in addition, that "the physical and chemical condition of the surface of the Earth, of the atmosphere, and of the oceans has been and is actively made fit and comfortable by the presence of life itself."

This notion is beginning to stir up a few signs of storm, and if it catches   9
on, as I think it will, we will soon find the biological community split into fuming factions, one side saying that the evolved biosphere displays evidences of design and purpose, the other decrying such heresy. I believe that students should learn as much as they can about the argument. In an essay in *Coevolution* (Spring 1981), W. F. Doolittle has recently attacked the Gaia Hypothesis, asking, among other things, ". . . how does Gaia know if she is too cold or too hot, and how does she instruct the biosphere to behave accordingly?" This is not a deadly criticism in a world where we do not actually understand, in anything like real detail, how even Dr. Doolittle manages the stability and control of his own internal environment, including his body temperature. One thing is certain: none of us can instruct our body's systems to make the needed corrections beyond a very limited number of rather trivial tricks made possible through biofeedback techniques. If something goes wrong with my liver or my kidneys, I have no advice to offer out of my cortex. I rely on the system to fix itself, which it usually does with no help from me beyond crossing my fingers.

Another current battle involving the unknown is between sociobiolo-   10
gists and antisociobiologists, and it is a marvel for students to behold. To observe, in open-mouthed astonishment, one group of highly intelligent, beautifully trained, knowledgeable, and imaginative scientists maintaining that all behavior, animal and human, is governed exclusively by genes, and another group of equally talented scientists asserting that all behavior is set and determined by the environment or by culture, is an educational experience that no college student should be allowed to miss. The essential lesson to be learned has nothing to do with the relative validity of the facts underlying the argument. It is the argument itself that is the education: we do not yet know enough to settle such questions.

One last example. There is an uncomfortable secret in biology, not   11
much talked about yet, but beginning to surface. It is, in a way, linked to the observations that underlie the Gaia Hypothesis. Nature abounds in instances of cooperation and collaboration, partnerships between species. There is a tendency of living things to join up whenever joining is possible: accommodation and compromise are more common results of close contact than combat and destruction. Given the opportunity and the proper circumstances, two cells from totally different species—a mouse cell and a human cell, for example—will fuse to become a single cell, and then the two nuclei will fuse into a single nucleus, and then the hybrid cell will divide to produce generations of new cells containing the combined genomes of both species. Bacteria

are indispensable partners in the fixation of atmospheric nitrogen by plants. The oxygen in our atmosphere is put there, almost in its entirety, by the photosynthetic chloroplasts in the cells of green plants, and these organelles are almost certainly the descendants of blue-green algae that joined up when the nucleated cells of higher plants came into existence. The mitochondria in all our own cells, and in all other nucleated cells, which enable us to use oxygen for energy, are the direct descendants of symbiotic bacteria. These are becoming accepted facts, and there is no longer an agitated argument over their probable validity; but there are no satisfactory explanations for how such amiable and useful arrangements came into being in the first place. Axelrod and Hamilton (*Science,* March 27, 1981) have recently reopened the question of cooperation in evolution with a mathematical approach based on game theory (the Prisoner's Dilemma game), which permits the hypothesis that one creature's best strategy for dealing repeatedly with another is to concede and cooperate rather than to defect and go it alone.

This idea can be made to fit with the mathematical justification based 12 on kinship already accepted for explaining altruism in nature—that in a colony of social insects the sacrifice of one individual for another depends on how many of the sacrificed member's genes are matched by others and thus preserved, and that the extent of the colony's altruistic behavior can be mathematically calculated. It is, by the way, an interesting aspect of contemporary biology that true altruism—the giving away of something without return—is incompatible with dogma, even though it goes on all over the place. Nature, in this respect, keeps breaking the rules, and needs correcting by new ways of doing arithmetic.

The social scientists are in the hardest business of all—trying to under- 13 stand how humanity works. They are caught up in debates all over town; everything they touch turns out to be one of society's nerve endings, eliciting outrage and cries of pain. Wait until they begin coming close to the bone. They surely will someday, provided they can continue to attract enough bright people—fascinated by humanity, unafraid of big numbers, and skeptical of questionnaires—and provided the government does not starve them out of business, as is now being tried in Washington. Politicians do not like pain, not even wincing, and they have some fear of what the social scientists may be thinking about thinking for the future.

The social scientists are themselves too modest about the history of 14 their endeavor, tending to display only the matters under scrutiny today in economics, sociology, and psychology, for example—never boasting, as they might, about one of the greatest of all scientific advances in our comprehension of humanity, for which they could be claiming credit. I refer to the marvelous accomplishments of the nineteenth-century comparative linguists. When the scientific method is working at its best, it succeeds in revealing the connection between things in nature that seem at first totally unrelated to each other. Long before the time when the biologists, led by Darwin and Wallace, were constructing the tree of evolution and the origin of species, the linguists were hard at work on the evolution of language. After beginning in

1786 with Sir William Jones and his inspired hunch that the remarkable similarities among Sanskrit, Greek, and Latin meant, in his words, that these three languages must "have sprung from some common source, which, perhaps, no longer exists," the new science of comparative grammar took off in 1816 with Franz Bopp's classic work "On the conjugational system of the Sanskrit language in comparison with that of the Greek, Latin, Persian and Germanic languages"—a piece of work equivalent, in its scope and in its power to explain, to the best of nineteenth-century biology. The common Indo-European ancestry of English, Germanic, Slavic, Greek, Latin, Baltic, Indic, Iranian, Hittite, and Anatolian tongues, and the meticulous scholarship connecting them was a tour de force for research—science at its best, and social science at that.

It is nice to know that a common language, perhaps 20,000 years ago, had a root word for the earth which turned, much later, into the technical term for the complex polymers that make up the connective tissues of the soil: humus and what are called the humic acids. There is a strangeness, though, in the emergence from the same root of words such as "human" and "humane," and "humble." It comes as something of a shock to realize that the root for words such as "miracle" and "marvel" meant, originally, "to smile," and that from the single root *sa* were constructed, in the descendant tongues, three cognate words, "satisfied," "satiated," and "sadness." How is it possible for a species to show so much wisdom in its most collective of all behaviors—the making and constant changing of language—and at the same time be so habitually folly-prone in the building of nation-states? Modern linguistics has moved into new areas of inquiry as specialized and inaccessible for most laymen (including me) as particle physics; I cannot guess where linguistics will come out, but it is surely aimed at scientific comprehension, and its problem—human language—is as crucial to the species as any other field I can think of, including molecular genetics.

But there are some risks involved in trying to do science in the humanities before its time, and useful lessons can be learned from some of the not-so-distant history of medicine. A century ago it was the common practice to deal with disease by analyzing what seemed to be the underlying mechanism and applying whatever treatment popped into the doctor's head. Getting sick was a hazardous enterprise in those days. The driving force in medicine was the need to *do* something, never mind what. It occurs to me now, reading in incomprehension some of the current reductionist writings in literary criticism, especially poetry criticism, that the new schools are at risk under a similar pressure. A poem is a healthy organism, really in need of no help from science, no treatment except fresh air and exercise. I thought I'd just sneak that in.

Questions for Discussion

1. In reflecting on the strangeness of termite social behavior in paragraph 3 and on how science is far from being able to explain it, Thomas observes that "this mystery is the best introduction I can think of to biological science in college . . . [for it teaches students] early in their careers about the uncertainties in science." Do the science courses you have had teach "the uncertainties in science" and encourage discussion of them? Do you agree that they should?

2. Thomas believes that science is full of mysteries. Does it seem to you that most people think of science as full of facts—cut, dried, and proved— rather than full of mysteries? Which of these views have been held by most of the science teachers you have known? Have you found that one view is more characteristic of good science teachers than the other view?

3. Do you agree with Thomas's opening sentence that "the greatest of all the accomplishments of twentieth-century science has been the discovery of human ignorance"? State your reasons.

4. Does the Gaia Hypothesis (¶8) sound like fact or fairy tale? Most great hypotheses in the history of science sounded like fairy tales (or sheer nuttiness) when they were first advanced. This does not necessarily argue in favor of the Gaia Hypothesis, but it does argue against the cliché that science progresses because scientists stick to what can be seen, measured, and proved. For example, when Copernicus suggested that the earth goes around the sun instead of the sun going around the earth, he was contradicting what everyone could "prove" simply by watching the sky every day. As Galileo later said, Copernicus performed "a rape upon the senses"; he asked people to believe in a theory that contradicted the "facts" of everyone's experience. Likewise, Newton asked people to rely more on their imaginations than on their own eyes. Since he could perform no laboratory tests to prove his theory of gravity, he asked everyone to picture gravity operating in a frictionless universe—a kind of universe no one on earth ever experiences. (Gravity still has not been defined or measured in any conclusive way.) And in our own century, Einstein had not performed one single laboratory experiment and could offer not a single fact to back up his claims when he proposed that mass and energy are equivalent at light speeds and that the speed of light is absolute. It took decades before *any* of his claims could be verified by observation, and most of them remain untested today.

    In light of the history of great scientific discoveries, what can you conclude about the nature of scientific inquiry? If Copernicus and Newton and Einstein were dreamers, surely they were informed dreamers; though they contradicted some of the "facts" of their day, they preserved what facts they could and thought out their reasons carefully, even when they had no laboratory experiments to support their hypotheses. What, then, is the role of facts in scientific inquiry, and what is the role of imagination? When Thomas opens his essay by praising modern science for accomplishing "the discovery of human ignorance," is he trying to spur us on to find more facts, or is he appealing to our imagination? Or both? (For the role of the imagination in inquiry, see Jacob Bronowski, "The Reach of Imagination," pp. 138–145.)

5. In paragraph 10 Thomas says that college students need to be exposed to the big controversies in science because "it is the argument itself that is the education." This assertion implies that *all* of education should be education-as-argument. Can you say what such an education would be? Are you getting such an education? Would you like to? How would you define its opposite?

Suggested Essay Topics

1. According to Thomas, "It is the admission of ignorance that leads to progress" (¶2). No doubt you have known teachers whose teaching did not reflect this view—teachers who never admitted ignorance or exposed their students to the "big arguments currently going on." Write a letter to one such teacher, arguing in support of Thomas's view of scientific education and imitating as well as you can Thomas's casual-seeming tone of geniality combined with hardheaded critical aggressiveness.

2. This is a tougher topic than the previous one and requires some library research. Picture yourself as a scientist in Copernicus' time, outraged at both the "unscientific method" and the content of Copernicus' new theory that the earth goes around the sun. Address a letter to Copernicus in which you try to persuade him of the scientific illegitimacy of contradicting so many proved facts. Point out just how well supported the accepted view of things is, and try to make him see that he is going to set science back 100 years if he gets people to believe in his nutty notions. Base your letter on library research. There *was* an enormous response to Copernicus' ideas; not only is reading some of this controversy firsthand a good introduction to the history of science, but writing about it is good practice at analysis.

Mary Midgley

In this probing and insightful essay, Mary Midgley (b. 1919) undertakes the arduous task of simultaneously defending and criticizing science, especially certain tendencies in evolutionary theorizing. While she contends that both the content and the methods of evolutionary science are important, she also criticizes the tendency of some evolutionary scientists to draw exaggerated conclusions about the character and destiny of the universe based on evolutionary postulates.

On the basis of facts as uncovered by evolutionary research, some scientists conclude that the world is a terrifying battleground dominated by each person's or society's inevitable drive to ensure survival and dominance. Other scientists, however, looking at the same data, draw no such pessimistic conclusions but see the world instead as the site of inevitable progressions that include the gradual improvement (sometimes, it is claimed, the perfection) of human nature itself and of society. The extreme forms of these pessimistic and optimistic pictures of the world are not, says Midgley, scientific in any sense and threaten both the prestige and the progress of science by claiming scientific legitimacy for views that can best be explained not as scientific theories but as moralistic, atheistic, or religious melodramas.

Midgley is not attacking the scientific impulse to draw big pictures of the world. She sees such pictures as the beginning point of all inquiries, whether scientific, religious, economic, or of some other kind. What she attacks is the tendency on the part of some scientists to claim that certain versions of the evolutionary picture are scientific conclusions, which they are not, or that they possess a scientific character in themselves.

In the end Midgley argues that the reliance on certain antitheses prevalent in modern discourse about both religion and science is dysfunctional to both. For the past century, for example, is has been common to divide the world up into a set of opposing characteristics that place science, rationality, and hard knowledge on one side of a dividing line and religion, spirituality, and intuition on the other. Midgley makes it clear that such antitheses as these are inadequate and in fact mask the way science works. She argues, for example, that scientific pictures of the world, including the evolutionary picture of human development, are attempts to stitch together a meaning for human existence; they are not simply the results of empirical research. No good scientist, she says, merely collects and and stores facts. Any good scientist collects facts to fit some big picture to which belief has already been committed. Instead of such beliefs being unscientific, they are in fact essential to scientific research and the maintenance of scientific energy.

Much of what Midgley says is, of course, controversial. Some scientists may feel that their objectivity is being impugned and that their scienticic research is being either trivialized or co-opted by a religious or at least unscientific point of view. But Midgley argues her case pointedly and cogently. Whether you agree or disagree, try to form your responses as cogently and concretely as she forms her arguments.

EVOLUTION AS A RELIGION

From Chapters 1, 8, and 12 of *Evolution as a Religion* (1985).

SCIENCE AND SYMBOLISM

The theory of evolution is not just an inert piece of theoretical science. It is, and cannot help being, also a powerful folk-tale about human origins. Any such narrative must have symbolic force. We are probably the first culture not to make that its main function. Most stories about human origins must have been devised purely with a view to symbolic and poetic fittingness. Suggestions about how we were made and where we come from are bound to engage our imagination, to shape our views of what we now are, and so to affect our lives. Scientists, when they find themselves caught up in these webs of symbolism, sometimes complain, calling for a sanitary cordon to keep them away from science. But this seems to be both psychologically and logically impossible.

Our theoretical curiosity simply is not detached in this way from the rest of our life. Nor do scientists themselves always want it to be so. Some of the symbolic webs are ones which they approve of, and promote as part of the ideal of science itself. For instance, Jacques Monod, as an atheistical biochemist, does not just rejoice at getting rid of the theistic drama. He at once replaces it by another drama, just as vivid, emotive and relevant to life, in which Sartrian man* appears as the lonely hero challenging an alien and meaningless universe:

> It is perfectly true that science attacks values. Not directly, since science is no judge of them and *must* ignore them; but it subverts every one of the mythical or philosophical ontogenies upon which the animist tradition, from the Australian aborigines to the dialectical materialists, has based morality, values, duties, rights, prohibitions.
>
> If he accepts this message in its full significance, man must at last wake out of his millenary dream and discover his total solitude, his fundamental isolation. He must realize that, like a gypsy, he lives on the boundary of an alien world; a world that is deaf to his music, and as indifferent to his hopes as it is to his sufferings or his crimes.[1]

But "discovering his total solitude" is just adopting one imaginative stance among many possible ones. Other good scientists, very differently, have used the continuity of our species with the rest of the physical world to reprove human arrogance and to call for practical recognition of kinship with other creatures. Many, like Darwin and the great geneticist Theodosius Dobzhansky,† have held that an attitude of awe and veneration for the wonders of the physical world is an essential condition for studying them properly. Others have talked in a more predatory way about the joys of the chase and the triumph of catching facts. Both motives, and many others, are evidently so habitual in science that they are only not mentioned because they are taken for granted.

It seems often to be assumed that they are therefore irrelevant, that Science itself is something so pure and impersonal that it ought to be thought of in complete abstraction from all the motives that might lead people to

---

*A reference to the French existential philosopher and novelist Jean-Paul Sartre (1905–1980), who portrayed individuals as pitted in lonely and isolated (but potentially heroic) opposition to a neutral universe, their job being to *assert* meaning in a world that possesses none intrinsically.
†Russian-born American geneticist (1900–1975), known especially for work on the philosophical implications of evolution.

practise it. This, unfortunately, cannot work because of the importance of world-pictures. Facts are not gathered in a vacuum, but to fill gaps in a world-picture which already exists. And the shape of this world-picture—determining the matters allowed for it, the principles of selection, the possible range of emphases—depends deeply on the motives for forming it in the first place.

Imagination, which guides thought, is directed by our attitudes. For instance, predatory and competitive motives tend to produce a picture dominated by competition and predation—one in which these elements do not only play their part, as they did for Darwin, but are arbitrarily and dogmatically isolated as sole rulers. Thus, in a familiar distortion which will concern us repeatedly, the sociobiologist M. T. Ghiselin flatly declares:

> The evolution of society fits the Darwinian paradigm in its most individualistic form. The economy of nature is competitive from beginning to end. Understand that economy, and how it works, and the underlying reasons for social phenomena are manifest. They are the means by which one organism gains some advantage to the detriment of another. No hint of genuine charity ameliorates our vision of society, once sentimentalism has been laid aside. What passes for co-operation turns out to be a mixture of opportunism and exploitation. The impulses that lead one animal to sacrifice himself for another turn out to have their ultimate rationale in gaining advantage over a third, and acts for the good of one "society" turn out to be performed for the detriment of the rest. Where it is in his own interest, every organism may reasonably be expected to aid his fellows. Where he has no alternative, he submits to the yoke of servitude. Yet, given a full chance to act in his own interest, nothing but expediency will restrain him from brutalizing, from maiming, from murdering—his brother, his mate, his parent, or his child. Scratch an "altruist" and watch a "hypocrite" bleed.[2]

As we shall see, this claim is essentially pure fantasy, not only unsupported by the empirical facts which are supposed to be its grounds, but actually contrary to them, such as they are. Is this a quite exceptional aberration? Some will suspect that it must be, not only because the world-picture involved is a bad one, but because scientists ought to be so impartial that they either do not have anything so unprofessional as a world-picture at all, or, if they have one, do not let it affect their work.

But this is a mistaken ideal. An enquirer with no such general map would only be an obsessive—someone who had a special motive for collecting facts indiscriminately. He would not be a person without an attitude, or without special motives, but one with motives so odd as to inhibit the kind of organizing activity which normally shapes people's ideas into some sort of coherent whole. Merely to pile up information indiscriminately is an idiot's task. Good scientists do not approximate to that ideal at all. They tend to have a very strong guiding imaginative system. Their world-picture is usually a positive and distinctive one, with its own special drama. They do not scrupulously avoid conveying any sense of dark and light, of what matters and what does not, of what is to be aimed at and what avoided at all costs. They use the lights and shadows to reveal the landscape. Like those who argue usefully on any other subject, they do their best work not by being neutral but by having strong preferences, being aware of them, criticizing them carefully, expressing them plainly and then leaving their readers to decide how far to share them.

Symbolism, then, is not just a nuisance to be got rid of. It is essential. 6 Facts will never appear to us as brute and meaningless; they will always organize themselves into some sort of story, some drama. These dramas can indeed be dangerous. They can distort our theories, and they have distorted the theory of evolution perhaps more than any other. The only way in which we can control this kind of distortion is, I believe, to bring the dramas themselves out into the open, to give them our full attention, understand them better and see what part, if any, each of them ought to play both in theory and in life. It is no use merely to swipe at them from time to time, like troublesome insects, while officially attending only to the theoretical questions. This will not make them go away, because they are a serious feature of life.

DARWIN'S BALANCE

The drama that attends a theory need not, then, be mere melodrama. 7 When sensationalism is present it is either irrelevant or—if it really belongs to a theory—shows that that theory is bad. The drama that goes with a good theory is simply the expressive aspect of the theory itself. In order of time, it is often conceived in advance of much of the supporting evidence. But when further facts accumulate, it ought to respond to them by refining and subtilizing its cruder outlines. This process usually makes it less extreme and one-sided, and so moves it away from the gratuitous sensationalism which marks melodrama. That does not make it less stirring or less important for life; it can make it more so. This imaginative and emotional deepening is part of the growth of a theory, not just a chance ornament. When the young Darwin immersed himself in the arguments about cosmic purpose in Paley's* theological textbook *The Evidences of Christianity,* and repeatedly read *Paradise Lost* on exploring trips from the *Beagle,* †[3] he was neither wasting his time nor distorting his scientific project. He was seriously working his way through a range of life-positions which lay on the route to the one he could finally use.

The result of this long preliminary pilgrimage was to make his own 8 picture unusually balanced and inclusive. To keep it so is, however, terribly hard. He himself made clear that he felt this difficulty deeply, and was constantly dissatisfied with his efforts, constantly changing his books to do

---

*William Paley (1743–1805), English theologian and utilitarian philosopher.
†The ship on which Darwin first visited the Galápagos Islands, where he observed many of the natural phenomena that supported his theory.

justice to some neglected angle. The vastness of the truth and the one-sidedness of formulae always haunted him. . . . The destructive message of [*Evolution as a Religion*] is a somewhat dismal one. It concerns the sort of trouble which arises when, with writers less careful than Darwin, the dramas take over. About evolution, theory itself has again and again been distorted by biases flowing from over-simple, unbalanced world-pictures. The trouble does not, of course, lie in mere wish-fulfilment of the obvious kind which paints the world as we should like it to be. It involves being obsessed by a picture so colourful and striking that it numbs thought about the evidence required to support it. Standards of proof then fall headlong. . . .

FALSE LIGHTS

There are two distortions in particular which will mainly concern us in this book, and they had better be indicated, however crudely, right away. Neither is new; both have often been denounced. But both persist, not just in the minds of outsiders ignorant of evolutionary theory, but also in those of many scientists who develop and expound it. The first is the better known and the more obviously pernicious. It is the "Social Darwinist" idea, expressed by Ghiselin, that life has been scientifically proved to be essentially competitive, in some sense which exposes all social feeling as somehow mere humbug and illusion. The phrase "survival of the fittest" has been used, ever since Herbert Spencer* first coined it, to describe an individualistic law showing such things as co-operation, love and altruism to be unreal, a law which (somewhat mysteriously) both demands and predicts that they should always give way to self-interest. This has often been exposed as nonsense. Since many very successful species of social animals, including our own, have evolved these traits, have survived by them and continue to live by them, their unreality cannot be the message of evolutionary theory. But because of its strong dramatic force, as well as various political uses, this notion persists through repeated attempts to correct it, and often twists up the ideas even of those who think they are helping to get rid of it. It is especially troublesome in the American sociobiology debate, a topic to which I shall have to give a rather disproportionate amount of attention, simply because its wide publicity makes it, just now, the most prominent hotbed of noisy errors about evolution.

The second main distortion may be called Panglossism,† or the Escalator Fallacy. It is the idea that evolution is a steady, linear upward movement, a single inexorable process of improvement, leading (as a disciple of Herbert Spencer's put it) "from gas to genius"[4] and beyond into some superhuman spiritual stratosphere. This idea, first put forward by Jean-Baptiste

*English philosopher (1820–1903) who, in a series of books beginning with *Principles of Psychology* (1855), applied Darwin's theory of evolution to social phenomena.

†Pangloss was the philosopher—ridiculed by Voltaire in his great satire *Candide* (1759)—who claimed that everything that happened was for the best and that the world was getting better and better.

Lamarck* at the beginning of the century,[5] convinced Spencer instantly and completely. It did not convince Darwin at all. He thought it vacuous, pointed out the obscurity of the metaphor "higher," and relied on no such paid-up cosmic insurance policy to bail out the human race. He developed his own view of selection on the humbler model of a bush—a rich radiation of varying forms, in which human qualities cannot, any more than any others, determine a general direction for the whole. Here too, however, what he rejected has been kept by many people as a central feature of the idea of evolution and seen as a key part of "Darwinism." Still unsupported by argument, it too continues to produce some extremely strange theorizing, and in its less obvious way also to do a great deal of damage. These two kinds of drama are, in fact, the shapes into which the two main strands of feeling about evolution naturally develop, if they are not held in balance and forced to correct each other. They are the hypertrophied forms of cosmic optimism and cosmic pessimism respectively. Since both these moods are common, theory-builders often oscillate between them rather casually, and produce views which owe something to both. Unluckily, this is not the same thing as the synthesis which Darwin attempted. It can merely give us the worst of both worlds. . . .

CLAIMS FOR THE FUTURE OF SCIENCE

Let us turn now to . . . [the] kind of prophecy, concerned mainly with the rosy future of science itself, but also indicating the route by which it is to bring about a general reform of life. It is from the sociobiologist Edward O. Wilson: 11

> When mankind has achieved an ecological steady state, probably by the end of the twenty-first century, the internalization of social evolution will be nearly complete. About this time biology should be at its peak, with the social sciences maturing rapidly . . . cognition will be translated into circuitry. Learning and creativeness will be defined as the alteration of specific portions of the cognitive machinery regulated by input from the emotive centers. Having cannibalized psychology, the new neurobiology will yield an enduring set of first principles for sociology. . . . Skinner's dream of a culture predesigned for happiness will surely have to wait for the new neurobiology. A genetically accurate and hence completely fair code of ethics must also wait.[6]

This means, however, that we shall get it in the end, once the neurobiologists have done their stuff. Wilson admits indeed that some of us may not like this future world when we get it, partly, it seems, because of worries about genetic

---

*French naturalist (1744–1829) and forerunner of Darwin, who proposed that changes in environment cause changes in animals and plants, resulting in adaptive modification, and that such acquired characteristics are then transmitted genetically to offspring.

engineering. But this will be due to our unscientific attitude. It affects neither the dogmatic confidence of the prediction nor the desirability of the outcome from the impersonal, scientific point of view.

The point about dogmatic confidence is interesting. Scrupulous modera- 12 tion in making factual claims is commonly seen as a central part of the scientific attitude. Julian Huxley, listing the bad habits which infest religion, naturally mentions "dogmatism" and "aspiring to a false certitude" among them and explains that science corrects these vices.[7] Remarks like those just quoted do not on the face of it seem to meet this standard.

When I have complained of this sort of thing to scientists, I have 13 sometimes met a surprising defence, namely, that these remarks appear in the opening or closing chapters of books, and that everybody knows that what is found there is not to be taken literally; it is just flannel for the general public. The idea seems to be that supplying such flannel constitutes a kind of a ritual. If so, it must surely strengthen our present unease, since addiction to ritual is another fault supposed to be the mark of religion. The point might of course just be the more practical one of selling books. But if grossly inflated claims to knowledge of the future are made for that reason, then there is either common dishonesty for personal profit, or an attempt to advance the cause of science by methods which disgrace it, and which (again) have always been considered a disgrace to religion. Putting these prophecies in a special part of the book does not disinfect them. It cannot be more excusable to peddle groundless predictions to the defenceless general public, who will take them to have the full authority of science, than to one's professional col- leagues, who know much better what bees infest one's bonnet. These bold prophecies of an escalating future are often combined, as they are here, with the vision of one's own Science in a gold helmet finally crushing its academic rivals: again, scarcely a monument to scientific balance and caution.

DRAWBACKS OF THE ESCALATOR MODEL

Is all this euphoria, however, actually dangerous? If the escalator myth 14 really has got out of hand, what harm does it do?

In one way, certainly, it does much less harm than the egoistic myth of 15 universal cut-throat competition. Optimism in general, even when it is mud- dled, tends to do less harm than pessimism. Faith in life, and in the human race, is certainly a better thing to have around than a supposedly science- based conviction of universal bloody-mindedness and hypocrisy. But once we are clear about that, we need to notice some objections, and as they have had much less attention than those which arise to the competitive myth, they may need more emphasis.

In the first place, faith in life and in the human race becomes much less 16 evident when we turn from those who rely on continued natural growth, like Teilhard* and Dobzhansky, to the champions of genetic engineering. Calling for surgical methods always shows less faith in the patient's constitution and more in the skills of the surgeon. The question, *in what do you put your faith?* is central to the whole enquiry. Those who put it in genetic engineering seem to give us what we now get so often here, an answer which misses the point of the question. They want us to put faith in certain techniques, or at most in the intellectual skills and capacities which make those techniques possible. But all these are means. What we need is to hear about aims, and about the faculties in all of us which reach out to those aims. What we get is a recommendation to entrust change to a certain set of experts, whose training has not called on them to pay any attention to conflicting aims at all.

The genetic engineering proposal, however, is not a necessary part of the escalator myth. Is there anything harmful about that myth itself, if we consider it in its more natural and consistent form as a simple prediction of steady, indefinite future human genetic progress to heights hitherto undreamed of?   17

I have already touched on the objection that this prediction, if it is taken as certain and infallible, gives a quite unwarranted sense of security, and can easily distract us from the need for other changes. If it is not taken as certain, but still as providing the only guideline towards safety, it admits the dangers but tells us, without argument, to rely on one particular way of escaping them rather than others, namely genetic engineering. And I think that those who do rely on it are in fact led by this way of thinking, not by any real evidence that this is a better prospect than other possible means of salvation. What, however, if no special question is raised about inevitability, but this progress is simply presented as the destiny offered to the human race? This somewhat vaguer picture is inspiring but a trifle dazzling. It may help us in assessing it to let the objector open the argument.   18

The central difficulty is that this story is arbitrarily human-centred, and that its view of humanity is at present arbitrarily intellect-centred. Its human-centredness distorts both evolutionary theory and our attitude to the natural world. By what right, and in what sense, can we consider ourselves as the directional pointer and aim-bearer of the whole evolutionary process? Does this mean what is often taken for granted today in controversy about the treatment of plants and animals, that all other organisms exist only as means to our ends? Kant and other philosophers have said this, many people believe it, yet it remains extremely obscure.[8] The idea that things are *there* for some external purpose seems to need a theological context, and this view did of course grow out of one. But that context will not subjugate everything to man. Certainly Judaeo-Christian thinking made the human race much more central than many other religions do, but it still considered man to be God's steward. Divine aims were always paramount, and God had created all his   19

---

*Teilhard de Chardin (1881–1955), French paleontologist and philosopher, who theorized that man is presently evolving, mentally and socially, toward a final spiritual unity.

creatures for his own purposes, not for man's. Non-human beings count in this picture as having their own special value. Redwoods and pythons, frogs, moles and albatrosses are not failed humans or early try-outs for humans or tools put there to advance human development.

When this is spelled out, people today usually accept it, yet the escalator 20 picture tends quietly and constantly to obscure it. Lamarck, who invented the escalator concept, did consider all non-human animals to be standing behind man, engaged on the same journey, and this still persisting idea does inevitably suggest that they are inferior and expendable. It obscures our enormous ignorance about their lives, about what it is like to be (say) a whale, a gorilla, an elephant, a mouse or a battery chicken, and supports our natural conviction that anything we don't do or experience can't have any value. The more we put aside this obviously hasty and inadequate myth, and notice the endless variety of existing creatures, the more we shall be driven to forget the linear metaphor of height, and return to the more Darwinian image of the radiating bush.

WHICH WAY IS UP?

Is there, however, still a fixed upward dimension? Does the bush have 21 a human tip? Are we in some sense the point of the whole? I have never myself felt the need to say this, but very many people do, and the point must be taken seriously. It may well be that any intelligent species, able to meditate on such things, must in some way think of itself as central in the whole world, because in its own world it is so. It may be morally necessary to treat our own destiny as the most important thing conceivable, if only because we cannot easily conceive anything greater. But this by no means licenses us to separate it from all others and pursue it at their expense, nor does it mean, as escalator-fanciers sometimes kindly suggest, that our duty to those behind us is to help them to become like ourselves as quickly as possible. The moral consequences of a serious attitude to our own destiny are excellent, but those of a contemptuous attitude to other destinies are quite another matter. The two should not be linked at all.

Turning from morals to theory, could this way of thinking license us to 22 predict that the next thing the bush will do is to grow taller? Change in human societies is now almost entirely a cultural, not a genetic matter, and it can as easily be for the worse as for the better. It is commonly recognized today that we badly need to be clear about this, since the belief in inevitable progress can be, and has been, used to justify bad changes which were preventable. Even, therefore, if we had reason to expect genetic change, this would not show that such change was good, nor that it was outside our control. And even if we had sound theoretical grounds for expecting the genetic development of our own species into something still greater and more distinctively human, this could scarcely show that we were the single supremely valuable object which gave point to the whole evolutionary process.

There does not have to be any such one object. And since there are no such theoretical grounds either—since this expectation has no place in Darwinian theory, and came to Lamarck and Spencer simply as a welcome, self-justifying hunch—it is very remarkable that scientifically educated people still continue to ask the question which stands as title to the last chapter of William Day's book, from which I have already quoted, the question "Where is evolution headed?"[9]

THE FUTURE AS MAGNIFYING MIRROR

How does this question arise? If we look at the literature which asks it 23 and attempts to give it answers, a very simple answer becomes almost unavoidable. It is a way of dramatizing morals. One can give a peculiar force to the praise and exaltation of particular ideals by presenting them as a piece of foresight, a glance at a real, attainable though perhaps distant future. This is an ancient, natural and legitimate device, which lies at the root of prophecy. Both bad and good futures can be used, but if the moral leverage is to work, both must be presented as only possible. There must still be time to work for this "future" or avert it. Both author and reader must therefore be clear that the vision is an imaginary one, and this literature must be kept separate from the relatively humdrum business of prediction. Sober predictions about the likely future development of terrestrial life would not carry any such moral message. They would not necessarily make human affairs central at all, but would refer to them only in so far as they seem likely to affect the development of ecosystems. But the prophecies which now concern us are not in the least like this. They are quite simply exaltations of particular ideals within human life at their own epoch, projected on to the screen of a vague and vast "future"—a term which, since Nietzsche* and Wells, is not a name for what is particularly likely to happen, but for a fantasy realm devoted to the staging of visionary dramas.

In their content, these dramas plainly depend on the moral convictions 24 of their author and of his age, not on scientific theories of any kind. Nietzsche, who laid down the ground-rules of this game, used Darwinian ideas and language as a pedestal for his own preferred ideal type, the unsocial, anarchic, creative individual, his enlarged and exalted self:

> Ye lonely ones of to-day; ye that stand apart, ye shall one day be a people; from you, that have chosen yourselves, a chosen people shall arise—and from it, the Superman. . . .
> And the Great Noon shall be when man standeth in the midst of his course between beast and Superman. . . . Dead are all gods; now will we that the Superman live.[10]

*Friedrich Wilhelm Nietzsche (1844–1900), German philosopher, poet, and philologist known for espousing the doctrine of the perfectibility of man through forcible self-assertion and for glorification of the superman or overman (übermensch).

And, more prosaically:

> The problem I raise here is not what ought to succeed mankind (the human being is an *end*) but what type of human being one ought to *breed*, ought to *will*, as more valuable, more worthy of life, more certain of the future.[11]

The mark of this favoured and expected type is not just that he is free from the trammels of existing religion and morality, but that he is a fully unified human being, free from the many bad habits which at present divide our nature. He is to reunite spirit and intellect, which now wither in pretentious isolation, with their strong roots in the body, the imagination and the passions. Although externally he is isolated, contemptuous of social links with his fellows, internally he balances this isolation by the strongest possible integration of his nature. Indeed Nietzsche's hostility to outward social bonds is largely a protest against their tendency to fragment the individual's being. And, among contemporary influences which promote this fatal division, he thinks the exaltation of the bare intellect, especially in its scientific form, every bit as pernicious as the Christian religion:

> The harsh helot condition to which the tremendous extent of science has condemned every single person to-day is one of the main reasons why education and *educators* appropriate to fuller, richer, *deeper* natures are no longer forthcoming. Our culture suffers from nothing *more* than it suffers from the superabundance of presumptuous journeymen and fragments of humanity.[12]

And again:

> *From a doctorate exam.*—"What is the task of all higher education?"—To turn a man into a machine—"By what means?" He has to learn how to feel bored. "How is this achieved?"—Through the concept of duty. . . . "Who is the perfect man?" The civil servant.[13]

Thus Nietzsche; do we like his future? If not, the Jesuit biologist Teilhard de Chardin offers us quite a different one, in which Nietzsche's twin abominations, physical science and Christianity, are both to be exalted and to find their final synthesis. It was Teilhard who invented the phrase "Omega man," using it to describe a future being, raised above us both spiritually and intellectually, whose destiny it is to complete the divine plan for this earth by perfecting it at the mental level—to add a noösphere, or intellectual realm, to the living realm, or biosphere, which is already present. (Teilhard seems also to have invented the term *biosphere*, and should be given the credit for that useful move.) In this ideal future, the idea of brotherly love and of the mystical union of individuals in the whole—an ideal which would have been pure ratsbane to Nietzsche—plays a central part, and traditional Christianity, however difficult it may be to fit in with this ambitious scheme, is certainly still conceived as the main guiding thread.

SCIENTISTS AS SUPERMEN

Do both these suggestions strike some readers today as a trifle crazy? 26 It cannot be too strongly emphasized how much this impression of craziness depends on current moral and intellectual habits. What will our own look like, to those who have ceased to share them? And what is actually in the minds of those who make parallel suggestions today?

I shall go on using William Day's book *Genesis on Planet Earth,* because 27 it seems to me to put exceptionally clearly ideas which are very widely accepted, and seldom as well expressed. Day writes throughout as if only one sort of improvement could possibly be in question, namely a rise in intelligence, and he treats *intelligence* as a term which could not possibly be ambiguous or need analysis. To increase this intelligence is, he says, the purpose of all life: an idea which he presents as needing no defence or explanation. His language about this is flagrantly teleological,* indeed vitalist:

> Life has endured, generation after generation, producing more than can live, sacrificing many that the most fit may survive. Species have followed species, rung after rung, in a continuous climb of the ladder called evolution. And in that long ascent, life has retained rapport with its surroundings by evolving its window on the universe—intelligence.[14]

What is meant by speaking of intelligence as a window, and why should such a window furnish the point of the whole? If windows matter so much, must it not be because what we see through them is important, and if it is, must there not be other valuable things besides intelligence? Windows are a means. Is the function we are talking about just the acquiring and ordering of information? or does it include certain deep ways of responding to it? Those who originally put this great stress on intelligence into European thought meant by it something enormously wider than mere ordered storage. Both Plato and Aristotle, who differed so much on countless other points, agreed in making the point of the whole intellectual enterprise consist in the contemplation to which it led: the awareness of a vast outer whole, within which human thought operates, and of which it can form only the faintest image. Day sees no such difficulty. Reality for him is what we make it through science:

> It is into all reality that life, led by man, is expanding. Reality is no longer restricted to the horizons of the senses, but extends to the far reaches conceived by the mind. Physical reality may or may not be finite, for what exists is what we perceive, or identify as reality, and how far we can extend reality is uncertain.[15]

*Purposeful, having a goal established by plan; not happening merely at random.

Resisting the temptation to go into all the implications of this—does it   28
actually mean that reality is what physicists say it is, and if so how do they
know what to say?—I stick to the point which now concerns us, namely that
the central business of the mind, the work for which "life" has evolved it,
is here physical science. Omega man emerges as quite simply a superscientist.
Only at one point does it look as if he might have any other interests: where
Day says that man's "intelligence has evolved where, unlike any other form
of life, he is touching on a new dimension. It is man's spirituality, psyche and
superego, and that part of man [sic] that makes him the forerunner of Omega
man."[16] But these mysterious dimensions have already been mentioned and
been explained as being simply physical: "real dimensions of time and space,
beyond our reach in size and perception."[17] Materialism is not being compromised. To settle that point finally, Day goes on [italics added]:

> A type of intelligence more evolved than man's could conceive of a
> reality *and exercise control over it* in a manner beyond our ability to compre-
> hend. What comprehension *and powers over nature* Omega man will be able
> to command can only be suggested by man's image of the supernatu-
> ral.[18]

The mention of spirituality proves to have been only a ritual one. The real
point of all this intelligence, and therefore of evolution itself, was, it turns
out, simply to put more physical power in the hands of the quasi-deified
human species, even though that species seems already to have a great deal
more physical power than it knows what to do with. . . .

BALANCING THE WORLD

I have been arguing that the contrast between science and religion is   29
unluckily not as plain, nor the relation between them as simple, as is often
supposed, and have been discussing some elements which can equally form
part of either. Thoughtful scientists have often mentioned this problem, but
a great many of their colleagues, and of the public generally, cling to the
reassuringly simple opposition. What often seems to happen is that a great
number of different antitheses are mixed up here, and used rather indiscriminately, as each happens to be convenient, to give colour to the idea of a
general crusade of light against darkness. We could group them roughly like
this:

			superstition
			partiality
			error
			magic
1	science	v	wish-fulfilment
			dogmatism
			blind conformism
			childishness

2   common sense ⎤   ⎧ intuition
    science   ⎥   v. ⎨ mysticism
    rationalism   ⎥   ⎩ faith
    logic   ⎦

                              ⎧ idealism
                              ⎥ animism
    materialism   v.   ⎨ vitalism
                              ⎥ mind-body dualism
                              ⎩ commonsense agnosticism

3   hard   v.   soft
    progress   v.   tradition
    determinism   v.   free will
    mechanism   v.   teleology
    empiricism   v.   ⎧ rationalism
                          ⎩ metaphysics
    scepticism   v.   credulity
    reason   v.   feeling or emotion
    objective   v.   subjective
    quantity   v.   quality
    physical science v.   the humanities
    realism   v.   reverence
    specialism   v.   holism
    prose   v.   poetry
    male   v.   female
    clarity   v.   mystery

SHIFTING PARADIGMS

A mental map based on this strange group of antitheses, a map which [30] showed them all as roughly equivalent and was marked only with the general direction "keep to the left," has for the last century usually been issued to English-speaking scientists with their first test-tube and has often gone with them to the grave. In spite of its wild incoherence, it still has great influence, though at least two recent developments within science itself have lately shaken it, and more are to be expected. The first shock is the series of changes whereby modern physics now shows indeterminacy as lying near the centre of causation, and solid matter as dissolving, on inspection, into non-solid energy. This is a severe upset to the crucial notions of mechanism and determinism. What perhaps cuts deepest, however, is something symbolic which looks more superficial and which would not matter at all if people were really only interested in facts and not in drama. It is the disturbance to the notion of "hardness," a metaphor whose application is entirely mysterious, but which has somehow served to keep the whole left-hand column together.

At present, this change results in a flow of popular books such as *The* [31] *Tao of Physics* by Fritdjof Capra and *The Dancing Wu Li Masters* by Gary Zukav,[19] which suggest that energy is spirit, and that what modern physics teaches is, give or take a mantra or two, very much what Zen masters and Hindu sages have been saying for centuries, or possibly millennia. Whatever else may be thought about this, it does at least point to the need to look again at our list of antitheses. On the face of things, these books do draw attention to the arbitrary narrow-mindedness which has been imposed on scientists, and call for science to look outward, though at times they also seem to convey the opposite message: science, especially physics, is already far more spiritual, and therefore more all-sufficient, than we have so far supposed. At least, however, the traditional set of antitheses is broken up. Serious physicists seem at present more aware than many biologists of its confusions and inadequacies. David Bohm's comment, extracts from which we saw earlier, deserves now to be quoted more fully:

> At the end of the nineteenth century, physicists widely believed that classical physics gave the general outlines of a complete mechanical explanation of the universe. Since then, relativity and quantum theory have overturned such notions altogether. It is now clear that no mechanical explanation is available, not for the fundamental particles which constitute all matter, inanimate and animate, nor for the cosmos as a whole (e.g. it is now widely accepted among cosmologists that in "black holes" there is a singularity, near which all customary notions of causally ordered law break down). So we are now in the strange position that whereas physicists are implying that, fundamentally and in its totality, inanimate matter is not mechanical, molecular biologists are saying that whenever matter is organized so as to be alive, it is completely mechanical.
>
> Of course, molecular biologists generally ignore the implications of physics, except when these implications support their own position. In this connection, it might be appropriate for them to consider that the nineteenth-century view of physics was enormously more comprehensively and accurately tested than is now possible for the current views of molecular biology. Despite this, classical physics was swept aside and overturned, being retained only as a simplification and an approximation valid in a certain limited domain. Is it not likely that modern molecular biology will sooner or later undergo a similar fate?
>
> What is needed for unrestricted objectivity is a certain tentative and exploratory quality of mind that is free of final conclusions. [Without this, there is an] ever-present danger that knowledge in broad and deep fields may give rise to the sort of "hubris" described above, in which there is an unquestioned belief in the complete validity of current forms of thinking. . . . If [this] is allowed to continue in science, this latter will in all probability eventually suffer the sort of decline of influence which has already befallen the religious view of the world. Indeed, there are already signs of such a trend.[20]

The second shock was delivered by recent discoveries about the functions of brain hemispheres. In its early days, this was often read, in a way which is itself a notable indicator of the underlying dramas expected, as a story about the "dominance" of one hemisphere, namely of course the calculating, articulate, scientific one, over the other, which was intuitive, humble

and not really very distinctively human. Further research, however, has
steadily shown more and more serious functions for the right-hand hemisphere, and has led increasingly to the acceptance of Kipling's picture expressed at the beginning of this chapter,* where it is utterly vital to have, and
to keep in balance, the two separate sides of one's head. The idea of the ruling
hemisphere had been just one more version of a simple but very powerful
hierarchical view of mental function which long dominated neurology, and
which Peter Reynolds, the comparative ethologist, has lately christened "the
Victorian brain."[21] This showed brain evolution dramatically as a series of
successive conquests, in which at each level of life a new brain area and its
faculties came in to rule the rest, culminating in man and the final victory of
the cerebral cortex, or some specially splendid part of it. To keep this dominance order clear, functions were neatly confined to particular structures, and
the belief that *Homo sapiens* possessed not just a better cortex but entirely
distinct organs to carry his higher faculties was at first hotly defended by
Owen† against Huxley.‡ Detailed neurological work has, however, worn
away almost every aspect of this seductive picture. As Stephen Walker, a
neurological psychologist, says,

> One still has a sense of regret that this charming and convincing tale must
> be discarded. The weight of evidence is now if anything more in favour
> of the unhelpful suggestion . . . that all the fundamental parts of the
> vertebrate brain were present very early on, and can be observed in
> lampreys.[22]

Moreover, new developments do not at all follow the simple pattern of
conquest and takeover. Functions are neither handed over wholesale to
grander organs nor fully determined by them; they seem to involve very
complex interactions between wide ranges of brain areas, in which it is
seldom safe to say either that any one area takes no part, or that any one
dominates or "rules" any others. No doubt each makes its own distinctive
contribution, to which adjectives like "higher" might sometimes usefully be
applied, but the only social metaphor which seems appropriate for these
transactions is co-operation. The brain, in short, works as a whole, and our
understanding of it has been very much held back by the fact that, as Walker
remarks, "there is a tendency to want to appoint some brain division as 'in
charge' of all the others, and this sets the stage for phylogenetic takeovers of
the executive position."

Brain evolution, in short, is not a simple success story establishing the   33
right of all left-hand members in our antitheses to subdue their partners.
Since the members of the two sets are in any case such a mixed lot as to make

*Midgley earlier quotes a Kipling poem, omitted here, in which the speaker says he would rather
suffer anything than "lose / Either side of my head."

†Sir Richard Owen (1804–1892), English anatomist and paleontologist, early opponent of Darwin's theory of evolution.

‡Thomas Henry Huxley (1825–1895), English biologist, who defended Darwin's theories so
persistently that he earned the nickname Darwin's Bulldog.

this wholesale arrangement impossible, we had better look at them separately on their merits.

FINDING THE RIGHT ENEMY

Which among these antitheses are really the ones we need, which of them give clear ground for a crusade? The ones in the first group seem the most promising for crusaders. In them science stands opposed to something undoubtedly bad. But in these cases it is certainly not the only opponent of the evils in question. Superstition and the rest find their opposites in clear thinking generally, and a particular superstition is as likely to be corrected by history or logic or common sense as by one of the physical sciences. The second group deals in ideas which are more ambitious, more interesting, but also much more puzzling, because we at once need definitions of the terms involved, and cannot easily give them without falling into confusion. The odd tendency of both rationalism and common sense to jump the central barrier is only one indication of the difficulties. In the third group, we have contrasts which are a good deal clearer. But they do not seem to provide material at all suitable for a crusade. They describe pairs of complementary elements in life and thought, both members of which are equally necessary, and indeed could scarcely be identified except in relation to each other as parts of a whole. We no longer want that truculent little "v." to divide them. They go very well together, and crusaders must avoid trying to set them at logger-heads. Thus it does not matter here that "reason" appears on both sides; we no longer want to reduce all these contrasts to a single underlying shape. The lines of division cross each other. Different distinctions are needed for different purposes.

How hard it is to relate these various antitheses clearly can be seen in Bertrand Russell's very interesting and influential paper "Mysticism and Logic." Russell's main enterprise here is an admirable attempt to move the whole debate into our group 3, to show apparently warring elements as both necessary and complementary:

> Metaphysics,* or the attempt to conceive the world as a whole by means of thought, has been developed, from the first, by the union and conflict of two very different human impulses, the one urging men towards mysticism, the other urging them towards science. . . . In Hume,† for instance, the scientific impulse reigns quite unchecked, while in Blake‡ a strong hostility to science co-exists with profound mystic insight. But the great-

---

*The study of things transcending physical nature, thus frequently associated with inquiries into the spiritual and the religious dimensions of reality.

†David Hume (1711–1776), Scottish philosopher whose skepticism restricted knowledge to what we learn from direct experience; strong opponent of all forms of metaphysics.

‡William Blake (1757–1827), English artist, poet, and mystic, violently opposed to science's "despiritualizing" effects.

est men who have been philosophers have felt the need both of science
and of mysticism; the attempt to harmonize the two was what made their
life, and what always must, for all its arduous uncertainty, make philosophy, to some minds, a greater thing than either science or religion. . . .
Mysticism, is, in essence, little more than a certain intensity and depth of
feeling in regard to what is believed about the universe. . . . Mysticism
is to be commended as an attitude towards life, not as a creed about the
world. The metaphysical creed, I shall maintain, is a mistaken outcome
of the emotion, although this emotion, as colouring all other thoughts and
feelings, is the inspirer of whatever is best in Man. Even the cautious and
patient investigation of truth by science, which seems the very antithesis
of the mystic's swift certainty, may be fostered and nourished by that
very spirit of reverence in which mysticism lives and moves.[23]

Russell has got a lot of things right here. He has "got in," as they say, 36
many items from the right-hand column of our antitheses in legitimate relation to science. He has got in emotion and poetry, indeed he has got in Blake,
with his criticisms of Newton.[*] He sees that emotion is so far from being an
opponent of science, or a menace to it, that emotion of a suitable kind is
necessary for science, and that part of that emotion can quite properly be
called "reverence." He sees that something of the sort is necessary for metaphysics too.

The word *metaphysics* here is not of course used in the abusive sense to 37
mean mere empty vapouring. It is used in its proper sense of very general
conceptual enquiry, covering such central topics as the relation of mind and
matter, free will and necessity, meaning, truth and the possibility of knowledge, all in an attempt (as Russell rightly says) to make sense of the world
as a whole. In this sense, naturally, views like materialism and empiricism,
and also sceptical enquiries like those of Hume, Ayer and Popper, are themselves part of metaphysics just as much as what they oppose or enquire into.
When A. J. Ayer began his book *Language, Truth and Logic*[24] with a chapter
called "The Elimination of Metaphysics," and went on to explain that the
word was for him virtually equivalent to "nonsense," he was, in any ordinary
sense of that word, simply doing metaphysics himself—expounding one theory of meaning among many others. Empty vapouring is *bad* metaphysics.
There is a lot of it about, but it cannot make the study unnecessary.

Russell, who had the advantage of having started his philosophical life 38
as a disciple of Hegel, was not tempted, as Hume and his disciples were, to
suppose that good metaphysics merely meant cutting down one's thoughts
on such topics to a minimum. He knew that, far from that, even highly
constructive metaphysicians like Plato and Heraclitus, Leibnitz and Hegel
often had something very important to say, especially about mathematics.
Yet he was now a convert to empiricism, and he wanted to set limits on the
thought-architecture of these bold rationalists. His solution was, on the

[*]Isaac Newton (1642–1727), English physicist and mathematician, who conceived the idea of
universal gravitation.

whole, to concentrate on the emotional function of this large-scale, constructive metaphysics, and on the intellectual function of science and of more
sceptical philosophy. Thus mystical, constructive metaphysics was to supply
the heart of the world-grasping enterprise, while science supplied the head.

THE MANY-SIDEDNESS OF SCIENCE

This is a bold and ingenious idea, but something has gone wrong with 39
it. He has fitted the head of one kind of enquiry on to the heart of another.
Constructive metaphysics has its own thoughts, and science its own motives.
If the word *science* means what it seems to mean here—primarily the search
for particular facts—then it is powered emotionally by the familiar motive of
detailed curiosity. If it means the building of those facts into a harmonious,
satisfying system, then it draws upon a different motive, the desire for intellectual order; which is also the motive for metaphysical endeavour. Without
this unifying urge, science would be nothing but mindless, meaningless collecting. At the quite ordinary scientific level, before any question of mysti-
cally contemplating the whole comes in, the system-building tendency, with
its aesthetic criteria of elegance and order, is an essential part of every science,
continually shaping the scrappy data into usable patterns. Scientific hypotheses are not generated by randomizers, nor do they grow on trees, but on the
branches of these ever-expanding thought systems.

This is why the sciences continually go beyond everybody's direct
experience, and do so in directions that quickly diverge from that of common
sense, which has more modest systems of its own. And because isolated
systems are always incomplete and can conflict with each other, inevitably
in the end they require metaphysics, "the attempt to conceive the world as
a whole," to harmonize them.

To what are interestingly called *lay* people, however, these intellectual
constructions present problems of belief which are often quite as difficult as
those of religion, and which can call for equally strenuous efforts of faith.
This happens at present over relativity, over the size and expansion of the
universe, over quantum mechanics, over evolution and many other matters.
Believers are—perhaps quite properly—expected to bow to the mystery,
admit the inadequacy of their faculties, and accept paradoxes. If a mystical
sense of reverence is, as Russell suggested, the right response to the vast and
incomprehensible universe, then science itself requires it, since it leads us on
directly to this situation. It cannot therefore be right to call mysticism and
science, as Russell does, two distinct, co-ordinate "human impulses." Mysticism is a range of human faculties; physical science, a range of enquiries
which can, at times, call these faculties into action. But long before it does
so, it has passed the limits of common sense, transcended experience and
begun to ask for faith.

At this stage, there is often a real problem about what kind of thinking 42
is going on, and whether it ought to be stopped. If, for instance, we ask

whether the universe is finite, are we still talking about anything at all? If so, do we know what it is? The most general concepts used by any science—concepts like life, time, space, law, energy—raise serious headaches, affecting their use in actual problems. To resolve these, however, we often need not more facts but a better way of fitting these concepts into their neighbours, of stating the wider problems which surround them, of "conceiving the world as a whole." Science quite properly calls on the whole range of our cognitive faculties, but it is not alone in doing so, nor can it define their whole aim. It is a part of our attempt to understand the universe, not the whole of it. It opens into metaphysics.

NOTES

All notes are Midgley's.

1. Jacques Monod, *Chance and Necessity,* trans. Austryn Wainhouse (London, Fontana, 1974), p. 160.

2. M. T. Ghiselin, *The Economy of Nature and the Evolution of Sex* (Berkeley, Cal., University of California Press, 1974), p. 247.

3. For both these influences see Gillian Beer's excellent discussions in *Darwin's Plots; Evolutionary Narrative in Darwin, George Eliot and Nineteenth Century Fiction* (London, Routledge & Kegan Paul, 1984), especially pp. 30–40 and 83–8.

4. Quoted by James Moore, *The Post-Darwinian Controversies; A Study of the Protestant Struggle to Come to Terms with Darwin in Great Britain and America 1870–1900* (Cambridge, Cambridge University Press, 1979), p. 167, from Edward Clodd.

5. In his *Philosophie Zoologique* (1809) and *Histoire Naturelle des Animaux sans Vertèbres* (1815–22).

6. Edward O. Wilson, *Sociobiology; The New Synthesis* (Cambridge, Mass., Harvard University Press, 1975), pp. 574–5.

7. Julian Huxley, *Religion without Revelation* (London, Benn, 1927), p. 372.

8. See for instance the essay on 'Duties towards animals and spirits' in Kant's *Lectures on Ethics,* trans. Louis Infield (London, Methuen, 1930). I have discussed these difficulties in *Beast and Man* (Brighton, Harvester Press, 1979), pts. 4 and 5, and in *Animals and Why They Matter* (Harmondsworth, Penguin, 1983) throughout.

9. William Day, *Genesis on Planet Earth; The Search for Life's Beginning* (2nd edn., New Haven, Conn., Yale University Press, 1984).

10. *Thus Spake Zarathustra,* pt. 1, 'Of virtue that giveth', trans. A. Tille and M. Bozman (London, Dent, Everyman edn., 1930), pp. 68–9.

11. *The Antichrist,* sec. 3, trans. R. J. Hollingdale (published with *Twilight of the Idols*) (Harmondsworth, Penguin, 1968), p. 116.

12. *Twilight of the Idols,* sec. 3, 'What the Germans lack', trans. R. J. Hollingdale (Harmondsworth, Penguin, 1968), p. 61.

13. Ibid., sec. 29, 'Expeditions of an untimely man', p. 83.

14. Day, op. cit., p. 381.

15. Ibid., p. 389.

16. Ibid., p. 391.

17. Ibid., p. 390.

18. Ibid., p. 391.

19. Fritdjof Capra, *The Tao of Physics* (London, Wildwood House, 1975) and Gary Zukav, *The Dancing Wu Li Masters* (London, Fontana, 1982).

20. In John Lewis (ed.), *Beyond Chance and Necessity* (London, Garnstone Press, 1974), pp. 128–35.

21. See Peter Reynolds, *On the Evolution of Human Behaviour* (Berkeley, Cal., University of California Press, 1981), pp. 35–6, 68 and 222–4.

22. Stephen Walker, *Animal Thought* (London, Routledge & Kegan Paul, 1983), p. 145.

23. Bertrand Russell, 'Mysticism and logic', reprinted in *Mysticism and Logic* (London, Allen & Unwin, 1917), pp. 9, 10 and 16.

24. London, Gollancz, 1936.

Questions for Discussion

1. Some people, says Midgley, hold to the "mistaken ideal" that "scientists ought to be so impartial that they either do not have anything so unprofessional as a world-picture at all, or, if they have one, do not let it affect their work" (¶4–5). Try to determine by class discussion how prevalent this view of scientific objectivity is among your classmates. How convincing or unconvincing do you and others find Midgley's description of scientific objectivity? What reasons would you use in arguing either for or against her views?

2. Summarize in your own words the positions of Herbert Spencer and Jean-Baptiste Lamarck (¶9–10) and Darwin's objections to their views. Can you and your classmates come up with references to evolutionary theory that you have heard that treat evolutionary theory as if it explains social relationships as well as biological development? Can you specifically recall hearing the phrase "survival of the fittest" applied to society, as if competition among corporations or countries could be explained by the model of biological competition? What does such an application mean? Did anyone in class know that this phrase was introduced by the sociologist Herbert Spencer, and not by Darwin?

3. Sift through Midgley's essay and copy in your notebook the metaphors used both by and about science and scientists, and note any repetitions. Discuss the possibility of substituting "literal" language for the metaphors? Can it be done, or do metaphors seem an essential part of scientific discourse? If so, what does this do to the conventional notion of scientific discourse as based solely on hard facts? If metaphors are not essential, should scientists make every attempt not to use them? Support your opinions with specific reasons.

4. Which sets of antitheses in paragraph 29 seem to you and your classmates a natural way of categorizing things? Why? Which, if any, do not seem natural? Why not? What diversity of opinions exists among members of

the class? Are there any discernible preferences for the right-hand list over the left-hand list (or vice versa)? If there are, on what grounds are the preferences explained or defended? Can you determine if religious believers tend to prefer one list and agnostics or atheists the other? If so, what does this suggest about the nature of the lists? If not, what does this suggest about deeply shared cultural values?

5. What does Bohm (¶31) mean by the term *hubris*, which appears near the end of the quoted passage? Does Midgley provide other examples of the kind of hubris he is referring to in other quotations?

6. In paragraph 30 Midgley says that two developments in the twentieth century have shaken people's faith in the validity of the antitheses that she outlines in paragraph 29. Explain in your own words the nature of these two developments. Which of the two was more widely known among your classmates?

7. Paraphrase Russell's point in the passage quoted in paragraph 35. Why does Midgley think Russell provides help in escaping the sterility of overdrawn antitheses? What is Midgley's criticism of Russell's point (¶39)?

Suggested Essay Topics

1. Write a précis: a summary of an argument that preserves the main points and structure of the original while condensing it greatly. Midgley's essay has 12 sections, each with its own heading. Using these headings and placing them in the same order as in Midgley's essay, write a three- or four-sentence summary of each subsection so that you wind up with a condensed but accurate paraphrase of her whole argument. This kind of exercise is not the same as doing original analysis, but when you are dealing with complex arguments such as Midgley's, it can be a useful way of making sure you understand what you are reading.

2. In an essay directed to your classmates, your instructor, a scientist, or a religious believer (whichever seems most appropriate to you), explain either the accuracy or the inaccuracy of the list of antitheses that Midgley lays out in paragraph 29. Whether the list seems to you helpful or unhelpful, right or wrong, explain (if you support the list) what it tells us about different kinds of knowledge, experience, or reality. If you do not support the list, explain why knowledge, experience, and reality cannot really be divided this way. If you choose this latter tack, you will have to show in addition that some other division would be better or that no divisions should be made at all.

IDEAS IN DEBATE

C. P. Snow
Loren Eiseley

C. P. Snow

The British writer C. P. Snow (1905–1980) could write about the distinctive character of the literary and scientific cultures because he not only knew them both intimately but spanned them in a distinguished and unusual way. He is thus an exception to the generalizations he makes about both the literary culture (or, as we in America would tend to say, the humanistic outlook or humanistic tradition) and the scientific culture (or scientific outlook). That he was himself an exception does not, of course, invalidate his generalizations; it simply underscores what a remarkable man he was. He spanned the two cultures by working professionally as both a trained scientist and a publishing novelist. He was a physicist at Cambridge from 1930 to 1950, and at the same time he wrote an 11-volume sequence of novels, collectively titled Strangers and Brothers *(1940–1970), that focuses on contemporary English society and documents the corrupting influence of power.*

The split between humanists and scientists that Snow described in 1956 has in the intervening decades both grown and shrunk. At the theoretical level the split has shrunk, but at the institutional level and in the eyes of the general public the split has grown. At the theoretical level the work of such theorists and philosophers of science as Jacob Bronowski, Loren Eiseley, Stephen Toulmin, Norwood Russell Hanson, Thomas Kuhn, Paul Feyerabend, Harold Brown, and Michael Polanyi has taught contemporary scientists to see that their modes of operation and those of the humanists are not as different as they were thought to be in 1956 when Snow published his original review, "The Two Cultures," in the New Statesman. *In the past 30 years scientists have become much less naïve about such issues as the status of a fact, the nature of objectivity, and the limits of empiricism. And humanists are probably much more knowledgeable now than Snow's literary colleagues were in 1956 about the general trends and controversies in scientific theory—though probably not much more knowledgeable about the details of scientific research. Generally, then, the two cultures have more of a speaking, or at least nodding, relationship today, at the theoretical level, than they had in the 1950s.*

At the institutional level, however, at the places where scientists actually conduct their research and humanists write their books, the specialization that Snow deplores has driven the two cultures even farther apart. In both the humanities and the sciences the topics of inquiry over the past three decades have become even more

427

specialized and thus more subdivided. The result is that a historian who has a general knowledge of trends in scientific theory these days will nevertheless be as ignorant as ever about the actual research that fuels theoretical controversy. What is more—and this is something new—humanists now find themselves in the same position of ignorance about research and theories, even those of other humanists. And in science today an organic chemist has a nearly impossible task trying to understand the work of a mathematical chemist. In other words, the split nowadays is not just between the humanists and the scientists but among the subdivisions within these two broad camps.

The split between scientists and humanists has also grown larger in the eyes of the general public since the 1950s. We have no statistical proof of this assertion, but it seems a logical consequence of the increasing specialization we just referred to. In the 1950s, as Snow reports, science was brash and optimistic. Since then science has had to endure a degree of suspicion and hostility that it once seemed immune to—primarily on occasions when technology has proved threatening, as in the near meltdown at the Three Mile Island nuclear facility, as in the injurious consequences of the Agent Orange defoliation of forests in Vietnam, or as in the deterioration of the ozone layer caused by atmospheric pollution. These problems, however, do not lead most people to reject science. Indeed, the remedies people look to are almost always scientific. Science is supposed to tell us how to make safer defoliants, more reliable nuclear power plants, more efficient, pollution-scrubbing smokestacks, and so on. And beyond that, most people still think of science as the source of the only true—or at least the most true—understanding of both the natural world and human nature.

While science has retained its prestige as a source of both true and useful knowledge, the humanities have lost prestige on this scale of measurement. Fewer people now seem to turn to the study of languages, history, literature, or philosophy for solving either social or personal problems. Thus in the more than 30 years since Snow's essay, science has maintained its position in society or even enhanced it, but the humanities have lost ground. B.A. degrees in the humanities and student enrollments in humanities courses have been steadily declining. In this and other ways, the split between the two cultures has become an even more formidable problem now than it was when Snow first called our attention to it.

As you read, try to extend and amplify Snow's reasons for thinking that the split between the sciences and the humanities is unfortunate and potentially disastrous. Also consider your own attitudes toward either culture in light of what you want out of your education or the qualities of mind you think a well-educated person should possess. If Snow is right, we should all share a common literacy in both science and the humanities. But as you know, science and humanities majors all too often not only avoid courses in the "other" culture (to whatever extent possible) but are downright hostile to them. Consider how far your own literacy (and that of your friends) extends in the sciences and humanities. Does it extend far enough? Far enough for what?

THE TWO CULTURES

From *The Two Cultures: And a Second Look* (1965).

It is about three years since I made a sketch in print of a problem which had been on my mind for some time.[1] It was a problem I could not avoid just because of the circumstances of my life. The only credentials I had to ruminate on the subject at all came through those circumstances, through nothing more than a set of chances. Anyone with similar experience would have seen much the same things and I think made very much the same comments about them. It just happened to be an unusual experience. By training I was a scientist: by vocation I was a writer. That was all. It was a piece of luck, if you like, that arose through coming from a poor home.

But my personal history isn't the point now. All that I need say is that I came to Cambridge and did a bit of research here at a time of major scientific activity. I was privileged to have a ringside view of one of the most wonderful creative periods in all physics. And it happened through the flukes of war—including meeting W. L. Bragg* in the buffet on Kettering station on a very cold morning in 1939, which had a determining influence on my practical life—that I was able, and indeed morally forced, to keep that ringside view ever since. So for thirty years I have had to be in touch with scientists not only out of curiosity, but as part of a working existence. During the same thirty years I was trying to shape the books I wanted to write, which in due course took me among writers.

There have been plenty of days when I have spent the working hours with scientists and then gone off at night with some literary colleagues. I mean that literally. I have had, of course, intimate friends among both scientists and writers. It was through living among these groups and much more, I think, through moving regularly from one to the other and back again that I got occupied with the problem of what, long before I put it on paper, I christened to myself as the "two cultures." For constantly I felt I was moving among two groups—comparable in intelligence, identical in race, not grossly different in social origin, earning about the same incomes, who had almost ceased to communicate at all, who in intellectual, moral and psychological climate had so little in common that instead of going from Burlington House or South Kensington to Chelsea,† one might have crossed an ocean.

In fact, one had travelled much further than across an ocean—because after a few thousand Atlantic miles, one found Greenwich Village‡ talking precisely the same language as Chelsea, and both having about as much communication with M.I.T.§ as though the scientists spoke nothing but Ti-

---

1

2

3

4

*Sir William Lawrence Bragg (1890–1971), Cavendish professor of experimental physics at Cambridge (1938–1954) and co-winner with his father of the 1915 Nobel Prize in physics.
†Chelsea has a long history as a literary and artistic section of London. In the eighteenth century Swift, Steele, and Smollett lived there. Later, Turner, Rossetti, Whistler, Leigh Hunt, and Carlyle lived there.
‡A famous literary and artistic section of New York City.
§Massachusetts Institute of Technology in Boston, a famous school of science and engineering.

betan. For this is not just our problem; owing to some of our educational and social idiosyncrasies, it is slightly exaggerated here; owing to another English social peculiarity it is slightly minimised; by and large this is a problem of the entire West.

By this I intend something serious. I am not thinking of the pleasant story of how one of the more convivial Oxford greats dons*—I have heard the story attributed to A. L. Smith—came over to Cambridge to dine. The date is perhaps the 1890's. I think it must have been at St John's, or possibly Trinity.† Anyway, Smith was sitting at the right hand of the President—or Vice-Master—and he was a man who liked to include all round him in the conversation, although he was not immediately encouraged by the expressions of his neighbours. He addressed some cheerful Oxonian chit-chat at the one opposite to him, and got a grunt. He then tried the man on his own right hand and got another grunt. Then, rather to his surprise, one looked at the other and said, "Do you know what he's talking about?" "I haven't the least idea." At this, even Smith was getting out of his depth. But the President, acting as a social emollient, put him at his ease by saying, "Oh, those are mathematicians! We never talk to *them.*"

No, I intend something serious. I believe the intellectual life of the whole of western society is increasingly being split into two polar groups. When I say the intellectual life, I mean to include also a large part of our practical life, because I should be the last person to suggest the two can at the deepest level be distinguished. I shall come back to the practical life a little later. Two polar groups: at one pole we have the literary intellectuals, who incidentally while no one was looking took to referring to themselves as "intellectuals" as though there were no others. I remember G. H. Hardy once remarking to me in mild puzzlement, some time in the 1930's: "Have you noticed how the word 'intellectual' is used nowadays? There seems to be a new definition which certainly doesn't include Rutherford or Eddington or Dirac or Adrian or me.‡ It does seem rather odd, don't y' know."[2]

Literary intellectuals at one pole—at the other scientists, and as the most representative, the physical scientists. Between the two a gulf of mutual incomprehension—sometimes (particularly among the young) hostility and dislike, but most of all lack of understanding. They have a curious distorted image of each other. Their attitudes are so different that, even on the level of emotion, they can't find much common ground. Non-scientists tend to think of scientists as brash and boastful. They hear Mr. T. S. Eliot,§ who just

---

*A don is a tutor in an English university.

†St. John's and Trinity are colleges at Cambridge University.

‡All great scientists: Ernest Rutherford (1871–1937) was awarded the 1908 Nobel Prize for chemistry, Arthur Stanley Eddington (1882–1944) was an English astronomer and Cambridge professor, P. A. M. Dirac (1902–1984) was instrumental in the development of quantum theory, and Edgar Douglas Adrian (1889–1977) was an English physiologist who won (with Sir Charles Sherrington) the Nobel Prize for medicine in 1932.

§Thomas Stearns Eliot (1888–1965) was a leading poet and critic for most of his career. He won the Nobel Prize for literature in 1948.

for these illustrations we can take as an archetypal figure, saying about his attempts to revive verse-drama that we can hope for very little, but that he would feel content if he and his co-workers could prepare the ground for a new Kyd or a new Greene.* That is the tone, restricted and constrained, with which literary intellectuals are at home: it is the subdued voice of their culture. Then they hear a much louder voice, that of another archetypal figure, Rutherford, trumpeting: "This is the heroic age of science! This is the Elizabethan age!" Many of us heard that, and a good many other statements beside which that was mild; and we weren't left in any doubt whom Rutherford was casting for the role of Shakespeare. What is hard for the literary intellectuals to understand, imaginatively or intellectually, is that he was absolutely right.

And compare "this is the way the world ends, not with a bang but a 8 whimper"†—incidentally, one of the least likely scientific prophecies ever made—compare that with Rutherford's famous repartee, "Lucky fellow, Rutherford, always on the crest of the wave." "Well, I made the wave, didn't I?"

The non-scientists have a rooted impression that the scientists are shal- 9 lowly optimistic, unaware of man's condition. On the other hand, the scientists believe that the literary intellectuals are totally lacking in foresight, peculiarly unconcerned with their brother men, in a deep sense anti-intellectual, anxious to restrict both art and thought to the existential moment. And so on. Anyone with a mild talent for invective could produce plenty of this kind of subterranean back-chat. On each side there is some of it which is not entirely baseless. It is all destructive. Much of it rests on misinterpretations which are dangerous. I should like to deal with two of the most profound of these now, one on each side.

First, about the scientists' optimism. This is an accusation which has 10 been made so often that it has become a platitude. It has been made by some of the acutest non-scientific minds of the day. But it depends upon a confusion between the individual experience and the social experience, between the individual condition of man and his social condition. Most of the scientists I have known well have felt—just as deeply as the non-scientists I have known well—that the individual condition of each of us is tragic. Each of us is alone: sometimes we escape from solitariness, through love or affection or perhaps creative moments, but those triumphs of life are pools of light we make for ourselves while the edge of the road is black: each of us dies alone. Some scientists I have known have had faith in revealed religion. Perhaps with them the sense of the tragic condition is not so strong. I don't know. With most people of deep feeling, however high-spirited and happy they are, sometimes most with those who are

*Robert Greene (c. 1558–1592) and Thomas Kyd (1558–1594) were relatively minor literary figures of the sixteenth century. Snow's point is that if Eliot and other literary people are content merely to prepare the way for minor writers, they are indeed motivated by a conservative impulse quite different from the high ambitions of the scientists.
†The last two lines of Eliot's poem "The Hollow Men."

happiest and most high-spirited, it seems to be right in the fibres, part of
the weight of life. That is as true of the scientists I have known best as of
anyone at all.

But nearly all of them—and this is where the colour of hope genuinely   11
comes in—would see no reason why, just because the individual condition
is tragic, so must the social condition be. Each of us is solitary: each of us dies
alone: all right, that's a fate against which we can't struggle—but there is
plenty in our condition which is not fate, and against which we are less than
human unless we do struggle.

Most of our fellow human beings, for instance, are underfed and die   12
before their time. In the crudest terms, *that* is the social condition. There is
a moral trap which comes through the insight into man's loneliness: it tempts
one to sit back, complacent in one's unique tragedy, and let the others go
without a meal.

As a group, the scientists fall into that trap less than others. They are   13
inclined to be impatient to see if something can be done: and inclined to think
that it can be done, until it's proved otherwise. That is their real optimism,
and it's an optimism that the rest of us badly need.

In reverse, the same spirit, tough and good and determined to fight   14
it out at the side of their brother men, has made scientists regard the
other culture's social attitudes as contemptible. That is too facile: some of
them are, but they are a temporary phase and not to be taken as representative.

I remember being cross-examined by a scientist of distinction. "Why do   15
most writers take on social opinions which would have been thought distinctly uncivilised and démodé at the time of the Plantagenets? Wasn't that
true of most of the famous twentieth-century writers? Yeats, Pound, Wynd-
ham Lewis, nine out of ten of those who have dominated literary sensibility
in our time—weren't they not only politically silly, but politically wicked?
Didn't the influence of all they represent bring Auschwitz* that much
nearer?"

I thought at the time, and I still think, that the correct answer was not   16
to defend the indefensible. It was no use saying that Yeats, according to
friends whose judgment I trust, was a man of singular magnanimity of character, as well as a great poet. It was no use denying the facts, which are
broadly true. The honest answer was that there is, in fact, a connection, which
literary persons were culpably slow to see, between some kinds of early
twentieth-century art and the most imbecile expressions of anti-social feeling.[3] That was one reason, among many, why some of us turned our backs
on the art and tried to hack out a new or different way for ourselves.[4]

But though many of those writers dominated literary sensibility for a   17
generation, that is no longer so, or at least to nothing like the same extent.

---

*One of Hitler's death camps in which millions of Jews were killed during World War II. The
scientist Snow quotes is suggesting that the political attitudes of the literary culture helped make
Auschwitz possible.

Literature changes more slowly than science. It hasn't the same automatic corrective, and so its misguided periods are longer. But it is ill-considered of scientists to judge writers on the evidence of the period 1914–50.

Those are two of the misunderstandings between the two cultures. I should say, since I began to talk about them—the two cultures, that is—I have had some criticism. Most of my scientific acquaintances think that there is something in it, and so do most of the practising artists I know. But I have been argued with by non-scientists of strong down-to-earth interests. Their view is that it is an over-simplification, and that if one is going to talk in these terms there ought to be at least three cultures. They argue that, though they are not scientists themselves, they would share a good deal of the scientific feeling. They would have as little use—perhaps, since they knew more about it, even less use—for the recent literary culture as the scientists themselves. J. H. Plumb, Alan Bullock and some of my American sociological friends have said that they vigorously refuse to be corralled in a cultural box with people they wouldn't be seen dead with, or to be regarded as helping to produce a climate which would not permit of social hope. 18

I respect those arguments. The number 2 is a very dangerous number: that is why the dialectic is a dangerous process. Attempts to divide anything into two ought to be regarded with much suspicion. I have thought a long time about going in for further refinements: but in the end I have decided against. I was searching for something a little more than a dashing metaphor, a good deal less than a cultural map: and for those purposes the two cultures is about right, and subtilising any more would bring more disadvantages than it's worth. 19

At one pole, the scientific culture really is a culture, not only in an intellectual but also in an anthropological sense. That is, its members need not, and of course often do not, always completely understand each other; biologists more often than not will have a pretty hazy idea of contemporary physics; but there are common attitudes, common standards and patterns of behaviour, common approaches and assumptions. This goes surprisingly wide and deep. It cuts across other mental patterns, such as those of religion or politics or class. 20

Statistically, I suppose slightly more scientists are in religious terms unbelievers, compared with the rest of the intellectual world—though there are plenty who are religious, and that seems to be increasingly so among the young. Statistically also, slightly more scientists are on the Left in open politics—though again, plenty always have called themselves conservatives, and that also seems to be more common among the young. Compared with the rest of the intellectual world, considerably more scientists in this country and probably in the U.S. come from poor families.[5] Yet over a whole range of thought and behaviour, none of that matters very much. In their working, and in much of their emotional life, their attitudes are closer to other scientists than to non-scientists who in religion or politics or class have the same labels as themselves. If I were to risk a piece of shorthand, I should say that naturally they had the future in their bones. 21

They may or may not like it, but they have it. That was as true of the 22
conservatives J. J. Thomson and Lindemann as of the radicals Einstein or
Blackett: as true of the Christian A. H. Compton as of the materialist Bernal:
of the aristocrats de Broglie or Russell as of the proletarian Faraday: of those
born rich, like Thomas Merton or Victor Rothschild, as of Rutherford, who
was the son of an odd-job handyman. Without thinking about it, they respond alike. That is what a culture means.*

At the other pole, the spread of attitudes is wider. It is obvious that 23
between the two, as one moves through intellectual society from the physi-
cists to the literary intellectuals, there are all kinds of tones of feeling on the
way. But I believe the pole of total incomprehension of science radiates its
influence on all the rest. That total incomprehension gives, much more perva-
sively than we realise, living in it, an unscientific flavour to the whole "traditional" culture, and that unscientific flavour is often, much more than we
admit, on the point of turning anti-scientific. The feelings of one pole become
the anti-feelings of the other. If the scientists have the future in their bones,
then the traditional culture responds by wishing the future did not exist.[6] It
is the traditional culture, to an extent remarkably little diminished by the
emergence of the scientific one, which manages the western world.

This polarisation is sheer loss to us all. To us as people, and to our 24
society. It is at the same time a practical and intellectual and creative loss, and
I repeat that it is false to imagine that those three considerations are clearly
separable. But for a moment I want to concentrate on the intellectual loss.

The degree of incomprehension on both sides is the kind of joke which 25
has gone sour. There are about fifty thousand working scientists in the country and about eighty thousand professional engineers or applied scientists.
During the war and in the years since, my colleagues and I have had to
interview somewhere between thirty to forty thousand of these—that is,
about 25 per cent. The number is large enough to give us a fair sample, though
of the men we talked to most would still be under forty. We were able to find
out a certain amount of what they read and thought about. I confess that even
I, who am fond of them and respect them, was a bit shaken. We hadn't quite
expected that the links with the traditional culture should be so tenuous,
nothing more than a formal touch of the cap.

As one would expect, some of the very best scientists had and have 26
plenty of energy and interest to spare, and we came across several who had
read everything that literary people talk about. But that's very rare. Most of
the rest, when one tried to probe for what books they had read, would
modestly confess, "Well, I've *tried* a bit of Dickens," rather as though Dickens
were an extraordinarily esoteric, tangled and dubiously rewarding writer,
something like Rainer Maria Rilke. In fact that is exactly how they do regard
him: we thought that discovery, that Dickens had been transformed into the

---

*In other words, differences of social class, political leaning, and wealth among the scientists are
all outweighed by common attitudes about the future based on scientific aspirations and outlook.

type-specimen of literary incomprehensibility, was one of the oddest results of the whole exercise.*

But of course, in reading him, in reading almost any writer whom we 27 should value, they are just touching their caps to the traditional culture. They have their own culture, intensive, rigorous, and constantly in action. This culture contains a great deal of argument, usually much more rigorous, and almost always at a higher conceptual level, than literary persons' arguments—even though the scientists do cheerfully use words in senses which literary persons don't recognise, the senses are exact ones, and when they talk about "subjective," "objective," "philosophy" or "progressive,"[7] they know what they mean, even though it isn't what one is accustomed to expect.

Remember, these are very intelligent men. Their culture is in many ways 28 an exacting and admirable one. It doesn't contain much art, with the exception, an important exception, of music. Verbal exchange, insistent argument. Long-playing records. Colour-photography. The ear, to some extent the eye. Books, very little, though perhaps not many would go so far as one hero, who perhaps I should admit was further down the scientific ladder than the people I've been talking about—who, when asked what books he read, replied firmly and confidently: "Books? I prefer to use my books as tools." It was very hard not to let the mind wander—what sort of tool would a book make? Perhaps a hammer? A primitive digging instrument?

Of books, though, very little. And of the books which to most literary 29 persons are bread and butter, novels, history, poetry, plays, almost nothing at all. It isn't that they're not interested in the psychological or moral or social life. In the social life, they certainly are, more than most of us. In the moral, they are by and large the soundest group of intellectuals we have; there is a moral component right in the grain of science itself, and almost all scientists form their own judgments of the moral life. In the psychological they have as much interest as most of us, though occasionally I fancy they come to it rather late. It isn't that they lack the interests. It is much more that the whole literature of the traditional culture doesn't seem to them relevant to those interests. They are, of course, dead wrong. As a result, their imaginative understanding is less than it could be. They are self-impoverished.

But what about the other side? They are impoverished too—perhaps 30 more seriously, because they are vainer about it. They still like to pretend that the traditional culture is the whole of "culture," as though the natural order didn't exist.† As though the exploration of the natural order was of no interest either in its own value or its consequences. As though the scientific edifice of the physical world was not, in its intellectual depth, complexity and articulation, the most beautiful and wonderful collective work of the mind

*This was "the oddest result" because Dickens is the last writer who could be justifiably accused or accurately described as being artistically incomprehensible. He was the most popularly admired and widely read author of the nineteenth century. Calling Dickens esoteric is like calling elevator music experimental.

†By "the natural order" he simply means "nature."

of man. Yet most non-scientists have no conception of that edifice at all. Even if they want to have it, they can't. It is rather as though, over an immense range of intellectual experience, a whole group was tone-deaf. Except that this tone-deafness doesn't come by nature, but by training, or rather the absence of training.

As with the tone-deaf, they don't know what they miss. They give a 31 pitying chuckle at the news of scientists who have never read a major work of English literature. They dismiss them as ignorant specialists. Yet their own ignorance and their own specialisation is just as startling. A good many times I have been present at gatherings of people who, by the standards of the traditional culture, are thought highly educated and who have with considerable gusto been expressing their incredulity at the illiteracy of scientists. Once or twice I have been provoked and have asked the company how many of them could describe the Second Law of Thermodynamics. The response was cold: it was also negative. Yet I was asking something which is about the scientific equivalent of: *Have you read a work of Shakespeare's?*

I now believe that if I had asked an even simpler question—such as, 32 What do you mean by mass, or acceleration? which is the scientific equivalent of saying, *Can you read?*—not more than one in ten of the highly educated would have felt that I was speaking the same language. So the great edifice of modern physics goes up, and the majority of the cleverest people in the western world have about as much insight into it as their neolithic ancestors would have had.

Just one more of those questions that my non-scientific friends regard 33 as being in the worst of taste. Cambridge is a university where scientists and non-scientists meet every night at dinner.[8] About two years ago, one of the most astonishing discoveries in the whole history of science was brought off. I don't mean the Sputnik*—that was admirable for quite different reasons, as a feat of organisation and a triumphant use of existing knowledge. No, I mean the discovery at Columbia by Yang and Lee. It is a piece of work of the greatest beauty and originality, but the result is so startling that one forgets how beautiful the thinking is. It makes us think again about some of the fundamentals of the physical world. Intuition, common sense—they are neatly stood on their heads. The result is usually known as the non-conservation of parity.† If there were any serious communication between the two cultures, this experiment would have been talked about at every High Table in Cambridge. Was it? I wasn't here: but I should like to ask the question.

There seems then to be no place where the cultures meet. I am not going 34 to waste time saying that this is a pity. It is much worse than that. Soon I shall

---

*In 1958 the Russians put the first man-made satellite, *Sputnik,* into orbit around the earth.

†Tsung-Dao Lee (b. 1926) and Chen Ning Yang (b. 1922) devised a set of experiments in 1956 that led to extensive revisions of basic theory in atomic and sub-atomic physics. For their accomplishments, generally known as the non-conservation of parity, they were awarded the Nobel Prize for physics in 1957.

come to some practical consequences. But at the heart of thought and creation we are letting some of our best chances go by default. The clashing point of two subjects, two disciplines, two cultures—of two galaxies, so far as that goes—ought to produce creative chances. In the history of mental activity that has been where some of the break-throughs came. The chances are there now. But they are there, as it were, in a vacuum, because those in the two cultures can't talk to each other. It is bizarre how very little of twentieth-century science has been assimilated into twentieth-century art. Now and then one used to find poets conscientiously using scientific expressions, and getting them wrong—there was a time when "refraction" kept cropping up in verse in a mystifying fashion, and when "polarised light" was used as though writers were under the illusion that it was a specially admirable kind of light.

Of course, that isn't the way that science could be any good to art. It has got to be assimilated along with, and as part and parcel of, the whole of our mental experience, and used as naturally as the rest. 35

I said earlier that this cultural divide is not just an English phenomenon: it exists all over the western world. But it probably seems at its sharpest in England, for two reasons. One is our fanatical belief in educational specialisation, which is much more deeply ingrained in us than in any country in the world, west or east. The other is our tendency to let our social forms crystallise. This tendency appears to get stronger, not weaker, the more we iron out economic inequalities: and this is specially true in education. It means that once anything like a cultural divide gets established, all the social forces operate to make it not less rigid, but more so. 36

The two cultures were already dangerously separate sixty years ago; but a prime minister like Lord Salisbury could have his own laboratory at Hatfield, and Arthur Balfour had a somewhat more than amateur interest in natural science. John Anderson* did some research in inorganic chemistry in Leipzig before passing first into the Civil Service, and incidentally took a spread of subjects which is now impossible.[9] None of that degree of interchange at the top of the Establishment is likely, or indeed thinkable, now.[10] 37

In fact, the separation between the scientists and non-scientists is much less bridgeable among the young than it was even thirty years ago. Thirty years ago the cultures had long ceased to speak to each other: but at least they managed a kind of frozen smile across the gulf. Now the politeness has gone, and they just make faces. It is not only that the young scientists now feel that they are part of a culture on the rise while the other is in retreat. It is also, to be brutal, that the young scientists know that with an indifferent degree they'll get a comfortable job, while their contemporaries and counterparts in English or History will be lucky to earn 60 per cent as much. No young scientist of any talent would feel that he isn't wanted or that his work is 38

*John Anderson (1882–1958) was chancellor of the exchequer, 1943–1945.

ridiculous, as did the hero of *Lucky Jim,* and in fact, some of the disgruntlement of Amis* and his associates is the disgruntlement of the under-employed arts graduate.

There is only one way out of all this: it is, of course, by rethinking our   39
education. In this country, for the two reasons I have given, that is more difficult than in any other. Nearly everyone will agree that our school education is too specialised. But nearly everyone feels that it is outside the will of man to alter it. Other countries are as dissatisfied with their education as we are, but are not so resigned.

The U.S. teach out of proportion more children up to eighteen than we   40
do: they teach them far more widely, but nothing like so rigorously. They know that: they are hoping to take the problem in hand within ten years, though they may not have all that time to spare. The U.S.S.R. also teach out of proportion more children than we do: they also teach far more widely than we do (it is an absurd western myth that their school education is specialised) but much too rigorously.[11] They know that—and they are beating about to get it right. The Scandinavians, in particular the Swedes, who would make a more sensible job of it than any of us, are handicapped by their practical need to devote an inordinate amount of time to foreign languages. But they too are seized of the problem.

Are we? Have we crystallised so far that we are no longer flexible at all?   41

Talk to schoolmasters, and they say that our intense specialisation, like   42
nothing else on earth, is dictated by the Oxford and Cambridge scholarship examinations. If that is so, one would have thought it not utterly impracticable to change the Oxford and Cambridge scholarship examinations. Yet one would underestimate the national capacity for the intricate defensive to believe that that was easy. All the lessons of our educational history suggest we are only capable of increasing specialisation, not decreasing it.

Somehow we have set ourselves the task of producing a tiny *élite*—far   43
smaller proportionately than in any comparable country—educated in one academic skill. For a hundred and fifty years in Cambridge it was mathematics: then it was mathematics or classics: then natural science was allowed in. But still the choice had to be a single one.

It may well be that this process has gone too far to be reversible. I have   44
given reasons why I think it is a disastrous process, for the purpose of a living culture. I am going on to give reasons why I think it is fatal, if we're to perform our practical tasks in the world. But I can think of only one example, in the whole of English educational history, where our pursuit of specialised mental exercises was resisted with success.

It was done here in Cambridge, fifty years ago, when the old order-of-   45
merit in the Mathematical Tripos† was abolished. For over a hundred years,

---

*Kingsley Amis's novel *Lucky Jim* (1953) satirizes the stuffiness and provinciality of the English educational system. The hero is a historian, not a scientist, and part of his problem is that he can't get a job.

†The Mathematical Tripos was the final examination instituted in the first half of the eighteenth century for honors in mathematics.

the nature of the Tripos had been crystallising. The competition for the top places had got fiercer, and careers hung on them. In most colleges, certainly in my own, if one managed to come out as Senior or Second Wrangler, one was elected a Fellow out of hand. A whole apparatus of coaching had grown up. Men of the quality of Hardy, Littlewood, Russell, Eddington, Jeans, Keynes, went in for two or three years' training for an examination which was intensely competitive and intensely difficult. Most people in Cambridge were very proud of it, with a similar pride to that which almost anyone in England always has for our existing educational institutions, whatever they happen to be. If you study the flysheets of the time,* you will find the passionate arguments for keeping the examination precisely as it was to all eternity: it was the only way to keep up standards, it was the only fair test of merit, indeed, the only seriously objective test in the world. The arguments, in fact, were almost exactly those which are used today with precisely the same passionate sincerity if anyone suggests that the scholarship examinations might conceivably not be immune from change.

In every respect but one, in fact, the old Mathematical Tripos seemed perfect. The one exception, however, appeared to some to be rather important. It was simply—so the young creative mathematicians, such as Hardy and Littlewood, kept saying—that the [Tripos] had no intellectual merit at all. They went a little further, and said that the Tripos had killed serious mathematics in England stone dead for a hundred years. Well, even in academic controversy, that took some skirting round, and they got their way. But I have an impression that Cambridge was a good deal more flexible between 1850 and 1914 than it has been in our time. If we had had the old Mathematical Tripos firmly planted among us, should we have ever managed to abolish it?

NOTES

All notes are Snow's.

1. "The Two Cultures," *New Statesman,* 6 October 1956.

2. This lecture was delivered to a Cambridge audience, and so I used some points of reference which I did not need to explain. G. H. Hardy, 1877–1947, was one of the most distinguished pure mathematicians of his time, and a picturesque figure in Cambridge both as a young don and on his return in 1931 to the Sadleirian Chair of Mathematics.

3. I said a little more about this connection in *The Times Literary Supplement,* "Challenge to the Intellect," 15 August 1958. I hope some day to carry the analysis further.

4. It would be more accurate to say that, for literary reasons, we felt the prevailing literary modes were useless to us. We were, however, reinforced in that feeling when it occurred to us that those prevailing modes went hand in hand with social attitudes either wicked, or absurd, or both.

5. An analysis of the schools from which Fellows of the Royal Society come tells its own story. The distribution is markedly different from that of, for example, members of the Foreign Service or Queen's Counsel.

*A flysheet is a small, loose advertising sheet, like a handbill; in this case it refers to campus leaflets espousing particular points of view.

6. Compare George Orwell's *1984*, which is the strongest possible wish that the future should not exist, with J. D. Bernal's *World Without War*.

7. *Subjective*, in contemporary technological jargon, means "divided according to subjects." *Objective* means "directed towards an object." *Philosophy* means "general intellectual approach or attitude" (for example, a scientist's "philosophy of guided weapons" might lead him to propose certain kinds of "objective research"). A "progressive" job means one with possibilities of promotion.

8. Almost all college High Tables contain Fellows in both scientific and non-scientific subjects.

9. He took the examination in 1905.

10. It is, however, true to say that the compact nature of the managerial layers of English society—the fact that "everyone knows everyone else"—means that scientists and non-scientists do in fact know each other as people more easily than in most countries. It is also true that a good many leading politicians and administrators keep up lively intellectual and artistic interests to a much greater extent, so far as I can judge, than is the case in the U.S. These are both among our assets.

11. I tried to compare American, Soviet and English education in "New Minds for the New World," *New Statesman*, 6 September 1956.

Questions for Discussion

1. Poll your class to see if the "two cultures" split is visible within it. Are the people who prefer humanities courses also fond of or excited by science courses? And vice versa? How many people enjoy switching back and forth equally?

2. In 1802 William Wordsworth (1770–1850), Romantic poet, wrote in his preface to *Lyrical Ballads:*

   The knowledge both of the poet and the man of science is pleasure; but the knowledge of the one cleaves to us as a necessary part of our existence, our natural and unalienable inheritance; the other is a personal and individual acquisition, slow to come to us, and by no habitual and direct sympathy connecting us with our fellow-beings. The man of science seeks truth as a remote and unknown benefactor; he cherishes and loves it in his solitude: the poet, singing a song in which all human beings join with him, rejoices in the presence of truth as our visible friend and hourly companion. Poetry is the breath and finer spirit of all knowledge; it is the impassioned expression which is in the countenance of all science.

   Discuss with your classmates what you think this passage means and whether you think it is true. Is Wordsworth privileging literary culture over scientific culture? Or does he simply see each kind of culture as covering a different domain of human knowledge and experience? Support your views with the best reasons you can create.

3. In 1821, a few years after Wordsworth wrote his preface, another Romantic poet, Percy Shelley (1792–1822), also undertook (in *A Defence of Poetry*) to compare literary culture with scientific culture. Looking about him at a world in which industrialization and economic expansion seemed to

be impoverishing at least as many people as it was enriching, he observed:

> We have more moral, political and historical wisdom, than we know how to reduce into practice; we have more scientific and economical knowledge than can be accommodated to the just distribution of the produce which it multiplies. The poetry in these systems of thought, is concealed by the accumulation of facts and calculating processes. . . . We want [i.e., lack] the creative faculty to imagine that which we know; we want the generous impulse to act that which we imagine; we want the poetry of life: our calculations have outrun conception; we have eaten more than we can digest. The cultivation of those sciences which have enlarged the limits of the empire of man over the external world, has, for want of the poetical faculty, proportionally circumscribed those of the internal world; and man, having enslaved the elements, remains himself a slave.

Is Shelley being fair to science by implying that the means by which men are making themselves rich are also impoverishing their social sympathies? Can you think of examples in which science has been used both ways— that is, to alleviate human suffering and to create it at the same time? And if both kinds of examples are plentiful, is science's failings the fault of science or of something else? If something else, what?

4. Twelve years after Shelley's *Defence,* in 1833, John Stuart Mill (1806– 1873)—philosopher, logician, and economist—wrote an essay called "What Is Poetry?" in which he asserts that the opposite of poetry is

> not prose, but matter of fact, or science. The one addresses itself to the belief; the other, to the feelings. The one does its work by convincing or persuading; the other, by moving. The one acts by presenting a proposition to the understanding; the other, by offering interesting objects of contemplation to the sensibilities.

How readily do you think this view of literary culture contributes to the popular notion that artists are impractical and irrational, guided by emotions and impulse rather than facts? Is this cliché true? Can you think of examples that contest it? Examples that support it? What do you think is the truth of the matter? Give reasons.

5. Fifty years after Mill's essay, in 1882, Matthew Arnold (1822–1888), poet and essayist, maintained in an essay titled "Literature and Science" that science yields important and true knowledge but cannot tell us what to do with such knowledge, cannot tell us how to relate it to the arenas of conduct and behavior. The humanities, he claims, are necessary for making these connections and therefore cannot be allowed to decline as science advances.

> Interesting, indeed, these results of science are, important they are, and we should all of us be acquainted with them. But what I now wish you to mark is, that we are still, when they are propounded and we receive them, we are still in the sphere of intellect and knowledge. And for the generality of men there will be found, I say, to arise, when they have duly taken in the proposition that their ancestor was "a hairy quadruped

furnished with a tail and pointed ears, probably arboreal in his habits," there will be found to arise an invincible desire to relate this proposition to the sense in us for conduct, and to the sense in us for beauty. But this the men of science will not do for us, and will hardly even profess to do. They will give us other pieces of knowledge, other facts, about other animals and their ancestors, or about plants, or about stones, or about stars; and they may finally bring us to those great "general conceptions of the universe, which are forced upon us all," says Professor Huxley, "by the progress of physical science." But still it will be *knowledge* only which they give us; knowledge not put for us into relation with our sense for conduct, our sense for beauty, and touched with emotion by being so put; not thus put for us, and therefore, to the majority of mankind, after a certain while, unsatisfying, wearying.

As you sit day after day in your college courses, do you ever experience the feeling that Arnold here attributes to "the generality of men," the feeling that you are learning more than you know how to use, more than you know the worth of, more than you can relate to the other pieces of knowledge you are learning in other classes? If so, has Arnold put the case accurately for you, or would you put the emphasis in different places? And what about the sense of beauty Arnold alludes to? What do you take him to mean by this? Do you need the sense that knowledge has to be somehow turned to the beautification of life before it has earned its way in the world? Can you provide examples one way or the other? How would you define *beauty* in this context?

6. After reading these selections by nineteenth-century figures on humanistic versus scientific culture, what changes, if any, in your view of Snow's version of the two cultures have been created? Is it possible that the two cultures he sees were at least a century in the making? How could you corroborate this statement by referring to the quotations? What counterexamples could you provide?

7. Some critics have noted that Snow's analysis simply ignores many areas of modern thought, particularly the social sciences. He has little to say about history, sociology, anthropology, and political science. Where do you think he would place these subjects, if he did include them in his twofold scheme? Do you think his analysis would have to be greatly modified if he wrote an essay on "the *three* cultures"?

Suggested Essay Topics

1. At the time of Snow's essay in the 1950s, he was right to see the humanists and scientists as constituting the two dominant constituencies in the university, but today there is another constituency separate from these two traditional groups: the people in the professional or pre-professional schools. People getting degrees in business, pharmacy, dance, theater, communications, and many other fields are in neither the humanities nor the sciences. The question is, should they be, or at least should they be

made to learn enough about the humanities and sciences as to achieve a minimal kind of literacy in both?

In an essay directed to your classmates, answer these questions with the best reasons you can find for either forcing people in professional programs to take humanities and science courses or exempting them from such requirements. State what you think the minimal requirements should be, and make clear what your criteria for "minimal" are. If, for example, you would only require them to take, say, three hours of literature, say why that is enough. Enough in relation to what?

2. Write an essay to your instructor in which you attack or support Arnold's claim that the knowledge of science cannot be related to the questions we most want answers to—questions about how to live, how to make life meaningful or beautiful—and that scientific knowledge will therefore always remain incomplete unless complemented by knowledge from the humanities (and possibly other sources as well).

Loren Eiseley

Loren Eiseley (1907–1977) both admits and contests C. P. Snow's assertion that the humanities and sciences form two antagonistic, mutually unintelligible cultures in today's world. He admits that as an institution, as a profession, science has separated itself from the methods and insights of religion, art, and speculation—the areas of human creativity studied by the humanities. He even provides examples of this split, as when he tells of the young science colleague who, when he finds Eiseley reading J. R. R. Tolkien, sneers, "I wouldn't waste my time with a man who writes fairy stories" (¶7). Eiseley is clear that science has become "a professional body, and with professionalism there tends to emerge a greater emphasis upon a coherent system of regulations" (¶20) that produce a "deliberate blunting of wonder" (¶19).

But Eiseley is also clear that this division is a product of misunderstanding, that it occurs only at superficial levels within both humanistic and scientific activity. It is an illusion—a dangerous illusion with potentially disastrous consequences, to be sure—but an illusion nevertheless. The molds that the humanists and scientists cast each other in, Eiseley says, "are always useful to the mediocre conformist" (¶22)— useful, that is, to the thinker who has no sense of wonder, no personal vision, and therefore nothing original to say. But "happily," he continues later, "the very great in science . . . have been singularly free of this folly" (¶38), and he goes on to cite Leonardo da Vinci, Newton, Darwin, and Einstein as great scientific thinkers who all "retained a simple sense of wonder . . . [and who] all show a deep humility and an emotional hunger which is the prerogative of the artist" (¶38). "Creation in science," says Eiseley, *"demands a high level of imaginative insight and intuitive perception"* (¶25), *which leaves us free to conclude, as indeed Eiseley implies, that the fence building, sloganeering, and sneering that go on between the mediocre professionals in both cultures are the opposite of creativity. Such hostility is stultifying and deadening, and it leads to that curious feature of the modern mind noted by Santayana, the mind that has "seemed to lose courage and to become ashamed of its own fertility"* (¶3).

As you read, ask yourself how much the conformist molds seem to characterize the thinking about scientists and humanists at your college or university. How much, and how uncritically, have you accepted such polarized, cliché-ridden thinking yourself? It would be odd if you had not accepted it, for, as both Snow and Eiseley agree, it pervades much of the thinking today not only about scientists and humanists but by scientists and humanists. Finally, ask yourself whether Snow and Eiseley have given you good reasons for re-thinking any prejudices you may have held and in what ways your education and society at large would both benefit if the rift between the two cultures were closed.

THE ILLUSION OF
THE TWO CULTURES

From *The American Scholar* (1964) and *The Star Thrower* (1978).

Not long ago an English scientist, Sir Eric Ashby, remarked that "to train young people in the dialectic between orthodoxy and dissent is the unique contribution which universities make to society." I am sure that Sir Eric meant by this remark that nowhere but in universities are the young given the opportunity to absorb past tradition and at the same time to experience the impact of new ideas—in the sense of a constant dialogue between past and present—lived in every hour of the student's existence. This dialogue, ideally, should lead to a great winnowing and sifting of experience and to a heightened consciousness of self which, in turn, should lead on to greater sensitivity and perception on the part of the individual.

Our lives are the creation of memory and the accompanying power to extend ourselves outward into ideas and relive them. The finest intellect is that which employs an invisible web of gossamer running into the past as well as across the minds of living men and which constantly responds to the vibrations transmitted through these tenuous lines of sympathy. It would be contrary to fact, however, to assume that our universities always perform this unique function of which Sir Eric speaks, with either grace or perfection; in fact our investment in man, it has been justly remarked, is deteriorating even as the financial investment in science grows.

More than thirty years ago, George Santayana* had already sensed this

*George Santayana (1863–1952), Spanish-American poet and philosopher and Harvard professor.

trend. He commented, in a now-forgotten essay, that one of the strangest consequences of modern science was that as the visible wealth of nature was more and more transferred and abstracted, the mind seemed to lose courage and to become ashamed of its own fertility. "The hard-pressed natural man will not indulge his imagination," continued Santayana, "unless it poses for truth; and being half-aware of this imposition, he is more troubled at the thought of being deceived than at the fact of being mechanized or being bored; and he would wish to escape imagination altogether."

"Man would wish to escape imagination altogether." I repeat that last   4
phrase, for it defines a peculiar aberration of the human mind found on both sides of that bipolar division between the humanities and the sciences, which C. P. Snow has popularized under the title of *The Two Cultures.* The idea is not solely a product of this age. It was already emerging with the science of the seventeenth century; one finds it in Bacon.* One finds the fear of it faintly foreshadowed in Thoreau. Thomas Huxley† lent it weight when he referred contemptuously to the "caterwauling of poets."

Ironically, professional scientists berated the early evolutionists such as   5
Lamarck and Chambers for overindulgence in the imagination. Almost eighty years ago John Burroughs observed that some of the animus once directed by science toward dogmatic theology seemed in his day increasingly to be vented upon the literary naturalist. In the early 1900s a quarrel over "nature faking" raised a confused din in America and aroused W. H. Hudson to some dry and pungent comment upon the failure to distinguish the purposes of science from those of literature. I know of at least one scholar who, venturing to develop some personal ideas in an essay for the layman, was characterized by a reviewer in a leading professional journal as a worthless writer, although, as it chanced, the work under discussion had received several awards in literature, one of them international in scope. More recently, some scholars not indifferent to humanistic values have exhorted poets to leave their personal songs in order to portray the beauty and symmetry of molecular structures.

Now some very fine verse has been written on scientific subjects, but,   6
I fear, very little under the dictate of scientists as such. Rather there is evident here precisely that restriction of imagination against which Santayana inveighed; namely, an attempt to constrain literature itself to the delineation of objective or empiric truth, and to dismiss the whole domain of value, which after all constitutes the very nature of man, as without significance and beneath contempt.

Unconsciously, the human realm is denied in favor of the world of pure   7
technics. Man, the tool user, grows convinced that he is himself only useful as a tool, that fertility except in the use of the scientific imagination is

---

*Francis Bacon (1561–1626), philosopher and author whose works were instrumental in furthering the development of modern science.

†Thomas Henry Huxley (1825–1895), English biologist, best known in his own day as "Darwin's bulldog" for his spirited defense and popularization of evolutionary theory.

wasteful and without purpose, even, in some indefinable way, sinful. I was reading J. R. R. Tolkien's great symbolic trilogy, *The Fellowship of the Ring,* a few months ago, when a young scientist of my acquaintance paused and looked over my shoulder. After a little casual interchange the man departed leaving an accusing remark hovering in the air between us. "I wouldn't waste my time with a man who writes fairy stories." He might as well have added, "or with a man who reads them."

As I went back to my book I wondered vaguely in what leafless land- 8 scape one grew up without Hans Christian Andersen, or Dunsany, or even Jules Verne.* There lingered about the young man's words a puritanism which seemed the more remarkable because, as nearly as I could discover, it was unmotivated by any sectarian religiosity unless a total dedication to science brings to some minds a similar authoritarian desire to shackle the human imagination. After all, it is this impossible, fertile world of our imagi- nation which gave birth to liberty in the midst of oppression, and which persists in seeking until what is sought is seen. Against such invisible and fearful powers, there can be found in all ages and in all institutions—even the institutions of professional learning—the humorless man with the sneer, or if the sneer does not suffice, then the torch, for the bright unperishing letters of the human dream.

One can contrast this recalcitrant attitude with an 1890 reminiscence 9 from that great Egyptologist Sir Flinders Petrie, which steals over into the realm of pure literature. It was written, in unconscious symbolism, from a tomb:

"I here live, and do not scramble to fit myself to the requirements of 10 others. In a narrow tomb, with the figure of Néfermaat standing on each side of me—as he has stood through all that we know as human history—I have just room for my bed, and a row of good reading in which I can take pleasure after dinner. Behind me is that Great Peace, the Desert. It is an entity—a power—just as much as the sea is. No wonder men fled to it from the turmoil of the ancient world."

It may now reasonably be asked why one who has similarly, if less 11 dramatically, spent his life among the stones and broken shards of the remote past should be writing here about matters involving literature and science. While I was considering this with humility and trepidation, my eye fell upon a stone in my office. I am sure that professional journalists must recall times when an approaching deadline has keyed all their senses and led them to glance wildly around in the hope that something might leap out at them from the most prosaic surroundings. At all events my eyes fell upon this stone.

Now the stone antedated anything that the historians would call art; it 12 had been shaped many hundreds of thousands of years ago by men whose faces would frighten us if they sat among us today. Out of old habit, since I like the feel of worked flint, I picked it up and hefted it as I groped for words

*Andersen (1805–1875), Edward Plunkett (1878–1957), eighteenth baron of Dunsany, and Verne (1828–1905) were all writers of fairy tales or adventure stories popular with children.

over this difficult matter of the growing rift between science and art. Certainly the stone was of no help to me; it was a utilitarian thing which had cracked marrow bones, if not heads, in the remote dim morning of the human species. It was nothing if not practical. It was, in fact, an extremely early example of the empirical tradition which has led on to modern science.

The mind which had shaped this artifact knew its precise purpose. It 13 had found out by experimental observation that the stone was tougher, sharper, more enduring than the hand which wielded it. The creature's mind had solved the question of the best form of the implement and how it could be manipulated most effectively. In its day and time this hand ax was as grand an intellectual achievement as a rocket.

As a scientist my admiration went out to that unidentified workman. 14 How he must have labored to understand the forces involved in the fracturing of flint, and all that involved practical survival in his world. My uncalloused twentieth-century hand caressed the yellow stone lovingly. It was then that I made a remarkable discovery.

In the mind of this gross-featured early exponent of the practical ap- 15 proach to nature—the technician, the no-nonsense practitioner of survival— two forces had met and merged. There had not been room in his short and desperate life for the delicate and supercilious separation of the arts from the sciences. There did not exist then the refined distinctions set up between the scholarly percipience of reality and what has sometimes been called the vaporings of the artistic imagination.

As I clasped and unclasped the stone, running my fingers down its 16 edges, I began to perceive the ghostly emanations from a long-vanished mind, the kind of mind which, once having shaped an object of any sort, leaves an individual trace behind it which speaks to others across the barriers of time and language. It was not the practical experimental aspect of this mind that startled me, but rather that the fellow had wasted time.

In an incalculably brutish and dangerous world he had both shaped an 17 instrument of practical application and then, with a virtuoso's elegance, proceeded to embellish his product. He had not been content to produce a plain, utilitarian implement. In some wistful, inarticulate way, in the grip of the dim aesthetic feelings which are one of the marks of man—or perhaps I should say, some men—this archaic creature had lingered over his handiwork.

One could still feel him crouching among the stones on a long-vanished 18 river bar, turning the thing over in his hands, feeling its polished surface, striking, here and there, just one more blow that no longer had usefulness as its criterion. He had, like myself, enjoyed the texture of the stone. With skills lost to me, he had gone on flaking the implement with an eye to beauty until it had become a kind of rough jewel, equivalent in its day to the carved and gold-inlaid pommel of the iron dagger placed in Tutankhamen's tomb.

All the later history of man contains these impractical exertions ex- 19 pended upon a great diversity of objects, and, with literacy, breaking even into printed dreams. Today's secular disruption between the creative aspect of art and that of science is a barbarism that would have brought lifted eyebrows in a Cro-Magnon cave. It is a product of high technical specialization, the deliberate blunting of wonder, and the equally deliberate suppression of a phase of our humanity in the name of an authoritarian institution, science, which has taken on, in our time, curious puritanical overtones. Many scientists seem unaware of the historical reasons for this development or the fact that the creative aspect of art is not so remote from that of science as may seem, at first glance, to be the case.

I am not so foolish as to categorize individual scholars or scientists. I am, 20 however, about to remark on the nature of science as an institution. Like all such structures it is apt to reveal certain behavioral rigidities and conformities which increase with age. It is no longer the domain of the amateur, though some of its greatest discoverers could be so defined. It is now a professional body, and with professionalism there tends to emerge a greater emphasis upon a coherent system of regulations. The deviant is more sharply treated, and the young tend to imitate their successful elders. In short, an "Establishment"—a trade union—has appeared.

Similar tendencies can be observed among those of the humanities 21 concerned with the professional analysis and interpretation of the works of the creative artist. Here too, a similar rigidity and exclusiveness make their appearance. It is not that in the case of both the sciences and the humanities standards are out of place. What I am briefly cautioning against is that too frequently they afford an excuse for stifling original thought or constricting much latent creativity within traditional molds.

Such molds are always useful to the mediocre conformist who instinc- 22 tively castigates and rejects what he cannot imitate. Tradition, the continuity of learning, are, it is true, enormously important to the learned disciplines. What we must realize as scientists is that the particular institution we inhabit has its own irrational accretions and authoritarian dogmas which can be as unpleasant as some of those encountered in sectarian circles—particularly so since they are frequently unconsciously held and surrounded by an impenetrable wall of self-righteousness brought about because science is regarded as totally empiric and open-minded by tradition.

This type of professionalism, as I shall label it in order to distinguish 23 it from what is best in both the sciences and humanities, is characterized by two assumptions: that the accretions of fact are cumulative and lead to progress, whereas the insights of art are, at best, singular, and lead nowhere, or, when introduced into the realm of science, produce obscurity and confusion. The convenient label "mystic" is, in our day, readily applied to men who pause for simple wonder, or who encounter along the borders of the known that "awful power" which Wordsworth characterized as the human imagination. It can, he says, rise suddenly from the mind's abyss and enwrap the solitary traveler like a mist.

We do not like mists in this era, and the word imagination is less and 24 less used. We like, instead, a clear road, and we abhor solitary traveling. Indeed one of our great scientific historians remarked not long ago that the literary naturalist was obsolescent if not completely outmoded. I suppose he meant that with our penetration into the biophysical realm, life, like matter, would become increasingly represented by abstract symbols. To many it must appear that the more we can dissect life into its elements, the closer we are getting to its ultimate resolution. While I have some reservations on this score, they are not important. Rather, I should like to look at the symbols which in the one case denote science and in the other constitute those vaporings and cloud wraiths that are the abomination, so it is said, of the true scientist but are the delight of the poet and literary artist.

Creation in science demands a high level of imaginative insight and 25 intuitive perception. I believe no one would deny this, even though it exists in varying degrees, just as it does, similarly, among writers, musicians, or artists. The scientist's achievement, however, is quantitatively transmissible. From a single point his discovery is verifiable by other men who may then, on the basis of corresponding data, accept the innovation and elaborate upon it in the cumulative fashion which is one of the great triumphs of science.

Artistic creation, on the other hand, is unique. It cannot be twice discov- 26 ered, as, say, natural selection was discovered. It may be imitated stylistically, in a genre, a school, but, save for a few items of technique, it is not cumulative. A successful work of art may set up reverberations and is, in this, just as transmissible as science, but there is a qualitative character about it. Each reverberation in another mind is unique. As the French novelist François Mauriac has remarked, each great novel is a separate and distinct world operating under its own laws with a flora and fauna totally its own. There is communication, or the work is a failure, but the communication releases our own visions, touches some highly personal chord in our own experience.

The symbols used by the great artist are a key releasing our humanity 27 from the solitary tower of the self. "Man," says Lewis Mumford, "is first and foremost the self-fabricating animal." I shall merely add that the artist plays an enormous role in this act of self-creation. It is he who touches the hidden strings of pity, who searches our hearts, who makes us sensitive to beauty, who asks questions about fate and destiny. Such questions, though they lurk always around the corners of the external universe which is the peculiar province of science, the rigors of the scientific method do not enable us to pursue directly.

And yet I wonder. 28

It is surely possible to observe that it is the successful analogy or symbol 29 which frequently allows the scientist to leap from a generalization in one field of thought to a triumphant achievement in another. For example, Progressionism in a spiritual sense later became the model contributing to the discovery of organic evolution. Such analogies genuinely resemble the figures and enchantments of great literature, whose meanings similarly can never be totally grasped because of their endless power to ramify in the individual mind.

John Donne gave powerful expression to a feeling applicable as much 30 to science as to literature when he said devoutly of certain Biblical passages: "The literall sense is alwayes to be preserved; but the literall sense is not alwayes to be discerned; for the literall sense is not always that which the very letter and grammar of the place presents." A figurative sense, he argues cogently, can sometimes be the most "literall intention of the Holy Ghost."

It is here that the scientist and artist sometimes meet in uneasy opposi- 31 tion, or at least along lines of tension. The scientist's attitude is sometimes, I suspect, that embodied in Samuel Johnson's remark that, wherever there is mystery, roguery is not far off.

Yet surely it was not roguery when Sir Charles Lyell* glimpsed in a few 32 fossil prints of raindrops the persistence of the world's natural forces through the incredible, mysterious aeons of geologic time. The fossils were a symbol of a vast hitherto unglimpsed order. They are, in Donne's sense, both literal and symbolic. As fossils they merely denote evidence of rain in a past era. Figuratively they are more. To the perceptive intelligence they afford the hint of lengthened natural order, just as the eyes of ancient trilobites† tell us similarly of the unchanging laws of light. Equally, the educated mind may discern in a scratched pebble the retreating shadow of vast ages of ice and gloom. In Donne's archaic phraseology these objects would bespeak the principal intention of the Divine Being—that is, of order beyond our power to grasp.

Such images drawn from the world of science are every bit as powerful 33 as great literary symbolism and equally demanding upon the individual imagination of the scientist who would fully grasp the extension of meaning which is involved. It is, in fact, one and the same creative act in both domains.

Indeed evolution itself has become such a figurative symbol, as has also 34 the hypothesis of the expanding universe. The laboratory worker may think of these concepts in a totally empirical fashion as subject to proof or disproof by the experimental method. Like Freud's doctrine of the subconscious, however, such ideas frequently escape from the professional scientist into the public domain. There they may undergo further individual transformation and embellishment. Whether the scholar approves or not, such hypotheses are now as free to evolve in the mind of the individual as are the creations of art. All the resulting enrichment and confusion will bear about it something suggestive of the world of artistic endeavor.

As figurative insights into the nature of things, such embracing concep- 35 tions may become grotesquely distorted or glow with added philosophical wisdom. As in the case of the trilobite eye or the fossil raindrop, there lurks behind the visible evidence vast shadows no longer quite of that world which we term natural. Like the words in Donne's Bible, enormous implications have transcended the literal expression of the thought. Reality itself has been superseded by a greater reality. As Donne himself asserted, "The substance of the truth is in the great images which lie behind."

It is because these two types of creation—the artistic and the scien- 36

---

*Lyell's (1795–1875) *Principles of Geology* (1830–1833) earned him the popular title of "father of geology."
†Fossils of Paleozoic marine arthropods.

tific—have sprung from the same being and have their points of contact even in division that I have the temerity to assert that, in a sense, the "two cultures" are an illusion, that they are a product of unreasoning fear, professionalism, and misunderstanding. Because of the emphasis upon science in our society, much has been said about the necessity of educating the layman and even the professional student of the humanities upon the ways and the achievements of science. I admit that a barrier exists, but I am also concerned to express the view that there persists in the domain of science itself an occasional marked intolerance of those of its own membership who venture to pursue the way of letters. As I have remarked, this intolerance can the more successfully clothe itself in seeming objectivity because of the supposed open nature of the scientific society. It is not remarkable that this trait is sometimes more manifest in the younger and less secure disciplines.

There was a time, not too many centuries ago, when to be active in 37 scientific investigation was to invite suspicion. Thus it may be that there now lingers among us, even in the triumph of the experimental method, a kind of vague fear of that other artistic world of deep emotion, of strange symbols, lest it seize upon us or distort the hard-won objectivity of our thinking—lest it corrupt, in other words, that crystalline and icy objectivity which, in our scientific guise, we erect as a model of conduct. This model, incidentally, if pursued to its absurd conclusion, would lead to a world in which the computer would determine all aspects of our existence; one in which the bomb would be as welcome as the discoveries of the physician.

Happily, the very great in science, or even those unique scientist-artists 38 such as Leonardo, who foreran the emergence of science as an institution, have been singularly free from this folly. Darwin decried it even as he recognized that he had paid a certain price in concentrated specialization for his achievement. Einstein, it is well known, retained a simple sense of wonder; Newton felt like a child playing with pretty shells on a beach. All show a deep humility and an emotional hunger which is the prerogative of the artist. It is with the lesser men, with the institutionalization of method, with the appearance of dogma and mapped-out territories, that an unpleasant suggestion of fenced preserves begins to dominate the university atmosphere.

As a scientist, I can say that I have observed it in my own and others' 39 specialties. I have had occasion, also, to observe its effects in the humanities. It is not science *per se;* it is, instead, in both regions of thought, the narrow professionalism which is also plainly evident in the trade union. There can be small men in science just as there are small men in government or business. In fact it is one of the disadvantages of big science, just as it is of big government, that the availability of huge sums attracts a swarm of elbowing and contentious men to whom great dreams are less than protected hunting preserves.

The sociology of science deserves at least equal consideration with the 40 biographies of the great scientists, for powerful and changing forces are at work upon science, the institution, as contrasted with science as a dream and an ideal of the individual. Like other aspects of society, it is a construct of men and is subject, like other social structures, to human pressures and inescapable distortions.

Let me give an illustration. Even in learned journals, clashes occasion- 41 ally occur between those who would regard biology as a separate and distinct domain of inquiry and the reductionists who, by contrast, perceive in the living organism only a vaster and more random chemistry. Understandably, the concern of the reductionists is with the immediate. Thomas Hobbes was expressing a similar point of view when he castigated poets as "working on mean minds with words and distinctions that of themselves signifie nothing, but betray (by their obscurity) that there walketh . . . another kingdome, as it were a kingdome of fayries in the dark." I myself have been similarly criticized for speaking of a nature "beyond the nature that we know."

Yet consider for a moment this dark, impossible realm of "fayrie." Man 42 is not totally compounded of the nature we profess to understand. He contains, instead, a lurking unknown future, just as the man-apes of the Pliocene contained in embryo the future that surrounds us now. The world of human culture itself was an unpredictable fairy world until, in some pre-ice-age meadow, the first meaningful sounds in all the world broke through the jungle babble of the past, the nature, until that moment, "known."

It is fascinating to observe that, in the very dawn of science, Francis 43 Bacon, the spokesman for the empirical approach to nature, shared with Shakespeare, the poet, a recognition of the creativeness which adds to nature, and which emerges from nature as "an art which nature makes." Neither the great scholar nor the great poet had renounced this "kingdome of fayries." Both had realized what Henri Bergson was later to express so effectively, that life inserts a vast "indetermination into matter." It is, in a sense, an intrusion from a realm which can never be completely subject to prophetic analysis by science. The novelties of evolution emerge; they cannot be predicted. They haunt, until their arrival, a world of unimaginable possibilities behind the living screen of events, as these last exist to the observer confined to a single point on the time scale.

Oddly enough, much of the confusion that surrounded my phrase "a 44 nature beyond the nature that we know" resolves itself into pure semantics. I might have pointed out what must be obvious even to the most dedicated scientific mind—that the nature which we know has been many times reinterpreted in human thinking, and that the hard, substantial matter of the nineteenth century has already vanished into a dark, bodiless void, a web of "events" in space-time.* This is a realm, I venture to assert, as weird as any

*In nineteenth-century physics, matter was viewed as determinate and predictable. It was thought that when physics finally succeeded in isolating the smallest particle of matter, the ultimate building block of reality would be revealed. Today, however, physics has given up the idea that there *is* an ultimate particle. Reality seems much more mysterious to physics today than it did 100 years ago. The smallest particles seem to be neither solid matter nor electromagnetic

we have tried, in the past, to exorcise by the brave use of seeming solid words. Yet some minds exhibit an almost instinctive hostility toward the mere attempt to wonder or to ask what lies below that microcosmic world out of which emerge the particles which compose our bodies and which now take on this wraithlike quality.

Is there something here we fear to face, except when clothed in safely 45 sterilized professional speech? Have we grown reluctant in this age of power to admit mystery and beauty into our thoughts, or to learn where power ceases? I referred earlier to one of our own forebears on a gravel bar, thumbing a pebble. If, after the ages of building and destroying, if after the measuring of light-years and the powers probed at the atom's heart, if after the last iron is rust-eaten and the last glass lies shattered in the streets, a man, some savage, some remnant of what once we were, pauses on his way to the tribal drinking place and feels rising from within his soul the inexplicable mist of terror and beauty that is evoked from old ruins—even the ruins of the greatest city in the world—then, I say, all will still be well with man.

And if that savage can pluck a stone from the gravel because it shone 46 like crystal when the water rushed over it, and hold it against the sunset, he will be as we were in the beginning, whole—as we were when we were children, before we began to split the knowledge from the dream. All talk of the two cultures is an illusion; it is the pebble which tells man's story. Upon it is written man's two faces, the artistic and the practical. They are expressed upon one stone over which a hand once closed, no less firm because the mind behind it was submerged in light and shadow and deep wonder.

Today we hold a stone, the heavy stone of power. We must perceive 47 beyond it, however, by the aid of the artistic imagination, those humane insights and understandings which alone can lighten our burden and enable us to shape ourselves, rather than the stone, into the forms which great art has anticipated.

Questions for Discussion

1. What logic or principle of development connects the first three paragraphs of Eiseley's essay with paragraph 4, in which he seems to focus on his thesis? What would be gained or lost if the first three paragraphs were dropped?

2. Once you are sure of the meanings of *dialectic, orthodoxy,* and *dissent,* do you

waves, yet they sometimes act like both. And the ultimate "facts" in particle physics seem not to be the predictable motion of solid particles but statistically "guessed at" *events.*

agree that "to train young people in the dialectic between orthodoxy and dissent is the unique contribution which universities make to society" (¶1)? Do you feel that this *should* be the aim of university teaching? Why or why not? Do you feel that this aim governs the teaching at your institution? If not, and if you think it should, what obstacles can you identify as blocking that aim? And finally, can you offer any remedies for the removal or at least the mitigation of these obstacles?

3. If you were the editor of this book and wanted to write a footnote explaining Eiseley's meaning in the first two sentences of paragraph 2, how could you make use of Jacob Bronowski's essay "The Reach of Imagination" (pp. 138–145) in writing a commentary? Is there a quotation in Bronowski's essay that amplifies and thus helps clarify Eiseley's point? Offer it to the rest of your class for discussion.

4. Do you agree with Santayana that people are so imprisoned by their notions of practicality that "the hard-pressed natural man will not indulge his imagination unless it poses for truth; and being half-aware of this imposition, he is more troubled at the thought of being deceived than at the fact of being mechanized or being bored" (¶3)? Can you provide examples of people who think of imaginative works as, if not downright deceiving, at least not leading to useful truth?

5. Eiseley's prose offers a flood of allusions to other writers and thinkers, including fairy-tale writers, philosophers, poets, anthropologists, literary critics, and, of course, natural scientists. The richness of his thinking seems directly related to the richness of this wide-ranging reading. How much of your own education is dominated by the desire to acquire something like this richness for yourself, to build it into the quality of your own mind? If this is not a personal goal for you, on what grounds do you reject or neglect it? Do most of your friends and peers hold to this goal? Do your teachers hold to it, either for themselves or for you? Should they? If those who do not hold to this goal were to adopt it, what differences would it make in their teaching and testing?

6. What fundamental traits in human nature does Eiseley see expressed in the decorative (or at least non-utilitarian) markings on the flint ax (¶16)? How does he use these markings as evidence in this argument that the division between the two cultures is merely an illusion?

Suggested Essay Topics

1. If you have ever had any teachers whose prejudiced views about either the sciences or the humanities have helped to reinforce the split between the two cultures, pick one such teacher now, either a scientist or a humanist, and address an essay in the form of a letter to that person, arguing that such prejudices are unreasonable and in the end deny to both the sciences and the humanities what is most creative in them. You will of course want to use Snow and Eiseley as sources for some of your ideas, but add any thinking of your own that will support the argument.

2. If you are majoring in neither the sciences nor the humanities but instead in some social science or pre-professional program such as business, nursing, accounting, or radio and television, and if you know that some of your peers or teachers in your field think that *both* the sciences and humanities are boring, irrelevant, or impractical, write an essay in the form of a letter to one of them arguing that people in the technical fields need the insights of the sciences and the humanities as much as anyone else; give the best reasons you can to support your claims.

❧ 11 ❧

RELIGIOUS PERSPECTIVES

Belief Versus Unbelief

We have just enough religion to make us hate, but not
enough to make us love one another.
Jonathan Swift

The fairest thing we can experience is the mysterious.
It is the fundamental emotion which stands at the cradle of true art
and true science. He who knows it not, who can no longer
wonder, can no longer feel amazement, is as good as dead,
a snuffed-out candle.
Albert Einstein

For my own part, the sense of spiritual relief which comes from
rejecting the idea of God as supernatural being is enormous. I see no
other way of bridging the gap between the religious
and the scientific approach to reality.
Julian Huxley

Incomprehensible? But because you cannot understand a
thing, it does not cease to exist.
Blaise Pascal

Religion is a passion for righteousness, and for the spread of
righteousness, conceived as a cosmic demand.
William Ernest Hocking

Many people . . . have been extremely religious and extremely wicked.
R. H. Thouless

Truth is the supreme God for me. Truth is God.
Gandhi

Religion . . . is the opium of the people.
Karl Marx

My country is the world, and my religion is to do good.
Thomas Paine

Elie Wiesel

Elie Wiesel (b. 1928), novelist and biblical commentator, winner of the Nobel Prize for literature, has written book after book since World War II, seeking a way to talk about religious questions while living with memories of the Nazi holocaust. How can a Jew—how can anyone—believe in and talk about God's loving care for his "chosen people" knowing that 6 million Jews and countless others were massacred? How can any sensitive person speak joyfully of "the sacred" after such an event? How can anyone have the courage or effrontery to affirm God's creation in the light of such horrors?

Wiesel has pursued such questions mainly in his novels, among them The Gates of the Forest, The Town Beyond the Wall, *and* A Beggar in Jerusalem. *Here we meet him in a different role, traditional in Jewish culture: that of the spiritual inquirer who wrestles with moral and spiritual problems by writing commentary on the mysterious stories in the Torah about the patriarchs, Israel's "founding fathers." In this essay, Wiesel comments on Genesis 22, in which God commands Abraham to sacrifice his son Isaac. This powerful story has always raised difficult questions, and Wiesel says the questions troubled him even as a child. Why do the innocent suffer? How can God ask of anyone such a terrible sacrifice as that of a son? How could Abraham have enough faith to accept such an awful command? And why is the story told just* this *way?*

Wiesel finds the story of Abraham and Isaac raising the same questions that are raised by the Nazi holocaust, and, as you might expect, he arrives at no simple, unambiguous reassurance about the meaning of evil and suffering in the world. But he does offer a path to the kind of spiritual insight, often humorous but always profound, that Jewish commentators have traditionally exhibited in the Midrash—a *term that refers both to a way of interpreting scripture and to the content of the accumulated stories and interpretations that the method has produced over millennia.*

It is important when reading commentary of this kind not to worry about the literal historical status of the stories themselves. Their value lies not in their factuality but in their meaning, and such meaning is always oblique and allusive, usually

*tentative, and sometimes downright puzzling—like the experience of evil and suffering
in life itself.*

THE SACRIFICE OF ISAAC

A Strange Tale About Fear, Faith, and Laughter

From "The Sacrifice of Isaac: A Survivor's Story," in *Messengers of God: Biblical Portraits and Legends*
(1976).

This strange tale is about fear and faith, fear and defiance, fear and laughter.   1

    Terrifying in content, it has become a source of consolation to those   2
who, in retelling it, make it part of their own experience. Here is a story that
contains Jewish destiny in its totality, just as the flame is contained in the
single spark by which it comes to life. Every major theme, every passion and
obsession that make Judaism the adventure that it is, can be traced back to
it: man's anguish when he finds himself face to face with God, his quest for
purity and purpose, the conflict of having to choose between dreams of the
past and dreams of the future, between absolute faith and absolute justice,
between the need to obey God's will and to rebel against it; between his
yearnings for freedom and for sacrifice, his desire to justify hope and despair
with words and silence—the same words and the same silence. It is all there.

    As a literary composition, this tale—known as the *Akeda*—is unmatched   3
in Scripture. Austere and powerful, its every word reverberates into infinity,
evoking suspense and drama, uncovering a whole mood based on a before and
continuing into an after, culminating in a climax which endows its characters
with another dimension. They are human—and more: forceful and real despite the metaphysical implications. At every step, their condition remains
relevant and of burning gravity.

    This very ancient story is still our own and we shall continue to be   4
bound to it in the most intimate way. We may not know it, but every one
of us, at one time or another, is called upon to play a part in it. What part?
Are we Abraham or Isaac? We are Jacob, that is to say, Israel. And Israel began
with Abraham.*

    Let us reread the text.   5

    Once upon a time there lived a man for all seasons, blessed with all   6
talents and virtues, deserving of every grace. His name was Abraham and his
mission was to serve as God's messenger among men too vain and blind to
recognize His glory. Tradition rates him higher than Moses—whose Law he
observed; higher even than Adam—whose errors he was asked to correct.

    Abraham: the first enemy of idolatry. The first angry young man. The   7
first rebel to rise up against the "establishment," society and authority. The

---

*Isaac's son, Jacob, received the name "Israel" when he strove with the angel and prevailed
(Genesis 32). The name later designated the 12 tribes, represented in Genesis by Jacob's 12 sons.

first to demystify official taboos and suspend ritual prohibitions. The first to reject civilization in order to form a minority of one. The first believer, the first one to suffer for his belief. Alone against the world, he declared himself free. Alone against the world, he braved the fire and the mob, affirming that God is one and present wherever His name is invoked; that one is the secret and the beginning of all that exists in heaven and on earth and that God's secret coincides with that of man.

8   And yet. Notwithstanding his total faith in God and His justice, His kindness as well, he did not for a moment hesitate to take God to task as he tried to save two condemned cities from destruction:* How can You—who embody justice—be unjust? He was the first who dared query God. And God listened and answered. For unlike Job, Abraham was protesting on behalf of others, not of himself. God forgave Abraham everything, including his questions. God is God and Abraham was His faithful servant; one was sure of the other. To test his will and vision, God had made him leave the security of his father's home, challenge rulers and engage their armies in battle, endure hunger and exile, disgrace and fire. His trust in God was never shaken. So loyal was he to God that he was rewarded with a son who became symbol and bearer of grace and benediction for generations to come.

9   Then one day God decided once more to test him—for the tenth and last time: Take your son and bring him to Me as an offering. The term used is *ola,* which means an offering that has been totally consumed, a holocaust. And Abraham complied. Without an argument. Without questioning or even trying to understand, without trying to stall. Without a word to anyone, not even his wife Sarah, without a tear; he simply waited for the next morning and left the house before she awakened. He saddled his donkey, and accompanied by his son and two servants, started on the road to Mount Moriah. After a three-day journey—which according to Kierkegaard† lasted longer than the four thousand years separating us from the event—father and son left the servants and donkey behind and began their ascent of the mountain. When they reached the top they erected an altar and prepared for the ritual. Everything was ready: the wood, the knife, the fire. Slaughterer and victim looked into each other's eyes and for one moment all of creation held its breath. The same fear penetrated the father and the son. A Midrash describes Isaac's fear. Stretched out on the altar, his wrists and ankles bound, Isaac saw the Temple in Jerusalem first destroyed and then rebuilt, and at the moment of the supreme test, Isaac understood that what was happening to him would happen to others, that this was to be a tale without an end, an experience to be endured by his children and theirs.‡ Never would they be spared the torture. The father's anguish, on the other hand, was not linked to the future; by sacrificing his son to obey God's will, Abraham knew that he was, in fact,

*Sodom and Gomorrah (see Genesis 18).

†Søren Kierkegaard (1813–1855), Danish philosopher and religious thinker.

‡The "Temple in Jerusalem" is Solomon's Temple, first built on the summit of Mt. Moriah where Abraham and Isaac's story takes place. Its history of repeated construction and destruction here symbolizes the history of the sufferings of the Jews.

sacrificing his knowledge *of* God and his faith *in* Him. If Isaac were to die, to whom would the father transmit this faith, this knowledge? The end of Isaac would connote the end of a prodigious adventure: the first would become the last. One cannot conceive of a more crushing or more devastating anguish: I shall thus have lived, suffered and caused others to suffer for nothing.

And the miracle took place. Death was defeated, the tragedy averted. The blade that could have cut the line—and prevented Israel from being born—was halted, suspended. 10

Was thus the mystery resolved? Hardly. As one plunges into Midrashic literature, one feels its poignancy. It leaves one troubled. The question is no longer whether Isaac was saved but whether the miracle could happen again. And how often. And for what reasons. And at what cost. 11

As a child, I read and reread this tale, my heart beating wildly; I felt dark apprehension come over me and carry me far away. 12

There was no understanding the three characters. Why would God, the merciful Father, demand that Abraham become inhuman, and why would Abraham accept? And Isaac, why did he submit so meekly? Not having received a direct order to let himself be sacrificed, why did he consent? 13

I could not understand. If God needs human suffering to be God, how can man foresee an end to that suffering? And if faith in God must result in self-denial, how can faith claim to elevate and improve man? 14

These were painful questions, especially for an adolescent, because they did not fit into the framework of the sin-punishment concept, to which all religious thought had accustomed us. 15

. . .

To me the *Akeda* was an unfathomable mystery given to every genera- tion, to be relived, if not solved—one of the great mysteries of our history, a mystery so opaque that it obscures not only the facts but also the names of the protagonists. 16

Why did Abraham, the would-be slaughterer, become, in our prayers, the symbol of *hesed:* grace, compassion and love? A symbol of love, he who was ready to throttle his son? 17

And Isaac, why was he called Isaac? *Yitzhak?* He who will laugh? Laugh at whom? At what? Or, as Sarah thought, he who will make others laugh? Why was the most tragic figure in Biblical history given such a bizarre name? 18

. . .

What do we know about his [Abraham's] life and his person? Many things told to us by the Bible and expounded upon by the Midrash. We are treated to an abundance of precise and picturesque details on both his private and public activities. We are informed about his habits, his moods, his busi- ness relationships, his difficulties with his neighbors, his servants and his concubines. He was rich, hospitable, friendly and giving; he invited strangers into his home without asking who they were or what the purpose of their 19 visit might be. He welcomed the hungry and helped the poor, angels and beggars alike, offering them both shelter and food.

. . .

He evidently was a restless man who could not stay idle long. He was 20 forever seeking new stimulation, new certainties; he abhorred all routine. He would go from Haran to Canaan, sometimes pushing as far as Damascus, in his search for worthy adversaries. He was an explorer of some stature who affronted kings and robbers, and enjoyed defeating them, exulting when he broke their pride.

Yet his greatest adventure was his encounter with God—an encounter 21 which was a result of deliberate choice on both sides. They addressed one another as equals. According to the Midrash, God said to Abraham: *Ani yekhidi veata yekhidi*—I am alone and you are alone, alone to know and proclaim it. From that moment on, their dialogue took place under the implacable sign of the absolute: they were to be both partners and accomplices. Before, says legend, God reigned only in heaven; it was Abraham who extended his rule unto the earth.

. . .

And one begins to wonder, since God and he loved one another so much 22 and collaborated so closely, why these tests? Why these ordeals and torture? Because God tests only the strong. The weak do not resist or resist poorly; they are of no consequence. But then, what good is it to resist, since God knows the outcome in advance? Answer: God knows, man does not.

Most commentators assume that Abraham was tested for his own good. 23 To serve as an example to the peoples of the world and to earn him their leaders' reverence. And also to harden him; to awaken in him an awareness of his own strength and potential.

Of course, this does not satisfy everyone: the idea that suffering is good 24 for Jews is one that owes its popularity to our enemies.

And indeed there is another explanation, though not a very original one, 25 that brings into the picture an old acquaintance, always present in moments of crisis and doubt: Satan. Source of all evil, supreme temptor. The easy, glib answer, the scapegoat. The crafty gambler, the unabashed liar. The servant who conveniently carries out the Master's dirty work, accepting all blame and anathema in His place. The sacrifice of Isaac? God had nothing to do with it; it was all Satan's doing. God did not want this test; Satan demanded it. The inhuman game was Satan's scheme and he bears full responsibility. Satan: the ideal alibi.

Just as he did with Job—who is frequently compared to Abraham for 26 more than one reason—Satan used gossip to distort and embellish history. On his return from an inspection tour on earth, he handed his report to the Almighty while telling Him his impressions. Thus he came to his surprise visit with Abraham, who was celebrating the birth of his beloved son Isaac. Rejoicing, sumptuous meals, public festivities, Satan did not spare the superlatives, as usual. And do You know, said he perfidiously, do You know that Your faithful servant Abraham has forgotten You—You? Yes indeed, his

good fortune has gone to his head; he forgot to set aside an offering for You.
He thought only of his joy, as though it did not come from You; he fed all
his guests, yet he neglected to offer You the youngest of his sheep, if only
as a modest token of his gratitude. God was not convinced. He answered: No,
no, you're wrong to suspect My faithful Abraham; he is devoted to Me, he
loves Me, he would give Me all that he possesses—he would give me his son
were I to ask him. Really? said Satan. Are You sure? I'm not. And God was
provoked and felt compelled to accept the challenge. The rest can be found
in Scripture.

   The Biblical narrative is of exemplary purity of line, sobriety and terse-   27
ness. Not one superfluous word, not one useless gesture. The imagery is
striking, the language austere, the dialogue so incisive, it leaves one with a
knot in one's throat.

   . . . *And, some time afterward, God put Abraham to the test. He said to him: Abraham.*   28
And he answered: Here I am. And He said: Take your son, your favored one, Isaac, whom
you love, and go to the land of Moriah and offer him there as a burnt offering on one of the
heights which I will point out to you.

   This time Abraham did not answer: *Here I am;* he did not answer at all.   29
He went home, lay down and fell asleep. The next morning he rose, awakened
his son and two of his servants, and started out on his journey. At the end
of three days—at the end of a silence that lasted three days—he saw the
appointed place in the distance. He halted, and instructed the servants: *You*
stay here with the ass. The boy and I will go up there; we will worship and we will return
to you.

   Abraham took the wood for the burnt offering and gave it to his son, Isaac. He himself   30
took the firestone and the knife; and the two walked away together.

   The last sentence gives us the key: one went to face death, the other to   31
give it, but they went together; still close to one another though everything
already separated them. God was waiting for them and they were going
toward Him together. But then Isaac, who until that moment had not opened
his mouth, turned to his father and uttered a single word: *Father.* And for the
second time Abraham answered: *Here I am.* Was it because of the silence that
followed this painfully hushed affirmation? Isaac began to feel uneasy; he
wanted to be reassured or at least understand.

   And Isaac said: Here is the firestone and the wood; but where is the sheep for the burnt   32
offering?

   Embarrassed, suddenly shy, Abraham tried to equivocate: *God will see to*   33
the sheep for His burnt offering, my son. And the two of them walked on together.

   The march continued. The two of them alone in the world, encircled by   34
God's unfathomable design. But they were *together.* Now the repetition renders a new sound while adding to the dramatic intensity of the narrative.

   And Isaac began to guess, to understand. And then he knew. And the   35
father and the son remained united. Together they reached the top of the
mountain; together they erected the altar; together they prepared the wood
and the fire. Everything was ready, nothing was missing. And Isaac lay on the
altar, silently gazing at his father.

And Abraham picked up the knife to slay his son. Then an angel of the Lord called 36
to him from heaven: Abraham, Abraham! And he answered: Here I am.

For the third time he answered: *Here I am.* I am the same, the same person 37
who answered Your first call; I answer Your call, whatever its nature; and
even were *it* to change, *I* would not.

And the angel said: Do not raise your hand against the boy or do anything to him. 38
For now I know that you fear God, since you have not withheld your son, your favored one,
from Me.

All is well that ends well. The sacrifice took place, yet Isaac remained 39
alive: a ram was slaughtered and burned in his stead. Abraham reconciled
himself with his conscience. And the angel, exulting, renewed before him
shining promises for the future: his children, as numerous as the stars reflected in the sea, would inherit the earth. Abraham once more plunged into
the magnificent dream which would always remind him of his covenant with
God. No, the future was not dead. No, truth would not be stifled. No, exile
would not go on indefinitely. Abraham should have returned home a happy
and serene man. Except that the tale ends with a strange sentence which
opens rather than heals the wounds: *Vayashav avraham el nearav*—And Abraham
returned to his servants. Note the singular: *Vayashav,* he returned. He, Abraham. Alone. And Isaac? Where was Isaac? Why was he not with his father?
What had happened to him? Are we to understand that father and son were
no longer together? That the experience they just shared had separated
them—albeit only *after* the event? That Isaac, unlike Abraham, was no longer
the same person, that the real Isaac remained there, on the altar?

These profoundly disquieting questions provoked passionate responses 40
in the Midrash, where the theme of the *Akeda* occupies as important a place
as the creation of the world or the revelation at Sinai.

The Midrash, in this case, does not limit itself to stating the facts and 41
commenting upon them. It delves into the very heart and silence of the cast
of characters. It examines them from every angle; it follows them into their
innermost selves; it goes so far as to imagine the unimaginable.

. . .

On the morning of the third day, says the Midrash, Abraham could 42
distinguish the appointed place from afar—just as the people did later before
Sinai. He turned to his son and asked: Do you see what I see? Yes, replied
Isaac, I see a splendid mountain under a cloud of fire. Then Abraham turned
to his two servants and asked: And you, what do you see? The servants,
passive onlookers, saw nothing but the desert. And Abraham understood that
the event did not concern them and that they were to stay behind. And that
the place was indeed the place.

And so the father and the son walked away together—*ze laakod veze léaked,* 43
the one to bind and the other to be bound, *ze lishkhot veze lishakhet,* the one to
slaughter and the other to be slaughtered—sharing the same allegiance to the
same God, responding to the same call. The sacrifice was to be their joint
offering; father and son had never before been so close. The Midrashic text

emphasizes this, as if to show another tragic aspect of the *Akeda*, namely, the equation between Abraham and Isaac. Abraham and Isaac were equals, in spite of their opposing roles as victim and executioner. But Abraham himself, whose victim was he? God's? Once more the key word is *yakhdav*, together: victims together. Together they gathered the wood, together they arranged it on the altar, together they set the stage for the drama to unfold. Abraham, says the text, behaved like a happy father preparing to celebrate his son's wedding, and Isaac like a groom about to meet his bride-to-be. Both were serene, at peace with themselves and each other.

But then, suddenly, for a brief moment, Isaac reentered reality and   44 grasped the magnitude and horror of what was to come: Father, what will you do, Mother and you, afterward? — He who has consoled us until now, answered Abraham, will continue to console us. — Father, Isaac went on after a silence, I am afraid, afraid of being afraid. You must bind me securely. And a little later: Father, when you shall speak to my mother, when you shall tell her, make sure she is not standing near the well or on the roof, lest she fall and hurt herself.

Our attention thereafter is centered on Isaac stretched out on the altar.   45 We watch him as Abraham gazes straight into his eyes. Abraham was weeping, his tears streaming into the eyes of his son, leaving a scar never to be erased. So bitterly did he weep that his knife slipped from his hands and fell to the ground. Only then, not before, did he shout in despair, and only then did God part the heavens and allow Isaac to see the higher sanctuaries of the *merkava*, of creation, with entire rows of angels lamenting: *Yakhid shokhet veyakhid nishkat*—Look at the slaughterer, he is alone and so is the one he is about to slaughter. All the worlds in all the spheres were in tumult: Isaac had become the center of the universe. He could not be allowed to die, not now, not like this. And die he would not. The voice of an angel was heard: Do not raise your hand against the boy, Abraham. Isaac must live.

Why did an angel intervene rather than God Himself? The Midrash   46 answers: God alone may order death, but to save a human life, an angel is enough.

A profoundly generous and beautiful explanation, but I have another   47 which I prefer. Mine allows me to do what until now I could not; namely, to identify not only with Isaac but also with Abraham.

The time has come for the storyteller to confess that he has always felt   48 much closer to Isaac than to his father, Abraham.

I have never really been able to accept the idea that inhumanity could   49 be one more way for man to move closer to God. Kierkegaard's too convenient theory of occasional "ethical suspension" never appealed to me. Kierkegaard maintains that Abraham concealed Isaac's fate from him in order to protect his faith in God; let Isaac lose faith in man rather than in man's Creator. These are concepts rejected by Jewish tradition. God's Law—we said it earlier—commits God as well; but while God cannot suspend His law, it is given to man—to man and not to God—to interpret it. However, faith in God is linked to faith in man, and one cannot be separated from the other.

Let us once again examine the question: Why didn't Abraham tell Isaac 50 the truth? Because he thought the *Akeda* was a matter strictly between himself and God; it concerned nobody else, not even Isaac.

Thus I place my trust in man's strength. God does not like man to come 51 to him through resignation. Man must strive to reach God through knowledge and love. God loves man to be clear-sighted and outspoken, not blindly obsequious. He respected Job because he dared to stand up to Him. Abraham had interceded on behalf of the two sinful cities long before the test with Isaac.

A double-edged test. God subjected Abraham to it, yet at the same time 52 Abraham forced it on God. As though Abraham had said: I defy You, Lord. I shall submit to Your will, but let us see whether You shall go to the end, whether You shall remain passive and remain silent when the life of my son—who is also Your son—is at stake!

And God changed his mind and relented. Abraham won. That was why 53 God sent an angel to revoke the order and congratulate him; He Himself was too embarrassed.

And suddenly we have another *coup de théâtre* [sudden dramatic turn of 54 events]. Abraham never ceases to astonish us: having won the round, he became demanding. Since God had given in, Abraham was not going to be satisfied with one victory and continue their relationship as though nothing had changed. His turn had come to dictate conditions, or else . . . he would pick up the knife—and come what may!*

Let us listen to the Midrash: 55

When Abraham heard the angel's voice, he did not cry out with joy or express his gratitude. On the contrary, he began to argue. He, who until now had obeyed with sealed lips, suddenly showed inordinate skepticism. He questioned the counterorder he had been hoping and waiting for. First he asked that the angel identify himself in due form. Then he demanded proof that he was God's messenger, not Satan's. And finally he simply refused to accept the message, saying: God Himself ordered me to sacrifice my son, it is up to Him to rescind that order without an intermediary. And, says the Midrash, God had to give in again: He Himself finally had to tell Abraham not to harm his son.

This was Abraham's second victory; yet he was still not satisfied.   56
Listen . . .   57

When Abraham heard the celestial voice ordering him to spare his son 58 Isaac, he declared: I swear I shall not leave the altar, Lord, before I speak my mind. — Speak, said God. — Did You not promise me that my descendants would be as numerous as the stars in the sky? — Yes, I did promise you that. — And whose descendants will they be? Mine? Mine alone? — No, said God, they will be Isaac's as well. — And didn't You also promise me that they

*The ellipses in paragraphs 54 and 57 are Wiesel's.

would inherit the earth? — Yes, I promised you that too. — And whose
descendants will they be? Mine alone? — No, said God's voice, they will be
Isaac's as well. — Well then, my Lord, said Abraham unabashedly, I could
have pointed out to You before that Your order contradicted Your promise.
I could have spoken up, I didn't. I contained my grief and held my tongue.
In return, I want You to make me the following promise: that when, in the
future, my children and my children's children throughout the generations
will act against Your law and against Your will, You will also say nothing and
forgive them. — So be it, God agreed. Let them but retell this tale and they
will be forgiven.

We now begin to understand why Abraham's name has become synon- 59
ymous with *hesed*. For indeed he was charitable, not so much with Isaac as
with God. He could have accused Him and proved Him wrong; he didn't. By
saying yes—almost to the end—he established his faith in God and His
mercy, thus bringing Him closer to His creation. He won and—so says the
Midrash—God loves to be defeated by His children.

But unlike God, Satan hates to lose. Unlike God, he takes revenge, 60
however and against whomever he can. Defeated by Abraham and Isaac, he
turned against Sarah, appearing before her disguised as Isaac. And he told her
the *true* story that was taking place on Mount Moriah. He told her of the
march, the ritual ceremony, the heavenly intervention. Barely had Satan
finished talking, when Sarah fell to the ground. Dead.

Why this legend? It has a meaning. Abraham thought that the *Akeda* 61
was a matter between himself and God, or perhaps between himself and his
son. He was wrong. There is an element of the unknown in every injustice,
in every adventure involving total commitment. One imposes suffering on a
friend, a son, in order to win who knows what battles, to prove who knows
what theories, and in the end someone else pays the price—and that someone
is almost always innocent. Once the injustice has been committed, it eludes
our control. All things considered, Abraham was perhaps wrong in obeying,
or even in making believe that he was obeying. By including Isaac in an
equation he could not comprehend, by playing with Isaac's suffering, he
became unwittingly an accomplice in his wife's death.

Another text, even more cruel, goes further yet. It hints that the tragic 62
outcome could, after all, not be averted. Hence the use of the singular verb:
Vayashav avraham el nearav. Yes, Abraham did return alone. One does not play
such games with impunity.

Of course, this hypothesis has been rejected by tradition. The ancient 63
commentators preferred to imagine Isaac shaken but alive, spending the
unaccounted-for years at a yeshiva or perhaps even in paradise, but eventually returning home.*

---

*A yeshiva is an academy for studying the Talmud, the body of Jewish law and tradition. The
notion of Isaac at a yeshiva is, of course, whimsical.

Yet popular imagination—collective memory—adheres rather to the ₆₄ tragic interpretation of the text. Isaac did not accompany his father on the way back because the divine intervention came too late. The act had been consummated. Neither God nor Abraham emerged victorious from the contest. They were both losers. Hence God's pangs of guilt on Rosh Hashana, when He judges man and his deeds. Because of the drama that took place at Mount Moriah, He understands man better. Because of Abraham and Isaac, He knows that it is possible to push some endeavors too far.

That is why the theme and term of the *Akeda* have been used, through- ₆₅ out the centuries, to describe the destruction and disappearance of countless Jewish communities everywhere. All the pogroms, the crusades, the persecutions, the slaughters, the catastrophes, the massacres by sword and the liquidations by fire—each time it was Abraham leading his son to the altar, to the holocaust all over again.

Of all the Biblical tales, the one about Isaac is perhaps the most timeless ₆₆ and most relevant to our generation. We have known Jews who, like Abraham, witnessed the death of their children; who, like Isaac, lived the *Akeda* in their flesh; and some who went mad when they saw their father disappear on the altar, with the altar, in a blazing fire whose flames reached into the highest of heavens.

We have known Jews—ageless Jews—who wished to become blind for ₆₇ having seen God and man opposing one another in the invisible sanctuary of the celestial spheres, a sanctuary illuminated by the gigantic flames of the holocaust.

. . .

But the story does not end there. Isaac survived; he had no choice. He ₆₈ had to make something of his memories, his experience, in order to force us to hope.

For our survival is linked to his. Satan could kill Sarah, he could even ₆₉ hurt Abraham, but Isaac was beyond his reach. Isaac too represents defiance. Abraham defied God, Isaac defied death.

What did happen to Isaac after he left Mount Moriah? He became a ₇₀ poet—author of the *Minha* service*—and did not break with society. Nor did he rebel against life. Logically, he should have aspired to wandering, to the pursuit of oblivion. Instead he settled on his land, never to leave it again, retaining his name. He married, had children, refusing to let fate turn him into a bitter man. He felt neither hatred nor anger toward his contemporaries who did not share his experience. On the contrary, he liked them and showed concern for their well-being. After Moriah, he devoted his life and his right to immortality to the defense of his people.

At the end of time, say our sages, God will tell Abraham: Your children ₇₁ have sinned. And Abraham will reply: Let them die to sanctify Your name. Then God will turn to Jacob and say: Your children have sinned. And Jacob will reply: Let them die to sanctify Your name. Then God will speak to Isaac:

*A daily afternoon liturgy.

Your children have sinned. And Isaac will answer: *My* children? Are they not also Yours? Yours as well?

It will be Isaac's privilege to remain Israel's *Melitz-Yosher,* the defender 72 of his people, pleading its cause with great ability. He will be entitled to say anything he likes to God, ask anything of Him. Because he suffered? No. Suffering, in Jewish tradition, confers no privileges. It all depends on what one makes of that suffering. Isaac knew how to transform it into prayer and love rather than into rancor and malediction. This is what gives him rights and powers no other man possesses. His reward? The Temple was built on Moriah. Not on Sinai.

Let us return to the question we asked at the beginning: Why was the 73 most tragic of our ancestors named Isaac, a name which evokes and signifies laughter? Here is why. As the first survivor, he had to teach us, the future survivors of Jewish history, that it is possible to suffer and despair an entire lifetime and still not give up the art of laughter.

Isaac, of course, never freed himself from the traumatizing scenes that 74 violated his youth; the holocaust had marked him and continued to haunt him forever. Yet he remained capable of laughter. And in spite of everything, he did laugh.

Questions for Discussion

1. Can you summarize Wiesel's point in one topic sentence (for example, "God is good, after all," or "The meaning of suffering is such-and-such or so-and-so")? If so, can you get your classmates to agree with your summary? If your summaries seem even less satisfactory than usual, why is that so?

2. Do you or any other members of your class know of interpretations of the story of Abraham and Isaac that Wiesel does not offer? If so, discuss how they differ from his.

3. For some religious thinkers, religion is best explained in full-fledged systematic *theologies,* organized accounts of the nature of God and God's creation (perhaps the most famous example is the *Summa Theologica* of St. Thomas Aquinas, a monumental intellectual inquiry running to thousands of pages). Neither the Torah nor the Christian Bible is like that. Like Wiesel, they seem to say that the truth about religion is expressed better in stories than in propositions or arguments. Do you think that there are some truths that are somehow "beyond" direct statement? That some genuine knowledge cannot be proved with argument? Or do you think that whatever cannot be stated in straightforward propositions must be something other than "truth" or "knowledge"—poetry, perhaps, or myth?

Suggested Essay Topics

1. Most of our suggested topics in this book have asked you to present an argument, a systematic defense of some belief, with your reasons worked out as fully as possible. Here is your chance to try a freer kind of exploration. Choose any story from the Torah or Bible (or any other scripture you may know) and tell it again, but more fully, adding your own hunches about the characters' motives or the probable outcomes. For example, you might dramatize the scene between Cain and Abel in Genesis 4, trying to understand the point of view of both characters. Or you might try the story of Mary and Martha in the New Testament (Luke 10:38–42). Try to tell your story in a tone that suggests, like Wiesel's, that you are engaged in a genuine search for meaning.

2. For Wiesel the holocaust was a supreme test of his religious faith, and he sees God's command to Abraham presenting a similar kind of supreme test. Can you think of experiences of evil or suffering in your own life that, though less grand in scale, presented to you the same *kind* of challenge? If so, write an essay in the form of a letter to someone you trust, recounting the argument with yourself (or perhaps the quarrel with God) that your experience produced. You may not want—or you may not be able—to settle the issues you raise, or you may feel ready to affirm or reject the religious views that were challenged by your experience. If you do take a settled position, however, try to give reasons for it. Merely asserting how you "feel" about God or religion will not make an interesting statement.

Walter T. Stace

Walter T. Stace (1886–1967), for many years a professor of philosophy at Princeton, undertakes here to define religion in the most basic terms possible. From his point of view, being religious has little to do with going to church, professing creeds, or believing conventionally in the existence of a personal God. Religion lies not in outward beliefs or activities but in an inner disposition of the soul that all human beings share. The "impulse [that] lies deep down in every human heart"—the religious impulse in its most basic form—is "the hunger of the soul for the impossible, the unattainable, the inconceivable" (¶6).

The most unattainable achievement for a human being—a creature—would be to enter a state beyond creatureliness: not by dying, for dying is in the nature of creatures, but by going beyond creaturely existence altogether. To exist but to have none of the transitory properties of existence—that is the impossible. Yet that condition is exactly what human beings most want—so argues Stace—even as they are aware that they will never achieve it.

Other aspects of conventional religion, such as moral codes and belief in a personal God, are not necessarily irrelevant to the religious impulse, but they are not synonymous with it. And religion is not to be debased by finding, or fabricating, "explanations" for it. Religion can be neither accounted for nor explained away by theories of social behavior, human psychology, logic, or reason. The fundamental characteristic of religion is an inescapable paradox: To be religious means knowing that I cannot have what I want, that I can never fully understand the mystery of what I want (cannot, at least, fully name it or explain it), and that I persist in longing for it against any hope of ever achieving it.

WHAT RELIGION IS

Chapter 1 of *Time and Eternity: An Essay in the Philosophy of Religion* (1952).

"Religion," says Whitehead, "is the vision of something which stands   1
beyond, behind, and within, the passing flux of immediate things; something which is real, and yet waiting to be realized; something which is a remote possibility, and yet the greatest of present facts; something which gives meaning to all that passes, and yet eludes apprehension; something whose possession is the final good, and yet is beyond all reach; something which is the ultimate ideal, and the hopeless quest."[1]

These words evidently express a direct intuition of the writer. They well   2
up from his own personal religious experience and therefore stir the depths in us who read. What he says is not a faded copy of what someone else has felt or thought or seen, as the majority of pious utterances are—hackneyed and wornout clichés, debased by parrot-like repetition, although they too, poor dead things, once issued fresh-minted from a living human soul. Here and there amid the arid hills of human experience are well-springs and fountain-heads of religious intuition. They are the original sources of all religion. They need not always be of great grandeur. They may be humble rivulets of feeling. Or they may give rise to great rivers of refreshment flowing through the centuries. But always, great or small, they bear upon themselves the stamp of their own authenticity. They need no external proof or justification. Indeed they are incapable of any. We know them because the God in us cries out, hearing the voice of the God in the other, answering back. The deep calls to the deep.

Whitehead's words are of this kind.   3

Note first their paradoxical character. To the "something" of which they   4
speak are attributed opposite characters which barely avoid, if they do avoid, the clash of flat contradiction. Each clause is a balance of such contradicting predicates. The meaning cannot be less than that paradox and contradiction are of the very essence of that "something" itself.

Note, too, the final words. That something which man seeks as his   5
ultimate ideal is the "hopeless quest." This is not a careless expression, an exaggeration, a loose use of words. It is not rhetoric. If this phrase had come at the beginning of the passage, it might have been toned down in the succeeding sentences. But it strikes the final note. It is the last word.

And one can see why. For religion is the hunger of the soul for the 6
impossible, the unattainable, the inconceivable. This is not something which
it merely happens to be, an unfortunate accident or disaster which befalls it
in the world. This is its essence, and this is its glory. This is what religion
means. The religious impulse in men *is* the hunger for the impossible, the
unattainable, the inconceivable—or at least for that which is these things in
the world of time. And anything which is less than this is not religion—
though it may be some very admirable thing such as morality. Let it not be
said that this makes religion a foolish thing, fit only for madmen—although
indeed from the world's point of view the religious man *is* a madman. For,
mad or not, this impulse lies deep down in every human heart. It is of the
essence of man, quite as much as is his reason.

Religion seeks the infinite. And the infinite by definition is impossible, 7
unattainable. It is by definition that which can never be reached.

Religion seeks the light. But it is not a light which can be found at any 8
place or time. It is not somewhere. It is the light which is nowhere. It is "the
light which never was on sea or land." Never was. Never will be, even in the
infinite stretches of future time. The light is non-existent, as the poet himself
says. Yet it is the great light which lightens the world. And this, too, the poet
implies.

Religion is the desire to break away from being and existence altogether, 9
to get beyond existence into that nothingness where the great light is. It is
the desire to be utterly free from the fetters of being. For every being is a
fetter. Existence is a fetter. To be is to be tied to what you are. Religion is
the hunger for the non-being which yet is.

In music sometimes a man will feel that he comes to the edge of break- 10
ing out from the prison bars of existence, breaking out from the universe
altogether. There is a sense that the goal is at hand, that the boundary wall
of the universe is crumbling and will be breached at the next moment, when
the soul will pass out free into the infinite. But the goal is not reached. For
it is the unspeakable, the impossible, the inconceivable, the unattainable.
There is only the sense of falling backward into time. The goal is only
glimpsed, sensed, and then lost.

One thing is better than another thing. Gold is perhaps better than clay, 11
poetry than push-pin. One place is pleasanter than another place. One time
is happier than another time. In all being there is a scale of better and worse.
But just because of this relativity, no being, no time, no place, satisfies the
ultimate hunger. For all beings are infected by the same disease, the disease
of existence. If owning a marble leaves your metaphysical and religious thirst
unquenched, so will owning all the planets. If living on the earth for three-
score years and ten leaves it unsatisfied, neither will living in a fabled Heaven
for endless ages satisfy it. For how do you attain your end by making things
bigger, or longer, or wider, or thicker, or more this or more that? For they will
still be *this* or *that.* And it is being this or that which is the disease of things.

So long as there is light in your life, the light has not yet dawned. There 12
is in your life much darkness—that much you will admit. But you think that
though this thing, this place, this time, this experience is dark, yet that thing,

that place, that time, that experience is, or will be, bright. But this is the great illusion. You must see that all things, all places, all times, all experiences are equally dark. You must see that all stars are black. Only out of the *total* darkness will the light dawn.

Religion is that hunger which no existence, past, present, or future, no   13
actual existence and no possible existence, in this world or in any other world, on the earth or above the clouds and stars, material or mental or spiritual, can ever satisfy. For whatever is or could be will have the curse on it of thisness or thatness.

This is no new thought. It is only what religious men have always said.   14
To the saint Narada the Supreme Being offered whatsoever boon his heart could imagine—abundance of life, riches, health, pleasure, heroic sons. "That," said Narada, "and precisely that is what I desire to be rid of and pass beyond." It is true that the things here spoken of—health, riches, even heroic sons—are what we call worldly, even material, things. But they are symbolic only. They stand for all things of any kind, whether material or non-material—for all things, at least, which could have an existence in the order of time, whether in the time before death or in the time after.

It is true that simple-minded religious men have conceived their goal   15
as a state of continued existence beyond the grave filled with all happy things and experiences. But plainly such happy things and experiences were no more than symbolic, and the happy heavens containing such things have the character of myth. To the human mind, fast fettered by the limits of its poor imagination, they stand for and represent the goal. One cannot conceive the inconceivable. So in place of it one puts whatever one can imagine of delight; wine and houris if one's imagination is limited to these; love, kindness, sweetness of spiritual living if one is of a less materialistic temper. But were these existences and delights, material or spiritual, to be actually found and enjoyed as present, they would be condemned by the saint along with all earthly joys. For they would have upon them the curse, the darkness, the disease, of all existent things, of all that is this or that. This is why we cannot conceive of any particular pleasure, happiness, joy, which would not *cloy*, which—to be quite frank—would not in the end be boring.

"In the Infinite only is bliss. In the finite there is no bliss," says the   16
ancient Upanishad.[2] And we are apt to imagine that this is a piece of rhetoric, or at least an exaggeration. For surely it is not strictly speaking true that in the finite there is no happiness at all. No doubt the saint or the moralist is right to speak disparagingly of the mere pleasures of sense. But is there, then, no joy of living? What of the love of man and woman, of parent and child? What of the sweetness of flowers, the blue of the sky, the sunlight? Is it not quite false that there is no bliss in these? And yet they are finite. So we say. But we fail to see that the author of the verse is speaking of something quite different from what we have in mind, namely of that ultimate bliss in God which is the final satisfaction of the religious hunger. And we think that this ultimate blessedness differs only *in degree* from the

happy and joyful experiences of our lives. Whereas the truth is that it differs *in kind.* The joys, not only of the earth, but of any conceivable heaven—which we can conceive only as some fortunate and happy prolongation of our lives in time—are not of the same order as that ultimate blessedness. We imagine any joyful, even ecstatic, experience we please. We suppose that the blessedness of salvation is something like this, only more joyful. Perhaps if it were multiplied a million times. . . . But all this is of no avail. Though we pile mountain of earthly joy upon mountain of earthly joy, we reach no nearer to the bliss which is the end. For these things belong to different orders; the one, however great, to the order of time; the other to the order of eternity. Therefore all the temporal joys which we pile upon one another to help our imaginations, are no more than symbolic, and the accounts of possible heavens mere myths.

Hence the religious soul must leave behind all things and beings, including itself. From being it must pass into Nothing. But in this nothing it must still be. Therefore also what it seeks is the being which is non-being. And God, who is the only food which will appease its hunger, is this Being which is Non-Being. Is this a contradiction? Yes. But men have always found that, in their search for the Ultimate, contradiction and paradox lie all around them. Did we not see that the words of Whitehead, with which we opened this chapter, must mean at least that contradiction and paradox lie at the heart of things? And is there any more contradiction here than we find—to give the most obvious example from traditional theology—in the doctrine of the Trinity? That, too, proclaims in unmistakable terms that there is contradiction in the Ultimate. The rationalizing intellect, of course, will not have it so. It will attempt to explain away the final Mystery, to logicize it, to reduce it to the categories of "this" and "that." At least it will attempt to water it down till it looks something like "common sense," and can be swallowed without too much discomfort! But the great theologians knew better. In the self-contradictory doctrine of the Trinity they threw the Mystery of God uncompromisingly in men's faces. And we shall see that all attempts to make religion a purely rational, logical, thing are not only shallow but would, if they could succeed, destroy religion. Either God is a Mystery or He is nothing at all.

NOTES

Both notes are Stace's.

[1] A. N. Whitehead, *Science and the Modern World,* chapter 12.
[2] Chandogya Upanishad.

Questions for Discussion

1. Do you agree with Stace's final assertion that "either God is a Mystery or He is nothing at all"? Do you think Stace argues this point convincingly? What parts of the supporting argument do you find particularly strong or weak?

2. According to Stace, the religious impulse "lies deep down in every human heart" (¶6). Granting Stace his definition of *religious impulse* as a paradoxical yearning for the unattainable, do you agree with the assertion that this impulse is universal? What forms of behavior in human beings do you think either confirm or contradict the assertion?

3. Can you confirm from your own experience or observation the assertion that people indeed "hunger for the impossible"? Is it your impression that people consistently yearn for some glimpse of or contact with something beyond and above creatureliness? Or does it seem to you that people generally accept the terms of human existence without much regret or complaint?

4. Keeping in mind the extreme claims for science that Midgley (pp. 404–424) cites, does it seem fair to suggest that some devotees of science have, as Midgley's title suggests, turned science itself into a religion? Can you think of ways in which modern science fits Stace's definition of religion as a yearning for the unattainable or for the absolute?

5. Do the devoutly religious people you know seem fairly or adequately described by Stace's analysis? If not, do you think, after reading Stace, that they are less religious than you formerly thought? Or do you think he has left important considerations out of his discussion? If the latter, what has he omitted?

Suggested Essay Topics

1. Describe an experience—preferably one that recurs often enough to form a pattern, but a unique one will do—in which you are aware of having "hungered for the impossible." (Make sure that you are talking about hungering for the impossible in the same sense that Stace means. Wanting new clothes for the weekend dance when you have only $10 does not qualify.) Then either use Stace's argument to explain this hunger as a religious impulse and the pursuit of its fulfillment as a religious experience or refute Stace's argument by explaining your hunger in non-religious terms. (You might want to say, for example, that your feelings were merely a product of psychological or social conditioning—a product of the way you've been raised. But you will not want to admit that your desire for the impossible has anything to do with seeking an escape from the limitations of creatureliness.)

2. Spend a Sunday morning listening to as many television evangelists and preachers as you can. Choose one who interests you and evaluate, as you think Stace would, the degree of genuine religiousness you find either in

the messages delivered or in the personality you can infer behind the messages.

It is important here not to slide from possible objections you may have to the surface opinions of the preachers into the automatic judgment that they are not genuinely religious. It is inherent in Stace's view that true religion can be expressed in many different—and no doubt often surprising—forms.

John Donne

Among many philosophers and religious believers the conviction persists—a consistent motif never quite drowned out by other views—that the profoundest truths cannot be expressed in straightforward propositions or declarative sentences but can only be hinted at, shadowed forth, in paradox. Such utterances contain contradictions, yet by their very perplexity seem to express the deepest truths more comprehensively, sensitively, and accurately than any other kind of formulation.

Whether or not John Donne (1572–1631) believed this as a general doctrine, his use of paradox is clear in "Batter My Heart." Only as God supports us can we approach Him; only as God loves us can we be made lovable. These are conventional Christian notions, not new and not especially powerful when summarized. What gives Donne's poem its power, freshness, and conviction is his imagery, which invests these notions with life and emotional power. Each ascending paradox is knottier and more emotionally laden than the last, until in the end the poet achieves a catharsis of intensity in picturing himself as freed by slavery, purified by rape.

BATTER MY HEART

From *Holy Sonnets* (1633).

> Batter my heart, three-personed God; for you
> As yet but knock, breathe, shine, and seek to mend.
> That I may rise and stand, o'erthrow me and bend
> Your force to break, blow, burn, and make me new.
> I, like an usurped town, to another due,   5
> Labor to admit you, but, oh, to no end;
> Reason, your viceroy in me, me should defend,
> But is captived and proves weak or untrue.

Yet dearly I love you and would be lovèd fain,
But am betrothed unto your enemy: 10
Divorce me, untie or break that knot again,
Take me to you, imprison me, for I,
Except you enthrall me, never shall be free,
Nor ever chaste, except you ravish me.

                                        1633

Questions for Discussion

1. What does Donne mean by "three-personed God" (l. 1)?

2. Does the extreme humility of the poet's voice strike you favorably? Does it seem to you to be the appropriate or correct stance for human beings to take before God? Or would you like to see the speaker showing more independence and spirit? Give reasons to support your view.

3. What is the root meaning of *enthrall*? How does the sense of this word that Donne is drawing on differ from the ordinary sense that the word usually possesses today?

4. For what is "town" a metaphor in line 5? Who is the usurper who holds the town captive at present?

Suggested Essay Topics

1. If you are an unbeliever, does Donne's poem lose force, interest, or relevance to you because you do not share with him the convictions upon which his own passionate emotional involvement is based? If so, you probably have little to say about the poem. But if you are an unbeliever who still finds the poem moving and powerful, as many unbelievers do, try to discover and discuss the reasons for the poem's success that are not based on shared religious beliefs with the reader. Write an essay directed to your instructor in which you discuss the reasons for the poem's success as a poem, quite apart from the Christian content of its message.

2. If you are a believer but are not a Christian, your reactions to this poem would be instructive to those of us who know only Christianity. For example, is paradox a common way in your religion of expressing the deep truths not containable in straightforward propositions? Does your religion posit an afterlife? If so, is that afterlife split into two versions, one of suffering for the sinful and one of blessedness for the virtuous? Does your religion insist on the self-abasement and humility that Donne exhibits in his poem? Would your religion understand Donne's emotions, his stance, even if it required belief in a different God?

   If you belong to a non-Christian religious tradition that can provide the kinds of comparisons suggested by these questions, write an essay directed to your classmates in which you begin by saying why Donne's kind of appeal to God would be intelligible or not intelligible to believers in your religion. Then go on to discuss other relevant differences that might help explain whether or not Donne's poem could have an appropriate counterpart in your religion. If not, why not?

IDEAS IN DEBATE

Bertrand Russell
C. S. Lewis

Bertrand Russell

*E*ach of the great world religions—Judaism, Christianity, Hinduism, Buddhism, Islam—has stimulated whole libraries of controversy. Over the centuries, theologians, church historians, and moralists have spent entire careers defending each faith against one or more of the others or arguing for specific interpretations within a given faith. Other scholars have spent lifetimes attacking alien traditions or attempting to purge a given tradition of errors and abuses. It is perhaps natural that some thinkers, viewing this enormous expenditure of energy and intelligence, have concluded that most of it, if not all, is sheer waste. Since questions about religious truth can never be finally settled and are certainly not subject to scientific testing, they feel that the whole tradition of religious controversy, like the entire religious enterprise, is all nonsense.

Bertrand Russell (1872–1970) was a skeptic of this kind, one who loved to show up the contradictions and follies of religious debate. Yet he was himself a kind of religious controversialist, often rising to prophetic fervor in recommending his own view of the values we should live by—for example, he titled one famous essay "A Free Man's Worship." Convinced that values are created only by human beings, not by any divinity, he defended his values passionately against a foolish and wicked world.

Russell's many attacks on Christianity are thus just one skirmish in what he saw as a lifetime war against human wickedness and folly, a war conducted by a tiny band of thinkers who favored reason and progress over superstition and sentimentality. Though his faith in the likelihood of intellectual and moral progress dimmed as he witnessed the carnage of two world wars, the horrors of Nazism, and then the threat of atomic annihilation, he never wavered in his conviction, arrived at in his youth, that Christianity in all of its manifestations had always been not only a fraud but a great obstacle to human happiness.

Russell's essay should be studied along with the essay that follows it: "What Christians Believe" by C. S. Lewis. The two were not addressed to each other, yet both authors write as if they were addressing and refuting the arguments of the opposing camp. As you read them, ask yourself what audience each author seems to be primarily addressing himself to and whether either one successfully enters what we

*might call the "argumentative field" of the other. Do they reconstruct their opponents'
arguments in a form that would make sense to those opponents? Do they both care
about the same issues, or do they for some reason simply talk past each other?*

WHY I AM NOT A CHRISTIAN

From *"Why I Am Not a Christian" and Other Essays on Religion and Related Subjects,* edited by Paul
Edwards (1957).

WHAT IS A CHRISTIAN?

Nowadays . . . we have to be a little more vague in our meaning of Christian-   1
ity [than were people in former times]. I think, however, that there are two
different items which are quite essential to anybody calling himself a Christian. The first is one of a dogmatic nature—namely, that you must believe in
God and immortality. If you do not believe in those two things, I do not think
that you can properly call yourself a Christian. Then, further than that, as the
name implies, you must have some kind of belief about Christ. The Mohammedans, for instance, also believe in God and in immortality, and yet
they would not call themselves Christians. I think you must have at the very
lowest the belief that Christ was, if not divine, at least the best and wisest
of men. If you are not going to believe that much about Christ, I do not think
you have any right to call yourself a Christian. Of course, there is another
sense, which you find in *Whitaker's Almanack* and in geography books, where
the population of the world is said to be divided into Christians, Mohammedans [Muslims], Buddhists, fetish worshipers, and so on; and in that sense we
are all Christians. The geography books count us all in, but that is a purely
geographical sense, which I suppose we can ignore. Therefore I take it that
when I tell you why I am not a Christian I have to tell you two different
things: first, why I do not believe in God and in immortality; and, secondly,
why I do not think that Christ was the best and wisest of men, although I
grant him a very high degree of moral goodness.

But for the successful efforts of unbelievers in the past, I could not take   2
so elastic a definition of Christianity as that. As I said before, in olden days
it had a much more full-blooded sense. For instance, it included the belief in
hell. Belief in eternal hell-fire was an essential item of Christian belief until
pretty recent times. In this country, as you know, it ceased to be an essential
item because of a decision of the Privy Council, and from that decision the
Archbishop of Canterbury and the Archbishop of York dissented; but in this
country our religion is settled by Act of Parliament, and therefore the Privy
Council was able to override their Graces and hell was no longer necessary
to a Christian. Consequently I shall not insist that a Christian must believe
in hell.

THE EXISTENCE OF GOD

To come to this question of the existence of God: it is a large and serious   3
question, and if I were to attempt to deal with it in any adequate manner I
should have to keep you here until Kingdom Come, so that you will have to
excuse me if I deal with it in a somewhat summary fashion. You know, of
course, that the Catholic Church has laid it down as a dogma that the existence of God can be proved by the unaided reason. That is a somewhat
curious dogma, but it is one of their dogmas. They had to introduce it because
at one time the freethinkers adopted the habit of saying that there were such
and such arguments which mere reason might urge against the existence of
God, but of course they knew as a matter of faith that God did exist. The
arguments and the reasons were set out at great length, and the Catholic
Church felt that they must stop it. Therefore they laid it down that the
existence of God can be proved by the unaided reason and they had to set
up what they considered were arguments to prove it. There are, of course, a
number of them, but I shall take only a few.

THE FIRST-CAUSE ARGUMENT

Perhaps the simplest and easiest to understand is the argument of the First   4
Cause. (It is maintained that everything we see in this world has a cause, and
as you go back in the chain of causes further and further you must come to
a First Cause, and to that First Cause you give the name of God.) That
argument, I suppose, does not carry very much weight nowadays, because,
in the first place, cause is not quite what it used to be. The philosophers and
the men of science have got going on cause, and it has not anything like the
vitality it used to have; but, apart from that, you can see that the argument
that there must be a First Cause is one that cannot have any validity. I may
say that when I was a young man and was debating these questions very
seriously in my mind, I for a long time accepted the argument of the First
Cause, until one day, at the age of eighteen, I read John Stuart Mill's Autobiography, and I there found this sentence: "My father taught me that the
question 'Who made me?' cannot be answered, since it immediately suggests
the further question 'Who made God?' " That very simple sentence showed
me, as I still think, the fallacy in the argument of the First Cause. If everything
must have a cause, then God must have a cause. If there can be anything
without a cause, it may just as well be the world as God, so that there cannot
be any validity in that argument. It is exactly of the same nature as the
Hindu's view, that the world rested upon an elephant and the elephant rested
upon a tortoise; and when they said, "How about the tortoise?" the Indian
said, "Suppose we change the subject." The argument is really no better than
that. There is no reason why the world could not have come into being
without a cause; nor, on the other hand, is there any reason why it should
not have always existed. There is no reason to suppose that the world had
a beginning at all. The idea that things must have a beginning is really due

to the poverty of our imagination. Therefore, perhaps, I need not waste any more time upon the argument about the First Cause.*

. . .

DEFECTS IN CHRIST'S TEACHING

Historically it is quite doubtful whether Christ ever existed at all, and if He did we do not know anything about Him, so that I am not concerned with the historical question, which is a very difficult one. I am concerned with Christ as He appears in the Gospels, taking the Gospel narrative as it stands, and there one does find some things that do not seem to be very wise. For one thing, He certainly thought that His second coming would occur in clouds of glory before the death of all the people who were living at that time. There are a great many texts that prove that. He says, for instance, "Ye shall not have gone over the cities of Israel till the Son of Man be come." Then He says, "There are some standing here which shall not taste death till the Son of Man comes into His kingdom"; and there are a lot of places where it is quite clear that He believed that His second coming would happen during the lifetime of many then living. That was the belief of His earlier followers, and it was the basis of a good deal of His moral teaching. When He said, "Take no thought for the morrow," and things of that sort, it was very largely because He thought that the second coming was going to be very soon, and that all ordinary mundane affairs did not count. I have, as a matter of fact, known some Christians who did believe that the second coming was imminent. I knew a parson who frightened his congregation terribly by telling them that the second coming was very imminent indeed, but they were much consoled when they found that he was planting trees in his garden. The early Christians did really believe it, and they did abstain from such things as planting trees in their gardens, because they did accept from Christ the belief that the second coming was imminent. In that respect, clearly He was not so wise as some other people have been, and He was certainly not superlatively wise. 5

THE MORAL PROBLEM

Then you come to moral questions. There is one very serious defect to my mind in Christ's moral character, and that is that He believed in hell. I do not myself feel that any person who is really profoundly humane can believe in everlasting punishment. Christ certainly as depicted in the Gospels did believe in everlasting punishment, and one does find repeatedly a vindictive fury against those people who would not listen to His preaching—an attitude which is not uncommon with preachers, but which does somewhat detract from superlative excellence. You do not, for instance, find that attitude in Socrates. You find him quite bland and urbane toward the people who would 6

*We omit Russell's examination of other arguments for the existence of God and move on to his examination of the character and teaching of Christ.

not listen to him; and it is, to my mind, far more worthy of a sage to take that line than to take the line of indignation. You probably all remember the sort of things that Socrates was saying when he was dying, and the sort of things that he generally did say to people who did not agree with him.

You will find that in the Gospels Christ said, "Ye serpents, ye generation 7
of vipers, how can ye escape the damnation of hell." That was said to people who did not like His preaching. It is not really to my mind quite the best tone, and there are a great many of these things about hell. There is, of course, the familiar text about the sin against the Holy Ghost: "Whosoever speaketh against the Holy Ghost it shall not be forgiven him neither in this World nor in the world to come." That text has caused an unspeakable amount of misery in the world, for all sorts of people have imagined that they have committed the sin against the Holy Ghost, and thought that it would not be forgiven them either in this world or in the world to come. I really do not think that a person with a proper degree of kindliness in his nature would have put fears and terrors of that sort into the world.

Then Christ says, "The Son of Man shall send forth His angels, and they 8
shall gather out of His kingdom all things that offend, and them which do iniquity, and shall cast them into a furnace of fire; there shall be wailing and gnashing of teeth"; and He goes on about the wailing and gnashing of teeth. It comes in one verse after another, and it is quite manifest to the reader that there is a certain pleasure in contemplating wailing and gnashing of teeth, or else it would not occur so often. Then you all, of course, remember about the sheep and the goats; how at the second coming He is going to divide the sheep from the goats, and He is going to say to the goats, "Depart from me, ye cursed, into everlasting fire." He continues, "And these shall go away into everlasting fire." Then He says again, "If thy hand offend thee, cut it off; it is better for thee to enter into life maimed, than having two hands to go into hell, into the fire that never shall be quenched; where the worm dieth not and the fire is not quenched." He repeats that again and again also. I must say that I think all this doctrine, that hell-fire is a punishment for sin, is a doctrine of cruelty. It is a doctrine that put cruelty into the world and gave the world generations of cruel torture; and the Christ of the Gospels, if you could take Him as His chroniclers represent Him, would certainly have to be considered partly responsible for that.

There are other things of less importance. There is the instance of the 9
Gadarene swine, where it certainly was not very kind to the pigs to put the devils into them and make them rush down the hill to the sea. You must remember that He was omnipotent, and He could have made the devils simply go away; but He chose to send them into the pigs. Then there is the curious story of the fig tree, which always rather puzzled me. You remember what happened about the fig tree. "He was hungry; and seeing a fig tree afar off having leaves, He came if haply He might find anything thereon; and when He came to it He found nothing but leaves, for the time of figs was not yet. And Jesus answered and said unto it: 'No man eat fruit of thee hereafter for ever' . . . and Peter . . . saith unto Him: 'Master, behold the fig tree which

thou cursedst is withered away.' " This is a very curious story, because it was not the right time of year for figs, and you really could not blame the tree. I cannot myself feel that either in the matter of wisdom or in the matter of virtue Christ stands quite as high as some other people known to history. I think I should put Buddha and Socrates above Him in those respects.

THE EMOTIONAL FACTOR

As I said before, I do not think that the real reason why people accept religion has anything to do with argumentation. They accept religion on emotional grounds. One is often told that it is a very wrong thing to attack religion, because religion makes men virtuous. So I am told; I have not noticed it. You know, of course, the parody of that argument in Samuel Butler's book *Erewhon Revisited.* You will remember that in *Erewhon* there is a certain Higgs who arrives in a remote country, and after spending some time there he escapes from that country in a balloon. Twenty years later he comes back to that country and finds a new religion in which he is worshiped under the name of the "Sun Child," and it is said that he ascended into heaven. He finds that the Feast of the Ascension is about to be celebrated, and he hears Professors Hanky and Panky say to each other that they never set eyes on the man Higgs, and they hope they never will; but they are the high priests of the religion of the Sun Child. He is very indignant, and he comes up to them, and he says, "I am going to expose all this humbug and tell the people of Erewhon that it was only I, the man Higgs, and I went up in a balloon." He was told, "You must not do that, because all the morals of this country are bound round this myth, and if they once know that you did not ascend into heaven they will all become wicked"; and so he is persuaded of that and he goes quietly away.

That is the idea—that we should all be wicked if we did not hold to the Christian religion. It seems to me that the people who have held to it have been for the most part extremely wicked. You find this curious fact, that the more intense has been the religion of any period and the more profound has been the dogmatic belief, the greater has been the cruelty and the worse has been the state of affairs. In the so-called ages of faith, when men really did believe the Christian religion in all its completeness, there was the Inquisition, with its tortures; there were millions of unfortunate women burned as witches; and there was every kind of cruelty practiced upon all sorts of people in the name of religion.

You find as you look around the world that every single bit of progress in humane feeling, every improvement in the criminal law, every step toward the diminution of war, every step toward better treatment of the colored races, or every mitigation of slavery, every moral progress that there has been in the world, has been consistently opposed by the organized churches of the world. I say quite deliberately that the Christian religion, as organized in its churches, has been and still is the principal enemy of moral progress in the world.

HOW THE CHURCHES HAVE
RETARDED PROGRESS

You may think that I am going too far when I say that that is still so. I do   13
not think that I am. Take one fact. You will bear with me if I mention it. It
is not a pleasant fact, but the churches compel one to mention facts that are
not pleasant. Supposing that in this world that we live in today an inexperienced girl is married to a syphilitic man; in that case the Catholic Church
says, "This is an indissoluble sacrament. You must stay together for life."
And no steps of any sort must be taken by that woman to prevent herself
from giving birth to syphilitic children. That is what the Catholic Church
says. I say that that is fiendish cruelty, and nobody whose natural sympathies
have not been warped by dogma, or whose moral nature was not absolutely
dead to all sense of suffering, could maintain that it is right and proper that
that state of things should continue.

That is only an example. There are a great many ways in which, at the   14
present moment, the church, by its insistence upon what it chooses to call
morality, inflicts upon all sorts of people undeserved and unnecessary suffering. And of course, as we know, it is in its major part an opponent still of
progress and of improvement in all the ways that diminish suffering in the
world, because it has chosen to label as morality a certain narrow set of rules
of conduct which have nothing to do with human happiness; and when you
say that this or that ought to be done because it would make for human
happiness, they think that has nothing to do with the matter at all. "What
has human happiness to do with morals? The object of morals is not to make
people happy."

FEAR, THE FOUNDATION OF
RELIGION

Religion is based, I think, primarily and mainly upon fear. It is partly the   15
terror of the unknown and partly, as I have said, the wish to feel that you
have a kind of elder brother who will stand by you in all your troubles and
disputes. Fear is the basis of the whole thing—fear of the mysterious, fear of
defeat, fear of death. Fear is the parent of cruelty, and therefore it is no
wonder if cruelty and religion have gone hand in hand. It is because fear is
at the basis of those two things. In this world we can now begin a little to
understand things, and a little to master them by help of science, which has
forced its way step by step against the Christian religion, against the
churches, and against the opposition of all the old precepts. Science can help
us to get over this craven fear in which mankind has lived for so many
generations. Science can teach us, and I think our own hearts can teach us,
no longer to look around for imaginary supports, no longer to invent allies
in the sky, but rather to look to our own efforts here below to make this world
a fit place to live in, instead of the sort of place that the churches in all these
centuries have made it.

WHAT WE MUST DO

We want to stand upon our own feet and look fair and square at the world—   16
its good facts, its bad facts, its beauties, and its ugliness; see the world as it
is and be not afraid of it. Conquer the world by intelligence and not merely
by being slavishly subdued by the terror that comes from it. The whole
conception of God is a conception derived from the ancient Oriental despo-
tisms. It is a conception quite unworthy of free men. When you hear people
in church debasing themselves and saying that they are miserable sinners, and
all the rest of it, it seems contemptible and not worthy of self-respecting
human beings. We ought to stand up and look the world frankly in the face.
We ought to make the best we can of the world, and if it is not so good as
we wish, after all it will still be better than what these others have made of
it in all these ages. A good world needs knowledge, kindliness, and courage;
it does not need a regretful hankering after the past or a fettering of the free
intelligence by the words uttered long ago by ignorant men. It needs a fearless
outlook and a free intelligence. It needs hope for the future, not looking back
all the time toward a past that is dead, which we trust will be far surpassed
by the future that our intelligence can create.

Questions for Discussion

1. Russell frequently addresses "you" and tells "you" what makes sense and
   what does not (for example, ¶1, sentence 4). Trace these seemingly direct
   addresses through the essay and decide whether they are all addressed to
   the same kind of reader. Is Russell addressing serious believers in Christianity, as he seems to be in paragraph 1? Or is he in fact ridiculing *those*
   "you's," at least part of the time, in order to produce an effect on some
   other kind of reader? In class discussion try to determine whether those
   of you who were already unsympathetic toward Christianity were more
   impressed by his arguments than were the Christian believers.

2. Readers sometimes mistakenly assume that when an author jokes about
   a subject he or she cannot be taking it seriously. But the world's finest,
   most "serious" writing is often cast in a tone of wit and humor, as you have
   no doubt noticed frequently in this book. By attending to the *kind* of jest
   an author offers, we can discover a good deal about how we are to read.
   Make a short list of some of Russell's jests and jibes (for example, the joke
   in ¶4; the bit about "Kingdom Come" in ¶3; the phrase "have *got going* on
   cause" in ¶4). Discuss the clues they provide about how we should view
   his arguments.

3. Russell's style, in what he called his "unpopular essays," is always simple
   and forceful, implying that the issues he deals with are quite clear, if only
   one will follow his logic. Choose any passage that seems to you especially

lively and read it aloud, dramatizing the tone of voice that the author might use if he delivered the piece as a lecture. (Try, for example, ¶7.) As he works to reinforce an air of simple clarity, does he in fact rely on devices that are really quite complicated, if not downright tricky? For example, how would you describe the tone of the sentence "It is not really to my mind quite the best tone" (¶7)? Or again, what is the force of the Hindu story about the tortoise (¶4)?

4. Russell seems to provide us with clues, in his subtitles, about how his logical organization runs. But if you consider the nature and especially the strength of his charges against Christianity as the essay progresses, you discover another organization: He advances from amiable, mild, jesting charges to angry, righteous indignation (¶12) and finally to a kind of visionary release from the chains of the past (¶15). Why do you think he organizes his effects in this way? What does this suggest about the kind of reader he hopes to influence?

Suggested Essay Topics

1. As we have seen, every written statement, regardless of its stated purpose, provides us with evidence about the kind of person who is responsible for writing in precisely *this* way. The sentence we are now writing, for example, implies authors who are *this* kind of people and not *that* kind. It tells you, most obviously, that we have chosen one certain "level of style" rather than any of many other possibilities, such as, "If you really gotta have us lay it out for you, we'll put it to you straight, but you oughta be able to figure it out for yourself—every time you open your yap you put your foot in it." But along with the choice of style we find suggestions about deeper matters of character; for example, what we have just said tells you that we care about certain "deeper matters," that we believe in the existence and importance of something called "character," and that we think it is important to learn how to "read" such matters in other people's prose.

   Write a description of the version of Bertrand Russell created by his essay. Using his character as projected by this essay, describe Russell as you would describe a new acquaintance. Give a word or two of evidence for each trait you attribute to him. (Don't worry, for now, about the flesh-and-blood author. He may or may not differ greatly from the self he chooses to present.) For example, "He is a man who would never voluntarily inflict pain on anyone. I know that is so because he shows so much feeling in portraying Christ's cruelty (¶7–8), and he explicitly hails 'kindliness' as a necessary quality in a virtuous man" (¶16).

2. This question is for those who have undergone at some time a major change of belief—either a conversion to or a deconversion from some religious creed. Russell asserts that in his experience religious people are no more virtuous than unbelievers; he implies in paragraph 11, in fact, that they are more vicious, and then, in paragraph 12, he says "quite deliber-

ately" that the Christian church "is the principal enemy of moral progress." Obviously no amount of evidence could prove or disprove this
charge, since our "sample" of virtuous or vicious believers or unbelievers
could never be more than a drop in the bucket. What we must do, then,
is accept Russell's implied invitation and consult our own experience.
Have you found that your beliefs about the world, or the beliefs of the
organized group you belong to, have or have not helped you develop the
"kindliness," courage, generosity, and honesty that Russell recommends?
Write a description of how your beliefs fortify—or fail to fortify—your
efforts to become a better person. Can you give an example of how your
beliefs enabled you to resist some temptation to do something that you in
fact disapprove of?

   Another possibility is to write an account of how the beliefs you
formerly held blocked your development. Think of examples of how your
former beliefs made you shortsighted, unreasonable, dogmatic, bossy, and
so on.

C. S. Lewis

                                    A widely recognized literary critic and his-
torian, C. S. Lewis (1898–1963) is now perhaps best known as an author of
children's stories (the "Narnia" tales) and as a witty, intelligent defender of Chris-
tianity.

   The task faced by all authors who set out to defend a given set of beliefs varies
greatly, depending on how sympathetic their readers are when they begin. For many
centuries, Christian authors writing in Europe or America could assume that most of
their readers were to some degree ready to take their arguments seriously. But from
the seventeenth century onward, the number of unbelievers increased rapidly. In our
century, Christian "apologists" (as defenders of the faith have traditionally been
called) have had to assume that most of their readers begin reading in either a skeptical
or a hostile frame of mind. As Lewis reports of himself in his autobiographical work
Surprised by Joy *(1955), proclaiming oneself an atheist in one's early youth became*
an almost automatic, normal step required of anyone with serious intellectual interests.

   Lewis's reconversion was by no means automatic, and the struggle between
doubt and belief that he fought with himself made him one of the best-informed and
most effective Christian writers of modern times. Because he had himself felt the force
of every conceivable argument against belief, he was able to meet doubting readers as
no "automatic" Christian could. In a series of satirical works (the best known is The
Screwtape Letters*), in science fiction (for example,* Perelandra*), and in direct*
argument of the kind we print here, he attempted to remind unbelievers that the issues
of belief and doubt are, as he says in paragraph 8, extremely complex and difficult—at
least as difficult as his proof for the existence of God (in ¶6). His chief target often

seems to be those who "put up a version of Christianity suitable for a child of six and make that the object of their attack" (¶9).

Be sure to read the preceding essay by Bertrand Russell for comparison with this one. Like Russell, Lewis is master of a style that seems to make complex issues crystal clear; they both suggest, in various ways, that if one does not accept their conclusions one must simply be too dull to follow a plain argument.

In reading Lewis, as in reading Russell, it is a good idea, at least the second time round, to have pencil in hand, tracing the connections between conclusions and reasons.

WHAT CHRISTIANS BELIEVE

From book 2 of *Mere Christianity* (1943, 1945, 1952).

THE RIVAL CONCEPTIONS OF GOD

I have been asked to tell you what Christians believe, and I am going to begin   1
by telling you one thing that Christians do not need to believe. If you are a Christian you do not have to believe that all the other religions are simply wrong all through. If you are an atheist you do have to believe that the main point in all the religions of the whole world is simply one huge mistake. If you are a Christian, you are free to think that all these religions, even the queerest ones, contain at least some hint of the truth. When I was an atheist I had to try to persuade myself that most of the human race have always been wrong about the question that mattered to them most; when I became a Christian I was able to take a more liberal view. But, of course, being a Christian does mean thinking that where Christianity differs from other religions, Christianity is right and they are wrong. As in arithmetic—there is only one right answer to a sum, and all other answers are wrong: but some of the wrong answers are much nearer being right than others.

The first big division of humanity is into the majority, who believe in   2
some kind of God or gods, and the minority who do not. On this point, Christianity lines up with the majority—lines up with ancient Greeks and Romans, modern savages, Stoics, Platonists, Hindus, Mohammedans [Muslims], etc., against the modern Western European materialist.*

Now I go on to the next big division. People who all believe in God can   3
be divided according to the sort of God they believe in. There are two very different ideas on this subject. One of them is the idea that He is beyond good and evil. We humans call one thing good and another thing bad. But according to some people that is merely our human point of view. These people would say that the wiser you become the less you would want to call anything good or bad, and the more clearly you would see that everything is good in one way and bad in another, and that nothing could have been different.

---

*A materialist believes only in the existence of matter. Thus spirit, including the divine, the materialist considers an illusion. [Our note]

Consequently, these people think that long before you got anywhere near the divine point of view the distinction would have disappeared altogether. We call a cancer bad, they would say, because it kills a man; but you might just as well call a successful surgeon bad because he kills a cancer. It all depends on the point of view. The other and opposite idea is that God is quite definitely "good" or "righteous," a God who takes sides, who loves love and hates hatred, who wants us to behave in one way and not in another. The first of these views—the one that thinks God beyond good and evil—is called Pantheism. It was held by the great Prussian philosopher Hegel and, as far as I can understand them, by the Hindus. The other view is held by Jews, Mohammedans and Christians.

And with this big difference between Pantheism and the Christian idea of God, there usually goes another. Pantheists usually believe that God, so to speak, animates the universe as you animate your body: that the universe almost *is* God, so that if it did not exist He would not exist either, and anything you find in the universe is a part of God. The Christian[s'] idea is quite different. They think God invented and made the universe—like a man making a picture or composing a tune. A painter is not a picture, and he does not die if his picture is destroyed. You may say, "He's put a lot of himself into it," but you only mean that all its beauty and interest has come out of his head. His skill is not in the picture in the same way that it is in his head, or even in his hands. I expect you see how this difference between Pantheists and Christians hangs together with the other one. If you do not take the distinction between good and bad very seriously, then it is easy to say that anything you find in this world is a part of God. But, of course, if you think some things really bad, and God really good, then you cannot talk like that. You must believe that God is separate from the world and that some of the things we see in it are contrary to His will. Confronted with a cancer or a slum the Pantheist can say, "If you could only see it from the divine point of view, you would realise that this also is God." The Christian replies, "Don't talk damned nonsense."* For Christianity is a fighting religion. It thinks God made the world—that space and time, heat and cold, and all the colours and tastes, and all the animals and vegetables, are things that God "made up out of His head" as a man makes up a story. But it also thinks that a great many things have gone wrong with the world that God made and that God insists, and insists very loudly, on our putting them right again.

And, of course, that raises a very big question. If a good God made the world why has it gone wrong? And for many years I simply refused to listen to the Christian answers to this question, because I kept on feeling "whatever you say, and however clever your arguments are, isn't it much simpler and easier to say that the world was not made by any intelligent power? Aren't

*One listener complained of the word *damned* as frivolous swearing. But I mean exactly what I say—nonsense that is *damned* is under God's curse, and will (apart from God's grace) lead those who believe it to eternal death. [Lewis's note.]

all your arguments simply a complicated attempt to avoid the obvious?" But then that threw me back into another difficulty.

My argument against God was that the universe seemed so cruel and unjust. But how had I got this idea of *just* and *unjust?* A man does not call a line crooked unless he has some idea of a straight line. What was I comparing this universe with when I called it unjust? If the whole show was bad and senseless from A to Z, so to speak, why did I, who was supposed to be part of the show, find myself in such violent reaction against it? A man feels wet when he falls into water, because man is not a water animal: a fish would not feel wet. Of course I could have given up my idea of justice by saying it was nothing but a private idea of my own. But if I did that, then my argument against God collapsed too—for the argument depended on saying that the world was really unjust, not simply that it did not happen to please my private fancies. Thus in the very act of trying to prove that God did not exist—in other words, that the whole of reality was senseless—I found I was forced to assume that one part of reality—namely my idea of justice—was full of sense. Consequently atheism turns out to be too simple. If the whole universe has no meaning, we should never have found out that it has no meaning: just as, if there were no light in the universe and therefore no creatures with eyes, we should never know it was dark. *Dark* would be without meaning.

THE INVASION

Very well then, atheism is too simple. And I will tell you another view that is also too simple. It is the view I call Christianity-and-water, the view which simply says there is a good God in Heaven and everything is all right—leaving out all the difficult and terrible doctrines about sin and hell and the devil, and the redemption. Both these are boys' philosophies.

It is no good asking for a simple religion. After all, real things are not simple. They look simple, but they are not. The table I am sitting at looks simple: but ask a scientist to tell you what it is really made of—all about the atoms and how the light waves rebound from them and hit my eye and what they do to the optic nerve and what it does to my brain—and, of course, you find that what we call "seeing a table" lands you in mysteries and complications which you can hardly get to the end of. A child saying a child's prayer looks simple. And if you are content to stop there, well and good. But if you are not—and the modern world usually is not—if you want to go on and ask what is really happening—then you must be prepared for something difficult. If we ask for something more than simplicity, it is silly then to complain that the something more is not simple.

Very often, however, this silly procedure is adopted by people who are not silly, but who, consciously or unconsciously, want to destroy Christianity. Such people put up a version of Christianity suitable for a child of six and make that the object of their attack. When you try to explain the Christian doctrine as it is really held by an instructed adult, they then complain that you are making their heads turn round and that it is all too complicated and that if there really were a God they are sure He would have made "religion" simple, because simplicity is so beautiful, etc. You must be on your guard against these people for they will change their ground every minute and only waste your time. Notice, too, their idea of God "making religion simple": as if "religion" were something God invented, and not His statement to us of certain quite unalterable facts about His own nature.

Besides being complicated, reality, in my experience, is usually odd. It 10 is not neat, not obvious, not what you expect. For instance, when you have grasped that the earth and the other planets all go round the sun, you would naturally expect that all the planets were made to match—all at equal distances from each other, say, or distances that regularly increased, or all the same size, or else getting bigger or smaller as you go farther from the sun. In fact, you find no rhyme or reason (that we can see) about either the sizes or the distances; and some of them have one moon, one has four, one has two, some have none, and one has a ring.

Reality, in fact, is usually something you could not have guessed. That 11 is one of the reasons I believe Christianity. It is a religion you could not have guessed. If it offered us just the kind of universe we had always expected, I should feel we were making it up. But, in fact, it is not the sort of thing anyone would have made up. It has just that queer twist about it that real things have. So let us leave behind all these boys' philosophies—these over-simple answers. The problem is not simple and the answer is not going to be simple either.

What is the problem? A universe that contains much that is obviously 12 bad and apparently meaningless, but containing creatures like ourselves who know that it is bad and meaningless. There are only two views that face all the facts. One is the Christian view that this is a good world that has gone wrong, but still retains the memory of what it ought to have been. The other is the view called Dualism. Dualism means the belief that there are two equal and independent powers at the back of everything, one of them good and the other bad, and that this universe is the battlefield in which they fight out an endless war. I personally think that next to Christianity Dualism is the manliest and most sensible creed on the market. But it has a catch in it.

The two powers, or spirits, or gods—the good one and the bad one—are 13 supposed to be quite independent. They both existed from all eternity. Neither of them made the other, neither of them has any more right than the other to call itself God. Each presumably thinks it is good and thinks the other bad. One of them likes hatred and cruelty, the other likes love and mercy, and each backs its own view. Now what do we mean when we call one of them the Good Power and the other the Bad Power? Either we are merely saying that we happen to prefer the one to the other—like preferring beer to cider—or else we are saying that, whatever the two powers think about it, and whichever we humans, at the moment, happen to like, one of them is actually wrong, actually mistaken, in regarding itself as good. Now if we mean merely that we happen to prefer the first, then we must give up talking about good and evil at all. For good means what you ought to prefer quite regardless of what you happen to like at any given moment. If "being good" meant simply joining the side you happened to fancy, for no real reason, then good would not deserve to be called good. So we must mean that one of the two powers is actually wrong and the other actually right.

But the moment you say that, you are putting into the universe a third   14 thing in addition to the two Powers: some law or standard or rule of good which one of the powers conforms to and the other fails to conform to. But since the two powers are judged by this standard, then this standard, or the Being who made this standard, is farther back and higher up than either of them, and He will be the real God. In fact, what we meant by calling them good and bad turns out to be that one of them is in a right relation to the real ultimate God and the other in a wrong relation to Him.

The same point can be made in a different way. If Dualism is true, then   15 the bad Power must be a being who likes badness for its own sake. But in reality we have no experience of anyone liking badness just because it is bad. The nearest we can get to it is in cruelty. But in real life people are cruel for one of two reasons—either because they are sadists, that is, because they have a sexual perversion which makes cruelty a cause of sensual pleasure to them, or else for the sake of something they are going to get out of it—money, or power, or safety. But pleasure, money, power, and safety are all, as far as they go, good things. The badness consists in pursuing them by the wrong method, or in the wrong way, or too much. I do not mean, of course, that the people who do this are not desperately wicked. I do mean that wickedness, when you examine it, turns out to be the pursuit of some good in the wrong way. You can be good for the mere sake of goodness: you cannot be bad for the mere sake of badness. You can do a kind action when you are not feeling kind and when it gives you no pleasure, simply because kindness is right; but no one ever did a cruel action simply because cruelty is wrong—only because cruelty was pleasant or useful to him. In other words badness cannot succeed even in being bad in the same way in which goodness is good. Goodness is, so to speak, itself: badness is only spoiled goodness. And there must be something good first before it can be spoiled. We called sadism a sexual perversion; but you must first have the idea of a normal sexuality before you can talk of its being perverted; and you can see which is the perversion, because you can explain the perverted from the normal, and cannot explain the normal from the perverted. It follows that this Bad Power, who is supposed to be on an equal footing with the Good Power, and to love badness in the same way as the Good Power loves goodness, is a mere bogy. In order to be bad he must have good things to want and then to pursue in the wrong way: he must have impulses which were originally good in order to be able to pervert them. But if he is bad he cannot supply himself either with good things to desire or with good impulses to pervert. He must be getting both from the Good Power. And if so, then he is not independent. He is part of the Good Power's world: he was made either by the Good Power or by some power above them both.

Put it more simply still. To be bad, he must exist and have intelligence 16 and will. But existence, intelligence and will are in themselves good. Therefore he must be getting them from the Good Power: even to be bad he must borrow or steal from his opponent. And do you now begin to see why Christianity has always said that the devil is a fallen angel? That is not a mere story for the children. It is a real recognition of the fact that evil is a parasite, not an original thing. The powers which enable evil to carry on are powers given it by goodness. All the things which enable a bad man to be effectively bad are in themselves good things—resolution, cleverness, good looks, existence itself. That is why Dualism, in a strict sense, will not work.

But I freely admit that real Christianity (as distinct from Christianity- 17 and-water) goes much nearer to Dualism than people think. One of the things that surprised me when I first read the New Testament seriously was that it talked so much about a Dark Power in the universe—a mighty evil spirit who was held to be the Power behind death and disease, and sin. The difference is that Christianity thinks this Dark Power was created by God, and was good when he was created, and went wrong. Christianity agrees with Dualism that this universe is at war. But it does not think this is a war between independent powers. It thinks it is a civil war, a rebellion, and that we are living in a part of the universe occupied by the rebel.

Enemy-occupied territory—that is what this world is. Christianity is the 18 story of how the rightful king has landed, you might say landed in disguise, and is calling us all to take part in a great campaign of sabotage. When you go to church you are really listening-in to the secret wireless from our friends: that is why the enemy is so anxious to prevent us from going. He does it by playing on our conceit and laziness and intellectual snobbery. I know someone will ask me, "Do you really mean, at this time of day, to re-introduce our old friend the devil—hoofs and horns and all?" Well, what the time of day has to do with it I do not know. And I am not particular about the hoofs and horns. But in other respects my answer is "Yes, I do." I do not claim to know anything about his personal appearance. If anybody really wants to know him better I would say to that person, "Don't worry. If you really want to, you will. Whether you'll like it when you do is another question."

THE SHOCKING ALTERNATIVE

Christians, then, believe that an evil power has made himself for the present 19 the Prince of this World. And, of course, that raises problems. Is this state of affairs in accordance with God's will or not? If it is, He is a strange God, you will say: and if it is not, how can anything happen contrary to the will of a being with absolute power?

But anyone who has been in authority knows how a thing can be in 20 accordance with your will in one way and not in another. It may be quite sensible for a mother to say to the children, "I'm not going to go and make you tidy the schoolroom every night. You've got to learn to keep it tidy on your own." Then she goes up one night and finds the Teddy bear and the ink and the French Grammar all lying in the grate. That is against her will. She would prefer the children to be tidy. But on the other hand, it is her will which has left the children free to be untidy. The same thing arises in any regiment, or trade union, or school. You make a thing voluntary and then half the people do not do it. That is not what you willed, but your will has made it possible.

It is probably the same in the universe. God created things which had free will. That means creatures which can go either wrong or right. Some people think they can imagine a creature which was free but had no possibility of going wrong; I cannot. If a thing is free to be good it is also free to be bad. And free will is what has made evil possible. Why, then, did God give them free will? Because free will, though it makes evil possible, is also the only thing that makes possible any love or goodness or joy worth having. A world of automata—of creatures that worked like machines—would hardly be worth creating. The happiness which God designs for His higher creatures is the happiness of being freely, voluntarily united to Him and to each other in an ecstasy of love and delight compared with which the most rapturous love between a man and a woman on this earth is mere milk and water. And for that they must be free. 21

Of course God knew what would happen if they used their freedom the wrong way: apparently He thought it worth the risk. Perhaps we feel inclined to disagree with Him. But there is a difficulty about disagreeing with God. He is the source from which all your reasoning power comes: you could not be right and He wrong any more than a stream can rise higher than its own source. When you are arguing against Him you are arguing against the very power that makes you able to argue at all: it is like cutting off the branch you are sitting on. If God thinks this state of war in the universe a price worth paying for free will—that is, for making a live world in which creatures can do real good or harm and something of real importance can happen, instead of a toy world which only moves when He pulls the strings—then we may take it it is worth paying. 22

When we have understood about free will, we shall see how silly it is to ask, as somebody once asked me: "Why did God make a creature of such rotten stuff that it went wrong?" The better stuff a creature is made of—the cleverer and stronger and freer it is—then the better it will be if it goes right, but also the worse it will be if it goes wrong. A cow cannot be very good or very bad; a dog can be both better and worse; a child better and worse still; an ordinary man, still more so; a man of genius, still more so; a superhuman spirit best—or worst—of all. 23

How did the Dark Power go wrong? Here, no doubt, we ask a question to which human beings cannot give an answer with any certainty. A reasonable (and traditional) guess, based on our own experiences of going wrong, can, however, be offered. The moment you have a self at all, there is a possibility of putting yourself first—wanting to be the centre—wanting to be God, in fact. That was the sin of Satan: and that was the sin he taught the 24 human race. Some people think the fall of man had something to do with sex, but that is a mistake. (The story in the Book of Genesis rather suggests that some corruption in our sexual nature followed the fall and was its result, not its cause.) What Satan put into the heads of our remote ancestors was the idea that they could "be like gods"—could set up on their own as if they had created themselves—be their own masters—invent some sort of happiness for themselves outside God, apart from God. And out of that hopeless attempt has come nearly all that we call human history—money, poverty, ambition, war, prostitution, classes, empires, slavery—the long terrible story of man trying to find something other than God which will make him happy.

The reason why it can never succeed is this. God made us: invented us 25 as a man invents an engine. A car is made to run on gasoline, and it would not run properly on anything else. Now God designed the human machine to run on Himself. He Himself is the fuel our spirits were designed to burn, or the food our spirits were designed to feed on. There is no other. That is why it is just no good asking God to make us happy in our own way without bothering about religion. God cannot give us a happiness and peace apart from Himself, because it is not there. There is no such thing.

That is the key to history. Terrific energy is expended—civilisations are 26 built up—excellent institutions devised; but each time something goes wrong. Some fatal flaw always brings the selfish and cruel people to the top and it all slides back into misery and ruin. In fact, the machine conks. It seems to start up all right and runs a few yards, and then it breaks down. They are trying to run it on the wrong juice. That is what Satan has done to us humans.

And what did God do? First of all He left us conscience, the sense of 27 right and wrong: and all through history there have been people trying (some of them very hard) to obey it. None of them ever quite succeeded. Secondly, He sent the human race what I call good dreams: I mean those queer stories scattered all through the heathen religions about a god who dies and comes to life again and, by his death, has somehow given new life to men. Thirdly, He selected one particular people and spent several centuries hammering into their heads the sort of God He was—that there was only one of Him and that He cared about right conduct. Those people were the Jews, and the Old Testament gives an account of the hammering process.

Then comes the real shock. Among these Jews there suddenly turns up 28 a man who goes about talking as if He was God. He claims to forgive sins. He says He has always existed. He says He is coming to judge the world at the end of time. Now let us get this clear. Among Pantheists, like the Indians, anyone might say that he was a part of God, or one with God: there would be nothing very odd about it. But this man, since He was a Jew, could not mean that kind of God. God, in their language, meant the Being outside the world Who had made it and was infinitely different from anything else. And when you have grasped that, you will see that what this man said was, quite simply, the most shocking thing that has ever been uttered by human lips.

One part of the claim tends to slip past us unnoticed because we have 29 heard it so often that we no longer see what it amounts to. I mean the claim to forgive sins: any sins. Now unless the speaker is God, this is really so preposterous as to be comic. We can all understand how a man forgives offences against himself. You tread on my toe and I forgive you, you steal my money and I forgive you. But what should we make of a man, himself unrobbed and untrodden on, who announced that he forgave you for treading on other men's toes and stealing other men's money? Asinine fatuity is the kindest description we should give of his conduct. Yet this is what Jesus did. He told people that their sins were forgiven, and never waited to consult all the other people whom their sins had undoubtedly injured. He unhesitatingly behaved as if He was the party chiefly concerned, the person chiefly offended in all offences. This makes sense only if He really was the God whose laws are broken and whose love is wounded in every sin. In the mouth of any speaker who is not God, these words would imply what I can only regard as a silliness and conceit unrivalled by any other character in history.

Yet (and this is the strange, significant thing) even His enemies, when 30 they read the Gospels, do not usually get the impression of silliness and conceit. Still less do unprejudiced readers. Christ says that He is "humble and meek" and we believe Him; not noticing that, if He were merely a man, humility and meekness are the very last characteristics we could attribute to some of His sayings.

I am trying here to prevent anyone saying the really foolish thing that 31 people often say about Him: "I'm ready to accept Jesus as a great moral teacher, but I don't accept His claim to be God." That is the one thing we must not say. A man who was merely a man and said the sort of things Jesus said would not be a great moral teacher. He would either be a lunatic—on a level with the man who says he is a poached egg—or else he would be the Devil of Hell. You must make your choice. Either this man was, and is, the Son of God: or else a madman or something worse. You can shut Him up for a fool, you can spit at Him and kill Him as a demon; or you can fall at His feet and call Him Lord and God. But let us not come with any patronising nonsense about His being a great human teacher. He has not left that open to us. He did not intend to.

Questions for Discussion

1. Lewis clearly sees that many of his readers will find some of his views shocking, perhaps most obviously his claim that Satan is literally real. Does he, like Russell, take any steps to lead his readers gently into the more controversial territory? Do the steps work? To put it another way, did you feel, by the end of the first few paragraphs, that the author could on the whole be trusted, even if you could not fully accept his arguments?

2. Russell tells us that he was once a believer who learned better. Lewis tells us that he was once an unbeliever who learned better (¶1). Do they increase their persuasiveness by making this kind of claim? Why or why not?

3. Lewis engages in much less obvious jesting than Russell, and he does not pause, like Russell, to relate illustrative anecdotes. (He does of course engage in frequent witty thrusts, but his tone is on the whole more serious.) Do you find his style heavy or pompous? How would you describe the "person" behind the writing here? Be as detailed as you can, giving both intellectual and moral qualities.

4. Work out in discussion with your classmates the exact line of argument in the section called "The Invasion." Give special attention to the logic in paragraph 12. When writers give us "only two possibilities," we should always be on our guard. Only if there *really* are no other possibilities must we accept their choice, and it is worth remembering that in most human issues the possibilities are not limited to two. Has Lewis played fair with his sharp choice between Christianity and Dualism? If you think of other possibilities, be sure that they are not merely other versions of one of his.

5. Later in the essay Lewis gives us a sharp choice among three possibilities: either Christ was who he said he was, or he was mad, or he was the Devil of Hell (¶31). What would Russell be likely to say about this choice? Again it is useful to ask yourself whether there are any other possibilities.

6. Whether we agree with them or not, both Russell and Lewis can teach us a good deal about how to present a case effectively. Lewis is especially skillful in this essay in organizing a body of difficult material into a clear sequence of steps. Trace those steps and ask about each of them: Why does he take it at *this* point? Once you have done that kind of reading of a variety of complicated essays, your own powers of organization will inevitably increase.

Suggested Essay Topics

1. If you consider yourself a Christian, write a letter to Lewis, explaining to him how his version of Christianity is similar to or different from yours. Your purpose, in the latter case, is not to convert him but to persuade him to see your view as something that he should take into account.

2. If you are an unbeliever in Christianity or a believer in some other religion, write a letter to either Lewis or Russell, disagreeing with any points in their arguments that seem faulty. Be sure that you have understood the point before trying to refute it.

~12~

ECONOMIC PERSPECTIVES

Capitalism Attacked and Defended

Money is indeed the most important thing in the world;
and all sound and successful personal and national morality should
have this fact for its basis.
George Bernard Shaw

But man has almost constant occasion for the help of his brethren,
and it is in vain for him to expect it from their
benevolence only. He will be more likely to prevail if he can
interest their self-love in his favour, and show them that it is for
their own advantage to do for him what he requires of
them. . . . It is not from the benevolence of the butcher, the brewer,
or the baker, that we can expect our dinner, but from
their regard to their own interest.
Adam Smith

A fool and his money are soon parted.
Old proverb

Money is like muck, not good except it be spread.
Sir Francis Bacon

You pays your money and you takes your choice.
Popular saying

The love of money is the root of all evil.
I Timothy 6:10

He that wants [i.e., lacks] money, means, and content
is without three good friends.
Shakespeare

Wine maketh merry: but money answereth all things.
Ecclesiastes 10:19

Joyce Carol Oates

In a chapter dealing with defenses of and attacks on capitalism, is it fair, does it make sense, to include a story? Many people would say that works of art have no definite political, moral, or economic messages to deliver. They would say that art and aesthetics are one kind of human activity and that politics and economics are another kind of activity and that the second kind is incompatible with the first kind. Admittedly, this story makes no explicit point about either politics or economics. Oates (b. 1938) indulges in no long sermons on economic doctrine such as we find in the novels of Ayn Rand, nor does she undertake any obvious kind of exposé such as Frank Norris's revelations about the meat-packing industry, nor does she focus with hostility on a certain group of persons as did Sinclair Lewis, whose novels openly attacked the lives and values of "main street" American businessmen.

Nonetheless, Oates's story carries a strong economic message. It is not about economic doctrine but about the way lives are lived, damaged, or destroyed among people whose economic level places them so far above other citizens that they have no view of how the poor, the desperate, and the deviants live or die. In addition, the "haves" in Oates's story have become so owned by their possessions and their positions that they can no longer see each other's emotional or spiritual needs, even when those needs belong to members of their own families. Affluence has swallowed them up, and they can see life only in monetary terms. The parents in the story think they are solving the problems of a shoplifting daughter, for example, by buying her the gloves she had stolen, completely failing to see—not really wanting *to see—that owning new gloves was never the issue.*

Thus the political and economic realities of the different characters in Oates's story are not present only as background, as they must always be for all of us, but also subtly emerge as determinative of the story's action, of the characters' understanding of themselves, and of their eventual destinies. In addition, the author implies a strong judgment about these political and economic realities, especially the economic ones, a judgment that challenges many of the most revered American dicta about the worthiness of making money, getting ahead in the world professionally, and having

*enough consumer goods, physical comfort, and social prestige to give one's neighbors
envious heartburn.*

HOW I CONTEMPLATED THE
WORLD FROM THE DETROIT
HOUSE OF CORRECTION AND
BEGAN MY LIFE OVER AGAIN

From *The Wheel of Love* (1965).

> Notes for an essay for an English class at Baldwin Country Day School;   1
> poking around in debris; disgust and curiosity; a revelation of the meaning
> of life; a happy ending. . . .

I. EVENTS

1. The girl (myself) is walking through Branden's, that excellent store. Suburb   2
of a large famous city that is a symbol for large famous American cities. The
event sneaks up on the girl, who believes she is herding it along with a small
fixed smile, a girl of fifteen, innocently experienced. She dawdles in a certain
style by a counter of costume jewelry. Rings, earrings, necklaces. Prices from
$5 to $50, all within reach. All ugly. She eases over to the glove counter,
where everything is ugly too. In her close-fitted coat with its black fur collar
she contemplates the luxury of Branden's, which she has known for many
years: its many mild pale lights, easy on the eye and the soul, its elaborate
tinkly decorations, its women shoppers with their excellent shoes and coats
and hairdos, all dawdling gracefully, in no hurry.

Who was ever in a hurry here?   3

2. The girl seated at home. A small library, paneled walls of oak. Someone   4
is talking to me. An earnest husky female voice drives itself against my ears,
nervous, frightened, groping around my heart, saying, "If you wanted gloves
why didn't you say so? Why didn't you ask for them?" That store, Branden's,
is owned by Raymond Forrest who lives on DuMaurier Drive. We live on
Sioux Drive. Raymond Forrest. A handsome man? An ugly man? A man of
fifty or sixty, with gray hair, or a man of forty with earnest courteous eyes,
a good golf game, who is Raymond Forrest, this man who is my salvation?
Father has been talking to him. Father is not his physician; Dr. Berg is his
physician. Father and Dr. Berg refer patients to each other. There is a connection. Mother plays bridge with. . . . On Mondays and Wednesdays our maid
Billie works at. . . . The strings draw together in a cat's cradle, making a net
to save you when you fall. . . .

3. *Harriet Arnold's.* A small shop, better than Branden's. Mother in her black   5
coat, I in my close-fitted blue coat. Shopping. Now look at this, isn't this cute,

do you want this, why don't you want this, try this on, take this with you to the fitting room, take this also, what's wrong with you, what can I do for you, why are you so strange . . . ? "I wanted to steal but not to buy," I don't tell her. The girl droops along in her coat and gloves and leather boots, her eyes scan the horizon which is pastel pink and decorated like Branden's, tasteful walls and modern ceilings with graceful glimmering lights.

4. Weeks later, the girl at a bus-stop. Two o'clock in the afternoon, a Tuesday, obviously she has walked out of school.   6

5. The girl stepping down from a bus. Afternoon, weather changing to colder. Detroit. Pavement and closed-up stores; grill work over the windows of a pawnshop. What is a pawnshop, exactly?   7

II. CHARACTERS

1. The girl stands five feet five inches tall. An ordinary height. Baldwin Country Day School draws them up to that height. She dreams along the corridors and presses her face against the Thermoplex Glass. No frost or steam can ever form on that glass. A smudge of grease from her forehead . . . could she be boiled down to grease? She wears her hair loose and long and straight in suburban teenage style, 1968. Eyes smudged with pencil, dark brown. Brown hair. Vague green eyes. A pretty girl? An ugly girl? She sings to herself under her breath, idling in the corridor, thinking of her many secrets (the thirty dollars she once took from the purse of a friend's mother, just for fun, the basement window she smashed in her own house just for fun) and thinking of her brother who is at Susquehanna Boys' Academy, an excellent preparatory school in Maine, remembering him unclearly . . . he has long manic hair and a squeaking voice and he looks like one of the popular teenage singers of 1968, one of those in a group, *The Certain Forces, The Way Out, The Maniacs Responsible.* The girl in her turn looks like one of those fieldsful of girls who listen to the boys' singing, dreaming and mooning restlessly, breaking into high sullen laughter, innocently experienced.   8

2. The mother. A midwestern woman of Detroit and suburbs. Belongs to the Detroit Athletic Club. Also the Detroit Golf Club. Also the Bloomfield Hills Country Club. The Village Women's Club at which lectures are given each winter on Genet and Sartre and James Baldwin, by the Director of the Adult Education Program at Wayne State University. . . . The Bloomfield Art Association. Also the Founders Society of the Detroit Institute of Arts. Also. . . . Oh, she is in perpetual motion, this lady, hair like blown-up gold and finer than gold, hair and fingers and body of inestimable grace. Heavy weighs the gold on the back of her hairbrush and hand mirror. Heavy heavy the candlesticks in the dining room. Very heavy is the big car, a Lincoln, long, and black, that on one cool autumn day split a squirrel's body in two unequal parts.   9

3. The father, Dr. ———. He belongs to the same clubs as # 2. A player of   10
squash and golf; he has a golfer's umbrella of stripes. Candy stripes. In his
mouth nothing turns to sugar, however, saliva works no miracles here. His
doctoring is of the slightly sick. The sick are sent elsewhere (to Dr. Berg?),
the deathly sick are sent back for more tests and their bills are sent to their
homes, the unsick are sent to Dr. Coronet (Isabel, a lady), an excellent psychiatrist for unsick people who angrily believe they are sick and want to do
something about it. If they demand a male psychiatrist, the unsick are sent
by Dr. ——— (my father) to Dr. Lowenstein, a male psychiatrist, excellent
and expensive, with a limited practice.

4. Clarita. She is twenty, twenty-five, she is thirty or more? Pretty, ugly,   11
what? She is a woman lounging by the side of a road, in jeans and a sweater,
hitchhiking, or she is slouched on a stool at a counter in some roadside diner.
A hard line of jaw. Curious eyes. Amused eyes. Behind her eyes processions
move, funeral pageants, cartoons. She says, "I never can figure out why girls
like you bum around down here. What are you looking for anyway?" An
odor of tobacco about her. Unwashed underclothes, or no underclothes, unwashed skin, gritty toes, hair long and falling into strands, not recently
washed.

5. Simon. In this city the weather changes abruptly, so Simon's weather   12
changes abruptly. He sleeps through the afternoon. He sleeps through the
morning. Rising he gropes around for something to get him going, for a
cigarette or a pill to drive him out to the street, where the temperature is
hovering around 35°. Why doesn't it drop? Why, why doesn't the cold clean
air come down from Canada, will he have to go up into Canada to get it, will
he have to leave the Country of his Birth and sink into Canada's frosty fields
. . . ? Will the F.B.I. (which he dreams about constantly) chase him over
the Canadian border on foot, hounded out in a blizzard of broken glass and
horns . . . ?

"Once I was Huckleberry Finn," Simon says, "but now I am Roderick Usher."   13
Beset by frenzies and fears, this man who makes my spine go cold, he takes
green pills, yellow pills, pills of white and capsules of dark blue and green
. . . he takes other things I may not mention, for what if Simon seeks me out
and climbs into my girl's bedroom here in Bloomfield Hills and strangles me,
what then . . . ? (As I write this I begin to shiver: Why do I shiver? I am now
sixteen and sixteen is not an age for shivering.) It comes from Simon, who
is always cold.

III. WORLD EVENTS

Nothing.   14

IV. PEOPLE AND CIRCUMSTANCES CONTRIBUTING TO THIS DELINQUENCY

Nothing.

15

V. SIOUX DRIVE

George, Clyde G. 240 Sioux. A manufacturer's representative; children, a dog; 16 a wife. Georgian with the usual columns. You think of the White House, then of Thomas Jefferson, then your mind goes blank on the white pillars and you think of nothing. Norris, Ralph W. 246 Sioux. Public relations. Colonial. Bay window, brick, stone, concrete, wood, green shutters, sidewalk, lantern, grass, trees, black-top drive, two children, one of them my classmate Esther (Esther Norris) at Baldwin. Wife, cars. Ramsey, Michael D. 250 Sioux. Colonial. Big living room, thirty by twenty-five, fireplaces in living room library recreation room, paneled walls wet bar five bathrooms five bedrooms two lavatories central air conditioning automatic sprinkler automatic garage door three children one wife two cars a breakfast room a patio a large fenced lot fourteen trees a front door with a brass knocker never knocked. Next is our house. Classic contemporary. Traditional modern. Attached garage, attached Florida room, attached patio, attached pool and cabana, attached roof. A front door mailslot through which pour *Time Magazine, Fortune, Life, Business Week, The Wall Street Journal, The New York Times, The New Yorker, The Saturday Review, M.D., Modern Medicine, Disease of the Month* . . . and also. . . . And in addition to all this a quiet sealed letter from Baldwin saying: *Your daughter is not doing work compatible with her performance on the Stanford-Binet.* . . . And your son is not doing well, not well at all, very sad. Where is your son anyway? Once he stole trick-and-treat candy from some six-year-old kids, he himself being a robust ten. The beginning. Now your daughter steals. In the Village Pharmacy she made off with, yes she did, don't deny it, she made off with a copy of *Pageant Magazine* for no reason, she swiped a roll of lifesavers in a green wrapper and was in no need of saving her life or even in need of sucking candy, when she was no more than eight years old she stole, don't blush, she stole a package of *Tums* only because it was out on the counter and available, and the nice lady behind the counter (now dead) said nothing. . . . Sioux Drive. Maples, oaks, elms. Diseased elms cut down. Sioux Drive runs into Roosevelt Drive. Slow turning lanes, not streets, all drives and lanes and ways and passes. A private police force. Quiet private police, in unmarked cars. Cruising on Saturday evenings with paternal smiles for the residents who are streaming in and out of houses, going to and from parties, a thousand parties, slightly staggering, the women in their furs alighting from automobiles bought of Ford and General Motors and Chrysler, very heavy automobiles. No foreign cars. Detroit. In 275 Sioux, down the block, in that magnificent French Normandy mansion, lives —— —— himself, who has the C—— account itself, imagine that! Look at where he lives and look at the enormous trees and chimneys, imagine his many fireplaces, imagine his wife and children, imagine his wife's hair, imagine her fingernails, imagine her bathtub of smooth clean glowing pink, imagine their embraces, his trouser pockets filled with odd coins and keys and dust and peanuts, imagine their ecstasy on Sioux Drive, imagine their income tax returns, imagine their little boy's pride in his experimental car, a scaled-down C——, as he roars around the neighborhood on the sidewalks frightening dogs and Negro maids, oh imagine all these things, imagine everything, let your mind roar out all over Sioux Drive and DuMaurier Drive and Roosevelt Drive and Ticonderoga Pass and Burning Bush Way and Lincolnshire Pass and Lois Lane.

When spring comes its winds blow nothing to Sioux Drive, no odors of 17 hollyhocks or forsythia, nothing Sioux Drive doesn't already possess, everything is planted and performing. The weather vanes, had they weather vanes, don't have to turn with the wind, don't have to contend with the weather. There is no weather.

VI. DETROIT

There is always weather in Detroit. Detroit's temperature is always 32°. Fast 18 falling temperatures. Slow rising temperatures. Wind from the north northeast four to forty miles an hour, small craft warnings, partly cloudy today and Wednesday changing to partly sunny through Thursday . . . small warnings of frost, soot warnings, traffic warnings, hazardous lake conditions for small craft and swimmers, restless Negro gangs, restless cloud formations, restless temperatures aching to fall out the very bottom of the thermometer or shoot up over the top and boil everything over in red mercury.

Detroit's temperature is 32°. Fast falling temperatures. Slow rising tem- 19 peratures. Wind from the north northeast four to forty miles an hour. . . .

VII. EVENTS

1. The girl's heart is pounding. In her pocket is a pair of gloves! In a plastic 20 bag! Airproof breathproof plastic bag, gloves selling for twenty-five dollars on Branden's counter! In her pocket! Shoplifted! . . . In her purse is a blue comb, not very clean. In her purse is a leather billfold (a birthday present from her grandmother in Philadelphia) with snapshots of the family in clean plastic windows, in the billfold are bills, she doesn't know how many bills. . . . In her purse is an ominous note from her friend Tykie *What's this about Joe H. and the kids hanging around at Louise's Sat. night? You heard anything?* . . . passed in French class. In her purse is a lot of dirty yellow Kleenex, her mother's heart would break to see such very dirty Kleenex, and at the bottom of her purse are brown hairpins and safety pins and a broken pencil and a ballpoint pen (blue) stolen from somewhere forgotten and a purse-size compact of Cover Girl Make-Up, Ivory Rose. . . . Her lipstick is Broken Heart, a corrupt pink; her fingers are trembling like crazy; her teeth are beginning to chatter; her insides

are alive; her eyes glow in her head; she is saying to her mother's astonished face *I want to steal but not to buy.*

2. At Clarita's. Day or night? What room is this? A bed, a regular bed, and a mattress on the floor nearby. Wallpaper hanging in strips. Clarita says she tore it like that with her teeth. She was fighting a barbaric tribe that night, high from some pills she was battling for her life with men wearing helmets of heavy iron and their faces no more than Christian crosses to breathe through, every one of those bastards looking like her lover Simon, who seems to breathe with great difficulty through the slits of mouth and nostrils in his face. Clarita has never heard of Sioux Drive. Raymond Forrest cuts no ice with her, nor does the C—— account and its millions; Harvard Business School could be at the corner of Vernor and 12th Street for all she cares, and Vietnam might have sunk by now into the Dead Sea under its tons of debris, for all the amazement she could show . . . her face is overworked, over-wrought, at the age of twenty (thirty?) it is already exhausted but fanciful and ready for a laugh. Clarita says mournfully to me *Honey somebody is going to turn you out let me give you warning.* In a movie shown on late television Clarita is not a mess like this but a nurse, with short neat hair and a dedicated look, in love with her doctor and her doctor's patients and their diseases, enamored of needles and sponges and rubbing alcohol. . . . Or no: she is a private secretary. Robert Cummings is her boss. She helps him with fantastic plots, the canned audience laughs, no, the audience doesn't laugh because nothing is funny, instead her boss is Robert Taylor and they are not boss and secretary but husband and wife, she is threatened by a young starlet, she is grim, handsome, wifely, a good companion for a good man. . . . She is Claudette Colbert. Her sister too is Claudette Colbert. They are twins, identical. Her husband Charles Boyer is a very rich handsome man and her sister, Claudette Colbert, is plotting her death in order to take her place as the rich man's wife, no one will know because they are *twins.* . . . All these marvelous lives Clarita might have lived, but she fell out the bottom at the age of thirteen. At the age when I was packing my overnight case for a slumber party at Toni Deshield's she was tearing filthy sheets off a bed and scratching up a rash on her arms. . . . Thirteen is uncommonly young for a white girl in Detroit, Miss Brook of the Detroit House of Correction said in a sad newspaper interview for the *Detroit News;* fifteen and sixteen are more likely. Eleven, twelve, thir-teen are not surprising in colored . . . they are more precocious. What can we do? Taxes are rising and the tax base is falling. The temperature rises slowly but falls rapidly. Everything is falling out the bottom, Woodward Avenue is filthy, Livernois Avenue filthy! Scraps of paper flutter in the air like pigeons, dirt flies up and hits you right in the eye, oh Detroit is breaking up into dangerous bits of newspaper and dirt, watch out. . . .

Clarita's apartment is over a restaurant. Simon her lover emerges from the cracks at dark. Mrs. Olesko, a neighbor of Clarita's, an aged white whisp of a woman, doesn't complain but sniffs with contentment at Clarita's noisy life and doesn't tell the cops, hating cops, when the cops arrive. I should give

more fake names, more blanks, instead of telling all these secrets. I myself am
a secret; I am a minor.

3. My father reads a paper at a medical convention in Los Angeles. There he   23
is, on the edge of the North American continent, when the unmarked detective put his hand so gently on my arm in the aisle of Branden's and said,
"Miss, would you like to step over here for a minute?"

And where was he when Clarita put her hand on my arm, that wintry   24
dark sulphurous aching day in Detroit, in the company of closed-down
barber shops, closed-down diners, closed-down movie houses, homes, windows, basements, faces . . . she put her hand on my arm and said, "Honey,
are you looking for somebody down here?"

And was he home worrying about me, gone for two weeks solid, when   25
they carried me off . . . ? It took three of them to get me in the police cruiser,
so they said, and they put more than their hands on my arm.

4. I worked on this lesson. My English teacher is Mr. Forest, who is from   26
Michigan State. Not handsome, Mr. Forest, and his name is plain unlike
Raymond Forrest's, but he is sweet and rodent-like, he has conferred with the
principal and my parents, and everything is fixed . . . treat her as if nothing
has happened, a new start, begin again, only sixteen years old, what a shame,
how did it happen?—nothing happened, nothing could have happened, a
slight physiological modification known only to a gynecologist or to Dr.
Coronet. I work on my lesson. I sit in my pink room. I look around the room
with my sad pink eyes. I sigh, I dawdle, I pause, I eat up time, I am limp and
happy to be home, I am sixteen years old suddenly, my head hangs heavy
as a pumpkin on my shoulders, and my hair has just been cut by Mr. Faye
at the Crystal Salon and is said to be very becoming.

(Simon too put his hand on my arm and said, "Honey, you have got to   27
come with me," and in his six-by-six room we got to know each other. Would
I go back to Simon again? Would I lie down with him in all that filth and
craziness? Over and over again.

a Clarita is being betrayed as in front of a Cunningham Drug Store she
is nervously eyeing a colored man who may or may not have money, or a
nervous white boy of twenty with sideburns and an Appalachian look, who
may or may not have a knife hidden in his jacket pocket, or a husky red-faced
man of friendly countenance who may or may not be a member of the Vice
Squad out for an early twilight walk.)

I work on my lesson for Mr. Forest. I have filled up eleven pages. Words   28
pour out of me and won't stop. I want to tell everything . . . what was the
song Simon was always humming, and who was Simon's friend in a very new
trench coat with an old high school graduation ring on his finger . . . ? Simon's
bearded friend? When I was down too low for him Simon kicked me out and
gave me to him for three days, I think, on Fourteenth Street in Detroit, an

airy room of cold cruel drafts with newspapers on the floor. . . . Do I really remember that or am I piecing it together from what they told me? Did they tell the truth? Did they know much of the truth?

VIII. CHARACTERS

1. Wednesdays after school, at four; Saturday mornings at ten. Mother drives   29
me to Dr. Coronet. Ferns in the office, plastic or real, they look the same. Dr. Coronet is queenly, an elegant nicotine-stained lady, who would have studied with Freud had circumstances not prevented it, a bit of a Catholic, ready to offer you some mystery if your teeth will ache too much without it. Highly recommended by Father! Forty dollars an hour, Father's forty dollars! Progress! Looking up! Looking better! That new haircut is so becoming, says Dr. Coronet herself, showing how normal she is for a woman with an I.Q. of 180 and many advanced degrees.

2. Mother. A lady in a brown suede coat. Boots of shiny black material, black   30
gloves, a black fur hat. She would be humiliated could she know that of all the people in the world it is my ex-lover Simon who walks most like her . . . self-conscious and unreal, listening to distant music, a little bowlegged with craftiness . . .

3. Father. Tying a necktie. In a hurry. On my first evening home he put his   31
hand on my arm and said, "Honey, we're going to forget all about this."

4. Simon. Outside a plane is crossing the sky, in here we're in a hurry.   32
Morning. It must be morning. The girl is half out of her mind, whimpering and vague, Simon her dear friend is wretched this morning . . . he is wretched with morning itself . . . he forces her to give him an injection, with that needle she knows is filthy, she has a dread of needles and surgical instruments and the odor of things that are to be sent into the blood, thinking somehow of her father. . . . This is a bad morning, Simon says that his mind is being twisted out of shape, and so he submits to the needle which he usually scorns and bites his lip with his yellowish teeth, his face going very pale. *Ah baby!* he says in his soft mocking voice, which with all women is a mockery of love, *do it like this—Slowly*—And the girl, terrified, almost drops the precious needle but manages to turn it up to the light from the window . . . it is an extension of herself, then? She can give him this gift, then? *I wish you wouldn't do this to me,* she says, wise in her terror, because it seems to her that Simon's danger— in a few minutes he might be dead—is a way of pressing her against him that is more powerful than any other embrace. She has to work over his arm, the knotted corded veins of his arm, her forehead wet with perspiration as she pushes and releases the needle, staring at that mixture of liquid now stained with Simon's bright blood. . . . When the drug hits him she can feel it herself, she feels that magic that is more than any woman can give him, striking the

back of his head and making his face stretch as if with the impact of a terrible sun. . . . She tries to embrace him but he pushes her aside and stumbles to his feet, *Jesus Christ,* he says. . . .

5. Princess, a Negro girl of eighteen. What is her charge? She is close- 33
mouthed about it, shrewd and silent, you know that no one had to wrestle her to the sidewalk to get her in here; she came with dignity. In the recreation room she sits reading *Nancy Drew and the Jewel Box Mystery,* which inspires in her face tiny wrinkles of alarm and interest: what a face! Light brown skin, heavy shaded eyes, heavy eyelashes, a serious sinister dark brow, graceful fingers, graceful wrist-bones, graceful legs, lips, tongue, a sugar-sweet voice, a leggy stride more masculine than Simon's and my mother's, decked out in a dirty white blouse and dirty white slacks; vaguely nautical is Princess's style. . . . At breakfast she is in charge of clearing the table and leans over me, saying, *Honey you sure you ate enough?*

6. The girl lies sleepless, wondering. Why here, why not there? Why Bloom- 34
field Hills and not jail? Why jail and not her pink room? Why downtown Detroit and not Sioux Drive? What is the difference? Is Simon all the difference? The girl's head is a parade of wonders. She is nearly sixteen, her breath is marvelous with wonders, not long ago she was coloring with crayons and now she is smearing the landscape with paints that won't come off and won't come off her fingers either. She says to the matron *I am not talking about anything,* not because everyone has warned her not to talk but because, because she will not talk, because she won't say anything about Simon who is her secret. And she says to the matron *I won't go home* up until that night in the lavatory when everything was changed. . . . "No, I won't go home I want to stay here," she says, listening to her own words with amazement, thinking that weeds might climb everywhere over that marvelous $86,000 house and dinosaurs might return to muddy the beige carpeting, but never will she reconcile four o'clock in the morning in Detroit with eight o'clock breakfasts in Bloomfield Hills . . . oh, she aches still for Simon's hands and his caressing breath, though he gave her little pleasure, he took everything from her (five-dollar bills, ten-dollar bills, passed into her numb hands by men and taken out of her hands by Simon) until she herself was passed into the hands of other men, police, when Simon evidently got tired of her and her hysteria. . . . *No, I won't go home, I don't want to be bailed out,* the girl thinks as a *Stubborn and Wayward Child* (one of several charges lodged against her) and the matron understands her crazy white-rimmed eyes that are seeking out some new violence that will keep her in jail, should someone threaten to let her out. Such children try to strangle the matrons, the attendants, or one another . . . they want the locks locked forever, the doors nailed shut . . . and this girl is no different up until that night her mind is changed for her. . . .

IX. THAT NIGHT

Princess and Dolly, a little white girl of maybe fifteen, hardy however as a   35
sergeant and in the House of Correction for armed robbery, corner her in the
lavatory at the farthest sink and the other girls look away and file out to bed,
leaving her. God how she is beaten up! Why is she beaten up? Why do they
pound her, why such hatred? Princess vents all the hatred of a thousand silent
Detroit winters on her body, this girl whose body belongs to me, fiercely she
rides across the midwestern plains on this girl's tender bruised body . . .
revenge on the oppressed minorities of America! revenge on the slaughtered
Indians! revenge on the female sex, on the male sex, revenge on Bloomfield
Hills, revenge revenge. . . .

X. DETROIT

In Detroit weather weighs heavily upon everyone. The sky looms large. The   36
horizon shimmers in smoke. Downtown the buildings are imprecise in the
haze. Perpetual haze. Perpetual motion inside the haze. Across the choppy
river is the city of Windsor, in Canada. Part of the continent has bunched up
here and is bulging outward, at the tip of Detroit, a cold hard rain is forever
falling on the expressway . . . shoppers shop grimly, their cars are not parked
in safe places, their windshields may be smashed and graceful ebony hands
may drag them out through their shatterproof smashed windshields crying
Revenge for the Indians! Ah, they all fear leaving Hudson's and being dragged to
the very tip of the city and thrown off the parking roof of Cobo Hall, that
expensive tomb, into the river. . . .

XI. CHARACTERS WE ARE FOREVER ENTWINED WITH

1. Simon drew me into his tender rotting arms and breathed gravity into me.   37
Then I came to earth, weighted down. He said *You are such a little girl,* and he
weighed me down with his delight. In the palms of his hands were teeth
marks from his previous life experiences. He was thirty-five, they said. Imagine Simon in this room, in my pink room: he is about six feet tall and stoops
slightly, in a feline cautious way, always thinking, always on guard, with his
scuffed light suede shoes and his clothes which are anyone's clothes, slightly
rumpled ordinary clothes that ordinary men might wear to not-bad jobs.
Simon has fair, long hair, curly hair, spent languid curls that are like . . .
exactly like the curls of wood shavings to the touch, I am trying to be exact
. . . and he smells of unheated mornings and coffee and too many pills coating
his tongue with a faint green-white scum. . . . Dear Simon, who would be
panicked in this room and in this house (right now Billie is vacuuming next
door in my parents' room: a vacuum cleaner's roar is a sign of all good things),

Simon who is said to have come from a home not much different from this, years ago, fleeing all the carpeting and the polished banisters . . . Simon has a deathly face, only desperate people fall in love with it. His face is bony and cautious, the bones of his cheeks prominent as if with the rigidity of his ceaseless thinking, plotting, for he has to make money out of girls to whom money means nothing, they're so far gone they can hardly count it, and in a sense money means nothing to him either except as a way of keeping on with his life. *Each Day's Proud Struggle,* the title of a novel we could read at jail. . . . Each day he needs a certain amount of money. He devours it. It wasn't love he uncoiled in me with his hollowed-out eyes and his courteous smile, that remnant of a prosperous past, but a dark terror that needed to press itself flat against him, or against another man . . . but he was the first, he came over to me and took my arm, a claim. We struggled on the stairs and I said, "Let me loose, you're hurting my neck, my face," it was such a surprise that my skin hurt where he rubbed it, and afterward we lay face to face and he breathed everything into me. In the end I think he turned me in.

2. Raymond Forrest. I just read this morning that Raymond Forrest's father, 38 the chairman of the board at ———, died of a heart attack on a plane bound for London. I would like to write Raymond Forrest a note of sympathy. I would like to thank him for not pressing charges against me one hundred years ago, saving me, being so generous . . . well, men like Raymond Forrest are generous men, not like Simon. I would like to write him a letter telling of my love, or of some other emotion that is positive and healthy. Not like Simon and his poetry, which he scrawled down when he was high and never changed a word . . . but when I try to think of something to say it is Simon's language that comes back to me, caught in my head like a bad song, it is always Simon's language:

> There is no reality only dreams
> Your neck may get snapped when you wake
> My love is drawn to some violent end
> She keeps wanting to get away
> My love is heading downward
> And I am heading upward
> She is going to crash on the sidewalk
> And I am going to dissolve into the clouds

XII. EVENTS

1. Out of the hospital, bruised and saddened and converted, with Princess's 39 grunts still tangled in my hair . . . and Father in his overcoat looking like a Prince himself, come to carry me off. Up the expressway and out north to home. Jesus Christ but the air is thinner and cleaner here. Monumental houses. Heartbreaking sidewalks, so clean.

2. Weeping in the living room. The ceiling is two storeys high and two   40
chandeliers hang from it. Weeping, weeping, though Billie the maid is *probably*
listening. I will never leave home again. Never. Never leave home. Never leave
this home again, never.

3. Sugar doughnuts for breakfast. The toaster is very shiny and my face is   41
distorted in it. Is that my face?

4. The car is turning in the driveway. Father brings me home. Mother   42
embraces me. Sunlight breaks in movieland patches on the roof of our
traditional contemporary home, which was designed for the famous auto-
motive stylist whose identity, if I told you the name of the famous car he
designed, you would all know, so I can't tell you because my teeth chatter at the thought of being sued . . . or having someone climb into my
bedroom window with a rope to strangle me. . . . The car turns up the
black-top drive. The house opens to me like a doll's house, so lovely in
the sunlight, the big living room beckons to me with its walls falling
away in a delirium of joy at my return, Billie the maid is *no doubt* listening
from the kitchen as I burst into tears and the hysteria Simon got so sick
of. Convulsed in Father's arms I say I will never leave again, never, why
did I leave, where did I go, what happened, my mind is gone wrong, my
body is one big bruise, my backbone was sucked dry, it wasn't the men
who hurt me and Simon never hurt me but only those girls . . . my God
how they hurt me . . . I will never leave home again. . . . The car is perpetually turning up the drive and I am perpetually breaking down in the
living room and we are perpetually taking the right exit from the expressway (Lahser Road) and the wall of the restroom is perpetually banging
against my head and perpetually are Simon's hands moving across my
body and adding everything up and so too are Father's hands on my
shaking bruised back, far from the surface of my skin on the surface of
my good blue cashmere coat (drycleaned for my release). . . . I weep for
all the money here, for God in gold and beige carpeting, for the beauty
of chandeliers and the miracle of a clean polished gleaming toaster and
faucets that run both hot and cold water, and I tell them *I will never*
leave home, this is my home, I love everything here, I am in love with everything
here. . . .

    I am home.
                                                               43

Questions for Discussion

1. Why does the girl in the story steal the gloves from Branden's store? Is her
parents' pulling of social strings—"fixing" things for her—the wrong or
right response to her act? Why?

2. What judgments about the mother and father are you led to make by paragraphs 9 and 10?

3. The Detroit weather seems to be used symbolically in this story—as a symbol of what? Is the symbolic treatment effective? Why or why not?

4. What do you learn about the central character when she lists "Nothing" under "III. World Events" (¶14)? You know from the story that the year is 1968—the year Robert Kennedy and Martin Luther King were assassinated, the year of the police riots at the Democratic national convention in Chicago, the year when anti-war protests against the Vietnam conflict were more vociferous than they had ever been, the year that an incumbent president was forced out of running for re-election because of his failure to end either the war or the protests against it, and the year in which it became clear that America was actually going to send a crew of astronauts to the moon (which happened the next year). In other words, 1968 was one of the most turbulent, dramatic, and vivid years the nation had experienced since the Second World War. Most people felt, at the very least, that it was impossible not to have opinions about public affairs, if not impossible to be acually involved firsthand. Yet to the central character of Oates's story, world events are "nothing." What does this blankness toward the outside world reveal about the girl, her upbringing, her problems, and possible solutions? Does it suggest any reasons that help explain her inability to understand why Princess and Dolly beat her up?

5. Why is the girl in the story so loyal to Simon? To what lengths does her loyalty carry her in helping to support his drug habit? Does paragraph 31 help you answer this question?

6. When the girl weeps (in the next-to-last sentence) "for all the money here, for God in gold and beige carpeting," what does she mean? In what sense is God in these things? For whom? And why does it make her weep?

7. Is the girl's homecoming happy or sad? Why? Will she be OK from now on? Why or why not?

Suggested Essay Topics

1. American society is full of double messages about money. On the one hand, we talk as if we were all convinced of money's limited importance as embodied in a whole cluster of clichés such as "Money can't buy love," "Money can't buy happiness," "You can't take it with you," "I'd rather be happy than rich," "Love of money is the root of all evil," "Easy come, easy go," and "Take time to smell the flowers." On the other hand, we also talk as if we were convinced that nothing is more important than money as embodied in a cluster of contrasting clichés that, revealingly, are not as explicit as the clichés against money. The clichés that laud money are more like code words or phrases. "Getting ahead," for example, makes no explicit reference to money, but everyone knows that money and the things money can buy are referred to. "Let's stick to the 'bottom line,'" a metaphor from accounting that is consistently applied to almost every area of

life, is more explicit but still refers to money only metaphorically. "Stick to practicalities" is even less direct but in many contexts translates into "Look at things from an economic point of view first." And most Americans are either proud or envious rather than shocked or outraged that some corporate executives are paid millions of dollars a year while other people in the same society are starving.

In light of all these double messages and contradictory attitudes about money (you can probably come up with other examples on your own), write an essay (using your classmates as an audience) in which you analyze the relationships among the family members and attempt to explain (a) why the girl acts as she does, (b) how the parents are to blame (or are blameless) for the girl's troubles, (c) how her difficulties might have been avoided, and (d) how money has played a role in the development of character and events.

2. Write about the events of the story from three different points of view, employing three different voices. The first voice is that of Simon, who was reared in a family much like the girl's own. He is speaking to the girl and evaluating people such as his own family and hers. The second voice is that of the girl's father, explaining to her, after her return home, why people such as Clarita and Simon are not fit companions and expressing his opinions about how they got where they are, why they live as they do, and what they should do with themselves. The third voice is your own as you attempt to reconcile the other voices, take sides with one or the other, or construct a view of the situation different from either. In your own voice, directed not to the girl but to a general reader (who you may assume has read the other two accounts), you are trying to sort out the rights and wrongs of this situation, determine who merits sympathy and who merits blame, and suggest changes that should be made.

IDEAS IN DEBATE

Paul Johnson
Herbert Schmertz
J. Robert Nelson
Eugene J. McCarthy
James Cone

Paul Johnson

Paul Johnson (b. 1928), British histo-
rian, author, and former editor of the New Statesman, *first delivered "Has Capi-*
talism a Future?" as a speech at a conference of bankers. Johnson's objective is to go
on the "ideological offensive" (¶37) and "to teach the world a little history" (¶38)
in order to defend capitalism against those he considers its five main enemies: aca-
demic leftists, ecological doomsayers, intrusive governments, union activists, and So-
viet totalitarianists. He measures the value of capitalism as an economic system
exclusively by the amount of national wealth it has generated. By comparing the
rate of national economic growth in later historical times (after capitalism's emer-
gence as the dominant economic system of the West) with the rate of economic
growth in earlier times, Johnson claims to have clearly assessed its value: "Industrial
capitalism, judged simply by its capacity to create wealth and to distribute it, is a
phenomenon unique in world history. One could argue that it is the greatest single
blessing ever bestowed on humanity" (¶11).

Following Johnson's essay are four responses (by Herbert Schmertz, J. Robert
Nelson, Eugene J. McCarthy, and James Cone) to his question "Has capitalism a
future?" Each respondent disagrees with parts of his position. It is clear that Johnson
has an ax to grind and that he is speaking as an advocate, but it is not so clear, at
least at first glance, whether his critics are simply looking for weaknesses in his
arguments or whether they are grinding their own axes in a biased way. It may be
helpful to know that Herbert Schmertz is a corporation executive; J. Robert Nelson is
a professor of theology; Eugene J. McCarthy is a former presidential candidate, former
senator, and author; and James Cone is a black theologian.

As you read, try to assess the validity of arguments raised on both sides of the
issues. Note that Johnson's facts are not disputed by any of his respondents, regardless
of whether they like or dislike his position. Once again we see that facts seldom
determine the positions that people take on issues. Everyone accepts Johnson's facts, yet

everyone has a different picture of their significance. The facts are not irrelevant— everyone clearly takes them seriously—but the point is that, in and of themselves, they are seldom conclusive.

HAS CAPITALISM A FUTURE?

This essay and the four responses to it are from *Will Capitalism Survive?* (1979), edited by Ernest W. Lefever.

Seen against the grand perspective of history, capitalism is a newcomer. I would date it, in its earliest phase in England, only from the 1780s. We now possess some knowledge of economic systems going back to the early centuries of the third millennium B.C. I could outline, for instance, the economic structure of Egypt under the Old Kingdom, about 2700 B.C. Our knowledge of how civilized societies have organized their economic activities thus covers a stretch of more than 4,600 years. And in only about two hundred of those years has industrial capitalism existed. As a widely spread phenomenon, it is barely one hundred years old.

(Before I go any further, let me define my term: by "capitalism" I mean large-scale industrial capitalism, in which privately financed, publicly quoted corporations, operating in a free-market environment, with the back-up of the private-enterprise money market, constitute the core of the national economy. This is a rather broad definition, but I think it will do.)

The next point to note is the remarkable correlation between the emergence of industrial capitalism and the beginnings of really rapid economic growth. Throughout most of history, growth rates, when we have the statistical evidence to measure them, have been low, nil, or minus. A century of slow growth might be followed by a century of decline. Societies tended to get caught in the Malthusian Trap: that is, a period of slow growth led to an increase in population, the outstripping of food supplies, then a demographic catastrophe, and the beginning of a new cycle.

There were at least three economic "Dark Ages" in history, in which a sudden collapse of the wealth-making process led to the extinction, or virtual extinction, of civilized living, and the process of recovery was very slow and painful. The last of these three Dark Ages extinguished Roman civilization in Western Europe in the fifth century A.D. Not until the thirteenth century were equivalent living standards achieved; the recovery thus took eight hundred years.

Society again fell into a Malthusian trap in the fourteenth century. Again recovery was slow, though more sure this time, as intermediate technology spread more widely and methods of handling and employing money became more sophisticated. As late as the first half of the eighteenth century, however, it was rare for even the most advanced economies, those of England and Holland, to achieve 1 per cent growth in any year. And there is a possibility that mankind would again have fallen into a Malthusian trap toward the end of the eighteenth century if industrial capitalism had not made its dramatic appearance.

And it *was* dramatic. By the beginning of the 1780s, in England, an unprecedented annual growth rate of 2 per cent had been achieved. During that decade, the 2 per cent was raised to 4 per cent. This was the great historic "liftoff," and a 4 per cent annual compound growth rate was sustained for the next fifty years. Since this English, and also Scottish, performance was accompanied by the export of capital, patents, machine tools, and skilled manpower to several other advanced nations, the phenomenon soon became international.

A few more figures are necessary to show the magnitude of the change that industrial capitalism brought to human society. In Britain, for instance, in the nineteenth century, the size of the working population multiplied fourfold. Real wages doubled in the half-century 1800–1850, and doubled again, 1850–1900. This meant there was a 1600 per cent increase in the production and consumption of wage-goods during the century. Nothing like this had happened anywhere before, in the whole of history. From the 1850s onward, in Belgium, France, Austria-Hungary, and above all in Germany and the United States, even higher growth rates were obtained; and feudal empires like Japan and Russia were able to telescope into a mere generation or two a development process that in Britain had stretched over centuries.

The growth rates of twelve leading capitalist countries averaged 2.7 per cent a year over the whole fifty-year period up to World War I. There was, it is true, a much more mixed performance between the wars. The United States, which in the forty-four years up to 1914 had averaged a phenomenal 4.3 per cent growth rate, and which in the seven years up to 1929 had increased its national income by a staggering 40 per cent, then saw its national income fall 38 per cent in a mere four years, 1929–1932.

But after World War II, growth was resumed on an even more impressive scale. In the 1950s, for instance, the twelve leading capitalist economies cited before had an average annual growth of 4.2 per cent. In Germany it was as high as an average of 7.6 per cent. In all the West European economies, the rate of investment in the 1950s was half again as high as it had ever been on a sustained basis. In several such countries it was over 20 per cent of the GNP; in Germany and the Netherlands it was 25 per cent, in Norway even higher. Moreover, this high capital formation took place not at the cost of private consumption but during a rapid and sustained rise in living standards, particularly of industrial workers. These tendencies were prolonged throughout the 1960s and into the 1970s. For the mature economies, the second industrial revolution—1945–1970—was entirely painless. This was also largely true in Japan, which achieved even higher investment and growth rates in an effort to catch up with the United States and Europe.

In short, after nearly five recorded millennia of floundering about in poverty, humanity suddenly in the 1780s began to hit on the right formula: industrial capitalism. Consider the magnitude of the change over the last two centuries or less. We all know the wealth of present-day West Germany. In the year 1800, in the whole of Germany fewer than 1,000 people had annual incomes as high as $1,000. Or again, take France. France now has more automobiles per capita even than Germany, and more second homes per family than any other country in Europe. In the 1780s, four-fifths of the French families spent 90 per cent of their incomes simply on buying bread— only bread—to stay alive.

In short, industrial capitalism, judged simply by its capacity to create 11 wealth and to distribute it, is a phenomenon unique in world history. One could argue that it is the greatest single blessing ever bestowed on humanity. Why, then, are we asking, "Has capitalism a future?" The answer is clear enough: because capitalism is threatened.

The idea has got around that industrial capitalism is unpopular and 12 always has been, that it is the work of a tiny minority who have thrust it upon the reluctant mass of mankind. Nothing could be further from the truth. The storage economies of remote antiquity were often hideously unpopular. So was the slave-based economy, combined with corporatism, of the classical world. Agricultural feudalism was certainly unpopular, and mercantilism had to be enforced, in practice, by authoritarian states.

But from the very start industrial capitalism won the approval of the 13 masses. They could not vote in the ballot box, but they voted in a far more impressive manner: with their feet. The poorest member of society values political freedom as much as the richest. But the freedom he values most of all is the freedom to sell his labor and skills in the open market, and it was precisely *this* that industrial capitalism gave to men for the first time in history. Hence it is a profound error of fact, in my view, to see what Blake called the "dark, satanic mills" of the industrial revolution as the enslavement of man. The factory system, however harsh it may have been, was the road to freedom for millions of agricultural workers. Not only did it offer them an escape from rural poverty, which was deeper and more degrading than anything experienced in the cities, but it allowed them to move from status to contract, from a stationary place in a static society, with tied cottages and semi-conscript labor, to a mobile place in a dynamic society.

That was why the common man voted for industrial capitalism with his 14 feet, by tramping from the countryside to the towns in enormous numbers, first in Britain, then throughout Europe. And tens of millions of European peasants, decade after decade, moved relentlessly across the Atlantic in pursuit of that same freedom, from semi-feudal estates and small holdings in Russia, Poland, Germany, Austria-Hungary, Italy, Ireland, Scandinavia, to the mines and factories and workshops of New York, Chicago, Pittsburgh, Cleveland, Detroit. It was the first time in history that really large numbers of ordinary people were given the chance to exercise a choice about their livelihood and destiny, and to move, not as members of a tribe or conscript soldiers, but as free individuals, selling their labor in the open market.

They voted for industrial capitalism with their feet not only because 15 they felt in their bones that it meant a modest prosperity for their children and grandchildren—and on the whole they have been proved abundantly right—but because they knew it meant a new degree of freedom for themselves. Indeed, the success of industrialization, despite all its evils, continues to persuade countless ordinary men and women, all over the world, to escape the poverty and restraints of the rural status society and to enter the free labor markets of the towns. Hence the growth of megalopolises all over the world—Calcutta and Bombay, Teheran and Caracas, Mexico City and Djakarta, Shanghai and Lagos, Cairo and Johannesburg. There are now literally scores of million-plus cities all over the Third World. This never-ending one-way flow from countryside to city is plainly a voluntary mass choice, for most governments fear and resent it, and many are attempting, sometimes savagely but always ineffectively, to halt or reverse it. It is more marked in the free-market economies, but it is noticeable everywhere.

Short of evacuating the cities by force and terror, as is now apparently 16 being practiced in parts of southeast Asia, there is no way to stop this human flood. There seems to be an almost irresistible urge in human beings to move away from the status society to contractual individualism, the central feature of industrial capitalism. This operates even in totalitarian societies, as witness the efforts, for instance, of the Chinese and Polish governments to limit the urban explosions they are experiencing.

If industrial capitalism is unique in its wealth-producing capacity and 17 also has the endorsement of the people, then why is it under threat? And who is threatening it?

THE INTELLECTUAL
AND MORAL BATTLE

Let me look at five principal elements. The *first,* and in some ways the most 18 important, is that *the free-enterprise idea is losing, if it has not already lost, the intellectual and moral battle.* Not long ago I went into Blackwell's, the great book shop at Oxford University. I wandered over the huge room that houses the books on politics and economics, and having been disagreeably surprised by what I saw there, I made a rough calculation. New books extolling the economic, social, and moral virtues of Communism and collectivism—and there were literally hundreds and hundreds from all over the world—outnumbered books defending free enterprise, or merely seeking to take an objective view of the argument, by between five and six to one. This overwhelming predominance of collectivism was not due to any sinister policy on the part of Blackwell's, which is a highly efficient capitalist enterprise. It was a marketing response to demand on the part of students and teachers. And this was not one of the new slum universities of recent years, some of which have been virtually shanghaied by Marxist factions, but Oxford University, one of the free world's greatest centers of learning, where the battle of ideas is fought under the best possible conditions.

There can be no doubt that the intellectual and moral assault on free 19 enterprise, and the exaltation of Marxist collectivism, that is such a striking feature of the 1970s is directly related to the huge expansion of higher education, put through at such cost to the capitalist economies in the 1960s. Now there is in this a huge and tragic irony. For in the 1950s, the decade when the university expansion was planned, it was the prevailing wisdom among the leading thinkers of the West that the growth of higher education was directly productive of industrial growth—that the more university graduates we turned out, the faster the GNPs of the West would rise. This was the thesis outlined by President Clark Kerr of Berkeley in his 1963 Godkin lectures at Harvard, and it was a thesis put forward in Britain with immense effect by Sir Charles, now Lord Snow. Kerr said: "What the railroads did for the second half of the last century, and the automobile for the first half of this century, may be done for the second half of the twentieth century by the knowledge industry: that is, to serve as the focal point for national growth." He added that more graduates would not only mean a bigger GNP but act as a reinforcement for middle-class democracy, with all its freedoms.

To speak of the "knowledge industry" was to ask for trouble. Knowl- 20 edge is not a manufactured commodity. There is knowledge for good and knowledge for evil, as the Book of Genesis says. The 1960s, during which most Western nations doubled and some even trebled their university places, did not reinforce democratic freedoms or enlarge the GNP or strengthen the free-enterprise system. They produced the students' revolts, beginning in Paris in 1968. They detonated the Northern Ireland conflict, which is still harassing Britain. They produced the Baader-Meinhoff Gang in West Germany, the Red Brigade in Italy, the Left Fascist terrorism of Japan. They produced an enormous explosion of Marxist studies, centered on the social sciences and especially sociology and on a new generation of school and university teachers who are dedicated, by a sort of perverted religious piety, to the spread of Marxist ideas.

There are ironies within the general irony. The new university of the 21 air, created in Britain at enormous expense to bring higher education to adults and therefore christened the Open University, has become virtually closed to any teacher not of proven Marxist opinions. Nuffield College, Oxford, founded by the great capitalist pioneer Lord Nuffield, who created the British automobile industry, has become a center of trade-union ideology, of the very ideas that slowly but surely are putting the British automobile industry out of world markets and out of business. Warwick University, created in the 1960s as a powerhouse of ideas and clever graduate executives for the West Midlands industrial complex, Britain's biggest, has become a seminary of Marxist and pseudo-Marxist agitators dedicated to the destruction of the wealth-producing machine that brought their university into existence.

I could go on. It is true, of course, that student unrest, as such, has 22 quieted down. But the steady diffusion of ideas hostile to our free system continues remorselessly. Industrial capitalism and the free-market system are presented as destructive of human happiness, corrupt, immoral, wasteful, inefficient, and above all, doomed. Collectivism is presented as the only way out compatible with the dignity of the human spirit and the future of our race. The expanded university threatens to become not the powerhouse of Western individualism and enterprise but its graveyard.

THE ECOLOGICAL PANIC

There is a *second* threat, what I have called *the "ecological panic."* This movement, 23 again, began with the best intentions. I well remember when Rachel Carson's book *The Silent Spring* first appeared in the *New Yorker.* The wave of concern that followed was justified. We were tending to ignore some of the destructive side effects of very rapid industrial expansion. The steps then taken, notably the clean-air policies and the policies for cleansing lakes and waterways, have been spectacularly successful. Thanks to smokeless fuel, London fogs, which were real killers, have been virtually eliminated; the last really serious one was in 1952. The Thames is now cleaner and has greater quantities of fish, and more varieties, than at any time since before the days of Spenser or Shakespeare. Similar successes are now being registered in the United States, which adopted such legally enforceable remedies somewhat later than Britain did. These are examples of what can be done by the thoughtful, unemotional, systematic, and scientifically justified application of conservation and anti-pollution policies.

But most of these were put in motion before the ecological panic started. 24 Once ecology became a fashionable good cause, as it did in the late 1960s, reason, logic, and proportion flew out the window. It became a campaign not against pollution but against growth itself, and especially against free-enterprise growth—totalitarian Communist growth was somehow less morally offensive. I highly recommend Professor Wilfred Beckerman's *In Defence of Economic Growth.* Beckerman is one of the best of our economists and was a member of the Royal Commission on Environmental Pollution; he knows the subject better perhaps than any other working economist, and his book is a wonderfully sane and lucid summary of it.

I have never yet been able to persuade any committed ecology cam- 25 paigner even to look at this book. Of course not. Such persons have a faith, and they do not want to risk it. One of the most important developments of our time is the growth, as a consequence of the rapid decline of Christianity, of irrational substitutes for it. These are not necessarily religious or even quasi-religious. Often they are pseudo-scientific in form, as for instance the weird philosophy of the late Teilhard de Chardin. The ecology panic is another example. It is akin to the salvation panic of sixteenth-century Calvinism. When you expel the priest, you do not inaugurate the age of reason—you get the witch doctor. But whereas Calvinist salvation panic may have contributed to the rise of capitalism, the ecology panic could be the death of it.

If the restrictions now imposed on industrial development had operated 26 in eighteenth-century England, the industrial revolution could not have taken place. It would in effect have been inhibited by law—as of course many landowners of the day wished it to be—and legal requirements would have eliminated the very modest profits by which it originally financed itself. We would still be existing at eighteenth-century living standards, and wallowing in eighteenth-century levels of pollution, which were infinitely worse than anything we experience today. (If you want to see what they were like, visit the slums of Calcutta or Djakarta.)

As it is, the ecology panic has been a potent destructive force. The 27 panic-mongers played a crucial role in persuading the Middle Eastern oil producers, especially Iran, to quadruple the price of oil in the autumn of 1973, the biggest single blow industrial capitalism has suffered since the Wall Street crash of 1929. That was the beginning of the profound recession from which we have not yet emerged. In the end, as was foreseeable at the time, the huge rise in oil prices did not do anyone any good, least of all the oil producers. But it ended the great post-war boom and robbed Western capitalism of its tremendous élan, perhaps for good. As Browning put it, "Never glad confident morning again!" And it is significant that the ecological lobby is now striving with fanatic vigor and persistence to prevent the development of nuclear energy, allegedly on the grounds of safety. Now it is a fact, a very remarkable fact in my view, that throughout the West (we have no figures for Russia or China) the nuclear power industry is the only industry, the *only* industry, which over a period of thirty years has not had a single fatal industrial accident. This unique record has been achieved by the efforts of the industry itself and the responsible governments, without any assistance from the ecolobby. But of course they would *like* a few fatal accidents. That would suit their purposes very well.

In Britain we had a long public enquiry, what we call a statutory en- 28 quiry, into whether or not it was right to go ahead with the enriched-uranium plant at Windscale. The enquiry was a model of its kind. The ecolobby marshalled all the scientific experts and evidence they could lay their hands on. At the end the verdict was that there was no reason whatever why the program should not proceed. Did the ecolobby accept the verdict? On the contrary. They immediately organized a mass demonstration and planned various legal and illegal activities to halt the program by force. It is notable that a leading figure in this campaign is the man who is perhaps Britain's leading Communist trade unionist, Mr. Arthur Scargill of the Mine-workers. He has never, so far as we know, campaigned against Soviet nuclear programs, peaceful or otherwise. It is true that most people in the movement in the United States, Britain, France, Germany, and Italy, so far as I have been able to observe, are not politically motivated; they are simply irrational. But irrationality is an enemy of civilized society, and it is being exploited by the politically interested.

BIG GOVERNMENT VS. THE MARKET

A *third* factor in the future of capitalism is *the growth of government.* Industrial 29 capitalism—or rather, the free-enterprise economy—and big government are natural and probably irreconcilable enemies. It is no accident that the industrial revolution took place in late eighteenth-century England, a time of minimum government. Of all the periods of English history, indeed of European history, it was the time when government was least conspicuous and active. It was the age, very short alas, of the Night Watchman state. As a matter of fact, the industrial revolution—perhaps the most important single event in human history—seems to have occurred without the English government's even noticing. By the time the government did notice, it was, happily, too late.

It is almost inevitable that government, particularly an active, interven- 30 tionist government, should view free enterprise with a degree of hostility, since it constitutes a countervailing power in the state. The tendency, then, is to cut free enterprise down to size, in a number of ways. In the United States the characteristic technique is government regulation and legal harassment, and this of course has been far more pervasive and strident since the ecolobby swung into action. In Britain the technique is both direct assault— nationalization—and slow starvation. In a way, nationalization is ineffective, since it allows the public to make comparisons between the performance of the nationalized sector and that of the free sector, nearly always to the latter's advantage.

Starvation is more insidious. By this I mean the progressive transfer of 31 resources, by taxation and other government policies, from the private to the public sector. In 1955, for instance, public expenditure in Britain as a proportion of the GNP was just over 40 per cent. By 1975, twenty years later, it had risen to nearly 60 per cent. This was accompanied by a record budget deficit of about $22 billion, itself a further 11½ per cent of the GNP. Of course, the tax money had to be provided, and the deficit serviced, by the private sector. We have, then, an Old Man of the Sea relationship in which the parasitical Old Man is growing bigger, and poor Sinbad smaller, all the time. The shrinking productive sector has to carry the burden of an ever-expanding loss-making public sector. Thus Britain's authorized steel industry will lose $1 billion this year, and it has been authorized by statute to borrow up to $7 billion, guaranteed by government and taxpayer. Now the interesting thing is that in Britain the public sector and the civil service generally are now paying higher wages, providing better conditions, and giving larger pensions—which in a growing number of cases are index-linked and thus inflation-proof—than the private sector can possibly afford. And of course they are financing these goodies out of tax-guaranteed deficits—that is, from the dwindling profits of the private sector. This is what I call the starvation technique. When a private firm goes bust, provided it is big enough, the state takes over, the losses are added to the taxpayer's bill, and the private sector has one more expensive passenger to carry.

In this technique, the *fourth* factor, *the trade unions,* play an important part. 32 In Britain it is demonstrably true that the legal privileges of the trade unions, which virtually exempt them from any kind of action for damages (including, now, libel), led directly to restrictive practices, over-manning, low productivity, low investment, low wages, and low profits. Thus trade-union action tends, in itself, to undermine the performance of industrial capitalism as a wealth-creating system. In Britain, the trade unions can rightly claim that capitalism is inefficient, because they make sure it is inefficient. Ford workers in Britain, using exactly the same assembly-line machinery as in West Germany, produce between 20 per cent and 50 per cent fewer automobiles. ICI Chemicals, one of the best companies in Britain, nevertheless has a productivity performance 25 per cent lower than its Dutch and German competitors. A recent analysis shows this is entirely due to over-manning and restrictive practices.

The private sector in Britain is now threatened by two further union 33 devices: the legally enforced closed shop, which compels workers to join designated unions on pain of dismissal without compensation or legal redress, and new plans to force firms to have up to 50 per cent worker directors, appointed not by the work force themselves nor even necessarily from among them but by and from the trade-union bureaucracy (Bullock Report). This has to be seen against the explicit policy of some groups within the unions of driving private-sector firms to bankruptcy by strikes and harassment, so that the state will then have to take them into the public sector.

What is happening in Britain will not necessarily happen elsewhere. But 34 there are many ways in which the present U.S. administration seems determined to follow Britain's example. The West Germans, too, are now beginning to adopt some of the institutions that flourish in British trade unionism, notably the shop stewards' movement. Businessmen all over the free world may despise the performance of British industry, but trade unionists all over the world admire and envy the power of British trade unionists and are actively seeking to acquire it for themselves.

THE TOTALITARIAN THREAT

Let me end on a word of warning. I have said nothing of the *fifth* threat to 35 industrial capitalism and the free-enterprise system—*the threat from without.* But this is bound to increase as the military superiority of the Soviet Union over the United States is reinforced. I have never thought that the Communist system would triumph by a direct assault. I have always assumed that it would first establish an overwhelming military predominance and then, by pressure and threats, begin to draw the political and economic dividends of it. If the United States opts out of the competitive arms race with the Soviet Union while supposedly providing merely for its own defense, then we must expect to see this fifth threat hard at work winding up industrial capitalism and free enterprise all over the world.

Therefore, when we ask, "Has capitalism a future?," I answer: It all 36 depends on the United States. West Germany and Japan, it is true, have strong free-enterprise economies; they also have a tradition of state capitalism, and would adapt themselves with surprising speed and readiness to a new collective order. France already has a huge public sector and a long tradition of *dirigisme* [state-controlled finance] or *étatisme* [state socialism]. All three are Janus-faced. Britain, I believe, is profoundly anti-collective and will remain so if it continues to be given the choice. But its private-enterprise system is now very weak, and its business and financial elites are demoralized and defeatist.

I myself think that capitalism will survive, because of its enormous 37 intrinsic virtues as a system for generating wealth and promoting freedom. But those who man and control it must stop apologizing and go on the ideological offensive. They must show ordinary people that both the Communist world and the Third World are parasitical upon industrial capitalism for their growth technology, and that without capitalism, the 200 years of unprecedented growth that have created the modern world would gradually come to an end. We would have slow growth, then nil growth, then minus growth, and then the Malthusian catastrophe.

Those who wish to maintain the capitalist system must endeavor to 38 teach the world a little history. They must remind it, and especially the young, that though man's achievements are great, they are never as solid as they look. If man makes the wrong choice, there is always another Dark Age waiting for him round the corner of time.

Herbert Schmertz

DEMOCRACY, TYRANNY, AND CAPITALISM

While I am all for capitalism and see many valid points in Paul Johnson's 1 argument, I get uneasy when I see it posed—as I think Johnson does—as the antithesis to Marxism or "Marxist collectivism." Marxism is at best a theory about history and at worst what the economist P. T. Bauer has called "an all-embracing secular messianic faith." Capitalism is neither. It is a historical phenomenon, as Johnson points out, but even by his own definition it is an economic system: a device, a means, a way to go about certain economic business. It is hardly a theory about history, and much less is it the force that must be set in the lists to combat the messianic faith of Marxist collectivism. I would guess that the faith of capitalists is invested in far more profound and transcendent realities than capitalism. What they see and fear in Marxist collectivism is not so much its menace to capitalism as its menace to freedom.

This distinction is important. There is some danger that readers of 2 Johnson's essay may come away believing that the struggle is between capitalism and Marxism. That is to wage the battle on Marxism's ground and in Marxism's terms, and it renders the contest deceptively simple. Marxism's argument is only superficially with capitalism: witness the cordiality of Marxist states when they are in need of high technology. At its essence,

Marxism's argument is about who shall make choices; it is a quarrel with freedom and democracy.

Given this perspective, I am somewhat hesitant about the broad scope 3 of Johnson's thesis. That the industrial revolution was an epochal event must be admitted, but Europe was by no means sick and poor when the industrial revolution began. Revolutionary economic changes had been initiated in the sixteenth century with the voyages of discovery and the considerable stimulation of trade, industry, and finance provoked by these discoveries. And—at least on this side of the ocean—we tend to assign even more importance to the revolution of ideas that might be said to have begun with the Magna Carta, developed in the Enlightenment, and culminated in the American Revolution: the idea that governments must answer to the people.

From such a perspective, the threats to capitalism outlined by Johnson 4 seem less formidable. We have seen that the university student's infatuation with collectivism tends to fade rather quickly once he begins to work within the capitalistic system and learns to recognize its virtues. We have seen, in the United States at least, a growing public realization that balance is necessary in questions that pit environmentalism against the need for energy, economic growth, and jobs; people are becoming more enlightened about the tradeoffs required in a progressive society. Americans have already begun a more careful definition of the role to be played by government in relation to enterprise and the market economy, as evidenced by the deregulation of airline fares and the movement toward decontrol of prices for natural gas and crude oil.

These are arguments that capitalism has begun to win on the basis of 5 facts and experience—on pragmatic, economic grounds. I would say that it is all very well to go on the "ideological offensive" but that one must be careful not to confuse ideology and economics, lest—as in Marxism—the one poison the other.

Many writers and scholars present capitalism as a scheme of social 6 organization, a remarkable fortress of ideology and philosophy concerning the right to private property, strict limitation of government power, and dedication to free markets or the market economy. Yet capitalism itself has displayed, in the main, a positive aversion to ideology, to declaring itself the one true way that men should live and work. Its claims—and demonstrated virtues—have mainly to do with the economic sphere. This is why multinational corporations are able to operate successfully and usefully in so many countries, with so many ideological shadings in their governments. For they enable economics to stand apart from politics.

Still, I suppose we are observing the phenomenon Bertolt Brecht de- 7 scribed when he said that to avoid ideology in our day is not to escape it. Presenting capitalism as a scheme of social organization gives the scholar a convenient rhetorical device to oppose to socialism or "Marxist collectivism." He can then argue private property vs. public ownership, market economy vs. centrally controlled economy, or limited government vs. all-pervasive government.

But the scheme of social organization in, say, the United States is not   8
capitalism but democracy. Americans, if asked, do not describe themselves as
capitalists. Capitalism, to the man in the street, is not the ideological fortress
underlying his liberties but an economic system that has worked rather well
(as Johnson points out) for almost every group or individual who got involved
with it. As long as we talk about capitalism in terms of what it is—an
economic device of proven value—it can generally hold its own in the public
dialogue. But we shall send people scurrying off in droves if we attempt to
load the nature and fate of Western civilization onto the back of capitalism.
I think Americans know very well that what Marxism can imperil is their
liberty, not their capitalism.

It is worth remembering that to offer a convincing catalogue of the   9
dangers or abject failures of socialism does not, in itself, convert one's listeners to capitalism. This seems to have mystified a fair number of capitalist
intellectuals; it is perhaps further evidence of the perils encountered when
ideology and economics are confused.

Can we look at capitalism without its ideological freight? Perhaps by   10
thinking of it as simply a "competitive market economy" we can consider it
as an economic system. As Johnson describes most forcefully, capitalism has
worked phenomenally well in achieving material abundance, the wide distribution of goods, and a steady increase in personal opportunity. I think we can
discern in the system of capitalism some sort of inner affinity with the human
desire to work, to make or build or accomplish something of one's own, and
an even deeper affinity with the human desire to change, to improve not only
one's self but also one's environment. Capitalism has not created these needs;
it has merely provided a marvelous means for fulfilling them. When critics
complain that capitalism has aggravated spiritual unease or restlessness in
Western civilization, they overlook the possibility that this very restlessness
has perhaps created and formed the civilization. Capitalism has been not a
primary cause but an efficient vehicle.

Johnson's warning that capitalism can be smothered, dismantled, and   11
destroyed is valid. I think there is some danger that this will happen in the
United States, but I am, on the whole, optimistic that it will not. Even in the
worst of times, many of us have persisted in believing that the American
public—given more information—would come to see that the market pros-
pers in liberty and atrophies under command.

That lesson of history is so clear that it cannot forever be ignored. It is   12
an idea that is currently in disfavor among many American intellectuals. But
the public is of a different mind. The public current is now running strongly
against big government and excessive, costly regulation—witness California's
Proposition 13* and similar tax revolts. The public demand is for change, for
a thorough pruning of the huge, remote bureaucracies that have been inter-

*The first of several state laws passed by referendum limiting the size of state budgets and
establishing limits on taxes.

fering so relentlessly not only with the free market but with almost everyone's life and work.

And even the intellectual community is beginning to resist the unnecessary interference of government in what had been an effective and highly successful market economy. In 1978 the new president of Yale University, A. Bartlett Giamatti, went to some length in his inaugural address to remind the Yale community of the dangers to Yale of "governmental intrusion" and to stress that private educational institutions "are an integral part of the private sector." He called for an end to the "ancient ballet of mutual antagonism" between private enterprise and private education, and said further: "There is a metaphor that informs the private business sector as it informs the private educational sector, and that is the metaphor of the free marketplace." 13

And of course there are other striking signs of the change in public opinion. Legislators themselves are becoming disenchanted with the unpredictable distortions and misallocations of resources that result from large-scale government interference in the operations of the market economy. They are coming to see the truth in Friedrich Hayek's observation that the competitive free market does not mean a national abdication from planning; rather, "competition means decentralized planning by many separate persons." 14

Inherent in the competitive market economy, in capitalism, there *is* a plan—a sort of unorchestrated harmony that represents not only the decisions of "many separate persons" but also the larger frame of public decisions and reasonable regulations that channel enterprise toward goals aligned with the democratic ideal. This is not true *laissez-faire* capitalism—if indeed there has ever been such a creature outside books—but rather a system in which the public sector takes pains to foster responsive, adaptable, innovative, and democratic markets. That system worked in an extraordinary, unprecedented way to advance the material well-being and range for personal autonomy of all those who took part in it. Today the public, much of the intellectual community, and many of the nation's political leaders show a growing appreciation of that system's worth—heartening evidence that capitalism does indeed have a future. 15

J. Robert Nelson

CAPITALISM:
BLESSING AND CURSE

Paul Johnson's description of the astounding effects of industrial capitalism within two hundred years reminds us of other remarkable developments in this relatively brief period. Except for some realms of philosophy, religion, 1 literature, and the arts—visual, auditory, and culinary—our present civilization is wholly different from that of the eighteenth century. He is probably correct in comparing the slums and peasants' hovels of Europe in that century to those in the poorest lands of the Southern Hemisphere today. In hundreds of respects our present world, whether brave or not, is certainly new. And for millions of people it is manifestly better in three broad categories—health, education, and welfare.

Johnson does not choose to argue that the capitalist economy had a great deal to do with the generally improved lot of countless human beings who, thanks to science and technology, will now live to maturity and old age. Before the advent of capitalism, utter poverty, malnutrition, and mortal diseases were common conditions; the primary question was not how to *enhance* life but how to *survive.* Industrial capitalism is sustaining growing numbers of human beings at a higher level of health and material well-being. No one can deny that this is largely the result of a sense of individual worth, initiative, aspiration, and competition. These human qualities had for centuries been denied and suppressed in the common people. They were like white roots and stems found under flat rocks. The plants are alive, but barely so; only when they are uncovered and exposed to sunlight can they grow and develop color. The use of technology to make a profit on invested capital, encouraged by increasingly democratic political societies, was like the lifting of a heavy stone from Western Europe and America.

Johnson does not overstate the case for crediting capitalism—both the ideology and the economic system—for much of what the developed countries enjoy and take for granted. He could have extended the catalogue of its good influences. But he could also have noted the conditions and strictures that have been imposed upon the exuberant free enterprise of the nineteenth century. Government regulation, brought about by democratically elected legislatures, shows that citizens recognized dangers and evils inherent in that economic system. They have seen capitalism for what it is: both a blessing and a curse.

Perhaps this perception of paradox derives from the religious force usually associated with the rise of capitalism—Calvinism. To those most conscious of being God's elect and most obedient to his will is attributed the famous work ethic. But whether or not they were Calvinists, many of the early capitalists were indeed tirelessly industrious, thrifty, and imbued with a sense of rightness and destiny. How could they avoid believing that divine and benign Providence had given to the British the nearly inexhaustible natural resources of a world empire and to Americans the unexplored and as yet unexploited North American continent (though the new Jerusalem they felt called to build in the green lands of England and New England turned out to be more commercial than heavenly).

The same Providence that gave them resources and inspired resourcefulness also required justice and mercy. While the early capitalists, who could be described as "God-fearing," had a limited concept of what justice required, they did give expression to mercy through acts of philanthropy that partially expiated their sin of acquisitiveness. Many colleges, universities, libraries, museums, charitable institutions, and foundations owe their existence in large measure to the "plagued conscience" of Christian and Jewish capitalists.

But this was not enough to offset the ill effects on the population of economic control by large corporations. As the era of robber barons gave way to the era of big business, the necessity of government regulation was apparent. Implicit in the motivation for regulation was a biblical teaching: the same heart of man that rejoices in the blessings of prosperity remains wicked and exceedingly self-centered. If there is any truth in the saying that there was more Methodism than Marxism in the rise of British socialism, a similar observation about religious influence is appropriate to America's willingness to accept the Rooseveltian reforms that rendered fully obsolete the concept of *laissez-faire.*

Paul Johnson's discussion of the relation between government and business is inadequate. It is merely contentious to say that industrial capitalism and big government are irreconcilable enemies. He has a legitimate complaint against *excessive* controls by government, but he goes much further and appears to preclude *proper* controls. He implies that the only alternative to big government's power over the economy is no control at all.

His discussion of labor unions leads to a similarly erroneous conclusion: better none at all than what we have in Britain and America today. This is unfortunate, since many who are sympathetic with Johnson's opposition to Marxism and Communism cannot believe that our national government and labor unions are equally perilous to a good society.

His polemic against the false gods and false hopes of Communism certainly is justified; but it would be more compelling if he had shown that the outrages of which industrial capitalism stands accused are easily matched, or exceeded, by those in socialist countries. These have to do with three kinds of exploitation: human, international, and ecological. Critics and dedicated opponents of capitalism have convincing reasons for faulting the corporate powers of free (or nearly free) enterprise. Countless workers and their dependents have suffered abuses and deprivations; natural resources of less developed countries have been pillaged for the profit of the rich ones; our air, water, and soil have been polluted. Johnson is not disposed to mention these vulnerable aspects of capitalist societies, which are the prime targets of both the academic Marxists and the pamphleteers. Neither does he admit the extent to which industrial capitalism is linked with, and dependent upon, the European and American production of military hardware and all the ancillary materials and services useful only to defense and warfare. Remembering that it was a representative of capitalist interests, President Eisenhower, whose last testament was a grave warning against the "military-industrial complex," we may find all the less convincing Johnson's generalization that industry and government are natural enemies.

These arguments can readily be turned back against Marxist apologists for socialist and Communist states and economies. When one thinks only of the Soviet Union's control over Eastern Europe, its expropriation of raw materials and manufactured products for itself, its spoliation of the natural environment, and its abysmal record of human degradation and oppression, it is obvious that the Communist pot has no basis for calling the capitalist kettle black. To make these points would strengthen the case for capitalism as an imperfect yet preferable mode of production and distribution.

Johnson's animosity toward what he calls the "ecolobby" is excessive 11 and perplexing. He gives the impression that he believes in industry's willingness and capability to care for the plundered planet by itself. Evidence abounds to show that this is an ill-founded belief—a point dramatized in March 1979 when the world turned horrified eyes on the Three Mile Island nuclear power reactor near Harrisburg, Pennsylvania. Although its malfunction and threatened explosion of radioactive materials were brought under control with no human death or injury, the catastrophic possibility was enough to negate such blithe cases for developing nuclear power as Johnson's.

Though his style is engaging and articulate, Johnson falls short of mak- 12 ing a satisfying apologia for industrial capitalism in our time. This is disappointing. There is merit in his trenchant observations about Marxists. He is right to point to the erosion of both the ideologically informed will and the political conditions that can make capitalism work as it should—i.e., for the common good. Not socialism but social mutuality and human solidarity must now determine our evaluation of any economic or political system.

Eugene J. McCarthy

CORPORATIONS HAVE CORRUPTED CAPITALISM

Little can be said against Paul Johnson's case for the productive power of 1 capitalism, whether a particular capitalist's motivation was to amass wealth (as the economist Carl Snyder observed years ago, "Deep as are our prejudices against avarice and greed, it cannot be denied that they have been great forces for the building of the modern economic world"), to demonstrate personal power and achievement (as in the case of empire-builders like Andrew Carnegie and James Hill), or to contribute to human welfare. Today the theoretical challenge, if it can properly be called that, is not to traditional capitalism but to capitalism as it is manifested in the corporation.

When economists began to write about the economics of "imperfect 2 competition," they signaled the end of the pure economics of Adam Smith and of capitalism. Today nearly 80 per cent of the productive activity in the United States is controlled by corporate organizations operating under charters granted by the states. These corporations are not free, competing entities but institutions given special privileges and advantages over individuals by legal social decision.

James Kent, in his *Commentaries on American Law,* published early in the   3
nineteenth century, observed that "the number of charters of incorporation" was increasing in the United States with a disturbing rapidity. "We are multiplying in this country to an unparalleled extent the institution of corporations," he said, "and giving them a flexibility and variety of purpose unknown to the Roman or to the English law."

Competition does not rule the economy of the United States today.   4
More and more, differences between the largest corporations and the government are settled not within a framework of law but by negotiation. For example, when Du Pont was ordered to divest itself of General Motors stock some seventeen years ago, the existing antitrust laws and penalties were not applied. Congress passed special legislation to work out the transition. In much the same way, the taxation of insurance companies and of oil companies has been settled by negotiation rather than by the application of public judgment and law.

The government's dealings with the steel industry in recent years dem   5
onstrate the same relationship. During the Korean War, when President Truman tried to prevent a slowdown in steel production by issuing an executive order to take over the industry, the independence of the industry was sustained by the Supreme Court.

Subsequent challenges to the industry were handled differently. The   6
Kennedy administration responded to a major increase in the price of steel not by attempting to apply the existing law or by executive order but by public denunciation and, according to some reports, by midnight calls from the FBI to steel-company officials.

In the Johnson administration, the presidents of steel companies were   7
called to the White House for "jawboning" sessions, generally approved by the press and politicians. The message was not that competition, the free economy, and the law of supply and demand should be allowed to prevail but that prices should be kept down. The steel-company officers, champions of free enterprise and of capitalism, surrendered, seeming to accept the idea that if prices were fixed in Pittsburgh, that would be an "action in restraint of trade." It was rather as if an English king had called in the nobles and said: "If you agree to these things in my presence, you will be able to do them. But if you agree to them among yourselves in Wales, you will be in deep trouble."

It has been suggested that the U.S. government seek the equivalent of   8
diplomatic representation on the boards of major corporations, especially those that are deeply involved in foreign business and finance.

What we have in America is not a free, competitive, capitalistic system   9
but a kind of corporate feudalism. In the feudal system, according to a schoolboy's definition, everyone belonged to someone and everyone else belonged to the king. In the modern order, nearly every worker belongs to

some corporation, and everyone else belongs to the government, federal, state, or local.

A corporately controlled economy has left us with a situation in which   10
there is widespread poverty, serious unemployment, the wasting of resources, shortages, and inflation. The corporation is not wholly responsible for these conditions. Undoubtedly outside policy or forces, such as war and government fiscal policies and regulations, have an adverse affect on the general economy and specifically on some institutions and businesses.

The concept of the corporation as an instrument for the conduct of   11
business and financial affairs is a valid one. But it is a concept that must prove its vitality in practice. If the corporation is to be privileged by law, as it is now, and if it is to control most of the powers on which the material well-being of the nation depends, then it must become more effective and more responsible, both socially and economically.

James Cone

CAPITALISM MEANS
PROPERTY OVER PERSONS

Some perspectives differ so radically from my own that I hardly know where   1
to begin in responding to them. Having read Paul Johnson's address several times, I still find it hard to believe that he can so uncritically support capitalism in the face of the vast human suffering arising from it. How should I respond to a point of view that seems completely insensitive to many human factors that I regard as important?

I will focus my comments on the *selective* character of Paul Johnson's   2
argument for industrial capitalism. Because I am a black American whose value system has been shaped in the historical context of an oppressed people's struggle for justice, I cannot avoid evaluating a given sociopolitical perspective in terms of how it helps or hinders that struggle. If one takes the general principle of "justice for the poor" as the criterion, Johnson's apology for capitalism is completely unconvincing. He shows little or no concern for oppressed humanity in Europe, the United States, and the Third World. It is as if they do not exist.

When a people's existence is not recognized, it means that their suffer-   3
ing is considered to have no bearing on the value of a given political system if that system continues to serve the interests of those for whom it was created. That was why white North Americans could speak of the United States as the "land of the free" while they held Africans as slaves. Similarly, Paul Johnson can speak of capitalism as "the greatest single blessing ever bestowed on humanity" even though the vast majority of people have been

victimized by it. He seems to be saying that as long as the white European and American ruling classes benefit from the profits of capitalism, its shortcomings in contributing toward the liberation of the poor from their poverty cannot count significantly against its value for humanity. Value is defined in terms of material profit for the rich, not economic and political structures for the benefit of all. It is this implication that makes his viewpoint reprehensible from my ethical perspective.

For whom does Johnson speak and for what purpose? I think the answer is obvious. He speaks for the haves and not the have-nots, for the rich and not the poor, for whites and not blacks, for the United States and Europe and not for Asia, Africa, and Latin America. His purpose is to show that recent threats to industrial capitalism arise not from the masses of people but rather from university intellectuals, trade unions, big government, ecology campaigners, and the Soviet Union. This selective focus and his caricature of the opponents of capitalism define the character of his address; he thereby limits the possibility of genuine dialogue with anyone whose perspective has been shaped by solidarity with the victims of industrial capitalism.

Johnson's defense of industrial capitalism centers on its ability to produce an "unprecedented annual growth rate" in Europe and North America. Aside from Japan, there is no mention in this connection of any country in the Third World. Nor does he say anything about the relation between the wealth of Europe and the United States and the poverty in Asia, Africa, and Latin America. Is he suggesting that this wealth is in no way connected with and dependent upon slavery and colonization in the Third World? Because the examples he gives of the value of industrial capitalism are almost exclusively limited to Europe and the United States, I am particularly interested in how he would explain the huge gap between the rich and the poor on both continents, but especially in Asia, Africa, and Latin America. And why does he not mention that though the United States has only 6 per cent of the world's population, it consumes over 30 per cent of the world's natural resources?

I contend that capitalism is under threat not because it has received a bad press from university intellectuals, ecology campaigners, and trade-union people, nor because of big government or even the outside danger of the Soviet Union, but because the so-called free-enterprise system is not free at all; it is actually controlled by multinational corporations.

I agree with Johnson that the capitalist economies of the United States and Europe have produced a lot of wealth. But I also know that the masses of people on both continents do not receive their just share of that wealth. While legislators in the United States enact laws almost yearly that appear to guarantee a fairer distribution, statistics show that the very rich still control a hugely disproportionate amount of the nation's wealth. This rich ruling class makes up only 0.5 per cent of the population but controls over one-fourth of the nation's privately held wealth and yearly income, including 50–86 per cent of all corporate stock (see Jonathan Turner and Charles Staines, *Inequality: Privilege and Poverty in America*, Goodyear, 1976).

When these economic factors are set in a racial context, the injustice is   8
even more striking. Blacks and other U.S. minorities are especially victimized,
because their color is an additional factor contributing to the economic injustice inflicted upon them. Aside from the small minority of black professionals
who are needed to create the appearance of equality in the United States,
blacks and other ethnic minorities are the last hired and often the first fired.
Their unemployment rate is always four to ten times higher than that of
whites. They are forced to live in urban ghettoes with no real opportunity to
participate in shaping the laws that affect their community.

People who share Paul Johnson's perspective like to delude themselves   9
into thinking that the poor enjoy living in poverty. They nourish this delusion by spending most of their time talking to rich capitalists and their
supporters rather than to the poor. Yet they like to claim that they know what
the poor think. What they label as the "poor" perspective is nothing but the
reinforcement of the ruling-class point of view. In the United States I have
met many white people who share Johnson's viewpoint. They were plentiful
during the civil-rights struggle in the 1950s and '60s, and today they are even
more vocal in advocating the essential justice of the American capitalist
system. When poor black people, during the 1960s, reacted in violent rebellion against intolerable economic conditions, white oppressors simply attributed such behavior to the influence of outside agitators and gave a military response that left many blacks dead in the streets.

Economic conditions in U.S. cities are no better today for the masses of   10
blacks than they were in the 1960s. But I am sure that urban police departments are better prepared for any disturbance that black people's poverty
may motivate them to create. People who share Paul Johnson's perspective
seem to be more concerned about eliminating social unrest through the power
of the police than about eliminating the economic conditions that create the
unrest.

Paul Johnson either is unaware of the gross injustices created by capital-   11
ism or has simply chosen to ignore them. If he thinks that the growth of
megalopolises all over the world is evidence of a popular endorsement of
capitalism, he is grossly mistaken. Poor people migrate to urban centers
because they are trying to survive in a situation of maldistributed wealth.
Whatever else may be said about the wealth that capitalism generates in the
United States, poor blacks and other minorities do not benefit from it.

When capitalism's wealth is viewed in an international context, the   12
injustice it creates appears even greater. The wealth of Europe and the United
States is directly determined by the poverty of the people of Asia, Africa, and
Latin America. This is the historical significance of slavery and colonization,
which today are continued in the economic domination of the Third World
by the United States and Europe. Despite the Western world's verbal defense
of human rights and freedom, its continued economic and military support
of the dictator governments of South Africa, South Korea, Chile, and many
other states completely invalidates what it says.

Although I am a Christian whose ethical perspective is derived pri-   13 marily from that tradition, I do not need to appeal to Christianity to demonstrate the gross immorality of economic arrangements defined by capitalism. One needs only to be sensitive to human beings and their right to life, liberty, and the pursuit of happiness to question seriously what Paul Johnson advocates. Capitalism is a system that clearly values property more than persons. That is why it is losing the moral and intellectual battle. And perhaps it is why Paul Johnson appeals to material statistics as evidence for the inherent value of capitalism rather than to the quality of life it makes possible for all people.

Questions for Discussion

1. In paragraph 15 of "Has Capitalism a Future?" Johnson pictures peasants and poor people all over the world going to the cities in a "never-ending one-way flow from [the] countryside." He calls this movement "plainly a voluntary mass choice." From what you know of poor people in cities either in the past or present, does this seem an accurate description of the urban poor?

2. Johnson calls the environmentalists' objections to industrial growth "ecological panic." What effect is the word *panic* designed to have on the reader?

3. Schmertz accuses Johnson of confusing capitalism as an economic system with democracy as a social system. Does this seem a well-placed criticism? Does Schmertz seem less or more eager than Johnson for capitalism to survive? Are Johnson and Schmertz appealing to the same *interests* in their readers? If so, what are they? If not, how do they differ?

4. Is McCarthy an opponent of capitalism? If not, what *does* he oppose? When he says that "competition does not rule the economy of the United States today" (¶4), is he saying that it should or should not? *Why* has competition disappeared from the American economy, and what should be done either to keep it out or to bring it back in?

5. What use does Nelson make of his observation that "the same heart of man that rejoices in the blessings of prosperity remains wicked and exceedingly self-centered" (¶6)? Does this remark provide support for Johnson's position? If so, how? If not, why not?

6. Nelson says that Johnson's attack on ecological advocates is "perplexing" (¶11). Does he really seem perplexed in the rest of the paragraph? If not, why do you think he uses this term? If you think his perplexity is genuine, what is he perplexed about?

7. Cone claims that Johnson "speaks for the haves and not the have-nots" (¶4). Do you think this is a fair accusation? Can you find evidence in Johnson's essay either to support or to refute it?

8. By putting Johnson's facts into the contexts of race and social class, Cone makes them look much less laudatory than Johnson does. Which writer do you think is being more careful with his facts? Are they speaking *at* each other or *past* each other?

Suggested Essay Topics

1. Select *one* of Johnson's respondents and make a list of three or four of his specific criticisms. Then write a letter to the critic in Johnson's name, addressing the criticisms in detail and answering them with information from "your" (Johnson's) essay, showing the critic that he has somehow failed to read you correctly.

2. Write a letter to Johnson, using evidence from all four of Johnson's respondents, to support a series of claims showing that Johnson has unfairly presented his argument for industrial capitalism.

Acknowledgments

St. Thomas Aquinas, "The Production of Woman." From *The Summa Theologica*. From *Basic Writings of Saint Thomas Aquinas*, edited by Anton C. Pegis. Copyright © 1945 by Random House, Inc. Reprinted by permission of the Estate of Anton C. Pegis.

W.H. Auden, "The Unknown Citizen." From *Collected Poems of W.H. Auden* edited by Edward Mendelson. Copyright © 1940, 1968 by W. H. Auden. Reprinted by permission of Random House, Inc., and Faber and Faber Ltd.

Bruno Bettelheim and Karen Zelan, "Why Children Don't Like to Read." From *On Learning to Read: The Child's Fascination with Meaning* by Bruno Bettleheim and Karen Zelan. Copyright © 1981 by Bruno Bettelheim and Karen Zelan. Reprinted by permission of Alfred A. Knopf, Inc.

Jacob Bronowski, "The Reach of Imagination." From *Proceedings of the American Academy of Arts and Letters and the National Institute of Arts and Letters*, 2d series, 17 (1967). Copyright © 1967 by the American Academy of Arts and Letters. Reprinted by permission of the American Academy and Institute of Arts and Letters.

James Cone, "Capitalism Means Property over Persons." From *Will Capitalism Survive?* edited by Ernest W. Lefever (Washington, D.C.: Ethics and Public Policy Center, 1979). Copyright © 1979 by the Ethics and Public Policy Center. Reprinted by permission of the publisher.

E. E. Cummings, "LIV" ("if everything happens that can't be done.") From *Complete Poems, 1913–1962* by E. E. Cummings. Copyright © 1923, 1925, 1931, 1935, 1938, 1939, 1940, 1944, 1945, 1946, 1947, 1948, 1949, 1950, 1951, 1952, 1953, 1954, 1955, 1956, 1957, 1958, 1959, 1960, 1961, 1962 by the Trustees for the E. E. Cummings Trust. Copyright © 1961, 1963, 1968 by Marion Morehouse Cummings. Reprinted by permission of Liveright Publishing Corporation.

Loren Eiseley, "The Illusion of the Two Cultures." From *The Star Thrower* by Loren Eiseley. Copyright © 1978 by the Estate of Loren C. Eiseley, Mabel L. Eiseley, Executrix. Reprinted by permission of Times Books, a Division of Random House, Inc.

Ralph Ellison, "Battle Royal." From *Invisible Man* by Ralph Ellison. Copyright © 1947, 1948, 1952 by Ralph Ellison. Reprinted by permission of Random House, Inc.

Francine Frank and Frank Ashen, "Of Girls and Chicks." From *Language and the Sexes* by Francine Frank and Frank Ashen. Copyright © 1983 by Francine Frank and Frank Ashen. Reprinted by permission of State University of New York Press.

Sigmund Freud, "Femininity." From *New Introductory Lectures On Psychoanalysis* by Sigmund Freud, translated and edited by James Strachey. Reprinted by permission of W. W. Norton & Company, Inc. Copyright © 1965, 1964 by James Strachey. Copyright 1933 by Sigmund Freud. Copyright renewed 1961 by W. J. H. Sprott.

Genesis 1–2:3, from *The Torah,* 2d ed. Copyright © 1962 by the Jewish Publication Society. Reprinted by permission of the publisher.

Pieter Geyl and Arnold J. Toynbee, "Can We Know the Pattern of the Past?" Reprinted from *The Pattern of the Past: Can We Determine It?* by Pieter Geyl, Arnold J. Toynbee, and Pitirim A. Sorokin. Copyright © 1949 by Beacon Press. Reprinted by permission of Beacon Press.

William Golding, "Thinking as a Hobby." Copyright © 1961, 1989 by William Golding. Reprinted by permission of Curtis Brown, Ltd. First printed in *Holiday* magazine.

Paul Goodman, "Utopian Thinking." From *Utopian Essays and Practical Problems* by Paul Goodman. Copyright © 1962 by Paul Goodman. Reprinted by permission of Random House, Inc.

Maxim Gorky, "On Books." From *On Literature* by Maxim Gorky, translated by Julius Katzer. Copyright © 1973 by University of Washington Press. Reprinted by permission of the publisher.

Edith Hamilton, "The Ever-Present Past" is reprinted from *The Ever-Present Past* by Edith Hamilton, by permission of W. W. Norton & Company, Inc. Copyright © 1958 by *The Saturday Evening Post.* Copyright © 1964 by W. W. Norton & Company, Inc.

Lorraine Hansberry, "In Defense of the Equality of *Men.*" Copyright © 1985 by Robert Nemiroff. Reprinted by permission of Robert Nemiroff. All rights reserved.

Adolf Hitler, "Is This a Jew?" From *Mein Kampf* by Adolf Hitler, translated by Ralph Manheim. Copyright © 1943, 1971 by Houghton Mifflin Company. Reprinted by permission of Houghton Mifflin Company and Century Hutchinson Publishing Group, Ltd.

Shirley Jackson, "Flower Garden." From *The Lottery and Other Stories* by Shirley Jackson. Copyright © 1948, 1949 by Shirley Jackson. Copyright © renewed 1976, 1977 by Laurence Hyman, Barry Hyman, Mrs. Sarah Webster and Mrs. Joanne Schnurer. Reprinted by permission of Farrar, Straus and Giroux, Inc.

Paul Johnson, "Has Capitalism a Future?" From *Will Capitalism Survive?* edited by Ernest W. Lefever (Washington, D.C.: Ethics and Public Policy Center, 1979). Copyright © 1979 by Paul Johnson. Reprinted by permission of the author.

Helen Keller, "The Key to Language." From *The Story of My Life* by Helen Keller. Copyright © 1902 by Helen Keller. Reprinted by permission of Doubleday Publishing Co., Inc.

Martin Luther King, Jr., "Letter from Birmingham Jail." From *Why We Can't Wait* by Martin Luther King, Jr. Copyright © 1963, 1964 by Martin Luther King, Jr. Reprinted by permission of Harper & Row, Publishers, Inc.

Ursula K. Le Guin, "Why Are Americans Afraid of Dragons?" Copyright © 1974 by Ursula K. Le Guin. Reprinted by permission of the author, the author's agent, Virginia Kidd, and the Putnam Publishing Group.

C. S. Lewis, "What Christians Believe." From *Mere Christianity* by C. S. Lewis. Copyright © 1943, 1945, 1952 by Macmillan Publishing Co., Inc. Copyright © 1943, 1945, 1952 by William Collins Sons & Co., Ltd. Reprinted by permission of William Collins Sons & Co., Ltd.

Malcolm X, "Freedom Through Learning to Read." From *The Autobiography of Malcolm X* by Malcolm X, with the assistance of Alex Haley. Copyright © 1964 by Alex Haley and Malcolm X. Copyright © 1965 by Alex Haley and Betty Shabazz. Reprinted by permission of Random House, Inc.

Eugene J. McCarthy, "Corporations Have Corrupted Capitalism." From *Will Capitalism Survive?* edited by Ernest W. Lefever (Washington, D.C.: Ethics and Public Policy Center, 1979). Copyright © 1979 by the Ethics and Public Policy Center. Reprinted by permission of the publisher.

Mary McCarthy, "Artists in Uniform." From *On The Contrary* by Mary McCarthy. Copyright © 1953 by Mary McCarthy. Reprinted by permission of the author.

Mary Midgley, "Evolution as a Religion." From *Evolution as Religion; Strange Hopes and Stranger Fears.* Copyright © 1985 by Mary Midgley. Reprinted by permission of Routledge, Chapman and Hall, Ltd.

Elaine Morgan, "The Man-made Myth." From *The Descent of Woman* by Elaine Morgan. Copyright © 1972 by Elaine Morgan. Reprinted by permission of Stein and Day Publishers and Souvenir Press Ltd.

J. Robert Nelson, "Capitalism: Blessing and Curse." From *Will Capitalism Survive?* edited by Ernest Lefever (Washington, D.C.: Ethics and Public Policy Center, 1979). Copyright © 1979 by the Ethics and Public Policy Center. Reprinted by permission of the publisher.

Friedrich Nietzsche, "The Ugliness of Woman." From *Beyond Good and Evil* by Friedrich Nietzsche, translated by Walter Kaufmann. Copyright © 1966 by Random House, Inc. Reprinted by permission of the publisher.

Joyce Carol Oates, "How I Contemplated the World from the Detroit House of Correction and Began My Life Over Again." From *The Wheel of Love.* Copyright © 1965 by Joyce Carol Oates. Reprinted by permission of Vanguard Press.

George Orwell, "Politics and the English Language." From *Shooting an Elephant and Other Essays* by George Orwell. Copyright © 1946, 1974 by Sonia Brownell Orwell. Reprinted by permission of Harcourt Brace Jovanovich, Inc., the estate of the late Sonia Brownell Orwell, and Martin Secker & Warburg, Ltd.

Plato, "Censorship." From *The Republic* in *The Dialogues of Plato,* translated by Benjamin Jowett, 4th ed. Copyright © 1953 by the Jowett Copyright Trustees. Reprinted by permission of Oxford: Clarendon Press.

Karl R. Popper, "Utopia and Violence." From *Conjectures and Refutations: The Growth of Scientific Knowledge* (2d ed., 1965.) Copyright © 1963, 1965 by Karl L. Popper. Reprinted by permission of the author.

Ayn Rand, "I Owe Nothing to My Brothers." From *Anthem* by Ayn Rand. Copyright © 1946 by Pamphleteers, Inc. Reprinted by permission of Dr. Leonard Peikoff, Executor, Estate of Ayn Rand.

Adrienne Rich, "Claiming an Education." From *On Lies, Secrets, and Silence: Selected Prose, 1966–1978* by Adrienne Rich. Copyright © 1979 by W. W. Norton & Co., Inc. Reprinted by permission of the publisher.

Theodore Roosevelt, "The Welfare of the Wage-Worker." From *The National Edition of Roosevelt's Works*, Vols. XV and XVI, by Theodore Roosevelt. Copyright © 1925 by Theodore Roosevelt. Originally published by Scribner Book Companies.

Phyllis Rose, "Heroic Fantasies, Nervous Doubts." From the *New York Times* "Hers" column of March 22, 1984. Copyright © 1984 by Phyllis Rose. Reprinted by permission of Georges Borchardt, Inc. and the author.

Betty Roszak, "The Human Continuum." From *Masculine/Feminine: Readings in Sexual Mythology and the Liberation of Women*, edited by Betty Roszak and Theodore Roszak. Copyright © 1969 by Betty Roszak. Reprinted by permission of Harper & Row, Publishers, Inc.

Bertrand Russell, "Happiness." Reprinted from *The Conquest of Happiness* by Bertrand Russell, by permission of Liveright Publishing Corporation. Copyright © 1930 by Horace Liveright, Inc. Copyright © 1958 by Bertrand Russell.

Bertrand Russell, "Why I Am Not a Christian." From *Why I Am Not a Christian and Other Essays on Religious and Related Subjects* by Bertrand Russell, edited by Paul Edwards. Copyright © 1957 by Allen & Unwin. Reprinted by permission of Simon & Schuster, a Division of Gulf & Western Corporation, and George Allen & Unwin, Ltd.

St. Paul, "I Corinthians 13." From *The New English Bible*. Copyright © by the Delegates of the Oxford University Press and the Syndics of the Cambridge University Press 1961, 1970. Reprinted by permission.

Margaret Sanger, "The Turbid Ebb and Flow of Misery." From *An Autobiography* by Margaret Sanger. Copyright © 1938 by W.W. Norton & Co., Inc. Reprinted by permission of Dr. Grant Sanger.

Herbert Schmertz, "Democracy, Tyranny, and Capitalism." From *Will Capitalism Survive?* edited by Ernest W. Lefever (Washington, D.C.: Ethics and Public Policy Center). Copyright © 1979 by the Ethics and Public Policy Center. Reprinted by permission of the publisher.

C. P. Snow, "The Two Cultures." From *The Two Cultures: And a Second Look*. Copyright © 1959 by C. P. Snow. Reprinted by permission of Cambridge University Press.

Stephen Spender, "In Railway Halls, on Pavements Near the Traffic." From *Collected Poems 1928–1953* by Stephen Spender. Copyright © 1934, 1962 by Stephen Spender. Reprinted by permission of Random House, Inc., and Faber & Faber, Ltd, from *Collected Poems* by Stephen Spender.

Walter T. Stace, "What Religion Is." From *Time and Eternity: An Essay in the Philosophy of Religion.* Copyright © 1952, renewed 1980 by Princeton University Press. Reprinted by permission of the publisher.

Lewis Thomas, "Debating the Unknowable." Originally published in *The Atlantic Monthly* (July 1981). Copyright © 1981 by *The Atlantic Monthly.* Reprinted in *Late Night Thoughts on Listening to Mahler's Ninth Symphony* by Lewis Thomas. Copyright © 1983 by Lewis Thomas. Reprinted by permission of *The Atlantic Monthly* and the Viking Press.

Alfred North Whitehead, "The Aims of Education." From *The Aims of Education and Other Essays* by Alfred North Whitehead. Copyright © 1929 by Macmillan Publishing Co., Inc., renewed © 1957 by Evelyn Whitehead. Reprinted by permission of Macmillan Publishing Co.

Elie Wiesel, "The Sacrifice of Isaac: A Strange Tale About Fear, Faith and Laughter." From *Messengers of God: Biblical Portraits and Legends* by Elie Wiesel, translated by Marion Wiesel. Copyright © 1976 by Elie Wiesel. Reprinted by permission of Random House, Inc.

Richard Wright, "The Library Card." Chapter XIII from *Black Boy* by Richard Wright. Copyright © 1937, 1942, 1944, 1945 by Richard Wright. Reprinted by permission of Harper & Row, Publishers, Inc.

Author Index

Rhetorical Index